A PRACTICAL APPROACH TO

REFERENCE

A PRACTICAL APPROACH TO
FAMILY LAW

NINTH EDITION

Jill Black DBE

Jane Bridge

Tina Bond

Liam Gribbin

Madeleine Reardon

OXFORD
UNIVERSITY PRESS

Great Clarendon Street, Oxford ox2 6DP
United Kingdom

Oxford University Press is a department of the University of Oxford.
It furthers the University's objective of excellence in research, scholarship,
and education by publishing worldwide. Oxford is a registered trade mark of
Oxford University Press in the UK and in certain other countries

© Jill Black, Jane Bridge, Tina Bond, Liam Gribbin, Madeleine Reardon 2012

The moral rights of the authors have been asserted

First Published Blackstone Press 1986; Ninth Edition 2012
Impression: 1

British Library Cataloguing in Publication Data
Data available

Library of Congress Cataloguing in Publication Data
2011945447

ISBN 978–0–19–969313–9

Typeset by Cenveo, Bangalore, India
Printed in Great Britain
on acid-free paper by
Ashford Colour Press Ltd, Gosport, Hampshire

Links to third party websites are provided by Oxford in good faith and
for information only. Oxford disclaims any responsibility for the materials
contained in any third party website referenced in this work.

PREFACE

This ninth edition has been a shared effort between Tina Bond, Madeleine Reardon and Liam Gribbin.

This edition contains a new chapter on forced marriages, the Forced Marriage (Civil Protection) Act 2007 coming into force in November 2008. We have also included all other relevant legislative changes within the pre-existing chapters. Examples of this are the Land Registration Act 2002, the Child Maintenance and Other Payments Act 2008, and the Domestic Violence, Crime and Victims Act 2004.

There have been sweeping changes brought about by the Family Procedure Rules 2010 which came into force on 6 April 2011 and these rules and their Practice Directions are also incorporated. They place mediation in an ever greater position of importance. We have reflected that by a revised chapter on mediation and other forms of alternative dispute resolution. The requirement that at least one party attends a Mediation Information and Assessment Meeting prior to an application to court is now a distinct procedural step in applications in respect of children and property.

We anticipate that before the next edition sweeping changes will occur within family law, particularly to private children applications within a court setting and the disappearance of legal aid for family cases. A review into family justice will shortly make its final recommendations to Parliament.

We are, as ever, grateful to our respective spouses, Barbara, Robert, and Chris, and assorted children who shared the ups and downs of us preparing a new edition for their support and patience. Tina would also like to acknowledge the enormous help of Dr Edna Smith in deciphering Tina's handwriting and making sense of countless pages of material. In addition, Liam thanks Sarah Giles of Regency Chambers in Peterborough for assistance with several chapters.

We also acknowledge with gratitude the help and support of Oxford University Press throughout the process of producing this book and liaising between the authors who live at opposite ends of the country.

The law is correct to 1 August 2011.

CONTENTS SUMMARY

CONTENTS

PART I FAMILY LAW PRACTICE

1 FAMILY LAW PRACTICE—SETTING THE SCENE, THE FIRST INTERVIEW, AND NEXT STEPS

2 PUBLIC FUNDING FOR FAMILY PROCEEDINGS

PART IV MONEY AND PROPERTY

22 THE HOME: PREVENTING A SALE OR MORTGAGE

23 KEEPING UP WITH THE MORTGAGE OR RENT

24 WELFARE BENEFITS

PART V DOMESTIC VIOLENCE

TABLE OF CASES

TABLE OF STATUTORY INSTRUMENTS

TABLE OF EUROPEAN LEGLISLATION

LIST OF FORMS

LAW SOCIETY'S FAMILY LAW
PROTOCOL 2010

LIST OF ABBREVIATIONS

ACA 2002	Adoption and Children Act 2002
ADR	Alternative dispute resolution
AJA 1999	Access to Justice Act 1999
Brussels IIR	Council Regulation (EC) No 2201/2003
CA 1989	Children Act 1989
CAA 1984	Child Abduction Act 1984
Cafcass	Children and Family Court Advisory and Support Service
CETV	cash equivalent transfer value
CMEC	Child Maintenance and Enforcement Commission
CMOPA 2008	Child Maintenance and Other Payments Act 2008
CPA 2004	Civil Partnership Act 2004
CPMCA 1978	Domestic Proceedings and Magistrates' Courts Act 1978
CPR 1998	Civil Procedure Rules 1998
CSA 1991	Child Support Act 1991
CSA 1995	Child Support Act 1995
CSPASSA 2000	Child Support, Pensions and Social Security Act 2000
CTC	child tax credit
DMPA 1973	Domicile and Matrimonial Proceedings Act 1973
DPMCA 1978	Domestic Proceedings and Magistrates' Courts Act 1978
DVCVA 2004	Domestic Violence, Crime and Victims Act 2004
DWP	Department for Work and Pensions
ECHR	European Convention for the Protection of Human Rights and Fundamental Freedoms
FDR	Financial Dispute Resolution
FHDRA	First Hearing Dispute Resolution Appointment
FLA 1986	Family Law Act 1986
FLA 1996	Family Law Act 1996
FM(CP)A 2007	Forced Marriage (Civil Protection) Act 2007
FMPO	Forced Marriage Protection Order
FP(AJ)D 2009	Family Proceedings (Allocation to Judiciary) Directions 2009
FPR 2010	Family Procedure Rules 2010
GRA 2004	Gender Recognition Act 2004
GRR	Gender Recognition Register
HFEA 1990	Human Fertilisation and Embryology Act 1990
HFEA 2008	Human Fertilisation and Embryology Act 2008
HRA 1998	Human Rights Act 1998
IA 1975	Inheritance (Provision for Family and Dependants) Act 1975
IPS	Identity and Passport Service
IRO	independent reviewing officer
LRA 2002	Land Registration Act 2002
LSC	Legal Services Commission

MCA 1973	Matrimonial Causes Act 1973
MEA 1991	Maintenance Enforcement Act 1991
MIAM	Mediation Information and Assessment Meeting
NACCC	National Association of Child Contact Centres
PCA 2002	Proceeds of Crime Act 2002
PFLRS	Private Family Law Representation Scheme
SOCA	Serious Organised Crime Agency
SRA	Solicitors Regulation Authority
TOLATA 1996	Trusts of Land and Appointment of Trustees Act 1996
WA 1837	Wills Act 1837
WRPA 1999	Welfare Reform and Pensions Act 1999
WTC	working tax credit

PART I

FAMILY LAW PRACTICE

1

FAMILY LAW PRACTICE—SETTING THE SCENE, THE FIRST INTERVIEW, AND NEXT STEPS

A   SETTING THE SCENE—PRELIMINARY POINTS

The scope of family law

1.01   Family law practice is becoming increasingly complex not only because of the sophisticated requirements of clients but because of the need to comply throughout with protocols, regulations, and the detailed rules of procedure. Public funding of family law cases faces an uncertain future, leading to a greater expectation that a client will be required to fund family proceedings out of his or her own pocket.

1.02   Traditionally, a 'family law case' concerned the position of parties to a marriage only. More recently, it has encompassed parties who are cohabiting (whether in an opposite-sex or same-sex relationship) and civil partners following the coming into force of the Civil Partnership Act 2004.

Family Procedure Rules 2010

1.03   The Family Procedure Rules 2010 ('FPR 2010', SI 2010/2955) came into force on 6 April 2011.

1.04   The rules 'provide a new code of procedure for family proceedings in the High Court, county courts and magistrates' court, and replace existing rules of court for family proceedings' (FPR 2010, Explanatory note). However, the rules do not extend to civil proceedings (eg proceedings under the Trusts of Land and Appointment of Trustees Act 1996 or the Inheritance (Provision for Family and Dependants) Act 1975) which are heard in a family court.

The overriding objective

1.05   The rules modernize many aspects of procedure and are modelled on the Civil Procedure Rules 1998 ('CPR 1998', SI 1998/3132). Hence, as with CPR 1998, the rules are supplemented by Practice Directions and forms and begin by stating the overriding objective as follows:

> (1) These rules are a new procedural code with the overriding objective of enabling the court to deal with cases justly, having regard to any welfare issues involved.
> (2) Dealing with a case justly includes, so far as is practicable—
>   (a) ensuring that it is dealt with expeditiously and fairly;
>   (b) dealing with the case in ways which are proportionate to the nature, importance and complexity of the issues;
>   (c) ensuring that the parties are on an equal footing;
>   (d) saving expense;
>   (e) allotting to it an appropriate share of the court's resources, while taking into account the need to allot resources to other cases. (r 1.1, FPR 2010)

The court must seek to give effect to the overriding objective when it exercises any power given to it by the rules or interprets any rule (r 1.2). Likewise the parties are required to help the court to further the overriding objective (r 1.3).

The principal changes

Set out below are some of the significant changes in the FPR 2010. The list is not intended to **1.06** be exhaustive. Reference is made to the relevant chapter where the changes are discussed in more detail:

(a) there is greater emphasis on the use of alternative dispute resolution, particularly mediation, in Part 3 and PD3A (Chapters 3, 18, and 30);
(b) PD5A contains a table of forms applicable to each type of proceedings;
(c) in divorce proceedings:
  (i)   the term 'special procedure' is abolished;
  (ii) the petition for divorce now contains numerous tick boxes for completion;
  (iii) a shorter statement of arrangements for children has been introduced;
  (iv) PD7A, para 2.1 actively discourages the naming of a co-respondent where the petition is based on the respondent's adultery;
  (v)   the costs rules now require that any party wishing to be heard on costs must serve written notice to this effect on every other party at least two days before the hearing (r 7.21(2)) (Chapters 4, 7, and 8);
(d) nullity proceedings which are undefended are to be heard without an oral hearing (Chapter 15);
(e) a statement of arrangements for children, a statement of information to support an application for a consent order dealing with financial provision, and a statement in support of an application for a non-molestation order and/or an occupation order under Part IV, Family Law Act 1996 are to be verified by a statement of truth (Chapters 8, 30, 36, and 37);
(f) provisions found in Part 33 relating to enforcement of orders made in family proceedings now enable a party seeking to enforce an order to apply for 'such method of enforcement as the court may consider appropriate' (r 33.3(2)), thus abolishing the need to select a method of enforcement which may not be appropriate (Chapter 33).

New terminology

There are important changes in terminology to be noted: **1.07**

(a) decrees of divorce, nullity, and judicial separation are now known collectively as 'matrimonial orders', although the old terminology is retained at various points in the rules;
(b) a decree of dissolution of a civil partnership becomes a 'civil partnership order';
(c) ancillary relief is now known as 'an application for a financial order/remedy';
(d) petitioner becomes 'applicant' (it should be noted, however, that there is no change to the wording of the Matrimonial Causes Act 1973 where the term 'petitioner' is found and the application form to seek a decree of divorce or judicial separation is still known as a 'petition');
(e) leave to apply is now to be referred to as 'permission to apply'.

The Family Law Protocol

All practitioners need to be aware of the third edition of the Family Law Protocol, published **1.08** by the Law Society in 2010. This offers invaluable guidance on dealing with commonly encountered family law problems together with good practical advice to avoid pitfalls. It also produces a range of guidance and online resources and contains a list of helpful contacts and addresses including Relate and National Family Mediation.

1.09 Copies of the Protocol are available from Law Society Publishing—tel: 0870 850 1422; email: lawsociety@prolog.uk.com; or online at <http://www.lawsociety.org.uk/bookshop>. Reference is made to the Protocol throughout the book and some of its guidance is quoted at length.

Solicitors Regulation Authority Handbook

1.10 From 6 October 2011 major changes to law firm regulation came into effect with the introduction of the Solicitors Regulation Authority Handbook ('SRA Handbook') and 'outcomes-focused regulation'. While it is not the purpose of this book to discuss the regulations in details, reference will be made to relevant provisions in this chapter.

1.11 Copies of the SRA Handbook and *A Practical Guide to Outcomes-focused Regulation* (to accompany the Handbook) are available from Law Society Publishing (see para 1.09).

B   THE FIRST INTERVIEW

1.12 The first interview with any client is extremely important. Family cases are no exception. It is important to recognize that, as far as the interviewee or prospective client is concerned, the first interview may have two distinct purposes:

(a) as a fact-finding exercise to obtain information from the solicitor as to the steps open to the interviewee to resolve the family problems he or she is experiencing. In addition, the interviewee will be assessing whether he or she feels comfortable with the solicitor and would have confidence in the solicitor if instructed to act on the interviewee's behalf;

or

(b) to give formal instructions to act on the interviewee's behalf. This assumes that the interviewee already has a clear idea of the outcome he or she is seeking.

1.13 In any event, prior to the first interview, it is important to obtain sufficient information from the interviewee to check that there is no conflict of interest with an existing client.

1.14 Chapter 3 of the SRA Handbook deals with the handling of conflict of interests. Solicitors are required to have in place systems that enable them to identify and deal with potential conflicts.

1.15 Solicitors are reminded that conflict of interests can arise between:

(a) the solicitor and current clients ('own conflict of interest'); and

(b) two or more current clients ('client conflict').

Solicitors are prohibited from acting for a client where there is a conflict, or a significant risk of conflict, between the solicitor and a client.

If there is a conflict, or a significant risk of a conflict, between two or more current clients, the solicitor may not act for all or both of them unless the matter falls within the scope of the limited exceptions set out in Outcome 3.6 of the Handbook. This states **1.16**

> where there is a client conflict and the clients have a substantially common interest in relation to a matter or a particular aspect of it you (that is, the solicitor) only act if:
>
> (a) you have explained the relevant issues and risks to the clients and you have a reasonable belief that they understand those issues and risks;
> (b) all the clients have given informed consent in writing to you acting;
> (c) you are satisfied that it is reasonable for you to act for all the clients and that it is in their best interests; and
> (d) you are satisfied that the benefits to the clients of you doing so outweigh the risks.

It is submitted that in family cases the nature of the conflict of interests are such that it would never be appropriate to act for both parties.

It is also necessary to give details in writing to the interviewee of the name and status of the person who is to conduct the interview. Information should be given as to whether the interview is free or available at a fixed cost or that the cost of the interview is at a reduced cost of £X per hour pro rata. The interviewee should also be given details of who to contact if the interviewee has a complaint. **1.17**

Interviewees should sign and date the document and both the interviewee and the solicitor should keep a copy of the signed document. **1.18**

After the interview, the solicitor should keep a note of the interview with the signed document. This should be filed and kept for record purposes. **1.19**

How should the solicitor approach the first interview?

The first interview provides the opportunity for the solicitor to gain the interviewee's confidence and to equip himself with much information which he will need if he is to act for the interviewee in the future. **1.20**

For example, the interviewee may have separated from her husband and not be receiving maintenance. It is for the solicitor to ascertain the interviewee's views, not only on her immediate problem, but also on related matters so that he may advise her properly. Where the interviewee has a maintenance problem, for instance, there are a number of different ways in which she might secure a maintenance order against her husband, one involving the issue of a divorce petition. In order to decide on the appropriate course of action, the solicitor needs to know whether the interviewee envisages getting divorced and whether there is any basis on which she can file a petition. **1.21**

It is important to recognize that the interviewee may be undecided about what she wants for the future and, in most cases, there is no harm in putting the options to her, explaining the implications of those options and suggesting that she go away and think things over for a few days, arranging another interview for the following week. **1.22**

1.23 Often the interviewee will be in a very distressed state at the first interview and care should be taken not to pressure her into a particular course of action. It must be remembered that when a marriage gets into difficulties, divorce is not the only option!

C   MATTERS TO BE COVERED WHEN TAKING INSTRUCTIONS

The basics

1.24 The guidance set out below assumes that the interviewee has decided to instruct you and will now be referred to as the client.

1.25 At the outset, the solicitor must comply with the requirements of the Money Laundering Regulations 2007 by asking the client to produce two forms of appropriate identification, one at least of which must confirm the client's home address. The client's passport and utility bills for the home address will usually suffice for these purposes.

Name, address, and telephone number

1.26 The client's full name and address must, of course, always be noted, as should her telephone number at home and at work so that she can be contacted urgently if necessary. It may also be necessary to note an address to which letters to a client may be sent, without the risk of the other party becoming aware of the contents.

1.27 Every firm has its own system for noting routine information of this type, often on the file itself, on a printed label attached to it, or on a computerized system. The client should be reminded to keep her solicitor up to date with any changes of address. If her address does change, the new address should be noted and the old address deleted from the file so that there is no danger of letters and documents being sent to the wrong address.

1.28 If the case is one where the client's address is to be kept secret from her spouse, cohabitant, or civil partner (eg because it is feared that otherwise there will be violence), this should be noted clearly on the file with the address so that no member of the solicitor's firm inadvertently discloses the address.

1.29 Clear instructions should be taken from the client as to leaving messages on an answerphone. Detailed messages may be accessed by the other party to the marriage, putting the client at considerable risk—the same may apply to the use of email.

The Community Legal Service scheme—Legal Help

1.30 The solicitor should find out whether the client is eligible for Legal Help. Before the client decides to accept Legal Help, the solicitor should clearly explain the Legal Services Commission's statutory charge (see Chapter 2). If the client decides to accept such advice, she must sign a form called Controlled Work 1.

1.31 The full details of the Community Legal Service scheme and the means of assessment are set out in Chapter 2. Note that there is an obligation on the solicitor to advise his client as to her eligibility for public funding generally whether or not his firm undertakes this work.

Where a client is financially eligible for public funding and certain types of work are contemplated, it may be necessary first to refer the client to mediation to determine whether the issue may be resolved by that process. **1.32**

Aspects of client care

Chapter 1 of the SRA Handbook sets out the requirements as to client care. **1.33**

The chapter explains how a solicitor is to provide a proper standard of service and client care which takes into account the individual needs and circumstances of each client. Outcomes and ways in which the solicitor may demonstrate that outcomes have been achieved are also set out. **1.34**

Once formal instructions are received, the solicitor should write two letters to the client: the retainer letter, confirming that the solicitor is to act for the client, and the very important client care letter. **1.35**

For the family law client, the client care letter should deal with the following: **1.36**

Level of service

Throughout the transaction the solicitor is required to provide an 'appropriate level of service' to the client. **1.37**

To achieve this initially the client care letter should: **1.38**

(a) provide in writing a summary of matters discussed clearly identifying the client's objectives in relation to the work to be undertaken;
(b) provide a summary of the options considered;
(c) summarize the specific advice given to date and the basis upon which that advice is given. It is sensible at this stage to:
    (i) give a clear indication of how long the proposed steps are likely to take. Be pessimistic as opposed to optimistic. Avoid unrealistic expectations on the part of the client;
    (ii) set out what steps the client needs to take. For example, it may be necessary for the client to compile relevant documents (especially in relation to financial matters or to obtain details of the value of his or her pension from the pension provider). Where appropriate, it should be emphasized that steps cannot be taken without further instructions or information from the client;
(d) record the specific instructions received from the client. This record must include an agreement as to the precise nature and scope of the work to be undertaken including, for example, the type and frequency of communication between solicitor and client.
    This means that one client may require the solicitor to provide regular written progress reports. Conversely, the client may wish to provide initial instructions and then hear no more until a particular point in the transaction has been reached. It goes without saying that the precise instructions will affect the costs estimate;
(e) clearly indicate what the solicitor will not be dealing with. For example, if tax is not the solicitor's area of expertise, the solicitor should let the client know that he will not be dealing with any tax matters in the work being undertaken but give help as to where

reliable advice might be obtained. Where, for instance, an accountant has already been instructed by the client, it is sensible to have a copy of the accountant's retainer letter to ensure that all aspects of the client's case are being dealt with.

Who is dealing with the case?

1.39 Chapter 1 of the SRA Handbook makes it clear that in providing services to the client it is important that the client is informed in the client care letter of the name and status of the person(s) dealing with the matter and the name and status of the person responsible for its overall supervision.

1.40 The need to indicate clearly the status of the person within the law firm who is to have conduct of the case was highlighted by the Court of Appeal in *Pilbrow* v *Pearless de Rougement* [1999] 2 FLR 139. Here the court held that there was total non-performance of the contract, thus relieving the client of the obligation to pay the bill of costs, where the client had asked to see a solicitor to discuss some personal problems and after the conclusion of the case learned that the person who had carried out the work on his behalf was not a solicitor.

Proceeds of Crime Act 2002 and the Money Laundering Regulations 2007

1.41 These are discussed in more detail at paras 1.51 ff but the solicitor should warn the client in the client care letter of the solicitor's duties under the 2002 Act and Regulations and the duties of disclosure of the client's financial affairs to the other party.

Costs

1.42 Chapter 1 of the SRA Handbook makes it clear that both in the client care letter and when appropriate as the matter progresses, the client should receive the best possible information about the likely overall cost of the case.

1.43 Further, the client must be informed of her right to challenge or complain about a bill and the circumstances in which she may be liable to pay interest on an unpaid bill.

1.44 As a minimum, at the outset the client must be informed of the overall likely cost of carrying out her instructions including a breakdown of fees, VAT, and disbursements and whether the charging rate is likely to be increased and, if so, when. The client is entitled to know the time likely to be spent in dealing with a matter, if time is a factor in the calculation of the fees.

1.45 Where it is not practicable to give a precise figure for the likely cost, an explanation of why this is the case should be given to the client together with as realistic an estimate as possible. This is especially relevant to a client involved in proceedings for financial provision where it is generally impossible to predict at the beginning of the case whether the matter may be dealt with by agreement or only by a full court hearing at a later stage.

1.46 The client care letter should reflect the discussions between the solicitor and the client as to whether the likely outcome will justify the expense or risk involved including, if relevant, the risk of having to bear an opponent's costs. Although the general principle in family cases is that each party is to be responsible for his or her own costs with limited opportunities to recover costs from the other party (the significance of this is explained in Chapters 8 and 30), costs may nevertheless be awarded against a party for litigation misconduct. However, even where such an award is made the client needs to understand that, in reality, such costs may never be recovered from the liable party.

In any event, the build-up of costs needs to be monitored throughout the proceedings, with the client being regularly updated, to ensure that, in proceedings relating to financial provision, the costs remain proportionate to the value of the claim: *Piglowska* v *Piglowski* [1999] 1 WLR 1360. **1.47**

Funding the case

Discussions as to how the case is to be funded should be confirmed in the client care letter. While it is important to remember that a solicitor is not permitted to enter into a conditional fee arrangement in family cases, sources of funding may include: **1.48**

(a) public funding—where this is likely to be available, the client must be informed that a contribution from the client to the cost of public funding may be required and that the statutory charge may apply at the conclusion of the proceedings (Chapter 2);
(b) insurance schemes;
(c) assistance through a trade union or employer arrangement.

Complaints handling

The client care letter must also inform the client of the right to complain and the procedure for making a complaint. (Chapter 1 of the SRA Handbook makes it clear that complaints must be dealt with promptly, fairly, openly, and effectively.) In addition to details about the law firm's internal complaints procedure, the client must be informed of the right to complain to the Legal Ombudsman, the time frame for doing so, and contact details for the Legal Ombudsman (email: enquiries@legalombudsman.org.uk; tel: 0300 555 0333). **1.49**

It is sensible to ensure that the client receives all the above information in duplicate with a request to retain one copy and return the other copy to the solicitor, duly signed and dated. **1.50**

Money laundering

Introduction

The Proceeds of Crime Act 2002 ('PCA 2002'; as amended by the Proceeds of Crime Act 2002 (Business in the Regulated Sector and Supervisory Authorities) Order 2007) has been the source of considerable uncertainty since it came into force in 2003. Fortunately, the Court of Appeal decision in *Bowman* v *Fells* [2005] EWCA Civ 226 sought to clarify many of these difficulties. **1.51**

The Act and the accompanying Regulations are complex and are largely beyond the scope of this book. What follows is intended to be a basic guide to those parts of PCA 2002 and the Regulations which are most likely to affect a lawyer working in family law. Additional guidance may be found in the Law Society Anti-Money Laundering Practice Note of 29 October 2009. It can be accessed at <http://www.lawsociety.org.uk/antimoneylaundering>. **1.52**

Becoming involved in 'an arrangement'—s 328, PCA 2002

Bowman confirms that the criminal offence of 'becoming involved in an arrangement' involving money laundering under s 328, PCA 2002 does not apply to the conduct of litigation in **1.53** general or to the settling of a dispute in a litigious context. Legal advisers involved in such work therefore no longer need to make an 'authorized disclosure' under PCA 2002 to the National Crime Agency.

1.54 The decision did not, however, consider 'transactional work' involving work outside a litigious setting, such as conveyancing. Section 328 continues to apply to such work although, following *Bowman*, it is now clear that common law legal professional privilege has not been overridden by PCA 2002, as had previously been thought. Useful and detailed guidance provided by the Law Society in relation to transactional work and s 328 in the light of *Bowman* can be found at <http://www.lawsociety.org.uk/productsandservices/antimoneylaundering. page>.

The duty to disclose in the 'regulated sector'—s 330, PCA 2002

1.55 Section 330, PCA 2002 continues to apply to those working in the 'regulated sector' and makes it a criminal offence to fail to disclose where the 'professional legal adviser' has knowledge or a suspicion of money laundering or reasonable grounds for suspicion. The 'regulated sector' is defined in para 2(2) of the Money Laundering Regulations 2003 (SI 2003/3075), as amended and updated by the Money Laundering Regulations 2007 (SI 2007/2157). The generally accepted view is that family solicitors and legal executives do fall within this category.

1.56 Section 330(6) provides a defence to a failure to disclose where the information came to the professional legal adviser in 'privileged circumstances'. It is important to note, however, that this exemption does not apply where the 'intention' behind the communication of the information is to 'further a criminal purpose' (s 330(11)). The 'purpose' can be that of either the client or a third party. This can place the legal adviser in a difficult position in knowing whether to protect the client's confidentiality and legal professional privilege or risk prosecution if the s 330(6) defence is not available. Amendments to s 330, PCA 2002 confirm that a legal adviser can speak openly with the firm's nominated money laundering officer without affecting the client's right to confidentiality. The Law Society guidance, referred to earlier, again provides a useful step-by-step guide in these circumstances. Guidance is also provided by the Law Society's Professional Ethics money laundering helpline (tel: 0870 606 2577).

Further general information

1.57 Having considered the client care matters above, the solicitor may find it helpful to use a checklist during the interview to ensure that all relevant matters are covered. The following checklist is merely a suggestion. No doubt the solicitor will need to add other matters which he regularly wishes to cover with clients.

Mediation and the Family Mediators Association have established centres nationwide and they operate under a common Code of Practice. These services provide a private and informal venue for separating couples to discuss issues relating to their children, property, and the divorce itself in the presence of a trained mediator or mediators.

Increasing use is now being made of the mediation process and therefore it is important for **1.67** the solicitor to understand how the process works and to be prepared to support it and recommend it where appropriate. In many instances it will now be necessary to refer a client to mediation and to establish the outcome of that process before a solicitor may make an application for public funding on his client's behalf or commence proceedings in court. The detailed provisions relating to mediation and public funding are discussed in Chapter 2. How mediation works in practice is explained in Chapter 3.

D   NEXT STEPS—TAKING ACTION ON THE CLIENT'S BEHALF

Possible courses of action

The matters covered in the checklist at para 1.57 above are fairly general. This general infor- **1.68** mation should enable the solicitor to decide what course of action might be appropriate. The following table is designed as a reminder of the principal remedies available for most of the problems commonly encountered in family work.

	Principal remedies available
Client's problem	*Remedies to be considered*
Wants divorce	Divorce proceedings (though bear in mind that very occasionally, nullity proceedings may be more appropriate)
Wants dissolution of civil partnership	Dissolution order under Civil Partnership Act 2004 ('CPA 2004')
Maintenance problems—self (married client or civil partner)	Welfare benefits Maintenance pending suit and periodical payments under Matrimonial Causes Act 1973 ('MCA 1973') if intending to seek divorce/nullity If not intending to seek divorce/nullity, consider judicial separation (same financial provision as divorce) *or* application to family proceedings court (formerly magistrates' court) under ss 2, 6, and 7, Domestic Proceedings and Magistrates' Courts Act 1978 ('DPMCA 1978') *or* s 27, MCA 1973 (county court) Please note that the DPMCA 1978 is not now included in this book because of its infrequent use in practice. Orders for civil partners under sch 5, CPA 2004
Maintenance problems—self (unmarried client or same-sex partnership where the partnership is not registered)	Welfare benefits. No court procedure for obtaining maintenance for self

(Continued)

	Principal remedies available
Client's problem	*Remedies to be considered*
Maintenance problems—children (married client)	Welfare benefits can include a sum in respect of children. Maintenance for child can be ordered in the course of divorce/ nullity/judicial separation proceedings or under ss 2, 6, and 7, DPMCA 1978 as it can for a spouse *alternatively* maintenance can be ordered in proceedings under sch 1, CA 1989 However, the effect of the Child Support Act 1991 ('CSA 1991') must be taken into account
Maintenance problems—children (unmarried client)	Welfare benefits. Maintenance orders can be made under sch 1, CA 1989 but most child maintenance is likely to be dealt with under the CSA 1991
Dispute over property (married client or civil partner)	Financial order under MCA 1973 if divorce/nullity being sought Section 17, Married Women's Property Act 1882 if divorce not intended Lump sums can be ordered under DPMCA 1978 and s 27, MCA 1973 For civil partner, if dissolution or nullity being sought, financial relief available under sch 5, CPA 2004 Schedule 6, CPA 2004 if dissolution or nullity not applied for Where children are involved, sch 1, CA 1989 enables the court to make periodical payments (in limited circumstances), lump sum orders and property adjustment orders
Dispute over property (unmarried client or same-sex partnership where the partnership is not registered)	Normal principles of contract, tort, trusts, and property law apply, eg proceedings under ss 14 and 15, Trusts of Land and Appointment of Trustees Act 1996 for order for sale of real property, proceedings for declaration of trusts, etc. Where children are involved, sch 1, CA 1989 enables the court to make periodical payments (in limited circumstances), lump sum orders, and property adjustment orders
Residence and contact (married client)	Can be resolved in course of divorce/nullity/judicial separation proceedings If financial order sought under DPMCA 1978, the court can exercise its powers under CA 1989 with respect to child *alternatively* CA 1989 *or* wardship (if unusual features, eg international element)
Residence and contact (civil partner) can be resolved in course of proceedings for dissolution, nullity, or separation order	If financial order sought under DPMCA 1978, the court can exercise its powers under CA 1989 with respect to child *alternatively* CA 1989 *or* wardship (if unusual features, eg international element)
Residence and contact (unmarried client or same-sex partnership not registered)	CA 1989 *or* wardship (if unusual features, eg international element)
Violence or molestation (married client or registered civil partner)	Non-molestation order under Part IV, Family Law Act 1996 ('FLA 1996')

(Continued)

| | *Principal remedies available* |
Client's problem	*Remedies to be considered*
Difficulties over occupation of home (married client or civil partner)	Occupation order under Part IV, FLA 1996
Difficulties over occupation of home (unmarried client or same-sex partnership not registered)	Occupation order under Part IV, FLA 1996

Note:
If there is agreement between the parties, the solicitor should not overlook the possibility of a separation/maintenance agreement as an alternative to proceedings. There is no reason why an unmarried couple should not make a binding agreement on matters such as maintenance, property, etc in just the same way as a married couple.

Preparing to commence proceedings

In some cases, the solicitor will have to commence proceedings without delay, for example where the client has been subjected to serious physical violence and requires a court order to prevent repetition. **1.69**

The solicitor should ensure that he takes down all further information from the client that he needs to start proceedings. One good way of ensuring that nothing is missed is for the solicitor to have in front of him at the interview a precedent of each of the documents required to commence proceedings. He then works through each document asking the client for the particulars required to draft each paragraph. So, for example, if divorce proceedings are to be commenced, the solicitor will work through a blank form of divorce petition and a blank statement of arrangements for children form with the client. **1.70**

The solicitor should also bear in mind what additional documents he will need to file when commencing proceedings so that he can ask the client for any required documents that may be in her possession. For example, in divorce cases the client must be asked for a copy of the marriage certificate. **1.71**

Negotiating

Although it is sometimes necessary to issue proceedings without delay (eg in a domestic violence case), it will not always be desirable to launch proceedings straight away. It is often a good idea to attempt to negotiate a settlement of disputed matters without proceedings first. Obviously some remedies, such as divorce or a dissolution order, can only be obtained through the courts. With other matters, such as maintenance, the solicitor may be open to criticism if he embarks upon proceedings without first seeing whether agreement can be reached. In the first place, the proceedings may place added strain on relations between the parties concerned and reduce the chances of settling things amicably. Secondly, the party commencing proceedings may find herself responsible for extra costs (of her own and possibly of the other side) as a result of her precipitate action. **1.72**

The solicitor is free to write to the other party, or to his solicitor if he is already represented, asking whether he is willing to consent to a particular course (eg to give his consent to a divorce decree based on two years' separation and consent) or to make his own proposals **1.73** for settlement (eg an offer of maintenance) or indeed, asking the other party to desist from a particular course of action (eg from harassing the client).

1.74   However, if the other party is not represented, it is good practice to suggest in the letter that he might like to seek independent legal advice, particularly if the issue is complex. A copy of the letter should be enclosed, to be passed on to any solicitor who is instructed.

1.75   The Family Law Protocol reminds solicitors of the need to communicate in a non-confrontational and constructive manner. The letter should be clear and free of jargon. Consideration should be given to the impact of any correspondence on its reader. It is sensible to send to the client a draft letter for checking before it goes to the other party. Indeed, copies of all but routine letters should be sent to the client for approval unless there is a specific reason not to do so: see Chapter 1 of the Protocol.

Letter writing

1.76   Apart from writing to the other party or his solicitor, there may also be other letters to be written. For example, if the client is being pressed for payment of gas and electricity bills or for mortgage instalments it can be helpful for the solicitor to write a letter on her behalf explaining the family difficulties and asking for forbearance until matters are resolved. There may be witnesses to contact (eg in support of an application for a non-molestation order) and reports to request (eg a medical report in relation to a child of the family who is disabled, for the purposes of considering the arrangements for the children under s 41, MCA 1973).

Advising the client

1.77   The client will no doubt be anxious about matters and have her own questions to ask. In particular she will want to know what is going to happen next. In addition to giving the client the information she requests, the solicitor should be alive to other matters of which the client will not be aware but of which she should be informed or warned. For example, a client seeking a divorce should be warned of the dangers of prolonged cohabitation in the run-up to the divorce (eg more than six months' cohabitation after discovering the respondent's adultery will debar the petitioner from relying on the adultery).

1.78   The client will be understandably nervous at the first interview and may forget to ask all the questions that she had intended to raise with the solicitor. The solicitor should therefore be prepared to clarify matters and to respond to questions at the second and subsequent interviews when the client feels more at ease.

Miscellaneous other steps

1.79   Depending on the nature of the case, the solicitor will find there are a number of other jobs to do. For example:

   (a)   If the family home is in the sole name of the other spouse or civil partner, he should register a Class F land charge or a notice to protect the client's home rights under Part IV, FLA 1996.
   (b)   He should consider whether to serve a notice of severance of joint tenancy if the parties are joint owners of the family home.

(c) He should consider the question of the client's will.

(d) He should advise on the availability of welfare benefits.

All these topics are covered in later chapters.

Other issues that may require consideration at an early stage include the need to consider **1.80** whether there is a risk that a child may be removed from England and Wales without the knowledge or consent of the client and the need to limit access to credit cards. The solicitor should also give relevant leaflets to the client as an aide-memoire, for example leaflets on public funding and court procedure.

Preparing a statement and proof of evidence

After the first interview with the client, it is customary to prepare a statement setting out all **1.81** the relevant information she has provided about the case in a readable manner for future reference.

Should it ever become necessary for the client to give oral evidence in court, it is good practice **1.82** to prepare a proof of evidence from the client's statement, setting out the matters that are relevant to the particular proceedings in a convenient order. The proof can then be used as an aide-memoire when taking the client through her evidence-in-chief.

Keeping the client up to date

It may be a statement of the obvious but clients become frustrated if they are not kept up to **1.83** date; a short telephone call or letter setting out the up-to-date position may avoid difficulties. Regular diary and file checks should ensure that cases are not forgotten.

E   KEY DOCUMENTS

The Family Law Protocol, 3rd edn (The Law Society, 2010) (<http://www.lawsocietyshop.org.uk>) **1.84**
Solicitors Regulation Authority Handbook (SRA, 2011)
Solicitors and Money Laundering: A Compliance Handbook, 3rd edn (The Law Society, 2009)
  (<http://www.lawsocietyshop.org.uk>)

2

PUBLIC FUNDING FOR FAMILY PROCEEDINGS

A   INTRODUCTION

General

This chapter explains the funding available through the Legal Services Commission (LSC)   **2.01**
to assist a client on a low income in meeting the costs of instructing a solicitor in family
proceedings.

2.02 Such funding is now known as 'public funding' following major changes set out in the Access to Justice Act 1999 ('AJA 1999'). It was previously known as 'legal aid' and this is the term still used by many clients.

2.03 As will become apparent in the chapter, there are various forms of public funding available to the family law client—which is most appropriate will depend upon the client's instructions and the circumstances of the case. In any event, it is essential to remember that the client must be financially eligible for public funding and, in many circumstances, must convince the LSC that the case is worth pursuing.

2.04 In addition, as is explained at paras 2.85 ff below, public funding is rarely free but should be seen as a loan to the client to be clawed back by the LSC from assets retained or won as a result of the proceedings.

2.05 This is a complex area but at the end of the chapter you should have an understanding of the public funding scheme and, most importantly, be able to identify the circumstances in which the client would be eligible for such help.

Specific changes affecting family practitioners

2.06 In recent years there have been three major developments of specific relevance to family practitioners. First, greater emphasis is now placed on the role of mediation as a means of resolving disputes. This means that as a precondition to obtaining various forms of public funding the client must take part in mediation and will only be eligible for such funding of services from a solicitor if mediation is found to be unsuitable or impractical.

2.07 Secondly, even where a solicitor does not undertake publicly funded family work, he must advise clients of their rights to public funding (where appropriate). Furthermore, if a client suffers financially as a result of the solicitor's failure to advise him as to the availability of public funding (eg as may be the case where he has to meet legal fees from his own pocket that could have been met from public funding), the solicitor may find himself sued successfully for negligence by the client.

2.08 Thirdly, in most family cases payment to solicitors is now by a system of fixed fees under a contractual arrangement with the LSC.

B   THE FUTURE OF PUBLIC FUNDING

2.09 As indicated in Chapter 1, public funding faces an uncertain future.

2.10 At the time of writing, the Legal Aid, Sentencing and Punishment of Offenders Bill contains provisions which would significantly affect the availability of public funding for the family law client. Essentially, it is proposed that public funding be removed from all family law cases except:

   (a)   those where domestic violence is involved: the term 'domestic violence' for these purposes includes not only physical abuse, but mental and sexual abuse, neglect, maltreatment, and exploitation; or

(b) where the application is for a prohibited steps order or a specific issue order under s 8, Children Act 1989 ('CA 1989') in circumstances where there is a risk that the child will be abducted.

This chapter sets out the essential elements of the *present* public funding scheme.

C   THE FUNDING CODE

The AJA 1999 established the statutory framework for the current public funding scheme but detailed guidance on the forms of funding available and the criteria for eligibility are found in regulations made under the Act and in the Funding Code.   **2.11**

The Code is divided into two Parts. Part 1 sets down the various levels of funding: the more complex the case becomes, the higher the level of funding that will be appropriate. The levels of funding which are relevant to family law cases are: **2.12**

(a)   Level 1—Legal Help
(b)   Level 2—Family Help (Lower)
(c)   Level 3—Family Help (Higher)
(d)   Level 4—Legal Representation

Funding is also available for Family Mediation. This is explained in Chapter 3, paras 3.36 ff.

The levels of funding are designed to recognize the different stages involved in dealing with family disputes. Initially a client may simply require advice but in more complex cases, court proceedings of some type may be necessary and a different level of service and method of funding would then become available.   **2.13**

The Funding Code defines 'family proceedings' as proceedings which arise out of family relationships, including proceedings in which the welfare of the children is determined (other than judicial review proceedings). Family proceedings are set out in the LSC's Category Definitions 2010 as referred to in the 2010 Standard Civil and Criminal Contracts. The information is updated from time to time and can be accessed by visiting the website at <http://www.legalservices.gov.uk>.   **2.14**

'Family proceedings' include all proceedings under any one or more of the following: **2.15**

(a)   Matrimonial Causes Act 1973 ('MCA 1973');
(b)   Inheritance (Provision for Family and Dependants) Act 1975;
(c)   Adoption Act 1976;
(d)   Domestic Proceedings and Magistrates' Courts Act 1978;
(e)   Part III, Matrimonial and Family Proceedings Act 1984;
(f)   Parts I to V, CA 1989;
(g)   Part IV, Family Law Act 1996 ('FLA 1996');
(h)   Adoption and Children Act 2002;
(i)   Civil Partnership Act 2004;
(j)   the inherent jurisdiction of the High Court in relation to children.

2.16 Other proceedings or matters also include, by way of example only:

(a) proceedings to enforce an order made in family proceedings;

(b) proceedings under s 20, Child Support Act 1995;

(c) proceedings under s 14, Trusts of Land and Appointment of Trustees Act 1996 where the proceedings are family proceedings;

(d) application for a parental order under the Human Fertilisation and Embryology Act 1990; and

(e) application to the court to change the name of a child.

2.17 Part II contains procedures for obtaining funding including granting, amending, and withdrawing certificates.

D   THE BASIC STRUCTURE OF THE SCHEME

Legal Help—Level 1

Generally

2.18 Legal Help does not cover the issue and conduct of court proceedings nor does it cover advocacy at court. Further, it does not cover the provision of mediation, although it does allow the solicitor to advise the client on issues arising from mediation. It essentially covers (under s 4(2), AJA 1999) 'advice and assistance' to the new client.

2.19 The following are examples of the type of work that can be handled under Legal Help:

(a) The solicitor can consider the client's problem and advise him on its legal implications and as to any practical steps that can be taken to sort it out.

Example The solicitor is consulted by a woman who complains that her husband is persistently violent towards her. Under the scheme, the solicitor advises her that she is entitled to the protection of an order from the family proceedings court under Part IV, FLA 1996, that proceedings will have to commence in the family proceedings court, and that meanwhile she is not obliged to continue to live with her husband if she would prefer not to do so. He might also suggest that she could take refuge temporarily in a hostel for victims of violence if there is one locally. He cannot commence the proceedings under the scheme. Before doing this he would have to make an application for funding under the Private Family Law Representation Scheme (PFLRS) introduced with effect from 9 May 2011.

(b) The solicitor can enter into correspondence on the client's behalf.

Example The solicitor is consulted by a woman who has got into difficulties with the mortgage instalments and other household bills relating to the family home since her husband left her. He advises her to write to the mortgage lender and other creditors explaining what has happened and asking them not to take any action yet as she will be seeking maintenance from her husband and therefore expects that her problems will be short-lived. He helps her with the terms of the letters. If necessary he could write the letters for her.

(c) The solicitor can negotiate for the client.

Example The solicitor writes on behalf of the woman in the previous example to her husband asking what proposals he makes for her maintenance and that of the children. If the husband makes an offer he can advise the wife as to whether she should accept it, and in the event of the husband's proposals being unacceptable, he can negotiate with the husband (or his solicitor if he has one) to obtain a better offer. If an agreement is reached he can advise the wife as to the best method of putting it into practice. If no agreement is reached he can advise the wife as to her rights to take the matter to court but he cannot commence proceedings for her until he has obtained funding for representation on her behalf.

(d) The solicitor can draft documents for the client.

   Example The solicitor drafts a separation or maintenance agreement on behalf of the client where earlier negotiations have achieved a level of agreement between the parties.

(e) The solicitor can make an application for further funding on the client's behalf if it is clear to him that he will need to take steps which are not covered by Legal Help.

Obtaining advice under Legal Help

To be eligible for Legal Help, the client must be financially eligible (see para 2.22) and satisfy the **2.20** sufficient benefit test. In essence, this means that Legal Help will not be provided where the client is seeking advice on a non-legal matter or where the claim is clearly hopeless from the outset.

Once the solicitor is satisfied that the client is financially eligible by completion of the **2.21** Controlled Work 1 Form, he may carry out work for which he will receive a fixed amount by way of fees. The current fee is £96. (Current fees and hourly rates are found in the Standard Contract Payment Annex available at <http://www.legalservices.gov.uk/civil/2010_civil_contract.asp>.)

Financial eligibility for Legal Help

A client is automatically entitled to Legal Help if in receipt of income support, income-based **2.22** jobseeker's allowance, or of a disposable income not exceeding £733 per month (the client's gross monthly income must not exceed £2,657 per month unless he or she has more than four children). No contribution is payable. However, Legal Help is not available if the client's disposable capital exceeds £8,000: reg 15, Community Legal Service (Financial) Regulations 2000, as amended. It is disposable income and capital that matter and they are calculated as follows:

(a) To arrive at disposable capital and income the solicitor starts by ascertaining:
   (i) all the client's capital resources at the date of assessment (including money owed to the client); *and*
   (ii) the total income from all sources (apart from housing benefit and some benefits and allowances, most commonly disability living allowance) which the client has received or may reasonably expect to receive in respect of the seven days up to and including the date of assessment.
   Note that the value of the subject matter of the claim in respect of which the client is seeking Legal Help is always left out of account.
(b) To these capital and income figures, the general rule is that the solicitor must add the capital and income resources of the client's partner. (Unmarried couples living together are to be treated for financial assessment purposes as spouses and civil partners.) However, this will not normally be necessary in the case of a client seeking advice about his family

problems, because the regulations provide that the partner's resources shall be left out of account if the spouse has a contrary interest in the matter in respect of which advice and assistance is being sought.

(c)　Various items should be left out of account or deducted when calculating disposable capital and income as follows:

Capital

(i)　the value of the main or only dwelling-house where the client resides. However, since 1 June 1996, the capital value of a client's home, which had previously been exempt in every case, may be taken into account in certain circumstances, as follows:

    (aa)　the capital value of the property (ie, market value less any amount outstanding on any mortgage debt or charge and cost of sale) will be taken into account insofar as it exceeds £100,000;

    (bb)　the capital amount allowed in respect of a mortgage debt or charge over the property cannot exceed £100,000;

    (cc)　where a client has a number of properties, the total amount of mortgage debt to be allowed for all the client's properties cannot exceed £100,000.

Example The applicant has a home worth £215,000. The mortgage is £200,000.

Value of home	£215,000
Deduct mortgage up to maximum allowable	£100,000
Deduct exemption allowance	£100,000
Deduct cost of sale (3% of the value)	£6,450
Amount to be taken into account in assessing financial eligibility	£8,550

In this case the client would be ineligible for public funding **unless the house formed the subject matter of the dispute** because the capital to be taken into account exceeds the £8,000 limit.

(ii)　the value of his household furniture and effects, personal clothing, and tools or implements of his trade;

(iii)　the subject matter of the problem with regard to which the client seeks Legal Help.

Income

(i)　income tax on the client's income;

(ii)　National Insurance contributions for the seven days up to and including the date of assessment;

(iii)　a reasonable sum for maintenance payments for an 'adequate' period for a former partner, a child, or a relative who is not a member of the client's household. The maintenance payments must be bona fide, and could include, for example, simply paying a former partner's household bills or mortgage;

(iv)　if the client and his partner are living together (regardless of whether her resources are aggregated with his or left out of account) a fixed allowance is made to take account of the maintenance of the partner and any children living with the client. The allowances from April 2011 are £167.53 per month for a partner and £271.58

per month for a child aged 15 or under. For a child aged 16 or over the allowance is similarly £271.58 per month;

(v) certain allowances can be made for rent or mortgage payments, including payments for any endowment policy linked to the mortgage arrangements. For a single applicant with no dependants, the maximum allowances for housing costs is £545 per month;

(vi) where the applicant and/or partner is receiving a wage or salary, there is a fixed allowance of £45 per month for *each* wage earner in the assessment to cover employment-related expenses such as travel costs. Actual childcare costs can also be deducted, but only to the extent that they are incurred because of work.

A Keycard (No 47) is to be found at the end of this chapter. It sets out the basic conditions as to financial eligibility.

Sufficient benefit test

In addition to the financial eligibility criteria being met for Legal Help, the solicitor must be satisfied that there is 'sufficient benefit' to the client, having regard to the circumstances of the matter, including the personal circumstances of the client, to justify the work being carried out. **2.23**

Legal Help in proceedings for divorce or dissolution of a civil partnership

In view of the fact that a certificate for Legal Representation is not usually available for proceedings for divorce or dissolution of a civil partnership, Legal Help has a particular importance in undefended cases. Provided the client is financially eligible, the solicitor will be able to give the client considerable help with the decree proceedings under the scheme. The following are examples of the work that a solicitor may be expected to carry out under the scheme: **2.24**

(a) preliminary advice on the basis for divorce or dissolution of a civil partnership, the effects of a decree or dissolution order on status, the future arrangements for the children, the income and assets of the family, and matters relating to housing and the family home;

(b) drafting the petition and the statement of the arrangements for the children and where necessary typing and writing the entries on the forms;

(c) advising on filing the documents at court and the consequential procedure, including service if no acknowledgment of service is filed;

(d) advising a client when the acknowledgment of service is received as to the procedure for applying for directions for trial, and typing or writing the entries on the form of affidavit of evidence;

(e) advising as to any attendance before the district judge to explain the arrangements for the children and advising on the court's powers under the CA 1989;

(f) advising on obtaining the decree absolute, in the case of divorce proceedings, or the final order where a civil partnership is to be dissolved.

It is important to remember that Legal Help cannot be used to cover the cost of attendance by the solicitor at court. **2.25**

2.26 Boiled down to essentials, this means that the solicitor can give the client all the help he could reasonably expect in relation to his divorce or dissolution of a civil partnership except that he cannot accompany him to court on any children's appointment that might be requested by the district judge (pursuant to s 41, MCA 1973) unless he agrees to do so as a favour without payment.

2.27 The current fee payable to the solicitor when advising a petitioner in a stand-alone divorce case is £162.

'Exceptional' cases

2.28 The solicitor will receive the same fixed fee irrespective of the amount of work he carries out on the client's behalf, unless the case becomes 'exceptional'. Generally this will happen when the solicitor's costs, if calculated on an hourly charging rate basis would amount to three times the fixed fee. For example, child abduction and domestic abuse cases could result in the case becoming 'exceptional' in which case the solicitor is paid by the LSC on an hourly charging rate basis.

Family Help (Lower)—Level 2

Scope of the funding

2.29 This form of funding enables the solicitor to provide ongoing assistance with a 'serious dispute'. This means the case must be one which, if unresolved, would result in family proceedings.

2.30 In regard to both children and finance, Family Help (Lower) covers all work up to the issue of proceedings (except proceedings to obtain a consent order dealing with financial provision where Family Help (Lower) can be used to cover the cost of such an application to court).

Application form

2.31 As with Legal Help, Family Help (Lower) is classified as Controlled Work and can be carried out under the law firm's contract. It does not require authorization by the LSC. Provided the client satisfies the financial eligibility criteria and the cost benefit test, the solicitor will tick the box at the bottom of page 5 of the original Controlled Work 1 Form to confirm that the criteria for Level 2 funding are met. This will be when all work which can be carried out under Legal Help has been completed and the matter can only progress by negotiation or other work under Family Help (Lower).

Financial eligibility

2.32 This is the same as for Legal Help (see para 2.22).

Cost benefit test

2.33 Family Help (Lower) may be provided only where the case satisfies the cost benefit test, that is, where the benefits to be gained for the client justify the likely cost such that a reasonable private paying client would be prepared to proceed and instruct a solicitor using his own funds.

Payment

2.34 The solicitor receives a fixed fee for the work carried out together with a settlement fee if the case is finally resolved at the Family Help (Lower) level.

The amount of the fixed fee and the settlement fee depends on the type of case: **2.35**

(a) for a children case: the fixed fee is £221.00
                            the settlement fee is £132.00
(b) for a finance case: the fixed fee is £231.00
                            the settlement fee is £139.00

In appropriate cases, all the above fees can be claimed together with the Legal Help—Level 1 fee of £96.00.

'Exceptional cases'

As with Legal Help (see para 2.28), the case can become 'exceptional' once the fees threshold **2.36** is reached.

Funding by way of a Certificate—Levels 3 and 4

A funding certificate authorizes the conduct of litigation and the provision of advocacy and **2.37** representation. It includes steps preliminary and incidental to proceedings, and steps to settle or avoid proceedings.

Private Family Law Representation Scheme

As indicated at para 2.19, this scheme came into effect on 9 May 2011. **2.38**

Under the scheme, there are two levels of funding: **2.39**

(a) Family Help (Higher)—Level 3; and
(b) Legal Representation—Level 4.

Family Help (Higher)—Level 3

This form of funding covers all work up to the preparation for a final hearing. In proceedings **2.40** for financial provision, for example, it would include making the application, preparation of documents (including disclosure), and attendance at the First Appointment and the Financial Dispute Resolution hearing.

Legal Representation—Level 4

This covers all work from preparation for a final hearing up to and including all work to con- **2.41** clude a case after a final hearing, for example implementing the terms of an order and advice on the merits of an appeal against a final order.

Application form

In order to obtain funding for Level 3 or Level 4 work, an application form (CLS APP3) must **2.42** be completed and submitted to the LSC.

The client will be required to attend an appointment with a mediator unless one of the excep- **2.43** tions applies. (The relationship between public funding and mediation is discussed at para

2.58.) Form CLS APP3 must therefore be accompanied by Form CLS APP7, certifying that the case is not suitable for mediation or that mediation has failed.

Financial eligibility

2.44 The financial eligibility conditions are the same as for other forms of public funding (see para 2.22). When public funding takes the form of a certificate for Family Help (Higher) or Legal Representation, in specified family proceedings a contribution may be payable for income and/or capital by the assisted person. 'Specified family proceedings' means family proceedings other than proceedings under Part IV, CA 1989 or Part IV, FLA 1996.

2.45 For Legal Representation the contribution regime is that an applicant with a disposable income of £316 or below per month and capital not exceeding £8,000 will not be required to pay any contributions. Where the applicant's monthly disposable income exceeds £316 but is less than £733, the contribution to be paid will be assessed as follows:

Band	Monthly disposable income	Monthly contribution
A	£316–465	¼ of income in excess of £311
B	£466–616	£38.50 + ⅓ of income in excess of £465
C	£617–733	£88.85 + ½ of income in excess of £616

2.46 The LSC determines whether the client is financially eligible for funding of this type by assessing the means form completed by the client and submitted with Form CLS APP3 and Form CLS APP7.

2.47 The Funding Code makes it clear that funding may be refused if alternative funding is available to the client. In particular where the dispute relates to finance and property the LSC has a discretion to refuse funding where it considers that the client should use savings or obtain a loan to cover the cost of the proceedings.

Merits test

2.48 **Merits Test, Stage 1—Prospects of success** On the application form (see para 2.42) the case must be put into one of three brackets describing the prospects of success:
(a) average or above;
(b) borderline or unclear (where the prospects are not poor but it is not possible to say that they are better than 50 per cent because of different disputes of fact, law, or expert evidence); or
(c) poor.

2.49 If prospects are poor or unclear, representation will be refused.

2.50 If prospects of success are borderline, representation will be refused unless there is a significant wider public interest or the case is of overwhelming interest to the client (eg because the case is about life, liberty, or a roof over his or her head).

2.51 **Stage 2—Cost–benefit/successful outcome** Representation will also be refused unless the likely benefits justify the likely cost, such that a reasonable private paying client would be prepared to take or defend the proceedings in all the circumstances (para 20.18 of the Funding Code).

Payment

Essentially, PFLRS introduces a fixed fee payable to the solicitor with separate standard fees **2.52** payable for advocacy under the Family Advocacy Scheme, also introduced on 9 May 2011.

The provisions of the Family Advocacy Scheme are set out in the Community Legal Service **2.53** Funding (Amendment No 2) Order 2010 (SI 2010/1109) and in section 7 of the 2010 Standard Contract Specification.

The fee payable varies according to whether the hearing is interim or final but, in any event, covers **2.54** all preparation for a hearing, travel to and waiting at court, and time spent on advocacy itself.

E FUNDING FOR MEDIATION

Mediation and funding for mediation are discussed in Chapter 3. **2.55**

This Part considers the funding of mediation from the solicitor's point of view. **2.56**

The importance of mediation

The LSC expects every effort to be made to resolve disputes through mediation rather than **2.57** through contested court proceedings.

Hence, before public funding is granted by the LSC for Level 3 or Level 4 work, a client will **2.58** have to attend an assessment meeting with a mediator to determine whether the use of mediation would be appropriate to resolve the family dispute.

Exemptions to the requirement to attend an assessment meeting

Attendance at an assessment meeting is not required where: **2.59**

(a) family proceedings are already in existence and the client is a respondent who has been notified of a court date which is within eight weeks of the date of notification;
(b) the client has a reasonable fear of domestic abuse from a partner or former partner (see Chapter 3, para 3.34);
(c) the client or other party cannot see a mediator (eg because bail conditions prevent contact with a spouse, former spouse, civil partner, or cohabitant, or where the client is in custody or in hospital or lives more than two hours away from the mediator);
(d) the other party is unwilling to attend mediation;
(e) emergency representation is required (eg to obtain a non-molestation order under Part IV, FLA 1996 or in a child abduction case).

Funding the assessment meeting and the mediation process

The mediator will determine whether the client is financially eligible for public funding for **2.60** mediation and whether mediation is suitable for the dispute.

2.61 The conditions for financial eligibility are set out in para 2.22. The form of public funding available to cover the cost of mediation is known as Family Mediation and is a separate level of service under the Funding Code.

2.62 For those eligible for such public funding, the cost of all mediation sessions will be covered. The mediator will agree a separate payment with the privately paying client.

The referral process

2.63 The Funding Code recognizes that the client may arrange his own meeting with a mediator but recommends that the solicitor takes responsibility for referring the client to a mediation service for a meeting with a mediator.

2.64 The mediation service is required to offer the client a meeting within 15 working days from the date they were first contacted. The service must inform the client that the meeting can take place either separately from or together with the other party. It is for the client to decide which type of meeting would be preferable.

2.65 Where both the client and the other party attend the same meeting with the mediator, the mediator is required to carry out domestic abuse screening interviews separately with each party before the meeting takes place.

The role of the solicitor

2.66 As is explained in Chapter 3, the solicitor continues to have a role in the mediation process either by acting as an advocate or observer in the mediation room or, and more usually, by advising the client on the implications of any proposed settlement achieved through the mediation process.

2.67 The cost of this may be funded through Family Help—Level 2, if the client is financially eligible.

Mediation and the statutory charge

2.68 A settlement achieved through the mediation process is exempt from the statutory charge.

F   EMERGENCY REPRESENTATION

Introduction

2.69 Emergency Representation is only available as part of Legal Representation and does not apply to any other level of service.

2.70 While a certificate for Emergency Representation should reduce the inevitable delay associated with the grant of a certificate for Legal Representation, it will be necessary not only to satisfy the standard criteria for Legal Representation, as set out above, but also to demonstrate that the certificate should be granted as a matter of urgency because it appears to be in the interests of justice to do so.

'Urgency and interests of justice': an explanation

The Funding Code states that: 2.71

> The application may be urgent if any of the following circumstances apply and there is insuf-
> ficient time for an application for a substantive certificate to be made and determined:
> (a) Representation (or other urgent work for which Legal Representation would be needed) is
>   justified in injunction or other emergency proceedings (for example for an injunction under
>   s. 37, MCA 1973 or for an order under Part IV of the Family Law Act 1996);
> (b) Representation (or other urgent work for which Legal Representation would be needed) is
>   justified in relation to an imminent hearing in existing proceedings; or
> (c) a limitation period is about to expire.

As far as 'in the interests of justice' is concerned, Emergency Representation is unlikely to be   2.72
granted unless

> the likely delay as a result of the failure to grant emergency representation will mean that
> either:
> (a) there will be a risk to the life, liberty or physical safety of the client or his or her family or the
>   roof over their heads; or
> (b) the delay will cause a significant risk of miscarriage of justice, or unreasonable hardship to
>   the client, or irretrievable problems in handling the case and, in either case, there are no
>   other appropriate options to deal with the risk.

G   THE ISSUE OF A CERTIFICATE FOR FAMILY HELP (HIGHER) AND/OR LEGAL REPRESENTATION

This is dealt with in Section 4 of Part 2 of the Funding Code.   2.73

Mechanics of issue where no contribution is payable

Where there is no contribution to be paid by the applicant or the application relates to special   2.74
CA 1989 proceedings, a certificate will be issued forthwith. The actual certificate will be sent
to the solicitor with a copy sent to the applicant.

Mechanics of issue where a contribution is payable

If the applicant is liable to pay a contribution, he will first be notified of the terms on which   2.75
a certificate is offered to him (ie, what his maximum and actual contributions would be,
the terms for payment, etc). If these terms are acceptable to the applicant, he must, within
14 days of being notified:

(a) complete the acceptance form (and a form of undertaking to pay the contribution
    required) and return them as directed; *and*

(b) if the contribution or any part of it is required to be paid before the certificate is issued (as is normally the case, for example, where a contribution from capital is required), make that payment accordingly.

When he has complied with these requirements, a certificate will be issued and sent to the solicitor and a copy will be sent to the applicant.

H   NOTIFICATION OF ISSUE OF A CERTIFICATE

2.76 If proceedings to which the client is a party have already been commenced by the time a certificate is granted, the solicitor should:

(a) serve all other parties to the proceedings straight away with notice of the issue of the certificate; *and*

(b) if any other person later becomes a party, serve him with a notice of issue also; *and*

(c) send the original certificate to the appropriate court office.

If the client is not yet a party to proceedings when he is granted the certificate, the solicitor's duty to notify other parties and to provide the court with a copy of the certificate arises as soon as his client does become a party to proceedings. It is not necessary (except in relation to appeals) to notify the other parties of any limitation on the certificate. The provisions as to notification and filing apply to both emergency and full certificates. The solicitor is also required to notify other parties of any amendment (other than financial) of the certificate, of the extension of an emergency certificate or its replacement with a full certificate, and of the revocation or discharge of a certificate. In addition he must send a copy of the amendment, notice of discharge, etc to the court.

I   THE EFFECT OF THE ISSUE OF A CERTIFICATE FOR FAMILY HELP (HIGHER) AND/OR LEGAL REPRESENTATION

Generally

2.77 Once a certificate is issued, the assisted person's legal expenses will be met from the Fund. Generally speaking, this means that he can be represented by a solicitor (and, if necessary, counsel) and given all such assistance as is usually given by a solicitor or counsel in the steps preliminary and incidental to any proceedings or in arriving at or giving effect to a compromise to avoid or bring to an end any proceedings.

2.78 The exact nature of what can be done for the client under this particular certificate depends on two things:

(a) the terms of the certificate itself;

(b) the provisions of the Funding Code which require special authorization to be obtained before certain steps are taken.

The terms of the particular certificate

The certificate will state what proceedings it covers and will set out any condition or limitation imposed by the LSC.   **2.79**

The solicitor should always be careful to note the terms of the certificate and particularly so in family cases where it is routine practice to impose a number of special restrictions on the scope of the certificate. Thus, for example, certificates issued in relation to *financial provision* in connection with divorce, nullity, judicial separation, or dissolution of a civil partnership are normally expressed to cover an application for all forms of financial provision except an order for the avoidance of a disposition or for variation. All financial provision certificates are limited, in the first instance, to the securing of one substantive order only. This means that the application for financial provision should be all-embracing and the order made should be as comprehensive as possible, since the wording of the certificate does not allow the client to have more than one 'bite at the cherry'.   **2.80**

The duty to act reasonably

The solicitor must remember that a certificate does not give him a free hand in relation to his client's case. Apart from the need to obtain specific authority before taking certain steps: **2.81**

(a) He must act with reasonable competence and expedition. If he wastes costs by not doing so, these costs may be reduced or even disallowed completely on assessment.
(b) He has an obligation to report to the LSC if he has reason to believe his client has required his case to be conducted unreasonably so as to incur unjustifiable expense to the Fund or has required unreasonably that the case be continued (eg when he has been competently advised that the only proper course is to settle on the terms offered and he refuses to do so). The LSC has power to discharge the certificate in cases such as this.

Solicitor not to accept payment other than from the Fund

Once a certificate has been granted, the solicitor must not take any payment from the client himself (or indeed from any other person) in respect of the client's legal costs. He must look only to the Fund for payment.   **2.82**

Costs in funded cases

The fact that one of the parties to the proceedings is publicly funded can affect the court's order for costs as follows: **2.83**

(a) Order for costs *against* a funded party: the court can order a funded party to pay the costs of the proceedings. Because of provisions contained in Section 21 of the Practice Direction About Costs (supplementing Parts 43–48 Civil Procedure Rules 1998) (now incorporated into the Family Procedure Rules 2010 (PD28A—Costs)), unsuccessful publicly funded family clients are subject to the same costs risks as privately paying family clients who become involved in litigation.

(b) Order for costs *in favour* of a funded party: the solicitor must not fall into the trap of think-
ing that, because his client is publicly funded there is no need to pursue an order for costs
with any great enthusiasm. First, he has a duty to the Fund to apply for costs in the same
situations as he would apply for costs on behalf of a private client. Secondly, he clearly has
a duty to his client to seek costs in order to reduce the effect of the statutory charge (see
below). The more of the client's costs that are paid by the other party to the proceedings,
the less the deficit to the Fund that the client will have to make up from his own pocket.

J   REIMBURSEMENT OF THE FUND AND THE STATUTORY CHARGE

Reimbursement of the Fund

2.84   Where public funding has been granted, the Fund will assume responsibility for paying the
legal costs of the funded person. The LSC will pay to the solicitor the costs approved following scrutiny of the solicitor's claim for costs by the court carrying out a detailed assessment.
Where the solicitor's claim for costs does not exceed £2,500 the LSC carries out the assessment
to check that the claim is reasonable. The LSC has a statutory duty to recoup for the Fund
whatever this costs. It does so as follows:

(a) From any payment made in the funded person's favour under any order or agreement for
costs with respect to the proceedings (s 11(4), AJA 1999).

Example 1   Mr and Mrs Robinson are divorced. Mrs Robinson is granted a certificate to be
heard in proceedings for financial provision. It is agreed that Mr Robinson will transfer
the house to Mrs Robinson and, in return, she will forgo all her remaining claims for
financial provision. Mr Robinson agrees to pay Mrs Robinson's legal costs in relation to
financial provision matters. The agreement is embodied in a consent order.
   Mr Robinson will pay an amount equal to his wife's legal costs to her solicitor who will
pay it on to the LSC. The LSC will use it to reimburse the Fund partially or wholly for the
cost of Mrs Robinson's public funding.

(b) If the costs recovered for the funded person are not enough to cover the cost of funding
the case, the LSC will also put the funded person's contribution towards the costs.

Example 2   Mr Robinson pays £700 of his wife's costs by agreement. Her costs are in fact
£1,000. The Fund therefore remains out of pocket in relation to Mrs Robinson's legal
costs. Mrs Robinson has paid a contribution towards her funding. This contribution is
retained by the LSC and put towards discharging the deficit.
   Note that if the total contribution made by an assisted person to the Fund is more than is
required to make up the deficit in the Fund the balance will be repaid to the funded person.

Example 3   Mrs Robinson's contribution towards her funding was £400. The deficit to the
Fund after Mr Robinson has paid his share of her costs is only £300. She is entitled to have
£100 repaid to her by the LSC in respect of her unused contribution.

(c) If the deficit to the Fund has still not been made good, subject to certain exceptions, the
LSC will look to any money or property recovered or preserved for the assisted person in

the proceedings to which the certificate relates to recoup the balance (s 10(7), AJA 1999). This is commonly called the LSC's statutory charge and is more fully described below.

Example 4 In proceedings for financial provision after divorce, Mr Sidebottom is ordered to pay his wife the sum of £50,000. Mrs Sidebottom is funded with a nil contribution. No order for costs is obtained against Mr Sidebottom. At the end of the proceedings, therefore, the Fund is out of pocket to the tune of the entire cost of Mrs Sidebottom's public funding, £8,000. £8,000 of Mrs Sidebottom's lump sum will therefore be applied in discharging the cost of her funding.

If the total of (a), (b), and (c) above still does not make good the Fund's deficit, the Fund will bear the balance of the deficit. If there is no order for costs, no property recovered or preserved, and no contribution paid by the assisted person, the Fund will, therefore, bear the entire costs of the proceedings.

K   SOLICITOR TO RECEIVE MONEYS DUE TO FUNDED PARTY

Regulation 18(1) of the Community Legal Service (Costs) Regulations 2000 (SI 2000/774) **2.85** requires that all moneys payable to a funded party by virtue of any agreement or order made in connection with the action, cause, or matter to which his certificate relates (whether made before or after proceedings were taken) must be paid to the funded party's solicitor. This includes sums due in respect of costs as well as sums due in settlement of the funded party's claim.

The solicitor is obliged forthwith: **2.86**

(a) to pay all moneys received by him by virtue of such an order or agreement to the LSC (though note the power of the LSC where the Fund would be sufficiently safeguarded by payment of a lesser sum to direct that only part of the moneys received by the solicitor should be paid to the LSC and the balance to the funded party himself); *and*

(b) to inform the LSC of any property recovered or preserved for the funded party and to send him a copy of the court order or agreement (reg 20(1)(a) and (b), ibid).

The purpose of reg 20 is, of course, to ensure that the question of reimbursement of the Fund can be dealt with before the funded party has a chance to spend any part of the money that may be required to reimburse the Fund.

L   THE STATUTORY CHARGE UNDER S 10(7), ACCESS TO JUSTICE ACT 1999

Generally

As we saw in para 2.84 above, the effect of s 10(7), AJA 1999 is that if the amount of costs **2.87** recovered for a funded party together with his own contribution towards his funding is not sufficient to cover the cost to the Fund of his legal expenses, the LSC can look to any property recovered or preserved for him in the proceedings to recoup the balance. Section 10(7) gives the LSC a first charge for the benefit of the Fund on any such property—this is commonly referred to as 'the statutory charge'.

2.88 The solicitor is obliged to notify the LSC of any property recovered or preserved and it is the LSC which then decides whether or not a charge arises. The considerations to be borne in mind in reaching such a decision are set out below. In practice the question will normally arise in connection with proceedings for financial provision following divorce, nullity, judicial separation, or proceedings to annul or dissolve a civil partnership and the remainder of Part L is therefore written with this in mind.

'Property' includes money

2.89 Although s 10(7) refers only to property, this does include money. Therefore the statutory charge can attach, for example, to a lump sum received by the funded party just as it can to a house recovered or preserved for him.

2.90 Further, the wording of s 10(7) makes it clear that the charge will arise whether the property was recovered or preserved by the funded party for himself or any other person.

Has any property been recovered or preserved?

2.91 This can be a very vexed question. The leading case is *Hanlon* v *Law Society* [1981] AC 124, [1980] 2 All ER 199. In this case the House of Lords held that property is 'recovered or preserved' if it was *in issue* in the proceedings and either the funded party made a successful claim in respect of it (in which case the property is recovered for him or for any other person) or successfully defended a claim in respect of it (in which case the property is preserved for him or for any other person). The fact that the court has a general discretion over all property and money belonging to the parties in proceedings for financial provision following a decree of divorce, nullity, judicial separation, or proceedings to annul or dissolve a civil partnership can be disregarded. What is important is whether the particular item that may be the subject of the charge has actually been in issue or not and this is a matter to be decided on the facts of each case by looking at the pleadings, the evidence, and the court's judgment or order.

Example (The facts of the *Hanlon* case.) The husband and wife were married in 1957. In 1963 a family home was purchased in the husband's name with a mortgage. Both parties contributed equally in money and work to the family and the marriage. The wife obtained funding to petition for divorce (this was in 1971 when such funding was still generally available for divorce), to apply for the equivalent of occupation and non-molestation orders and to take proceedings under s 17, Married Women's Property Act 1882. She made a small contribution towards her funding.

The wife was granted a divorce, given custody of the two children of the marriage, and granted a property adjustment order requiring the husband to transfer the family home to the wife absolutely. The equity in the home was worth about £10,000.

The wife's costs were £8,025 (£925 for the divorce and applications for the occupation and non-molestation orders, £1,150 for the equivalent of residence and contact applications, and £5,950 in respect of the property adjustment order). The husband was funded also and no order for costs was made against him. Clearly, therefore, the Fund was substantially out of pocket in relation to the wife's legal costs and the question arose as to whether the Law Society (now replaced by the LSC) had a charge on the house in respect of the wife's costs.

The House of Lords held that the whole house had been in issue. It was pointed out that, if the husband had agreed at the outset that the wife had at least a half share in the house, then only the husband's half share would have been in issue (and therefore recovered by the wife and subject to the charge). However, in this case in the original pleadings each spouse was claiming the transfer of the other's interest in the house to themselves and this position was never altered by agreement or concession that the wife was entitled to at least part of the house. Thus the entire house was property recovered by the wife (the husband's interest) or preserved for her (her own interest) and therefore the whole house was subject to the charge.

The *Hanlon* case concerned an issue over *title* to property. The case of *Curling* v *Law Society* [1985] 1 All ER 705, carries the charge a stage further. In that case the family home was bought in joint names. The husband petitioned for divorce and sought a property adjustment order in respect of the home. The wife was publicly funded. She sought an order that the house be sold. The husband did not dispute the wife's entitlement to a half share in the property (so her title to half the house was never in issue). However, he did wish to remain in the house and negotiations led to an agreement whereby the husband would buy out the wife's interest in the house. The wife argued that as the title to the house had never been in issue in the proceedings, the sum she received for her interest in it could not be regarded as property recovered or preserved and therefore could not be the subject of the statutory charge. The Court of Appeal held that the ownership of the house could not be looked at in isolation when considering whether the wife had recovered or preserved property in the proceedings. The fact that a party recovers in the proceedings that to which he is already entitled in law does not by itself prevent the attachment of the statutory charge. The property has been in issue in the proceedings if the party's right to realize his share in the property is contested just as much as if his rights of ownership had been disputed. Thus, because the parties had been in dispute over whether the house should be sold forthwith enabling the wife to realize her share in it, her interest in the property had been in issue and the sum paid by the husband in respect of her interest was therefore property recovered by her and subject to the charge.

The statutory charge will apply to a property co-owned by two unmarried parents where an   **2.92**
action has been compromised so that a sale of the property is postponed in order that the
mother and child may live there, since the mother gains exclusive possession of the property
over a long period and thus has the benefit of a 'property right' within the meaning of s 10(7),
AJA 1999 despite the fact that the parties' respective beneficial interests were never in issue
(*Parkes* v *Legal Aid Board* [1997] 1 FLR 77).

In summary, and subject to para 2.96 below, the following propositions are put forward on   **2.93**
the question of whether property has been recovered or preserved:

(a) Property can have been recovered or preserved only if it has been 'in issue' in the proceedings (*Hanlon*).
(b) Whether particular property has been in issue must be determined as a matter of fact from the statements, the evidence, the court's judgment/order (*Hanlon*), and, as in *Curling*, the correspondence.
(c) If there has been an argument over ownership of the property, the property has been in issue (*Hanlon*).

(d) However, it is necessary to look specifically to see whether the whole title to the property was in dispute or just part. If the person defending the claim conceded from the outset that part of the property belonged to the claimant as a matter of prior entitlement, the title to that part of the property was never in issue (*Hanlon*).

(e) Although there has been no dispute over ownership of the property in question, that property can still have been in issue if there has been conflict over whether a party should be allowed to realize his share in the property within a certain time or not (*Curling*). Thus, if the parties agree that the matrimonial home is owned, say, equally, but one party seeks a prompt sale and equal division of the proceeds (or a lump sum payment from the other party in respect of his interest) and the other seeks an order which provides for a postponement of the sale, the property has been in issue.

(f) Again, where there is no dispute over the beneficial entitlements in the property but a dispute over possession, the charge may apply if, as a result of the court order, one party preserves the right to remain in possession of the property and resists an application by the co-owner for an order for the immediate sale of the property (see *Parkes*, para 2.92 above).

Recovery or preservation for any other person

2.94 The wording of s 10(7), AJA 1999 is wider than the previous provisions contained in s 16, Legal Aid Act 1988 and now the charge will arise whether the property is recovered or preserved for the funded party or *for any other person* (such as a child of the family).

Charge applicable to property recovered/preserved as a result of a compromise

2.95 Section 10(7) makes it quite clear that property recovered or preserved includes any property paid to the funded party by way of a compromise arrived at to avoid or bring to an end the proceedings as well as property recovered or preserved as a result of a judgment or order of the court. Thus, the funded party cannot avoid the charge by settling a claim out of court even if he does so before proceedings are commenced.

Exemptions from the charge

2.96 Regulation 44 of the Community Legal Service (Financial) Regulations 2000, as amended, provides that certain property is exempt from the charge. The exemptions include:

(a) periodical payments of maintenance for a spouse or former spouse, civil partner or former civil partner, or child;

(b) sums ordered to be paid under Part IV, FLA 1996 (eg a compensating lump sum on transfer of a tenancy);

(c) pension sharing orders;

(d) where the family home is recovered or preserved or a lump sum received and the only funding received by the client has been Legal Help or Family Help (Lower) (however, in some circumstances the charge will apply, but only to costs above the exceptional case threshold (see para 2.28 above));

(e) a lump sum received by way of a pension attachment order or attachment of death-in-service benefits (under ss 25B and 25C, MCA 1973 (reg 24, Community Legal Service (Financial) (Amendment) Regulations 2007 (SI 2007/906)).

What costs form part of the charge?

It is the outstanding cost of 'the proceedings' that is the subject of the charge. This means **2.97** that the charge is not confined to the cost of the part of the proceedings which resulted in the recovery or preservation of the property in question. It extends to the cost of the whole cause, action, or matter covered by the certificate (*Hanlon v Law Society*; see paras 2.91 and 2.93). The facts of the *Hanlon* case illustrate this principle. There, the wife's certificate covered the divorce suit and the proceedings for financial provision arising out of it in relation to property adjustment and the equivalent of residence and contact orders in relation to the children. The charge on the family home therefore comprised not only the cost of the property adjustment proceedings themselves but also the cost of the divorce proceedings and the equivalent of residence and contact proceedings.

Where the client first receives Legal Help and Family Help (Lower) but then goes on to obtain **2.98** a certificate for Family Help (Higher) and Legal Representation in relation to the same proceedings, the cost of the Legal Help and Family Help (Lower) will be added to the overall costs incurred by the funded party in determining the cost to the Fund of the case.

Example Mrs Wetherby petitions for divorce. Her solicitor advises her under the Legal Help scheme in relation to the divorce and drafts the petition. She then obtains a certificate for proceedings for financial provision. She has a nil contribution. Her husband is ordered to pay her £70,000 in the proceedings for financial provision but no order for costs is obtained against him in relation to those proceedings or the divorce itself. The LSC will look to Mrs Wetherby's lump sum for payment of all the funding provided.

Settlement obtained through the mediation process

It is important to remember that where property is recovered or preserved by a settlement **2.99** achieved through the use of mediation and funded by a certificate for Family Mediation the costs incurred are exempt from the statutory charge.

Similarly, costs incurred by a solicitor in putting the terms of a mediated settlement into **2.100** effect, for example by drafting and obtaining a consent order, are also exempt from the statutory charge *provided* that such work is funded by Family Help.

Enforcement of the charge

The charge vests in the LSC which is entitled to enforce it in just the same way as anyone **2.101** else entitled to a charge. If the charge affects land, it can be registered as a charge against the property (reg 52, Community Legal Service (Financial) Regulations 2000). If both cash and a dwelling-house are recovered or preserved, the charge will first be enforced against the cash and the balance only against the property.

2.102   The LSC can agree to postpone the charge in appropriate cases. In practice this means that, if the charge relates to the funded party's home, the LSC will accept a registered charge over the property. Thus, the funded party will not be forced to sell the property straight away to repay the LSC's charge. However, when he does decide to sell of his own accord he will be bound to repay the LSC out of the proceeds of the sale and the LSC may agree to transfer the charge to his next house. If the funded party wishes the charge to be transferred in this way, application should be made to the LSC.

2.103   Where the only property recovered or preserved is a sum of money which by order of the court or under the terms of the agreement reached is to be used for the purpose of purchasing a home for himself or his dependants, then the LSC may agree to defer enforcing its charge over the sum if:

   (a)   the funded party wishes to purchase a home in accordance with the order or agreement, and agrees that the new home will itself be subject to a charge; *and*
   (b)   the LSC is satisfied that the new property will provide adequate security for the amount in question.

2.104   Where the charge is postponed for any reason interest will accrue to be paid when the charge is redeemed. The calculation of interest is explained at para 2.106.

2.105   In order to try to ensure that the LSC will agree to the postponement of the charge the order for ancillary relief should contain the following provision:

> And it is certified for the purposes of reg 52(1)(a) of the Community Legal Service (Financial) Regulations 2000 [that the lump sum of £x has been ordered to be paid to enable the petitioner/ respondent to purchase a home for himself/herself (or his/her dependants)] [that the property (address) has been preserved/recovered for the petitioner/respondent for use as a home for him- self/herself (or his/her dependants)].

Calculation of interest

2.106   Interest runs from the date on which the charge is registered and will continue until the outstanding costs are paid: reg 53, Community Legal Services (Financial) Regulations 2000.

2.107   The annual interest rate is 8 per cent. Simple, not compound, interest will accrue.

Waiver of the charge

2.108   In certain circumstances the charge may be waived. Where relevant property has been recov- ered or preserved under the Legal Help or Family Help (Lower) schemes, the solicitor may apply to the LSC to waive the charge in part or in full if enforcement would cause to the client grave hardship or distress or would be unreasonably difficult to enforce because of the nature of the property.

2.109   In determining whether the client would suffer grave hardship, the LSC will consider the personal and financial circumstances of that party compared to the value of the property recovered or preserved. Further, the LSC will consider the nature of the property recovered or preserved. Where, for example, the funded party is in receipt of income support and the item of property recovered is an essential item, such as a cooker, the LSC may agree to waive the charge. Similarly where the item is of genuine sentimental value (eg a wedding ring) and enforcement would cause grave distress, the LSC may agree to waive the charge.

As for the problem of enforcement, this may arise because the property is outside the jurisdic- **2.110** tion and leads to waiver of the charge. However, where enforcement is likely to be inconvenient or slow this will not in itself justify waiver.

M DUTY TO MAKE THE CLIENT FULLY AWARE OF THE POTENTIAL IMPACT OF THE CHARGE

It is imperative that the client is made fully aware of the existence of the statutory charge **2.111** and of its potential impact in his particular case. The client cannot be reminded of the charge too frequently. It is suggested that, at minimum, the solicitor should explain it to him comprehensively:

(a) in the client care letter;
(b) when the client receives Legal Help; *and*
(c) when application is made for a Family Help (Higher) certificate; *and*
(d) when any settlement is being considered which would produce cash or property which might be affected by the charge.

Clients have a knack, as all solicitors are aware, of forgetting that unpalatable advice has ever been given. It is not unknown, therefore, for a client to turn round when, for example, a large part of his lump sum is eaten up by the statutory charge and say that he was never warned that this would happen. It is important that, in addition to explaining the charge to the client orally and giving the short explanatory leaflet provided by the LSC, the solicitor writes to the client giving a further brief explanation so that there is a record of his advice. Such advice should be updated in writing as the case progresses and costs increase.

Solicitors should be aware that, in order for the client to appreciate properly how the charge **2.112** may affect him in practice, he must be given an estimate of the likely costs of the proceedings in just the same way as a privately paying client. For example, in financial provision proceedings the client must be informed of the costs estimates lodged at the court at each hearing (see Chapter 30).

N MINIMIZING THE EFFECTS OF THE CHARGE

The obvious way to *avoid* the impact of the charge completely is to achieve a settlement **2.113** through mediation, as explained earlier.

Failing that, the most effective way to *minimize* the charge is to seek to recover the client's costs **2.114** from the other party to the proceedings. However, this is rarely possible in family cases.

2.115   As we have seen earlier, the charge will only attach to property that has been in issue. Another way in which to minimize the charge is therefore for the issues involved in the proceedings to be narrowed down as far as possible *at the outset*.

Example Mrs Hill consults her solicitor with a view to a divorce. The family home is in joint names and Mrs Hill thinks that her husband accepts that she is entitled to half of it. She wishes to claim the entire house (in which there is an equity of about £80,000) in proceedings for financial provision. She then proposes to sell the house and buy a smaller property. The solicitor writes to Mr Hill's solicitor asking him to confirm that Mr Hill accepts his wife's entitlement to half the house and that the dispute between the parties is only over the other half share. Mr Hill's solicitor confirms this. Mrs Hill files a divorce petition making a comprehensive claim for financial relief and property adjustment and, in particular, claiming the transfer of the house to her. She obtains funding for proceedings for financial provision. The district judge ultimately orders that the house should be transferred to her.

Mrs Hill's half of the house was never in issue. The statutory charge in relation to her costs will only attach to the half share in the house which she has recovered from her husband in the proceedings. Mrs Hill does sell the house immediately after the proceedings are over. The LSC is not prepared to take a charge over her new house—it requires immediate repayment of its charge. Broadly speaking, her debt to the LSC will be as follows:

Equity in house	£80,000
Property recovered by Mrs Hill in the proceedings is therefore half this figure	£40,000
Property subject to the charge	£40,000

Mrs Hill's costs amounted to £8,000. She paid no contribution to her funding and no order for costs was obtained against Mr Hill. The Fund is therefore out of pocket by £8,000. Mrs Hill will be required to pay £8,000 to the LSC in respect of her costs.

Note that, had the whole of the house been in issue in the proceedings, Mrs Hill would have recovered half of it and preserved the remainder. Thus the entire equity of £80,000 would have been open to the charge.

If possible, not only the correspondence but also the statements and other documents filed should make clear what property is and what property is not in dispute.

O   OTHER METHODS OF FUNDING

2.116   There are occasions where a client is not eligible for public funding but has few resources, if any, to pay the solicitor on a private paying basis.

2.117   Since a solicitor is not allowed to enter into a conditional fee agreement with a client in respect of family proceedings, other methods of funding have to be considered. These may include, for example:

(a) an application to the court for an order for maintenance pending suit under s 22, MCA 1973 (see Chapter 29);

(b) a 'Sears Tooth' agreement. Held to be valid in *Sears Tooth (A Firm)* v *Payne Hicks Beach (A Firm) and Others* [1997] 2 FLR 116, this is an arrangement whereby solicitors can take a charge on any property recovered or preserved in the proceedings usually by an assignment of rights under an order dealing with property or capital (but no maintenance);

(c) a personal loan from a bank or credit card company;

(d) a loan from relatives or friends—it is important in these circumstances to show that there is an enforceable contract for repayment of the loan, otherwise the court may not be prepared to take it into account when quantifying liabilities; or

(e) funding under an insurance scheme.

P   CHAPTER SUMMARY

1. Where the client has limited financial resources, public funding may be available to enable the client to pay for legal advice and representation.   **2.118**

2. There are various 'levels of service' which a publicly funded client may receive. These are:
    (a) Legal Help—Level 1;
    (b) Family Help (Lower)—Level 2;
    (c) Family Help (higher)—Level 3;
    (d) Legal Representation—Level 4.

3. Except in public law children cases, the client will need to satisfy the means and merits tests to be eligible for public funding.

4. Public funding is not free—a contribution may be payable as the case progresses.

5. Public funding is often described as 'a loan not a gift' and will need to be repaid from property or capital 'recovered or preserved'. This is known as 'the statutory charge'.

6. Where public funding is not available, other methods of funding should be considered.

Q   KEY DOCUMENTS

Legal Aid Handbook 2011/12 (Legal Action Group, 2011)   **2.119**

R   USEFUL WEBSITES

LSC's website <http://www.legalservices.gov.uk/aboutus/publications.asp#subscribe>   **2.120**
Civil and family eligibility guidance is found in vols 2 and 3 of the LSC Manual which may be downloaded at <http://www.legalservices.gov.uk/civil/civil_legal_aid_eligibility.asp>
The Funding Code may be downloaded at <http://www.legalservices.gov.uk/civil/what_cases_do_we_fund.asp>

Community Legal Service
KEYCARD NO 47- Issued April 2011

General

This card is intended as a quick reference point only when assessing financial eligibility for those levels of service for which the supplier has responsibility including Legal Help.

A full list of the relevant levels of service and guidance on the assessment of means is set out in Part E of Volume 2 of the Legal Services Commission Manual. References in this card to volume and section numbers e.g. volume 2E-section 1 are references to the relevant parts of that guidance. Suppliers should have regard to the general provisions set out in guidance volume 2E-section 2, particularly those set out in sub paragraphs 3-5 and further guidance in section 12 regarding the documentation required when assessing means. This keycard and the guidance are relevant to all applications for funding made on or after 11 April 2011.

Eligibility Limits

The summary of the main eligibility limits from 11 April 2011 are provided below:

Level of Service	Income Limit	Capital Limit
All Levels of Service*: o Legal Help; o Help at Court; o Family Mediation; o Family Help (Lower), and o Legal Representation before the Immigration and Asylum Chamber of the First-tier Tribunal, and Immigration and Asylum Chamber of the Upper Tribunal (except where the Tribunal is exercising its judicial review jurisdiction under s15 of the Tribunals, Courts and Enforcement Act 2007); o Legal Representation in respect of Specified Family Proceedings before a Magistrates' Court (other than proceedings under the Children Act 1989 or Part IV of the Family Law Act 1996).	Gross income not to exceed £2657** per month Disposable income not to exceed £733 per month. Passported if in receipt of Income Support, Income Based Job Seekers' Allowance, Income Based Employment and Support Allowance or Guarantee Credit. [Also passported for Legal Help, Help at Court and Legal Representation (asylum and immigration matters only), if in receipt of NASS Support].	Disposable Capital not to exceed £3000 (CLR immigration matters) £8000 (All other levels of service) Passported if in receipt of Income Support, Income Based Job Seekers' Allowance, Income Based Employment and Support Allowance or Guarantee Credit. [Also passported for Legal Help, Help at Court and Legal Representation (asylum and immigration matters only), if in receipt of NASS Support].

* May be subject to contribution from income and/or capital (see volume 2E-section 3.2 paras 1 to 5)
** A higher gross income cap applies to families with more than 4 dependant children. Add £222 to the base gross income cap shown above for the 5th and each subsequent dependant child.

Additional information regarding the financial eligibility criteria is also provided in guidance volume 2E-section 3

STEP BY STEP GUIDE TO ASSESSMENT

Step One Determine whether or not the client has a partner whose means should be aggregated for the purposes of the assessment (see guidance in volume 2E-section 4.2 paras 1-5).

Step Two Determine whether the client is directly or indirectly in receipt of a 'passporting' benefit in order to determine whether the client automatically satisfies the relevant financial eligibility test, as indicated by the 'passported' arrangements stated in the eligibility limits summary table.

Step Three For any cases which are not 'passported' determine the gross income of the client, including the income of any partner, (see guidance in volume 2E-section 5). Where that gross income is assessed as being above £2,657 per month, then the client is ineligible for funding for all levels of service and the application should be refused without any further calculations being performed. Certain sources of income can be disregarded and a higher gross income cap applies to families with more than 4 dependant children (see guidance in volume 2E-section 3).

Step Four For those clients whose gross income is not more than £2,657 per month assess disposable income. Fixed allowances are made for dependants and employment expenses, and these are set out in the table below. Other allowances can be made for: tax; national insurance; maintenance paid; housing costs; child-care incurred because of work; and criminal legal aid contributions. If the resulting disposable income is above the relevant limit then funding should be refused across all levels of service without any further calculations being necessary.

Fixed rate allowances (per month) from 11 April 2011	
Work related expenses for those receiving a wage or salary	£45

Dependants Allowances
        Partner
        Child aged 15 or under
        Child aged 16 or over
	£167.53
	£271.58
	£271.58

Housing cap for those without dependants	£545

Step Five Where a client's disposable income is below the relevant limit then it is necessary to calculate the client's disposable capital (see guidance in volume, 2E-section 7). If the resulting capital is above the relevant limit, then the application should be refused.

Step Six For those clients whose disposable income and disposable capital have been assessed below the relevant limits then for all levels of service other than Legal Representation in Specified Family Proceedings, the client can be awarded funding.

Step Seven For Legal Representation in Specified Family Proceedings, it is necessary to determine whether any contributions from either income or capital (or both) should be paid by the client (see guidance in volume 2E-section 3.2 paras 1 to 5). For ease of reference the relevant income contribution table is reproduced below. Such contributions should be collected by the supplier (see guidance in volume 2E-section 3.2 para 4).

Band	Monthly disposable income	Monthly contribution
A	£316 to £465	1/4 of income in excess of £311
B	£466 to £616	£38.50 + 1/3 of income in excess of £465
C	£617 to £733	£88.85+ 1/2 of income in excess of £616

3

FAMILY MEDIATION AND
COLLABORATIVE LAW

A INTRODUCTION

This chapter will discuss mediation, the form of alternative dispute resolution most com- **3.01**
monly employed to resolve family law disputes. The meaning of mediation, the different
mediation models now available, and its enhanced importance following the introduction of
the Family Procedure Rules 2010 ('FPR 2010', SI 2010/2955) will be explained.

Funding for mediation will be considered along with the guidance set out in Part 2, Family **3.02**
Law Protocol 2010. The mediation process will be described.

Finally, reference will be made to collaborative family law, a process which is developing **3.03**
rapidly in England and Wales and involves a lawyer-led process to facilitate agreement with
limited court involvement.

B THE MEANING OF MEDIATION

The Law Society Code of Practice for Family Mediation (July 2009) describes family mediation **3.04**
as a process in which:

    1.1 a couple or other family members

    1.2 whether or not they are legally represented

    1.3 and at any time, whether or not there are or have been legal proceedings

    1.4 agree to the appointment of a neutral third party (the mediator)

    1.5 who is impartial

    1.6 who has no authority to make any decisions with regard to their issues

    1.7 which may relate to separation, divorce [relationship breakdown, dissolution of civil
        partnership], children's issues, property and financial questions or any other issues they
        may raise

1.8 but who helps them reach their own informed decisions

1.9 by negotiation

1.10 without adjudication.

3.05 Normally mediation will take place between a single mediator and the parties involved in the family dispute. Sometimes other family members (eg new partners, step-parents, and the like) may become involved in the mediation process with the agreement of the parties and the mediator.

3.06 It is unusual for children to be seen by a mediator or for children to participate actively in the process. If this is to occur, the mediator must be specifically trained in the involvement of children in the process and the same requirement as to confidentiality applies to consultations with children as to the rest of the process (para 2.2.7, Family Law Protocol).

Mediation is not arbitration

3.07 Arbitration is 'the settlement of a question at issue by one to whom the parties agree to refer their claims in order to obtain an equitable decision' (*Oxford English Dictionary*). In mediation, solutions or settlement are not imposed on the parties. The mediator does not make findings of fact. The mediator's function is more limited. It is to assist the parties to come to a settlement themselves.

Mediation is not reconciliation

3.08 The process of reconciliation is 'to bring a person again into friendly relations with another after an estrangement' (*Oxford English Dictionary*). Mediation does not have as its prime object the aim of reconciling estranged parties. However, mediation may indirectly promote reconciliation because its process may require the parties to address some of the issues which initially led to the breakdown of their marriage. Mediation can help to reduce tension, hostility, and misunderstandings and hence improve communication between the parties. A mediator must be aware throughout the process of mediation of the possibility of reconciliation between the couple concerned. Where there is such a possibility the mediator must ensure that the couple are given proper information about marriage counselling.

Mediation is not conciliation

3.09 Conciliation is 'to gain good will by acts which induce friendly feeling' (*Oxford English Dictionary*). Conciliation is just one of the tools used in mediation. For example, in the course of mediation one of the parties may make a concession over a particular issue in dispute. The other party may interpret that concession as a gesture of goodwill and therefore be encouraged to make further progress in the negotiation process. However, there are many other tools which may be used in the course of mediation. A mediator may work through a wide range of strategies before finding the one which fits the nature of the parties needing assistance.

C MEDIATION MODELS

As well as the traditional mediation model described in para 3.04 other mediation models **3.10** include:

Co-mediation

This is where two mediators, usually one of each gender and often from different disciplines **3.11** (eg counselling therapy, psychology, or social work), work together to provide effective mediation. This will be particularly appropriate, for example, where there are higher than usual levels of conflict and/or complexity, a foreign element, or significant issues of culture or ethnicity.

Anchor mediation

Here, there is an explicit arrangement with the parties that the mediation may take place with **3.12** one or two mediators, as the circumstances of the mediation require.

However, one mediator (the 'anchor mediator') will be present throughout the mediation **3.13** process, the second mediator taking part from time to time as may be helpful (para 2.2.2.1, Family Law Protocol).

Mediation with legal representative in the mediation room

Although this arrangement is unusual, there is no reason in principle why a legal representa- **3.14** tive may not be present during the mediation process. The role of the legal representative will be determined for the individual mediation: the legal representative may be there to provide advice, to undertake mediation advocacy, or simply to observe and offer advice away from the mediation room.

As for the public funding of a legal representative in the mediation room, see para 3.36. **3.15**

Shuttle mediation

Usually both parties meet the mediator at the same time. However, some mediators offer **3.16** 'shuttle mediation' where the mediator shuttles between the parties who are each in separate rooms with the intention of ultimately working with the parties in the same room. During shuttle mediation all information will be shared. If the parties never meet together during the process, it is difficult to consider that what has occurred amounts to effective mediation (para 2.2.27, Family Law Protocol).

Caucusing mediation

While this is much more common in commercial mediation, it may occur in family media- **3.17** tion when more conventional mediation techniques seem to stall. Again, separate meetings are held by the mediator with each of the parties in an attempt to defuse tension. In this process, not all information is shared and the mediator may hold secrets (para 2.2.28, Family Law Protocol).

3.18 Given the overall need for disclosures and transparency in family cases, this form of mediation will only occur in exceptional circumstances.

D   MEDIATION, THE FAMILY LAW PROTOCOL, AND THE FAMILY PROCEDURE RULES 2010

The Family Law Protocol

3.19 The Family Law Protocol states 'Increasingly there is an expectation on the part of the family justice system that mediation will have been tried unless there are good reasons to the contrary' (Part 2, para 2.2.29(8)).

Part 3, Family Procedure Rules 2010

3.20 The above principle is reinforced by provisions found in Part 3, FPR 2010 which came into force on 6 April 2011. Part 3 sets out the court's powers to encourage the parties to use alternative dispute resolution (ADR) both before and after an application has been made to the court (r 3.1(1)). For family cases, mediation will be the form of ADR most commonly used.

Parties' agreement required

3.21 While the court is obliged by r 3.2 to consider, at every stage in the proceedings, whether ADR is appropriate, the rules make it clear that mediation has to involve the agreement of both parties: the court's role is therefore limited to 'encouraging' the use of mediation.

Adjournment for mediation

3.22 Where the court considers that ADR is appropriate, it may direct that the proceedings or a hearing in the proceedings be adjourned for such specified period as it considers appropriate:

(a) to enable the parties to obtain information and advice about ADR; and
(b) **where the parties agree**, to enable alternative dispute resolution to take place (r 3.3(1)(a) and (b)).

3.23 The court may at the same time give directions about the timing and method by which the parties must tell the court if any of the issues in the proceedings have been resolved (r 3.3(3)) and give further directions as to the management of the case if the parties fail to keep the court informed (r 3.3(4)).

Practice Direction 3A—Pre-Application Protocol for Mediation Information and Assessment

Further, where a client is considering making an application for an order in certain family **3.24** proceedings, PD3A—Pre-Application Protocol for Mediation Information and Assessment sets out a procedure to encourage the parties to undertake mediation in an attempt to resolve the dispute *before* court proceedings are commenced.

The 'family proceedings' to which the Pre-Application Protocol applies are as follows: **3.25**

(a) private law proceedings under the Children Act 1989 ('CA 1989') (eg for a parental responsibility order under ss 4, 4ZA, and 4A, CA 1989; for a contact order, prohibited steps order, residence order, and specific issue order under s 8, CA 1989);
(b) for proceedings for a financial remedy (eg under Part II, Matrimonial Causes Act 1973 ('MCA 1973')) (Annex B of the Pre-Application Protocol).

Paragraph 4.1 of the Pre-Application Protocol states that before making an application to **3.26** court the parties will be expected to have followed the steps set out in the Protocol.

These require a potential applicant to consider with a mediator whether the dispute may be **3.27** capable of being resolved through mediation. Further, the Pre-Application Protocol expects any respondent to have attended a Mediation Information and Assessment Meeting (MIAM) if invited to do so.

If court proceedings are subsequently taken, the court will wish to know at the first hearing **3.28** whether mediation has been considered by the parties.

The court will take into account any failure to comply with the Protocol and may refer the **3.29** parties to a meeting with a mediator before the proceedings continue.

Mediation procedure

Annex A of the Pre-Application Protocol sets out the procedure to be followed by the applicant **3.30** or the applicant's legal representative to ensure compliance with the terms of the Protocol.

The procedure includes: **3.31**

(a) contacting a family mediator (information can be obtained from local family courts, from the Community Legal Advice Number—CLA Direct (tel: 0845 345 4345) or at <http://www.direct.gov.uk>);
(b) providing the mediator with contact details for the other party or parties to the dispute;
(c) attendance by the applicant at a MIAM. This meeting may also be attended by the other party or separate meetings may be held. (The mediator is required to consider with the party or parties whether public funding may be available to cover the cost of the meeting and, if not, the cost will be the responsibility of the party or parties attending.)

If the applicant then makes an application to court in respect of the dispute, the applicant **3.32** should at the same time file a completed Family Mediation Information and Assessment Form (Form FM1) confirming attendance at the meeting or giving reasons for not attending.

3.33 Form FM1 must be completed and signed by the mediator and countersigned by the applicant or the applicant's legal representative, where either:

(a) the applicant has attended a MIAM; or

(b) the applicant has not attended a MIAM; and

    (i) the mediator is satisfied that mediation is not suitable because another party to the dispute is unwilling to attend a MIAM to consider mediation;

    (ii) the mediator determines that the case is not suitable for a MIAM; or

    (iii) a mediator has made a determination within the previous four months that the case is not suitable for a MIAM or for mediation.

In all other circumstances, Form FM1 must be completed and signed by the applicant or the applicant's legal representative.

In what circumstances is mediation inappropriate?

3.34 There will of course be circumstances where the applicant is not expected to attend a MIAM before making an application to court. These are dealt with in Annex C of the Pre-Application Protocol.

3.35 In addition to points (b)(i), (ii), and (iii) in para 3.33 above, an applicant is not expected to attend a MIAM where:

(a) there have been allegations of domestic abuse by one party against the other and this has resulted in a police investigation or the issuing of civil proceedings for the protection of any party within the last 12 months;

(b) the dispute concerns financial issues and the applicant or another party is bankrupt;

(c) the parties are in agreement and there is no dispute to mediate;

(d) the proposed application is for an order in relevant family proceedings which are already in existence and are continuing;

(e) the proposed application is to be made without notice to the other party;

(f) the proposed application is urgent, meaning:

    (i) there is a risk to life, limb, or physical safety of the applicant or his or her family or his or her home; or

    (ii) any delay caused by attending a MIAM would cause a risk of significant harm to a child, a significant risk of a miscarriage of justice, unreasonable hardship to the applicant, or irretrievable problems in dealing with the dispute (eg irretrievable loss of significant evidence).

E   PUBLIC FUNDING FOR MEDIATION

3.36 Public funding for family mediation is available for parties who come within the relevant eligibility criteria. The Legal Services Commission (LSC) administers Civil Legal Aid and, as has already been mentioned in this chapter, greater emphasis is now placed on mediation as a means of resolving disputes generally. Chapter 2 deals comprehensively with Civil Legal Aid and therefore only a brief outline is given here to guide the practitioner to the appropriate sources. 'Family Mediation' is a separate level of funding under the Funding Code, authorizing mediation of a family dispute and an assessment of whether mediation appears suitable to the dispute, the parties, and all the circumstances (see Chapter 2, paras 2.55 ff). In certain circumstances a client must attend an assessment of suitability with a recognized mediator before an application can be made for Family Help (Higher) (see Chapter 2, para 2.40) and for Legal Representation (see Chapter 2, paras 2.43 ff) where the following family proceedings are contemplated:

(a) MCA 1973 (except s 37);
(b) Domestic Proceedings and Magistrates' Courts Act 1978;
(c) private law applications and financial relief proceedings under the CA 1989.

There are a number of categories of proceedings for which it will not be necessary for the client to attend an appointment to be assessed for suitability for mediation (see Chapter 2, para 2.59).   **3.37**

Non-contributory public funding at Family Help—Level 2 is available to enable the client to receive advice from a solicitor during the mediation process. The advice will usually relate to the legal implications of the proposed settlement achieved in mediation.   **3.38**

The funding will extend to implementing the outcome of mediation into a legally binding court order (by consent) if required.   **3.39**

Further LSC Funding (at Level 2) is available to remunerate legal representatives present in the mediation room, as explained at para 3.14 above.   **3.40**

F   FAMILY LAW PROTOCOL

Aims of the Protocol

Part 2 of the Family Law Protocol covers best practice in all aspects of private family law disputes. It is worth repeating here that the Protocol places an emphasis upon the importance of mediation, family dispute resolution, and the interests of children in the family.   **3.41**

Part I, paras 1.5.1 and 1.5.3 of the Protocol reminds solicitors to encourage the use of mediation and other methods of dispute resolution (including negotiation between the parties' solicitors) and collaborative law (see para 3.59 below).   **3.42**

Screening for mediation (Part 2, paras 2.2.8–2.2.11)

The Protocol emphasizes that it is important that only suitable cases are referred to mediation. At an early stage solicitors must, unless it is clearly inappropriate to do so, explain the mediation process and advise clients on the benefits and/or limitations of mediation in their case, as well as the role of solicitors in supporting the mediation process (para 2.2.9). Family mediation usually involves both parties meeting with the mediator at the same time. It can resolve or narrow issues in dispute. However, sometimes the issues may make mediation inappropriate, for example (para 2.2.11):   **3.43**

(a) where domestic abuse has occurred or is still occurring. If clients still wish to mediate, the solicitor should discuss the risks with them and decide whether any action can be taken to make them feel safe in the mediation, for example by first obtaining a non-molestation order through the court;

    (b) where the imbalance in power between the parties is likely to be beyond the capacity of the mediators to address;

    (c) where relationship counselling or marital therapy may be more appropriate.

Selecting a mediator (Part 2, paras 2.2.12–2.2.15)

3.44 It is useful for solicitors to keep details of mediators who are trained and accredited with an established organization. Solicitors should advise publicly funded clients of the availability of publicly funded mediation and that the statutory charge (explained in Chapter 2) does not apply to work done in respect of mediation.

The benefits of mediation (Part 2, para 2.2.29)

3.45 Solicitors should explain to their clients the benefits of mediation, which include:

    (a) When parties divorce or separate, it is generally better if both parties can sort out together the practical arrangements for the future.

    (b) The aim of mediation is to help parties to find a solution that meets the needs of all involved, especially the children, and that both parties feel is fair. At the end of mediation, those involved should feel that there has been no 'winner or loser' but that together they have arrived at sensible, workable arrangements.

    (c) Mediation can help to reduce tension, hostility, and misunderstandings and so improve communication between parties. This is especially important if children are involved, as parties may need to cooperate over their care and upbringing for some years to come.

    (d) Mediation can offer general costs savings as parties have only one professional assisting them. Clients who are able to agree will incur lower fee levels.

    (e) Mediation may have economic benefits because if a party is eligible for publicly funded mediation, he or she will not be required to make any contribution towards the cost of the mediation. If a party is eligible for mediation he or she will also be eligible for legal advice in respect of that mediation during and at the end of mediation and will not need to make a contribution to this.

The timing of the referral to mediation (Part 2, paras 2.2.30–2.2.33)

3.46 In publicly funded cases, there is a requirement to consider mediation at the commencement of the matter and before Level 3 Public Funding or Legal Representation can be obtained. Even if a case is unsuitable initially for mediation, the solicitor must keep under review the possibility of a referral to mediation as public funding might be available at that later stage. In private cases, the solicitor must give careful consideration to the timing of mediation. The requirements of Part 3, FPR 2010 (see paras 3.19 ff above) must also be borne in mind.

Supporting clients in mediation (Part 2, para 2.2.34)

3.47 Mediation usually works best when supported by independent legal advice. When a solicitor refers a client to mediation he should explain that:

    (a) the mediation process should be supported by independent legal advice;

(b) public funding is available for mediation for those eligible;

(c) no financial agreement is directly binding between the parties until it has been approved by the court as a consent order or made legally binding in some other manner;

(d) parties may consult their solicitors at any stage in mediation, but this is particularly important when financial disclosure and settlement proposals are being considered; and

(e) seeking advice from solicitors between mediation sessions can be positively helpful in assessing whether proposals are appropriate.

The role of solicitors during mediation (Part 2, para. 2.2.36)

The support offered by a solicitor during the mediation process is very important. Solicitors should: **3.48**

(a) assist clients to provide financial disclosure where necessary and assess the disclosure which takes place in mediation;

(b) give advice about settlement proposals as and when required, bearing in mind the long-term interests of clients and/or any children;

(c) give advice about other options;

(d) facilitate the obtaining of third party input or information, for example welfare benefits advice, expert valuation, or accountancy advice;

(e) bear in mind the respective costs of mediation as opposed to mainstream legal proceedings including, in particular, the likely costs of court proceedings;

(f) give advice about any untenable or unsustainable position either clients or their partners may be adopting;

(g) help clients to reach a decision and encourage clients to raise issues in mediation as appropriate;

(h) remind clients to raise issues in mediation as appropriate;

(i) encourage clients to 'stick with the process' unless inappropriate.

The role of solicitors following mediation (Part 2, paras 2.2.37–2.2.40)

It is important that it is made clear to parties that proposals made in mediation are not legally binding between them and that each of them should have access to independent legal advice when proposals are made. Where mediation does not result in firm proposals between the parties the solicitor should: **3.49**

(a) discuss with the client the reasons for the discontinuation of the mediation;

(b) note what has been achieved; and

(c) discuss what options for progression now arise.

Where the parties have produced interim proposals, the solicitor should discuss the position and any potential difficulties, including the need to apply for any interim court orders. Where proposals for settlement have been made then solicitors should follow the guidance in the main protocol. Where it is appropriate to draft a consent order dealing with finances, the guidance on consent orders should be followed (discussed in Chapter 30, para 30.120).

G   THE MEDIATION PROCESS

3.50 Mediation can address children's issues, property, and financial issues, or all issues. It is for the clients to decide which areas they wish to be the subject of mediation. Sometimes clients will be asked to fill in a referral form prior to the first mediation appointment setting out basic details about the length of the marriage or cohabitation, the date of any separation, the names and ages of the parties and their children, the living arrangements, the stage of any legal proceedings, preliminary information about employment, housing, and an outline of their financial position. Each party will be invited to state on the form briefly what they hope to settle through mediation. The form often includes a question about the possibility of reconciliation. Finally, the form often includes questions about domestic abuse/imbalance of power between the parties so that the mediator can be alerted at the earliest opportunity to the possible existence of such issues. If there are any, the mediator will usually take steps to see each party separately at the First Appointment to check out those issues with a view to deciding whether it would be appropriate for mediation to take place at all. In other cases, instead of using a referral form the mediator will gather the information verbally from the parties at the First Appointment.

3.51 The mediation process is divided into five major stages. These are discussed in turn.

Establishing the arena

3.52 Once the mediator has gathered the preliminary information from the parties he will then establish from them whether or not they are willing to take part in mediation. The mediation process and its ground rules will be explained. The mediator will invite the parties to share any concerns they may have about the process. If they wish to proceed then they will be asked to sign the Agreement to Mediate, confirming their commitment to the process. It is made clear at every stage that mediation is a voluntary process and that the parties are free to terminate it at any point. Likewise, the mediator has power to terminate mediation if it becomes inappropriate for any reason.

Clarifying the issues

3.53 The next step is for the mediator to establish with the parties which issues they wish to discuss in mediation. The issues are defined and often the mediator will write them on a flipchart, explaining that others can be added if necessary as mediation proceeds. In this way the mediator helps the parties to set the agenda for mediation and to work out the order/priority in which they wish to tackle the issues. For example, the arrangements for children may need immediate discussion. In finance and property mediation and all issues mediation, the mediator explains to the parties how financial information is to be gathered. A substantial financial questionnaire, based on Form E used in proceedings for financial provision, is distributed to the clients and they are asked to complete it before the next mediation session and to bring supporting documentation, with sufficient copies for each other and the mediator. By explaining the way in which the process works the mediator helps to establish the parties' trust in the process and in the mediator.

Exploring the issues

At the next mediation appointment, time will be allocated to cover the issues on the parties'   **3.54**
agenda. If there are issues concerning the children, the parties may wish to discuss them first.
The mediator will enquire about the existing arrangements for the children and the parents'
views and concerns about them. This will include exploring the parents' perception of each
child's position, feelings, and point of view. There may be discussion about the sharing of
parental responsibility and exploration of the options, taking account of the child's feelings
and needs. The mediator will consider with the parties whether they will talk further to the
children or whether the children themselves should be involved in the mediation. If so, then
the parties will need to decide when and how this should take place. Interim arrangements
may be agreed and tried out, while longer term arrangements are considered.

Where financial information has been provided by both parties this is shared and discussed   **3.55**
and is written up on the flipchart to provide an overview. The mediator enquires about missing information, clarifies discrepancies, and gives information as required to help the parties
to ensure that the whole financial picture has been given. If further information and supporting documentation is required, the mediator will help the parties to identify this and to
establish a time frame for it to be supplied. The mediator will try to discover each party's self-
interest in the dispute, increase the parties' motivation to solve their problems, develop trust,
and establish motivation for them to build agreements between themselves where possible.

Developing options

The mediator will help the parties to identify, create, and develop various options for solving   **3.56**
their problems. This is done by developing communication between the parties and seeking their respective ideas for possible solutions. The mediator will help them to look at the
advantages and disadvantages of each option and test the consequences of their not reaching
agreement. It is part of the mediator's job to understand the underlying needs and fears of
the parties and to recommend that they seek independent legal and/or financial advice from
solicitors, accountants, and other experts. The mediator may prepare an interim mediation
summary to assist them in seeking advice. Further discussions about the children will take
place if needed.

Securing agreement

The mediator will help the parties to clarify their proposals for settlement and the issues that   **3.57**
remain outstanding. He will seek detailed financial proposals and help the parties to compare the
proposals with their needs, budgets, and so forth. The mediator will help the parties to quantify
the differences between them to establish the size of any gap between their respective positions
and needs. He will explore the scope for reaching agreement and invite further proposals from
both parties. The mediator will encourage joint decision making where possible and help the parties to fit together the different elements of their proposals and reality-test them. The mediator
helps the parties to record their proposals and brings the process to a close.

Where the parties have reached proposals for settlement the mediator will usually draw up   **3.58**
a legally privileged document incorporating them. Where the proposals relate to financial

issues, the mediator will, in addition, draw up an 'open' statement of financial information, summarizing the information disclosed during the process, which is not legally privileged and which may be used in court if necessary. Different mediation bodies have different precedents for these documents, but the basic content of each will be similar. Both parties will be encouraged to seek legal advice on the proposals and any outstanding issues. Further negotiations may take place between legal advisers over the drafting of formal agreements or consent orders. If there are still substantial differences between the parties or the parties need to review arrangements or deal with changed circumstances they may return to mediation to work out further solutions.

H   COLLABORATIVE LAW

3.59   Collaborative family law is a process by which family lawyers and their clients agree in writing to reach settlement in relation to the issues involved and agree not to go to court. They agree to work together to resolve children and financial issues arising out of their separation and/ or divorce. They may enlist the help of experts, such as child specialists, family therapists, financial specialists, and mediators, as part of the team. Collaborative family lawyers use their skills in representation, negotiation, and problem-solving to help their clients to shape agreements appropriate to their circumstances. Settlement is reached by means of 'four way' face-to-face meetings involving the two clients and their respective lawyers. All information and disclosure is provided in the collaborative process. Collaborative law has many benefits, in particular as regards the emotional management of the parties to the dispute. However, the cost is unlikely to be very different from the conventional process of settlement by inter-solicitor negotiation. The clients remain in control of the process but have their lawyers present throughout for legal advice and guidance. As with mediation, it will not be suitable for everyone, but is a useful process for some clients and may help them to manage the breakdown of their relationship more easily. However, if no settlement can be reached then the collaborative lawyers must withdraw from acting for their clients and new lawyers must be instructed to take the matter forward by way of court proceedings. Additional information on the operation of collaborative law can be found in Part 2.3, Family Law Protocol. It should be noted that para 7.58 of the 2010 Standard Civil Contract Specification provides that Family Help (Lower) may be appropriate to fund collaborative law cases.

3.60   The Collaborative Family Law Group (<http://www.collabfamilylaw.org.uk>) has been under the auspices of Resolution (formerly the Solicitors Family Law Association).

I   KEY DOCUMENTS

3.61   *The Family Law Protocol*, 3rd edn (The Law Society, 2010).
Resolution Family Disputes Handbook (The Law Society, 2010)

J   USEFUL CONTACTS AND WEBSITES

Family Mediators Association   **3.62**
Glenfinnan Suite
Braeview House
9/11 Braeview Place
East Kilbride G74 3XH
Tel: 01355 244 594
Email: info@thefma.co.uk
<http://www.thefma.co.uk>

National Family Mediation
Margaret Jackson Centre
4 Barnfield Hill
Exeter EX1 1SR
Tel: 0300 4000 636
Fax: 01392 271945
Email: general@nfm.org.uk
<http://www.nfm.org.uk>

College of Mediators
3rd Floor, Alexander House
Telephone Avenue
Bristol BS1 4BS
Tel: 0845 65 85 258
Email: admin@collegeofmediators.co.uk
<http://www.collegeofmediators.co.uk>

Family Mediation Council
PO Box 593
Exeter EX1 9HG

PART II
FAMILY LIFE

4

THE GROUND FOR DIVORCE AND
THE FIVE FACTS

The present law of divorce is contained in the Matrimonial Causes Act 1973 ('MCA 1973')

A   A NOTE ON TERMINOLOGY

4.01 The party seeking a divorce is described as 'the petitioner' in the Matrimonial Causes Act 1973 ('MCA 1973') and 'the applicant' in the Family Procedure Rules 2010 ('FPR 2010', SI 2010/2955) which govern the procedure to obtain the decree of divorce.

4.02 In this and subsequent chapters dealing with aspects of divorce, the term 'applicant' will be used unless specific reference is made to the wording in the MCA 1973.

B   THE GROUND FOR DIVORCE

4.03 There is only one ground for divorce, that is that the marriage has irretrievably broken down: s 1(1), MCA 1973.

4.04 A decree absolute of divorce terminates the marriage and radically changes the status of the parties, especially in relation to eligibility for certain state benefits and pensions.

C   THE FIVE FACTS

The court cannot hold that the marriage has irretrievably broken down unless the petitioner   **4.05**
satisfies the court of one or more of the five facts set out in s 1(2), MCA 1973. These are:

(a)   that the respondent has committed adultery and the petitioner finds it intolerable to live
with the respondent;

(b)   that the respondent has behaved in such a way that the petitioner cannot reasonably be
expected to live with the respondent;

(c)   that the respondent has deserted the petitioner for a continuous period of at least two
years immediately preceding the presentation of the petition;

(d)   that the parties to the marriage have lived apart for a continuous period of at least two
years immediately preceding the presentation of the petition and the respondent consents to a decree being granted (two years' separation and consent);

(e)   that the parties to the marriage have lived apart for a continuous period of at least five
years immediately preceding the presentation of the petition (five years' separation).

Because of the requirement that one of the five facts should be proved, it is possible for a situ-   **4.06**
ation to arise where the marriage has undoubtedly broken down irretrievably but no divorce
can yet be granted because neither party can establish any of the five facts.

Example A couple separate by mutual consent simply because they have found that they are
incompatible. Neither has committed adultery or behaved in such a way that the other cannot reasonably be expected to live with them. Although the marriage has irretrievably broken
down, they are not able to obtain a divorce during the first two years of their separation as
none of the five facts can be established. When two years are up, assuming they both wish to
be divorced, it will be possible to establish two years' separation and consent (s 1(2)(d)) and one
or other party will be able to seek a decree.

D   IRRETRIEVABLE BREAKDOWN

No link necessary between s 1(2) fact and irretrievable breakdown

It is not necessary for the applicant to show that the irretrievable breakdown of the marriage   **4.07**
has been caused by the s 1(2) fact on which she relies (*Stevens* v *Stevens* [1979] 1 WLR 885;
Buffery v *Buffery* [1988] 2 FLR 365 (CA)).

Example (The facts of *Stevens* v *Stevens*.) The applicant established that the respondent's behaviour was such that she could not reasonably be expected to live with him: s 1(2)(b). The marriage had irretrievably broken down but in fact it was established that it was the applicant's
own behaviour that had caused the breakdown.

The applicant was nevertheless entitled to a decree.

Proving irretrievable breakdown

4.08   Section 1(4), MCA 1973 provides that if the court is satisfied that one of the s 1(2) facts is proved, unless it is satisfied on all the evidence that the marriage has not broken down irretrievably it shall grant a decree of divorce (subject to the provisions of s 5, MCA 1973, see Chapter 12). In other words, once one of the facts is established, a presumption of irretrievable breakdown is raised. In an undefended case, there is not normally any evidence to displace the presumption and the court therefore accepts the applicant's statement in her petition that the marriage has irretrievably broken down without further enquiry.

4.09   However, it is open to the respondent to challenge the applicant's assertion of irretrievable breakdown by filing an answer denying that the marriage has irretrievably broken down. In this event, the suit will become defended and it will be up to the court to determine on the basis of all the evidence at the hearing whether or not the marriage has irretrievably broken down by that date (see *Ash* v *Ash* [1972] 1 All ER 582; *Pheasant* v *Pheasant* [1972] 1 All ER 587).

Adjournment with a view to reconciliation

4.10   If at any stage in the divorce proceedings the court feels that there is a reasonable possibility of a reconciliation between the parties, the court may adjourn the proceedings for whatever period it thinks fit to enable attempts at reconciliation to take place: s 6(2), MCA 1973.

E   ADULTERY: S 1(2)(a)

Two separate elements to prove

4.11   There are two matters that the applicant must prove:

(a)   that the respondent has committed adultery; *and*
(b)   that she finds it intolerable to live with him.

The adultery may be the reason why the applicant finds it intolerable to live with the respondent but it is not necessary for there to be any link between the two matters (*Cleary* v *Cleary* [1974] 1 All ER 498, followed in *Carr* v *Carr* [1974] 1 All ER 1193).

Example   (The facts of *Cleary* v *Cleary*.) The respondent wife committed adultery. The applicant husband took her back afterwards but things did not work out because the wife corresponded with the other man, went out at night, and then went to live at her mother's and did not return. The applicant said that he could no longer live with the respondent because there was no future for the marriage. Although it was the respondent's conduct after the adultery and not the adultery itself that had made it intolerable for the applicant to live with her, he had satisfied both limbs of s 1(2)(a) and was entitled to a decree.

Meaning of adultery

4.12   Adultery is voluntary sexual intercourse between a man and woman who are not married to each other but one of whom at least is a married person (*Clarkson* v *Clarkson* (1930) 143 LT 775).

Proof of adultery

It would be quite extraordinary if the applicant were able to produce a witness who had actually **4.13**
seen the respondent committing adultery. Proof is therefore normally indirect.

Examples of the type of evidence commonly used are set out in the following paragraphs. **4.14**

Confessions and admissions

It used to be routine practice for a confession statement to be obtained from the respondent **4.15**
(and if possible the co-respondent as well) admitting adultery and setting out briefly the
circumstances in which it took place.

Nowadays, the acknowledgment of service forms used by respondents and co-respondents **4.16**
in adultery cases ask the question 'Do you admit the adultery alleged in the petition?' If the
respondent answers this question in the affirmative and signs the form, the court can accept
this as sufficient evidence of adultery. Depending on the nature of the case and the practice
of the particular court in which proceedings are pending, it may or may not still be necessary
for the old style of confession statement or other evidence of adultery (see paras 4.20 and 4.21
below) to be obtained as well.

In circumstances where there is some doubt as to whether the respondent will admit the **4.17**
adultery in his acknowledgment of service form, it is sensible to obtain a signed confession in
any event before commencing divorce proceedings. To do otherwise may result in costs being
incurred without any prospect of a divorce being obtained because the applicant cannot
prove the fact of adultery in any other way.

If the respondent denies adultery and proceeds to file an answer, the case will be defended and **4.18**
the court will have to consider whether, on all the evidence available at the hearing, adultery
is proved.

If the respondent does not admit (or even denies) adultery in the acknowledgment of service **4.19**
but does not go so far as to file an answer, his lack of cooperation will not necessarily be fatal
to the applicant's case. She will simply have to attempt to prove adultery by other evidence.

Circumstantial evidence

The following are examples of the type of evidence from which the court can be asked to infer **4.20**
adultery:

(a) Evidence that the respondent and another woman are living together as man and wife.
    The applicant may be able to state this from her own observations. Alternatively she
    may be able to produce an independent witness of her own to the fact (eg the next-door
    neighbour of the respondent and his cohabitant). If necessary an enquiry agent can be
    instructed to watch the respondent and collect evidence of cohabitation.
(b) Evidence that the respondent and another woman had the inclination and the oppor-
    tunity to commit adultery, for example that they had formed an intimate relationship
    (eg they may have been seen kissing or holding hands in public or the applicant may
    have obtained copies of 'love letters' passing between them) and had spent the night
    together in the same bedroom or alone together in the same house. Again, the applicant
    may be able to supply this evidence herself but, if not, an enquiry agent may be able to help.

Indeed, in the case of evidence of the type set out in both points (a) and (b), the court may *require* independent evidence before it is satisfied of adultery.

(c) Evidence that the wife has given birth to a child of which the husband is not the father. Normally it is presumed that a child born during the marriage is legitimate. However, this presumption can be displaced, for example, by evidence that the parties did not have any contact with each other during the time in which conception must have taken place (eg where the husband has been working overseas continuously for a prolonged period). A birth certificate can be admitted as prima facie evidence of the facts required to be entered on it. This can be useful where the wife has registered the birth and named someone other than the husband as the father of the child.

Findings in other proceedings

4.21 Findings made by a court in other proceedings may be admissible as evidence of adultery by the party against whom the finding had been made, for example:

(a) where the husband has been found to be the father of a child in proceedings brought by the mother of the child under sch 1, Children Act 1989, for a lump sum order or transfer of property order;

(b) where the husband has been found to be the father of a child in proceedings brought by the Child Support Agency for maintenance for the child;

(c) where a finding of adultery has been made against either party in family proceedings;

(d) where the husband had been convicted of rape;

(e) where the applicant has already been granted a decree of judicial separation on the basis of the adultery on which she relies in the divorce proceedings, the court may treat the decree of judicial separation as sufficient proof of the adultery (s 4(2), MCA 1973): see Chapter 12.

4.22 The solicitor has to consider whether the co-respondent should be named where the petition is based on the respondent's adultery and the identity of the co-respondent is known to the applicant.

4.23 As a general rule, the co-respondent should not be named unless the applicant seeks an order for costs against the co-respondent. This approach is reinforced by para 2.1, PD7A, FPR 2010 which states that the co-respondent should not be named unless the applicant believes that the proceedings are likely to be defended.

Intolerability

4.24 Normally, at least in an undefended case, the applicant's statement in her petition that she finds it intolerable to live with the respondent will be accepted at face value.

4.25 However, further evidence may be required in support of her contention if either:

(a) the information supplied by the applicant in the petition itself and in support of the petition raises doubts in the mind of the court as to whether the applicant finds it intolerable to live with the respondent; *or*

(b) the respondent files an answer challenging the applicant's assertion, in which case the divorce will become defended and the court will hear evidence from both parties on the issue.

The test to be applied when an issue arises over whether the applicant finds it intolerable to live with the respondent is a subjective one (*Goodrich* v *Goodrich* [1971] 2 All ER 1340), that is, 'does *this applicant* find it intolerable to live with the respondent' and not 'would *a reasonable applicant* find it intolerable to live with the respondent?'

Living together

In some cases the applicant can be prevented from relying on adultery because she has lived **4.26** with the respondent after she discovered his adultery. This matter is dealt with at para 4.61 below.

F   BEHAVIOUR: S 1(2)(b)

The test for behaviour

The test as to whether the respondent has behaved in such a way that the applicant cannot **4.27** reasonably be expected to live with him is a cross between a subjective and an objective test. The formula used in the case of *Livingstone-Stallard* v *Livingstone-Stallard* [1974] Fam 47 seems to have been accepted (see *Birch* v *Birch* [1992] 1 FLR 564), that is:

> Would any right-thinking person come to the conclusion that *this* husband has behaved in such a way that *this* wife cannot reasonably be expected to live with him, taking into account the whole of the circumstances and the characters and personalities of the parties?

Thus, not only must the court look at the respondent's behaviour but also at the applicant's **4.28** behaviour (eg asking whether she provoked the respondent deliberately or simply by her own anti-social conduct). Consideration must also be given to what type of people the applicant and respondent are (eg asking whether the applicant is particularly sensitive and vulnerable) and to the whole history of the marriage. The court must then evaluate all this evidence and decide objectively whether, in these particular circumstances, it is reasonable to expect the applicant to go on living with the respondent.

Examples of behaviour

Violent behaviour

It is quite common for applicants to rely on violent behaviour on the part of the respondent. **4.29** One serious violent incident may entitle the applicant to a decree (eg an unprovoked attack upon the applicant causing her an unpleasant injury for which she required medical treatment). If the violence used is relatively minor (eg the occasional push and shove), more than one incident will be required or it will be necessary for the applicant to show that there was other behaviour as well as the violence.

Other behaviour

The respondent's behaviour need not be violent to entitle the applicant to a decree. All sorts of **4.30** other anti-social behaviour can be sufficient as the following examples show. Incidents which are relatively trivial in isolation can amount to sufficient behaviour when looked at as a whole, particularly if the applicant is especially sensitive to the respondent's behaviour for some reason.

Example 1 (The facts of *Livingstone-Stallard* v *Livingstone-Stallard*, para 4.27 above.) The husband was 56, the wife 24. The marriage was unsatisfactory from the start. The wife's complaints about her husband's behaviour included the following matters. The husband criticized the wife over petty things—her behaviour, her friends, her way of life, her cooking, her dancing—and was abusive to her, called her names, and, on one occasion, spat at her. Once he tried to kick her out of bed. On one occasion he criticized her for leaving her under-clothes soaking in the sink overnight (although he did the same himself) and said that it was indicative of the way she had been brought up. He made a fuss when she drank sherry with a photographer who had brought round their wedding photographs, forbidding her to give refreshment to 'trades-people' again (on the basis that if she drank sherry with a tradesman it might impair her faculties so that the tradesman might make an indecent approach to her). The wife left after the husband had bundled her out of the house on a cold evening and locked her out, throwing water over her when she tried to get back in. She suffered bruising and was in a very nervous state for six weeks, needing sedation.

    Although many of these complaints were trivial themselves, the wife was entitled to a decree.

Example 2 (The facts of *Birch* v *Birch*, para 4.27 above.) The parties had lived together for more than 27 years. The wife's main complaint against the husband was that he was dogmatic and dictatorial with nationalistic, male chauvinistic characteristics, which she had resented for many years. The judge found that, in contrast, the wife was sensitive, taking a passive role and putting her own interests aside until the children had grown up and left home.

    The wife was entitled to a decree.

Note that although Examples 1 and 2 are taken from the facts of decided cases they are not intended to be looked on as *precedents* of what is and is not sufficient behaviour; every case is different and must be decided on its own facts. The examples are only intended to show the type of conduct which is relevant in establishing behaviour.

4.31   Other matters which can constitute behaviour include excessive drinking leading to unpleas-ant behaviour, unreasonably refusing to have sexual intercourse or making excessive sexual demands, having an intimate relationship (falling short of adultery) with another person, committing serious criminal offences, and keeping the other party unreasonably short of money.

Where the respondent is mentally ill

4.32   The fact that the respondent's behaviour is the result of his mental illness does not necessarily prevent it from being sufficient to entitle the applicant to a decree. However, the fact that he is mentally ill will be a factor for the court to take into account in determining whether s 1(2)(b) is satisfied (*Katz* v *Katz* [1972] 3 All ER 219 and see also *Richards* v *Richards* [1972] 3 All ER 695 and *Thurlow* v *Thurlow* [1975] 2 All ER 979).

Behaviour which is not sufficient

Section 1(2)(b) will not be satisfied if all that is proved is that the applicant became disen-   **4.33**
chanted with the respondent or bored with marriage.

Simple desertion cannot amount to behaviour; the applicant must wait for two years to elapse   **4.34**
from the date of desertion and apply on the basis of s 1(2)(c) (*Stringfellow* v *Stringfellow* [1976]
2 All ER 539).

The relevance of living together despite the behaviour

In some cases the petitioner may not be able to prove sufficient behaviour because she and   **4.35**
the respondent have continued to live together; see paras 4.63 ff.

G   ESTABLISHING AS A MATTER OF FACT THAT THE PARTIES ARE LIVING APART

The facts set out in s 1(2)(c) to (e) all require cohabitation to have ceased and the parties to   **4.36**
have lived apart for a period of time.

Living apart for the purposes of s 1(2)(d) and (e)

'Living apart' is defined for the purposes of s 1(2)(d) and (e) (the two-year and five-year separa-   **4.37**
tion facts) in s 2(6), MCA 1973. This provides that a husband and wife shall be treated as living
apart unless they are living with each other in the same household.

It is usually possible to pinpoint a time at which the spouses began to live apart in the sense   **4.38**
required by the Act. This is normally the time when one or the other moves out of the family
home to live in his own accommodation elsewhere and the parties start to lead separate lives.
However, difficulties can arise:

(a) When the parties have been living separately in any event, not because the marriage has
broken down but for some reason, for example because one spouse has gone to look after
his or her invalid parents or because they are working in different cities or because one
is working abroad. Although as a matter of fact they are living separately, this physical
separation is not sufficient; they will not be counted as living apart within the meaning
of the MCA 1973 until at least one of them has decided that the marriage is at an end
(*Santos* v *Santos* [1972] 2 All ER 246). It is not necessary for that spouse to communicate
this decision to the other spouse. Of course, it is easier to prove that the requisite state
of mind did exist if something was said to the other spouse but in other cases, a decision
that the marriage is at an end can be inferred from conduct, for example where the party
living away ceases to contact the other party or to return home for holidays or sets up
home with someone else.

     Example 1 The husband is posted abroad. To begin with, he and his wife email each
other frequently and he spends his periods of leave at home with her and the children.

After he has been abroad for a year, contact between him and his wife ceases and he does not answer her emails. In April 2011 he writes to his mother saying that he does not see any future in the marriage and does not intend to come home when his posting is over. Two years later the wife wishes to apply for a divorce; the husband consents to a decree. She can rely on s 1(2)(d). It can be seen from the husband's conduct and his letter to his mother that he had decided in 2011 that the marriage was over. The two-year separation period therefore began to run from that date.

Example 2 The husband is sentenced to a period of six years' imprisonment. To begin with the wife intends to stand by him. However, after six months she meets another man whom she wishes, ultimately, to marry and with whom she starts to live. The parties will be treated as having separated at this point because it is then that the wife recognizes that the marriage has no future.

(b) When the parties continue to live under the same roof but contend that they are actually living there separately. Whether or not the court will accept in these circumstances that there has been a sufficient degree of separation will depend on the living arrangements. To establish that the parties have been living apart it must be shown that the normal relationship of husband and wife has ceased and that they have been leading separate existences. The position is best illustrated by an example.

Example (The facts of *Mouncer* v *Mouncer* [1972] 1 All ER 289.) The husband and wife slept in separate bedrooms in the matrimonial home. They shared the rest of the house. They continued to take meals (cooked by the wife) together and shared the cleaning of the house making no distinction between one part of the house or the other. The wife no longer did any washing for the husband. The only reason the husband went on living in the house was his wish to live with and help to look after the children.

The parties had not been living apart.

If the parties in *Mouncer* had lived in separate parts of the house, had not shared cleaning and had taken meals separately, no doubt the court would have found that they were not living in the same household, albeit that they were living under the same roof, and would have accepted therefore that they were living apart.

Living apart in desertion cases

4.39 Section 2(6) applies only to s 1(2)(d) and (e). However, if a question were to arise in a desertion case as to whether cohabitation had ceased, there is no doubt that similar principles would be applied (see *Smith* v *Smith* [1940] P 49). In addition, recognition that the marriage is at an end must be communicated to the other party: *Beeken* v *Beeken* [1948] P 302 (CA).

H   DESERTION: S 1(2)(c)

4.40 Under s 1(2)(c), the applicant must show not only that the respondent has deserted her but also that this state of affairs has gone on for a continuous period of at least two years immediately preceding the presentation of the petition.

Desertion rarely relied on

It is rare these days for an applicant to rely on desertion. No doubt the reason for this is that **4.41** if the respondent has seen fit to desert the applicant, he is usually sufficiently disenchanted with the marriage to consent to a decree of divorce being granted. Thus, the applicant need not struggle with the technicalities of desertion but can base her petition much more conveniently on two years' separation and consent (s 1(2)(d)). Furthermore, if the respondent has committed adultery, the applicant need not even wait for two years' separation; she can apply for a divorce immediately on the basis of the adultery.

It should never be necessary to rely on *constructive* desertion (ie, behaviour by the respondent **4.42** causing the applicant to withdraw from cohabitation). In such cases, the petition should be based on behaviour under s 1(2)(b). Apart from being more straightforward than desertion, the behaviour fact has the marked advantage that the applicant need not wait for two years' separation to have elapsed before applying as she must with desertion.

Desertion is thus only likely to be used where adultery and behaviour cannot be made out and **4.43** where, despite having walked out in the first place, the respondent is not prepared to consent to a decree being granted or where he has simply disappeared and cannot therefore be asked to consent to a decree.

What is desertion?

The law relating to desertion is detailed and rather technical. This book outlines the main **4.44** provisions; it does not deal with the intricacies. A fuller picture of the law can be found in standard practitioners' works on divorce.

The essentials of desertion are as follows: **4.45**

(a) The respondent must have withdrawn from cohabitation with the intention of bringing cohabitation permanently to an end.
 (i) *Cessation of cohabitation*: it is vital that cohabitation should have ceased. The applicant cannot say that the respondent has deserted her if he is, in fact, still living with her, even if he contributes virtually nothing to family life. See paras 4.36 ff as to when the parties will be taken to be living apart.
 (ii) *Intention*: the respondent must intend to bring cohabitation permanently to an end.

Example 1 As far as the wife is concerned, she and her husband have been living together in the matrimonial home perfectly happily. One day, the husband packs his suitcase and departs to live in his own flat, saying that the wife has done nothing wrong but that he needs his freedom and does not intend to live with her ever again. The husband has thus withdrawn from cohabitation with the intention of bringing it permanently to an end. He has, in fact, deserted the wife.

This example deals with a couple who are living in the same house at the time that the desertion occurs. While this is the normal situation, it is not always the case. It is quite possible for one party to desert the other at a time when they are living in different places anyway (*Pardy v Pardy* [1939] 3 All ER 779). It is not the actual packing up and leaving that is important. What is important is the change in the respondent's state of mind so that he no longer regards himself as a married man with all the normal obligations of married life (including, ultimately, returning to live with the applicant), but decides that he will never resume cohabitation with the applicant and therefore regards himself as a free agent.

Example 2 The husband and wife live together. The husband gets a job in Saudi Arabia and, with the wife's consent, he goes off for a year's contract. Just before he is due to come home, he decides that he is not going to return to live with his wife and he telephones to tell her so. The physical separation of the parties would, up to now, have had no consequence as far as divorce proceedings were concerned. At this point, however, the husband starts to be in desertion. If this state of affairs continues for two years, the wife will be able to apply for a divorce on the basis of this desertion.

It does seem, however, that where the original separation was consensual, a party cannot be in desertion simply because he subsequently makes up his mind privately not to resume cohabitation at the end of the agreed period as originally planned. He will not be in desertion until he communicates this to the other party or until the agreed period of separation expires and he does not return (*Nutley* v *Nutley* [1970] 1 All ER 410).

In other cases, there is no need for an express statement by the respondent of his intentions. It can be inferred from his conduct that he intends to bring cohabitation permanently to an end. In Example 1, therefore, the husband would have been just as much in desertion if he had said nothing to his wife but had merely departed with all his belongings to live in his own flat, with no intention of resuming cohabitation.

Because the respondent's state of mind is the essence of desertion, he will not be in desertion if he is forced to live separately from his wife against his will, for example if he is imprisoned. However, if he is already in desertion when the involuntary separation supervenes (eg he is sentenced to a period of imprisonment after he has deserted his wife), the desertion will be presumed to continue throughout the period of involuntary separation (*Williams* v *Williams* [1938] 4 All ER 445). The court may treat the respondent as having been in desertion during a period in which he was excluded from the matrimonial home by a court order (ie, an occupation order made under Part IV, Family Law Act 1996).

(b) The applicant does not consent to the respondent's withdrawal from cohabitation. If the applicant consented to the respondent's withdrawal from cohabitation, she cannot allege that he has deserted her. Consent can be expressed (eg where a separation agreement is drawn up providing for immediate separation) or can be implied from what the applicant says or does.

Example (The facts of *Spence* v *Spence* [1939] 1 All ER 52.) For a fortnight before she left home, the wife engaged in open preparations for her departure. Her husband was perfectly aware of her intentions and they discussed the division of their household goods. The husband did not make any attempt to deter his wife from going or to delay her departure.

The husband was held tacitly to have consented to his wife's departure.

However, the mere fact that the applicant breathes a sigh of relief when the respondent has gone does not mean that she has consented to his departure.

The following situations may arise:

    (i) Consent can pre-date the respondent's departure, in which case desertion never begins.

    (ii) On the other hand, the applicant may decide to consent to the separation after the event, in which case her consent can bring the respondent's desertion to an end (*Pizey* v *Pizey* [1961] 2 All ER 658).

    (iii) Consent may be to a limited period of separation (eg while the respondent works abroad). Such consent comes to an end when that period ends; thereafter, the respondent can be in desertion (*Shaw* v *Shaw* [1939] 2 All ER 381).

    (iv) If consent is given to an unlimited period of separation, it can be withdrawn and either party can seek a resumption of cohabitation. If the other party, without just cause, refuses to resume cohabitation, he will be in desertion (*Fraser* v *Fraser* [1969] 3 All ER 654). Furthermore, if the parties originally separate contemplating that they will get back together eventually (even though no time may be fixed) and one of them then decides never go back to live with the other and communicates this to the other, he will be in desertion from that point unless, of course, the other spouse is agreeable to the permanent separation (*Nutley* v *Nutley*, above).

(c) The respondent must not have any reasonable cause to withdraw from cohabitation.

Normally, if the respondent has reasonable cause to leave, this will arise from the behaviour of the applicant although there would seem to be no reason, in principle, why some cause unconnected with the applicant should not be sufficient justification for the respondent going (eg where it is shown that it is imperative for his health that he should leave the applicant permanently). Where the applicant's conduct is relied on, it must be shown to be 'grave and weighty' and not merely part of the ordinary wear and tear of married life (*Dyson* v *Dyson* [1953] 2 All ER 1511).   **4.46**

There are no recent authorities on the point but it would seem logical to suggest that the type of behaviour that would form the basis of a petition under s 1(2)(b) would also constitute reasonable cause in a desertion case. Furthermore, a reasonable belief that the applicant has committed adultery will give the respondent reasonable cause to leave even though the adultery cannot be proved (*Glenister* v *Glenister* [1945] 1 All ER 513).   **4.47**

Termination of desertion

The ways in which desertion can be brought to an end include the following: **4.48**

(a) By the parties subsequently agreeing to live apart (*Pizey* v *Pizey*, para 4.45 above).

(b) By the granting of a decree of judicial separation. Once a decree of judicial separation has been granted, neither party has any further obligation to live with the other and cannot therefore be in desertion by failing to do so. However, if the decree of judicial separation was based on two years' desertion, the applicant can subsequently issue a divorce petition based on the same desertion (s 4(1), MCA 1973). The desertion will be deemed to have taken place immediately prior to the issue of the divorce petition if the parties have not resumed cohabitation since the judicial separation decree was granted and the decree of judicial separation has continued in force since it was granted (s 4(3)). Furthermore, the court may treat the decree as sufficient proof of desertion in the divorce proceedings: s 4(2) (see further Chapter 12, paras 12.12 ff).

(c) By the resumption of cohabitation for a prolonged period (certain periods of cohabitation are disregarded, however, in determining whether there has been a continuous period of desertion; see paras 4.65 ff).

(d) By the deserting spouse making a genuine offer to resume cohabitation which the deserted spouse unreasonably refuses (*Ware* v *Ware* [1942] 1 All ER 50).

(e) By the deserted spouse subsequently providing the deserter with reasonable cause to stay away, for example where she commits adultery which comes to the notice of the deserter.

Living together during a period of desertion

4.49   In determining whether the period of desertion is continuous, certain periods of cohabitation can be ignored, see paras 4.65 ff.

I   TWO YEARS' SEPARATION AND CONSENT: S 1(2)(d)

Two separate matters to prove

4.50   There are two matters which the applicant must prove:

(a) that she and the respondent have lived apart for a continuous period of at least two years immediately preceding the presentation of the petition; *and*

(b) that the respondent consents to a decree being granted.

Living apart

4.51   As to what is meant by living apart, see paras 4.36 ff. Certain periods of cohabitation can be disregarded in considering whether the parties have lived apart *continuously*, see para 4.65 below.

Respondent's consent

4.52   The respondent normally signifies his consent to the court on the acknowledgment of service form (which must be signed by him personally and, if he is represented by a solicitor, his solicitor as well; see r 7.12(4) and (6), FPR 2010), and see Chapter 8.

4.53   The respondent can make his consent conditional, for example giving his consent provided that the applicant does not seek an order for costs of the divorce (*Beales* v *Beales* [1972] 2 All ER 667).

4.54   Whether his consent is unqualified or conditional, the respondent can withdraw it at any stage before the decree is pronounced (*Beales* v *Beales*, para 4.53 above). If s 1(2)(d) is the only basis for the petition, the petition will then have to be stayed (r 7.12 (13) and (14), FPR 2010).

If decree nisi is granted solely on the basis of two years' separation and consent, the respondent can apply at any time before the decree is made absolute to have the decree rescinded if he has been misled by the applicant (intentionally or unintentionally) about any matter which he took into account in deciding to give his consent (s 10(1), MCA 1973).   **4.55**

Section 10(2), Matrimonial Causes Act 1973

Under s 10(2), the respondent may seek to hold up decree absolute until his financial position after the divorce has been considered by the court, see Chapter 11.   **4.56**

J   FIVE YEARS' SEPARATION: S 1(2)(e)

Establishing the five years' separation

If the applicant can establish that she and the respondent have been living apart for a continuous period of at least five years immediately preceding the filing of the petition, she is entitled to a decree whether or not the respondent consents to a divorce (subject only to the respondent's right to raise a defence under s 5, MCA 1973 of grave financial or other hardship, see Chapter 11).   **4.57**

Cohabitation during the five-year period

Certain periods of cohabitation can be disregarded in determining whether the five-year period is continuous, see para 4.65 below.   **4.58**

Section 10(2), Matrimonial Causes Act 1973

As with s 1(2)(d), the respondent can seek to hold up decree absolute by an application under s 10(2) to have his financial position considered, see Chapter 11.   **4.59**

K   THE EFFECT OF LIVING TOGETHER IN RELATION TO THE FIVE FACTS: S 2

Section 2 deals with the relevance of the parties having lived with each other when considering whether any of the five facts have been made out. Section 2(6) provides that the parties are to be treated as living apart unless they are living together in the same household.   **4.60**

Cohabitation after adultery

Cohabitation exceeding six months is a total bar

Section 2(1) provides that the applicant cannot rely for the purpose of s 1(2)(a) on adultery committed by the respondent if the parties have lived with each other for a period exceeding   **4.61** or periods together exceeding six months after the applicant learned that the respondent had committed adultery.

Example 1 Mr Brown commits adultery on one occasion only in June 2011. On 1 July 2011 Mrs Brown learns of this. She and her husband continue to live together as man and wife as before although they bicker constantly. In March 2012 Mrs Brown decides that the marriage is doomed and consults a solicitor with a view to applying for a divorce on the basis of her husband's adultery. She cannot do so. She has cohabited for a period exceeding six months since she learned of the adultery on 1 July 2011 and he has not committed further acts of adultery since then.

If the respondent commits adultery on more than one occasion, time will not begin to run until after the applicant learns of the last act of adultery.

Example 2 Mr Green begins an affair with his secretary at the office party at Christmas 2010. He first commits adultery with her on 23 December 2010. The affair continues until April 2011. Mrs Green learns almost straight away of the adultery on 23 December 2010 but thinks that that is the only occasion on which adultery took place. She discovers the true facts about the continuing adultery on 1 August 2011. She continues to live with her husband until 1 September 2011 when she leaves him because relations have become so strained. Mrs Green will be able to petition for divorce on the basis of her husband's adultery. The last act of adultery was in April 2011, she learned of it on 1 August 2011 and she only cohabited with her husband for one month thereafter.

Cohabitation of six months or under to be disregarded

4.62 Section 2(2) provides that where parties have lived together for a period or periods not exceeding six months in total after it became known to the applicant that the respondent had committed adultery, the cohabitation is to be disregarded in determining whether the applicant finds it intolerable to live with the respondent. Thus, in Example 2 above, it could not be said against Mrs Green that she did not find it intolerable to live with her husband because she had in fact lived with him for a month after finding out about his last act of adultery. This period of cohabitation would be disregarded in determining the question of intolerability.

Cohabitation and behaviour

Cohabitation of six months and under to be disregarded

4.63 Section 2(3) provides that the fact that the applicant and the respondent have lived with each other for a period or periods not exceeding six months in total after the last incident of behaviour proved, is to be disregarded in determining whether the applicant cannot reasonably be expected to live with the respondent.

Example 1 The last incident of behaviour proved by the applicant was on 3 January 2011 when the respondent beat her over the head with a snow shovel. She did not leave the respondent until the middle of February 2011. The period of cohabitation from 3 January 2011 until mid-February 2011 will be disregarded.

The behaviour on which the applicant relies may be continuous in which case time will only start to run against the applicant if she cohabits with the respondent after the particular behaviour ceases.

Example 2 The applicant makes several allegations of violence on the part of the respondent during 2011. She continues to live with the respondent until shortly before decree nisi is granted. No specific incidents are detailed in relation to the period after 2011. However, the applicant alleges generally that the respondent continually criticizes and belittles her, keeps her short of money, and prevents her from having any contact with her friends and family. Her cohabitation for more than six months since the last specific incidents in 2011 will not prejudice her entitlement to a divorce because the other behaviour of which she complains continued up to the day when she left and time therefore never started to run against her.

Cohabitation of more than six months

If the applicant continues to live with the respondent for a period or periods exceeding six **4.64** months in total, the cohabitation will be taken into account in determining whether the applicant can reasonably be expected to live with the respondent. The longer the applicant goes on living with the respondent after the last incident of behaviour, the less likely the court is to find that it is not reasonable to expect her to live with the respondent unless she can give a convincing reason for her continued cohabitation. However, cohabitation for more than six months is not an absolute bar in a behaviour case as it is in a case of adultery (*Bradley* v *Bradley* [1973] 3 All ER 750).

Example (The facts of *Bradley* v *Bradley* above.) The wife applied for a divorce on the basis of the husband's behaviour, alleging many incidents of violence. She was still living with the husband. The parties lived in a council house with four bedrooms with seven of their children. The wife said she had no alternative but to continue to sleep with the husband, cook his meals, etc because she was too frightened of him to do anything else. She could not be rehoused by the council whilst she was still married. The wife was not prevented from relying on s 1(2)(b) by reason of her continued cohabitation. She was entitled to have her case investigated on its merits and to call evidence to show that, although she was still living with her husband, she could not reasonably be expected to continue to do so.

Cohabitation and s 1(2)(c) to (e)

Section 2(5) provides that in considering whether a period of desertion or living apart has **4.65** been continuous, no account is to be taken of a period or periods not exceeding six months in total during which the parties resumed living with each other. However, no period or periods during which the parties lived with each other can be counted as part of the period of desertion or separation.

Example Husband and wife started living apart exactly two years ago. However, they have lived with each other for two periods of a month during this time. Neither can apply for a divorce therefore until two years and two months have elapsed since the initial separation.

It should be noted that s 2(5) is dealing with the question of *continuity* of the period of separation. It does not say that the periods of cohabitation should be disregarded for other purposes. A short period of cohabitation (six months or less) may therefore be relevant in determining, for example, whether desertion has been terminated or whether, in the case of either separation fact, there has been the sort of decision required by *Santos* v *Santos*, para 4.38 above, that the marriage is at an end.

4.66   Although the statute does not say so expressly, it must be the case that a period or periods of cohabitation in excess of six months *will* automatically break the continuity of the separation.

4.67   In drafting the petition, details of the date of separation must be specified in the statement of case. Where there has been a period of resumed cohabitation, no matter how short, details of this should also be included.

The rationale behind the cohabitation rule

4.68   The provisions of s 2 are designed to facilitate a reconciliation between the parties and to give them an opportunity to reflect on the state of their marriage without prejudicing proceedings for divorce if such proceedings become necessary at a later stage. It is vital that the solicitor understands the practical effect of the s 2 provisions and warns the client from the outset about the rules which are relevant to the client's particular circumstances.

L   CHAPTER SUMMARY

4.69   1. The only ground for divorce is that the marriage has broken down irretrievably.
2. The applicant must prove one or more of the following 'facts' on the balance of probabilities:
    Fact A: respondent's adultery and the applicant finding it intolerable to live with the respondent.
    Fact B: respondent's behaviour.
    Fact C: respondent's desertion for a continuous period of at least two years.
    Fact D: applicant and respondent have lived apart for a continuous period of at least two years and the respondent consents to the decree being granted.
    Fact E: the applicant and the respondent have lived apart for a continuous period of at least five years.
3. Care is needed where the parties have resumed cohabitation as laid down in s 2, MCA 1973.

M   KEY DOCUMENTS

4.70   Matrimonial Causes Act 1973

5

BAR ON FILING DIVORCE PETITIONS WITHIN ONE YEAR OF MARRIAGE

A   ABSOLUTE ONE-YEAR BAR

Proceedings for divorce cannot be commenced within the first year of marriage (s 3(1), **5.01** Matrimonial Causes Act 1973 ('MCA 1973')).

This bar is absolute and means that no matter how difficult the circumstances the applicant **5.02** must wait for at least one year before she may apply for a divorce (*Butler* v *Butler, The Queen's Proctor Intervening* [1990] 1 FLR 114).

In many circumstances, alternative steps need to be taken to give the client immediate assist- **5.03** ance and these are listed below with reference to the relevant chapter where the provisions are described in greater detail.

In practice, the solicitor is most likely to be required to provide advice on protection from **5.04** domestic abuse and help in resolving disputes relating to children.

B   BAR NOT APPLICABLE TO NULLITY PETITIONS

It is important to remember that the one-year bar does not apply to nullity petitions. Indeed, **5.05** in the case of certain voidable marriages, far from there being a time bar which prevents the applicant from filing a petition too *soon* after the marriage, there is a bar which prevents her from applying if she leaves it too *long* after the marriage (in these cases, the petition must usually be filed within three years of marriage, see Chapter 15). If there are grounds on which the marriage is void or voidable (see Chapter 15) a petition for nullity can therefore be filed without delay, even within days of the wedding in an appropriate case.

C   ALTERNATIVE COURSES OF ACTION FOR THE FIRST YEAR OF MARRIAGE

5.06   The wish to remarry is of course one of the reasons why people seek divorces. Unless there are grounds for seeking a nullity decree, the absolute bar on divorce within the first year of marriage means that there is nothing the solicitor can do to enable a client to remarry during that period. However, even though divorce is temporarily out of the question, the chances are that something can be done to help a client. The main options are as follows:

(a)   The client can be advised that she is free to look for alternative accommodation if things are not working out—although she must remain married, no one can force her to cohabit with her spouse.

(b)   Judicial separation (see further at Chapter 12): there is no restriction on the filing of petitions for judicial separation in the first year of marriage. However, now that the bar on divorce proceedings is so short it is questionable whether it is worth applying for a decree of judicial separation on behalf of a client who has made up her mind that she wants a divorce and is only prevented from seeking one by the one-year bar. Bearing in mind that it will take at least several weeks to obtain a decree of judicial separation, unless the solicitor is consulted only a short time after marriage, he may find that no sooner has he obtained a decree of judicial separation than the one year is up and proceedings have to be commenced all over again to obtain the decree of divorce that the client really wants. Consideration should therefore be given to whether, whilst waiting for the year to elapse, time would be better spent in concentrating on alleviating the client's immediate problems by means of other proceedings in the family proceedings court or county court.

(c)   Section 27, MCA 1973 (see further at Chapter 26).

(d)   Domestic Proceedings and Magistrates' Courts Act 1978.

(e)   Children Act 1989 (see further at Chapters 17 and 18).

(f)   Proceedings under Part IV, Family Law Act 1996 for a non-molestation order and/or an occupation order (see further at Chapters 36 and 37).

(g)   Section 17, Married Women's Property Act 1882 proceedings (see further at Chapter 28): it should be noted that under s 17, the court only has power to declare existing property rights and not to vary them. Should a divorce subsequently take place it will be open to the court to override any declaration already made under s 17 and adjust the parties' rights in the property under s 24, MCA 1973. Therefore, in the case of a client who intends to apply for a divorce as soon as she is allowed to do so, careful consideration should be given to whether a s 17 application is worthwhile. It may be better to advise the client to wait to have any property disputes determined in the aftermath of the divorce. It will usually be difficult to justify the costs involved in the two sets of proceedings in any event.

D   WHEN THE FIRST YEAR IS UP

As soon as the first year of marriage is up it is open season for divorce. In practice, only peti-   **5.07**
tions based on adultery (s 1(2)(a), MCA 1973) and behaviour (s 1(2)(b), MCA 1973) will be
feasible for at least another year as the other s 1(2) facts depend on there having been at least
two years' separation.

Even though the temptation is to shelve the question of divorce entirely until the first year   **5.08**
has elapsed, in fact there is no reason why the case should not be prepared (marriage certificate obtained, divorce petition drafted, etc) before the end of the year so that the petition can
be filed at the earliest possible opportunity.

Section 3(2), MCA 1973 makes it clear that a divorce petition may be based wholly or partly on   **5.09**
matters which occurred during the first year of marriage even though it cannot be presented
during that year. Thus, for example, once the year is over a decree could be sought on the basis
of adultery that occurred during the year and a period of separation upon which reliance is
placed under s 1(2)(c) to (e) can start to run during the first year.

E   CHAPTER SUMMARY

1. Proceedings for divorce cannot begin until one year after the marriage takes place.   **5.10**
2. Proceedings for a decree of judicial separation or nullity can begin at any time after the
   date of the marriage.
3. Other courses of action for the first year of marriage are outlined in the chapter.

F   KEY DOCUMENTS

Matrimonial Causes Act 1973   **5.11**

6

JURISDICTION IN DIVORCE, NULLITY, JUDICIAL SEPARATION, AND PROCEEDINGS TO DISSOLVE A CIVIL PARTNERSHIP

A   INTRODUCTION

6.01 One important requirement in commencing proceedings for divorce is to be able to demonstrate that the court has jurisdiction to entertain a petition for divorce. Simply because an individual is living in England does not give a court the power to deal with their family difficulties.

The relevant law is found in s 5, Domicile and Matrimonial Proceedings Act 1973 ('DMPA 1973'), as amended, and is now largely based on one or both spouses being habitually resident in England and Wales. Where 'habitual residence' cannot be demonstrated, it may be possible to base jurisdiction on one of the parties being domiciled in England and Wales. **6.02**

The position may be unclear at times and it will be necessary to take careful instructions from the client to be sure that the court does in fact have jurisdiction. Hence, the characteristics of both 'habitual residence' and 'domicile' are explained in this chapter. **6.03**

It should be noted that reference is made at para 6.32 to the jurisdiction position where a civil partnership is to be dissolved. **6.04**

B JURISDICTION FOR DIVORCE: S 5, DOMICILE AND MATRIMONIAL PROCEEDINGS ACT 1973

Council Regulation (EC) No 2201/2003 of 27 November 2003 now governs the jurisdiction conditions to be fulfilled to petition for a decree of divorce by amending s 5(2), DMPA 1973. The Council Regulation is known as Brussels IIR. It came into force on 1 March 2005. **6.05**

Section 5(2) now provides as follows: **6.06**

> The court shall have jurisdiction to entertain proceedings for divorce or judicial separation if (and only if):
> (a) the court has jurisdiction under the Council Regulation; or
> (b) no court of a Contracting State has jurisdiction under the Council Regulation and either of the parties to the marriage is domiciled in England and Wales on the date when the proceedings are begun.

The purpose of the Council Regulation, amongst other things, is to enact provisions to unify the rules of conflict of jurisdiction in family matters and provides that, in such matters, jurisdiction shall lie with the courts of the Member State in whose territory: **6.07**

(a)
   (i) the spouses are habitually resident, or
   (ii) the spouses were last habitually resident, insofar as one of them still resides there, or
   (iii) the respondent is habitually resident, or
   (iv) in the event of a joint application, either of the spouses is habitually resident, or
   (v) the applicant is habitually resident if he or she resides there for at least one year immediately before the application was made, or
   (vi) the applicant is habitually resident if he or she resided there for at least six months immediately before the application was made and is either a national of the member state in question or, in the case of the United Kingdom and Ireland, has his 'domicile' there;
(b) both spouses are nationals or, in the case of the United Kingdom and Ireland, it is the place of 'domicile' of both spouses.

The above list under the Council Regulation is designed to offer a multiple choice of jurisdictional factors to determine whether the court has authority to entertain the petition for divorce: the list is not intended to be hierarchical. Provided that one criterion is met, the court of the Contracting State has jurisdiction. It will be noted that it is based principally on the habitual residence of the parties as distinct from their domicile. 'Habitual residence' is discussed more fully in paras 6.10 ff below.

6.08   Where no court of a Contracting State has jurisdiction under the Council Regulation, a petition for divorce may properly be lodged in a court in England and Wales where either party is domiciled in England and Wales on the date when the proceedings are begun. 'Domicile' is explained in paras 6.17 ff.

6.09   How the amendments to s 5, DMPA 1973 affect the drafting of the divorce petition and the completion of the acknowledgment of service is explained in Chapters 7 and 8.

C   THE MEANING OF HABITUAL RESIDENCE

6.10   Until 1985, habitual residence had not been defined for the purposes of s 5, DMPA 1973. However, in the case of *Kapur v Kapur* [1985] 15 Fam Law 22, Bush J held that habitual residence is essentially the same as ordinary residence (a concept with which the courts are familiar in other areas of the law). He therefore held that habitual residence means voluntary residence with a degree of settled purpose; that a limited purpose such as education could be a settled purpose and the husband was held to have satisfied the requirement of 12 months' habitual residence.

6.11   In *Ikimi v Ikimi* [2001] 2 FLR 1288, the Court of Appeal considered the term 'habitual residence'. Here Thorpe LJ held that to be 'habitually resident' meant the same as to be 'ordinarily resident'. Accordingly, it was possible to be habitually resident in England and Wales for the purpose of divorce proceedings even if residence in the country amounted to 161 days in the relevant year only and the applicant had at the same time been habitually resident in Nigeria. More recently in *Armstrong v Armstrong* [2003] 2 FLR 375, however, the court held that living in England for 71 days per year with little evidence of a settled intention to remain did not amount to 'habitual residence'. The decree nisi was rescinded because the court did not have jurisdiction.

6.12   On the other hand, in *Mark v Mark* [2004] 1 FLR 1069, the Court of Appeal held that the applicant wife who had not obtained indefinite leave to remain in the United Kingdom at the time of the divorce proceedings (and, therefore, was categorized as an 'over stayer'), was nevertheless habitually resident and domiciled in England and Wales. Hence, the court had jurisdiction to entertain the petition for divorce.

6.13   Thorpe LJ indicated that to deny the wife access to the court amounted to a breach of Art 6 of the European Convention for the Protection of Human Rights and Fundamental Freedoms 1950.

6.14   He also confirmed that the court had a margin of discretion in determining whether or not an element of illegality tainted the stay of the applicant and thus precluded the acquisition of domicile of choice and the right to invoke the court's jurisdiction. This decision was subsequently confirmed by the House of Lords at [2005] UKHL 42.

For a more recent case where the concept of habitual residence was considered in the context of divorce proceedings by Singer J, see *L-K* v *K* [2007] 2 FLR 729. **6.15**

It is suggested that, in summary, the practical position as to habitual residence is as follows: **6.16**

(a) There should not normally be any difficulty in establishing jurisdiction on the basis of 12 months' or 6 months' habitual residence if one or the other party has been living in England and Wales for, for example, business, education, family reasons, health, or even simply love of the country, throughout the whole year immediately preceding the presentation of the petition.

(b) Temporary or occasional short absences, for example on holiday abroad, will not prevent an individual from establishing habitual residence.

(c) Even rather more prolonged absences will not necessarily disrupt an individual's habitual residence.

(d) It is irrelevant that the individual's real home is outside England, or that he intends or expects to live outside England in the future.

(e) The illegality of the stay may not necessarily mean that the court does not have jurisdiction.

D   THE MEANING OF DOMICILE

Determining a person's domicile can be very tricky. This book provides only a very broad outline of the law of domicile. Should a problem over domicile be encountered, reference should be made to standard practitioners' works on family law and also to textbooks on private international law. **6.17**

What is domicile?

Domicile is essentially a legal concept used to link an individual with a particular legal system. The concept of domicile is primarily used to determine which country's law should govern questions of an individual's personal status. Domicile and nationality are two quite separate matters; it is not possible to find out where a person is domiciled merely by finding out his nationality. Neither is it possible to ascertain a person's domicile simply by finding out where he lives; residence and domicile are not the same thing. **6.18**

Key points

(a) A person must be domiciled in a place which has only one legal system. This means that it is not possible to be domiciled in the British Isles—a person is domiciled in England and Wales, or in Scotland or in Northern Ireland. **6.19**

(b) Every person has a domicile.

(c) It is not possible to have more than one domicile at one time.

(d) However, it is possible for an individual's place of domicile to change as his personal circumstances alter throughout his life.

Determining where a person is domiciled

6.20 There are three types of domicile: domicile of origin, domicile of dependence, and domicile of choice.

Domicile of origin

6.21 The law attributes a domicile to every newborn baby. This is his domicile of origin.

6.22 Normally a child of married parents will take as his domicile that of his father at the time of his birth, whereas the child of the unmarried family will take that of his mother. Domicile of the relevant parent determines the domicile of the child, not the actual place of birth.

6.23 An individual must never be without a domicile. Therefore, he retains his domicile of origin throughout his life. At times it may be overtaken by a different domicile of dependence or domicile of choice, but in the absence of any other domicile it will always revive.

Domicile of choice

6.24 **Residence and intention** Once an individual reaches the age of 16, he will be able to acquire a domicile of choice. An individual acquires a domicile of choice by living in a country other than the country of his domicile of origin with the intention of continuing to reside there permanently, or at least indefinitely.

    (a) *Residence*
For a domicile of choice to be acquired in a country, the individual must actually take up residence there. It is not enough for him to make up his mind in his freezing flat in north London that he will emigrate to Australia, or even for him to buy his airline ticket or board his plane. He must actually arrive in the country.

    (b) *Intention*
An individual cannot acquire a domicile of choice in a country until he decides to live there permanently, or for a settled period of time. Thus a domicile of choice will not be acquired in Saudi Arabia by someone simply posted there by his employers or spending some time there on holiday. See *Cramer* v *Cramer* [1987] 1 FLR 116 where Stephen Brown LJ stated that the burden of establishing a change of domicile (from a domicile of origin to a domicile of choice) is 'a heavy one'.

This point was reinforced in *R* v *R (Divorce: Jurisdiction: Domicile)* [2006] 1 FLR 389. In holding that the respondent wife in divorce proceedings had not acquired a domicile of choice in France, Philip Sapsford QC indicated that what would need to be demonstrated, on a standard of proof which went beyond a mere balance of probabilities, was a fixed and settled intention to abandon her English domicile of origin and to settle permanently in France. A change of domicile could not be established simply by making declarations to that effect or by acquiring a home in a different country. In particular, the fact that the wife's driving licence, passport, nationality, bank accounts, credit cards, and medical insurance were all English undermined her argument that she had acquired a domicile of choice in France. For more recent guidance, see *M* v *M (Divorce) (Domicile)* [2011] 1 FLR 919.

Examples of domicile of choice

Example 1 Mr Maynard has always lived in England as had his father before him. His domi- **6.25**
cile of origin is English (taken from that of his father when he was born). He becomes a
famous writer and decides to investigate the possibility of living in Switzerland. He goes to
stay in Switzerland to look at property. At this stage, his domicile of origin is still operative as
he has not yet made up his mind whether to live in Switzerland. He returns home and
decides that he will move permanently to Switzerland. He has still not acquired a domicile
of choice there as he has not taken up residence there. He sells his house and winds up his
business in England and travels to Switzerland. He has now acquired a domicile of choice in
Switzerland.

Example 2 Mr Connor, a man of 35, has always lived in the United States. He has a domicile
of origin in Texas. He comes to England to work for an English company. He buys a house in
England and moves his family over. However, he intends to return to the United States when
he retires. He does not acquire a domicile of choice in England because he lacks the required
intention to live here at least indefinitely.

Loss of domicile of choice In contrast with the domicile of origin, a domicile of choice can be **6.26**
lost forever. Although there is a question mark over the exact nature of the intention required,
it would seem that a domicile of choice will be lost if the individual gives up residence in the
country in question and ceases to have the intention to reside there permanently or at least
indefinitely. Both elements must be present. Intention to leave the country without actually
leaving is not sufficient, neither is leaving without any change in the original intention to live
there permanently or indefinitely.

An individual may acquire a new domicile of choice immediately the old one is abandoned. **6.27**
However, if he does not do so, for example if he gives up his home in one country and then
travels around whilst making up his mind where to settle for the future, his domicile of origin
will revive to fill the gap.

Proof of intention The individual concerned may not have formulated his intentions as to **6.28**
the future explicitly. His intention can, however, be inferred from all the circumstances of the
case—what he did, what he said, etc.

Domicile of dependence

Until a child is 16 and can acquire an independent domicile of choice, he has a domicile of **6.29**
dependence on one or other of his parents. To begin with, this is the same as his domicile
of origin, but if the domicile of his relevant parent changes, so will the child's domicile of
dependence.

Thus, the domicile of a child of married parents will normally change with that of his father, **6.30**
or, if his father dies, with that of his mother. If, however, the child's parents are separated and
he is living with his mother, his domicile will change with that of his mother: s 4, DMPA 1973.
A child of the unmarried family will have a domicile of dependence on his mother.

6.31 When the child becomes capable of acquiring an independent domicile at 16, he will retain his domicile of dependence until he acquires a domicile of choice.

Example Mr and Mrs Hall are happily married. Mrs Hall gives birth to a baby daughter, Sarah. Sarah takes her domicile of origin from her father who is domiciled in England at this time. Subsequently, Mr and Mrs Hall decide to go and live in France and take up residence there. They therefore acquire domiciles of choice in France and Sarah thus has a domicile of dependence in France. Mr and Mrs Hall then encounter marital problems and separate. Mrs Hall goes to live with her mother in Scotland, intending to stay there permanently and taking Sarah with her. Sarah's domicile is now dependent on her mother as her parents are living apart and she has her home with her mother. She is therefore domiciled in Scotland. This is still the case after her sixteenth birthday until, at the age of 23, she marries and goes to live permanently in Northern Ireland. She now has a domicile of choice in Northern Ireland.

E   JURISDICTION FOR DISSOLUTION OF A CIVIL PARTNERSHIP

6.32 A combination of s 219, Civil Partnership Act 2004 and Civil Partnership (Jurisdiction and Recognition of Judgments) Regulations 2005 (SI 2005/3334) makes it clear that jurisdiction for the termination of a civil partnership is as for divorce adopting the grounds prescribed in Brussels IIR.

F   RECOGNITION OF FOREIGN DECREES

Recognition of divorce and separation decrees

6.33 There are detailed statutory rules as to the recognition of foreign decrees of divorce and separation. These are set out in the Family Law Act 1986 ('FLA 1986').

6.34 A distinction is made between decrees granted under the law of any part of the British Isles and divorces and separations obtained overseas. A further distinction is made between an overseas divorce or separation obtained by means of proceedings, on the one hand, and one obtained otherwise than by means of proceedings, on the other. The rules relating to recognition of a decree obtained otherwise than by means of proceedings are particularly stringent. The details are set out in s 46, FLA 1986. Note that a decree of divorce or judicial separation granted under the law of any part of the British Isles must be recognized throughout the United Kingdom: s 44(2), FLA 1986.

Recognition of nullity decrees

6.35 The recognition of foreign nullity decrees is governed by ss 45 to 48, FLA 1986.

Entitlement to financial provision in English courts after foreign divorce, nullity, or legal separation

Part III, Matrimonial and Family Proceedings Act 1984 gives the English courts jurisdiction   **6.36**
to grant financial relief after an overseas divorce, annulment, or legal separation obtained by
means of proceedings and which is recognized in this country as valid. Such an application for
financial provision can be made whether the decree in a foreign country was made before or
after the 1984 Act came into force (*Chebaro* v *Chebaro* [1987] 2 FLR 456). Permission of the
court is required before such a financial relief application can be made. More recent case law
includes *A* v *S (Financial Relief after Overseas US Divorce and Financial Proceedings)* [2003] 1 FLR 431
and *M* v *L (Financial Relief after Overseas Divorce)* [2003] 2 FLR 425.

G   CHAPTER SUMMARY

1. The English court will only have jurisdiction to deal with petitions for divorce (or for   **6.37**
   application for dissolution of a civil partnership) if one of the grounds in Brussels IIR is
   satisfied.
2. Jurisdiction is based on one party's habitual residence or domicile.

H   KEY DOCUMENTS

Domicile and Matrimonial Proceedings Act 1973   **6.38**
Family Law Act 1986
Part III, Matrimonial and Family Proceedings Act 1984
Council Regulation (EC) No 2201/2003
Civil Partnership (Jurisdiction and Recognition of Judgments) Regulations 2005 (SI
   2005/3334)

7

DRAFTING A DIVORCE PETITION

A INTRODUCTION

7.01 Chapters 7 and 8 describe one of the most common tasks for the family law practitioner—drafting the divorce petition and the procedure to be followed to obtain the decree absolute of divorce.

7.02 Before drafting the petition, it is helpful to check the following matters to ensure that your client will obtain a decree of divorce.

(a) Are the parties validly married? If not, the court has no jurisdiction to grant a decree of divorce but instead nullity proceedings may be appropriate.

(b) Have the parties been married for at least one year (see Chapter 5)?

(c) Does the court have jurisdiction to entertain a petition for divorce (see Chapter 6)?

(d) Are you satisfied, following full discussions with the client, that the marriage has irretrievably broken down and hence the ground for divorce can be demonstrated?

(e) Can you prove, on the balance of probabilities, the statutory fact to be relied on? For example, will the respondent admit to the adultery to be alleged or consent to a divorce based on two years' separation? If there are any doubts, the potential difficulties should be resolved at this stage otherwise time and money will be wasted. Where it is known, for instance, that the respondent is unlikely to admit to the adultery to be alleged, consider whether the alternative fact of 'behaviour' might be appropriate as the basis for the divorce. The respondent's specific admission or consent will not be required.

The relevant rules of procedure governing the conduct of divorce proceedings are found in the Family Procedure Rules 2010 ('FPR 2010', SI 2010/2955).

Every application for divorce is commenced by petition (FPR 2010, PD5A). The petition is the **7.03** central document in the case. It is filed by the spouse seeking the divorce ('the applicant') and served on the other spouse ('the respondent').

The petition informs the respondent and the court of the basis on which the applicant claims **7.04** to be entitled to a decree and of the other orders that she will be seeking as part of the divorce process, for example in relation to periodical payments, property, and provision for the children.

The solicitor normally prepares the petition on behalf of the client. If the client is receiving **7.05** Legal Help, the solicitor will be entitled to payment for doing this under the scheme. The private client must meet the cost personally. In some cases it may be possible to recover at least part of the cost of the proceedings from the respondent or co-respondent if there is one (see Chapter 8, para 8.82).

B   THE CONTENTS OF THE PETITION

The petition for divorce in Form D8 sets out the information required to commence the **7.06** divorce proceedings. Form D8 (Notes) provides guidance on completing a petition for divorce. Copies of both documents are reproduced at the end of this chapter.

The information to be given in the petition is as follows: **7.07**

(a) the name of the applicant and the type of application (ie, for a decree of divorce or a decree of judicial separation);
(b) details of the name, address, date of birth, occupation, and gender of the applicant and the respondent;
(c) the date and place of the marriage;
(d) the address at which the parties to the marriage last lived together as husband and wife;
(e) the grounds on which the court has jurisdiction to deal with the application for divorce (see Chapter 6);
(f) details of any other proceedings in any court in England and Wales or elsewhere with reference to the marriage or to any children of the family or between the applicant and the respondent with reference to any property of either or both of them;
(g) where the fact on which the petition is based is five years' separation, whether any, and if so what, agreement or arrangement has been made or is proposed to be made between the parties for the support of the applicant and any child of the family;
(h) confirmation of the nature of the application and, in the case of divorce, that the marriage has irretrievably broken down;

(i) the fact alleged by the applicant for the purposes of s 1(2), Matrimonial Causes Act 1973 ('MCA 1973'). The 'facts' are printed on the petition and the applicant must tick the relevant one;

(j) details in support of the fact relied on but not the evidence by which it is to be proved;

(k) details of the children of the family including full names and dates of birth together with details of whether the child is aged 16 but under 18 and in education, training, or working full time, whether the child is a child of both parties or a child of the family in some other way;

(l) details of children (including full names and dates of birth) who are children of either party but who are not children of the family;

(m) service details including information as to whether the applicant is represented by a solicitor and, if so, the name and address of the solicitor;

(n) details of the co-respondent if any.

7.08 Every petition for divorce shall conclude with a prayer setting out particulars of the remedy claimed. The prayer should set out any claim for costs and any application for financial provision which it is intended to claim.

7.09 A carefully drafted petition will go a long way towards ensuring that a decree of divorce is obtained swiftly and smoothly. The solicitor should therefore bear in mind the following notes when drafting the petition.

C   NOTES ON DRAFTING THE PETITION

7.10 These notes refer to the printed petition form and the supporting notes for guidance reproduced at the end of this chapter.

7.11 Note that details of the name of the court, the case number, date received by the court, date issued, and time issued are completed by the court before service of the petition on the respondent.

7.12 The applicant must on page 1 of the petition give her full name and confirm what she is applying for.

Part 1—Details of the applicant and the respondent

7.13 Here the applicant must give the full names by which she and the respondent are currently known, together with the address, date of birth, and occupation of each party. The gender of each party must also be stated. The notes for guidance recognize that the applicant may not have up-to-date details of the respondent (eg she may no longer know his current occupation) but she is required to give the current details as fully as she knows them.

7.14 The applicant may leave blank details of her address or that of her children if she feels threatened by the respondent knowing where she is living or because there is a history of domestic violence (r 29.1(1), FPR 2010). In these circumstances she is required to file Form C8 containing confidential contact details for use by the court.

The contact details will not be revealed to the respondent unless the court directs otherwise **7.15** (r 29.1(1)).

Part 2—Details of the marriage

The details of the marriage should be taken exactly from the marriage certificate. The place of **7.16** the marriage should be fully stated: forms of wording are set out in the notes for guidance. The court is likely to reject any petition where the details of the marriage are incorrectly given.

Part 3—Jurisdiction

This Part is concerned with the basis for the court's jurisdiction. The basis on which a court **7.17** may have jurisdiction to deal with a petition for divorce is laid down in s 5(2), Domicile and Matrimonial Proceedings Act 1973, discussed in Chapter 6. Part 3 now requires the applicant to indicate by ticking the appropriate box on what ground the court has jurisdiction under Art 3(1) of Council Regulation (EC) No 2201/2003 Concerning Jurisdiction and the Recognition and Enforcement of Judgments in Matrimonial Matters and the Matters of Parental Responsibility of 27 November 2003. It is a matter of ticking the box which most accurately reflects the particular circumstances of the applicant and the respondent setting out in the space provided the ground on which the applicant seeks to rely to demonstrate that the court has jurisdiction. The grounds are set out fully in the notes for guidance at the end of the chapter.

If none of the grounds applies, the court may still have jurisdiction on an alternative basis **7.18** (known as the residual jurisdiction). For example, in matrimonial proceedings the court has jurisdiction on this basis if:

(a) no court in any European Union Member State has jurisdiction under Council Regulation 2201/2003; and
(b) either the applicant or the respondent is domiciled in England and Wales on the date when the petition is issued.

Part 4—Other proceedings or arrangements

In this Part details must be given of *all* court proceedings in relation to the marriage or the **7.19** children of the family or between the applicant and the respondent in relation to their property. In particular, details of the name of the court in which the proceedings took place and details of the order(s) which were made must be given. If there are proceedings related to the marriage, the applicant must also state whether she and the respondent resumed living together as husband and wife after the order was made.

The information must include completed proceedings and those which were abandoned **7.20** without a final decision or order being made. Details of proceedings in both England and Wales and those taking place elsewhere must be given.

It is unusual for proceedings to be taking place outside England and Wales. An example of **7.21** the type of proceedings to which reference should be made would be foreign divorce proceedings.

7.22 It should be noted that Council Regulation 2201/2003 provides that where a party issues proceedings in a jurisdiction of one of the Contracting States (these are set out in Chapter 6), the court of the state in which proceedings are first issued shall have exclusive jurisdiction. Proceedings issued in another Contracting State for the same remedy must be stayed. There is little scope for the exercise of discretion save for some limited exceptions including that a stay would be manifestly contrary to public policy.

7.23 What this means in practice is that if divorce proceedings are validly issued in, say, Spain, any divorce proceedings subsequently commenced in England must be stayed. Arguments as to fairness and convenience will carry no weight. The party to the marriage who commences the divorce proceedings first will be able to secure the jurisdiction of his or her choice.

7.24 More commonly, applications to a court under Part IV, Family Law Act 1996 for a non-molestation order and/or an occupation order and under s 17, Married Women's Property Act 1882 must obviously be mentioned. Practitioners sometimes overlook the fact that if any of the children of the family have been adopted, details of the adoption proceedings must be given.

7.25 This Part of the petition also requires the applicant, where the petition is based on five years' separation, to indicate whether the parties have reached an agreement for the support of the applicant and for any child of the family. It is understood that the wording here is to change in the near future to refer also to details of any agreement to support the respondent.

Part 5—The facts

7.26 This Part requires the applicant, by completion of two tick boxes, to confirm:

(a) that the marriage has irretrievably broken down (the sole ground for divorce); and
(b) the fact relied on under s 1(2), MCA 1973 to prove that she is entitled to a decree of divorce.

Part 6—Statement of case

7.27 The applicant must set out in this Part the allegations which she is relying on to prove the fact given in Part 5. It is important to remember that the onus of proof lies on the applicant, the standard of proof being the civil standard, that is, on the balance of probabilities.

7.28 The notes for guidance encourage brevity in completing this Part and make the point, for example, that where it is alleged that the respondent has committed adultery, the co-respondent need not be named unless the allegation is likely to be contested (r 7.10(3)).

7.29 The following guidelines should also help:

(a) Adultery cases: if possible, give the date(s) and place(s) of the adultery (or, where adultery has taken place frequently over a period of time, the dates between which it was committed). If the respondent and the other party to the adultery have been cohabiting, the dates and place of cohabitation should be given. If there has been a child as a result of the adultery, this should be stated. As indicated above, it is no longer necessary for the co-respondent to be named in the petition even if his identity is known to the applicant. However, if the applicant seeks to make a claim for costs against that person it will be necessary to name the person and make him a party to the proceedings (ie, as co-respondent).

(b) Behaviour cases: as a rule of thumb, where the applicant's statement clearly discloses sufficient evidence of behaviour and there is no reason to believe that the petition will be defended, it should be sufficient to set out about six allegations/incidents. Generally it is appropriate to include the first, the worst, and the last incident of behaviour during the marriage. Incidents should be described in chronological order wherever possible. A long narrative is not required. The date of the incident should be given as precisely as possible together with sufficient information to identify the incident the applicant has in mind and to see why it is alleged to constitute behaviour. The allegations should not be 'hopelessly general' (*Butterworth* v *Butterworth* [1997] 2 FLR 336). If the applicant suffered an injury to health as a result of the incident or was otherwise affected, this should be stated. It is quite common to include a general paragraph summarizing the characteristics of the respondent's behaviour.

(c) Desertion cases: the date and circumstances of the respondent's departure should be given in sufficient detail to show that the respondent intended to bring cohabitation to an end permanently. Part 6 should also state that the applicant did not consent to the respondent's departure and gave him no cause to leave.

(d) Consensual separation cases: the date and brief circumstances of the separation should be given. Care must be taken in cases where the parties have continued to live in the same house to give sufficient information to establish that they did maintain separate households under the same roof.

(e) Five years' separation cases: details should be given as in consensual separation cases.

It should be made clear in all cases in the statement of case whether the applicant and respondent **7.30** have ceased to cohabit and, if so, when. The provisions of s 2, MCA 1973 as to cohabitation (see Chapter 4) should be borne in mind when drafting the statement and any relevant periods of cohabitation should be referred to.

Example The applicant and respondent separated on 4 May 2006. The petition alleges five years' separation. The parties have, in fact, resumed living together for two periods, from 1 August to 22 September 2007 and from 3 February to 8 April 2008. These periods do not together exceed six months, therefore they will be disregarded in determining whether the applicant should get a decree. However, they should be referred to in the details of separation thus:

> The applicant and the respondent have lived apart for a continuous period of at least five years immediately preceding the presentation of this petition, namely from 4 May 2006 when, after unhappy family difficulties, the applicant left the respondent, save that the applicant and the respondent have resumed living together for two periods not exceeding six months in all, namely from . . . In the circumstances, no account should be taken of the said periods.

Part 7—Details of the children

This Part requires the details of all living children of the family to be given. **7.31**

'Child of the family' in relation to the parties to a marriage is defined in s 52, MCA 1973 as: **7.32**

(a) a child of both of those parties; and

(b) any other child, not being a child who is placed with those parties as foster parents by a local authority or voluntary organisation, who has been treated by both of those parties as a child of their family.

A child will qualify as a child of the family on the basis that he is a child of both parties to the marriage even if he was born to them before the marriage took place or after it broke down or was adopted by them rather than being their natural child.

7.33   A child can become a child of the family by virtue of the second limb of the definition even though he is the child of only one party to the marriage or, indeed, where he is the child of neither of the parties. It is not always easy to determine whether a child has become a child of the family by virtue of treatment. It is a broad question of fact which must be decided by the court looking at all the circumstances of the case. The test is objective.

7.34   The following points should also be borne in mind:

(a)   The exclusion of children boarded out with the parties automatically prevents children such as foster children becoming children of the family no matter how long the child has lived with the family.

(b)   A child can only be treated as a child of the family once it is born so a generous attitude towards a forthcoming baby on the part of a husband during his wife's pregnancy by another man will not lead to the baby becoming a child of the family. It is only if he continues to treat the child as a child of the family once it is born that it will achieve the status of a child of the family (*A v A (Family: Unborn Child)* [1974] 1 All ER 755).

(c)   The family can cease to exist before a divorce takes place if the parties to the marriage separate permanently. Where this happens and the wife gives birth to a child by another man after the separation, it is not possible for that child to be treated as a child of the family (*M v M* [1980] 2 FLR 39).

(d)   If a child has been treated as a child of the family, the fact that the husband only behaved in this way towards the child because he believed, mistakenly as it turns out, that the child was his own will not prevent the child being classed as a child of the family (*W(RJ) v W(SJ)* [1971] 3 All ER 303).

(e)   The definition can include a child brought up by its grandparents in circumstances where the evidence suggests that the natural parents have handed over responsibility for the care of the child. Here, the child became 'a child of the family' to be considered in divorce proceedings following the breakdown of the marriage of the grandparents: *Re A (Child of the Family)* [1998] 1 FLR 346 (CA).

Example 1   Susan is the natural child of Mr and Mrs Smith born whilst they were living together before they got married. She is automatically a child of their family.

Example 2   Mr and Mrs Smith get divorced. Mrs Smith subsequently remarries. Susan lives with Mrs Smith and her new husband, Mr Jones. Mr Jones welcomes Susan as his own daughter and takes an interest in all that she does. For example, he regularly attends parents' evenings at Susan's school with Mrs Smith, he supports Mrs Smith in matters of discipline, and he provides Susan with pocket money. Although Susan's natural father pays £100 per week towards her maintenance, the housekeeping that Mr Jones gives to Mrs Smith is used to feed the family as a whole including Susan. Susan addresses Mr Jones as John. There is little doubt that Susan is a child of the family of Mrs Smith and Mr Jones.

Example 3   The wife has a child by her first marriage. The child goes to live with her grandparents when the first marriage breaks down. The wife remarries. The child visits the wife and her new husband to stay at weekends and for substantial periods during the school holidays (about 50–60 days a year in all). She has her own room at their house and the new husband buys her a pony which he expects her to groom and muck out. He also reproves her is she does not keep her bedroom clean.

In the case of *A v A* (above), a child in this situation was held not to be a child of the family—her home was with her grandparents and the husband's behaviour towards her did not amount to treating her as a child of his and the mother's family.

Example 4 Mrs Brown remarries after the death of her first husband. Her son Sam is at boarding school. He spends the holidays living with Mrs Brown, her new husband, and the new husband's two children by his previous marriage who live with their father permanently. He has his own room at their house and all three children are treated in exactly the same way by both Mrs Brown and her new husband. It is likely that all three children are children of the family.

The petition should state the full names (including surnames) of all living children whom the applicant alleges are children of the family. If the child is not the natural or adopted child of both parents it is good practice to state his paternity and that he has been treated as a child of the family. It is open to the respondent subsequently to deny that a child is a child of the family. It may be necessary for him to do this, for example, in order that he should be excused from any financial liability for the child. **7.35**

If the children are under the age of 18, their dates of birth should be given. **7.36**

If the children are 18 or over this should be stated. The court has a duty under s 41, MCA 1973 to look after the interests not only of minor children but also of those children over 18 who have special needs (see Chapter 8). Therefore, if there is a child of the family who is over 18 but is still dependent on his parents and unable to look after his own interests, for example because of learning disability, brief details should also be given of his circumstances to enable the court to decide whether it needs to look more closely at the arrangements for him in accordance with s 41. **7.37**

The petition requires the applicant to indicate whether a statement of arrangements for children is to be attached to the petition (see Chapter 8) and goes on to require the applicant also to give details of children who are not children of the family, but are children of either party to the marriage (for example, children living with another parent). **7.38**

Part 8—Special assistance or facilities at court

This Part provides the applicant with the opportunity to warn the court if special assistance or facilities would be required if the applicant or the respondent were to attend court. The notes for guidance indicate that the court would find it helpful to know if, for example, the applicant or the respondent would require large print documents, wheelchair access, a hearing loop, or a sign language interpreter. **7.39**

Part 9—Service details

In this Part, the applicant must confirm whether she is acting in person, is not represented by a solicitor but is receiving advice from a solicitor (this will apply where the applicant is receiving **7.40**

Legal Help from a solicitor but is deemed to be acting in person), or is represented by a solicitor (because she is either paying privately or is in receipt of a certificate for Legal Representation for the divorce proceedings). She may then indicate to which address documents should be sent. She must also give the respondent's address for service (and that of the co-respondent if there is one). This will be the address of the last-known residence of the respondent (and co-respondent) unless the applicant's solicitors have been notified that the respondent (or co-respondent) is represented by solicitors who will accept service of the petition on his behalf.

Part 10—Prayer

7.41 As the notes for guidance make clear, the prayer in the petition is the applicant's request to the court.

Prayer for dissolution of marriage

7.42 This is a standard prayer which takes the same form in all divorce petitions.

Prayer for costs

7.43 Careful consideration should be given to whether the costs of obtaining a decree should be claimed from the respondent or the co-respondent. A claim for costs will normally be included where the applicant is receiving full public funding or is paying privately for the services of her solicitor. Whether costs will be ordered is a matter within the discretion of the court (see Chapter 8, paras 8.82 ff). The general view is that costs should *not* normally be claimed where the applicant is receiving Legal Help. There seem to be two reasons for this. First, the financial benefit of a claim for costs will inevitably be small as the applicant will only be entitled to costs as a litigant in person in any event. Secondly, the prayer for costs can sometimes prove to be the last straw that decides the respondent not only to contest the issue of costs but also to oppose the granting of a divorce.

7.44 It must be said, however, that quite a number of practitioners do nevertheless claim costs in Legal Help cases and some district judges continue to grant costs although the practice seems to vary around the country. It may be that the reason for solicitors continuing to claim costs is to reduce the potential impact of the statutory charge, or to save the trouble of amending the petition later to claim costs should the case be defended.

7.45 A sensible approach, therefore, is to word the prayer for costs to read as follows: 'That the respondent may be ordered to pay costs of the divorce should the proceedings become defended or should the statutory charge apply.'

7.46 If a prayer for costs is included, it is open to the respondent/co-respondent to contest his liability to pay. He will do this initially by notifying the court of his objection on the acknowledgment of service form. For the subsequent procedure, see Chapter 8.

Prayer for financial provision

7.47 It will normally be advisable to include a prayer for all available forms of financial provision. This is because the applicant is obliged to make any claims that she wishes to make on her own behalf for maintenance pending suit, periodical payment orders, property adjustment, and pension orders in the petition (r 9.4, FPR 2010; Chapter 29). If she fails to include all her claims in the petition at the outset, she will not be able to make them at all unless either:

(a) if the omission is discovered before a decree is granted, the petition is amended to include the appropriate claims. The petition can be amended without the court's permission before it is served but thereafter the permission of the court is required for amendments; as to amendment, see further Chapter 9, *or*

(b) if the omission is not discovered until after a decree has been granted, then the court's permission to make the application is necessary. The only exception to this is that if the parties are agreed as to the terms of the order, the applicant can make an application for the agreed order without the court's permission.

If the omission is not discovered until after the applicant has remarried, she will be debarred from making any claim at all (whereas a lump sum or property adjustment claim made *before* remarriage can be pursued after remarriage).

> **Example** Mr and Mrs Williams have been married for many years. They have always lived in a council house and, as far as Mrs Williams is aware, they have no savings. Mrs Williams leaves her husband and seeks a divorce. She obtains a flat from a housing association so she does not want a transfer of the council house nor does she want any of the contents of the house which have had their day. She does not even want maintenance because she has met someone she intends to marry. When her petition is filed, all the claims for financial provision are struck out of the prayer. After decree absolute comes through, Mrs Williams remarries. She then discovers that her husband had been saving a meaningful sum from his earnings throughout the marriage without telling her. He has amassed savings of over £100,000 over the years. Mrs Williams consults her solicitor with a view to claiming a share. She cannot do so because no claim for a lump sum or property adjustment order was included in her petition and she is debarred from making one now by her remarriage. Had her petition included a comprehensive prayer for financial provision, she could have proceeded with a claim in relation to the savings despite her remarriage.

Although claims for financial provision for children can be made at any time, it will generally   **7.48** be convenient to include full claims on their behalf in the petition as well (remembering, of course, that the court's jurisdiction has been curtailed following the coming into force of the Child Support Act 1991, see Chapter 35).

Signature

Where the applicant is receiving advice under the Legal Help scheme, she should sign the   **7.49** petition herself.

If the solicitor is acting for the applicant in receipt of full public funding (ie, a certificate for   **7.50** Legal Representation) or on a private basis, the petition should be signed by the solicitor in his own or the firm's name (r 17.2(6), FPR 2010).

Dissolution of a civil partnership

7.51 This chapter has examined the way in which a petition for divorce should be drafted. It should be noted that the petition and the notes for guidance also refer to dissolution of a civil partnership and should be read accordingly.

D   KEY DOCUMENTS

7.52 Family Procedure Rules 2010 (SI 2010/2955)

Divorce/dissolution/
(judicial) separation petition

To be completed by the Court	
Name of court	
Case No.	
Date received by the court	
Date issued	
Time issued	

Notes to Petitioners

- This form should be used if you are making an application to the court for divorce/dissolution to end your marriage or civil partnership or (judicial) separation from your spouse or civil partner.

- Before completing this form, please read the supporting notes for guidance on completing the form.

- Please answer all questions. If you are unsure of the answer to any question, or you do not think that it applies to you, please indicate this on the form.

- If there is not enough room on the form, you may continue on a separate sheet. Please put your name, the Respondent's (your spouse/civil partner) name, and the number of the Part the information relates to, at the top of your continuation sheet.

- If completing this form by hand, please use **black ink and BLOCK CAPITAL LETTERS** and tick the boxes that apply.

See the supporting notes for guidance

I, [   ] (please state your full name)

apply for a ☐ divorce

☐ dissolution

☐ (judicial) separation

in respect of my ☐ marriage

☐ civil partnership

and give the following details in support of my application.

continued over the page ⇨

Part 1 About you (the Petitioner) and the Respondent (your spouse/civil partner)

See the supporting notes for guidance

Petitioner	Respondent
My current name is First name(s) (in full)	**The Respondent's current name is** First name(s) (in full)
[ ]	[ ]
Last name	Last name
[ ]	[ ]
My address is (including postcode)	The Respondent's address is (including postcode)
Postcode [ ][ ]	Postcode [ ][ ]
My date of birth is D D / M M / Y Y Y Y	The Respondent's date of birth is D D / M M / Y Y Y Y
My occupation is	The Respondent's occupation is
I am [ ] male [ ] female	The Respondent is [ ] male [ ] female

Part 2 Details of marriage or civil partnership

See the supporting notes for guidance

On the   day of   [19   ] [20   ]

(insert your name exactly as it appears on your marriage/civil partnership certificate)

[ ]

[ ] married   [ ] formed a civil partnership with

(insert the name of the Respondent exactly as it appears on your marriage/civil partnership certificate)

[ ]

at

(insert the place where the marriage/civil partnership was formed, exactly as it appears on your marriage/civil partnership certificate)

[ ]

A certified copy of your marriage/civil partnership certificate must be sent to the court with this completed petition (see supporting notes for guidance).

Part 3 Jurisdiction

See the supporting notes for guidance

The Respondent and I last lived together as ☐ husband and wife ☐ civil partners at

> Address

The court has jurisdiction to hear this case under

☐ Article 3(1) of the Council Regulation (EC) No 2201/2003 of 27 November 2003

or

☐ the Civil Partnership (Jurisdiction and Recognition of Judgments) Regulations 2005

on the following grounds

    ☐ The Petitioner and Respondent are both habitually resident in England and Wales

    ☐ Other (please state any other connection(s) on which you wish to rely)

or

☐ The court has jurisdiction other than under the Council Regulation on the basis that no court of a Contracting State has jurisdiction under the Council Regulation and the ☐ Petitioner ☐ Respondent is domiciled in England and Wales on the date when this application is issued

or

☐ The court has jurisdiction other than under the Civil Partnership (Jurisdiction and Recognition of Judgments) Regulations on the basis that no court has, or is recognised as having jurisdiction as set out in the Regulations, and

either:

    ☐ the ☐ Petitioner ☐ and/or the Respondent is domiciled in England or Wales

or

    ☐ the Petitioner and Respondent registered as civil partners of each other in England or Wales and it would be in the interests of justice for the court to assume jurisdiction in this case.

continued over the page ⇨

3

Part 4 Other proceedings or arrangements

See the supporting notes for guidance

☐ There are and/or have been

  ☐ proceedings in any court in England and Wales or elsewhere with reference to the

    ☐ marriage

    ☐ civil partnership

    ☐ or to any child of the family

    ☐ or between the Petitioner and Respondent with reference to any property of either or both of them

    (please enter details below)

  or

  ☐ no other proceedings in any court in England and Wales or elsewhere.

☐ This is an application based on five years' separation and

  ☐ agreement has been made or is proposed to be made between the parties for the support of the Petitioner (and any child of the family)

  (please enter details below)

  or

  ☐ no agreement has been made or is proposed to be made.

Part 5 The fact(s)

See the supporting notes for guidance

I apply for a

☐ divorce on the ground that the marriage has broken down irretrievably, or

☐ dissolution on the ground that the civil partnership has broken down irretrievably, or

☐ (judicial) separation

and

I rely on the following fact(s) in support of my application:

☐ The Respondent has committed adultery and the Petitioner finds it intolerable to live with the Respondent (this fact is not applicable in relation to a civil partnership)

☐ The Respondent has behaved in such a way that the Petitioner cannot reasonably be expected to live with the Respondent

☐ The Respondent has deserted the Petitioner for a continuous period of at least two years immediately preceding the presentation of this petition

☐ The parties to the marriage/civil partnership have lived apart for a continuous period of at least two years immediately preceding the presentation of the petition and the Respondent consents to a decree/order being granted

☐ The parties to the marriage/civil partnership have lived apart for a continuous period of at least five years immediately preceding the presentation of the petition.

Part 6 Statement of case

See the supporting notes for guidance

(in all cases, please state briefly any relevant details about the fact(s) on which you rely)

Part 7 Details of the children

See the supporting notes for guidance

Children of the family

Full names of the children of the family	Gender male	Gender female	Date of birth (or state if over 18)	Over 16 but under 18 and in education, training or working full time	(a) Child of both parties	(b) Other child of the family
	☐	☐	D D / M M / Y Y Y Y	☐	☐	☐
	☐	☐	D D / M M / Y Y Y Y	☐	☐	☐
	☐	☐	D D / M M / Y Y Y Y	☐	☐	☐
	☐	☐	D D / M M / Y Y Y Y	☐	☐	☐
	☐	☐	D D / M M / Y Y Y Y	☐	☐	☐
	☐	☐	D D / M M / Y Y Y Y	☐	☐	☐

Statement of arrangements for children
See the supporting notes for guidance

☐ I attach a completed statement of arrangements in respect of those children of the family who are either aged under 16, or aged under 18 and at school, college, or in training for a trade, profession or vocation

or

☐ No statement of arrangements is attached, because there are no children of the family, or no children of the family are either aged under 16 or aged under 18 and at school, college, or in training for a trade, profession or vocation.

5

Children of either party who are not children of the family

Full names of the children of either party who are not children of the family	Gender male female	Date of birth (or state if over 18)	Born to or adopted by Petitioner	Born to or adopted by Respondent
	☐ ☐	D D / M M / Y Y Y Y	☐	☐
	☐ ☐	D D / M M / Y Y Y Y	☐	☐
	☐ ☐	D D / M M / Y Y Y Y	☐	☐
	☐ ☐	D D / M M / Y Y Y Y	☐	☐
	☐ ☐	D D / M M / Y Y Y Y	☐	☐
	☐ ☐	D D / M M / Y Y Y Y	☐	☐

Part 8 Special assistance or facilities if you attend court

See the supporting notes for guidance

If you are required to attend court during these proceedings will you need any special assistance or facilities?

☐ Yes (please supply details below)   ☐ No

continued over the page ▯⇨

Part 9 Service details

See the supporting notes for guidance

☐ I am not represented by a solicitor in these proceedings

☐ I am not represented by a solicitor in these proceedings but am receiving advice from a solicitor

☐ I am represented by a solicitor in these proceedings and all documents for my attention should be sent to my solicitor whose details are as follows:

Box 1 Solicitor's details

Name of solicitor			
Name of firm			
Address to which all documents should be sent for service		Telephone no.	
		Fax no.	
		DX no.	
Postcode ☐☐☐ ☐☐☐		Your ref.	

E-mail	

Box 2 Petitioner's address for service

Address (including postcode)	
	Postcode ☐☐☐ ☐☐☐

Box 3 Respondent's address for service

Address (including postcode)	
	Postcode ☐☐☐ ☐☐☐

Box 4 Co-Respondent's details, if any

☐ There is no Co-Respondent

☐ There is a Co-Respondent whose details are as follows:

First Name	
Last Name	
Address (including postcode)	
	Postcode ☐☐☐ ☐☐☐

Part 10

See the supporting notes for guidance

Prayer

The Petitioner therefore prays

(1) The application

☐ That the ☐ marriage ☐ civil partnership be dissolved

or

☐ That the Petitioner be (judicially) separated from the Respondent.

(2) Costs (if you wish to claim costs from the Respondent or Co-Respondent)

☐ That the ☐ Respondent ☐ Co-Respondent shall be ordered to pay the costs of this application

(3) Financial Order (if you wish to make an application for a Financial Order)

☐ (a) That the Petitioner may be granted the following Financial Order(s):

☐ an order for maintenance pending suit

☐ periodical payments order

☐ secured provision order

☐ lump sum order

☐ property adjustment order

☐ order under section 24B, 25B or 25C of the Act of 1973 (Pension Sharing/Attachment Order)

☐ (b) **For the children**

☐ a periodical payments order

☐ a secured provision order

☐ a lump sum order

☐ a property adjustment order

Signed [   ]   Dated [D D] / [M M] / [Y Y Y Y]

Supporting notes for guidance on completing a divorce/dissolution/(judicial) separation petition

Important
You should complete this petition if you wish to make an application to the court to dissolve a marriage or civil partnership or if you wish to obtain a (judicial) separation from your spouse or civil partner. You can only apply for a divorce/dissolution if you have been in your marriage or civil partnership for at least one year.

In this form any reference to a marriage certificate or civil partnership certificate means a certified copy of the entry in the Register of Marriages or Register of Civil Partnerships. If you do not have the original marriage/civil partnership certificate, you can apply for a certified copy from the General Register Office or from the relevant Register Officer. Please see leaflet **D183 – About Divorce/ Dissolution** or **D192 – About (Judicial) Separation** for more details, copies of which can be obtained from either a family county court or by going to www.justice.gov.uk.

If you entered into a religious marriage as well as a civil marriage, these divorce proceedings may not dissolve the religious part of your marriage. It is important that you contact the relevant religious authority which authorised the marriage to see whether or not you should take steps to dissolve that marriage. If you do not dissolve the religious marriage, this could have consequences for you and your children.

In cases of urgent applications it may be possible for you to provide an undertaking to the court to deliver the original or a certified copy of the marriage/civil partnership certificate to the court at a later date.

If you are attaching any order of the High Court or a county court to your petition, it must be a sealed copy of the order (that is, a copy that has been stamped with the seal of the court). If you are attaching an order made by a Family Proceedings Court/magistrates' court, it must be a certified copy (a copy certified by a court officer to be a true copy of the original order), or a copy that has been stamped with the seal of the originating court. If you are in any doubt about what is needed, please contact the court where you are applying for assistance.

Take or send the completed application form to the court together with the court fee and any documents you are attaching in support of your application. You will also need to give the court a copy of the petition and documents for each Respondent. If you are not sure about the court fee payable for your petition, or you think that you may be exempt from paying all or part of the fee, you can go to www.justice.gov.uk or contact the court for more information.

Complete the form as fully as you are able. If the form is not fully completed the court may be unable to issue your petition and this may delay your case.

Assistance in completing the form
The notes below will help you to complete the form. However if you are unsure about any of the questions or how to answer them you may wish to seek legal advice.

Page 1: Insert the full name by which you are currently known, and then confirm what you are applying for by ticking the appropriate box.

Part 1: About you (the Petitioner) and the Respondent

You are known as the Petitioner. Your spouse or civil partner is known as the Respondent. You should enter your current details and the Respondent's current details as fully as you know them, making sure you enter the names by which you are both currently known.

If you do not wish to disclose your or your child(ren)'s address, for example because you may feel threatened by the Respondent knowing where you live, or because there is a history of domestic violence, you can leave the details blank and complete Confidential contact details, form **C8**.

Occupation

Please give your occupation and that of the Respondent. If you are not in current employment, please state 'Unemployed/retired/carer' or some other description of your situation.

Part 2: Details of marriage/civil partnership

It is important that the details are entered **exactly** as they are shown on your marriage or civil partnership certificate.

You should attach a certified copy of the marriage/civil partnership certificate together with any other supporting documents regarding any change of name (such as a certified copy of a change of name deed). Photocopies cannot be accepted. If you married or entered into a civil partnership in a foreign country and your marriage/civil partnership certificate is in the language of that country, you must provide a translation of the certificate into English, or Welsh in a court in Wales, from an authorised person (a person authorised for translations). The translation should be signed by a notary public or be authenticated by a statement of truth.

When giving the place at which the marriage/civil partnership was formed you should write the exact words contained in the marriage/civil partnership certificate, including both the printed and written words, which come after the phrase 'Marriage solemnised at' or 'Civil Partnership formed at'.

For example:

- For a marriage in a Register Office: 'The Register Office, in the District of .... in the County of ....'
- For a marriage which took place in a church: ' .... Church, in the Parish of .... in the County of ....'
- For a civil partnership: '.................... in the Registration Authority of ....'

Part 3: Jurisdiction

It is important to be sure that the court has jurisdiction (is able as a matter of law) to deal with your application. Jurisdiction depends on you and/or the Respondent having a specific connection to England and Wales, which may be a connection listed in one of the Regulations referred to below, or a connection which gives rise to the court's 'residual jurisdiction'. It is possible for you to have a connection under more than one option.

Jurisdiction under the Council Regulation or Civil Partnership Regulations

The principal connections that give the court jurisdiction are set out in the following provisions:

- for matrimonial proceedings, Article 3(1) of Council Regulation (EC) No 2201/2003 of 27 November 2003; and
- for civil partnership proceedings, the Civil Partnership (Jurisdiction and Recognition of Judgments) Regulations 2005.

If you consider that the court has jurisdiction to hear the case under one of these provisions you should
- tick the appropriate box to show which of these provisions applies; and
- then state the connection(s) ('the grounds') on which you rely to show that the court has jurisdiction.

The relevant connections are set out below. These connections depend on where you or the Respondent have your 'habitual residence' or your 'domicile'.

Habitual Residence – This is the country where you live voluntarily and for settled purposes (such as work, training, family life), apart from temporary or occasional absences. You must spend a substantial amount of time in a place to be habitually resident there.

Domicile – This is the country which you consider to be your permanent home.

Note: If your spouse/civil partner lives in or is a national of another country, they may have the option of issuing proceedings abroad, and this could prevent your case from continuing here.

The relevant connections
The court will have jurisdiction to hear your case under the Council Regulation or the Civil Partnership Regulations if any of the following connections applies on the date on which your petition is issued. You should state which of the connections matches your situation. You do not need to specify more than one, but if more than one connection applies, you may state more if you wish. **If your spouse/civil partner is not, or may not be, habitually resident in England and Wales, you should state all the connections that apply.**

The connections are that:

- The Petitioner and the Respondent are habitually resident in England and Wales.

- The Petitioner and Respondent were last habitually resident in England and Wales and the [Petitioner*] [or] [the Respondent*] still reside there (*specify as appropriate).

- The Respondent is habitually resident in England and Wales.

- The Petitioner is habitually resident in England and Wales and has resided there for at least a year immediately prior to the presentation of the petition.

- The Petitioner is domiciled and habitually resident in England and Wales and has resided there for at least six months immediately prior to the petition.

- (in a matrimonial case only) The Petitioner and Respondent are both domiciled in England and Wales.

If you and the Respondent are both habitually resident in England and Wales, you should tick the box next to that statement.

If this does not apply to you, or if you wish to rely on any additional or alternative connection(s), please tick 'other' and write in the box any of the other connections on which you rely.

Residual jurisdiction
If none of the above applies, the court may still have jurisdiction on an alternative basis (known as the residual jurisdiction) outside the Regulations. The connection which will give such residual jurisdiction will depend on whether the proceedings are matrimonial or civil partnership proceedings.

For matrimonial proceedings, the court has jurisdiction on a residual basis if:

- no court in any Contracting State (that is, no court in an EU Member State) has jurisdiction under the Council Regulation (because neither the Petitioner nor Respondent is habitually resident in any other Contracting State, nor is there any Contracting State of which they are both nationals, or in the case of the UK and Ireland, in which they are both domiciled); and
- either the Petitioner or the Respondent is domiciled in England and Wales on the date when the petition is issued.

If this option matches your situation you should tick the box next to the appropriate statement and state whether the Petitioner or the Respondent is domiciled in England and Wales.

For civil partnership proceedings, the court has jurisdiction on a residual basis if no court has, or is recognised as having, jurisdiction under the Civil Partnership (Jurisdiction and Recognition of Judgments) Regulations, and either:

- the Petitioner or the Respondent is domiciled in England or Wales

or

- the Petitioner and the Respondent registered as civil partners of each other in England and Wales and it would be in the interests of justice for the court to assume jurisdiction in this case.

If either option matches your situation, you should:

- tick the box next to the appropriate statement; and
- then tick the box by the connection which matches.

If none of the connections described above, whether under the Regulations or residual jurisdiction, matches your situation, the court will not have jurisdiction to deal with your application.

If you are completing this form and need help in deciding which connection applies, you should seek legal advice particularly in international cases.

Part 4: Other proceedings or arrangements

You should indicate, if there have been other proceedings in England and Wales, or elsewhere, concerning:

- your marriage/civil partnership
- any child of the family
- any property belonging to either you or to the Respondent.

This includes any proceedings relating to the marriage/civil partnership, or to any child of the family even if the proceedings have now finished or were abandoned without a final decision being made.

You should give details of the name of the court in which the proceedings took place, details of the order(s) which were made, details of any future hearings and, if proceedings were about your marriage/civil partnership, say whether you and the Respondent resumed living together as husband and wife/civil partners after the order was made.

If there have been proceedings in a court outside England and Wales which have affected the marriage/civil partnership, or may affect it, please give the name of the country and the court in which they are taking/have taken place, the date the proceedings were begun and the names of the parties, details of the order(s) made and if no order has yet been made, the date of any future hearing(s).

If your application is based on five years' separation you should answer the second question as appropriate and enter full details of any arrangements made.

Part 5: The fact(s)

Tick the appropriate box to indicate whether you are applying for a divorce (in the case of a marriage) or a dissolution (in the case of a civil partnership), or for a (judicial) separation in respect of your marriage/ civil partnership. Delete the words that do not apply within the statements.

If you are applying for a divorce/dissolution, at least one year must have passed since you married/ entered into a civil partnership before you issue the application.

If you are relying on the facts of two years' desertion, two years' separation with consent or five years' separation, the relevant time period must have passed before you issue the application at the court. E.g. separation or desertion was on 1 March 2010, the first day that an application can be issued is 2 March 2012 (or 2015 in the case of 5 years separation).

Tick the appropriate box(es) to indicate the fact(s) you intend to rely on to prove your application.

Part 6: Statement of case

This space is provided for you to give details of the allegations, which you are using to prove the facts given in Part 5. In most cases one or two sentences will do.

In the case of marriage only, if you have alleged adultery give:

- the date(s) and place(s) where the adultery took place.

You do not have to name the person with whom your spouse is alleged to have committed adultery unless the allegation is likely to be disputed.

If you have alleged unreasonable behaviour give:

- details of a course of conduct, or, particular incidents, including dates, but it should not be necessary to give more than about half a dozen examples of the more serious incidents, including the most recent.

If you have alleged desertion give:

- the date of desertion
- brief details of the circumstances of the desertion
- confirmation that you have lived separately since the date of desertion.

If you have alleged either two or five years' separation give:

- the date of separation
- brief details of how the separation came about
- (in the case of two years' separation) confirmation that the Respondent consents to a decree/order being granted.

In all cases, please give any other relevant details about the fact(s) on which you rely.

If you need more space, you may continue on a separate sheet. You must put your name, the Respondent's name and Part 6 Statement of Case at the top of the continuation sheet.

5

Part 7: Details of the children

This part asks for details of children of the family. 'Children of the family' includes:

(a) Children born to both you and the Respondent or adopted by both of you;

(b) Other children treated by both of you as children of the family: for example your own or the Respondent's children, or children adopted by one of you;

Any children in these categories should be included on your petition.

For each child you should state:

- their full names, including surname
- their gender
- their date of birth, or you must if applicable state that they are over 18
- if the child is over 16 but under 18 you must state whether he or she is at school or college, or training for a trade, profession or vocation, or is working full time
- whether they fall under (a) or (b) above.

Statement of arrangements for children

If you or the Respondent have any children of the family:

- under 16
- over 16 but under 18 if they are at school or college, university or are training for a trade, profession or vocation

you **must** complete the statement of arrangements for children form. This form is available from the court and online at www.justice.gov.uk.

Before you send your divorce/dissolution/(judicial) separation petition to the court you should try to reach an agreement with your spouse/civil partner about the proposals for the children's future. There is space for your spouse/civil partner to sign at the end of the statement of arrangements for children form if agreement is reached. If your spouse/civil partner does not agree with the proposals they will have the opportunity at a later stage to state why and make their own proposals.

The completed statement of arrangements for children must be signed by you and, if it is agreed, by the Respondent as well. You will need to submit a copy of the completed form whether or not the Respondent has signed it, when you send your divorce/dissolution/(judicial) separation petition to the court together with a copy for the Respondent. If you are attaching health reports please supply one additional copy of the reports (2 copies in total).

You should enter details of all children who are not children of the family e.g. any children who have been born to or adopted by either you or the Respondent, in the table provided.

If there are no children of the family, or no children under the ages specified please tick the second box.

Part 8: Special assistance or facilities if you attend Court

If you or the Respondent need special assistance and/or special facilities due to a disability or impairment, please set out your requirements in full. The court staff will need to know, for example, if you want documents to be supplied in an alternative format, such as Braille or large print. They will also need to know about any specific requirements you may have on the day of the hearing, such as wheelchair access, a hearing loop, or a sign language interpreter. If you require a foreign language interpreter and are unable to provide your own, you may request that one is booked by the court.

The court staff will get in touch with you about your requirements. It is important that you make the court aware of all your needs. If you do not, any hearing may have to be delayed or adjourned to another date.

Part 9: Service details

Throughout the divorce/dissolution/(judicial) separation process, the court will be required to send documents to either one or all of the parties in the case, depending on the stage which the proceedings have reached. This is known as service of the documents.

Please complete the boxes in this section as follows:

Box 1 – If you have a solicitor acting for you, you must insert their details here.

Box 2 – This is the address to which the court will send all documentation for the Petitioner. If you have solicitors acting for you then enter 'as above'.

Please note that if you indicate that you have a solicitor acting for you the Court will only correspond with them. Any questions that you may have about your case should be directed to your solicitor.

Box 3 – This is the address to which the court will send all documentation for the Respondent. If the Respondent does not live in England and Wales, they may be given extra time to file documents. Please check with the court for more details.

Box 4 – Any additional people in the case, for example if you name another person in a case of adultery or an improper association with another person, that person will be known as a Co-Respondent and their address for service of all court documents should be entered here. You do not have to name the person with whom your spouse is alleged to have committed adultery unless the allegation is likely to be disputed. In addition, unless you have permission from the court, you should not name a Co-Respondent if they are under the age of 16 or are the alleged victim of rape committed by the Respondent (see Paragraph 2.1 of Practice Direction 7A).

Part 10: Prayer

The prayer of the petition is your request to the court. You should consider carefully the claims which you wish to make. You should adapt the prayer to suit your claims.

(1) The application

Confirm what you are applying for.

(2) Costs

If you wish to claim that the Respondent or Co-Respondent pay your costs you must do so in your petition. It is not possible to make a claim after a decree/order has been granted. The court will not normally make a costs order where the application is based on 5 years separation.

(3) Financial Order

If you need the court to resolve any dispute over finances you can apply for a financial order. This can deal with property, maintenance, a lump sum payment and/or pensions. An application for a financial order for yourself can only be made before you remarry or enter into a new civil partnership. For more details please see leaflet **D190 – I want to apply for a financial order**.

If you do not complete this section now, but later decide to apply for a financial order, you may be at a financial disadvantage.

If you wish to apply for any of these orders, you should indicate which orders you seek.

You are advised to consult a solicitor if you are unsure about completing this section or about which order(s) you require.

If you complete this section or you later decide to apply for a financial order, you will need to complete and file a Form A to proceed with your application when you are ready to do so.

You can apply to the court for a financial order for any child(ren) of the family in connection with the divorce/dissolution/(judicial) separation proceedings, but the court may only make a periodical payments order for a child if:

- you and the respondent have made a written agreement about child maintenance;
- the child is a stepchild of the Respondent;
- the child or the person with care of the child or the absent parent of the child is **not** habitually resident in the United Kingdom;
- payments are sought in addition to child support maintenance paid under a Child Support Agency calculation;
- the payments are to meet expenses arising from a child's disability;
- the payments are to meet expenses incurred by a child in being educated or training for work;
- the Child Support Agency does not have power to make a maintenance calculation due to the age of the child.

If none of the above applies to you, you should make an application for child maintenance to the Child Support Agency; the court cannot make an order for child maintenance in your case.

If you are not sure whether the court can hear your application please consult a solicitor; a member of the court staff may be able to assist you with the form, but cannot give you legal advice. Leaflet **D190 – I want to apply for a financial order** is also available.

What must I send to the court?

☐ Your completed divorce/dissolution/(judicial) separation petition – one for the court records and one service copy for the Respondent (and one service copy for the Co-Respondent, if applicable). You should keep a copy for your records.

☐ One original or certified marriage/civil partnership certificate – photocopies will not be accepted. (In cases of urgent applications it may be possible for you to provide an undertaking to the court to deliver the original or a certified copy of the marriage/civil partnership certificate to the court at a later date.)

☐ Your completed statement of arrangements for children, if applicable – one for the court records and one service copy for the Respondent. You should keep a copy for your records.

☐ The appropriate issue fee. Please see leaflet **EX50 – Civil and Family Court fees** for details on the fees payable and whether or not you have to pay them.

8

UNDEFENDED DIVORCE: PROCEDURE FOR OBTAINING THE DECREE

A   DOCUMENTS REQUIRED

8.01 The following documents should be prepared/assembled for filing at court. A copy should be kept for the solicitor's own file of all documents that are to be filed at court.

The application for divorce (the petition)

8.02 For notes on drafting the petition, see Chapter 7. To assist you in understanding the procedure to obtain a divorce, a flowchart is to be found at the end of this chapter.

8.03 Part 7, Family Procedure Rules 2010 ('FPR 2010') sets out the procedure to obtain a divorce (known in the terminology of the FPR 2010 as a 'matrimonial order').

8.04 The proceedings are commenced in the Family Division of the High Court or in any divorce county court: r 7.5(1), FPR 2010. The application must be made in Form D8 (the divorce petition), discussed in detail in Chapter 7.

8.05 The petition must be accompanied by documents prescribed in the form itself. (These include, for example, a certified copy of the marriage certificate.)

8.06 The court will require the applicant to provide the original petition plus one copy for each party who is to be served. Therefore, the solicitor must always have ready the original petition plus one copy for the respondent. Where there is a co-respondent, a further copy will be required. It is possible for there to be more than one co-respondent if the petition makes several allegations of adultery. In this event, one further copy of the petition is required for each additional co-respondent.

The marriage certificate

The marriage certificate must be filed with the petition. If the client does not have a mar- **8.07** riage certificate one can be obtained by post or by personal attendance from the office of the Superintendent Registrar of Marriages for the district where the marriage took place. A standard fee is usually payable, presently £7.00. Alternatively, a copy can be obtained by post from:

> General Register Office
> Smedley Hydro
> Trafalgar Road
> Southport PR8 2HH
> (tel: 01704 569824)

The fee is £23.40.

If the client is receiving Legal Help, the cost of obtaining the certificate can be met under Legal **8.08** Help. However, the financial limit on this advice is little enough as it is and some solicitors request the client to obtain a copy of the certificate herself. If it is necessary for the solicitor to obtain the certificate for the client, the possibility of seeking or authorizing an extension of the Legal Help limit should be borne in mind if costs are nearing the normal limit.

Only one copy of the marriage certificate is required. It is kept on the court file and is not **8.09** usually returned to the applicant if the divorce proceedings do not go ahead or are dismissed. An application for the return of the marriage certificate, granted at the court's discretion, is required where the parties subsequently become reconciled.

Where the marriage certificate is in a foreign language, the court will usually require a certi- **8.10** fied translation of the certificate to be filed as well (para 3.1(b), PD7A, FPR 2010).

The statement as to arrangements for children (Form D8A)

Generally

Where there is a child of the family who is: **8.11**

(a) under 16; or
(b) over 16 but under 18 and receiving instruction at an educational establishment or undergoing training for a trade or profession,

then the applicant is required to file a Form D8A setting out the arrangements for those children. In 'exceptional circumstances' the district judge can direct that a decree not be made absolute until matters in respect of the children have been resolved (s 41(2), Matrimonial Causes Act 1973 ('MCA 1973')).

The Notes for Guidance recommend that the statement of arrangements for children be **8.12** agreed with the respondent (and provision is made for this in Part 4 of the statement of arrangements Form D8A). If this is not practicable, then it would appear that the applicant cannot be compelled to comply with the requirement. If the respondent's agreement has not been or cannot be obtained, then it would be good practice to provide a letter of explanation for the court when the Form D8A is filed (see also r 7.12(7), FPR 2010 which deals with the respondent's statement in response to the applicant's statement).

8.13 The statement of arrangements should be signed by the applicant personally as a statement of truth (even where a solicitor is acting for her), giving background information about each child, for example where he is to live after the divorce, details of his school, health, etc. This statement is the core of the information available to the district judge when he considers the arrangements for the children.

8.14 The statement of arrangements form can be obtained from the offices of divorce county courts, from law stationers, or online. Where there is more than one child to whom s 41, MCA 1973 applies, then details in relation to all the children can be given on one form. See paras 8.102 ff below for a more detailed analysis of the way in which the procedures for s 41, MCA 1973 operate.

Completing Form D8A

8.15 Completing the form is a relatively straightforward matter. A blank copy of Form D8A appears on pp 126–131. The solicitor should take care to give as much information as possible on the form. The court will require the original statement as to arrangements plus one copy for service on the respondent, together with the original and a copy of any medical report that is attached to the form. The arrangements for the children are of no concern to the co-respondent and he is not provided with a copy of Form D8A.

8.16 There are two particularly important features of the statement of arrangements for children:

(a) Where the applicant has or intends to apply for an order under s 8, Children Act 1989 ('CA 1989') (eg for a residence or contact order) in respect of a child of the family, this must be indicated in the statement (para 17).

(b) The applicant must indicate whether a maintenance calculation has been carried out by the Child Support Agency in respect of a child of the family as a result of which payments are being made for the benefit of the child (para 15), if not then the applicant must indicate whether or not she will make an application through the Child Support Agency (para 15).

Medical reports

8.17 If a child has a long-standing illness or suffers from a disability, this must be stated in Form D8A. If there is an up-to-date medical report, it should be attached to Form D8A. If there is not, consideration should be given as to whether a report or at least a letter should be obtained from the doctor responsible for the child. In a relatively straightforward case (eg where a child was born with a disability, such as the lack of a finger on one hand, which does not need treatment and with which the child has learned to cope) no report or letter may be required. In more complex cases, for example where the child is currently receiving regular treatment of more than a routine nature (as where the child is undergoing a series of surgical operations), a report will be necessary in order that the district judge is sufficiently well informed about the child to decide whether he can grant a s 41 declaration.

8.18 If no report is provided and the district judge decides when giving directions for trial that a report is necessary, he can give a direction to that effect: see r 7.25(4), FPR 2010 (see para 8.108 below).

8.19 The cost of obtaining a medical report is covered by the Legal Help scheme. However, as this will increase the applicant's costs of obtaining the divorce, the solicitor should bear in mind that it may become necessary to authorize or to apply for an extension at some stage.

Where children are not living with applicant

Where the children are not living with the applicant, she may not be able to give all the information required by Form D8A. It would be good practice for the respondent in such a case to file a statement in Form D8A together with his acknowledgment of service without any prompting. However, this is not always done. **8.20**

Where the applicant is not able to give the necessary information and the respondent has not supplied it voluntarily, it is likely that the court will ask the respondent to file a statement giving information about the children in the form of a letter or in Form D8A. However, there does not appear to be any power to require the respondent to provide information and, if he fails to do so by the time the district judge considers the arrangements for the children, the proper course would appear to be for the district judge to direct that a report by an officer of the Children and Family Court Advisory and Support Service (Cafcass) be prepared giving details of the respondent's arrangements for the children (see para 8.108 below). **8.21**

Certified copies of court orders

Where there have been previous proceedings relating to the parties to the marriage, or children of the family, the court will usually expect the applicant to file at the court certified copies of previous court orders so that the district judge may have as full a picture as possible of the history of the marriage. **8.22**

Public funding

Public funding in its form of a certificate for Legal Representation is not normally granted for the decree proceedings as opposed to proceedings in relation to ancillary matters such as applications made under the CA 1989 and property (see Chapter 2). If a certificate is granted, however, it must be filed with the court and a notice of issue served on the respondent and co-respondent, if applicable. **8.23**

B   COMMENCEMENT OF PROCEEDINGS

Divorce proceedings are commenced by the filing of the divorce petition and supporting documents at court. **8.24**

The solicitor will normally find it most convenient to commence the divorce proceedings in his local divorce county court or the divorce county court nearest to where the applicant lives. The petition and supporting documents listed in paras 8.01 ff above must be filed at the court office of the chosen county court. They can be handed in personally over the counter in the court office or sent by post. **8.25**

Statement of arrangements for children

To be completed by the parties	
Name of court	Case No. (if known)
Name of Petitioner	
Name of Respondent	

To the Petitioner

You must complete this form if you or the Respondent have any children under 16 or any children under 18 who are at school or college or are training for a trade, profession or vocation.

The Petitioner is only required to complete Parts 1, 2, 3 and the Statement of Truth. Please use **black ink and BLOCK CAPITAL LETTERS**.

Before you issue a divorce/dissolution/(judicial) separation or nullity petition try to reach an agreement with your spouse or civil partner over the proposals for the children's future. There is space for them to sign at the end of this form if agreement is reached.

If your spouse/civil partner does not agree with the proposals, they will have the opportunity at a later stage to state why they do not agree and will be able to make their own proposals.

You should take or send the completed form together with a copy to the court when you issue your divorce/dissolution/(judicial) separation or nullity petition.

To the Respondent

The Petitioner has completed Part 1, 2 and 3 of this form.

Please read all parts of the form carefully.

If you agree with the arrangements and proposals for the children you should sign Part 4 of the form. If completing this form by hand, please use **black ink and BLOCK CAPITAL LETTERS** and tick the boxes that apply. You should return the form to the Petitioner or their solicitor.

If you do not agree with all or some of the proposals, **do not sign this form.** You will be given the opportunity of explaining your position when you receive the divorce/dissolution/(judicial) separation or nullity petition.

To the Petitioner and Respondent

If you wish to apply for any of the orders which may be available to you under Part I or II of the Children Act 1989 please see leaflet CB1 'Making an application - children and the family courts'. If you are unsure of which application you require, you are advised to see a solicitor or go to a Citizens Advice Bureau.

Addresses of solicitors and advice agencies can be obtained from the Yellow Pages and the Solicitors' Regional Directory which can be found at Citizens Advice Bureaux, Law Centres and any local library.

The Court will only make an order if it considers that an order will be better for the child(ren) than no order.

Part 1 Details of the children

1. Are the details of the children as stated in Part 7 of the divorce/dissolution/(judicial) separation or nullity petition correct?

    ☐ Yes   ☐ No

    If No, please give further information in the box below

Part 2 Arrangements for the children of the family

Please give details for each child, if arrangements are different. If necessary, continue on another sheet and attach it to this form.

Living arrangements

2. Where and with whom do the children live?

Name of child(ren)	Resides with	At address

3. Is this arrangement agreed by both the Petitioner and Respondent?

    ☐ Yes   ☐ No

    If No, please give details in the box below.

4. What are the contact arrangements between the child(ren) and the non-resident parent?

5. Have you (the Petitioner) and Respondent agreed to these contact arrangements?

    ☐ Yes   ☐ No

    If No, please give details in the box below.

2

6. Who will care for the child(ren) on a day to day basis?

    [   ]

7. Have you (the Petitioner) and Respondent agreed to who will care for the child(ren) on a daily basis?

    ☐ Yes   ☐ No

    If No, please give details in the box below.

    [   ]

Education

8. Give the name(s) of the school, college or place of training attended by the child(ren).

Name of child	Name of school, college or place of training

9. Will there be any change in these arrangements as a result of your divorce/dissolution/(judicial) separation or annulment?

    ☐ Yes   ☐ No

    If Yes, please give details in the box below (include any changes to payment of school fees).

    [   ]

10. Do any of the children have any special educational needs?

    ☐ Yes   ☐ No

    If Yes, please give details in the box below.

    [   ]

continued over the page ⇨

3

Details of health

11. Are the children generally in good health and do not have any special health needs?

    ☐ Yes   ☐ No

    If No, please give details of any serious disability, chronic illness, or the care needed and how it is to be provided, in the box below.

12. Do any of the children have any special health needs?

    ☐ Yes   ☐ No

    If Yes, please give details of the care needed and how it is to be provided, in the box below.

Details of care and other court proceedings

13. Are the children in the care of the local authority, or under the supervision of a social worker or probation officer?

    ☐ Yes   ☐ No

    If Yes, please give details in the box below. Please include information about any current proceedings in the youth or family courts.

14. Are any of the children the subject of a Child Protection Plan?

    ☐ Yes   ☐ No

    If Yes, please give details in the box below, including the name of the local authority and the date of registration.

15. Are there, or have there been, any proceedings in any court involving the children, for example;

    a) residence or contact proceedings?

    b) care or supervision?

    c) adoption or wardship?

    ☐ Yes   ☐ No

If Yes, please give details in the box below and attach a copy of any order(s) which you have.

```



```

☐ A maintenance calculation has been made under the Child Support Act 1991, or, an application has been made for a maintenance calculation, but it has not yet been determined, and the details are as follows:

```



```

☐ The following agreement has been reached in relation to child maintenance:

```



```

☐ No agreement has been reached and no application has been made for a maintenance calculation.

16. Are there, or have there been, any proceedings in any court which may impact on the children, for example non-molestation orders, or criminal proceedings relating to domestic violence?

☐ Yes   ☐ No

If Yes, please give details in the box below.

```



```

Part 3 To the Petitioner

Mediation

17. If you are not agreed as to the arrangements for the children, are you intending to:

- seek to resolve matters with the Respondent directly?

  ☐ Yes   ☐ No

- propose the use of Alternative Dispute Resolution such as mediation?

  ☐ Yes   ☐ No

  If No, would you agree to do so?

  ☐ Yes   ☐ No

- make an application to the court?

  ☐ Yes   ☐ No

5

Statement of Truth

I believe that the facts stated in this statement of arrangements for children are true

Print full name

Signed   Dated D D / M M / Y Y Y Y

(Petitioner)

Proceedings for contempt of court may be brought against a person who makes or causes to be made, a false statement in a document verified by a statement of truth.

Part 4 Agreement of Respondent

☐ I agree with the arrangements and proposals contained in Part 1 and 2 of this form.

☐ I do not agree with the arrangements and proposals contained in Part 1 and 2 of this form.
If you do not agree would you be prepared to see a mediator?

☐ Yes   ☐ No

Signed   Dated D D / M M / Y Y Y Y

(Respondent)

C   FEE

8.26   There is a court fee of £340 payable when the petition is filed. If the applicant is in receipt of Legal Help or is receiving income support or otherwise on a low income (providing, in the latter two cases, that she is not also receiving full public funding), she is entitled to exemption from the fee. A form applying for exemption is obtainable from the court and should be completed on the applicant's behalf. The fee will almost certainly be payable when the applicant is paying privately for her solicitor's services. Where the applicant (in exceptional circumstances) is publicly funded by certificate from the outset, a fee is payable when the petition is filed.

D   ADDITIONAL MATTERS WHERE THE SOLICITOR IS ACTING

When is the solicitor acting?

8.27   The solicitor *is not* acting in the divorce proceedings if his client is receiving only Legal Help in relation to them. Such a client is looked upon as a litigant in person for the purposes of the decree proceedings. This is unaffected by any certificate that may have been granted in the client's favour in relation to other family matters. The solicitor *is* acting in the divorce proceedings if his client is paying privately for his services or if a certificate has been granted in relation to these proceedings.

Additional duties

8.28   The solicitor must file a statement of reconciliation in Form D6 (one copy only required) with the petition (r 7.6, FPR 2010). This states whether or not he has discussed with the applicant the possibility of a reconciliation and given her the names and addresses of persons qualified to help to effect a reconciliation (see Chapter 1, paras 1.58 ff for further details of such persons). There is not, in fact, any requirement that the solicitor *must* discuss reconciliation with the client. However, the fact that he must file Form D6 ensures that he will at least turn his mind to the question and, unless it is clearly inappropriate in the client's particular circumstances, it will usually be good practice to discuss the possibility of reconciliation with the client. In any event, this would be necessary to establish that the marriage has in fact irretrievably broken down.

E   ENTRY IN COURT BOOKS

8.29   When the court receives the petition, it enters the cause in the books of the court and a file number is allocated to it. The solicitor will be notified of the number. This is the official identity tag for the case and must be quoted on all correspondence with the court and used on all documents connected with the divorce and with related matters.

F SERVICE OF THE PETITION

Before the divorce can go any further the petition must be served on the respondent and any **8.30** co-respondent (Part 6, FPR 2010) or, in exceptional circumstances, service may be dispensed with (r 6.20).

Tracing a missing respondent

The applicant may have lost touch with the respondent and be unable to provide an address **8.31** for him. Efforts will have to be made to trace him in order that the petition can be served either by post or personally. Apart from the normal enquiries that can be made of the respondent's former employers, his relations and friends, his clubs and trade union, there are various special ways of tracing a missing respondent. These are set out fully in *Practice Direction* [1989] 1 All ER 765, [1989] 1 WLR 219, as amended by Practice Direction of 20 July 1995 and reproduced in FPR 2010 at PD6C. In summary, if the petition is filed by a wife and includes a claim for maintenance for her or the children or there is an existing maintenance order in favour of the applicant or children which the applicant is seeking to enforce, the court can request a search to be made on behalf of the applicant for the respondent's address from the records of the Department for Work and Pensions (DWP) or, failing that, of the Passport Office. Application should be made to the district judge for a search to be requested. If the respondent is known to be serving or to have served recently in the Armed Forces, the applicant's solicitor can request an address for service on the respondent from the appropriate service department.

It is also useful to know that if the applicant is making or seeking to enforce a maintenance **8.32** claim, the DWP is often willing to provide the applicant's solicitor with an address for the respondent when requested to do so simply by a letter from the solicitor. This should be tried before asking the district judge to request this information. The DWP will also forward a letter to a party's last known address in all cases. The respondent's bank may be prepared to do the same. The DWP can be contacted at:

NICB Special Section A
Newcastle-upon-Tyne NE98 1YU

Court to effect service

Rule 6.5, FPR 2010 makes is clear that primary responsibility for service on the respondent **8.33** now lies with the applicant. However, the applicant may request the court to effect service and this will be done by first class post.

The administrative procedure followed by the court office is as follows: **8.34**

(a) Each copy of the petition for service has annexed to it:
   (i) a notice of proceedings (Form D9) which explains to the respondent that a petition for divorce has been filed and instructs him to complete the acknowledgment of service. It also contains notes on completing the acknowledgment of service;
   (ii) a form of acknowledgment of service (Form D10);
   (iii) if there is a certificate for Legal Representation, notice of issue of the certificate.

(b) The respondent's copy of the petition also has annexed to it a copy of the statement as to arrangements for the children, if any, plus a copy of any medical report attached to it.

(c) A copy of the petition and the documents annexed to it is served, on request, on the respondent by the court. Normally service is effected by the court simply by posting the documents to the respondent at the address given for him by the applicant at the foot of the petition (known as 'postal service'). The court is required to note in the court records the date of posting; or leaving with, delivery to, or collection by the relevant service provider (r 6.18(1), FPR 2010).

(d) If the acknowledgment of service is then completed and signed by the respondent (or his solicitor on his behalf if this is appropriate) and returned to the court, the petition is taken to have been duly served (r 6.15(1), FPR 2010).

Alternatives to postal service by the court

General

8.35 Postal service through the court is not always successful or appropriate. All sorts of problems can arise over service, for example the applicant may not be able to provide an address for service on the respondent or the respondent may fail to return the acknowledgment of service after the documents have been posted to him.

8.36 There are various alternatives to postal service by the court. What is appropriate depends on the nature of the problem that has arisen. The various methods of service are described in para 8.38. Common problems and suggested solutions are dealt with in paras 8.54 ff below.

8.37 Case law makes it clear that the rules preceding FPR 2010 were designed to ensure that the respondent has direct personal knowledge of the change in status which the applicant is seeking to achieve through divorce proceedings. Hence, in *Akhtar v Rafiq* [2006] 1 FLR 27 the decrees nisi and absolute of divorce were held to be void because there had been no proper service of the divorce papers on the respondent wife—the address given for service of the documents was not that of the wife and the husband had asserted that the thumb print on the acknowledgment of service was that of the wife without knowing it to be so. Bodey J indicated that it was not good enough to say after the event that, although the petition had not been duly served, the respondent in fact knew all about the proceedings. A similar approach is adopted in FPR 2010.

Alternative methods of service

8.38 **Personal service by the court bailiff** The district judge can direct bailiff service on the applicant's request made in writing on the prescribed form (D89). There is an extra fee payable for this service (currently £105) unless the applicant is 'fees exempt'.

8.39 The applicant must provide some means whereby the bailiff can identify the respondent, normally a photograph. Paragraph 11.4, PD6A, FPR 2010 makes it clear that where the applicant is represented by a solicitor, service by a bailiff will rarely be granted and it will be necessary for the solicitor to show why service by bailiff is required rather than service by a process server. This does not, of course, apply in Legal Help cases.

8.40 Service is effected by the bailiff delivering a copy of the petition to the respondent personally. He will attempt to get the respondent to sign for the papers.

Once the bailiff has served the respondent personally he files a certificate to this effect, stating **8.41** how he identified the respondent. If the respondent returns the acknowledgment of service to the court, this will prove service. Where the acknowledgment of service is not returned it will be necessary for the applicant in her affidavit in support of the petition to identify the respondent's signature for the documents or to identify the respondent in the photograph used by the bailiff. Together with the bailiff's certificate, this will be sufficient proof of service: para 12.2, PD6A.

Service through the applicant The applicant can request that service be carried out through **8.42** her (r 6.5(1), FPR 2010). The applicant herself must never effect personal service of the documents (r 6.5(3)) but her solicitor can serve the respondent or an enquiry agent can be instructed to do so. Some means of identification must be provided by the applicant as with bailiff service, usually a photograph.

Personal service through the applicant has an advantage over bailiff service in that the bailiff **8.43** cannot be expected to search for the respondent if the applicant cannot supply a definite address or if the respondent is not at his address when the bailiff calls whereas an enquiry agent can be instructed to do so.

Where personal service through the applicant is required, the solicitor will probably need to **8.44** obtain an extension of the Legal Help financial limit to cover the cost of service. Normally the solicitor will be able to extend the initial financial limit where it is reasonable and appropriate to do so. The sufficient benefit test should be re-applied before any extension is granted. The person serving the petition should attempt to get the respondent to sign for the documents. If no acknowledgment of service is returned to the court office, the server will be required to file a certificate of service stating the date and time of personal service (r 6.17(2), FPR 2010). In her affidavit in support of the petition, the applicant will then identify the respondent's signature for the documents or identify the photograph used by the server as a photograph of the respondent, as with bailiff service.

Deemed service Where the acknowledgment of service has not been returned to the **8.45** court but the district judge is nevertheless satisfied that the petition has been received by the respondent, he can direct that service is deemed to have been effected (r 6.16(1), FPR 2010).

An application in Form D11 should be sent to the district judge with the applicant's request for **8.46** directions for the decree nisi to be granted (see para 8.77 below) asking for service to be deemed. A fee of £45 is payable unless the applicant is 'fees exempt'. The district judge will need some evidence that the respondent has received the petition; a sworn statement should therefore be filed from someone who can give evidence to this effect, exhibiting documentary evidence that the respondent has received the petition. The person who can give evidence that the respondent has received the petition is often the applicant herself. However, to deem service effective on the basis of the applicant's evidence alone carries an obvious danger in that an unscrupulous applicant could, by giving false evidence on this point, ensure that the respondent knew nothing of the divorce proceedings. Some district judges may therefore be reluctant to agree on the basis of the applicant's uncorroborated evidence that service should be deemed.

Example 1 The applicant and respondent continue to live in the same house even after divorce proceedings have been commenced. The applicant is present when the respondent picks up the divorce papers which have arrived in the post, opens the envelope, glances at the contents, and deposits them in the dustbin. The applicant's sworn statement to this effect *may* be sufficient to satisfy the district judge that the respondent has received the documents.

Example 2 After receiving the petition the respondent consults a firm of solicitors who write an open letter to the applicant's solicitors concerning the petition but the respondent then fails to return the acknowledgment of service, terminates his instructions to his solicitors, and disappears into thin air. The district judge deems service to have been effected in view of the letter from his ex-solicitors.

8.47 There is an important qualification to r 6.16(1) which is set out in r 6.16(2) and which states that where:

(a) the petition alleges two years' separation and the respondent consents to the decree being granted; and

(b) none of the other facts mentioned in s 1(2), MCA 1973 is alleged,

then the petition will not be deemed to have been served unless the court is satisfied that the respondent has received notice of the proceedings and the applicant produces a written statement signed by the respondent containing the respondent's consent to the grant of the decree.

What this means in practice is that an order for deemed service will not be made in cases relying on s 1(2)(d) unless some evidence can be produced to the court to demonstrate that the respondent previously consented to a decree of divorce being granted.

8.48 **Alternative service** Where all the applicant's efforts to trace the respondent have failed, the applicant will have to ask either for an order for alternative service or for service to be dispensed with (see para 8.52 below).

8.49 An order for alternative service directs that the petition be served in some way other than postal or personal service. It will only be permitted where the applicant has made proper attempts to trace and serve the respondent by post or personally. The alternative method of service permitted will be clearly specified in the order.

Example 1 The respondent is known to visit a relative regularly but efforts to effect personal service at that address have failed. Alternative service by posting the documents to that address could be authorized.

Example 2 Where it is known that the respondent uses a particular telephone number, alternative service may take the form of sending an SMS text message or leaving a voicemail message on that number saying where the petition and accompanying documents are to be found for collection by the respondent.

8.50 One method of alternative service is by advertisement. However, no order for service by advertisement will be given unless it appears to the district judge that there is a reasonable possibility that the advertisement will come to the knowledge of the person concerned. Indeed, in practice, the district judge is unlikely to permit any form of alternative service unless he is satisfied that it has a reasonable chance of bringing the proceedings to the knowledge of the person concerned. If the district judge considers that service by an alternative method should be authorized, he must specify the method or place of service, the date on which the petition is deemed to be served, and the period for filing an acknowledgment of service (r 6.19(3), FPR 2010).

Application for alternative services should be made to the district judge, without notice to **8.51** the respondent, by filing an application setting out the grounds on which the application is made (para 6.2, PD6A, FPR 2010).

Dispensing with service If all else fails, the district judge may be asked to make an order **8.52** dispensing with the need for service of the petition. He will do this where in his opinion it is impracticable to serve the petition or for other reasons it is necessary or expedient to dispense with service (r 6.20, FPR 2010). Clearly it can be a serious matter for the district judge to dispense with service as it means that the respondent may be divorced without even knowing that divorce proceedings have been commenced. The district judge will therefore have to be satisfied that exhaustive enquiries have been made to trace the respondent (see para 8.31 above) and that alternative service would not be appropriate.

Example The applicant has no idea where the respondent is. Enquiries of his relatives suggest that he has gone to work abroad but no one knows where. Enquiries of his past employers, past landlady, the DWP, the passport office, etc draw a blank. The district judge may be inclined to dispense with service.

The district judge can make an order dispensing with service altogether or dispensing with further service once one final method of service is tried.

An application for service to be dispensed with should be made, in the first instance, with- **8.53** out notice to the respondent by way of an affidavit in Form D13B setting out the grounds of the application (the attempts made to serve the respondent, the enquiries made as to his whereabouts, etc) but the district judge can require the attendance of the applicant when he decides the application (r 6.20(3) FPR 2010).

Common problems and solutions

Problem 1 From the outset the applicant is not able to give a definite address for service for **8.54** the respondent. The court cannot attempt to effect service.

Solution **8.55**
(a) Check that enquiries of the nature outlined in para 8.31 above have been made. If they have not, they should be set in motion; they may produce an address at which postal service can be effected.
(b) If the applicant is able to provide information as to where the respondent may be found (although she cannot provide an address as such), it may well be appropriate to request *personal service through the applicant* so that an enquiry agent can be instructed to trace the respondent and serve him with the petition personally.
(c) If an address or information as to the respondent's whereabouts is still not forthcoming, apply for *alternative service* or for *service to be dispensed with*. Personal service by the court bailiff or through the applicant will be impossible as the respondent cannot be traced. Deemed service is obviously inappropriate as the applicant cannot even attempt to serve the petition on the respondent so he clearly cannot be deemed to have received it.

8.56   **Problem 2** The applicant thinks she knows where the respondent is and provides an address for service. The acknowledgment of service is not returned.

8.57   **Solution**

    (a)   If the court office has not received the acknowledgment after seven days from the date they posted the petition to the respondent they may automatically inform the applicant's solicitor that the acknowledgment of service has not been returned and invite the solicitor to consider alternative methods of service.

         On the other hand some courts do not automatically inform the applicant's solicitors of non-receipt of the acknowledgment, so the applicant's solicitor should remember (he would be well advised to make a diary note to remind himself) to review the case after the respondent has had a reasonable period to return the acknowledgment (which will probably be not less than two weeks from the date of filing the petition). If at this stage no copy acknowledgment has been received from the court, the solicitor should confirm with the court office that nothing has been received by them and should then take the appropriate steps to deal with service.

    (b)   If the applicant still reasonably believes that the respondent is resident at the address given or can give another address, *bailiff service* should be requested (provided that the applicant is not legally represented).

    (c)   If the applicant is no longer confident about the respondent's address but still thinks she knows where he can be found (eg he regularly visits a certain public house), *personal service through the applicant* should be requested.

    (d)   If the applicant no longer has any idea where the respondent is, an application should be made for *alternative service* or for *service to be dispensed with*.

    (e)   Should the applicant be able to provide evidence that despite his silence the respondent has received the petition, an application should be made for *service to be deemed* as a substitute for alternative service or dispensing with service.

8.58   **Problem 3** Bailiff service is attempted and fails.

8.59   **Solution** If the applicant has any real idea of the whereabouts of the respondent and there is a prospect of him being traced by an enquiry agent, *personal service through the applicant* should be requested. Otherwise, application should be made for *alternative service* or for *service to be dispensed with*. *Deemed service* is an alternative where appropriate as in Problem 2.

8.60   **Problem 4** Personal service is attempted and fails.

8.61   **Solution** Apply for *alternative service* or for *service to be dispensed with*. *Deemed service* is an alternative.

Service on a party under a disability

8.62   The court does not carry out service where the party to be served is under a disability, that is, he is under 18 or a protected party ('protected party' for these purposes means a person who lacks capacity within the meaning of the Mental Capacity Act 2005 to conduct proceedings) (r 2.3, FPR 2010). Service must be through the applicant and there are special rules as to the method of service and as to procedure generally (rr 6.28–6.33, FPR 2010).

Service on a co-respondent

The procedure for serving a co-respondent with the petition is the same as for the respondent. **8.63** The routine practice is for the court to attempt postal service. The copy of the petition for service has annexed to it a notice of proceedings in Form D9 and a form of acknowledgment of service in Form D10 and, if there is a funding certificate, a notice of issue of the certificate. The co-respondent does not, however, receive a copy of the statement as to arrangements for the children.

If postal service fails, bailiff service or personal service through the applicant will normally **8.64** be tried. Application can be made for service to be deemed or dispensed with or alternative service ordered as in the case of service on the respondent. As the divorce will not affect the status of the co-respondent, it may be easier to persuade the court to dispense with service where difficulty is experienced than it is in relation to service on a respondent.

Service outside England and Wales

Rule 6.41, FPR 2010 allows any document in family proceedings (including a divorce petition) **8.65** to be served outside England and Wales *without* the court's prior permission either in accordance with the FPR 2010 (ie, by prepaid first class post or personally or by alternative service).

Rule 6.47(1), FPR 2010 requires the documents to be accompanied by a translation in the **8.66** official language of the country in which they are to be served unless the documents are to be served in a country where English is the official language or the person on whom the documents are to be served is able to read and understand English (r 6.47(4) and (5), FPR 2010).

G RETURN OF THE ACKNOWLEDGMENT OF SERVICE

Filling in the acknowledgment of service

The acknowledgment of service is straightforward. It is in question and answer form and the **8.67** respondent is given extra guidance in Form D9 (notice of proceedings) on how to complete the form.

The solicitor can sign the acknowledgment for the respondent unless either: **8.68**

(a) in adultery cases, the acknowledgment contains an admission of adultery; *or*
(b) in cases of two years' separation and consent, the acknowledgment is used to signify the respondent's consent to the decree (r 7.12(4) and (5), FPR 2010).

In both these cases, the respondent must sign the acknowledgment personally. The solicitor will also sign the acknowledgment of service if he is representing the respondent (as opposed to advising and assisting him under the Legal Help scheme).

Note that the fact that the respondent states in the acknowledgment that he intends to **8.69** defend the divorce does not amount to a formal step towards defending. The respondent's statement merely ensures that the divorce will be held up to give him time to file an answer (see Chapter 10). However, if he fails to do so within the proper time, the case will proceed undefended as if he had not raised any objection.

8.70 Note also that what the respondent states about his intention when filling in the acknowledgment of service in no way binds him. He may, for example, indicate that he intends to defend and then do nothing about it, or indicate that he has no intention of seeking a CA 1989 order in respect of the children and then change his mind and make an application.

8.71 In addition, the respondent is required to indicate whether there are any proceedings continuing in any country outside England and Wales which relate to the marriage or are capable of affecting its validity and substance, and to give details of any such proceedings. If such proceedings have already been commenced in another EU state, it is likely that subsequent proceedings issued in England and Wales will be automatically stayed. Secondly, the respondent is now required to indicate in which country he is (a) habitually resident and (b) domiciled. He must also state of which country he is a national. He must indicate whether he objects to paying the applicant's costs, if claimed (see paras 8.88 ff below). Lastly, he must indicate whether he agrees with the statement of the applicant as to the grounds of jurisdiction set out in the petition. If he does not agree, he must specify his reasons.

Returning the acknowledgment of service

8.72 The acknowledgment of service must be returned (normally by post) to reach the court within seven days after the respondent received the divorce papers (r 7.12(1), FPR 2010).

8.73 The respondent and co-respondent can normally be relied upon to return the acknowledgment of service at least with a little prompting from the court, which may send a reminder and a new copy of the acknowledgment of service if the first one is not returned within a reasonable period.

8.74 If the acknowledgment of service is returned:

(a) The court sends a photocopy of it to the applicant's solicitor. This triggers the necessary steps to obtain the decree nisi of divorce (see para 8.77 below).

(b) If the respondent or co-respondent indicates in the acknowledgment of service that he intends to defend the case, matters will automatically be held up for a period of 28 days from the date he received the divorce petition to give him the opportunity to file an answer (r 7.12(8)) (see Chapter 10 for further details concerning the filing of an answer). If neither the respondent nor the co-respondent files an answer within this period, the case will proceed as an undefended matter unless, at any time, the respondent or co-respondent gets permission of the court to file an answer out of time (see Chapter 10).

(c) If, as is more likely, the respondent and co-respondent indicate that they do not intend to defend the case, the next step will usually be for the applicant's solicitors to request the district judge to give directions for trial.

8.75 If the acknowledgment of service is not returned, the applicant's solicitor will have to decide what further steps are to be taken in relation to service of the petition (see above).

H   WHEN DECREE NISI CAN BE GRANTED

The district judge can give directions for the grant of the decree nisi if he is satisfied of the **8.76** following matters:

(a) *Due service*: the district judge must be satisfied that a copy of the petition has been duly served on every party required to be served (r 7.19(1), FPR 2010). Where there is a respondent and a co-respondent, service on both will be required. Where the acknowledgment of service has been returned by a respondent or co-respondent, this will be taken as proof of due service of the petition on that party provided:

    (i) that it is signed by that party or by a solicitor on his behalf; *and*

    (ii) where the form purports to be signed by the respondent, the signature is proved to be that of the respondent—this is usually proved by the applicant identifying the signature as the respondent's in her D80A–D80E affidavit which she files in support of the petition when the decree nisi is applied for (see para 8.77 below) (r 7.19(1)); *and*

(b) *Case undefended*: the district judge must be satisfied that the case can be classed as undefended, that is, either:

    (i) the respondent and co-respondent have informed the court (almost certainly in the acknowledgment of service) that they do not intend to defend the case; *or*

    (ii) no notice of intention to defend has been given by either the respondent or any co-respondent and the time for giving such a notice has expired; *or*

    (iii) if notice of intention to defend has been given by any party, the time allowed him for filing an answer has expired, that is, 28 days from the date on which the respondent or co-respondent received the petition inclusive of the day of receipt (r 7.12(8)); *and*

(c) *Consent given if s 1(2)(d) case*: where the petition is based on two years' separation and consent, the district judge must be satisfied that the respondent has given notice to the district judge that he consents to the decree being granted (r 7.12(4) and (6)). This consent is normally given in the acknowledgment of service.

I   APPLYING FOR THE DECREE NISI

The district judge will not grant the decree nisi automatically. It is up to the applicant's solicitor **8.77** to make a written application that he should do so (r 7.19(1), FPR 2010). This is done by filing:

(a) a standard form of application (in Form D84) for the decree nisi signed personally by the applicant or by the solicitor if fully representing the applicant (this form can be obtained from the court office if necessary); *and*

(b) an affidavit from the applicant in support of the petition (r 7.19(4)). There is a standard printed form of affidavit suited to each of the s 1(2), MCA 1973 facts (Forms D80A–D80E). These affidavits are in question and answer form and may now be affirmed instead of being sworn. Great care should be taken in completing the affidavit. The following points should be borne in mind:

(i)   The affidavit requires the applicant to swear that everything stated in the petition is true. If there are errors in the petition these must be resolved before the affidavit is sworn. If the corrections or amendments required are minor (eg the date of birth of one of the children of the family is wrongly stated or, more commonly, the address of one party has changed since the petition was filed), they can be set out in the relevant paragraph of the affidavit. The district judge will then, in most cases, treat the petition as amended in these respects without any requirement that it should be re-served in its amended form on the respondent or co-respondent.

However, if the alterations required are more serious (eg if the applicant wishes to add an allegation of behaviour in a petition based on s 1(2)(b), MCA 1973), the proper course will be to apply to the district judge for permission to amend the petition which will then have to be re-served on the respondent (and co-respondent if there is one) before the applicant will be able to apply for the decree nisi and file her affidavit in support of the petition. See Chapter 9 for further details as to amendment of the petition.

(ii) It is this affidavit that provides the district judge with evidence of the fact relied on in the petition and of irretrievable breakdown of the marriage. It also replaces the need to attend court and to give oral evidence in front of the district judge. There are five different versions of Form D80 because each is tailored to one of the facts in s 1(2) so that the applicant is prompted to provide information relevant to the fact on which she relies. The solicitor has a great advantage over an applicant filling in the affidavit without Legal Help because he knows the case law on the subject and he can therefore give an informed answer to each question ensuring that all the information that the applicant can give in support of her case is given. It is most important for the solicitor to keep the substantive law as to divorce (set out in Chapter 4) in mind, so that this advantage is not thrown away.

(iii) Where the applicant and respondent have lived in the same household since the matters complained of, care should be taken in stating the period(s) of this cohabitation and the reason why it occurred. Certain periods of cohabitation can be disregarded in considering whether the applicant is entitled to a decree (see Chapter 4); cohabitation in excess of this may bar the applicant from obtaining a decree unless she is able to give a good reason for it. If the applicant and the respondent are still living together at the time the affidavit is completed, it would be prudent to give a reason for this in case it raises doubts in the district judge's mind as to whether the marriage has truly broken down.

(iv) Where the applicant is relying on s 1(2)(c) to (e) (all facts where a period of separation is required) and it is alleged that the parties have been living apart under the same roof, great pains should be taken to show that the parties were indeed maintaining two separate households (giving details of which rooms were used by which party, whether meals were shared, washing done by one for the other, etc); *and*

(c) Any corroborative evidence on which the applicant intends to rely. It is not always easy to decide when the district judge will be satisfied with the applicant's evidence alone and when further independent evidence will be required. There are no rules about this; it depends on the standards of the district judge who considers the case and the best guide is therefore experience of the practice of the local district judges. However, the following points may be helpful:

   (i) The object of the exercise is, of course, to satisfy the district judge that the applicant is entitled to a decree. The district judge has a two-part decision to make when considering whether he is satisfied with the applicant's case: first, he must decide whether the details contained in the petition, *if true*, would entitle the applicant to a decree; and secondly, whether the details contained in the petition *are in fact true*. The first stage is a question of law and if the district judge is not satisfied on the law no amount of evidence provided by the applicant to corroborate what she says in the petition will change his mind.

   The second stage is a question of fact and corroborative evidence can help the district judge to be satisfied as to the truth of the petition. While the district judge must be satisfied as to the evidence, this duty must be measured against the need for proportionality as stated in the overriding objective set out in r 1.1, FPR 2010.

   (ii) The majority of the facts stated in the petition do not need any further support than the evidence of the applicant in her Form D80 affidavit. However, corroboration may be required of the s 1(2), MCA 1973 fact alleged and the particulars given in relation to it.

It should be emphasized that practice varies enormously from one county court to another and it is most important to check the particular requirements of the court where the petition has been filed. In the authors' experience, specific corroboration will be required in adultery cases (usually provided by the respondent's personally signed acknowledgment of service admitting the adultery).

(d) Costs: it often happens that an applicant claims costs against the respondent in her divorce petition without giving much thought as to whether she really wishes to pursue that claim. The respondent often files an acknowledgment of service objecting to the payment of costs, sometimes giving reasons and sometimes not. When the applicant then goes on to file her D80 affidavit it will be of great assistance to the court if she makes it clear whether she still wishes to claim costs in spite of the respondent's objections.

(e) It should be noted that Forms D80 A–D contain three additional clauses at the end which ask the applicant whether she has read the statement of arrangements and whether she wishes to alter anything contained in that statement or in the petition itself. It also requires the applicant to identify the signature at the bottom of Part 4 of the statement of arrangements and to confirm that it is that of the respondent, assuming that this has been returned to the court by the respondent.

J   GRANTING THE DECREE NISI

The role of the district judge

8.78   Once the application for the decree nisi (in Form D84) and the appropriate affidavit in support have been filed at court, the district judge will consider the application. This task is undertaken in box work not in open court.

8.79   First, the district judge will check that the petition has been served on the respondent or that service has been dealt with in one of the ways described in paras 8.35–8.61 above.

8.80   Next, the district judge will read the petition for divorce and the affidavit in support (described in detail at para 8.77 above) to determine:

(a)   that the case is undefended; and

(b)   that the applicant is entitled to a decree nisi.

District judge satisfied

8.81   If satisfied as to these two matters, the district judge must grant a certificate to this effect and direct that the application be listed before the court for the making of the decree nisi at the next available date (r 7.20(2)(a), FPR 2010).

8.82   The district judge will then deal with the question of costs.

8.83   If the applicant claims costs in her petition the district judge considers her claim and, if he is satisfied that she is entitled to the costs of obtaining the divorce, he includes in his certificate a statement to that effect (r 7.20(3), FPR 2010). Whether costs are ordered is a matter within the discretion of the court. If there are any general rules, they are as follows:

(a)   behaviour and desertion cases: respondent pays the costs;

(b)   adultery cases: respondent and/or co-respondent pay the costs unless they show that this would be unjust because the adultery took place after the breakdown of the marriage or was brought about by the applicant's own conduct or, in the case of the co-respondent, because he/she did not know and could not have been expected to know that the respondent was married;

(c)   consensual separation cases: applicant and respondent pay half the costs each. However, it is open to the respondent to prevent this by refusing to give his consent to the decree unless the entire costs are borne by the applicant;

(d)   five years' separation cases: no order as to costs. This means that the respondent's solicitor's bill is likely to be noticeably less than that of the applicant's solicitor.

8.84   Where the district judge is not satisfied that the applicant is entitled to costs, the court may make no direction as to costs (r 7.20(3), FPR 2010).

8.85   It is open, however, to the applicant who has been deprived of costs to make representations at the hearing for the grant of the decree nisi as to why an order for costs should be made in the applicant's favour. Paragraphs 8.89 and 8.90 below describe the procedure.

8.86   Where the respondent and/or co-respondent do not inform the court at any stage of any objection to paying costs, many districts judges will grant the applicant costs without question.

However where the solicitor is instructed by the respondent and/or co-respondent that **8.87** he does not object to paying the applicant's costs in principle, it is sensible to do one of the following:

(a) agree a figure for the costs with the solicitor advising the applicant, such figure to include disbursements and VAT so that the extent of the respondent's liability is clear. It can then be stated in the acknowledgment of service form that the respondent has agreed to pay costs in the amount specified;

(b) ensure that the respondent indicates that he will be responsible for the costs if and only if the decree absolute is granted. Two benefits arise from this. First, the respondent knows that his liability for costs will only arise if the marriage is in fact dissolved. Secondly, he knows at what point his liability to pay arises.

If on the other hand, the respondent and/or co-respondent do wish to object to paying the **8.88** applicant's costs, the appropriate place is normally in the acknowledgment of service. The district judge will then bear in mind their objections in deciding the question of costs.

As indicated in para 8.85, the applicant may attend court and be heard on the question of **8.89** costs (r 7.21(1)). A similar opportunity is given to the respondent and/or co-respondent.

However r 7.21(2) FPR 2010 makes it clear that neither party will be heard unless the object- **8.90** ing party has not less than two days before the hearing, served on every other party written notice of his or her intention to attend the hearing and apply for, or oppose, the making of an order for costs. The hearing will take place on the date on which the decree nisi is granted. (It would appear that there is no requirement to notify the court of an intention to attend court on that date.)

District judge not satisfied

If the district judge is not satisfied that the applicant is entitled to a decree he must do one **8.91** of two things:

(a) He can direct the applicant to provide such further information or to take such other steps as the court may specify (r 7.20(2)(b)(i), FPR 2010). He may direct that the further information be verified by an affidavit (r 7.20(5), FPR 2010). More unusually, the applicant could be required to attend court to give oral evidence before the district judge.

   Example The district judge reads the statement of case in the petition setting out the allegations of the respondent's behaviour where the petition is based on s 1(2)(b) and considers the allegations to be insufficiently detailed. He may direct the applicant to prepare and file an affidavit giving greater detail of the allegations made.

   Once the applicant has complied with the district judge's direction, the district judge will reconsider the case and decide whether to grant his certificate that the applicant is entitled to a decree nisi.

(b) Alternatively, the district judge may direct that the case be listed for a case management hearing (r 7.20(2)(b)(ii), FPR 2010). The case management hearing is explained at para 8.95 below.

It is important to realize that no order that the district judge makes can amount to a final refusal of a decree. It is only the judge who can finally dismiss the petition and in practice he will rarely find it necessary to do this.

K   PRONOUNCEMENT OF DECREE NISI

8.92   If the district judge has certified that the applicant is entitled to a decree, decree nisi will be granted by a judge or district judge on the day fixed by the district judge.

8.93   The pronouncement of the decree is unexciting. It is quite likely that all that will happen is that the clerk of the court or the judge or district judge himself will read out a list of cases and ask if there are any applications in these cases (eg objections as to costs or attempts by respondents to prevent the pronouncement of the decree by having the district judge's certificate set aside and seeking permission to file an answer). Once any applications are dealt with, the judge or district judge will then announce that decrees are pronounced in all the cases listed and that other relief is granted in accordance with the district judge's certificate. When the judge or district judge grants other relief in accordance with the district judge's certificate, this means that if the district judge has certified that the applicant is entitled to costs or that the applicant or respondent is entitled to agreed financial provision an order of the court is automatically made to that effect. This saves the judge or district judge the trouble of going through all the cases on his list ordering costs here and financial provision there as appropriate.

8.94   Both parties can attend the granting of the decree nisi if they wish but it is not normally necessary for either to attend (r 7.18 FPR 2010) unless either wishes to be heard on the question of costs (see paras 8.85–90 above).

L   CASES REFERRED TO THE JUDGE

8.95   It can happen that the district judge is not satisfied as to the applicant's case. In these circumstances, as explained in para 8.91 above, the district judge may direct that the case be listed for a case management hearing.

8.96   Rule 7.22(3), FPR 2010 sets out what must happen next. First, the court must consider what further evidence is required properly to dispose of the proceedings and give directions about the filing and service of such evidence. Secondly, the court must give directions for the future conduct of the proceedings including directing either that on compliance with any directions given at the case management hearing a further application should be made under r 7.19, FPR 2010 for the decree nisi now to be granted or (and more rarely) direct that the case is not suitable to be dealt with in that way.

Where such a direction is given the court must determine how the case is to proceed in future. **8.97**
Rule 7.22(4), FPR 2010 states that the court may then give directions as to the filing and service
of evidence, deal with disclosure and inspection of documents and give directions as to
the conduct of the final hearing and the attendance of witnesses.

Alternatively, the court may direct that the case be listed for a further hearing at which such **8.98**
directions will be given.

The object of the further directions is to attempt to resolve the difficulty which originally **8.99**
led to the district judge not being satisfied that the applicant was entitled to a decree nisi of
divorce in the first place. If, having complied with the further directions, the applicant is still
unable to persuade the district judge that she is entitled to a decree nisi, the case will need to
be listed for a final hearing at which the judge will consider the evidence.

The applicant will be required to attend the final hearing and give evidence on oath in **8.100**
support of her petition. A certificate for Legal Representation may be available for such
hearings (see Chapter 2) so that the applicant will normally be represented by her solicitor
or by counsel. Public funding will only be available if the circumstances of the particular
case justify representation and there are sufficient prospects of obtaining a decree nisi
of divorce.

 The district judge may decide to grant the decree nisi there and then, in which case the **8.101**
applicant will be able to obtain the decree absolute of divorce in due course (see para 8.117
below). However, the judge may dismiss the petition. Apart from the possibility of an
appeal against the judge's order under Part 30, FPR 2010 this is the end of the petition as far
as the applicant is concerned. In any event, the judge will make whatever order as to costs he
thinks fit.

M CONSIDERATION OF ARRANGEMENTS FOR THE CHILDREN OF THE FAMILY

Rule 7.25, FPR 2010 places the main burden of 'considering' those arrangements on the district **8.102**
judge.

Section 41, MCA 1973 requires that in any proceedings for divorce, judicial separation, or **8.103**
nullity the court must *consider*, at the date on which the court considers the arrangements:

(a) whether there is any child of the family who has not reached the age of 16; and
(b) whether there is a child who has reached 16 in respect of whom it should direct that s 41
      should apply.

In practice this duty will usually be carried out by the district judge when deciding whether
the applicant is entitled to a decree nisi of divorce where there is no application for an order
under the CA 1989 pending in respect of a child of the family.

Where there is no application for an order under the Children Act 1989 pending

8.104   The district judge will consider the arrangements that are proposed for the upbringing and welfare of the children immediately after making his certificate of entitlement to decree nisi under r 7.20(2)(a), FPR 2010. He will then consider whether he should exercise any of his powers under the CA 1989 with respect to any of the children of the family. He will do this by a close examination of Form D8A which has been filed with the divorce petition. Usually it is the applicant who has submitted it. The respondent is perfectly entitled to file a Form D8A if he wishes, but it is rare to find this in practice.

8.105   In examining Form D8A the district judge will look for anything in the proposed arrangements which may be unsatisfactory so far as the children are concerned. He will look to see that there is, for example, adequate accommodation, education, health care, and financial provision for the child.

8.106   If the district judge considers, pursuant to s 41(2), MCA 1973, that:

(a) the exercise of his powers is, or is likely to be, necessary but the court is not in a position to exercise them without further consideration, *and*
(b) there are *exceptional* circumstances which make it desirable in the interests of the child to do so,

then he may direct that a decree of divorce or nullity not be made absolute, or a decree of judicial separation not be granted, until the court orders otherwise.

8.107   If, however, the court is satisfied, pursuant to r 7.25(3), FPR 2010, that either:

(a) there are no children of the family to whom s 41 applies, or
(b) there are such children, but that the court need not exercise its powers or make a direction under s 41,
(c) then the district judge must give a certificate to that effect.

What happens if the district judge is not satisfied with the proposed arrangements?

8.108   If the district judge is not satisfied with the proposed arrangements for the children then he may give one of the following directions, pursuant to r 7.25(4), FPR 2010:

(a) that the parties, or any of them, must file further evidence as to the arrangements for the children (the exact nature of the information required may be specified, eg a medical report);
(b) that a welfare report on the children or any of them be prepared;
(c) that the parties, or any of them, attend before him.

8.109   Rule 7.25(5), FPR 2010 requires that where the court makes a direction under r 7.25(4) above, the court must state in writing:

(a) its reasons for doing so; and
(b) in the case of a relevant direction, the exceptional circumstances which make it desirable in the interests of the child that the court should make such a direction.

Example 1 Form D8A filed by Mrs Plum revealed that the 3-year-old child of the family, Tracy, was living with Mrs Plum and was suffering from leukaemia. However, the form gave no information as to whether or not the child was still being treated for the illness.

The district judge then asked the applicant to file a medical report in relation to the child. The medical report showed that the child's treatment was being satisfactorily undertaken by the hospital and that the parents were cooperating with the treatment programme. The district judge decided there was no need to look any further into the matter.

Example 2 The facts are as in Example 1 above but Mrs Plum failed to file any medical report. The district judge asked Mr and Mrs Plum to attend at court for an appointment with him so that he could find out from them the reasons for their failure to give the information requested. The parties failed to attend the appointment. The district judge decided to order a Cafcass officer's report in respect of Tracy. He was reluctant to take this step unless it was absolutely necessary because he knew that generally it took two or three months for such a report to be compiled. However, there appeared to be no other way of obtaining proper information about Tracy.

Example 3 The facts are as in Example 2 above. The Cafcass officer tried to make an appointment with Mr and Mrs Plum on many occasions but they refused to see her on any basis. The Cafcass officer reported the difficulties to the court. The district judge applied the cumulative test in s 41(2), MCA 1973 and found that the circumstances of the case might require the court to exercise some of its powers under the CA 1989: s 41(2)(a), MCA 1973 (eg to ask the local authority to investigate the case and to report to the court as to whether it wished to take any action in relation to the child: s 37, CA 1989). Applying the next limb of the test (s 41(2)(b), MCA 1973), the district judge considered that he was not in a position to exercise that power without giving further consideration to the case. He wished to extend to the parties a final invitation to attend court for an appointment with him, along with a clear warning as to the consequences that might follow if they refused. He then applied the third, cumulative, part of the test in s 41(2) and considered that there were 'exceptional circumstances' in this case which made it desirable in the interests of Tracy that he should direct that the decree was not to be made absolute until the outstanding problems had been resolved.

It seems clear from the wording of s 41(2) that the intention of Parliament was that decree absolute should not be withheld lightly. The cumulative requirements of s 41(2) make it clear that it should be a power used only in 'exceptional circumstances'. In practice many district judges recognize the limited resources available to Cafcass or the local authority to assist and determine that there are 'exceptional circumstances' justifying refusal of the decree absolute. The onus is then placed on the parties to provide the court with the relevant information in order to satisfy the district judge about the arrangements and ultimately to obtain the decree absolute.

General examples of matters which might cause the district judge to consider whether the court is, or is likely to be, required to exercise any of its powers under the CA 1989 are as follows: **8.110**

Accommodation Where the parties are living in cramped accommodation (eg three children with the applicant and her parents and brother in a two-bedroomed flat), or in unsuitable accommodation (eg a rented flat with no bathroom over a nightclub), or where there is doubt as to the applicant's security of tenure over the accommodation (eg where she has been served with notice to quit). In such circumstances the district judge may want the Cafcass officer to look at the accommodation, or he may require documentary evidence that the applicant   **8.111**

will soon be able to provide suitable accommodation, for example a letter from the council promising her accommodation within a limited period of time. Sometimes the district judge will require an updated statement of arrangements to be filed at court once the applicant has moved to suitable accommodation.

8.112   **Disputes over residence of and contact with the child**   If it is clear that the parents are in dispute as to where the child should live and how much contact, if any, he should have with the parent with whom he is not residing, then it is likely that one or other of the parties will apply for a s 8 order. If no application has yet been made for a s 8 order by the time the district judge comes to consider the arrangements for the children then the district judge may arrange an appointment for the parties to come to court and see him. He might point out to them the relevant applications they might make to resolve the issue. If a s 8 application is then made, the issue will automatically fall to be determined by the judge in any event, and the district judge need not consider the issue further.

8.113   If, however, the parties do not take any steps to seek a s 8 order it is not clear to what extent the district judge will enquire further into the matter. If, in due course, the parents make it clear that neither of them wishes to make an application, and all of the other circumstances relating to the child appear satisfactory, then the authors would tentatively submit that the court is unlikely to take the view that it should interfere further. In that case, the court will certify under r 7.25(3)(b), FPR 2010 that there is no need for the court to exercise any of its powers under the CA 1989 or to give any direction under s 41(2), MCA 1973.

Where an application for an order under the Children Act 1989 is pending

8.114   Where an application for an order under the CA 1989 is pending then it will not be necessary for the district judge to consider the arrangements for the children because they will be fully considered in due course by the court which disposes of the application. The fact that an intention to make an application, for example for a residence or contact order, is merely indicated in Form D8A would not be sufficient to relieve the district judge of the duty to consider the arrangements for the children. There must be an actual notice of application before the district judge is no longer required to consider the arrangements.

8.115   Where an application for an order under the CA 1989 is pending in a family proceedings court prior to the commencement of the divorce proceedings then the usual practice would be for the magistrates to transfer the application to a county court so that all matters could be heard together. In that case the district judge would not be required to consider the arrangements for the children, since they would be dealt with in the disposal of the application.

N   DECREE ABSOLUTE

The need for decree absolute

8.116   The first decree granted to an applicant is a decree nisi. This does not free the applicant or the respondent from the marriage. The marriage is only dissolved once decree absolute is obtained.

Application for decree absolute

A decree nisi normally may not be made absolute before the expiration of six weeks from the **8.117** date on which it is granted (s 1(5), MCA 1973 as varied). There is power to expedite decree absolute but it is rarely used (see paras 8.127 ff below).

As soon as the six-week period expires, the applicant can apply for decree absolute by filing **8.118** with the district judge a notice in Form D36 (r 7.32(1), FPR 2010) together with the prescribed fee (currently £45) unless the applicant is 'fees exempt'. There is no need to give the respondent notice of the application.

When he receives Form D36, the district judge searches the court records in relation to the **8.119** case. He has to satisfy himself on various matters which are set out in full in r 7.32(2), FPR 2010. In brief, he must be sure:

(a) that the court has complied with the duty to consider the arrangements for the children under s 41, MCA 1973 and has not given any direction under s 41(2) that requires the decree not to be made absolute;
(b) that no one is trying to upset the decree nisi by means of an appeal or an application for rescission of the decree nisi;
(c) that the provisions of s 10(2) to (4), MCA 1973 (consideration of the respondent's financial position after the divorce) either do not apply or have been complied with.

If the district judge is satisfied as to the matters set out in r 7.32(2), FPR 2010, he will make the decree absolute.

Both the applicant and the respondent will be sent a certificate in Form D37 certifying that **8.120** the decree nisi has been made absolute and giving the date on which this was done.

As soon as the decree is made absolute, the applicant and respondent are both released from **8.121** the marriage and are free to remarry should they wish to do so.

Application by respondent

If the applicant does not apply to have the decree made absolute, once three months have **8.122** elapsed from the earliest date on which the applicant could have applied for decree absolute, the respondent may make application for decree absolute (s 9(2), MCA 1973). The earliest that the respondent can apply is therefore three months and six weeks after the pronouncement of decree nisi.

The respondent's application may be made to a judge or to a district judge (r 7.33, FPR 2010). **8.123** A fee of £90 is payable. Notice of the application must be served on the applicant not less than three clear days before the day on which the application is heard. A short hearing usually takes place, affording the applicant an opportunity to explain why she has not applied for the decree absolute. The usual reason for delay by the applicant is because she wishes to have the security of orders for financial provision in place before forfeiting her right, for example, to share in the respondent's pension arrangements. She would normally lose such a right following her change of status on the grant of the decree absolute. The decree absolute was refused for those reasons and because of the respondent husband's devious approach to proceedings for financial provision in *Wickler* v *Wickler* [1998] 2 FLR 326.

8.124   Conversely, the respondent husband's application for the decree nisi to be made absolute will not be refused simply because proceedings for financial provision are not yet concluded. To prevent the husband's application from succeeding, the wife must show not only significant non-disclosure of financial assets but also the probability that the husband will leave the jurisdiction and take no further part in the ancillary relief proceedings: *Re G (Decree Absolute: Prejudice)* [2003] 1 FLR 870.

District judge can require affidavit

8.125   If application is not made to have the decree made absolute until after 12 months have elapsed after decree nisi was granted, the notice in Form D36 must be accompanied by a written explanation giving reasons for the delay, stating whether the parties have lived together since decree nisi and, if so, between what dates, and stating (if the wife is the applicant) whether the wife has given birth to any child since the decree or (if the husband is the applicant) whether the husband has reason to believe that the wife has given birth to such a child and, in either case, if so, stating the relevant facts and whether it is alleged that the child is or may be a child of the family.

8.126   The district judge may require the explanation to be verified by an affidavit from the applicant and may make such order on the application as he thinks fit. In particular he must ensure that s 41, MCA 1973 has been complied with where it appears that there is, or may be, a child of the family born since decree nisi (r 7.32(3) and (4), FPR 2010).

Expediting decree absolute

8.127   If there is some urgency about obtaining decree absolute, it is possible to apply for a special order giving permission to expedite decree absolute. However, the normal six-week waiting period between decree nisi and decree absolute is so short that it should very rarely be necessary to do.

8.128   It is suggested that, in urgent cases, rather than attacking the problem after decree nisi, the solicitor should make efforts to speed things up at an earlier stage. Naturally this means him dealing with his own part of the case (drafting the petition, etc) expeditiously. It is also suggested that the solicitor should write a letter to the court to accompany the applicant's Form D80 affidavit explaining the urgency and asking the court to ensure that the district judge deals with the application as soon as possible and fixes an early date for the pronouncement of decree nisi. Paragraph 8 of PD7A, FPR 2010 gives guidance on this point.

Declaration that the decree absolute is void

8.129   There are a number of circumstances where an application may be made for a declaration that the decree absolute is void.

8.130   Such circumstances include: (a) where it emerges that the court does not have jurisdiction; (b) where a fundamental irregularity undermines the entire proceedings; or (c) where there has been a failure to comply with the statutory requirements which are conditions precedent to the right to a decree. This latter situation was described as 'controversial' by Holman J in

Krenge v *Krenge* [1999] 1 FLR 969 and did not cover the situation where the respondent had applied for the decree absolute to be set aside because the decree nisi and decree absolute had been sent to him in the same envelope. The judge's decision was based on the fact that the respondent had received the certificate of entitlement to a decree nisi on an earlier occasion and therefore was well aware of the stage the proceedings had reached.

O PROCEDURE FOR DISSOLUTION OF A CIVIL PARTNERSHIP

The procedure described above, together with the guidance on drafting the petition in Chapter 7, also applies where a civil partnership is to be dissolved. **8.131**

As might be expected, the wording of the petition reflects the fact that a civil partnership has been formed and requires details of the date and place. **8.132**

Throughout the petition, reference is made to a civil partnership instead of a marriage. **8.133**

Orders for dissolution will be conditional in the first instance (the equivalent of the decree nisi in divorce proceedings) and may not be made final (the equivalent of the decree absolute in divorce proceedings) until six weeks from the date of the conditional order. **8.134**

P KEY DOCUMENTS

Family Procedure Rules 2010 (SI 2010/2955) **8.135**

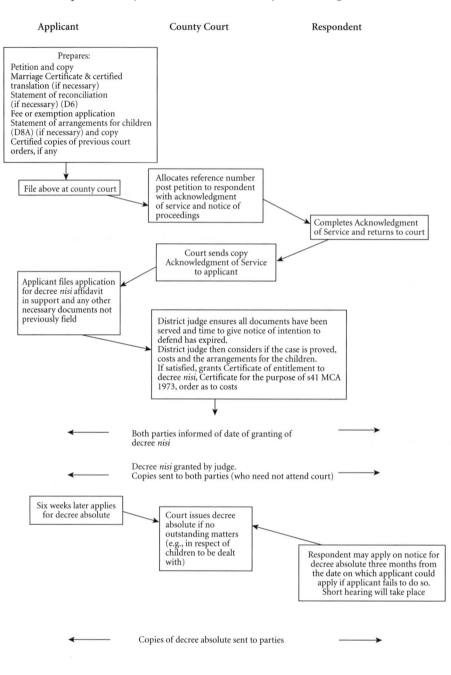

9

AMENDED, SUPPLEMENTAL, AND NEW PETITIONS

A INTRODUCTION

On rare occasions the divorce petition will require amendment (eg to give details of previous **9.01** family proceedings not recited in the original petition) or to be replaced by a new petition where the applicant wishes to rely on a new s 1(2), Matrimonial Causes Act 1973 ('MCA 1973') fact that has occurred only since the date of the original petition. This chapter briefly explains the relevant procedure.

B AMENDMENT, SUPPLEMENTAL PETITION, OR FRESH PETITION?

It is important to recognize which matters can be the subject of an amendment of the petition **9.02** and which necessitate the filing of a supplemental petition or of a completely fresh petition.

Addition of s 1(2), Matrimonial Causes Act 1973 facts

(a) Where the new facts arose *before* the date of the petition: if the applicant wishes to add to **9.03** the petition an additional s 1(2) fact which arose before the date of the original petition, she may do so by means of a straightforward amendment.

Example 1 In October 2011 the wife discovers that her husband had committed adultery at Christmas. His behaviour towards her has been violent and unpleasant since the beginning of the marriage and this is the last straw. She leaves him immediately and files a petition based on his adultery. Contrary to expectations the respondent indicates that he intends to deny the allegation of adultery and the applicant's solicitors decide that it would be prudent to add an allegation of behaviour under s 1(2)(b). This can be done by amendment of the original petition because the behaviour alleged occurred before the date of the original petition.

(b) Where the new fact arose *after* the date of the petition: a petition cannot be amended to add new s 1(2) facts that have arisen after the date of the original petition. This rules out not only straightforward amendments to the original petition but also the filing of a supplemental petition which (although a separate document) is, in effect, another means of amending the original petition. The applicant wishing to add a s 1(2) fact that has arisen (or, in the case of a separation fact, has been completed) since the date of the original petition must therefore file a fresh petition.

Example 2 In October 2011 the applicant leaves the respondent and files a petition based on his adultery. The respondent defends the petition and the matter drags on into 2012. By this time the parties have been separated for two years and the respondent is prepared to consent to a decree. The applicant now wishes to seek a decree on the basis of s 1(2)(d) (two years' separation and consent). She cannot do this by amendment of the original petition because the two years' separation were not complete at the date of the original petition nor, for the same reason, can she file a supplemental petition. She must file a fresh petition based on s 1(2)(d).

Addition or amendment other than the addition of new s 1(2) facts

9.04 (a) To take account of matters arising before the date of the petition: this can be done by means of a straightforward amendment to the original petition or, in the case of very minor corrections, in special procedure cases, through the applicant's Form D80 affidavit.

Example 1 The applicant files a petition based on s 1(2)(b) without first consulting a solicitor. She then seeks legal advice before obtaining decree nisi. It is clear to her solicitor that her petition is inadequate as it stands and that there are other allegations of behaviour on the part of the respondent before the date of the petition which should properly be added. This can be done by amendment of the petition.

Example 2 In the petition the date of birth of one of the children is given incorrectly as 1 June 2008. It should be 2 June 2008. This is a minor correction and can be dealt with by means of the applicant's Form D80 affidavit.

(b) To take account of matters arising after the date of the petition: certain matters arising after the date of the petition can be dealt with by means of a straightforward amendment, for example the petition can be amended to add details of a child born after the date of the petition.

However, if the applicant wishes to add further allegations to the statement of the case in support of the s 1(2) fact on which the petition is based in respect of incidents which arose after the date of the petition, she will have to file a supplemental petition.

Example In October 2010 the applicant files a petition based on the respondent's behaviour (s 1(2)(b)). The parties continue to live together after the petition is filed and nothing is done about the divorce. However, in July 2011 the applicant leaves the respondent because of his unpleasant and violent behaviour which has continued since the date of the divorce petition. She wishes to proceed with the divorce. If the applicant attempts to proceed on the basis of the petition as it stands she will find herself in difficulty in view of the long period of cohabitation that has followed the last incident of behaviour alleged (well in excess of the six-month period that s 2(3) says should be disregarded). She cannot amend the petition to add further incidents of behaviour that have arisen between 2010 and 2011 as these post-date the petition. She will have to file a supplemental petition alleging further incidents of behaviour during this period.

C PROCEDURE FOR AMENDMENT

In theory amendments can be made up until the date of decree absolute. In practice it will **9.05** rarely be necessary or appropriate to make amendments after decree nisi.

The standard procedure for amendment is set out in r 7.13, Family Procedure Rules 2010 **9.06** ('FPR 2010'). The solicitor should prepare an amended petition with the amendments clearly shown in red:

(a) Where no application has been made for the decree nisi under r 7.19(1) nor an answer filed a petition may be amended without the court's permission (r 7.13(1), FPR 2010).

    The amended petition should then be filed at court together with the appropriate number of copies for service (see Chapter 8, para 8.03). It will be served on the respondent (and co-respondent) in the normal way (r 7.13(3), FPR 2010).

(b) Once an application for the decree nisi or an answer has been filed, permission is required. A copy of the amended petition should first be sent to the respondent (and co-respondent if necessary) with a covering letter asking whether he would be prepared to consent to the proposed amendment. If he is prepared to consent in writing to the amendment an application to the district judge for permission should be made without notice to the other side (r 7.13(4)(a), FPR 2010). If either the respondent or the co-respondent is not prepared to consent to the amendment, an application for permission will have to be made on notice to the district judge. If the district judge grants permission the amended petition must be filed at the court office with a copy for re-service on the respondent (and co-respondent). The district judge will make any further directions that have become necessary as a result of permission being granted, for example where the respondent (or co-respondent) has given notice that he wishes to defend he will need time to amend his answer if he has already filed one or to file an answer to the amended petition if not, so the district judge will fix the time within which he must do this.

As already explained, where only a minor amendment to the petition is required (eg the date of birth of a child of the family has been wrongly stated), it is not likely to be necessary to go through the standard procedure for amendment. It will usually be acceptable if the amendment is detailed in the applicant's Form D80 affidavit. The district judge will almost certainly give permission for the petition to stand corrected as outlined in the affidavit without the need for re-service on the respondent or co-respondent. He will then proceed to consider the case as if the petition had originally been filed as corrected.

D   SUPPLEMENTAL PETITIONS

9.07   A supplemental petition is a separate document filed at some stage after the petition itself. It is not a new petition; it is part of the original petition and is used to make amendments to this where it is inappropriate to do so by means of a straightforward amendment in red of the original document.

9.08   A supplemental petition may be filed without permission of the court at any time before an application for the decree nisi or answer is filed, but thereafter only with the court's permission (r 7.13(1) and (2), FPR 2010).

E   FRESH PETITIONS

9.09   As we have seen at para 9.01 above, where alterations required to the original petition cannot be accomplished by means of amendment or supplemental petition, a fresh petition will be required. The most frequent use of a fresh petition is probably where the applicant wishes to rely on a new s 1(2) fact that has only arisen since the date of the original petition.

9.10   The procedure for filing a fresh petition depends on whether the original petition is still extant.

9.11   If the original petition has been withdrawn (either because it has been discontinued by the applicant before service (r 7.9, FPR 2010) or dismissed after service on the applicant's application or after adjudication, or otherwise disposed of by final order), a fresh petition can be filed in the normal way without the court's permission.

9.12   It is quite likely, however, that the applicant will not want to burn her boats by seeking to discontinue the first petition or to have it dismissed and will prefer to file a fresh petition whilst the original petition still stands. To do this she will require permission of the court (r 7.7(1), FPR 2010)). She will have to show good reason why two petitions should be on the go at the same time.

Example   Reference should be made to Example 2 given in para 9.03 above. The applicant in that example may wish to preserve the first adultery petition until after she has obtained decree nisi on the s 1(2)(d) petition just in case the respondent should decide to withdraw his consent to the decree before decree nisi. If the s 1(2)(d) decree is granted without difficulty, the first petition should be dismissed at the same time. However, should the respondent withdraw his consent, the applicant could resurrect the adultery petition and go on to attempt to prove adultery and obtain a decree on that basis.

F CHAPTER SUMMARY

1. Where the applicant wishes to rely on a s 1(2), MCA 1973 fact, which arose *before* the peti- **9.13**
   tion was filed at court, the original petition may be amended.
2. Where the applicant wishes to rely on a s 1(2), MCA 1973 fact, which arose *after* the petition was filed, a fresh divorce petition will be required.
3. Where minor amendments are required, for example to rectify the spelling of a name or a
   date, this may be done by giving the correct information in the affidavit in support of the
   petition.

10

DEFENDED DIVORCES

A GENERAL

10.01 Gone are the days of the sensational divorce proceedings reported in detail on the front page of the national papers and attended by everyone who was anyone. Nowadays it is rare to see a divorce contested to the bitter end.

10.02 Partly this is due to the shift in emphasis in family law from looking for a culprit when a marriage breaks down to enabling the parties to extricate themselves from their unfortunate situation with the minimum of distress. There is no doubt, however, that it is also due to financial considerations (the cost of a defended suit can be enormous) and to the attitudes of judges and district judges concerned with divorce cases who will encourage the parties time and again to look for alternative ways of resolving their differences.

10.03 This book aims to deal with the routine family practice. Therefore, while the procedure for an undefended divorce is described in great detail in Chapter 8, the procedure in relation to defended divorce suits will be described in outline only in this chapter.

B PUBLIC FUNDING FOR DEFENDED DIVORCES

For the respondent

10.04 The respondent who consults a solicitor wishing to defend a divorce petition will find that the first hurdle he must overcome is the cost of the whole affair.

If the respondent is not financially eligible for public funding his decision on cost is simple— **10.05**
can he afford to defend the case bearing in mind that he may not recover his costs, even if he
is successful in having the petition dismissed?

The fact that the respondent *is* financially eligible for public funding does not mean he can **10.06**
ignore the cost of the divorce:

(a) Despite the respondent's financial eligibility, public funding will only be granted to him
    to defend the case if he satisfies the Legal Services Commission (LSC) that there is a sub-
    stantial defence with sufficient prospects of success and there are substantial practical
    benefits to be gained by avoiding the decree.

(b) If he is granted public funding to defend, it will be limited to all steps up to and includ-
    ing disclosure of documents and thereafter obtaining counsel's opinion on the merits
    of the case continuing as a contested case. This means that he can only go so far on his
    initial certificate. If he wants to go on from disclosure of documents to a full contested
    hearing of the case, the papers will have to be sent to counsel for an opinion on
    the merits. Application will then have to be made to the LSC to have the limitation on
    the certificate removed. The LSC is only likely to agree to this if counsel's opinion is
    favourable.

(c) Even if he is granted public funding to cover the entire proceedings, a large part of the
    ultimate bill is likely to be met by the respondent himself out of his share of the family
    property because of the LSC's statutory charge (Chapter 2, para 2.87).

For the applicant

The applicant will not have had public funding when she filed her petition; at most, she will **10.07**
have received Legal Help (see Chapter 2). If the respondent files an answer and the applicant
wishes to proceed with the petition, she will have to consider the cost of a defended case just
as the respondent must.

As soon as an answer is filed, the case is looked upon as defended and public funding is, there- **10.08**
fore, theoretically available. However, if the applicant is to be granted public funding, she
must satisfy the LSC that it is reasonable for her to continue with the proceedings.

The statutory charge will also affect the applicant. Thus if she loses (ie, her petition is dis- **10.09**
missed) or if she obtains a decree but fails to recover her costs, she too may find herself footing
a large part of the public funding provided to her from her share in the family property.

Is it reasonable to defend/proceed with the case?

Whether the LSC will be prepared to accept that it is reasonable for the respondent or the **10.10**
applicant to defend the petition or to proceed with the petition after an answer has been filed
will depend on the particular facts of the case. Public funding will not, however, be granted/
continued if there is a suitable alternative way of proceeding with the case.

Example A petition is filed based on behaviour (s 1(2)(b), Matrimonial Causes Act 1973
('MCA 1973')). The applicant is not publicly funded. The respondent is publicly funded. He
obtains funding to file an answer denying the behaviour and cross-petition on the basis of

the applicant's adultery. The applicant denies the adultery. Although it is clear that both parties want a divorce, the case drags on with both parties maintaining their positions.

Eventually two years elapse, during which the parties have lived apart. It would therefore be possible for one or the other party to obtain a decree on the non-contentious basis of two years' separation and consent. Both parties are willing to present a petition based on s 1(2)(d) but neither party is willing to give consent to the other party obtaining the decree—each wants to obtain the decree *himself*. At this point, it is necessary for the respondent to seek counsel's opinion as disclosure of documents has taken place and he needs to have the limitation on his certificate lifted before he can go any further with the case. Counsel advises that the only reasonable course is for a decree to be obtained on the basis of s 1(2)(d). In all probability, therefore, the respondent's certificate will be terminated and he will be forced, by financial considerations, to agree to a divorce on the basis of s 1(2)(d).

C   OUTLINE OF PROCEDURE IN A DEFENDED CAUSE

10.11 (a) Notice of intention to defend: the respondent/co-respondent returns the acknowledgment of service giving notice of his intention to defend. The time for giving notice of intention to defend is seven days from service of the petition, inclusive of the day of service (r 7.12(1), Family Procedure Rules 2010 ('FPR 2010')).

     (b) Filing an answer—the normal procedure: a respondent/co-respondent who wishes to defend the petition or dispute any of the facts alleged in it, or a respondent who wishes to make in the proceedings any charge against the applicant in respect of which the respondent seeks a remedy, or to oppose the grant of a decree on the basis of s 5(1), MCA 1973 (grave financial or other hardship), must file an answer in Form D8B within 21 days after the expiration of the time limit for giving notice of intention to defend, that is, within 28 days after service of the petition inclusive of the day of service (r 7.12(8), FPR 2010). A fee of £230 is payable. Normal service rules apply (Part 6, FPR 2010).

Note:

     (i) an answer may be filed even though the party concerned has not given notice of his intention to defend (r 7.12(10), FPR 2010);

     (ii) no answer is necessary merely to contest the applicant's claim for costs (for the procedure for contesting costs, see Chapter 8, paras 8.78–90 and r 7.12(9), FPR 2010), or to contest the applicant's application for an order under Part I or Part II, Children Act 1989 or in relation to financial provision.

     (c) Filing an answer—after directions for the grant of the decree nisi are given: it is not unknown for the respondent/co-respondent to make up his mind that he wants to defend only after the court has certified that the applicant is entitled to a decree nisi. The case will have proceeded in the usual way (see Chapter 8) and the chances are that the district judge will therefore have granted his certificate that the applicant is entitled to a decree (see Chapter 8, para 8.81). The district judge's certificate is tantamount to decree nisi (*Day v Day* [1979] 2 All ER 187). To enable the respondent/co-respondent to defend, it will therefore be necessary for him to make an application to the court for an extension of time to file an answer (rr 7.13(4) and 7.14(1) and (2) FPR 2010).

It may be an uphill battle to persuade the district judge to make the necessary orders to permit the respondent/co-respondent to defend.

(d) Transfer to High Court: when the answer is filed, the district judge may order the case to be transferred to the High Court (s 39, Matrimonial and Family Proceedings Act 1984). Transfer to the High Court is no longer mandatory. The detailed provisions are found in r 7.24, FPR 2010.

(e) Subsequent procedure: once an answer is filed, the case becomes defended and the court is required to direct that the case be listed for a case management hearing (r 7.20(4), FPR 2010). The court must:

(i) decide the place of hearing (r 7.22(2)(a)). Hearings will normally take place in public (r 7.16(1)). An application may be made under Part 18, FPR 2010 for the hearing to be held in private, if one of the following conditions is met:

(aa) publicity would defeat the object of the hearing;

(bb) it involves matters relating to national security;

(cc) it involves confidential information (including information relating to personal financial matters) and publicity would damage that confidentiality;

(dd) a private hearing is necessary to protect the interests of any child or protected party;

(ee) it is a hearing of an application made without notice and it would be unjust to any respondent for there to be a public hearing; or

(ff) the court considers it to be necessary, in the interests of justice (r 7.16(3)).

(ii) set a timetable for the filing and service of evidence (r 7.22(2)(b)). The court may, for example, order either party to clarify any matter which is in dispute in the proceedings or to give additional information in relation to either the petition for divorce or the answer (r 7.15(1));

(iii) make orders for the disclosure and inspection of documents (r 7.22(2)(c)). Part 21, FPR 2010 gives detailed guidance on disclosure and inspection;

(iv) give directions as to the conduct of the final hearing and the attendance of witnesses.

At the final hearing the judge will examine the evidence given by both parties and any **10.12** witnesses and decide whether a decree of divorce should be granted. This give the impression that a defended divorce will be resolved one way or another speedily and clinically. The chances are, on the contrary, that the proceedings will be fraught with emotion and protracted over a long period of time.

There are now few reported cases dealing with a defended divorce. However, the case of **10.13** *Butterworth v Butterworth* [1997] 2 FLR 336 is an example in which the Court of Appeal (Butler-Sloss LJ) made it clear that a defended divorce should be heard by a circuit judge and not a recorder. She also made it clear that the respondent should be made fully aware of the allegations made against him: 'hopelessly general' allegations were unacceptable.

D   KEY DOCUMENTS

Family Procedure Rules 2010 (SI 2010/2955). **10.14**

11

PROTECTION OF RESPONDENTS IN SEPARATION CASES: SECTIONS 5 AND 10, MATRIMONIAL CAUSES ACT 1973

A INTRODUCTION

11.01 The Matrimonial Causes Act 1973 ('MCA 1973') provides two statutory protections for the respondent to a divorce petition.

11.02 First, s 5 enables a respondent to defend a divorce based on the fact of five years' separation. While rarely relied on now in practice, it may still be helpful in limited circumstances.

Secondly, s 10 contains a procedure to enable the court to scrutinize the financial position **11.03** of the respondent as it will be on dissolution of the marriage *before* the decree absolute is granted. The procedure applies where the petition is based on s 1(2)(d) or s 1(2)(e) and provides protection for the vulnerable respondent since the decree absolute will not usually be granted until satisfactory financial arrangements have been put in place for his or her benefit.

Solicitors often fail to recognize the tactical advantages in invoking s 10—it can exert consid- **11.04** erable pressure on an applicant anxious to remarry.

Applications under ss 5 and 10, MCA 1973 are normally made by wives. Therefore this **11.05** chapter departs from the practice adopted in much of the rest of the book and assumes that the wife is the respondent.

B   SECTION 5, MATRIMONIAL CAUSES ACT 1973—GRAVE FINANCIAL OR OTHER HARDSHIP

Provisions of s 5(1)

Where a divorce petition is based on five years' separation (s 1(2)(e), MCA 1973), the respond- **11.06** ent may oppose the granting of a decree on the ground that the dissolution of the marriage will result in grave financial or other hardship to her and that it would in all the circumstances be wrong to dissolve the marriage (s 5(1)).

Effect of s 5 defence

Where the only fact on which the applicant is entitled to rely is s 1(2)(e), the court will have **11.07** to dismiss the petition if it finds that the respondent's s 5 defence is made out (s 5(2)). There is no point, however, in the respondent raising a defence under s 5 where the applicant relies on and can establish alternative s 1(2) facts as well. The s 5 defence only operates in relation to s 1(2)(e); therefore the applicant would be able to go on to obtain a decree on the basis of one of the alternative facts despite the respondent's objection.

Hardship

Generally

Whether the respondent relies on financial hardship or some other form of hardship, she **11.08** must show:

(a) that it would be grave: divorce almost inevitably causes a certain amount of hardship— the hardship must be very serious; *and*

(b) that it would result from the dissolution of the marriage: if the respondent's hardship arises, in fact, from the breakdown of the marriage rather than from the divorce, she will not be able to establish a s 5 defence.

Section 5(3) specifically provides that hardship shall include the loss of the chance of acquiring any benefit which the respondent might acquire if the marriage were not dissolved (eg widow's pension benefits).

Financial hardship

11.09   In deciding whether the respondent will suffer grave financial hardship, the court is entitled to look not only at what the respondent will lose as a result of the divorce (eg a substantial widow's pension because of her change in status following decree absolute) but also at what she will gain (eg income support) (*Reiterbund* v *Reiterbund* [1974] 2 All ER 455, confirmed by Court of Appeal [1975] 1 All ER 280 and *Jackson* v *Jackson* [1993] 2 FLR 848).

11.10   Where the respondent sets up a prima facie case of hardship, the applicant will usually seek to put forward proposals to alleviate the hardship and the court will then decide whether the proposals are sufficient. If the applicant's best proposals are not sufficient to remove the hardship, the petition will be dismissed (see, eg, *Le Marchant* v *Le Marchant* [1977] 3 All ER 610).

11.11   Because of the availability of pension attachment and pension sharing orders (see Chapter 29) the defence is less likely to succeed on the financial hardship ground than was the case in the past. Further, the defence will not succeed where the respondent has substantial capital: *Archer* v *Archer* [1999] 1 FLR 327.

Other hardship

11.12   Most reported cases on 'other hardship' have concerned foreign wives who have claimed hardship on social and religious grounds (see, eg, *Banik* v *Banik* [1973] 3 All ER 45). Their efforts to defend on this basis have generally met with failure.

Wrong in all the circumstances to dissolve the marriage

11.13   It is possible for the court to grant a decree despite the fact that the respondent has established grave hardship. This is because the court will dismiss the petition only if it considers it would be wrong in all the circumstances to dissolve the marriage.

11.14   Section 5(2) provides that the circumstances the court must consider include the conduct of the parties to the marriage and the interests of those parties and of any children or other persons concerned. The court can also consider any other relevant circumstances, for example that the applicant intends to remarry, and can consider the broader aspect of the case, that is, whether a marriage which has hopelessly broken down long ago should be preserved or whether it is not right in the public interest to terminate it (see, eg, *Mathias* v *Mathias* [1972] 3 All ER 1 and *Brickell* v *Brickell* [1973] 3 All ER 508).

Procedure

11.15   If the respondent wishes to raise a s 5 defence, she must do so by filing an answer setting out her contentions (see Chapter 10).

11.16   She would be well advised to make a claim under s 10(2), MCA 1973 (a less radical provision) as an alternative (see paras 11.18 ff below).

Indeed a failure to file an application under s 10 could form the basis of an action for breach   **11.17**
of duty and negligence: *Griffiths* v *Dawson and Co* [1993] 2 FLR 315. Here, Ewbank J held,
amongst other things, that even if there had been no specific instructions to do so, it would
have been negligent for the solicitor for the respondent wife not to have filed an application
under s 10. The exception would be where the respondent understood the consequences of
not making the application and gave clear instructions not to do so.

C   SECTION 10, MATRIMONIAL CAUSES ACT 1973

Section 10(2): prevention of decree absolute pending consideration of respondent's financial position

When can s 10(2) be used?

Where the petition is based on two years' separation and consent or on five years' separation,   **11.18**
the respondent is entitled to apply to the court for consideration of her financial position after
the divorce (s 10(2)). The court will not consider the respondent's position under s 10 where
a finding has been made as to any other fact mentioned in s 1(2), MCA 1973 (ie, adultery,
behaviour, or desertion) as well as a finding under s 1(2)(d) or (e).

The time for consideration of the respondent's position is between decree nisi and decree   **11.19**
absolute—the court has no power, if the case is proved, to refuse to grant the decree nisi.

Section 10(3) and (4)

Section 10(3) provides that, where the respondent makes an application under s 10(2), the   **11.20**
court shall not make the decree absolute unless it is satisfied:

(a) that the petitioner should not be required to make any financial provision for the
respondent; *or*
(b) that the financial provision made by the petitioner for the respondent is reasonable and
fair or the best that can be made in the circumstances.

Section 10(4) relaxes the provisions of s 10(3) slightly by providing that the court can make
the decree absolute notwithstanding the requirements of s 10(3) if:

(a) it appears to the court that there are circumstances making it desirable that the decree
should be made absolute without delay; *and*
(b) the court has obtained a satisfactory undertaking from the petitioner that he will make
such financial provisions for the respondent as the court may approve.

Note that the terminology of 'petitioner' is retained here in line with the wording under
MCA 1973.

Circumstances to be considered

The court hearing a s 10(2) application must consider all the circumstances including the age,   **11.21**
health, conduct, earning capacity, financial resources, and financial obligations of each of the
parties and the financial position of the respondent as, having regard to the divorce, it is likely
to be after the death of the petitioner, should the petitioner die first (s 10(3)).

11.22 It is clear that the court is not restricted to looking only at the financial needs or obligations arising after the divorce, but can also refer to past obligations which have not been fulfilled.

Section 10(2)—a delaying tactic, not a defence

11.23 The respondent cannot prevent a divorce being granted by making an application under s 10(2). What she can do is substantially delay the granting of decree absolute, thus, assuming that the applicant is anxious to have the divorce made final as soon as possible (eg so that he can remarry), putting pressure on the applicant to make acceptable financial arrangements for her.

Example The husband, who wishes to remarry, files a petition based on five years' separation. He is a wealthy man. The wife has very little in her own right. The parties are unable to reach any agreement over property and finance. The wife makes an application under s 10(2) for consideration of her financial position after the divorce. Decree nisi is granted on the basis of five years' separation. The husband cannot obtain decree absolute until after the question of the wife's finances is resolved. Therefore, in view of his wish to remarry, he is put under pressure to come up with a sensible offer of a settlement.

In a sense, of course, in a s 1(2)(d) case (two years' separation and consent), s 10(2) merely reinforces the bargaining power which the respondent already has in that she can withhold her consent until financial matters are resolved to her satisfaction. In a s 1(2)(e) case, however, the respondent has no bargaining power and s 10(2) can be used to give her a valuable lever over the applicant.

Procedure

11.24 A s 10(2) application must be made by notice in Form B.

11.25 The considerations taken into account by the court are very similar to those listed in s 25, MCA 1973 for consideration on applications for financial provision. In practice, the respondent will usually make her s 10(2) application together with a comprehensive application for financial provision under ss 23, 24, 24B, 25B, and 25C, MCA 1973 and the two applications will normally be heard at the same time. It is convenient for one financial statement in Form E to be filed in support of both applications.

11.26 It would seem that the same approach should be adopted in respect of both applications (see, eg, *Krystman* v *Krystman* [1973] 3 All ER 247). Thus it is likely that the hearing of the applications will be virtually indistinguishable from a normal financial remedy hearing except that, as well as making orders for financial provision, the court will be asked to make an order under s 10(3) approving the financial provision so as to enable the applicant to go on to obtain decree absolute.

Rule 7.29 requires the court in these circumstances to make a written record of the reasons for deciding to grant the decree absolute.

Section 10(1): rescission of decree nisi under s 1(2)(d)

11.27 By virtue of s 10(1), where the court has granted a decree nisi of divorce on the basis only of two years' separation and consent, the court may rescind the decree on the respondent's application if it is satisfied that the applicant misled the respondent (whether intentionally

or unintentionally) about any matter which the respondent took into account in deciding to give his consent.

The respondent must apply before the decree is made absolute. The procedure is set out in **11.28** r 7.28, FPR 2010. The application will be made in Form D11, will follow the Part 18 procedure, and will be heard in open court.

Section 10A: divorce and dissolution of religious marriages

Background to the provisions

Section 10A was introduced into the MCA 1973 by the Divorce (Religious Marriages) Act 2002 **11.29** and came into force on 24 February 2003. The provisions are similar in function to those set out above at paras 11.18 ff but operate in the circumstances described below.

The aim of the provisions is to remedy a disadvantage suffered by Jewish men and women **11.30** who are prevented from remarrying because of the refusal of their former spouses to grant or accept a religious divorce, known as a 'get'.

In Jewish law, an individual cannot be married or divorced against his or her will. For a divorce **11.31** obtained under the MCA 1973 to be recognized as effective in Jewish law, a 'get' must also be obtained. This is a divorce under Jewish law where the mutual cooperation of the parties is required. To obtain a 'get', the husband has to go before a Beth Din court to obtain the divorce, deliver it to his wife, and she is obliged to accept it. In the absence of this procedure, the wife is not permitted to remarry in Jewish law although the husband may be able to do so. Hence, a Jewish woman who remarries under the civil law but in the absence of a 'get' will be stigmatized in the Jewish community, being considered an adulteress and any children born as a result of the second marriage will be regarded as illegitimate in Jewish law.

The provisions of s 10A, Matrimonial Causes Act 1973

The provisions enable the county court to make an order refusing to grant the decree absolute **11.32** of divorce until a declaration by both parties is produced to the court to the effect that they have taken such steps as are required to dissolve the marriage (in accordance with the usages of the Jews, or any other prescribed religious usages): s 10A(2), MCA 1973.

The order preventing the grant of the decree absolute will only be made if the court is satisfied **11.33** that, in all the circumstances of the case, it is just and reasonable to do so and the order may be revoked at any time: s 10A(3)(a) and (b), MCA 1973.

In effect, the wife may use these provisions to exert pressure on the husband to obtain a 'get' **11.34** thus enabling her to remarry free of stigma.

Incidentally, it should be noted that, while the Act is presently confined in its scope to the **11.35** Jewish community, it empowers the Secretary of State to extend the provisions by order to other faiths so it could provide relief in similar cases in the Islamic community.

The procedure

Unlike the position under the Family Proceedings Rules 1991, no specific means of making **11.36** the application for an order refusing the decree absolute is laid down in the FPR 2010. It is assumed therefore that the application is made in Form D11 following the procedure laid down in Part 18.

11.37   As for the timing of the application, it may be made by the respondent once the decree nisi has been granted (it cannot be made before that date) and before the decree absolute has been obtained by the applicant.

11.38   Rule 18.7(1) FPR 2010 requires that the application notice must state the order sought and, briefly, the grounds for the order. A draft of the order must be attached to the application notice (r 18.7(2) FPR 2010). The application notice should be accompanied by a copy of any written evidence in support, to be verified by a statement of truth, as prescribed by Part 17, FPR 2010.

11.39   A copy of the application notice and evidence in support must be served on the other party or parties to the proceedings. The recipient is entitled to at least seven days' notice of the hearing.

11.40   As for the later declaration (to lift the bar on the grant of the decree absolute) r 7.30(1) requires that it:

(a)   be made and signed by both parties to the marriage concerned;

(b)   gives particulars of the proceedings in which the order under s 10A(2) was made;

(c)   confirms that the steps required to dissolve the marriage in accordance with the religious usages appropriate to the parties have been taken;

(d)   unless the court directs otherwise, be accompanied by:

    (i)   a certificate from a relevant religious authority that all such steps have been taken; or

    (ii)   such other documents showing the relevant steps have been taken as the court may direct; and

    (iii)   be filed at the court either before or together with an application to make the decree nisi absolute.

11.41   Rule 7.32(2)(h) FPR 2010 provides that the court records must be checked to ensure that any order made in respect of a religious divorce has been complied with before the decree absolute of divorce is granted.

D   RESCISSION OF THE DECREE NISI IN OTHER CIRCUMSTANCES

11.42   In rare circumstances, application may be made to the court for rescission of the decree nisi of divorce under s 9(2), MCA 1973. An example of such a case is *S v S (Rescission of Decree Nisi: Pension Sharing Provision)* [2002] 1 FLR 457 which demonstrated that the parties may, *by consent*, seek the rescission of a decree nisi granted before 1 December 2000, and never having been made absolute, in order then to lodge a new petition which would include an application for a pension sharing order (see Chapter 29). Singer J held that rescission of the decree was not contrary to public policy nor was it an attempt to outwit the intention of Parliament: it was a practical attempt to arrange family affairs to best advantage.

E   PROTECTION FOR RESPONDENT CIVIL PARTNERS

11.43   Sections 47 and 48, Civil Partnership Act 2004 provide similar protection for civil partners to that found in ss 5 and 10, MCA 1973.

F   CHAPTER SUMMARY

1. Section 5(1), MCA 1973 provides a defence to a divorce based on the parties having lived   **11.44**
   apart for five years. The respondent must prove that the decree of divorce would result in
   the respondent suffering grave financial or other hardship and that it would be wrong to
   dissolve the marriage.
2. Section 10(2), MCA 1973 enables the respondent in divorce proceedings based on two
   or five years' separation to ask the court to consider his or her financial position after the
   divorce—the decree absolute is delayed until the court is satisfied as to these matters.

G   KEY DOCUMENTS

Matrimonial Causes Act 1973   **11.45**
Divorce (Religious Marriages) Act 2002
Family Procedure Rules 2010 (SI 2010/2955)

12

JUDICIAL SEPARATION

A WHAT IS A DECREE OF JUDICIAL SEPARATION?

12.01 In essence this decree relieves the parties to a marriage from the duty to cohabit and enables either or both of them to apply to the court for orders for financial provision (discussed fully in Chapter 29).

B   THE GROUNDS FOR JUDICIAL SEPARATION: S 17, MATRIMONIAL CAUSES ACT 1973

A petition for judicial separation may be presented to the court by either party to a marriage **12.02** on the ground that any of the facts mentioned in s 1(2), Matrimonial Causes Act 1973 ('MCA 1973') exists (see Chapter 4 for a full discussion of the law concerning the s 1(2) facts).

The provisions of s 2, MCA 1973 concerning the effect of cohabitation in relation to the s 1(2) **12.03** facts apply as they do in the case of divorce (see Chapter 5).

C   THE APPLICATION OF SS 6 AND 7, MATRIMONIAL CAUSES ACT 1973 TO JUDICIAL SEPARATION

By virtue of s 17(3), the provisions of s 6, MCA 1973 apply as they do with divorce.   **12.04**

Section 6(1) provides that rules of court shall be made requiring a solicitor *acting* for an **12.05** applicant to file a statement as to whether he has discussed the possibility of a reconciliation with the applicant. Rule 7.6, Family Procedure Rules 2010 provides that such a statement of reconciliation shall be filed in Form D6.

Section 6(2) enables the court to adjourn the proceedings at any stage for reconciliation **12.06** attempts if there appears to be a reasonable possibility of a reconciliation.

D   NO TIME RESTRICTION ON PETITION

Section 3, MCA 1973 (the one-year bar on divorce petitions) does not apply to judicial separation **12.07** petitions. There is therefore no restriction on when a petition for judicial separation can be presented—if one of the s 1(2) facts can be made out, a petition can be filed the day after the wedding.

E   SECTION 5, MATRIMONIAL CAUSES ACT 1973 NOT APPLICABLE

Section 5 (see Chapter 11) does not apply to petitions for judicial separation. It is therefore not **12.08** possible for the respondent to defend the proceedings on the basis that a decree would result in grave financial or other hardship to him. The best that he can do if he is worried about his financial position is to make an application for financial provision under ss 23, 24, 25B, and 25C, MCA 1973. It should be noted that pension sharing orders are not available in proceedings for a decree of judicial separation.

F   SECTION 10, MATRIMONIAL CAUSES ACT 1973 NOT APPLICABLE

12.09   Section 10 (see Chapter 11) does not apply either. The respondent cannot therefore seek to have the judicial separation decree granted on the ground of s 1(2)(d) (two years' separation and consent) rescinded on the basis that the applicant misled the respondent into giving his consent. Nor can the respondent in a case based on s 1(2)(d) or s 1(2)(e) (five years' separation) hold up the granting of a decree, as he can in divorce proceedings, by applying to have his financial position considered by the court.

G   THE PROCEDURE FOR SEEKING A DECREE OF JUDICIAL SEPARATION

12.10   The procedure for seeking a decree of judicial separation is virtually the same as the procedure for seeking a decree of divorce: see Chapter 8. The following points should be noted, however:

(a)   There is only *one* decree of judicial separation as opposed to the two decrees (decree nisi and decree absolute) in divorce proceedings. There is therefore no need to apply to have the decree of judicial separation made absolute.

(b)   Although the petition in a judicial separation case will look almost the same as a divorce petition, irretrievable breakdown of the marriage will not be alleged and the prayer will be for judicial separation instead of dissolution of the marriage. Other documents such as the applicant's Form D80 affidavit will also be amended accordingly.

(c)   Whereas, with divorce, decree nisi will not be made absolute until the district judge has considered the proposed arrangements for any relevant child of the family, in the case of judicial separation no decree will be granted at all until the district judge has considered the s 41 arrangements.

(d)   The funding position is the same as it is with divorce cases: see Chapter 2. Public funding is therefore only available in a limited class of judicial separation cases; the majority of cases will be dealt with under the Legal Help scheme.

H   THE EFFECT OF THE DECREE: S 18, MATRIMONIAL CAUSES ACT 1973

12.11   Where a decree of judicial separation is granted it does not terminate the marriage but it does have the following important consequences:

(a)   The applicant is no longer bound to cohabit with the respondent (s 18(1)). Of course, no one can force the applicant to cohabit with the respondent even when there is no decree of judicial separation, so at first sight s 18(1) seems to be stating the obvious. However, what it is designed to do is make it clear that neither the applicant nor the respondent can be in desertion after the decree is granted by virtue of the fact that she or he declines thereafter to live with the other party.

(b)   If either party dies intestate whilst the decree is in force and the separation is continuing, his or her property devolves as if the other party to the marriage were dead (s 18(2)).

Note, however, that in contrast with the position on divorce, wills are unaffected by a decree of judicial separation. If the client has made a will leaving property to her spouse, she should therefore be advised that he will benefit under the will despite the judicial separation. If she does not wish this to happen, a new will should be made.

(c) The court can make orders for financial provision under ss 23, 24, 25B, and 25C, MCA 1973. Note that, as with divorce, the court can also make orders for maintenance pending suit in respect of the period between the filing of the petition and pronouncement of the decree. See Chapter 29 for full details of the court's powers in relation to these matters.

(d) Orders under Parts I and II, Children Act 1989 can be made by the court, pursuant to s 41, MCA 1973 (see Chapters 17 and 18).

I SUBSEQUENT DIVORCE: S 4, MATRIMONIAL CAUSES ACT 1973

Judicial separation no bar to divorce

The parties are free to apply for divorce even after they have been granted a decree of judicial **12.12** separation (s 4(1)).

Procedure for seeking subsequent divorce

The most convenient way in which a subsequent divorce can be sought is for the divorce **12.13** petition to be filed by the spouse who applied for the decree of judicial separation on the basis of the same facts. The court may then treat the decree of judicial separation as sufficient proof of the fact by reference to which it was granted.

The applicant will have to establish irretrievable breakdown of the marriage which would **12.14** not, of course, have been established at the time of the judicial separation decree. In practice, however, irretrievable breakdown is normally presumed once a s 1(2) fact is proved so this should not present a problem (see Chapter 4).

The applicant must give evidence in support of her divorce petition in the normal way **12.15** (usually in her Form D80 affidavit in support of her petition) even where the petition follows an earlier judicial separation (s 4(2)).

One situation to watch out for is where the parties have resumed cohabitation since the date **12.16** of the judicial separation decree. Where this has happened, the provisions of s 2, MCA 1973 must be borne in mind. Note that it will not necessarily be only the period(s) of cohabitation that has/have taken place since the date of the decree that will be relevant. Reference must be made to the terms of the section in order to ascertain which period of cohabitation is relevant in relation to which s 1(2) fact.

In some cases it will not be possible or desirable for the divorce petition to be put on the same **12.17** basis as the judicial separation petition, for instance it may now be the other party who wishes to apply for the divorce. In such situations the right approach is to examine the facts in the normal way to see whether any of the s 1(2) facts can be made out independently of the judicial separation decree. The only bearing that the judicial separation decree has on this is that it prevents either party being in desertion after it has been granted.

Example In 2011 the wife obtains a decree of judicial separation on the basis of her husband's adultery. The reason why the husband had committed adultery was, in fact, that the marriage had broken down owing to the wife's thoroughly unpleasant behaviour. In 2012 the husband decides that he wishes to apply for a divorce. He cannot apply on the basis of his own adultery but he can file a petition based on his wife's behaviour (s 1(2)(b)).

J   REASONS FOR SEEKING JUDICIAL SEPARATION

12.18   Although judicial separations are fairly rare these days, from time to time a case will arise in which it is appropriate to seek a decree of judicial separation. Judicial separation does have the following advantages over divorce:

(a)   There is no restriction as to when the petition can be presented. Judicial separation may therefore be useful during the first year of marriage when divorce is not permitted. If the client really wishes to be divorced and is contemplating judicial separation as second-best, it will often be better for her to wait patiently until the first year of marriage is up rather than devote several months of that year to obtaining a decree of judicial separation only to spend more time the next year having it converted into a decree of divorce.

(b)   There are less likely to be religious objections on the part of either party to judicial separation than to divorce.

(c)   Some people find it less traumatic to accept the halfway house of a judicial separation than to sever their ties with their spouse completely by a divorce. Judicial separation enables them to have their cake and eat it—the fact that judicial separation does not enable them to remarry is of no consequence to them because they are in no state of mind to do so anyway and they *are* able to take advantage of the same wide powers of the court in relation to financial provision as they could after a divorce.

(d)   If the choice is between judicial separation and other methods of seeking financial relief during the marriage, for example an application under s 27, MCA 1973 (see Chapter 26), judicial separation has the advantage that the court's powers in relation to finances and property are more comprehensive. For example, the court can make orders for sale of the matrimonial home or transfer of specific assets from one party to the other after a judicial separation, whereas under s 27, MCA 1973 the court can only grant periodical payments and lump sum orders.

However, for most clients seeking financial relief during the marriage, judicial separation will not fit the bill either because they are unable to make out any of the s 1(2) facts and therefore cannot apply anyway, or because judicial separation seems too drastic a step.

Insoluble problems over property can be dealt with during the marriage by an application under s 17, Married Women's Property Act 1882 (see Chapter 28), although in practice such applications are to be avoided where possible.

K   CHAPTER SUMMARY

1. A decree of judicial separation may be granted by establishing one of the five facts in   **12.19**
   s 1(2), MCA 1973.
2. The decree relieves the parties from the duty to cohabit but does not terminate the
   marriage.
3. The court may make orders for financial provision (except pension sharing orders) in
   judicial separation proceedings.

13

COHABITANTS

A   INTRODUCTION

13.01   Cohabitation is widespread and is becoming ever more common. The 2001 Census recorded that there were over two million cohabiting couples in England and Wales, an increase of 67 per cent in just ten years. The number of such households where one or more children are present has doubled in the same period. The Government Actuary's Department predict that by 2031 there will be 3.8 million cohabiting couples.

13.02   In some respects the law relating to cohabitation has struggled to keep pace with such changing times. As a result, parts of the legal framework are complex and piecemeal.

13.03   Throughout this book we have tried to refer to the position of cohabitants when referring to that of parties to a marriage or registered civil partners. While attempting to avoid unnecessary repetition the purpose of this chapter is to summarize the principal legal consequences of cohabitation and to refer to the various chapters where a full explanation is provided.

This chapter concentrates on opposite-sex cohabitation but reference will be made to same-sex **13.04** cohabitants where appropriate.

Before going further, it may be useful to consider what the term 'cohabitation' means. **13.05**

There is no statutory definition, but a helpful and generally accepted interpretation was given **13.06** by HHJ Norris QC in *Churchill* v *Roach* [2003] All ER (D) 348, as follows:

> It seems to me to have elements of permanence, to involve a consideration of the frequency and
> intimacy of contact, to contain an element of mutual support, to require some consideration of
> the degree of voluntary restraint upon personal freedom which each party undertakes, and to
> involve an element of community of resources. None of these factors is of itself sufficient, but
> each may provide an indicator.

Same-sex cohabitation no doubt has the same characteristics. A definition of such a relation- **13.07** ship was offered by Baroness Hollis of Heigham during the passage of the Civil Partnership Bill through Parliament as 'two people of the same sex are to be regarded as living together as if they were civil partners if, but only if, they would be regarded as living together as husband and wife were they instead two people of the opposite sex': Hansard HL Grand Committee, col GC 490.

B PROTECTION FROM VIOLENCE

As will be seen in Chapters 36 and 37, cohabitants and former cohabitants may seek occupa- **13.08** tion orders or non-molestation orders in their favour under Part IV, Family Law Act 1996 ('FLA 1996'). The definition of 'cohabitant' in s 62, FLA 1996 has been extended to include same-sex cohabitants who are not registered civil partners. Further, the term 'associated person' now includes a former civil partner, a same-sex cohabitant, or former cohabitant, a relative of a civil partner, and a party to a civil partnership agreement.

It will be recalled that the duration of occupation orders is dependent upon the question of **13.09** whether the cohabitant is entitled to occupy the dwelling-house in the first place. By contrast, non-molestation orders are not subject to a strict limit unless the court directs otherwise.

C INHERITANCE

So far as an opposite-sex or same-sex cohabitant is concerned there is no entitlement in the **13.10** event of intestacy. It is essential therefore that the cohabitants consider whether to make appropriate provision for each other by making wills. These may need amendment on the breakdown of the relationship.

Insofar as they hold property as beneficial joint tenants, the doctrine of survivorship will **13.11** ensure that on the death of one, the other will obtain the property absolutely. Thus, on breakdown of the relationship, severance of the joint tenancy should be considered. Where property is vested in the sole name of the deceased, it may be that as a result of the application of the principles of the law of trusts (see Chapter 28), the survivor can establish an interest enforceable against the personal representatives.

13.12   Although a cohabitant has no entitlement on intestacy, he may nevertheless benefit from the estate if the deceased leaves no relatives within the statutory list (as contained in s 46(1), Administration of Estates Act 1925). In such circumstances, the deceased's estate will devolve to the Crown as *bona vacantia*. The Crown is empowered to provide out of the estate for 'dependants, whether kindred or not, of the intestate, and other persons for whom the intestate might reasonably have been expected to make provision'.

13.13   In the event of no will being made (and the deceased dying intestate), or a will being proved which does not make reasonable financial provision for the surviving cohabitant, the survivor may apply to the court for financial provision pursuant to the Inheritance (Provision for Family and Dependants) Act 1975 ('IA 1975'), as amended by the Law Reform (Succession) Act 1995 and the Civil Partnership Act 2004 ('CPA 2004'). In these circumstances the survivor of opposite or same-sex cohabitation may apply to the court for financial provision from the deceased's estate. The 'financial provision' contemplated here is 'such financial provision as it would be reasonable in all the circumstances of the case for the applicant *to receive for his maintenance*': s 1(2)(b), IA 1975 (emphasis added).

13.14   It should be noted that this is in contrast with the 'financial provision' contemplated for spouses or civil partners which is defined as 'such financial provision as it would be reasonable in all the circumstances of the case for a husband and wife (or a civil partner) to receive, whether or not that provision is required for his or her maintenance': s 1(2)(a) and (aa), IA 1975, as amended. In these cases, the court is to have regard to what the survivor would have been awarded in financial remedy proceedings.

13.15   Under previous statutory provisions, the surviving cohabitant had to satisfy the court that immediately before the death of the deceased he or she had been wholly or partly maintained by the deceased: under the 1995 Act there is no need to prove such a dependency. However, the claiming cohabitant has to show that during the whole period of two years prior to the death of the deceased he or she was living in the same household as the deceased as the husband or wife of the deceased. The death in question must have occurred on or after 1 January 1996: ss 1(1)(ba) and 1(1A).

13.16   Several recent cases have interpreted the requirement for cohabitation under s 1(1)(ba). In *Churchill* v *Roach* [2003], for example, the applicant was found not to have lived in the same household as the deceased for the required two years because the parties had lived in separate properties for all but the final year of their relationship. Their relative independence from each other led the judge to conclude that there were 'two separate domestic economies'.

13.17   However, the claim did not fail in its entirety since the applicant had been partly maintained by the deceased before his death and she could thus demonstrate the necessary dependency under s 1(1)(e), IA 1975.

13.18   Occasional periods of separation will not prevent the court from holding that the couple were 'living in the same household' provided that the separations are 'transitory' and there is evidence to suggest that, had the deceased lived, the relationship would have continued: *Gully* v *Dix* [2004] 1 WLR 1399.

What does it mean to 'live together as husband and wife'? This aspect of the requirements **13.19** of the Act was explored in *Re Watson (Deceased)* [1999] 1 FLR 878, Neuberger J recognizing 'the multifarious nature of marital relationships' so that the fact that the sexual relationship between the applicant and the deceased had ended some time ago did not mean that the application failed. It was sufficient that the parties regarded each other as important in their lives.

If the court is satisfied that the conditions under s 1 are established, it may make an order **13.20** under the terms of s 2 of the 1975 Act.

The powers of the court are wide and include the possibility of orders for periodical payments, **13.21** lump sums, transfers of property, settlements of property, and variation of settlements. Further, the court may require the acquisition of property for the benefit of the survivor using assets of the estate to fund the purchase.

When the court is deciding whether it should make an order for financial provision and, if so, **13.22** the terms of the order, it must consider:

(a) the age of the applicant and the length of the period during which the applicant lived as the husband or wife of the deceased and in the same household as the deceased; and

(b) the contribution made by the applicant to the welfare of the family of the deceased, including any contribution made by looking after the home or caring for the family: s 3(2A), IA 1975.

Where the applicant is unable to satisfy the requirements of s 1(1)(ba), IA 1975, he may still **13.23** have a claim under s 1(1)(e) of the Act for provision as a dependant of the deceased but the general view is that it is likely that he would be awarded less, the calculation being based on the values of his lost dependency.

In any event, it would seem from guidance given by Robert Walker J in *Graham* v *Graham* **13.24** [1997] 1 FLR 860 that the court will be concerned to meet the applicant's reasonable future needs (in this case, for modest accommodation) rather than to match the higher standard of living enjoyed by him during the period of cohabitation.

See also Chapter 25, which deals in more detail with aspects of wills and inheritance. **13.25**

D   STATUS OF CHILDREN

The law relating to children is dealt with in Chapters 17 to 21. However, it is important to **13.26** remember some of the distinctions which apply to a child born to married parents in comparison with one born to unmarried parents. Whereas parental responsibility is vested in both married parents, an unmarried mother has parental responsibility exclusively irrespective of the stability of her relationship with the unmarried father: s 2(2), Children Act 1989 ('CA 1989').

However, the unmarried father may acquire parental responsibility in one of a number of **13.27** ways:

(a) by marrying the mother;

(b) by entering into a parental responsibility agreement with the mother. This agreement must be in writing and in a prescribed form: s 4(1)(b) and (2), CA 1989;

(c) by obtaining a parental responsibility order. The application would normally be made to the family proceedings court but it may be made to the county court or High Court. The mother may deny that the applicant is the father of the child and the issue of paternity would then have to be dealt with as a preliminary matter. In determining the application the court must have regard to the child's welfare as its paramount consideration (s 1(1), CA 1989), it must have regard to the principle that delay in determining the issue is likely to prejudice the welfare of the child (s 1(2), CA 1989) and must not make an order unless it considers that doing so would be better for the child than making no order at all (s 1(5), CA 1989). Curiously the court is not obliged to have specific regard to the so-called 'welfare checklist' in s 1(3) but no doubt will consider these matters indirectly to seek to promote the child's welfare (see further Chapter 17).

(d) by being appointed as the guardian of the child by the court: s 5, CA 1989. The unmarried father may appoint a testamentary guardian provided he has parental responsibility for the child in question at the date of his death. However, the appointment will only be effective if the unmarried mother is already dead;

(e) by obtaining a residence order in his favour. Section 12(1), CA 1989 provides that in these circumstances the court shall also make a s 4 parental responsibility order in favour of the unmarried father unless he has already otherwise acquired parental responsibility;

(f) s 111, Adoption and Children Act 2002 came into force on 1 December 2003. Where a child is born to unmarried parents after this date, the father will automatically acquire parental responsibility when he is registered on the birth certificate as the father. The provision is not, however, retrospective in effect.

13.28   It should be noted also that the unmarried father is treated as a 'parent' for the purpose of applying for one or more of the s 8 orders, irrespective of whether or not he has parental responsibility for the child in question. The significance of this is that the unmarried father need not seek the court's permission to pursue his application.

E   FINANCIAL PROVISION AND THE SIGNIFICANCE OF THE CHILD SUPPORT ACT 1991

13.29   It should be noted that, subject to the provisions of the Child Support Act 1991 ('CSA 1991'), cohabitants have no obligation to provide financial support for each other and are unable to apply for periodical payments orders for their own benefit. Further, the cohabitant may not apply for a pension sharing or pension attachment order under s 24B, 25B, or 25C, Matrimonial Causes Act 1973 ('MCA 1973').

13.30   Section 15 and sch 1, CA 1989 provide a range of orders which may be sought against the parent of the child, for the benefit of the child of the unmarried family, by a parent or guardian of the child, or by any person in whose favour a residence order is in force with respect to the child.

13.31   Of particular relevance now is the availability of an order for a lump sum payment of up to £1,000 in the family proceedings court, and orders for lump sum payments of any amount and for settlement of property orders for the benefit of the child in the county court or High Court.

However, note that property adjustment orders will not ordinarily be made under s 15 and sch 1, CA 1989, to provide benefits for the child after he has attained independence, unless there are exceptional circumstances: *A* v *A (A Minor: Financial Provision)* [1994] 1 FLR 657.

The position so far as financial support for the child is concerned has been affected by the   **13.32**
CSA 1991. The Act created the Child Support Agency which quickly became mired in delay and complexity. Reforms were made in 1998 to simplify the formula used to calculate a parent's liability. The performance of the Agency, however, remained poor and following further reforms the Child Maintenance and Enforcement Commission (CMEC) was created by virtue of the Child Maintenance and Other Payments Act 2008.

Child Support Act 1991—the basic principles

As has been stated in previous chapters, the aim of the legislation is to establish a regime to   **13.33**
ensure that the non-resident parent (whether or not married) makes a significant contribution to the financial support of his or her natural child.

The Act empowers CMEC to trace non-resident parents, to investigate their means, and calcu-   **13.34**
late, collect, and enforce child maintenance payments. The Act is discussed in further detail in Chapter 35.

The position of the unmarried father

The unmarried father who is a non-resident parent has a statutory obligation to maintain his   **13.35**
natural child. This is irrespective of whether he has parental responsibility for the child or has had his parental responsibility for the child terminated by a court order: *R* v *Secretary of State for Social Security, ex p West* [1999] 1 FLR 1233.

The man in question may, of course, deny paternity, in which case the CSA 1991 provides   **13.36**
that a maintenance calculation may not be made against him unless the case falls into certain categories: s 26(1).

Where one of the categories applies, a maintenance calculation will be carried out despite a   **13.37**
denial of paternity: in other words, parentage will be assumed and liability to pay will arise.

Those categories include registration of the father on the birth certificate, where there has   **13.38**
been a previous parentage declaration under s 55A, Family Law Act 1986 or where the parent has already been adjudged to be the father in other relevant court proceedings.

Where parentage is disputed and none of the above categories applies, s 27(1) and (1A), CSA 1991   **13.39**
enables the Secretary of State or carer parent to apply to the family proceedings court, in the first instance, for a declaration of parentage. Such a declaration has effect only for the purposes of the CSA 1991.

The court may direct that scientific tests be undertaken to determine parentage, may draw   **13.40**
inferences from a refusal to undertake such tests, and may consent to the carrying out of the testing on behalf of the child where the carer parent objects: s 21(3), Family Law Reform Act 1969. The court must be satisfied that the tests are in the child's best interests.

F   OWNERSHIP AND OCCUPATION OF PROPERTY

Ownership

13.41   The position relating to ownership of property and opposite-sex or same-sex cohabitants is discussed in Chapter 22.

13.42   Briefly, it should be recalled that there are no provisions akin to those found in s 24, MCA 1973 to assist a cohabitant: he can only rely on the trust principles discussed in Chapter 28. The first step in advising a cohabitant on aspects of ownership is to check the title deeds to determine the extent to which ownership of legal and equitable interest in property is expressly dealt with there. In the absence of such express declaration the position is as follows. Where a cohabitant was engaged to be married, they may apply for a declaration of ownership under the terms of s 17, Married Women's Property Act 1882.

13.43   Furthermore, where there is evidence that they made a substantial contribution to the improvement of the property, they may seek a share or enlarged share of the property because of that contribution (s 37, Matrimonial Proceedings and Property Act 1970) provided that they were parties to an agreement to marry. Reliance on these provisions is permitted under s 2(1) and (2), Law Reform (Miscellaneous Provisions) Act 1970.

13.44   It should be noted that a combination of ss 66, 67, 68, and 74, CPA 2004 creates rights similar to those set out above for the benefit of either civil partners or parties to a civil partnership agreement.

13.45   However, where a cohabitant was neither engaged to be married nor a party to a civil partnership agreement he must apply to the court for a declaration of a resulting, implied, or constructive trust in his favour under s 53(2), Law of Property Act 1925 and a sale under s 14, Trusts of Land and Appointment of Trustees Act 1996. In other words the cohabitant must fall back entirely on the principles of land law. In the recent case of *Thomson* v *Humphrey* [2010] 2 FLR 107 it was held that a common intention that a man provide a home for the woman and children was not sufficient to establish the common intention that she should also have a share in the property. That approach is, however, to be contrasted with the recent and important Supreme Court judgment in *Jones* v *Kernott* [2011] UKSC 53 where the justices went to some lengths to encourage courts hearing such cases to make the necessary inferences from the behaviour of the parties to satisfy a finding that a shared intention did in fact exist.

Procedure

13.46   The procedure to pursue such an application is governed by the Civil Procedure Rules 1998 ('CPR 1998').

13.47   The application is commenced by issuing a claim under Part 8, CPR 1998 using the Part 8 claim form, N208. The Chancery Division of the High Court may be used or the county court for the area where the defendant lives or the property is situated.

13.48   Concise relevant details should be included on the claim form with a more detailed history set out in the supporting witness statement. The concise details should include, therefore, the declaration as to beneficial interest sought by the claimant (remembering that this may also relate to personal property and interests in endowment policies, etc), a declaration that Part 8,

CPR 1998 applies to the claim, and some details as to the legal basis of the claim (eg contribution or detrimental reliance, if a declaration of a constructive trust is sought).

As for the contents of the witness statement, these should be as comprehensive as possible **13.49** and separate headings are recommended in order to separate different aspects of the case and make it easier for the judge to locate relevant material.

It is suggested that the following matters should be dealt with in chronological order: **13.50**

(a) the background to the relationship;
(b) the history of the acquisition of the asset(s);
(c) the agreement or arrangement which the parties had as to ownership, including the reasons for a particular agreement and the words used in such discussions;
(d) the financial arrangements between the parties both at the time of acquisition and subsequently;
(e) the contribution made both in money and money's worth as well as contribution to improvements to the property, if any;
(f) details of acts of detriment and/or reliance on the conduct of the other party; and
(g) concluding paragraph restating the remedies sought.

Once the claim form and witness statement have been filed at the court, the court will issue and seal the claim form and fix a date for directions.

Copies of the claim form, witness statement, and notice of the directions hearing will be served **13.51** by the claimant's solicitor on the defendant who must file an acknowledgment of service in Form N210 within 14 days indicating whether he objects to the use of the Part 8 procedure, seeks a different remedy from that of the claimant, or wishes to take part at any hearing. The defendant must serve any written evidence on which he wishes to rely with his acknowledgment of service. At the first directions hearing the case will be allocated to the multi-track and directions given for the future conduct of the case (eg as to additional witness statements, valuations, etc) with provision for a further case management conference prior to a final hearing, if necessary.

Transfer of tenancies

By virtue of sch 7, FLA 1996, as amended by sch 9, para 13, CPA 2004, the court has power **13.52** to make an order effecting the transfer of the following tenancies between opposite-sex and same-sex cohabitants whether or not they are joint tenants at any time after they cease to live together. The tenancies to which the Act applies are:

(a) a protected or statutory tenancy within the meaning of the Rent Act 1977;
(b) a statutory tenancy within the meaning of the Rent (Agriculture) Act 1976;
(c) a secure tenancy within the meaning of s 79, Housing Act 1985;
(d) an assured tenancy or assured agricultural occupancy within the meaning of Part I, Housing Act 1988.

The court may make the order in circumstances where one cohabitant is entitled to occupy the dwelling-house by virtue of a relevant tenancy and the cohabitants cease to live together. The order may be made at any time *after* the relationship comes to an end (sch 7, para 3).

The order may be made in respect of a dwelling-house which is or was a home in which they **13.53** cohabited (sch 7, para 4).

13.54 The criteria to be applied by the court in determining the application are discussed in para 31.97. However, where only one cohabitant is a tenant, the court must have regard to the further matters set out in s 36(6)(e) to (h) of the Act.

Occupation

13.55 It is crucial to appreciate that a cohabitant does not enjoy home rights such as are provided for parties to a marriage or registered civil partners under the FLA 1996 with the provisions to register home rights so as to be effective against the claims of third parties.

13.56 The principal ways in which a cohabitant who is not solely and beneficially entitled to the property may remain in occupation are as follows:

(a) By obtaining an occupation order against the other party. It will be recalled that this is likely to be a temporary arrangement.

(b) By establishing a licence to occupy. It may be possible for the cohabitant to establish a contractual licence to occupy by pointing to the existence of all the elements necessary to create a valid contract the terms of which are sufficiently clear. Alternatively, the court may declare the existence of a licence to occupy through application of the principles of equitable estoppel. This will arise where:

  (i) one partner has spent money or otherwise acted to his or her detriment;

  (ii) there is a belief that he owned an interest in the property which justified the spending of money or that he would thereby obtain such an interest; and

  (iii) the other partner actively encouraged that belief or took no steps to disabuse their partner of that belief.

(c) A beneficial interest is established in the proceeds of sale which carries with it a right to occupy: *Bull v Bull* [1955] 1 QB 234.

(d) There is a transfer of the property to the cohabitant, to be held for the benefit of a minor child, under sch 1, CA 1989 (although note that property adjustment orders will not ordinarily be made under sch 1 to provide benefits for the child after he has attained independence, unless there are exceptional circumstances: *A v A (A Minor: Financial Provision)* [1994] 1 FLR 657).

G   COHABITATION CONTRACTS

13.57 The proposition that cohabitants have fewer rights and less protection than parties to a marriage or civil partners is generally accepted. However, where cohabitants enter into a valid cohabitation contract they are likely to have the reassurance that the terms will be implemented. Hence, it could be argued that they enjoy more control over their financial affairs than is available to married couples or civil partners who face the court's discretion in proceedings for a financial remedy. Indeed, even if matters are settled by a consent order, the terms are limited by the scope of the court's powers.

13.58 In what circumstances, therefore, will a cohabitation contract be valid and enforceable? This question was examined at length by Hart J in *Sutton v Mishcon de Reya and Gawor & Co* [2003] EWHC 3166.

In essence, the following principles must be observed to ensure that the contract will be **13.59** regarded as lawful and valid:

(a) the parties must demonstrate an intention to create legal relations;
(b) there should be no reference to the provision for payment for sexual services or relations (where there is no consideration as such, the terms should be incorporated in a deed);
(c) the terms of the contract should be clear and unambiguous with financial terms being separated from non-financial ones; and
(d) there must be nothing about the circumstances in which the contract was entered into which would lead to its being set aside (eg because of evidence of duress, undue influence, or misrepresentation) arguably making essential the need for each party to receive independent legal advice before signing the document.

H   COHABITATION—THE FUTURE?

In 2006 the Law Commission were invited to make recommendations about reforming the **13.60** law of cohabitation and the July 2007 report *Cohabitation: The Financial Consequences of Financial Breakdown* (Law Com No 307) was the careful and detailed result.

In the report the Law Commission set out the case for reform. They quote survey results **13.61** which confirmed that a substantial majority of people think cohabitants should have access to financial relief on relationship breakdown. They felt that merely trying to increase public awareness about the absence of such relief was not enough. At the same time, to provide all remedies available to married couples was probably to go too far.

What was proposed was a 'middle path' whereby some cohabitants should be able to obtain **13.62** financial relief in the event of separation. Typically, those cohabitants would have satisfied certain eligibility requirements such as having had a child together or being together for a certain number of years. A further proposed requirement was that the couple had not agreed to disapply the scheme. Finally, a cohabitant seeking a financial remedy would have to show a 'qualifying contribution' such as the presence of an economic disadvantage or the other partner retaining some form of economic benefit.

The Law Commission's hope was that the scheme would respond more comprehensively **13.63** than the current law to the economic impact of a separation upon such couples. Where children were present, it was felt that the scheme would enable a more effective remedy to be provided to the principal carer, thereby directly benefitting children.

Proposals similar to these were enacted in Scotland in 2006 and it was initially the govern- **13.64** ment's view that a period of monitoring the success of the Scottish reforms was necessary before a concluded view could be expressed on the Law Commission's final proposals.

However, a subsequent change in government and a new legislative programme has, at the **13.65** present time, rendered the chance of any meaningful reform to this area of law as slim.

14

CIVIL PARTNERSHIP ACT 2004

A INTRODUCTION

14.01 The Civil Partnership Act 2004 ('CPA 2004') was ground-breaking legislation which places same-sex partners who register their partnership in virtually the same legal position as different sex partners who enter into marriage.

14.02 For the family lawyer the principal areas of interest are those of formation, dissolution, and termination of a civil partnership. The Act's application to children and domestic violence is also important.

B FORMATION OF A CIVIL PARTNERSHIP

Eligibility

14.03 To be eligible to enter into a civil partnership the parties must be of the same sex, must not already be in a civil partnership or marriage, must be aged 16 or over, and not within the prohibited degrees of relationship. The prohibited degrees of relationship are set out in Part 1, sch 1 and mirror those that apply in the case of marriage.

Where a prospective civil partner is aged 16 or 17 the consent of an 'appropriate person' must **14.04** be obtained before the young person and the other person can register the civil partnership (s 4(1)). 'Appropriate person' is defined in Part 1, sch 2 and includes any parent of the child with parental responsibility, special guardians, and, where the young person is in care, the relevant local authority or prospective adopters. Where consent is refused by an appropriate person the young person may then seek the court's consent (sch 2, para. 4).

Registration

The Act contains three ways in which civil partnerships may be registered, namely the stand- **14.05** ard, modified, and special procedures.

Whichever procedure is followed, the prospective partners are regarded as having registered **14.06** their civil partnership once each of them has signed the 'civil partnership schedule' in the presence of a civil partnership registrar and in the presence of each other and two witnesses (s 2(1)). In the case of the standard and modified procedures, the place of registration should be open to the public.

Both partners must have resided in England and Wales for at least seven days immediately **14.07** before giving notice and must make a solemn declaration in writing that there is no impedi- ment of kindred or affinity or other lawful hindrance to the formation of the civil partnership (s 8(4)). Upon being given notice of the proposed civil partnership the 'registration author- ity' (a local council) publicizes the relevant information for a period of 15 days. Assuming no objections are made during this period, the registration authority then issues a Civil Partnership Schedule which must be signed within one year by the proposed civil partners and their witnesses. The signing of the Schedule creates and registers the civil partnership.

The modified procedure mirrors provisions in the Marriage Act 1983 enabling persons who **14.08** are housebound or detained to register their civil partnerships. The detailed requirements are set out in ss 18 and 19.

The special procedure recreates the procedure of the Marriage (Registrar General's Licence) **14.09** Act 1970 and enables a prospective civil partner to register the partnership when he or she is seriously ill and not expected to recover. The procedure is set out in ss 21 to 27.

In the case of all three procedures no form of words is prescribed for the registration itself and, **14.10** strictly speaking, the process is one that is purely paper-based. Local authorities are therefore free to offer their own choice of words or ceremonies.

By virtue of s 202, Equality Act 2010 places of worship will be allowed to conduct civil partner- **14.11** ships although they cannot be compelled to.

Registration by a former spouse, one of whom has changed sex

Where a certificate under the Gender Recognition Act 2004 ('GRA 2004') has been issued **14.12** to a spouse of a marriage which has been dissolved, the former spouses can apply under a fast-track procedure in sch 3 of the Act for the registration of a civil partnership. In this instance there is no 15-day waiting period although the Civil Partnership Schedule must be signed by each spouse and their witnesses within one month or it will otherwise be void.

C   TERMINATION OF CIVIL PARTNERSHIPS

Dissolution orders

14.13   CPA 2004 mirrors the provision of the Matrimonial Causes Act 1973 ('MCA 1973') in that a civil partnership may not be dissolved for a period of 12 months following its creation. After this period it must be shown that the civil partnership has broken down irretrievably and that one of four 'facts' listed in s 44(5) exists. The 'facts' are unreasonable behaviour, two years' separation with consent to a dissolution order, five years' separation without such consent, and desertion for a period of two years. The one difference is that while spouses may rely upon adultery to establish an irretrievable breakdown of their marriage, this option is not open to a civil partner. In this instance, such a person may seek to rely upon the adultery as 'behaviour' under s 44(5)(a).

14.14   As with divorce, dissolution orders are, in the first instance, conditional and are then made final after a period of six further weeks.

14.15   Similarly, the case law that has developed in relation to divorce will apply to civil partnership dissolution orders.

Nullity orders

14.16   Section 49 sets out the circumstances in which a civil partnership is void and these, in the main, relate to breaches of the various formal requirements, such as non-fulfilment of the eligibility criteria. In this instance the civil partnership will be void *ab initio* and treated as if it had never existed.

14.17   Section 50 lists the grounds on which a civil partnership is voidable. These bear some similarities to the equivalent grounds in marriage, including there having been no valid consent (by way of duress, mistake, or unsoundness of mind), where at the date of its formation the respondent was pregnant by some person other than the applicant (presumably only applicable in cases of gender change), and where an interim certificate has been issued under the GRA 2004. The CPA 2004 does not, however, render a partnership voidable on the basis of non-consummation or where one of the parties was suffering from venereal disease at the date of the civil partnership.

14.18   Nullity orders under s 50 must be sought within three years of the date of formation except where the ground relied upon is an interim certificate issued under the GRA 2004. In this instance an application for nullity must be made within six months of the certificate.

Separation orders

14.19   Separation orders equate to judicial separation between spouses (see Chapter 13).

D   FINANCIAL RELIEF UPON TERMINATION

Schedule 5, CPA 2004 is designed to mirror the provisions for spouses under the MCA 1973. **14.20** Civil partners are therefore provided with the full range of financial relief that can be utilized by spouses including property adjustment orders, periodical payments orders, interim maintenance, sale of property orders, and pension sharing orders.

In considering any such application the court must have regard to the criteria contained in **14.21** Part 5, sch 5 which are similar to ss 25 and 25A, MCA 1973. For obvious reasons, therefore, the case law that has developed in respect of applications for financial orders will apply to financial relief upon the termination of civil partnerships.

As with applications for financial orders, entry into a subsequent civil partnership or marriage **14.22** is a bar to any application for financial provision.

E   CHILDREN

The CPA 2004 amended s 4 of the Children Act 1989 ('CA 1989') to enable a civil partner to **14.23** obtain parental responsibility for a child in the same way that it is granted to a step-parent who marries a parent either by an order or by agreement.

A civil partner is also entitled to apply for contact, residence, prohibited steps, specific issue, **14.24** and special guardianship orders without obtaining the leave of the court whether or not a civil partnership is currently subsisting.

Schedule 1, CA 1989 is also extended to enable civil partners to apply for financial provision **14.25** for children.

F   CIVIL PARTNERSHIP HOMES AND DOMESTIC VIOLENCE

Schedule 9, CPA 2004 places civil partners in the same position as spouses as far as rights of **14.26** occupation of their shared home are concerned and in respect of remedies available to them under Part 4, Family Law Act 1996. 'Matrimonial home rights' are therefore now known as 'home rights'. Similarly, as far as applications for occupation orders are concerned, the status accorded to civil partners is the same as spouses and is therefore greater than the status of same-sex couples who have not registered a civil partnership.

15

NULLITY

A INTRODUCTION

15.01 In the eyes of the law some marriages suffer from impediments which lead to them being either void or voidable. In relation to marriages celebrated after 31 July 1971 the grounds on which a marriage is void or voidable are contained in ss 11 and 12, Matrimonial Causes Act 1973 ('MCA 1973'). The solicitor will rarely be called upon to deal with a marriage celebrated before this date.

B THE NEED FOR A NULLITY DECREE

Void marriages

A void marriage is void from the beginning and can, in theory, be treated by both parties as **15.02** never having taken place without the need for a decree of nullity. However, it is almost always advisable to seek a decree even where the marriage clearly appears to be void. One reason for this is that most clients will wish to take advantage of the court's powers under the MCA 1973 to grant financial provision. These powers are only exercisable if a decree of nullity is granted. Another reason is that possession of a nullity decree puts the status of both parties beyond doubt (which is particularly important where one party does not agree that the marriage is void), thus avoiding complications that could arise, for example, when one party seeks to remarry.

Voidable marriages

Because a voidable marriage is valid unless and until a decree of nullity has been granted, a **15.03** decree is essential.

C VOID MARRIAGES: S 11

A marriage shall be void on the following grounds only: **15.04**

(a) That it is not a valid marriage under the provisions of the Marriage Acts 1949, 1983, and 1994, that is, where:
  (i) the parties are within the prohibited degrees of relationship (which can be relationship by blood or by marriage), for example where they are father and daughter, brother and sister, son and step-mother; *or*
  (ii) either party is under the age of 16; *or*
  (iii) the parties have intermarried in disregard of certain requirements as to the formation of marriage, for example where they marry according to the rites of the Church of England in a place which is not a church or other building in which banns may be published or without observing the requirements as to banns, licences, etc, both being aware of the irregularity at the time of the marriage. (Note that the Marriage Act 1994 permits civil ceremonies of marriage to take place on premises approved by local authorities, thus considerably increasing the number of venues available for marriage ceremonies.)
(b) That at the time of the marriage either of the parties was already lawfully married or a civil partner (amended by Civil Partnership Act 2004 ('CPA 2004'). The onus of proof, on the balance of probabilities, lies on the party asserting that the marriage is void: *Wicken v Wicken* [1999] 1 FLR 293. Here the husband's claim that the marriage was void because the wife was already lawfully married failed because documentary evidence of a divorce had been produced and the parties had gone through a marriage ceremony. Further, both had asserted that the wife was free to marry. The parties had cohabited for a number of years during which they had held themselves out as validly married.
(c) That the parties are not respectively male and female. In *Bellinger v Bellinger (Validity of Marriage: Transsexual)* [2003] 1 FLR 1043, the House of Lords followed the decision in *Corbett v Corbett* [1970] 1 All ER 33 and dismissed the appeal of a male-to-female transsexual

(Mrs Bellinger) against the refusal of the Court of Appeal to declare her marriage to a man to be valid and subsisting. The marriage was void on the grounds laid down in s 11(c), MCA 1973 because the parties were not 'respectively male and female'. The court did not accept that, as a result of gender-reassignment treatment, Mrs Bellinger was 'female' at the time the marriage was celebrated.

The provisions of the subsequent Gender Recognition Act 2004 ('GRA 2004') are fully explained in Chapter 16.

(d) In the case of polygamous marriage entered into outside England and Wales, that either party was at the time of the marriage domiciled in England and Wales.

D   VOIDABLE MARRIAGES: S 12

15.05 A marriage shall be voidable on the following grounds only:

(a) that it has not been consummated owing to the incapacity of either party to consummate it;

(b) that it has not been consummated owing to the wilful refusal of the respondent to consummate it;

(c) that either party to the marriage did not validly consent to it whether in consequence of duress, mistake, unsoundness of mind, or otherwise;

(d) that at the time of the marriage either party, though capable of giving a valid consent, was suffering (whether continuously or intermittently) from mental disorder within the meaning of the Mental Health Act 1983 of such a kind or to such an extent as to be unfitted for marriage;

(e) that at the time of the marriage the respondent was suffering from venereal disease in a communicable form;

(f) that at the time of the marriage the respondent was pregnant by someone other than the petitioner;

(g) that an interim gender recognition certificate under the GRA 2004 has, after the marriage, been issued to either party to the marriage;

(h) that the respondent is a person whose gender at the time of the marriage had become the acquired gender under the GRA 2004.

Grounds (g) and (h) were inserted into s 12, MCA 1973 by the GRA 2004 and their significance is explained in Chapter 16.

E   BARS TO RELIEF WHERE THE MARRIAGE IS VOIDABLE: S 13, MATRIMONIAL CAUSES ACT 1973

Absolute bar applicable to all voidable marriages

15.06 The court shall not grant a nullity decree on the grounds that the marriage is voidable if the respondent satisfies the court:

(a) that the petitioner, knowing that she could have the marriage annulled, so conducted herself in relation to the respondent as to lead the respondent reasonably to believe that she would not seek to do so; *and*

(b) that it would be unjust to the respondent to grant the decree (s 13(1)).

Bars applicable only to certain voidable marriages

Limitation period

There is a 'limitation period' for the institution of proceedings for a decree on the grounds set **15.07** out in s 12(c), (d), (e), (f), and (h) (see para 15.05 above), that is, lack of consent, mental disorder, venereal disease, pregnancy by someone else, and where, at the time of the marriage, the respondent is a person whose gender had become the acquired gender under GRA 2004. The court shall not grant a decree on any of these grounds unless it is satisfied that proceedings were instituted within three years from the date of the marriage (s 13(2)). However, there is an exception to this rule: by virtue of s 13(4), a judge may grant permission to institute proceedings on any of these grounds after the three-year period if:

(a) he is satisfied that the petitioner has at some time during the three-year period suffered from a mental disorder within the meaning of the Mental Health Act 1983; *and*
(b) he considers that in all the circumstances of the case it would be just to grant permission for the institution of proceedings.

An application for permission can be made even if the three-year period has already expired (s 13(5)).

Where the proceedings are based on s 12(g) the decree will be refused unless the petition is **15.08** filed within six months from the date on which the interim gender recognition certificate was granted: s 13(2A).

Knowledge of petitioner

The court shall not grant a decree on the grounds set out in s 12(e), (f), or (h) (venereal disease, **15.09** pregnancy, and acquisition of acquired gender) unless it is satisfied that at the time of the marriage the applicant was ignorant of the fact alleged (s 13(3)). This is an absolute bar.

F   PROCEDURE FOR A DECREE OF NULLITY

As with divorce proceedings (see Chapter 8), the procedure to obtain a decree of nullity in **15.10** respect of a void or voidable marriage is now governed by Part 7, Family Procedure Rules 2010 ('FPR 2010').

In brief, the proceedings are commenced by filing at court Form D8N (the petition for a decree of nullity). Supporting notes for guidance on completing the petition are found in Form D8N.

The case proceeds by the applicant filing an affidavit in support of the petition (Form D80F in the case of a void marriage and Form D80G in the case of a voidable marriage).

The terminology of the Rules refers to an application for a 'matrimonial order' which includes proceedings for a nullity order (or a decree of nullity).

In consequence, unopposed applications for a decree of nullity will be treated in the same way as unopposed applications for a decree of divorce and wherever possible will be dealt with without a hearing (r 7.19, FPR 2010).

The following points should be noted:
(a) PD7B, FPR 2010 sets out detailed provisions relating to medical examinations in nullity proceedings (relevant where the petition is based on s 12(a) or 12(b), MCA 1973);

(b) PD7C, FPR 2010 sets out additional requirements to be fulfilled where either party to the marriage is, or has during the course of the marriage, been married to more than one person;

(c) PD7D, FPR 2010 deals with the provision of gender recognition certificates under the GRA 2004 (see Chapter 16) and explains how parties to proceedings for a decree of divorce or nullity or judicial separation should be described in any court list or court document (to reflect the changes brought about by GRA 2004). In particular, titles (eg Mr, Mrs, Miss) should be omitted and the parties should be described by the initials and surname of their current names only.

(d) Public funding is available for nullity proceedings. Since nullity proceedings no longer involve a hearing, public funding is available as for divorce (see Chapter 2).

(e) There are two decrees, decree nisi and decree absolute, as there are with divorce.

(f) Section 41, MCA 1973 (arrangements for children of the family) applies as it does in divorce cases (see Chapter 8, paras 8.102 ff).

G   EFFECT OF A DECREE OF NULLITY

On status

Voidable marriages

15.11   A decree of nullity granted in respect of a voidable marriage operates to annul the marriage only from after the date of decree absolute. The marriage is treated as if it had existed up to that time (s 16, MCA 1973 and see *Ward* v *Secretary of State for Social Services* [1990] 1 FLR 119). Because the marriage existed until the decree, children of the union are automatically legitimate. Remarriage can take place after the decree absolute. Provision in a will by one spouse for the other will lapse (Wills Act 1837, s 18A, added by the Administration of Justice Act 1982, s 18(2)). Neither spouse will be able to claim on the other's intestacy.

Void marriages

15.12   A void marriage is a nullity from the very start and the nullity decree simply declares this fact. Children of a void marriage are treated as legitimate by virtue of s 1, Legitimacy Act 1976 if, at the time of conception or insemination (or the celebration of the marriage if this is later) both or either of the parents *reasonably* believed the marriage was valid and the father was domiciled in England and Wales at the time of the birth or, if he died before the birth, was so domiciled immediately before his death.

Other effects

15.13   The full range of orders for financial provision under the MCA 1973 in relation to children, property, capital, and pensions are available in connection with proceedings for nullity just as they are with a divorce.

H   NULLITY PROCEEDINGS AND CIVIL PARTNERSHIP

A nullity order is available for civil partnerships under ss 49 and 50, CPA 2004. The position   **15.14**
is explained fully in Chapter 14.

I   CHAPTER SUMMARY

1. A decree of nullity is available where a marriage is void or voidable.   **15.15**
2. A void marriage is one that never existed despite the parties going through a ceremony of marriage. The grounds on which a marriage is void are set out in s 11, MCA 1973.
3. A voidable marriage exists until steps are taken to set it aside. The grounds to do so are set out in s 12, MCA 1973.
4. In certain circumstances, parties to a voidable marriage may be barred from obtaining a decree of nullity. The bars are set out in s 13, MCA 1973.
5. The court may make orders for financial provision where a decree of nullity has been granted.

16

GENDER RECOGNITION ACT 2004

A INTRODUCTION

16.01 The Gender Recognition Act 2004 ('GRA 2004') came fully into force on 4 April 2005 and provides for gender recognition certificates to be issued to enable transsexual people to be recognized, for legal purposes, in their acquired gender. This brought the law of England and Wales into line with the European Convention on Human Rights.

The recognition process

16.02 In order for a transsexual to obtain legal recognition of their acquired gender, an application for a full gender recognition certificate has to be made to a Gender Recognition Panel.

16.03 The Panel determines applications in private; no hearing takes place unless the Panel considers it to be necessary. Reasons for the decision must be communicated to the applicant.

Grounds for the application

Section 2(1) provides that a full gender recognition certificate must be granted if the Gender **16.04** Recognition Panel is satisfied that the applicant (who must be aged at least 18 years: s 1(1)(a)):

(a) has or has had gender dysphoria;
(b) has lived in the acquired gender throughout the period of two years ending with the date on which the application is made;
(c) intends to continue to live in the acquired gender until death;
(d) complies with the evidential requirements imposed by s 3.

The meaning of gender dysphoria

Gender dysphoria is a complex condition. People who have it believe that they were some- **16.05** how born into the wrong body and often prefer to live as a member of the opposite sex.

The Act provides that the term 'gender dysphoria' means the disorder 'variously referred to as **16.06** gender dysphoria, gender identity disorder and transsexualism' (s 25).

It is important to recognize, however, that there is no requirement for the applicant to have **16.07** undergone gender reassignment surgery in order to succeed in the application. Applications are often made by those who have undergone hormone therapy.

The evidence requirements

Section 3 deals with the evidence requirements in support of the application. **16.08**

The application must be supported by: **16.09**

(a) a report by a registered medical practitioner or registered psychologist practising in the field of gender dysphoria together with a report by another registered medical practitioner (who need not be such a specialist). The report must include details of the diagnosis of the applicant's gender dysphoria from the specialist practitioner (s 3(2)) and details of the treatment undergone, prescribed, or planned (s 3(3));
(b) a statutory declaration by the applicant that he or she satisfies the requirements of s 2(1)(b) and (c) (see para 16.04);
(c) a statutory declaration as to whether or not the applicant is married (see paras 16.11 ff);
(d) any further information or evidence that the Secretary of State or Panel may require or that the applicant may wish to submit.

The medical practitioner practising in the field who supplies the report should include details **16.10** of the process followed and evidence considered over a period of time to make the diagnosis in the applicant's case. It is not enough to merely use the broad phrase 'gender reassignment surgery' without indicating what surgery has been carried out. Reference should be made to each individual procedure. All other relevant treatments should also be included, such as hormone therapy. This information will assist the Panel with evaluating whether the requirements of s 2 are met.

The issue of the certificate

16.11   Unless the applicant is married or a civil partner, the Panel must issue a full gender recognition certificate: s 4(2). Where the applicant is already validly married or a civil partner, a successful application will lead to the grant of an interim recognition certificate which is of limited effect.

The interim gender recognition certificate

16.12   As discussed in Chapter 15, the issue of an interim gender recognition certificate provides a ground for nullity proceedings to be instituted under s 12, Matrimonial Causes Act 1973 ('MCA 1973'). The proceedings must, however, be commenced within six months of the issue of the interim gender recognition certificate: s 13(2A), MCA 1973.

16.13   Once the decree of nullity is made absolute, the court granting the decree must issue a full gender recognition certificate and send a copy to the Secretary of State (s 5(1), GRA 2004).

16.14   Where the applicant's marriage is subsequently terminated by divorce or nullity proceedings (on a ground other than the issue of an interim gender recognition certificate) within six months of the date of the issue of the interim certificate, the interim certificate may be converted to a full gender recognition certificate by application to the Panel: s 5(2), GRA 2004. Such application must be made within six months of the termination of the marriage: s 5(3), GRA 2004.

16.15   Where the marriage is terminated by death within a period of six months from the date of issue of the interim certificate, the interim certificate may be similarly converted to a full certificate by application to the Panel within six months of the date of the death: s 5(2) and (3), GRA 2004.

16.16   It follows that a full gender recognition certificate will not be granted until any existing marriage or civil partnership to which the applicant is a party is terminated or annulled.

The Gender Recognition Register

16.17   Schedule 3, GRA 2004 requires the Registrar General to maintain a Gender Recognition Register ('GRR'). Once a full gender recognition certificate has been granted, the Secretary of State must send a copy to the Registrar General: s 10(1), GRA 2004. On receipt, the Registrar is required to make an entry in the GRR, mark the birth register entry, and make a traceable connection between the entries. It is then possible to obtain certified copies of the entries in the GRR and short certificates of birth compiled from it. Neither must disclose that the entry or compilation is from the GRR: sch 3, para 3, GRA 2004.

16.18   The GRR is not available for public inspection and the applicant's confidentiality is protected throughout the application and registration process by provisions set out in detail in s 22, GRA 2004.

Rejection of the application and appeal

Section 8, GRA 2004 deals with the position when the application is rejected. First, the applicant may appeal to the High Court on a point of law against the Panel's decision. The appeal must be heard in private if the applicant so requests. The High Court may allow the appeal and issue the certificate, allow the appeal and refer the matter back to the Panel or another Panel for reconsideration, or dismiss the appeal. **16.19**

Where rejected, the applicant may not make a further application until a period of six months has elapsed from the date on which the application was rejected. **16.20**

Referral to the High Court

Where a certificate is granted but the Secretary of State considers that the decision to grant the certificate was secured by fraud, he may refer the case to the High Court which must quash or confirm the decision: s 8(6). **16.21**

The consequences of the issue of a full gender recognition certificate

Section 9(1) provides that, once a full gender recognition certificate has been granted, 'the person's gender becomes for all purposes the acquired gender'. **16.22**

The subsection goes on to state 'if the acquired gender is the male gender, the person's sex becomes that of a man and, if it is the female gender, the person's sex becomes that of a woman'. **16.23**

Crucially, this means that where a full gender recognition certificate has been issued, the recipient whose acquired gender is now that of a man, will be treated as a 'male' for the purposes of s 11(c), MCA 1973 and will be able to contract a valid marriage with a woman, thus dealing with the longstanding difficulty highlighted by the case of *Corbett v Corbett* [1970] 2 WLR 1306, discussed in Chapter 15. **16.24**

As with most other legislation, however, the provisions are not retrospective in effect and will not, for example, validate a marriage between a same-sex couple. **16.25**

Two further points need to be mentioned here. First, the Marriage Act 1949 is amended to incorporate a conscientious objection clause. Section 5B states that 'a clergyman is not obliged to solemnize the marriage of a person if the clergyman reasonably believes that the person's gender has become the acquired gender under the Gender Recognition Act 2004'. **16.26**

Secondly, as explained in Chapter 15, the grounds on which a marriage may be voidable have been further extended by adding para (h) to s 12, MCA 1973. This makes a marriage voidable if, at the time of the marriage, the respondent is a person whose gender had become the acquired gender under the GRA 2004. **16.27**

While outside the scope of this book, it should be noted that the GRA 2004 makes consequential amendments in areas such as welfare benefits and pensions (sch 5) and sex discrimination (sch 6). **16.28**

What the acquired gender does not affect

16.29   There are certain areas of law and activity which remain unaffected by the fact that an individual has an acquired gender. These include, for example, succession rights and the responsibilities of a personal representative (ss 15, 16, and 17, GRA 2004), certain sports activities (s 19, GRA 2004), and gender-specific offences involving sexual activity (s 20, GRA 2004).

16.30   Critically, however, for family lawyers, s 12, GRA 2004 provides that the acquired gender does not affect the status of the person as the father or mother of a child.

> **Example**   Helen is unmarried at the time when she gives birth to her daughter, Octavia. She has parental responsibility for Octavia by virtue of s 2(2)(a), Children Act 1989 ('CA 1989').
>
> Helen is then granted a full gender recognition certificate and is to be treated as a man (s 9(1), GRA 2004), becoming known as Paul. However, because Paul was a woman when Octavia was born, parental responsibility for the child is not lost on the issue of the full gender recognition certificate.
>
> Paul then forms a relationship with Stacey but does not marry her. Paul and Stacey together receive treatment at a clinic licensed by the Human Fertilisation and Embryology Authority. Stacey is inseminated by donor sperm and subsequently gives birth to a child, William.
>
> Stacey is William's mother (s 27(1), Human Fertilisation and Embryology Act 1990 ('HFEA 1990')) and Paul is treated, by virtue of s 28(3), HFEA 1990, as the child's father. Because the parties are unmarried, Paul will not automatically have parental responsibility for William (s 2(2)(b), CA 1989) and will have to acquire it by one of the ways prescribed in s 4, CA 1989.

Gender recognition and civil partners

16.31   Where an individual seeking a gender recognition certificate is a registered civil partner, the Panel may grant an interim gender recognition certificate (assuming that the grounds for the certificate are made out) only until the civil partnership is annulled or dissolved: s 4(3), GRA 2004.

16.32   Provisions similar to those set out in paras 16.11 ff and found in s 5A, GRA 2004 would then apply in order for the applicant to obtain a full gender recognition certificate.

16.33   Termination of a civil partnership is discussed in Chapter 14.

Guidance for clients

16.34   A Gender Recognition Helpline has been established and may be contacted on 01473 252749.

B   KEY DOCUMENTS

16.35   Gender Recognition Act 2004

President's Guidance No 1 of December 2005—evidential requirements for medical practitioners

C   USEFUL WEBSITES

Gender dysphoria: information on NHS website <http://www.nhs.uk>   **16.36**
Gender Recognition Panel: site includes forms, procedure, and medical information <http://www.grp.gov.uk>

PART III
CHILDREN

17

THE CHILDREN ACT 1989: GENERAL PRINCIPLES, PARENTAL RESPONSIBILITY ORDERS IN FAMILY PROCEEDINGS, SECTION 8 ORDERS, GUARDIANSHIP ORDERS, AND FINANCIAL PROVISION AND PROPERTY ADJUSTMENT FOR CHILDREN

A   INTRODUCTION

The Children Act 1989: an overview

The Children Act 1989 ('CA 1989') came into force on 14 October 1991.   **17.01**

The public law (eg care orders, supervision orders, emergency protection orders) and the   **17.02**
private law (eg residence orders, contact orders, prohibited steps orders, specific issue orders)
relating to children are contained in the same statute. The Act provides a clear and consistent
code for the whole of child law. It also aims to protect families from unwarranted state interference and to promote the basic principle that parents and local authorities should be free to
work together in 'voluntary partnership' for the benefit of the children concerned.

B   GENERAL PRINCIPLES

There are certain general principles contained in the CA 1989 which apply both to private law   **17.03**
and public law proceedings alike. Those principles will be set out in this chapter.

The paramountcy of welfare

Section 1(1), CA 1989 states that: **17.04**

when a court determines any question with respect to:

(a) the upbringing of a child; or
(b) the administration of a child's property or the application of any income arising from it,

the child's welfare shall be the court's paramount consideration.

17.05 The welfare principle will not apply to the determination of other questions which are out-side the ambit of s 1(1) even though they indirectly affect the child, for example whether the court should make an occupation order under Part IV, Family Law Act 1996 ('FLA 1996')—see *Richards v Richards* [1984] AC 174; *Gibson v Austin* [1992] 2 FLR 437; *G v J (Ouster Order)* [1993] 1 FLR 1008—or whether blood tests should be taken in an attempt to ascertain paternity—*S v McC* [1972] AC 24. Maintenance is excluded from the definition of 'upbringing' in the Act (see s 105(1)) and orders relating to maintenance after divorce are not subject to the welfare test in s 1(1) but to the requirement in s 25(1), Matrimonial Causes Act 1973 ('MCA 1973') to give 'first consideration' to the welfare of the child.

17.06 *'Child'* is defined as anyone under the age of 18 (s 105, CA 1989), but the court's power to make s 8 orders is restricted to children under 16 unless the case is exceptional (s 9(7), CA 1989). Likewise, the court may not make a care or supervision order in respect of a child who has reached the age of 17 (or 16 if the child is married): s 31(3), CA 1989.

17.07 *'Paramount'* means that 'the welfare of the child should come before and above any other consideration in deciding whether to make an order': Hansard HL, vol 502, col 1167. There is no provision which indicates how the court should approach cases involving more than one child where the welfare of each conflicts. However, in *Birmingham City Council v H (No 3)* [1994] 1 FLR 224 the House of Lords considered a case in which the child who was the subject of care proceedings was a baby but the mother was herself under the age of 18. They held that the question which had to be determined was as to the upbringing of the child in care and it was the welfare of that child which must be the court's paramount consideration. The fact that the parent is also a child does not mean that both the parent's and the child's welfare are paramount and that each has to be balanced against the other, since no question was to be determined as to the parent's upbringing.

17.08 *'Welfare'* is not defined by the CA 1989. However, the checklist set out in s 1(3) indicates some of the issues which might be relevant.

17.09 Note that the Human Rights Act 1998 ('HRA 1998') came into force on 2 October 2000 and it brings with it some tension between the paramountcy of welfare principle in s 1(1), CA 1989 and the way the interests of children are balanced with the interests of others in the family, under the principles set out in the European Convention for the Protection of Human Rights and Fundamental Freedoms ('ECHR').

17.10 There is potential tension between the way in which the interests of the child concerned in private law or public law proceedings are treated under domestic law when compared with the way they are treated under the ECHR. Article 8 makes it clear that the starting point when considering decisions which affect the private and family lives of individuals is that all family members have a right to respect for their private and family life; the interests of children are not said to be paramount. However, European case law indicates that the European Court of Human Rights is gradually moving towards the paramountcy principle when deciding cases which affect the upbringing of children (*Hoppe v Germany* [2003] 1 FLR 384; *Yousef v The Netherlands* [2003] 1 FLR 210; *CF v Secretary of State for the Home Department* [2004] 2 FLR 517).

The welfare checklist

Section 1(3), CA 1989 requires the court to have regard to a 'welfare checklist' whenever it is **17.11** considering the following matters:

(a) whether to make, vary, or discharge a s 8 order, and the making, variation, or discharge of the order is opposed by any party to the proceedings: s 1(4)(a); or
(b) whether to make, vary, or discharge a special guardianship order or an order under Part IV, CA 1989, that is, a care or supervision order: s 1(4)(b). (Note: the use of the list is not mandatory where the court is considering an emergency protection order.)

There would be nothing to prevent a court from referring to the welfare checklist for guidance in any other type of case. Its use is only *mandatory* for the categories of proceedings in points (a) and (b) above.

The checklist consists of the following factors, which are not listed by the statute in any order **17.12** of importance:

(a) the ascertainable wishes and feelings of the child concerned (in light of his age and understanding);
(b) his physical, emotional, and educational needs;
(c) the likely effect on him of any change in his circumstances;
(d) his age, sex, background, and any characteristics of his which the court considers relevant;
(e) any harm which he has suffered or is at risk of suffering;
(f) how capable each of his parents, and any other person in relation to whom the court considers the question to be relevant, is of meeting his needs;
(g) the range of powers available to the court under the CA 1989 in the proceedings in question.

The list aims to guide the court and to achieve consistency across the country as well as **17.13** informing legal advisers and helping parties to concentrate on the issues that affect their children. In *B v B (Residence Order: Reasons for Decision)* [1997] 2 FLR 602, the Court of Appeal reminded judges of the importance of taking the welfare checklist fully into account, commenting that it ensured that all relevant matters were considered and that it could be useful in helping to clarify the reasons for the decision.

The wishes and feelings of the child (s 1(3)(a))

Where a child expresses a wish to reside with a particular parent or to have contact with a **17.14** parent then the court must give due weight to that factor. The court will consider the age and maturity of the child when deciding how much weight to attach to such wishes. The court will be aware that the child is likely to be influenced, consciously or not, by the views of the parent with whom he resides. He may be afraid to voice (or even to form) his own opinion for fear of hurting one or the other parent. Even if he obviously does have strong wishes of his own, they may not be in his own interests.

The child's wishes may become known to the court in a variety of ways (eg by the parents **17.15** giving evidence of what he has said to them). The best evidence of a child's wishes is through the welfare report (see Chapter 18, para 18.45). The children and family reporter will normally mention in his report anything that the child has said to him about his wishes; with older children, he may actually ask the child what he feels about the case.

17.16 Examples of cases in which an issue arose as to the weight to be attached to the wishes and views of the children are as follows:

(a) In *Re S (Change of Surname)* [1999] 1 FLR 672, the two girls, now aged 15 and 16, were made subject to a care order as a result of the father's abuse of the older girl and the risk he posed to the younger girl. Both girls applied for leave to change their surname to that of their mother. The older girl was successful at first instance and the younger girl (who was assessed as *Gillick* competent) was successful after the refusal of the first instance court was overturned on appeal.

(b) In *Re S (Contact: Children's Views)* [2002] 1 FLR 1156, the court paid due regard to the clear wishes and feelings of a 16- and a 14-year-old, emphasizing that if young people are to be brought up to respect the law, the law has to respect them and their wishes, even to the extent of allowing them, as occasionally they may do, to make mistakes.

(c) In *Re S (Intractable Contact Dispute)* [2010] 2 FLR 1517 the Court of Appeal overturned an order which permitted two children, aged 12 and 13, to decide on each occasion whether they wished to take up contact or not, holding that the children were too young to have the burden of such a decision imposed on them and they needed an external authority to set out the contact arrangements.

As these cases illustrate, the issue of what weight is to be given to a child's views is case-specific and will vary depending on the children's ages, the nature of the decision, and the particular dynamics and circumstances of the family.

17.17 The HRA 1998 implements the ECHR. Article 6 guarantees, among other things, the right to a fair hearing, including the right of access to a court, and is relevant to the question of the extent to which children should participate directly in proceedings which affect them.

17.18 The European Court of Human Rights has interpreted Art 6 as conferring an effective right of access to a court in the determination of civil rights and obligations (*Golder* v *UK* (1975) 1 EHRR 524, paras 35 and 36). In UK domestic law there are restrictions on the right of access to the court in certain circumstances, for example where defined categories of applicants (including the child who is the subject of the proceedings) must seek permission of the court before bringing proceedings in private or public law child cases: ss 10 and 34, CA 1989. Any application by a child to participate directly in proceedings must be considered in the light of Art 6, and the issue of how the child's views are to be put before the court involves a consideration of the child's Art 6 rights: *Mabon* v *Mabon* [2005] 2 FLR 1011 (see para 17.23 below).

17.19 **Should the judge see the child?** A judge's decision whether or not personally to interview a child is entirely a matter for the exercise of his judicial discretion. The judge should hear submissions from the parties first. The judge must decide who should be present at the interview: normally at least the child's guardian, if one has been appointed, and/or the child's solicitor will be present, and the judge must communicate the matters discussed to the parties: *B* v *B (Minors) (Interviews and Listing Arrangements)* [1994] 2 FLR 489; *Re W (Leave to Remove)* [2008] 2 FLR 1170.

The Family Justice Council has issued *Guidelines for Judges Meeting Children who are subject* **17.20**
to Family Proceedings, reported at [2010] 2 FLR 1872. It is a matter for the judge's discretion
whether he meets the child. If he does decide to do so, the judge should explain to the child
that he cannot keep the child's views confidential, and that the decision taken is the responsibility of the judge and not that of the child.

Should magistrates see the child in private? The position as to whether it is desirable for **17.21**
magistrates to see a child privately is unclear. There were suggestions in some of the older
cases that this would generally be inappropriate: *Re M (A Minor) (Justices' Discretion)* [1993] 2
FLR 706. However, the Family Justice Council guidelines, approved by the President of the
Family Division, include magistrates within their scope and do not differentiate between
magistrates and judges.

The ability of a child to participate as a party The general rule is that a child is automati- **17.22**
cally a party to the proceedings, and is represented by a solicitor, in public law proceedings. In
private law proceedings the child will not be a party unless he is joined to the proceedings by
the court because the court considers that this is in his best interests (r 16.2, Family Procedure
Rules 2010 ('FPR 2010')).

In either case the child will be represented by a children's guardian, from whom his solicitor **17.23**
will take instructions, unless the solicitor considers that the child is able, with regard to his
understanding, to instruct his solicitor directly (r 16.6, FPR 2010). Where there is an issue
between the child and his solicitor as to his ability to conduct the proceedings without a
children's guardian, the court will determine the issue and must grant an application for permission if it considers that the child has 'sufficient understanding': r 16.6(6), FPR 2010. See
also *Re S (A Minor) (Independent Representation)* [1993] 2 FLR 437; *Re CT (A Minor) (Wardship:*
Representation) [1993] 2 FLR 278. In *Mabon v Mabon* [2005] 2 FLR 1011, the Court of Appeal
recognized the growing acknowledgement of the autonomy and consequential rights of children to participate in decision-making processes that fundamentally affect their family life
and allowed three boys aged 17, 15, and 13 to participate directly in a dispute about residence
between their parents.

Where the child is not the subject of the proceedings, but is a party (eg a parent who is himself **17.24**
a child, or a sibling) he must have a 'litigation friend' to conduct proceedings on his behalf,
unless his solicitor considers that he is able, having regard to his understanding, to give
instructions or the court grants him permission to instruct his solicitor directly: r 16.6(5) and
(6), FPR 2010.

The following cases involved children seeking to instruct a solicitor directly rather than **17.25**
through a children's guardian (formerly 'guardian ad litem' in private law proceedings):

(a) In *Re H (A Minor) (Care Proceedings: Child's Wishes)* [1993] 1 FLR 440, a boy aged 15 years
    and eight months had sufficient understanding to instruct his own solicitor in care
    proceedings where he disagreed with the proposals being put forward on his behalf by his
    guardian. Thorpe J held that in those circumstances the solicitor instructed by the guard-
    ian should have put forward the instructions given to him by the boy rather than those
    given to him by the children's guardian.

(b) In *Re M (Minors) (Care Proceedings: Child's Wishes)* [1994] 1 FLR 749 the wishes of a 12-year-
    old boy conflicted with the views of his guardian and he was separately represented.

However, the guardian had taken no steps to seek directions or the leave of the court to secure separate representation for himself. Wall J held that it was important that the guardian should inform the court where it appeared to him that the child was instructing his own solicitor directly, or that he intended to conduct or was capable of conducting the proceedings on his own behalf. The involvement of the court was important because there might be an issue about the capacity of the child to give coherent instructions which should be resolved by the court.

(c) In *Re S (A Minor) (Independent Representation)* [1993] 2 FLR 437 an 11-year-old boy lacked sufficient understanding to participate as a party in emotionally complex and highly fraught private law proceedings in which his parents each sought a residence order in respect of him.

The child's physical, emotional, and educational needs (s 1(3)(b))

17.26 The fact that one parent has greater material prosperity or offers more pleasant surroundings than the other carries very little weight in a dispute as to where a child is to live. In any event, the courts are often able to go some way towards equalizing the differences between parents in this respect by making a maintenance order in favour of the carer parent or, where there is a decree of divorce, nullity, or judicial separation, by means of financial orders.

17.27 If, however, there is evidence that the accommodation offered by a parent is undesirable in some way, this will have a bearing on the decision as to where the child lives. This information will be provided by the welfare report although both parents are also likely to have some comments to make on the question when giving evidence. Naturally, the court will be reluctant to entrust the care of a child to a parent who is presently in unsatisfactory accommodation and has no definite plans about obtaining something better. Where a parent is not housed, the court should not make an order which seeks to put pressure on the local authority housing department to provide accommodation, and should not 'conjure up resources where none exist': *Holmes-Moorhouse v London Borough of Richmond upon Thames* [2009] UKHL 7.

17.28 What is likely to be more important than accommodation is the standard of day-to-day care the parents offer. It is rare that one finds a parent against whom no criticism can be levelled. The court will not therefore go into all the minor grumbles that one parent has about the other's care of the children (eg they do not go to bed until 8 pm and they should be in bed at 7 pm, or they are allowed to get down from the meal table before everyone has finished eating). However, if there is evidence, for example, that the children are often dirty, or hungry, or unsupervised, or that the parent does not or cannot exercise discipline, this will be relevant to the issue as to where the child is to live.

17.29 Another factor which the court will consider is the need of a child for regular medical treatment. It may be that one of the parents lives in an area where the provision of treatment is significantly better. In those circumstances the 'physical needs' of the child might be a deciding factor in determining where the child is to live. Where the child has special needs (eg because of a physical or learning disability), the court will take this into account and will look to see who is best equipped to deal with the child in terms of accommodation, experience, patience, motivation, and so forth.

17.30 In considering the child's emotional needs the court will place weight upon the closeness of the child's ties with one or other of his parents, or with his brothers and sisters, and the trauma consequent upon a breaking of those ties. The court is reluctant to split brothers and sisters: *Re P (Custody of Children: Split Custody Order)* [1991] 1 FLR 337. However, there are, very occasionally, special cases where such an order is justified: see, for example, *Re S (Children)* [2011] EWCA Civ 454, where the children's different ages meant that the judge should have assessed their needs separately rather than taking it as read that they should be treated the same.

It is now generally understood within the family justice system as a whole that a child's emotional needs include the need to have an enduring relationship with both his parents. Where one parent is unwilling or unable to support the child's relationship with the other, this factor may be of great importance in deciding where the child is to live. For consideration of this issue, see para 17.162 below. **17.31**

Where one parent is working and the other is not, the parent who can be at home full time for the children has a considerable advantage. This is especially the case where the children are below school age. As they get older and spend time at school and with their own friends, the question of work becomes less decisive provided the arrangements proposed by the working parent for after school, school holidays, and illnesses are satisfactory. **17.32**

In the past there have been few cases where the *educational* needs of the child have proved decisive. In its widest sense 'educational needs' could cover almost anything to do with the upbringing of the child. However, education in the sense of 'schooling' may still be a significant factor, particularly if one parent is moving away from the area at a time which is especially important (eg when the child is about to take his GCSEs). In those circumstances the parent who will continue to live in proximity to the child's current school may be at an advantage in any dispute over residence. The younger the child is, the less weight is likely to be attached to a temporary disruption of his schooling whilst he moves from his old home to the new one. If the child needs a special school for some reason then this will be an important factor, whatever the age of the child. **17.33**

The likely effect on the child of a change in circumstances (s 1(3)(c))

The court is always very reluctant to remove a child from his present home unless there is a strong reason to do so. It follows that the parent who is looking after the child at the time of a dispute as to where the child is to live starts with a considerable advantage over anyone else. The longer that situation continues, the greater the advantage will become. This is commonly referred to as the 'status quo' argument. For example, faced with two parents of equal merit, one of whom has been caring for the child for a considerable time already, the court will almost inevitably grant a residence order to that parent. **17.34**

The child's age, sex, background, and any relevant characteristics (s 1(3)(d))

The *age* of a child will often be an important factor in deciding what is in his best interests. For example, a young baby's needs will usually be best satisfied by living with his mother, whereas a 15-year-old will generally be considered sufficiently mature to make up his own mind as to where he would like to live: *Re W (A Minor) (Residence Order)* [1992] 2 FLR 332. The age and maturity of the child will be important when the court decides what weight to attach to the child's wishes, as already discussed in para 17.25. **17.35**

The *sex* of the child is another factor to be placed in the balance, although in most cases this factor will not carry significant weight. In the older authorities, importance was often **17.36** attached to the needs of girls, particularly those approaching their teenage years, to be in the care of their mothers. In recent years, however, and in line with changing societal norms, it has become much more common for fathers to take on the primary care of children of all ages, both boys and girls, and therefore many of the older cases must be treated with caution.

17.37   The child's *background* can cover a multitude of different factors, for example his religious upbringing, his family environment, and so forth.

17.38   Likewise, the child's relevant characteristics could cover a broad spectrum of matters, for example a disability or a severe illness. It could also cover religious, sporting, or intellectual factors.

17.39   Where the child's parents are from a particular cultural or ethnic background, the court must take into account the attitudes and habits prevalent in that culture in deciding any question that arises in relation to the child's upbringing.

17.40   Where a child is of mixed race, the court will take into account the differences between the parents' cultures and look to see how the child has been brought up so far. If he has been brought up, for example, in the mother's English way of life, the court will be reluctant to grant a residence order to the father who is now living the Indian way of life in an Indian community. However, the court will be inclined to require generous contact in such cases in order that the child should be able to maintain his links with the cultures of both parents. The court's approach will normally be to preserve, as far as possible, elements of both cultures until the child is of an age where he is able to make decisions for himself. The same approach applies to disputes about religion: *Re S (Specific Issue Order: Religion: Circumcision)* [2005] 1 FLR 236.

Any harm which the child has suffered or is at risk of suffering (s 1(3)(e))

17.41   The word 'harm' is a deliberately wide-ranging term. It covers both physical injury and psychological trauma. The Adoption and Children Act 2002 ('ACA 2002') has extended the meaning of 'harm' in s 31(9), CA 1989 to include, for example, impairment suffered by hearing or seeing the ill-treatment of another.

How capable are the parents and any other relevant person of meeting the child's needs (s 1(3)(f))?

17.42   The court will have to assess the capability for childcare of the persons who apply to look after children. If the dispute is between two parents who are equally committed and able to care for the child then the deciding factor may be that one works full time whereas the other is available all day.

17.43   Clearly, if a parent has ill-treated the child in the past, this will be a very important factor in the dispute as to with whom the child should live. His claim will also be prejudiced if he has ill-treated another child.

17.44   Other matters that may be taken into account include:

   (a)   *The criminal record/criminal conduct of a parent*—to what extent criminal conduct will affect the outcome of a dispute over the care of a child depends very much on the particular circumstances of the case. If both parents have been regularly involved in crime, it is unlikely that the application of either will be affected by this factor (although it must be remembered that the court does have power under s 37(1), CA 1989, to order the local authority to look into the circumstances of the family to ascertain whether the local authority wishes to apply for a care or supervision order where the court feels that it is undesirable for the child to be in the care of either parent or any other individual). On the other hand, if one parent is a law-abiding citizen and the other has a criminal record or is known to commit criminal offences, this will prejudice that parent's application for the care of the child. The court will be particularly reluctant to place the child in an environment where he will be subjected to bad influences in his day-to-day life (eg where there is evidence that a parent takes drugs, regularly commits offences of dishonesty, etc). Furthermore, the court will have to take account of the fact that a parent who commits criminal offences jeopardizes the stability of the home he offers in that he is at risk of being imprisoned, in which case other arrangements would have to be made for the care of his child.

(b) *Mental and physical illness*—the mental illness of a parent is relevant to a dispute over the care of a child. However, whether it will have any bearing on the outcome of the case depends on the nature of the mental illness. If there is evidence that the illness causes the parent concerned to behave in a way that may be harmful to the children's physical or mental state, or if the parent is likely to need regular in-patient treatment in hospital for the condition, obviously this will be an important consideration. If the question of mental illness is raised and the parent concerned feels that he or she is, in fact, perfectly well or has been treated successfully, it would be advisable to obtain medical evidence to this effect. Physical illness will only have a bearing on the case if it prevents the parent from looking after the children properly, for example because he or she is bedridden or disabled or has to return for prolonged stays in hospital.

(c) *Religious views*—the religious views of a parent are rarely of much importance in a case relating to the care of children. However, the court is likely to be reluctant to grant the care of a child to a parent who belongs to an extreme religious sect if there is evidence that the influence of this sect may be harmful to the child. It is worth bearing in mind that the court has wide powers to attach conditions to s 8 orders and it may be possible in this way to ensure that the child is not exposed to harmful aspects of the parent's faith. For example, when granting a residence order to a parent who belongs to a sect that is against blood transfusions, the court may be able to impose a condition that the child should be allowed to have a transfusion if it becomes necessary for his health or life.

(d) *Domestic violence*—domestic violence perpetrated by one parent on another is itself a serious failure in parenting. Where domestic violence is admitted or proved, this is likely to affect the court's assessment of the perpetrator's capacity to care for the child. Domestic violence is discussed in more detail at para 17.163 below.

17.45 The court is also enjoined to consider the capability 'of any other person in relation to whom the court considers the question to be relevant'. This would include, for example, the new partner of one of the spouses, the child's grandparents or other members of the child's family, child minders, nannies, and nurseries.

17.46 Not infrequently the child will be in regular contact with someone other than the parent with care of the child. For example, either parent may be sharing accommodation with relatives for the foreseeable future, or may propose that the child is cared for by a nanny or by a relative whilst he is out at work, or may have formed a relationship with a new partner or intend to remarry. In these circumstances it is most important that the court should be informed about anyone else who will be in regular contact with the child and that any welfare report prepared should include an assessment of that person's likely role in the child's life.

Example 1 After the parties separate, the mother returns to live with her own father and mother. She is available full time to look after the child. However, she does not dispute that of her three brothers who also live in the family home, two are regularly in trouble with the police and one is a glue-sniffer. The child's father lives with his sister who has two young children and proposes that, while he is at work, his sister will look after the children. The court hears from the mother and her own father and from the child's father and his sister. A residence order is awarded to the father in view of the undesirable family circumstances of the mother.

The range of powers available to the court (s 1(3)(g))

17.47　It is of particular importance for the practitioner to note the factor in s 1(3)(g) which requires the court to have regard to the range of powers available to it in the relevant proceedings. Thus, the court is able to choose the appropriate order for a case, even where no one has made an application for that particular order. For example, the court can grant *anyone* a s 8 order, even without a formal application having been made to the court: s 10(1)(b), CA 1989; this might happen, for example, where it becomes clear in the course of a hearing that a grandparent, rather than either of the parents, would be the most appropriate person to care for the child whose residence is in dispute: *Re J (Leave to Issue Application for Residence Order)* [2003] 1 FLR 114. Another example might arise where a parent makes an application for a residence order but during the course of the hearing the court considers that a care or supervision order may be appropriate. In that situation the court has power to adjourn the case and to direct the local authority to investigate the circumstances of the child with a view to deciding whether it would be appropriate for them to apply for an order: s 37(1), CA 1989; in an urgent case, where the welfare of the child requires it, the court can make an interim care order without hearing from the local authority.

Preventing further applications under s 91(14)

17.48　The court also has power to prevent further applications being made to the court without leave for any type of order under the CA 1989, for example for parental responsibility (s 4), guardianship (s 5), contact, residence, specific issue, and prohibited steps (s 8).

17.49　Initially s 91(14) was used mainly to deal with those cases where applications have been made too frequently or where the previous applications were vexatious or frivolous, and the parties, including the children, are seen to be suffering or likely to suffer if such applications are allowed to continue. However, there is now emerging a new category of cases to which s 91(14) may apply. In *C v W (Contact: Leave to Apply)* [1999] 1 FLR 916, a s 91(14) restriction was imposed upon a parent who could not be described as a vexatious or obsessive litigant; in that case, it was the father's 'complete disregard' for the requirements of the court and for the welfare of his child which made the court conclude that the restriction was appropriate. In *Re M (Section 91(14) Order)* [1999] 2 FLR 553, the mother's children were in care with no prospect of rehabilitation to her, but due to the delay by the local authority in formulating a long-term plan for the children she had had a high level of contact with them. Once the local authority had formulated a plan, it was necessary to reduce the level of contact and the court imposed a s 91(14) restriction for a period of 12 months in order to give the children time to settle in their new home and to give the mother time to accept the situation. Helpful guidelines dealing with the use of s 91(14) are to be found in *Re P (S 91(14) Guidelines) (Residence and Religious Heritage)* [1999] 2 FLR 573, as follows:

(a) Section 91(14) is to be read in conjunction with s 1(1) (the paramountcy of the welfare of the child).

(b) The court's power under s 91(14) is an exercise of its discretion.

(c) The use of s 91(14) amounts to a significant statutory intrusion into a party's rights to bring proceedings before the court.

(d) The power must be used carefully and sparingly and should be the exception rather than the rule.

(e) Section 91(14) is a useful weapon of last resort in cases of repeated and unreasonable applications.

(f) In exceptional circumstances the court could use s 91(14) in other types of cases to those in point (e) above provided there is clear evidence of need and the welfare of the child demands it.

(g) In cases under point (f) above the court must be satisfied that:
  (i) the facts go beyond the normal settling-in time and temporary hostility that can follow where a regime has been ordered by the court; and
  (ii) there is a serious risk that without a s 91(14) restriction the child or his primary carers will be subject to strain.

(h) The court can impose a s 91(14) restriction of its own motion, provided that the parties have been given an opportunity to be heard.

(i) A s 91(14) restriction can be imposed without limit of time (see also *Re B (Section 91(14) Order: Duration)* [2004] 1 FLR 871).

(j) The court should specify the extent of the restrictions and the type of application to be restrained as well as the duration of the order. The degree of restriction should be proportionate to the harm that it is intended to avoid (see also *Re G (Contempt: Committal)* [2003] 2 FLR 58).

(k) It is undesirable to make an order without notice first having been given to the other side (ie, *ex parte*) unless there are exceptional circumstances.

The term of an order under s 91(14) must be proportionate and consistent with the child's **17.50** welfare and the court's primary aim to promote the relationship between the parent and the child. Such orders must be made only after careful consideration and having given the party involved an opportunity to make full submissions. This is particularly important where the party is a litigant in person.

Lifting the s 91(14) bar on future applications

When the court considers an application for leave to lift a bar imposed under s 91(14), the test **17.51** to be applied when considering whether such leave should be granted is simply:

(a) does the application demonstrate that there is any need for renewed judicial investigation?;

(b) if 'yes', then leave should be granted.

The court considers the statements supporting the application and the contents of any court welfare officer's report and in appropriate cases the application may be determined at a directions appointment if these statements etc indicate that the application should go no further: *Re A (Application for Leave)* [1998] 1 FLR 1. Wherever possible, all interested parties should receive notice of such hearings so that the court can consider representations from all of them when considering the application. Such orders should not be made against a litigant in person at short notice unless the circumstances are exceptional: *Re C (Prohibition on Further Applications)* [2002] 1 FLR 1136.

Civil restraint orders

17.52 The FPR 2010 introduced a new power, available to the county court and High Court, to make a civil restraint order preventing a person from making unmerited applications in family proceedings: r 4.8, FPR 2010. A limited civil restraint order may be imposed by any judge, where a party has made two or more applications that have been judged to be 'totally without merit'; it prevents that party from making any further application within the proceedings without the permission of an identified judge. An extended civil restraint order may only be made by a High Court judge, where a party has 'persistently made applications which are totally without merit'. This order prevents the party from making any further applications in any matter related to the proceedings without permission of an identified judge. A general civil restraint order is intended for the most persistent and vexatious of litigants: again such an order may be made only by a High Court judge, and only in circumstances where an extended civil restraint order is not sufficient. This order prohibits the party from making any application in any court without the permission of a named judge, and can last for a maximum of two years.

Presumption of no order

17.53 Section 1(5), CA 1989 provides that:

> where a court is considering whether or not to make one or more orders under this Act with respect to a child, it shall not make the order or any of the orders unless it considers that doing so would be better for the child than making no order at all.

17.54 The importance of this principle to the practitioner cannot be too greatly stressed. Increasingly, the courts are showing a tendency, where parties meet at court and reach a compromise in what was until then a dispute about their children, to make no order at all. If the court takes the view that the parties are now agreed as to what should happen then it may decide that it would be better for the child for those agreed arrangements to prevail between the parties rather than embodying them in a court order. Such a solution may prevent a parent from feeling bitter that he has had arrangements imposed upon him by the court (albeit in a consent order). The less bitter the parents feel about the arrangements made for the children, the easier it is likely to be for them to cooperate with each other in future, with the consequence that the children will suffer less upset as a result. It is a principle running throughout the CA 1989 that wherever possible the courts should not interfere with the arrangements made by parents in respect of their children unless it is necessary in the interests of the children to do so.

17.55 Of course, it may happen that the agreed arrangements break down in any event with the result that the case has to return to court and an order has to be made. However, at least the parties will have had every possible opportunity to achieve a solution without the interference of the court.

There will be circumstances in which an order will need to be made, despite an agreement **17.56** between the parties concerned. An example is where it is agreed that the grandmother is to care for the child. Parental responsibility may be conferred on a grandmother only as part of a residence order: s 12, CA 1989. A residence order will therefore be necessary to ensure that the grandmother acquires *locus standi* in relation to the child and is able, for example, to give consent to medical treatment: *B v B (A Minor) (Residence Order)* [1992] 2 FLR 327. Another such example is to be found in the case of *G v F (Contact and Shared Residence: Applications for Leave)* [1998] 2 FLR 799 where two women cohabited in a lesbian relationship for five years and a child was born by artificial insemination. During their cohabitation the applicant played a full part in raising the child and continued to do so after the couple separated. It was accepted that a shared residence order was the appropriate means of conferring parental responsibility on the applicant (since she had no right to apply for parental responsibility in its own right in the way in which an unmarried father could do under s 4, CA 1989). See also *Re H (Shared Residence: Parental Responsibility)* [1995] 2 FLR 883 which concerned the conferral of parental responsibility on a stepfather by way of a shared residence order. However, there must be an element of residence in a shared residence order; it cannot be used merely as a vehicle to confer equal status on parents: *Re A (Shared Residence)* [2002] 1 FCR 177—where the child was not only not going to reside with the other parent, but was not even going to visit him, thus making a shared residence order inappropriate.

The delay principle

Section 1(2), CA 1989 requires the court 'in any proceedings in which any question with **17.57** respect to the upbringing of the child arises' to have regard 'to the general principle that any delay in determining the question is likely to prejudice the welfare of the child'.

Once again, this provision is of great importance. The practitioner must be very aware of the **17.58** court's desire to hear applications in respect of children as soon as possible. In order to put the provision into proper effect s 11 (in relation to s 8 orders) and s 32 (in relation to care and supervision orders), CA 1989 require the court to draw up a timetable for the progress of the case with a view to eliminating undue delay in the proceedings.

Rule 12.13(1), FPR 2010 requires the court to fix the next hearing date on transfer; when a **17.59** hearing is postponed or adjourned; or at the conclusion of any hearing at which the proceedings are not finally determined. Specific provision for timetabling public law cases is contained in FPR 2010, PD12A; and for private law cases in PD12B. The court will expect the timetable to be adhered to and will take steps to enforce adherence to it. This may sometimes mean, for example, that the court will proceed to hear a case without a welfare report if it decides that the advantage to the child of a speedy hearing outweighs the disadvantage to him of proceeding without a welfare report.

The Public Law Proceedings Guide to Case Management, set out in FPR 2010, PD12A, has as **17.60** its main aim to ensure that care cases are dealt with as justly, expeditiously, and fairly as possible. The key principles underlying the Practice Direction are that there should be judicial continuity, active case management by the court, consistency by the standardization of steps to be taken in preparation, and a case management conference in each care case to enable the judge to identify the issues and fix the timetable for all further directions and hearings.

17.61   The HRA 1998 implements the ECHR. Article 6(1) requires that cases be heard within a reasonable time and underlines the importance of rendering justice without delays which might jeopardize its effectiveness and credibility.

17.62   Time usually starts to run when the proceedings are instituted (*Darnell* v *UK* (1993) 18 EHRR 205), although it may be earlier in certain circumstances. Time ends with the final decision disposing of the matter, including any appeal. In deciding on the reasonableness of the duration the court takes into account the complexity of the case, the conduct of the applicant, the way in which the matter was dealt with by the administrative and judicial authorities, and the importance of what is at stake for the applicant. In *H* v *UK* (1988) 10 EHRR 95, the European Court of Human Rights made it clear that the obligation is on the state to ensure that the systems in place for hearing cases run effectively and efficiently. In every case relating to children, the ECHR obligation to bring proceedings within a reasonable time must therefore be considered in addition to the existing principle in s 1(2), CA 1989.

C   PARENTAL RESPONSIBILITY

17.63   Parental responsibility is a concept introduced by the CA 1989 and it emphasizes the importance of responsibility *for* children, rather than rights *over* children. For the rules relating to the court's jurisdiction to make parental responsibility orders, see para 17.70 below.

17.64   The concept of parental responsibility is defined in s 3(1), CA 1989 as 'all the rights, duties, powers, responsibilities and authority which by law a parent of a child has in relation to the child and his property'. However, no further definition is attempted since the Law Commission took the view that the list would be changing constantly 'to meet differing needs and circumstances' (Law Com No 172, para 2.6). It was decided in *R* v *Tameside Metropolitan Borough Council* [2000] 1 FLR 942 that parental responsibility includes the right to decide where a child lives. In that case the local authority were providing the child with accommodation with the consent of his parents (rather than by way of a care order, which would have conferred parental responsibility). The local authority had no power to arrange for the child to be transferred out of a residential institution and into foster care without the permission of the child's parents.

17.65   A person with parental responsibility may not surrender or transfer any part of that responsibility: s 2(9), CA 1989. However, he may arrange for some part, or all, of that responsibility to be met by one or more other persons, for example schools, local authorities, churches, etc. The exercise of parental responsibility will often be qualified in some way by agreement between the parents or by order of the court. For example, the father of a child may agree that the child should live with the mother, in which case the mother has a greater degree of day-to-day 'parental responsibility' than does the father. He agrees to his parental responsibility being curtailed and thus his ability to exercise it is subject to his agreement with the mother (or, in default of agreement, subject to the order of the court). The parent involved would not be permitted to do anything which was incompatible with the court order: s 2(8).

17.66   In addition, the CA 1989 allows those having parental responsibility for the child to act alone and without the other (or others) in meeting that responsibility. However, if a particular statute requires the consent of another person, then this must be obtained in the manner prescribed: s 2(7); for example, the Child Abduction Act 1984 prohibits the removal of children from the United Kingdom without the consent of all those who have parental responsibility for the child.

Parental responsibility and the child

Parental power and responsibility to make decisions for and on behalf of children necessarily **17.67** varies according to the nature of the decision and the age of the child. When a child reaches an age and stage of maturity where he is competent to take a particular decision for himself, then his right to do so must be respected. Plainly, whether the child is competent will be issue-specific: a child of 15 may be competent to make decisions about the practical arrangements for contact, but not competent to make life-changing decisions about medical treatment.

In *Gillick* v *West Norfolk and Wisbech Area Health Authority* [1986] AC 112, the House of Lords **17.68** held that a child under 16 was capable of giving consent to medical treatment if he was capable of understanding what was proposed and of expressing his own wishes. '*Gillick* competence' is the term now used to describe this concept.

It has been held that the court may disregard the wishes of even a *Gillick*-competent child **17.69** if his welfare requires it, although these wishes will carry significant weight: *Re W (A Minor) (Medical Treatment: Court's Jurisdiction)* [1993] 1 FLR 1; see also *Re Roddy (A Child) (Identification: Restriction on Publication)* [2004] 2 FLR 949. The courts have been prepared to authorize life-saving medical treatment of *Gillick*-competent 16- and 17-year-olds, notwithstanding that there would be no power to impose such treatment on a competent, non-consenting adult: *Re P (Medical Treatment: Best Interests)* [2004] 2 FLR 1117.

Who has parental responsibility?

Under the CA 1989 there is a wide variety of people who may acquire parental responsibility **17.70** for a child in different ways.

(a) Parental responsibility is conferred automatically on the mother of a child, irrespective of her marital status: s 2(1).
(b) If the father was married to the mother at the time of the child's birth he will automatically have parental responsibility: s 2(3).
(c) After 1 December 2003, a father who was not married to the mother at the time of the child's birth has parental responsibility if his name is placed on the birth certificate at registration or re-registration of the birth under the Births and Deaths Registration Act 1953: s 4(1)(a).
(d) If the father was not married to the mother at the time of the child's birth then he may acquire parental responsibility by agreement with the mother or by order of the court (s 4), or by obtaining a residence order: s 12(1).
(e) Where a lesbian couple have a child together through assisted reproduction, the mother's partner will have parental responsibility if she is registered as a parent on the child's birth certificate or enters into an agreement with the child's mother, or if the women are in a civil partnership: ss 42 and 43, Human Fertilisation and Embryology Act 2008 ('HFEA 2008').

(f) A step-parent who is married to or the civil partner of one of the child's parents may acquire parental responsibility by agreement, or by order of the court: s 4A(1), CA 1989.

(g) Guardians will acquire parental responsibility for children, so that they are equated with natural parents: s 5(6).

(h) Local authorities may acquire parental responsibility, for example on the making of a care order (s 33(3)) or a placement order: s 25(2), ACA 2002.

(i) A person who has been granted an emergency protection order will acquire parental responsibility for the duration of the order: s 44(4), CA 1989.

(j) A person who has been granted a residence order will automatically have parental responsibility for the duration of the order: s 12(1) and (2).

(k) When a child becomes a ward of court then the court itself will acquire parental responsibility: see para 17.209 below.

(l) When a child is placed for adoption or adopted, his (prospective) adoptive parents will acquire parental responsibility (and the natural parents will lose it): ss 25(3) and 46(1), ACA 2002.

(m) Whilst a special guardianship order is in force the special guardian has parental responsibility for the child in respect of whom it is made and is able to exercise that responsibility to the exclusion of any other person with parental responsibility (save for another special guardian): s 14C(1).

17.71 There is no limit on the number of people who can have parental responsibility for a child at any one time, and a person does not lose parental responsibility merely because someone else acquires it. Although on the making of a care order or a placement order a local authority obtains parental responsibility for a child, the parents will not lose it and it will be 'shared', although the local authority has the power to determine the extent to which any other person may exercise it: s 33(3).

17.72 It is unusual for a person to lose parental responsibility, other than via an adoption or a parental order (an order made in favour of surrogate parents under s 54, HFEA 2008). These are the only circumstances in which a mother or a married father may lose parental responsibility. The parental responsibility of others may be removed by the court, but this is rare: see, for example, the circumstances of *Re P (Terminating Parental Responsibility)* [1995] 1 FLR 1048.

Meaning of 'father' and 'mother'

17.73 There is no definition of either 'father' or 'mother' within the CA 1989. Generally it can be assumed that references in the CA 1989 to 'father' and 'mother' are intended to denote the natural parents of the child: that is, the birth mother and the biological father. The HFEA 2008 defines the parents of a child born as a result of assisted reproduction. Regardless of whether or not she is a biological parent, 'the woman who is carrying or has carried a child as a result of the placing in her of an embryo or of sperm and eggs, and no other woman is to be treated as the mother of the child': s 33(1). Where a child is born to a married woman as a result of her having been artificially inseminated with donor sperm, then her husband is to be treated as the father of the child unless it is shown that he did not consent to his wife's insemination. The same rule applies where the woman who receives treatment is in a civil partnership, in that her partner will be a second (female) parent of the child unless it is shown that she did not consent to the treatment. Where a couple (heterosexual or homosexual) undergo treatment together, and each consents formally to the mother's partner being treated as a parent of the child, that person, male or female, will be the child's second parent and will be entitled to be registered as such on the birth certificate.

In *Re G (Children)* [2006] 2 FLR 629, the House of Lords identified three ways in which a person **17.74** may become a natural parent: biological, gestational, and social/psychological. Distinct from these concepts is the status conferred by legal parenthood, which may be defined by statute or common law depending on the nature of the proceedings.

Automatic parental responsibility

Parental responsibility is conferred automatically on the mother of a child irrespective of her **17.75** marital status. Whether the father also has parental responsibility depends on whether he was married to the mother at the time of the child's birth: s 2(1). If he was so married then he will also have automatic parental responsibility. Even if the father was not lawfully married to the mother at the time of the birth he may still be treated as so married in particular circumstances (s 2(3), importing s 1, Family Law Reform Act 1987), for example if the child is subsequently legitimated. The only way in which a parent can be divested of 'automatic' parental responsibility is upon the child being adopted or upon a parental order being made.

Unmarried fathers

If the father was not married to the mother at the time of the child's birth and does not come **17.76** within the extensions to this concept then on the face of it he will not have parental responsibility for the child. However, he may acquire parental responsibility in one of several ways:

(a) After 1 December 2003, a father not married to the mother at the time of the child's birth has parental responsibility if his name is placed on the birth certificate at registration or re-registration of the birth under the Births and Deaths Registration Act 1953 (s 4(1)(a)). However, in reality, an unmarried father will not be able to register his name without the consent of the mother. If he does acquire parental responsibility by registration of his name on the birth certificate then that responsibility can only be removed by order of the court, on application by any person with parental responsibility for the child or, with leave, on the application of the child himself (if he has sufficient understanding).

(b) By applying for and obtaining a residence order, using Form C100 to make the application (s 12(1)); if the court makes a residence order in favour of a father, it must at the same time make a parental responsibility order under s 4 (which will then continue in force even if the residence order is later revoked).

(c) By applying to the court for a parental responsibility order, using Form C1 to make the application (s 4(1)(a)), in which case the order will last until discharged by the court (s 4(3)).

(d) By making a 'parental responsibility agreement' with the mother in the prescribed form (s 4(1)(b)), which will last until discharged by the court (s 4(3)). The form which such an agreement must take is prescribed by the Parental Responsibility Agreement Regulations 1991.

Article 8(1), ECHR guarantees a right to family life but it does not place an unmarried father **17.77** in the same position as a married father or an unmarried mother. The CA 1989 does not automatically give unmarried fathers parental responsibility for their children. It does, however, provide a vehicle by which unmarried fathers may acquire parental responsibility.

17.78 **Factors to be considered in making parental responsibility order** There is now a substantial body of case law which sets out the various factors which the court must consider when deciding whether to make a parental responsibility order. In *Re H (Illegitimate Children: Father: Parental Rights) (No 2)* [1991] 1 FLR 214 the test to be applied was summarized as follows:

(a) The welfare of the child is the court's paramount consideration: s 1(1), CA 1989.

(b) Was the association between the parties sufficiently enduring?

(c) Has the father by his conduct during and since the application shown sufficient commitment to the child to justify giving him a legal status equivalent to that which he would have had if the parties had been married?

(d) How great is the degree of attachment which exists between the father and the child?

(e) The court must pay due attention to the fact that a number of parental rights would, if conferred upon the father by a parental responsibility order, be unenforceable. However, although this is a relevant consideration, it is not an overriding one.

(f) What are the father's reasons for applying for the parental responsibility order?

17.79 In *Re P (A Minor) (Parental Responsibility Order)* [1994] 1 FLR 578, Wall J made some very useful observations as to the nature of a parental responsibility order. He said (at p 584): 'It is important to be quite clear that an order for parental responsibility to the father does not give him a right to interfere in matters within the day-to-day management of the child's life.' He went on to say (at p 585):

> It is to be noted that on any view an order for parental responsibility gives the father no power to override the decision of the mother, who already has such responsibility: in the event of disagreement between them on a specific issue relating to the child, the court will have to resolve it. If the father were to seek to misuse the rights given him under s. 4 such misuse could, as a second to last resort, be controlled by the court under a prohibited steps order against him and/or a specific issue order. The very last resort of all would presumably be the discharge of the parental responsibility order.

17.80 The case of *C and V (Contact and Parental Responsibility Order)* [1998] 1 FLR 392, confirmed that the unmarried father's failure to obtain a contact order in his favour should not mean that his application for a parental responsibility order would also fail. The Court of Appeal reminded practitioners that a parental responsibility order was designed to enable the actual father to have the same status of fatherhood which he would have enjoyed if he had been married to the child's mother.

17.81 Even where the child of an unmarried father has already been received into the care of the local authority it may still be right to make a parental responsibility order in favour of the father, provided that he has shown commitment to the child and that his reasons for making the application are proper ones; the fact that the father is awkward, difficult, and thoroughly unresponsive to the social workers involved will not necessarily prevent the making of an order: *Re G (A Minor) (Parental Responsibility Order)* [1994] 1 FLR 504.

17.82 The theme of current case law seems to be that the making of parental responsibility orders will generally be the norm rather than the exception when a father has shown a wish to be involved in his child's life: for example, *Re J-S (Contact: Parental Responsibility)* [2003] Fam Law 65; and contested parental responsibility applications are now quite rare. This is consistent with the change in the law which has meant that unmarried fathers named on the child's birth certificate after December 2003 have parental responsibility, and the consequent emphasis on parental responsibility as an important means of conferring the status of parent-hood, even when the father's contact with the child is quite limited.

There are very few reported cases in which a refusal to make a parental responsibility order has **17.83** been upheld. However, the following cases (all of which were decided prior to the change in the law in December 2003) are examples of such refusal: in *Re T (A Minor) (Parental Responsibility: Contact)* [1993] 2 FLR 450, the father had used serious violence against the mother and had been guilty of cruel behaviour towards the child; in *Re P (Minors: Parental Responsibility Order)* [1997] 2 FLR 722, the father was serving sentences of imprisonment for robbery, had begot-ten one of the children concerned during a period of home leave in the course of which he committed a further offence for which he was sentenced to imprisonment. The lack of a responsible attitude towards the child or evidence that the exercise of parental responsibility will be used to interfere with or undermine the mother's care of the child may result in the court refusing to make a parental responsibility order: *Re H (Parental Responsibility)* [1998] 1 FLR 855; *Re P (Parental Responsibility)* [1998] 2 FLR 96.

The unmarried father who does not seek parental responsibility will still remain liable to main- **17.84** tain his child: s 3(4), CA 1989. However, where a father refuses to pay maintenance for his child, the court should not use the weapon of withholding a parental responsibility order to obtain from the father his financial dues: *Re H (Parental Responsibility: Maintenance)* [1996] 1 FLR 867.

Nature of a parental responsibility agreement As already mentioned in para 17.70, one **17.85** way in which an unmarried father can obtain parental responsibility is by entering into a parental responsibility agreement with the mother, using the form prescribed in the Parental Responsibility Agreement Regulations 1991. The case of *Re X (Parental Responsibility Agreement: Children in Care)* [2000] 1 FLR 517 held that where two children were subject to care orders and the local authority wanted to place them for adoption, the local authority had no power to stop the mother from entering into a parental responsibility agreement with the unmar-ried father in respect of the children even though the children were subject to care orders. The court decided that to create a parental responsibility agreement both parents must act *in unison* and sign the agreement and therefore entering into the agreement was not in itself an exercise of parental responsibility; the unmarried father does not have parental responsibility when he signs the agreement and therefore the mother cannot be said to be exercising paren-tal responsibility when she signs it either.

Termination of parental responsibility agreements and orders A parental responsibility **17.86** order or agreement will automatically end upon the child attaining the age of 18: s 91(7) and (8), CA 1989. The order or agreement could be discharged by the court before the child attains 18 if the court is satisfied on the 'welfare' test contained in s 1(1) that it would be better for the child if the court were to discharge it rather than refuse to do so: s 4(3). Any person with parental responsibility may apply to discharge the order or agreement, as indeed may the child himself if he is of sufficient age and understanding: s 4(3)(b) and (4). However, paren-tal responsibility cannot be removed from a father in whose favour a residence order exists: s 12(4). Indeed, where a residence order has been made in favour of a person who is not a parent or guardian of the child, that person must also continue to have parental responsibility while the residence order remains in force: s 12(2).

17.87 An example of a case where a parental responsibility agreement was terminated is *Re P (Terminating Parental Responsibility)* [1995] 1 FLR 1048. Here the unmarried parents entered into such an agreement shortly after the birth of the child. Later the father caused injuries to the child leaving the child physically and mentally disabled. In response to the father's application for a contact order the mother applied for termination of the agreement. Singer J indicated that the normal presumption was that once an agreement was entered into, it would remain in force until the welfare of the child warranted its termination. In order to determine whether the agreement would be terminated, the court had to consider whether it would have made a parental responsibility order in favour of the father if he did not already have parental responsibility. On the facts, there was no aspect of parental responsibility which the unmarried father could exercise in a way which would be beneficial to the child. Accordingly, the agreement would be terminated.

Step-parents

17.88 Step-parents may acquire parental responsibility for a child of their spouse:

(a) by agreement between the step-parent and the parents with parental responsibility for the child, or by order of the court: s 4A(1). Such an agreement will constitute a 'parental responsibility agreement' within the definition of s 4(2) (see para 17.70 above), and can only be terminated by the court on application by any person with parental responsibility for the child or, with leave, on application by the child himself (provided he has sufficient understanding);

(b) by the making of a residence order in his favour, parental responsibility being retained for as long as the order remains in force: s 12(2). However, the rights enjoyed by natural parents in relation to adoption and guardianship will not apply to him: s 12(3);

(c) by the making of an adoption order in his favour.

17.89 A step-parent will be responsible for the maintenance of a child insofar as the step-parent is a party to the marriage (whether or not subsisting) in relation to which the child concerned is a child of the family: sch 1, para 16. (For a definition of 'child of the family' see s 105(1).) This will be the case irrespective of whether the step-parent has 'parental responsibility' or not: s 3(4)(a).

17.90 A step-parent who has care of a child may do what is reasonable in all the circumstances of the case for the purpose of safeguarding or promoting the child's welfare: s 3(5).

Civil partners

17.91 By virtue of s 75(2), Civil Partnership Act 2004, civil partners may apply for parental responsibility for the children of their civil partners, using the same mechanism as is used for the acquisition of parental responsibility by step-parents after marriage under s 4A(1), CA 1989 (see para 17.88, above).

Person with de facto care of child

17.92 Where a person has de facto care of a child but no parental responsibility for him then that person may do whatever is reasonable to safeguard and promote the child's welfare: s 3(5).

D   GUARDIANSHIP

Central to the role of guardians under the CA 1989 is the conferment upon them of parental **17.93** responsibility for the child in question: s 5(6).

Appointment of a guardian

A guardian may be appointed for a child under 18 in the following ways: **17.94**

(a) by the court in family proceedings, with or without an application:
    (i)   where the child has no parent with parental responsibility for him: s 5(1)(a); or
    (ii) where a residence order has been made with respect to the child in favour of a parent
        or guardian of his who has died while the order was in force: s 5(1)(b);
(b) by a parent with parental responsibility: s 5(3);
(c) by an existing guardian: s 5(4).

When a court decides whether to appoint a guardian it must apply the 'welfare' principle set **17.95** out in s 1(1). As with applications for a parental responsibility order, it is not mandatory for the court to use the statutory checklist of factors in s 1(3) unless it is making the decision in the course of hearing a contested application for a s 8 order, care order, or supervision order. However, in practice the court is likely to refer to the checklist in any event, and in addition to consider the relationship between the child in question and the proposed guardian, the recorded wishes of the deceased parent, the wishes of the child's nearest relative, and other such matters.

A parent who has parental responsibility, or a guardian, may appoint a guardian to assume **17.96** parental responsibility on the death of the appointor: s 5(3) and (4). Two or more persons may join together to make such an appointment: s 5(10). Any such appointment need not be made by will or by deed. It was felt that such formalities may deter people from making an appointment. Instead, it will be sufficient for the appointment to be in writing, dated and signed at the direction of the person making the appointment in his presence and in the presence of two witnesses. Unmarried fathers will be able to make appointments if they have obtained parental responsibility or been appointed as guardians.

The appointment of a guardian will not take effect on the death of the appointor unless either **17.97** the child has no parent with parental responsibility for him, or at the time of the appointor's death a residence order in his favour was in effect: s 5(7).

Revocation of guardianship

Revocation of guardianship can be achieved in the following ways: **17.98**

(a) by a later appointment of a guardian, unless it is clear that the later appointment is of an
    additional guardian: s 6(1);
(b) by a written, signed, and dated instrument revoking the appointment: s 6(2);

(c) by the destruction of the document in question with the intent of revoking the appointment, except in the case of a will or codicil: s 6(3);

(d) by the revocation of the will or codicil that contains the appointment: s 6(4).

17.99   Where the initial appointment of a guardian was by way of court order then the court retains jurisdiction to terminate the appointment at any time in the following ways: s 6(7):

(a) on the application of anyone with parental responsibility for the child;

(b) on the application of the child himself;

(c) by the court's own motion in the course of any family proceedings if the court considers it should be brought to an end even though no application has been made.

If the appointment is not terminated earlier it will end on the child reaching the age of 18, as will any court order made under s 5(1): see s 91(7) and (8).

Disclaimer of guardianship

17.100   A guardian appointed other than by way of a court order may disclaim his appointment by making an instrument in writing to this effect, provided that he does so within a reasonable time of first knowing that the appointment has taken effect: s 6(5) and (6).

E   SPECIAL GUARDIANSHIP ORDERS

17.101   Section 115, ACA 2002 has inserted ss 14A–14D into the CA 1989 to introduce special guardianship orders. These orders will be particularly suitable for cases concerning older children where, although adoption might otherwise be in the best interests of the child, it is important that he keeps in touch with his natural parents and that the parents are not deprived of parental responsibility.

17.102   The following categories of people may apply for a special guardianship order:

(a) any guardian of the child;

(b) anyone else who has a residence order for the child;

(c) anyone who has the consent of all those who hold residence orders for the child;

(d) a local authority foster parent with whom the child has lived for one year preceding the application;

(e) anyone who comes within the categories set out in s 10(5)(b) or (c), CA 1989 (see Chapter 18, para 18.35);

(f) anyone else with the local authority's consent, if the child is the subject of a care order.

17.103   Applicants for a special guardianship order must give three months' notice of their intention to apply and must be vetted by the local authority. The local authority has a duty to compile a report dealing with the suitability of the applicant for the use of the court considering the order: s 14A(8), CA 1989. Once appointed, the special guardian can exercise parental responsibility to the exclusion of all others who have parental responsibility apart from other special guardians (subject to any order of the court to the contrary): s 14C(1)(b). The natural parents will retain their parental responsibility but it will be curtailed severely as a result of the order. The court will have power to vary or discharge a special guardianship order on application by defined categories of applicants: s 14D(1). The first reported special guardianship order was made in the case of *A Local Authority* v *Y Z and Others* [2006] 2 FLR 41. The judge approved special guardianship orders in respect of three children who had been placed with members of their extended family. The two older children had lived with an aunt and uncle for two years and the youngest child, aged 5, had lived with another aunt and her partner for almost two years. The court held that the children required the permanence, stability, and security that special guardianship provided. It was preferable to the alternatives available under the CA 1989 and adoption was neither sought nor was desirable.

F ORDERS IN FAMILY PROCEEDINGS

Introduction

The needs and circumstances of children are constantly changing and therefore it is right **17.104** that the orders that regulate the arrangements for their upbringing are sufficiently flexible to reflect those changes as and when it becomes necessary.

The orders available under the CA 1989 encourage the move away from the tendency of par- **17.105** ents to feel that they have *rights over* children towards an acknowledgement by them of their *responsibilities for* their children. The principle of 'parental responsibility' under the CA 1989 has already been discussed at paras 17.63 ff.

An important aim of the CA 1989 is to ensure that wherever possible orders relating to the **17.106** upbringing of children can be made in the course of existing proceedings in respect of the same family, so as to avoid the necessity for several sets of proceedings to run concurrently. For example, where the occupation of the matrimonial home is in dispute the needs of the children are frequently an important factor in determining the relief sought. The court has wide powers to regulate the occupation of the home in conjunction with residence and contact orders in order to stabilize the home situation as swiftly as possible.

The court is able to make a s 8 order in the course of any 'family proceedings'. For the purposes **17.107** of the CA 1989 'family proceedings' are defined in s 8(3) and (4) as any proceedings under:

(a) the inherent jurisdiction of the High Court in relation to children;
(b) Parts I, II, and IV, CA 1989;
(c) the MCA 1973;
(d) the Adoption Act 1976;
(e) the Domestic Proceedings and Magistrates' Courts Act 1978;
(f) Part III, Matrimonial and Family Proceedings Act 1984;
(g) proceedings under FLA 1996;
(h) Schedule 5 to the Civil Partnership Act 2004;
(i) Schedule 6 to the Civil Partnership Act 2004;
(j) the ACA 2002;
(k) sections 11 and 12 of the Crime and Disorder Act 1998.

Jurisdiction: the Family Law Act 1986 and Brussels IIR

17.108 Council Regulation (EC) No 2201/2003 (known as 'Brussels IIR') applies to civil matters relating to (a) divorce, legal separation, or marriage annulment and (b) parental responsibility. The scope of the term 'parental responsibility' is wide and includes most public law and private law children proceedings, but not proceedings relating to adoption or maintenance of the child.

17.109 The central concept used to found jurisdiction under Brussels IIR is the child's habitual residence. Unless the facts are absolutely clear and/or undisputed, establishing 'habitual residence' in the context of Art 8 of Brussels IIR will involve a fact-based enquiry into the child's degree of integration into a social and family environment within the Member State in question. For the purposes of Brussels IIR a child can have only one habitual residence.

17.110 Section 2(1), FLA 1986 provides that a court in England and Wales cannot make a s 8 order (other than an order varying or discharging such an order) unless either:

(a)   the court has jurisdiction under Brussels IIR; or

(b)   Brussels IIR does not apply, but the question of making the order arises in matrimonial or civil partnership proceedings in England and Wales, which are continuing (proceedings are treated as continuing until the child's 18th birthday, unless they are dismissed);

(c)   Brussels IIR does not apply and on the relevant date the child is either habitually resident in England and Wales or present in England and Wales, provided that the child is not habitually resident in another part of the United Kingdom and there are not continuing matrimonial or civil partnership proceedings in another part of the United Kingdom.

17.111 The jurisdiction to make an order under the court's inherent jurisdiction is a little wider. Jurisdiction is founded on the same basis as the jurisdiction to make a s 8 order, save that the court has an additional power to make orders based purely on the child's physical presence where Brussels IIR does not apply and the court is satisfied that the immediate exercise of its powers is necessary for the child's protection: s 2(3), Family Law Act 1986 ('FLA 1986').

Example 1 Emma and Lucy are in a civil partnership. They have one child, Joshua. The family lived in France until two months ago, when the parents separated and Emma and Joshua returned to London. Emma applies in England for a residence order. Lucy argues that Joshua is still habitually resident in France. The court will have to carry out an enquiry into the facts, as required by Brussels IIR, to determine whether Joshua is habitually resident in London and whether the English court can assume jurisdiction.

Example 2 Michael has always lived in the United States with his mother, Alison. His parents separated two years ago and his father, Harry, moved to England; Harry stays with him each school holiday. Harry petitioned for divorce in England and the divorce proceedings are continuing. Michael comes to stay with his father for the summer and an issue arises about whether he should have medical treatment before he returns. The court does not have jurisdiction under Brussels IIR because Michael is not habitually resident in England and Wales. However, the court may assume jurisdiction based either on the continuing divorce proceedings or on Michael's physical presence within the jurisdiction.

G   SECTION 8 ORDERS

Section 8, CA 1989 creates the following orders: **17.112**

(a) A residence order: this settles the arrangements to be made as to the person with whom a child is to live.
(b) A contact order: this requires the person with whom a child lives to allow the child to visit or stay with the person named in the order, or for that person and the child to otherwise have contact with each other.
(c) A prohibited steps order: this orders that no step which could be taken by a parent in meeting his parental responsibility for a child, and which is of a type specified in the order, shall be taken by any person without the consent of the court.
(d) A specific issue order: this gives directions for the determination of a specific question which has arisen, or which may arise, in connection with any aspect of parental responsibility for a child.

Any reference to 'a s 8 order' means any of the above orders and any order varying or discharging such an order: s 8(2).

When a court is hearing *contested* proceedings in relation to a s 8 order it *must* have regard to   **17.113**
the following:

(a) the principle that the child's welfare is the paramount consideration: s 1(1);
(b) the statutory checklist of factors ('the welfare checklist'): s 1(3);
(c) the principle that it must not make any order unless it considers that doing so would be better for the child than making no order at all: s 1(5).

See para 17.11 above for a detailed discussion of these principles.

Who can apply for s 8 orders?

The court can make s 8 orders in two ways: **17.114**

(a) in the course of existing family proceedings: s 10(1); 'family proceedings' are defined in s 8(3). Note: they include care proceedings and adoption proceedings;
(b) as a result of a specific self-contained application to the court for a s 8 order: s 10(2).

In each case certain persons are 'entitled to apply' for s 8 orders as of right whilst anyone else may only do so with leave of the court.

Persons 'entitled to apply' for s 8 orders

There is a distinction between those entitled to apply: **17.115**

(a) for a residence or contact order; and
(b) for a specific issue or prohibited steps order.

The class of persons entitled to apply for the orders in point (a) is wider than the class of those who are entitled to apply for the orders in point (b).

17.116   The following are the class of persons who can apply for *any* s 8 order:

(a) any parent, guardian, or special guardian of the child: s 10(4)(a);

(b) any person who by virtue of s 4A has parental responsibility for the child: s 10(4)(aa);

(c) any person in whose favour a residence order is in force with respect to the child: s 10(4)(b).

17.117   The persons who are entitled to apply to the court for a residence or contact order are *extended* by s 10(5) and (5A) to include:

(a) any party to the marriage (whether or not subsisting) in relation to whom a child is a child of the family (as defined in s 105(1));

(b) any civil partner in a civil partnership (whether or not subsisting) in relation to whom the child is a child of the family: s 10(5)(aa);

(c) any person with whom the child has lived for a period of at least three years (as defined in s 10(10)): s 10(5)(b);

(d) any person who (s 10(5)(c):

(i)   in any case where a residence order is in force with respect to the child, has the consent of each of the persons in whose favour the order was made;

(ii) in any case where the child is in the care of the local authority, has the consent of that authority; or

(iii) in any other case, has the consent of each of those (if any) who have parental responsibility for the child;

(e) a local authority foster parent, or a relative of the child, is entitled to apply for a residence order with respect to a child if the child has lived with him for a period of at least one year immediately preceding the application: s 10(5A) and (5B);

(f) if a special guardianship order is in force with respect to a child, an application for a residence order may only be made with leave: s 10(7A).

Note that this list is *in addition* to those persons set out in s 10(4), and that it may be further extended by rules of court (s 10(7)).

Obtaining leave of the court

17.118   Any person who does not fall within the categories set out in para 17.117 above must apply to the court for leave to make a s 8 application. If the child himself applies for leave then the court may grant leave only if it is satisfied that the child has sufficient understanding to make the proposed application: s 10(8). If the person applying for leave is someone other than the child then the court must consider the specific matters set out in s 10(9) when making its decision, that is to say:

(a) the nature of the proposed application for the s 8 order;

(b) the applicant's connection with the child;

(c) any risk there might be of that proposed application disrupting the child's life to such an extent that he would be harmed by it; and

(d) where the child is being looked after by a local authority:

(i)   the authority's plans for the child's future; and

(ii) the wishes and feelings of the child's parents.

17.119   In *Re A and W (Minors) (Residence Order: Leave to Apply)* [1992] 2 FLR 154, it was held that, since on an application for leave to apply for a residence order no question with regard to the child's upbringing is determined, and since s 10(9) stipulates particular matters to which the court must have regard in determining such an application, s 1(1) does not apply. However, the court may take into account additional factors where they are relevant, including the wishes of the child: *Re A (A Minor) (Residence Order: Leave to Apply)* [1993] 1 FLR 425. The court must take into account all the circumstances of the case, including the likely outcome of the substantive hearing if the application for leave is granted: *Re M (Care: Contact: Grandmother's Application)* [1995] 2 FLR 86. However, it is essential that the court gives proper weight to the statutory criteria and does not place too great an emphasis on the merits of the substantive application: *Re J (Leave to Issue Application for Residence Order)* [2003] 1 FLR 114.

In *Re F and R (Section 8: Grandparent's Application)* [1995] 1 FLR 57, leave was granted on **17.120** appeal because the grandparent visited the children and already had close contact with them. However, there is no presumption in favour of grandparents obtaining leave. Leave will not be granted where, because of the level of disharmony between the applicant and the child's parents, the substantive application is likely to fail; nor will leave be granted if it would be harmful to the child because of the disruption which would be caused: *Re A (A Minor) (Section 8 Order: Grandparent's Application)* [1995] 2 FLR 153.

In exceptional circumstances the court will entertain an oral application for leave, particu- **17.121** larly where the circumstances dictate that the application be made on an *ex parte* basis: *Re O (Minors) (Leave to Seek Residence Orders)* [1994] 1 FLR 172.

Factors in request for leave by child Where the person applying for leave is the child, **17.122** the factors in s 10(9) do not specifically apply and there is no equivalent checklist which applies instead. Section 10(8) requires the court to be satisfied that the child has 'sufficient understanding' to make the application. However, even if that test is satisfied the court still has a discretion as to whether to allow the application, and the child's welfare is not para-. mount: *M v Warwickshire County Council* [2008] 1 FLR 1093. The court should approach such applications with caution, particularly in private law cases where there is a risk of the child being drawn into a conflict between warring parents, and particularly where the child is also seeking to act without a children's guardian: *Re N (Contact: Minor Seeking Leave to Defend and Removal of Guardian)* [2003] 1 FLR 652. Applications are covered by r 12.12, FPR 2010.

The meaning of 'sufficient understanding' has been considered by the courts in a number of **17.123** different contexts. In *Re S (A Minor) (Independent Representation)* (paras 17.23 and 17.25 above), an 11-year-old boy was held not to have sufficient understanding to participate as a party in a bitter and protracted dispute between his parents as to with which of them he should live. At p 444H, Sir Thomas Bingham said:

> Different children have differing levels of understanding at the same age. An understanding is not absolute. It has to be assessed relatively to the issues in the proceedings. Where any sound judgement on these issues calls for insight and imagination which only maturity and experience can bring, both the court and the solicitor will be slow to conclude that the child's understanding is sufficient.

Foster parents

Section 9(3), CA 1989 restricts a local authority foster parent from applying for leave to apply **17.124** for s 8 orders unless:

(a) he has the consent without the consent of the local authority;

(b) he is a relative of the child; or

(c) the child has lived with him for at least one year preceding the application.

17.125 If the foster parent of a child in care has the consent of the local authority, or has cared for the child for one year, he may apply for a residence or contact order without first applying for leave (s 10(5)(c)). However, leave will be required if he wishes to apply for a specific issue or prohibited steps order.

Duration of s 8 orders

17.126 The main provisions which govern the duration of s 8 orders are as follows:

(a) As a general rule s 8 orders other than residence orders will continue unless discharged by the court or otherwise, until the child reaches the age of 16: s 91(10).

(b) The court must not make a contact order, specific issue order, or prohibited steps order which is to have effect for a period which will end after the child has reached 16, unless it is satisfied that the circumstances of the case are exceptional: s 9(6).

(c) A residence order will continue until the child reaches the age of 18, unless before then it is varied or discharged: s 91(11).

(d) The court must not make a s 8 order, other than one varying or discharging a s 8 order, once the child has reached 16, unless it is satisfied that there are exceptional circumstances: s 9(7).

(e) If an order is extended beyond, or made after, the child reached 16, then it comes to an end when he reaches 18: s 91(11).

(f) The making of a care order will discharge all current s 8 orders (s 91(2)), as will the making of certain orders in adoption proceedings.

H   RESIDENCE ORDERS

17.127 Residence orders settle the arrangements to be made as to the person or persons with whom the child lives. They aim to cater for a wider range of situations than a custody order was able to do.

17.128 A residence order does not have any effect on the parental responsibility of either parent; it is intended to settle the child's living arrangements and no more.

17.129 The Court of Appeal has confirmed in *Re E (Residence: Imposition of Conditions)* [1997] 2 FLR 638 that it is not permissible to attach to a residence order a condition that the mother live with the child at a specified address. If the mother was considered to be suitable and a residence order was made in her favour, attaching such a condition was an unjustified interference with her right to choose where to live in the United Kingdom. However, there may be circumstances which justify preventing a residential parent from moving to a different part of the United Kingdom: *Re S (A Child) (Residence Order: Condition) (No 2)* [2003] 1 FCR 138—where the mother was prevented from moving with her 9-year-old Down's syndrome child from London to Cornwall; *Re H (Children) (Residence Order: Condition)* [2001] 2 FLR 1277, where the father was prevented from moving with the children from England to Northern

Ireland; *B v B (Residence: Condition Limiting Geographical Area)* [2004] 2 FLR 979, where the court attached to the mother's residence order a condition that she reside in a defined area of southern England as she had no good reasons for her proposed move to Newcastle other than to be distanced further from the father.

Shared and joint residence orders

A residence order can be made in favour of more than one person. Where those persons are **17.130** living together, the order is known as a 'joint' residence order. Where they are not living together then the order may specify the periods to be spent in each household (s 11(4)); these are commonly known as 'shared' residence orders.

The history of the cases on shared residence since the CA 1989 came into force demonstrates **17.131** a significant shift in judicial approach.

When shared residence orders first became available, courts made them relatively rarely, since **17.132** it was thought that giving a child two competing homes would often lead to confusion and stress. However, in *D v D (Shared Residence Orders)* [2001] 1 FLR 495, the Court of Appeal took a more relaxed approach to shared residence orders and endorsed a move away from any 'exceptional circumstances' requirement. Where the basic arrangements for the children are settled, the existence of a continuing dispute about the detail does not prevent the making of a shared order. The Court of Appeal questioned whether it is necessary to demonstrate a positive benefit, as long as the order can be shown to be in the child's interests. This approach was continued in the case of *Re F (Shared Residence)* [2003] 2 FLR 397, in which the Court of Appeal held that the fact that the parents' homes might be separated by a considerable distance did not preclude a shared residence order. The children would be based at their father's home during most school half terms and holidays and based with their mother during term time. In *Re G (Leave to Remove)* [2008] 1 FLR 1587 a shared residence order was made in respect of children who were to divide their time between their parents' homes in two different countries after their mother's relocation to Germany. In *A v A (Shared Residence)* [2004] 1 FLR 1195, Wall J held that the fact that the parents were incapable of working in harmony was no bar to making a shared residence order; in fact, it made the order more appropriate because it reinforced the message that the parents were equal in the eyes of the law and had equal duties and responsibilities. The court will in the appropriate case use a shared residence order to convey the message that 'neither parent is in control and that the court expects parents to cooperate with each other for the benefit of their children': *Re P (Shared Residence Order)* [2006] 2 FLR 347.

A shared residence order should only be made if there is an element of 'residence'. In *Re A* **17.133** *(Children) (Shared Residence)* [2002] 1 FCR 177 a shared residence order had been made at first instance in order to recognize the equal status of each parent. On appeal, the Court of Appeal held that where the child was not only not going to reside with the other parent, but was refusing even to visit her, a residence order was not appropriate.

Shared residence to confer parental responsibility

It is now well established that a limited use of a shared residence order is to confer paren- **17.134** tal responsibility on a person who would not otherwise have it. In the case of *Re H (Shared*

Residence: Parental Responsibility) [1995] 2 FLR 883, a shared residence order was made principally to give parental responsibility to the (separated) stepfather of a child whom the stepfather had treated as a child of the family and the court felt that it was of great therapeutic importance for the child to have this formal relationship with his stepfather. *In Re G (Children)* [2006] 2 FLR 629, the House of Lords upheld a shared residence order in respect of the children of former partners of the same sex, partly in order to confer parental responsibility and as a safeguard against the marginalization by the biological mother of her former partner. See also *Re A (Joint Residence/Parental Responsibility)* [2008] 2 FLR 1593 where a shared residence order was used to give parental responsibility to the mother's former partner who had believed, until the separation, that he was the child's father.

Residence orders made without notice

17.135   A residence order made without notice first having been given to the other side should be for a limited period and should only be made in exceptional circumstances where it is necessary for the protection of the child, for example in a 'snatch' situation or a child abduction. There are two competing considerations: the children's long-term welfare and their short-term protection. In ordinary circumstances the court will be extremely reluctant to disturb the status quo pending a full investigation into a residence dispute. However, there may be those comparatively rare cases in which it is more important for the children to stay temporarily with the parent who has removed them, rather than that they should be returned to the parent with whom they had lived previously, pending the outcome of investigations into the circumstances of the removal. In most cases, however, where the order is not in fact intended to settle the children's living arrangements for anything but the very short term, the court is more likely to make a prohibited steps order preventing the children from being removed from the care of the applicant pending a hearing on notice to the other party.

17.136   See *Re P (A Minor) (Ex Parte Interim Residence Order)* [1993] 1 FLR 915 for an example of a case in which the Court of Appeal set aside a without notice interim residence order because the judge should have adjourned the matter to hear both sides. Where a party who was absent when a without notice order was made wishes to challenge the order, the appropriate course is for him to apply to the judge who made it to vary or rescind the order. This should be done on short notice unless the case is wholly exceptional: *Re P (A Minor) (Ex Parte Interim Residence Order)* (above).

Restriction on change of name

17.137   Section 13(1), CA 1989 states that where a residence order is in force with respect to a child then no person may cause the child to be known by a new surname without first obtaining either:

(a)   the written consent of every person with parental responsibility for the child; or

(b)   the leave of the court.

17.138   If a person with a residence order does wish to change the child's surname then he should first contact the other persons who have parental responsibility to see if they will consent in writing to the change. If so, the change of name can go ahead as planned. If no consent is forthcoming then the court's leave will be necessary. An application for leave should be made using the appropriate prescribed form. In a case where a residence order is in force, an application to change a child's name is a free-standing application under s 13, rather than one for a specific issue order under s 8.

Given the principle of non-intervention in s 1(5), there will be many occasions when a residence order is not made and the provisions of s 13(1) will not apply. In these circumstances the application should be made under s 8. Whether the application will be for a specific issue order or a prohibited steps order will depend on the circumstances. An application under s 13 is not appropriate in a case where no residence order is in force. **17.139**

In *Dawson* v *Wearmouth* [1999] 1 FLR 1167 the House of Lords reviewed the principles to be applied to a change of name application. The proper course in all cases in which a change of name is contemplated is: **17.140**

(a) Consult anyone with parental responsibility, whether or not there is a residence order in force.
(b) Consult the unmarried father without parental responsibility. It is not certain the extent to which the consent of an unmarried father without parental responsibility is material to a change of name. Section 13 only requires the consent of those with parental responsibility and so it is possible to infer that there is no need to consult an unmarried father without parental responsibility. However, if the unmarried father finds out about the change of name and disagrees with it, he could apply to the court for a specific issue order under s 8. Therefore, it is probably sensible to consult the unmarried father even if he has no parental responsibility for the child: see *Re C (Change of Surname)* [1998] 2 FLR 656.
(c) If consent is obtained from the relevant people, ensure that it is put in writing.
(d) If the change of name is disputed, the matter must be referred to the court for determination as follows:
   (i) if there is a residence order in force, under s 13;
   (ii) if there is no residence order in force, under s 8.

Butler-Sloss LJ laid down further guidelines for cases concerning the change of a child's name in *Re W, Re A, Re B (Change of Name)* [1999] 2 FLR 930 with the warning that the guidelines do not purport to be exhaustive. Each case must be decided on its own facts with the welfare of the child the paramount consideration and all the relevant factors weighed in the balance by the court at the time of the hearing. The summary (at p 933F) is as follows: **17.141**

(a) If parents are married, they both have the power and the duty to register their child's names.
(b) If they are not married, the mother has the sole duty and power to do so.
(c) After registration of the child's names, the grant of a residence order obliges any person wishing to change the surname to obtain the leave of the court or the written consent of all those who have parental responsibility.
(d) In the absence of a residence order, the person wishing to change the surname from the registered name ought to obtain the relevant written consent or the leave of the court by making an application for a specific issue order.
(e) On any application, the welfare of the child is paramount and the judge must have regard to the s 1(3) criteria.

(f)   Among the factors to which the court should have regard is the registered surname of the child and the reasons for the registration, for instance recognition of the biological link with the child's father. Registration is always a relevant and an important consideration but it is not in itself decisive. The weight to be given to it by the court will depend upon the other relevant factors or valid countervailing reasons which may tip the balance the other way.

(g)   The relevant considerations should include factors which may arise in the future as well as the present situation.

(h)   Reasons given for changing or seeking to change a child's name based on the fact that the child's name is or is not the same as the parent making the application do not generally carry much weight.

(i)   The reasons for an earlier unilateral decision to change a child's name may be relevant.

(j)   Any changes of circumstances of the child since the original registration may be relevant.

(k)   In the case of a child whose parents were married to each other, the fact of the marriage is important and there would have to be strong reasons to change the name from the father's surname if the child was so registered.

(l)   Where the child's parents were not married to each other, the mother has control over registration. Consequently, on an application to change the surname of the child, the degree of commitment of the father to the child, the quality of contact, if it occurs, between father and child, the existence or absence of parental responsibility are all relevant factors to take into account.

Use of both parents' surnames

17.142   It may be appropriate in some cases in which there is a dispute about which surname the child is to be known by for both parents' surnames to be used: *Re R (Surname: Using Both Parents')* [2001] 2 FLR 1358. In *Re R* the child of unmarried parents had been registered under the father's name, but after they separated the mother used the name of her new husband (the child's stepfather) instead. It was agreed that the mother could move to Spain with her new husband, but the Court of Appeal held that the mother must retain the father's surname for the child. In Spain it is the custom to have one surname from the father and one from the mother and the Court of Appeal hoped that the mother would adopt this practice in order to ease the child's adjustment to a life in that culture. Hale LJ said (at p 1363) 'parents and courts should be much more prepared to contemplate the use of both surnames in an appropriate case, because that is to recognise the importance of both parents'.

Change of first name

17.143   The law is more relaxed in relation to the use of first names for children than for surnames. In *Re H (A Child)* [2002] 1 FLR 973 the parents separated before the child was born and had no contact with each other. On the child's birth the father registered the birth with his choice of first names. The mother subsequently registered the birth in her choice of names, but her later registration was cancelled. The mother sought a declaration that she could use her own choice of first names for the child. It was held that no order of the court could prevent the mother from using the first name of her choice within the home. Furthermore, she was entitled to use her choice of first name in any dealings with external authorities, provided that she always recognized that the child had an immutable series of names by statutory registration.

Restriction on removal from the jurisdiction

Section 13(1), CA 1989 also dictates that where a residence order is in force with respect to a **17.144** child then no person may remove him from the United Kingdom without either:

(a) the written consent of every person with parental responsibility for the child; or
(b) the leave of the court.

However, the person with the residence order is permitted to remove the child from the jurisdiction for a period of less than one month without having to comply with the two requirements set out above. The idea is to allow for short holiday trips. However, there is no restriction on the number of trips that may be taken.

Furthermore, the court can give a general direction at the time it makes the residence order to **17.145** allow the removal of the child from the jurisdiction generally or for specified purposes. This can be in favour of the person with the residence order or any other person. This can be very useful in that it avoids repeated minor applications to the court. For instance, where the non-residential parent (say, the father) lives abroad and it is envisaged that the child will visit him regularly twice each year the court can make a direction that the father have leave to remove the child from the jurisdiction twice each year.

Permission to remove permanently from the jurisdiction

If it is proposed that the children should emigrate permanently but the other persons with **17.146** parental responsibility refuse to consent then the permission of the court must be sought. In considering whether to give leave to take a child out of the jurisdiction permanently, the welfare of the child is the paramount consideration. The leading case is *Payne* v *Payne* [2001] 1 FLR 1052, in which the Court of Appeal laid down guidelines in relation to such applications:

(a) the welfare of the child is paramount;
(b) there is no presumption created by s 13(1)(b) in favour of the applicant parent;
(c) the reasonable proposals of the parent with a residence order wishing to live abroad carry great weight;
(d) consequently, the proposals have to be scrutinized with care and the court needs to be satisfied that there is a genuine motivation for the move and not the intention to bring contact between the child and the other parent to an end;
(e) the effect on the applicant parent and the new family of the child of a refusal of leave is very important;
(f) the effect on the child of the denial of contact with the other parent, and in some cases his family, is very important;
(g) the opportunity for continuing contact between the child and the parent left behind may be very significant.

The Court of Appeal emphasized that the implementation of the HRA 1998 has not affected **17.147** the principles the courts should apply in dealing with these difficult issues. For two cases in which permission was given to remove children permanently from the jurisdiction, see *L* v *L (Leave to Remove Children from Jurisdiction: Effect on Children)* [2003] 1 FLR 900 and *Re C (Permission to Remove from Jurisdiction)* [2003] 1 FLR 1066. However, where removal from the jurisdiction will cause a significant loss to the child in relation to emotional and educational issues leave may be refused (*Re Y (Leave to Remove from Jurisdiction)* [2004] 2 FLR 330—where the child had been brought up to be bilingual in Welsh and English and the parents had shared his care since separation, the court refused the mother's application for leave to remove him from Wales to the United States).

Residence orders and parental responsibility

17.148 The granting of a residence order in favour of anyone automatically gives them parental responsibility for the child: s 12(2). Where a father who does not have parental responsibility applies for a residence order and the court grants one in his favour, then the court must make an order under s 4 giving the father parental responsibility: s 12(1). The s 4 order can only be ended by an order of the court, and must not be revoked while the residence order is still in effect: ss 12(4) and 4(3). However, s 12(3) prevents those with residence orders who are not parents or guardians from giving consent to adoption, freeing for adoption, and appointing a guardian for the child.

Restriction on local authorities applying for residence orders

17.149 A local authority may not apply for a residence order or have one made in its favour: s 9(2). However, a residence order may be made in favour of any child, even one subject to a care order (s 9(1)), although in such a case the residence order will have the effect of discharging the care order (s 91(1)).

Enforcement of residence orders

17.150 The committal of a parent to prison for failure to comply with a s 8 order is likely to be harmful to the child and to the future relationship of the child with the parent who applied for committal. Therefore, although committal may be available as a remedy where a s 8 order is injunctive (ie, where it requires a person to do, within a specified time, or to abstain from doing, an act) it should be a remedy of last resort. There are other methods which should be tried first.

17.151 Section 14, CA 1989, provides that if a person is in breach of the arrangements settled by a residence order (whether it be the person in whose favour the order has been made or some other person who is in breach), then the person with the residence order can enforce it under s 63(3), Magistrates' Courts Act 1980, as if it were an order requiring the other person to produce the child to him. In order to enforce it he must first serve a copy of the residence order on the other person. This remedy does not prevent him from pursuing any other remedy that may be open to him.

17.152 Another way in which a residence (or indeed a contact) order may be enforced is by using s 34, FLA 1986. The object of s 34, FLA 1986 is to give effect to the decision of the court that a child should be given up into the care of a person in accordance with the residence order (or that a child be given up to a person for a period of contact). The effect of s 34 is that 'the court may make an order authorising an officer of the court or a constable to take charge of the child and deliver him to the person concerned'.

Discharge of residence orders

(a) A residence order will end upon the child in question attaining the age of 18: s 91(11). **17.153**

(b) If a residence order is made in favour of parents, each of whom have parental responsibility for the child, it will cease to have effect if they live together for a continuous period of more than six months: s 11(5).

(c) If a care order is made in respect of a child, then any residence order (together with any other s 8 orders) will be discharged automatically: s 91(2). Conversely, if a child in care is made the subject of a residence order then the care order will be discharged automatically: s 91(1).

I CONTACT ORDERS

Contact orders require the person with whom the child is living to allow the child to visit or **17.154** stay with the person named in the order, or for that person and the child otherwise to have contact with each other. Where the parties are unable to agree over the degree of contact which the non-residential parent should have with the child either party may ask the court to determine the contact arrangements. This is called making an application for 'defined contact'. Normally applications are for definition of regular contact visits but, even where the normal contact visits are working satisfactorily, the court can be asked to resolve a particular issue over contact (eg whether there should be contact on Christmas Day).

Maintaining the relationship through contact

It is an important principle of case law that contact should not be refused between parent **17.155** and child unless absolutely necessary in the child's interests: see *Re B (Minors: Access)* [1992] 1 FLR 140 and *Re H (Minors: Access)* [1992] 1 FLR 148. *In Re O (A Child) (Contact: Withdrawal of Application)* [2004] 1 FLR 1258, Wall J said:

> Unless there are cogent reasons against it, the children of separated parents are entitled to know and have the love and society of both their parents. In particular the courts recognise the vital importance of the role of non-resident fathers in the lives of their children, and only make orders terminating contact when there is no alternative.

Contact and human rights

The denial of contact between parent and child can amount to a breach of the parent's right **17.156** to respect for family life as guaranteed by Art 8, ECHR: *Hokkanen v Finland* (1995) 19 EHRR 139. Under the ECHR, the parent's right to contact with his child is not an absolute right, but the public authorities (which includes the court) are under a duty to take all necessary steps to facilitate reunion as can be taken in the circumstances.

There has been a series of cases in which fathers have complained that the refusal of **17.157** the court to grant them contact with their children constitutes a breach of their right to family life. These complaints were upheld in the cases of *Elsholz v Germany* [2000] 2 FLR 486,

Ciliz v *The Netherlands* [2000] 2 FLR 469, *Elsholz* v *Italy* [2000] Fam Law 680. However, the father's complaint was rejected in *Glaser* v *UK* [2001] 1 FLR 153. In *S and G* v *Italy* [2000] 2 FLR 771 a mother's complaint that the authorities had prevented her from having contact with her children was upheld as constituting a breach of Art 8. In *Bove* v *Italy* [2005] Fam Law 752, the failure of the court to enforce the father's access rights had infringed Art 8. The key question to be asked is whether the national authority has taken all steps that are reasonable in the circumstances (*Zawadkaw* v *Poland* [2005] 2 FLR 897).

17.158   In public law childcare cases the obligation on the authorities to promote reunification between parents and children is not absolute. The authorities must do their utmost to facilitate reunification but the rights of all parties concerned must be considered and the best interests of the child must be taken into account (*Hokkanen* v *Finland* [1996] 1 FLR 289; *KA* v *Finland* [2003] 1 FLR 696). In *Re F (Care Proceedings: Contact)* [2000] Fam Law 708, litigants were warned that where care orders have been made under s 31, together with contact orders under s 34(4) authorizing the local authority to terminate contact with the parents of the child concerned, it would be disappointing if the ECHR were to be routinely used as a make-weight ground of appeal, or if there were in every case to be extensive citation of authorities from the European Court of Human Rights.

Parent's hostility to contact

17.159   In *Re H (A Child) (Contact: Mother's Opposition)* [2001] 1 FCR 59 the court held that where a parent objects to contact, it should first evaluate whether that opposition is with or without objective foundation. Where it is without objective foundation the court should not give up the prospect of achieving contact at too early a stage. Rather than use its coercive powers, the court should work with local agencies for counselling and mediation to achieve contact where possible.

17.160   A parent's hostility to contact is itself likely to put the child at risk of harm, either because the level of conflict is extreme or because the child himself takes on the negative attitudes of the resident parent, or both. In *Re M (Contact: Welfare Test)* [1995] 1 FLR 274 it was held that it is helpful for the court to consider whether in the particular case, the fundamental emotional need of every child to have an enduring relationship with both parents is outweighed by the depth of harm which the child will be at risk of suffering if a contact order is made.

17.161   Where the resident parent's hostility is so extreme that it has instilled in the child a 'false and distorted' belief system, the court may consider that the interim threshold for a care order has been met and use its powers under ss 37 and 38 to remove the child to a foster placement or to change residence: *Re M (Intractable Contact Dispute: Interim Care Order)* [2003] 2 FLR 636.

17.162   As a last resort, the court will consider transferring residence to the other parent if this is the only way that the child can maintain a relationship with both parents. In *Re G (Children)* [2006] 2 FLR 629 Baroness Hale commented that these orders were becoming more common. However, the court should always remember that the child's welfare is paramount and any order made must follow this principle and not be designed to punish the resident parent. Such orders may be enforced using the 'stepping stone' of a foster placement or, exceptionally, by use of the Tipstaff: *Re S (A Child)* [2010] EWCA Civ 219.

Domestic violence

Domestic violence in itself involves a significant failure in parenting. Where there has been **17.163** serious domestic violence, a parent may be so traumatized by the effect of the other's behaviour that the distress caused by the prospect of contact may mean that the child's welfare would be likely to suffer as a result of contact taking place. The leading case is *Re L; Re V; Re M; Re H* [2000] 2 FLR 865, in which the Court of Appeal considered four appeals raising the issue of the impact of domestic violence/abuse on contact decisions:

(a) Courts need a heightened awareness of the existence and consequences on children of exposure to inter-parental violence.
(b) Allegations of violence made in the course of a contact application must be adjudicated upon and determined. (Note that where a court holds a preliminary hearing focusing on the issue of domestic violence, the final hearing must be held before the same Bench as the case is, effectively, part-heard: *M v A (Contact: Domestic Violence)* [2002] 2 FLR 921.)
(c) There is no prima facie barrier of no contact if violence is proved.
(d) In assessing the impact of past violence on the contact issue, the ability of the violent party to recognize his past conduct, to be aware of the need to change, and to make a genuine effort to do so are likely to be important considerations.
(e) When making an interim order, before adjudication on factual allegations, the court should ensure that the safety of the child and the residential parent is secured before and after any contact occasion.

Even in cases where the residential parent has a genuine and intense phobia of the other **17.164** parent there may still be justification for ordering indirect contact instead: *Re L (Contact: Genuine Fear)* [2002] 1 FLR 621; *Re S (Violent Parent: Indirect Contact)* [2000] 1 FLR 481. For a case in which the mother's genuine fear of the father did justify the termination of contact, see *Re H (Contact Order) (No 2)* [2002] 1 FLR 22. When considering whether to terminate contact between a parent and child, the judge has to weigh more than the child's happiness in the balance; he also has to ensure that the child's needs will be satisfied not only in the present, but also in the medium and the long term, if contact were terminated: *Re J-S (A Child) (Contact: Parental Responsibility)* [2002] 3 FCR 433.

A court considering whether or not to list a fact-finding hearing in a private law case where **17.165** there are allegations of domestic violence must follow FPR 2010, PD12J—Residence and Contact Orders: Domestic Violence and Harm.

Child's objections to contact

Finally, there are also cases in which the child himself may have strong objections to the **17.166** exercise of contact by his natural father, in which case the older the child is the more weight the court will attach to his wishes. In *Re S (Contact: Children's Views)* [2002] 1 FLR 1156, three children with learning difficulties, aged 16, 14, and 12, expressed views about contact which led to the court making no order regarding the elder two children, and a defined contact order in relation to the youngest child. The court held that if young people are to respect the law, the law has to respect them and their wishes, even if it sometimes means young people making mistakes. The judge so worded the preamble to the order as to underline that the court considered contact to be desirable, but to reassure the children that it would not be imposed on them against their will. Rather, the children would be free to agree to have contact with their father and their mother would not discourage this.

Indirect contact

17.167 In certain cases the court may order that a parent be allowed to maintain contact with the children indirectly, by post and/or by way of telephone calls, email, Skype, or other electronic communication (see, eg, *Re O (Contact: Imposition of Conditions)* [1995] 2 FLR 124; *A v L (Contact)* [1998] 1 FLR 361; *Re M (Contact: Family Assistance: McKenzie Friend)* [1999] 1 FLR 75; *Re P (Contact: Indirect Contact)* [1999] 2 FLR 893). However, the court should be careful to define the frequency of such contact in the order and a 'not more than' formula is often useful, for example that the parent be allowed to write to the child not more than four times in each calendar year, or, that the parent be allowed to telephone the child not more than once every two weeks. In *Re M (A Minor) (Contact: Conditions)* [1994] Fam Law 252 it was decided that the court may order the mother to comply with an order for contact by post by reading messages to a child who cannot read provided that the mother agrees, but the court cannot order the mother to read to the child the contents of any letter addressed to the child, since she must be permitted to censor the contents of such letters where appropriate. The judge also held that the court cannot order the mother to write progress reports on the child to the father because it is not within the court's powers in making contact orders to order the parents to have contact with each other. Furthermore, the court does not have power to make injunctive orders dressed up as contact orders (see *D v N (Contact Order: Conditions)* [1997] 2 FLR 797, where the Court of Appeal held that the first instance court had no jurisdiction under s 11(7), CA 1989 to impose conditions in the manner of injunctions in order to protect a parent from molestation by the other parent).

Contact centres

17.168 Where families need a neutral meeting place for contact to take place and are unable to find one, the National Association of Child Contact Centres (NACCC) may be able to help. The NACCC is a loose federation of centres which each operate independently but which subscribe to a common Code of Practice. The NACCC can be contacted at:

> Minerva House
> Spaniel Row
> Nottingham NG1 6EP
> Tel: 0845 4500 280
> <http://www.naccc.org.uk>

17.169 The NACCC has produced a Protocol for the referral of families to Child Contact Centres (revised 2 July 2010.) It provides guidance as to which categories of cases are suitable for this service, and the practical steps to be taken in order to get in touch with an appropriate centre and has suggested wording for court orders requiring the attendance of parties and children at the centre. Practitioners should be aware of the difference between supported contact, offered by contact centres, and supervised contact. Most contact centres will provide a safe place for contact, staffed by volunteers who will provide practical assistance and a 'watchful eye'. If, in fact, a more intensive level of supervision is required (eg because of relevant issues of violence or substance misuse by a parent) then a supported contact centre is unlikely to be appropriate.

Relevance of biological parenthood in contact disputes

The relevance of a blood tie in contact disputes has been explored in *Re C* [1992] 1 FLR 306. **17.170** The applicant for access was not the child's father, although the child had believed him to be her father at one time. The mother had formed a relationship with another man (who was not the child's father either). The recorder refused the application on the basis that in the long term it would be disruptive to the child and contrary to her welfare. The Court of Appeal upheld the decision, rejecting the applicant's claim that because he had lived with the child for a period of time as her father there must be a compelling reason to justify denying him access. The Court of Appeal held that the existence of a blood tie was an important factor because children, as they grow up, are likely to want to get to know their natural parents. Thus, in such a case although the short-term prognosis for contact might indicate that it would not be beneficial the long-term considerations might prevail. These long-term considerations were not present where there was no blood relationship and therefore its absence was a significant factor to be examined when assessing the course most appropriate for the welfare of the child. On the other hand, where two people have agreed jointly to raise a child, and the child views each as his parent (eg where a child is conceived within a marriage but using fertility treatment and donor sperm), the absence of a biological link with one parent is unlikely to carry weight.

The Supreme Court has confirmed in *Re B (A Child)* [2010] 1 FLR 551 that welfare is always **17.171** paramount and 'it is only as a contributor to the child's welfare that parenthood assumes any significance'. There is no question of a 'natural parent presumption'.

What may a person without parental responsibility do to safeguard the welfare of the child while he is in his care?

If the child visits or stays with someone without parental responsibility for him (eg a grand- **17.172** parent) then that person may take such action as is reasonable to safeguard or promote the child's welfare: s 3(5). Any person with parental responsibility may exercise it insofar as this is not incompatible with any order under the CA 1989: s 2(8).

Restrictions on the making of contact orders

(a) The court must not make a contact order in respect of a child who has reached the age of **17.173** 16 unless there are exceptional circumstances: s 9(7).

(b) Contact orders cannot be made in respect of children who are in local authority care by virtue of a care order, and local authorities may not apply for contact orders nor have them made in their favour: s 9(2). However, s 34 does provide a special scheme whereby orders can be made which allow or refuse contact with children in care (see Chapter 20, para 20.75).

(c) A contact order requiring one parent to allow the child to visit the other will lapse automatically if the parents live together for a continuous period of more than six months: s 11(6).

(d) The making of a care order will discharge a contact order (and any other s 8 order): s 91(2).

'No contact' orders

17.174   An order that there is to be no contact between the child and a named person falls within the general concept of contact, and it falls within the definition of 'contact order' in s 8(1) (per Sir Stephen Brown P in *Nottinghamshire County Council v P* [1993] 2 FLR 134 at p 143). Thus, it is not appropriate to apply for a prohibited steps order when in reality the party seeks a 'no contact' order, since to do so is to use a prohibited steps order as a 'back door' method of achieving a contact order in a way which is prohibited by s 9(5)(a).

Enforcement of contact orders

17.175   The 'menu' of options for enforcement of a contact order is as follows:

(a) An order under s 34, FLA 1986 (the same procedure as may be used to enforce a residence order: see para 17.173 above).

(b) Committal for contempt of court if the order is breached.

(c) An enforcement order under s 11J, CA 1989.

(d) An order requiring the person in breach of the order to pay financial compensation: s 11O, CA 1989.

17.176   When a court makes or varies a s 8 contact order it must attach to the order a notice warning of the consequences of failing to comply with the contact order.

Committal

17.177   A contact order may only be enforced by way of committal proceedings if it is specifically defined: *D v D (Access: Contempt: Committal)* [1991] 2 FLR 34. The courts have expressed different views on the appropriateness of committal proceedings as a means of enforcing contact orders. Plainly, any order must be both necessary and proportionate, as it involves an interference with the parent's rights under Art 5, ECHR and (usually) Art 8. Where the parent in breach of the order is caring for young children, the court must evaluate the effect of a committal order on them and on their family life: *B v S (Contempt: Imprisonment of Mother)* [2009] 2 FLR 1005. However, it is not correct to say that a committal order is an order of 'last resort' and therefore the court must of necessity try all other options before committing a contemnor to prison: *A v N (Committal: Refusal of Contact)* [1997] 1 FLR 533; see also *Re S (A Child) (Contact Dispute: Committal)* [2005] 1 FLR 812.

Enforcement under Children Act 1989, s 11J or 11O

17.178   The court has the power, when satisfied beyond reasonable doubt that a person has failed to comply with a contact order without reasonable excuse, to make an enforcement order requiring the person to carry out an unpaid work requirement. Before making the order, the court must be satisfied that the order is necessary to secure compliance with the contact order, and that the likely effect on the person of making the enforcement order is proportionate to the seri-ousness of the breach: s 11L(1). The court is obliged to receive a report (prepared by the Children and Family Court Advisory and Support Service (Cafcass), which will liaise with the National Probation Service) about the likely effect of the enforcement order on the person in breach.

If a breach of a contact order, without reasonable excuse, has caused another person (usually **17.179** the person in whose favour the order was made) financial loss, for example due to a holiday being missed because the child was not available, the court may make an order requiring the person in breach of the order to pay financial compensation for the loss: s 11O(1). The court must take into account the financial circumstances of the person in breach and also the welfare of the child concerned. If an order is made, it is recoverable as a civil debt.

Contact activity directions and conditions

Section 11A, CA 1989 permits the court to make a 'contact activity direction' within proceed- **17.180** ings when it is considering whether to make, vary, or discharge a contact order. Such a direc-tion may only be made at an interim stage in the proceedings. A contact activity direction requires a party to participate in 'an activity that promotes contact with the child concerned'. The activities that may be directed include:

(a) Programmes, classes, and counselling or guidance sessions (eg a 'Parenting Information Programme').
(b) Programmes to address a person's violent behaviour.
(c) Sessions in which information or advice is giving about making or operating contact arrangements, including mediation information sessions.

There is no power to direct a person to undergo any form of medical or psychiatric assessment or treatment, or to take part in mediation.

Section 11C, CA 1989 permits the court to make a 'contact activity condition' at the same **17.181** time as it makes a contact order. The activities that may be included in a contact activity con-dition are the same as those available to the court when making a contact activity direction. The difference is that a contact activity condition may be made at the same time as making a contact order which concludes the proceedings.

In either case, the court must satisfy itself that the activity specified is appropriate and can be **17.182** provided in a location where the party/parties can reasonably be expected to travel. This infor-mation is requested from Cafcass prior to making the direction or condition. The court must also obtain information about the party and the likely effect of the direction or condition on him.

The court may require Cafcass to monitor implementation of a contact order for up to one **17.183** year: s 11H.

J   PROHIBITED STEPS ORDERS

A prohibited steps order directs that no step which could be taken by a parent in meeting **17.184** his parental responsibility for a child, and which is of a type specified in the order, may be taken by a person without the consent of the court. The order can be made either on its own or together with a residence or contact order. It might be used, for example, in a case where no residence order is in force, to restrain one parent from removing the child of the family from the jurisdiction without the consent of the other parent. The following are examples of circumstances in which a prohibited steps order is *not* appropriate:

(a) Where a parent wishes to apply for an order that an abducted child be returned to live with her at home, then she should apply for a residence order (possibly with conditions and directions attached), rather than a specific issue order seeking the return of the child together with a prohibited steps order to prevent further removal: see dicta of Butler-Sloss LJ in *Re W (A Minor) (Residence Order)* [1992] 2 FLR 332.

(b) A prohibited steps order cannot be used to prohibit the parents from contacting each other, since this does not fall within the statutory definition of 'a step which could be taken by a parent in meeting his parental responsibility for a child': *Croydon LBC v A (No 1)* [1992] 2 FLR 341.

(c) A local authority cannot apply for a prohibited steps order to exclude a parent from the family home in circumstances in which he poses a threat to the children of the family, since that is a 'back door' method of achieving a residence order (by regulating who could live in the household) or contact order (by regulating the contact between the father and the children) and local authorities are prohibited from applying for a residence or contact order by the terms of s 9(2): *Nottinghamshire County Council v P* [1993] 2 FLR 134; *Re S (Minors) (Inherent Jurisdiction: Ouster)* [1994] 1 FLR 623. Indeed, in *Nottinghamshire County Council v P* (above), Sir Stephen Brown P expressed doubt as to whether a prohibited steps order could ever be used as an 'ouster' order. This view was confirmed in *Re D (Prohibited Steps Orders)* [1996] 2 FLR 273, where the court overturned an order preventing the father from staying overnight in the matrimonial home, since in this case it operated as an 'ouster' by the 'back door' in circumstances which did not warrant it (but see Chapter 21, para 21.26 for details of the court's new statutory power to include an exclusion requirement in an emergency protection order in certain circumstances).

(d) Where a court wishes to order that a named person shall have 'no contact' with a child then the order falls within the definition of a 'contact' order in s 8(1), and it is not appropriate to make a prohibited steps order preventing contact (*Nottinghamshire County Council v P* (above); *Re H (Prohibited Steps Order)* [1995] 1 FLR 638).

Restrictions on the use of prohibited steps orders

17.185 (a) A prohibited steps order may not be made in respect of children over the age of 16, save in exceptional circumstances: s 9(7).

(b) A prohibited steps order can only relate to an action which is within the power of a parent and does not (unlike wardship) appear to bind the child or give the court control over the decisions which the child is entitled to take for himself.

(c) A prohibited steps order cannot be made in respect of a child in the care of a local authority pursuant to a care order: s 9(1).

(d) A prohibited steps order cannot be used as a 'back door' method of achieving a result which could have been achieved by the making of a residence or contact order: s 9(5)(a).

(e) A prohibited steps order cannot be used in any way which is denied to the High Court by s 100(2) in the exercise of its inherent jurisdiction with respect to children, for example to commit a child to care, to require a local authority to accommodate a child, or to give the local authority power to make decisions about children. The order could not be used to prevent the child's removal from care where there is no care order, but it could be used to prevent someone from visiting the child in a foster home in such circumstances: see ss 100(2) and 9(5)(b).

(f) The making of a care order will discharge a prohibited steps order: s 91(2).

K   SPECIFIC ISSUE ORDERS

Specific issue orders, like prohibited steps orders, are designed to be made either on their **17.186** own or together with a residence or contact order. They enable the court to give directions to determine a specific issue which has arisen, or which may arise, in connection with any aspect of parental responsibility for a child, for example the decision to change the child's surname, choice of schools, religious upbringing, medical treatment. However, note that where a residence order is in force an application to change a child's surname is by way of a free-standing application under s 13 and not by way of a specific issue order: *Dawson* v *Wearmouth* (para 17.140 above); *A* v *Y (Child's Surname)* [1999] 2 FLR 5. For a more detailed discussion of the considerations involved in an application to change a child's surname, see paras 17.137 ff.

Some examples of cases in which specific issue orders were used are as follows: **17.187**

(a) *Re K (Specific Issue Order)* [1999] 2 FLR 280—where the father applied for a specific issue order that the mother tell their child of the father's existence and of his true paternity, but the order was refused since on the facts there were cogent reasons to deny the child's right to know his paternity.

(b) *Re R (A Minor) (Blood Transfusion)* [1993] 2 FLR 757—where the court held that it was appropriate for the local authority to apply for a specific issue order to authorize a blood transfusion to the 10-month-old child of parents who were Jehovah's Witnesses.

(c) *Re HG (Specific Issue Order: Sterilisation)* [1993] 1 FLR 587—where it was appropriate to deal with a case concerning the sterilization of a child by way of a specific issue order. In such cases there will be a need for the child to be granted party status and to be legally represented: see para 17.22 above.

(d) *Re C (HIV Test)* [1999] 2 FLR 1004—where the court made a specific issue order authorizing blood testing of a baby girl with a view to determining whether she was infected with HIV.

(e) *Re M (Medical Treatment: Consent)* [1999] 2 FLR 1097—where a specific issue order was sought in a case in which it was proposed to carry out a heart transplant on a 15-year-old girl against her wishes.

(f) *Re P (Parental Dispute: Judicial Determination)* [2003] 1 FLR 286—where parents seek a specific issue order to determine which school the children should attend, the court must make the final decision and must not abdicate that responsibility by simply appointing one parent with absolute responsibility for the decision.

17.188 The use of specific issue orders extends to disputes involving non-parents, including some involving local authorities, for example sterilization or abortion in relation to a child in care. The court could either take the relevant decision itself or direct that it should be determined by others, for example that a child be treated as a specified doctor deems appropriate.

Restrictions on the making of specific issue orders

17.189 The restrictions are the same as those described for prohibited steps orders at para 17.184 above.

L   INTERIM ORDERS AND SUPPLEMENTARY PROVISIONS

17.190 The supplementary provisions set out in s 11(3) and (7), CA 1989 are intended to preserve the greatest possible flexibility of the court's powers in relation to s 8 orders so that the court can make interim orders, delay implementation of orders, or attach other special conditions to orders where the circumstances call for it. The court can, for example, direct that the order be made to have effect for a specified period, or contain provisions which are to have effect for a specified period.

When will an interim application be appropriate?

17.191 Section 11(3), CA 1989 states that where the court has power to make a s 8 order, it may do so at any time during the course of the proceedings in question even though it is not in a position to dispose finally of those proceedings.

17.192 The solicitor should always consider applying for an interim order where the parties are unable to agree about residence or contact. The longer the period that elapses during which the client does not have residence/contact, the more damage is done to his long-term application and an interim application should therefore be made if it is felt that it will secure residence/contact for the client in advance of the full hearing. However, it should be stressed that the normal approach of the court on an interim residence hearing is to maintain the status quo unless there are strong reasons against this. (See paras 17.34 ff above.) Thus where one party has in fact had the child residing with him for some time (even if not by virtue of a court order), the court is unlikely to order the child to be transferred to the other party pending the full hearing.

Example 1 Mr and Mrs Jones separate. They are in the process of a divorce. The children remain in the matrimonial home with Mr Jones. Six months later Mrs Jones manages to secure a flat for herself and wishes the children to live with her. She intends to make an application for a residence order and wishes to seek an interim residence order meanwhile. Her interim application will almost certainly fail, on the basis that a decision involving a change in the status quo should be taken after a full investigation of the facts and arguments at a final hearing.

Example 2 The facts are as in Example 1. Fed up with waiting, Mrs Jones fails to return the children after a contact visit and keeps them at her flat. Mr Jones makes an application for an interim residence order in respect of the children. The court takes the view that the children should be returned to Mr Jones pending a final hearing as this was the status quo before the snatch. He is therefore granted an interim residence order.

The court is more likely to make an interim order defining contact than transferring the residence of the children. If a parent who wishes to seek a long-term order for residence or contact is being denied any, or any regular, contact with the children, application should usually be made for interim contact in order to ensure that his full application will not be prejudiced because he has lost touch with the children.

Example 3 The facts are as in Example 1 above. Mrs Jones is being refused any contact with the children. Although Mrs Jones is unlikely to be granted an interim residence order in respect of the children, she should apply for interim contact in an attempt to preserve close contact with the children. Depending on the reasons that Mr Jones puts forward for her attitude, the chances are that an interim contact order will be made.

It can also be very valuable for the court hearing a final contact application if a few interim visits have taken place during the run-up to the case in order that their effect can be assessed. If there is real concern as to the children's attitude to contact, the court may order these visits to be supervised by a children and family reporter who can then report to the court.

If a parent with a residence order in respect of the children has been ordered to afford contact   **17.193** to the other parent, she should not thereafter stop contact visits of her own accord. If she does so she will be in breach of the contact order and liable to be brought before the court with a view to committal for contempt (although other methods of enforcing orders are preferred to committal proceedings except as a last resort). The proper course if she is worried about contact continuing is for her to make an application to have contact stopped and, in the meanwhile, to seek an interim order to this effect. In practice, a parent who is genuinely worried about the effect of contact on the children will normally simply refuse to let the children go, leaving it up to the other party to decide whether to take the matter back to court to obtain an order for defined contact or to enforce the existing defined contact arrangements. A parent who has stopped contact or is contemplating doing so must, however, be warned that it will weigh heavily against her in any applications concerning the children if it is found that she has done so without good reason.

Use of other supplementary provisions

Section 11(7)(a), CA 1989, allows the court to make a s 8 order which contains directions   **17.194** about how it is to be carried into effect. Section 11(7)(b) permits the court to make a s 8 order which imposes conditions:

which must be complied with by any person:

    (a) in whose favour the order is made;
    (b) who is a parent of the child concerned;
    (c) who is not a parent of his but who has parental responsibility for him; or
    (d) with whom the child is living and to whom the conditions are expressed to apply.

There are numerous ways in which the court may make use of these provisions to give effect to s 8 orders.

Example Mr and Mrs Jones are divorcing. Mr Jones has moved to Coventry. Each of them applies for a residence order in respect of their son, Tom, aged 12. Tom is presently at school near to the former matrimonial home in Exeter where Mrs Jones still lives. The court hears the dispute in May 2011 and decides that Tom should move to live with his father. Tom is just about to take his school examinations. Therefore the court *delays implementation* of the order to allow Tom to finish the school term at his present school. The court directs that the residence order will take effect on 1 August 2011.

17.195   The court could also, for example, use the supplementary provisions to order a gradual build-up of contact in circumstances where a child had not seen the person concerned for a long time. For an example of a contact order containing conditions as to the exercise of indirect contact by the father to his child, see *Re O (Contact: Imposition of Conditions)* [1995] 2 FLR 124 and *Re P (Contact: Indirect Contact)* [1999] 2 FLR 893.

17.196   Conditions and directions under s 11(7) may only be attached to ensure that the s 8 order works effectively. The provisions cannot be used to impose conditions unrelated to the issue of contact, but aimed at protecting the other parent from harassment: *D v N (Contact Order: Conditions)* (para 17.167 above).

M   SETTLING RESIDENCE AND CONTACT DISPUTES

17.197   It is of the utmost importance that the parties should be encouraged to resolve their differences over residence and contact. Bitter disputes between parents cause a great deal of distress to children, particularly if a full court hearing has to be held to delve into all the issues.

17.198   It should be remembered at all times that one of the fundamental principles of the CA 1989 is that the court should make no order unless it considers that to make an order would be better for the child than making no order at all (s 1(5)). If, therefore, the parties do reach a compromise and the court takes the view that there is a realistic possibility of it working then the court may question the necessity for embodying the agreement in any form of court order, whether by consent or otherwise.

Mediation

17.199   It is becoming more common for parents to use family mediation as a method of negotiating an agreement in relation to the issues surrounding their separation and/or divorce. This method of alternative dispute resolution is particularly suitable for disputes in relation to the arrangements as to where a child will live and how he will share time between his parents after the separation. For further discussion of this see Chapter 3.

17.200   As of 6 April 2011, a party who applies for a private law order in respect of a child, except for enforcement proceedings, must comply with the Pre-Application Protocol for Mediation Information and Assessment contained in FPR 2010, PD3A. The Protocol requires the applicant to contact a family mediator prior to issuing his application in order to attend a Mediation Information and Assessment Meeting ('MIAM'), and to provide the mediator with the other party's contact details so that he or she can be invited to a MIAM either together with the applicant or separately.

The applicant is not required to attend a MIAM if the mediator determines that the case is not **17.201** suitable or if mediation is not locally available; if there is a background of domestic abuse or child protection concerns; if there is an agreement between the parties; or if the prospective application is to be made without notice or is urgent.

N   VARIATION OF S 8 ORDERS

The court has power to make new s 8 orders from time to time and to vary or discharge exist- **17.202** ing orders. A party who seeks to vary an existing order must file the appropriate application form and apply for a hearing. Normally the court will not make a new order if nothing has changed since the original order was made.

O   FAMILY ASSISTANCE ORDERS

The CA 1989 introduced the 'family assistance order' which is designed to involve a Cafcass **17.203** officer (or officer of the local authority) for a period of up to six months in helping a family at a time of marital breakdown. The officer is required to advise, assist, and (if appropriate) befriend any person named in the order.

Family assistance orders may only be made with the agreement of all those involved (except **17.204** the child): s 16(3) and (7). There is no need for the court to make a s 8 order as a prerequisite to granting a family assistance order (s 16(1)), but the supervisor may be asked to report back to the court if there is a s 8 order in force (s 16(6)). Where the case is referred back to court then the court may make any s 8 order (s 10(1)(b)), subject to the restrictions contained in s 9; the officer would not need to make an application. When the officer is concerned about the child's well-being he should refer the case to the local authority for investigation under s 47(1)(b).

Before making a family assistance order, the court must obtain the opinion (verbally or in **17.205** writing) of the appropriate officer about whether he or she believes it would be in the best interests of the child for an order to be made and, if so, how the order should operate and for what period. Any person who is proposed to be named in the order must be given the oppor- tunity to comment on what is proposed: FPR 2010, PD12M.

Family assistance orders are still comparatively rare. Importantly, there is no power under **17.206** s 11(7), CA 1989 to make orders against a local authority in private law proceedings requiring that authority to supervise contact as part of a family assistance order: *Re E (Family Assistance Order)* [1999] 2 FLR 512.

In *S v P (Contact Application: Family Assistance Order)* [1997] 2 FLR 277, Callman J in the Family **17.207** Division refused to grant the father's application for a family assistance order. The father was in prison and he asked the court to make a family assistance order to require the local authority to provide an escort to bring the children to prison to visit him. The court held that it was not appropriate to make the order for this purpose.

17.208 For further comment on family assistance orders see the cases of *Re M (Contact: Supervision)* [1998] 1 FLR 727, *Re M (Contact: Family Assistance: McKenzie Friend)* (para 17.167 above), and *Re K (Supervision Orders)* [1999] 2 FLR 303.

P WARDSHIP AND THE COURT'S INHERENT JURISDICTION

17.209 The inherent jurisdiction is the exercise by the High Court of the powers of the Crown as *parens patriae*. It is based upon the duty of the Crown to protect all those subjects who owe allegiance to the Crown, and it extends to both adults and children within the areas of civil and criminal law. In children cases the High Court may exercise its inherent jurisdiction by making a minor a ward of court; the effect of this is that no significant step in the child's life may be taken without the permission of the High Court. However, where a decision of the court is sought in relation to a single issue (eg whether to authorize a particular type of medical treatment) then a free-standing application under the inherent jurisdiction may suffice.

17.210 The use of the inherent jurisdiction in relation to children is theoretically without limit, but in practice is limited by statute and case law, most significantly by the CA 1989. The court may not use the inherent jurisdiction (s 100):

(a) to place the child in the care of a local authority;
(b) to require a child to be accommodated on behalf of a local authority;
(c) to make a child who is subject to a care order a ward of court.

The use of the inherent jurisdiction is also limited by case law. In particular, the court should not make use of the inherent jurisdiction where the same result could be achieved under the CA 1989: the inherent jurisdiction is there to deal with lacunae in statute, not as an alternative to the court's statutory powers.

17.211 A local authority's ability to invoke the use of the inherent jurisdiction is limited. Any such application requires leave, which will only be granted if the court is satisfied that the result which the local authority wishes to achieve cannot be achieved by making any other type of order, and that there is reasonable cause to believe that if the inherent jurisdiction is not exercised the child is likely to suffer significant harm: s 100(3)(4).

17.212 Some examples of the exercise of the inherent jurisdiction are as follows:

(a) To authorize a blood transfusion for a child who is seriously ill and whose parents do not consent to such treatment: *Re O (A Minor) (Medical Treatment)* [1993] 2 FLR 149.
(b) To override the refusal of a minor to submit to assessment and medical examination and treatment, notwithstanding that she was of sufficient understanding to make an informed decision about medical examination or psychiatric examination or other assessment: *South Glamorgan County Council v W and B* [1993] 1 FLR 574.
(c) To grant an application of the local authority under s 100 to prevent a film company and Channel 4 television from continuing to film five children on the streets, some of

whom were subject to care orders or interim care orders, on the basis that the filming was exploiting vulnerable children and was having a detrimental effect on their upbringing: *Nottingham City Council* v *October Films Ltd* [1999] 2 FLR 347.

Q   FINANCIAL PROVISION AND PROPERTY ADJUSTMENT FOR CHILDREN

Section 15, CA 1989, together with sch 1, set out the provisions whereby the court can order **17.213** financial provision for children. The provisions do not replace those in the MCA 1973 or the Domestic Proceedings and Magistrates' Courts Act 1978. The effect of the Child Support Act 1991 ('CSA 1991') on those provisions is set out in paras 17.221 ff.

'Financial provision' comes within definition of 'family proceedings'

An application for financial provision comes within the definition of 'family proceedings' **17.214** for the purposes of the CA 1989. Therefore, a court hearing such an application may make residence or contact orders (or any other s 8 order) if it considers such orders should be made: s 10(1).

Who is under an obligation to pay?

The obligation to pay lies only upon parents and step-parents. **17.215**

'Parents' include the child's natural mother and father and also any party to a marriage **17.216** (whether or not subsisting) in relation to whom the child concerned is a child of the family and any civil partner in a civil partnership (whether or not subsisting) in relation to whom the child concerned is a child of the family (sch 1, para 16(2)). An order cannot be made against a person who has not been married to the applicant and is not the natural parent of the child concerned: *J* v *J (A Minor) (Property Transfer)* [1993] 2 FLR 56, even when that person has parental responsibility and a shared residence order is in force: *T* v *B* [2010] EWHC 1444.

'Child' includes a child over 18 where an application is made under sch 1, para 2 or 6: sch 1, **17.217** para 16(1).

'Child of the family' is defined in s 105(1) as being, in relation to the parties to a marriage: **17.218**

(a)   a child of both those parties;
(b)   any other child, not being a child who is placed with those parties as foster parents by a local authority or voluntary organization, who has been treated by both of those parties as a child of their family.

When deciding whether to exercise its powers against a person who is not the mother or **17.219** father of the child (ie, a step-parent who is or was married to or in a civil partnership with the child's parent), the court must have regard to:

(a)   whether that person had assumed responsibility for the maintenance of the child and, if so, the extent to which and basis on which he assumed that responsibility and the length of period during which he assumed that responsibility and the length of the period during which he met that responsibility;

(b)   whether he did so knowing that the child was not his child;

(c)   the liability of any other person to maintain the child.

Who can apply for payment?

17.220   Parents, including unmarried mothers, unmarried fathers without parental responsibility, guardians, special guardians, and people with a residence order will be able to apply for a range of orders in relation to children: sch 1, para 1(1).

What orders are available?

17.221   The CSA 1991 restricts the court's jurisdiction to make unsecured or secured periodical payments orders for the benefit of a child. The court retains jurisdiction to make such orders where:

(a)   the child is the step-child of the prospective payer, provided that the child has been treated as a child of the family by him; or

(b)   the person applying for the order is the guardian of the child; or

(c)   the person applying for the order is not the parent of the child but is a person in whose favour a residence order has been made in respect of the child;

(d)   any one of the parent with care, the non-resident parent, or the child is resident outside the jurisdiction;

(e)   the order is required to meet education or training expenses (eg school fees), or expenses referable to a child's disability.

17.222   In addition, the court has jurisdiction to make a 'top-up' order where a Child Maintenance and Enforcement Commission (CMEC) maximum assessment is in force, that is, where the paying parent's net weekly income exceeds the CMEC maximum (currently £2,000 per week): s 8(6), CSA 1991.

17.223   Otherwise, where financial provision is sought against the natural parent of the child then in normal circumstances it will be necessary to apply to CMEC for a maintenance assessment to be carried out. The courts do not have jurisdiction to make periodical payments orders in these circumstances: s 8, CSA 1991. An alternative, where the carer parent is not in receipt of state benefits, may be for the parents to enter into a maintenance agreement for the support of the child. For further details of the CSA 1991, see Chapter 35.

17.224   However, it is important to remember that the courts retain jurisdiction to make lump sum and property settlement and property transfer orders as follows:

(a)   Family proceedings court: lump sum order up to a maximum of £1,000.

(b)   High Court and county court:

(i)   lump sum order of unlimited amount;

(ii)   settlement of property order for the benefit of the child;

(iii)   transfer of property order to or for the benefit of the child.

17.225   As a general rule orders for financial provision will end when the child attains the age of 17. However, provision can be made for orders to extend until the child reaches 18 or beyond: sch 1, paras 2 and 3.

The court will only make a lump sum order to provide for a particular item of capital expendi- **17.226**
ture: lump sum orders will not be made in such a way as to provide for the regular support of
the child even though the Child Support Agency had made a nil assessment and the respondent father lived in a house worth £2.6 million and had motor vehicles valued at £190,000:
Phillips v Peace [1996] 2 FLR 237.

What matters will the court consider when making an order for financial provision?

The list of factors to which the court must have regard in considering whether to order financial **17.227**
provision for a child are set out in sch 1, para 4. The factors include the income, earning capacity, property, and other financial resources of the parents, the applicant, and any other person
in whose favour the court proposes to make the order, together with their financial needs,
obligations, and responsibilities; the financial needs of the child; the income, earning capacity,
property, and other financial resources of the child; any physical or mental disability of the
child; the manner in which the child was being, or was expected to be, educated or trained.

In a suitable case the court has power to transfer a council tenancy from the joint names of the par- **17.228**
ties into the sole name of one of them for the benefit of the children; the word 'benefit' is not limited to cases where a financial benefit is to be conferred on the child: *K v K (Minors: Property Transfer)*
[1992] 2 FLR 220; *Re F (Minors) (Parental Home: Ouster)* [1994] 1 FLR 246; *B v B (Transfer of Tenancy)*
[1994] Fam Law 250. However, it seems that s 1(1), CA 1989 does not apply to applications under
sch 1: *J v C (Child: Financial Provision)* [1999] 1 FLR 152. Section 105, CA 1989 expressly excludes
maintenance from the definition of the 'upbringing' of a child; it is unlikely that Parliament
intended that an application for a property transfer should be governed by the principle that the
child's welfare is paramount when applications for periodical payments are expressly excluded
from that principle. Furthermore, in *K v H (Child Maintenance)* [1993] 2 FLR 61 Sir Stephen Brown
P held that the provisions of sch 1 deal comprehensively with financial provision and should not
be confused with applications relating to the upbringing of a child or the administration of the
child's own property. Nonetheless, the welfare of the child is a relevant consideration, even if not
paramount or the first consideration: *J v C (Child: Financial Provision)* (above).

It is clear that property adjustment orders should not ordinarily be used to provide benefits **17.229**
for the child after he has attained independence: *J v C (Child: Financial Provision)* (para 17.228
above). Thus, the transfer of property to a child absolutely would be an exceptional order to
make: *A v A (A Minor: Financial Provision)* [1994] 1 FLR 657. Furthermore, where an unmarried
father is ordered to purchase a house on trust for sale for the children, with sale to be postponed until the youngest child reaches 21 or until all of the children have ceased full-time
secondary or tertiary education, it is wrong to give the children beneficial interests in the
proceeds of sale since this would make provision for them beyond their dependency: *T v S*
[1994] 1 FCR 743 (FD).

In the case of *Re P (Child: Financial Provision)* [2003] 2 FLR 865 the father was extremely **17.230**
wealthy and the court made an award to the mother which drew a balance between seeking
to give the child a standard of living bearing some relationship with the father's resources and
lifestyle, and yet avoiding the provision of support to the mother as if it had been spousal
maintenance. However, it is important for the court to guard against unreasonable claims
made on behalf of the child but with a disguised element of providing for the mother's
independent benefit. It is noteworthy that *Re P (Child: Financial Provision)* places more weight

on the welfare of the child in sch 1 proceedings than was the case in *J* v *C (Child: Financial Provision)* (para 17.228 above).

17.231   In an appropriate case the court may make an award under sch 1 to provide for a parent's legal costs of pursuing or defending proceedings where this is of benefit to the child: *MT* v *T* [2007] 2 FLR 925.

Variation of orders for financial relief

17.232   The provisions for variation of periodical payments are contained in sch 1, para 6.

Interim orders

17.233   The court has power to make interim orders for financial provision in respect of a child and the relevant provisions are to be found in sch 1, para 9. There are no time limits imposed by the statute upon interim orders and provision is made for orders to be renewed from time to time. This reflects the principle that all orders are really interim because the needs and circumstances of children are always changing. The court is given power to make further orders for periodical payments and lump sums after the original application has been determined. However, property adjustment orders remain a 'once and for all' provision.

R   KEY DOCUMENTS

17.234   **Statutes**
Adoption and Children Act 2002
Children Act 1989
Civil Partnership Act 2004
Human Rights Act 1998
Matrimonial Causes Act 1973

Statutory Instruments
Parental Responsibility Agreement Regulations 1991 (SI 1991/1478)
Family Procedure Rules 2010 (SI 2010/2955)

Practice Directions/Practice Notes
Practice Note 'Official Solicitor: Appointment in Family Proceedings' [2001] 2 FLR 155
Practice Direction (Representation of Children in Family Proceedings pursuant to Family Proceedings Rules 1991, Rule 9.5) [2004] 1 FLR 1188
CAFCASS and the National Assembly for Wales Practice Note (Appointment of Guardians in Private Law Proceedings) [2006] 2 FLR 143
The President's Private Law Programme

S   USEFUL WEBSITES

17.235   Network of Access and Child Contact Centres (NACCC) <http://www.naccc.org.uk>

18

PROCEDURE FOR ORDERS UNDER THE CHILDREN ACT 1989

A   THE COURTS—JURISDICTION AND ALLOCATION OF PROCEEDINGS

18.01   In addition to streamlining and codifying the law relating to children, the Children Act 1989 ('CA 1989') creates a unified structure of the High Court, county courts, and family proceedings court. The structure is as follows:

(a) High Court tier: staffed by Family Division judges;

(b) county court tier: staffed by selected circuit judges and district judges sitting at designated trial centres. There are different classes of county court:

  (i)   divorce county courts;

  (ii) family hearing centres;

  (iii) care centres;

  (iv) adoption centres;

  (v)   intercountry adoption centres;

  (vi) forced marriage county courts.

(c) family proceedings court: staffed by magistrates and district judges.

The criteria that govern which court is the most appropriate venue are contained in the Allocation and Transfer of Proceedings Order 2008 and the *Practice Direction: Allocation and Transfer of Proceedings* [2009] 1 FLR 365. The Order specifies types of proceedings which must be started in a magistrates' court. Proceedings may be transferred between courts in accordance with the criteria set out in arts 13 to 19 of the Order.

18.02   The general rule about transfer is that the court must have regard to the need to avoid delay: art 13(1). Transfer may occur at any stage in the proceedings, and a case may be transferred more than once.

Commencement of proceedings

Proceedings to be commenced in magistrates' court

18.03   Proceedings with a public law element will, generally speaking, commence in the magistrates' court and will be governed by the public law protocol for care cases (see further Chapter 17, para 17.200). However, there is provision for them to move horizontally within the same tier of courts or vertically up and down from one tier to another. Therefore, criteria have been created to ensure that cases are allocated to the most appropriate venue for the hearing. Article 5 of the Allocation Order sets out those proceedings which *must* be commenced in the magistrates' court. These include non-agency domestic adoptions, Child Support Act appeals, and applications for parental orders under the Human Fertilisation and Embryology Act 2008.

In addition, the following CA 1989 proceedings must be commenced in the magistrates' **18.04** court, unless they concern a child who is subject to pending proceedings in the county court or High Court:

(a) s 4 or 4A: free-standing applications for parental responsibility under s 4 or 4A, CA;

(b) s 25: secure accommodation orders;

(c) s 31: care and supervision orders;

(d) s 33(7) (leave to change name of or remove from United Kingdom child in care);

(e) s 34 (parental contact with children in care);

(f) s 36 (education supervision orders);

(g) s 43 (child assessment orders);

(h) s 44 (emergency protection orders);

(i) s 45 (duration of emergency protection orders etc);

(j) s 46(7) (application for emergency protection order by police officer);

(k) s 48 (powers to assist discovery of children etc);

(l) s 50 (recovery orders);

(m) s 102 (powers of constable to assist etc);

(n) para 19, sch 2 (approval of arrangements to assist child to live abroad).

Applications by a child for leave to apply for an order, and international adoption applica- **18.05** tions, must be issued in the county court: art 6.

All other applications (including applications for s 8 orders) may be issued in any court. **18.06** However, proceedings may be started in the High Court only where the proceedings are exceptionally complex; the outcome of the proceedings is important to the public in general; or there is another substantial reason for the proceedings to be started in the High Court: art 7. Paragraph 5.1 of the Practice Direction sets out factors to be taken into account when considering whether the criteria apply. These include the death of a child in the family, a parent having committed a grave crime, and cases with a complex international element (unrecognized foreign adoptions and removal to a non-Hague country). The likely length of hearing, number of experts, standard human rights issues, and the celebrity of the parties are not issues which will normally justify the hearing of a case in the High Court.

Transfer of proceedings

The requirement to have regard to delay means that where the decision whether to transfer **18.07** is finely balanced, the proceedings should not be transferred if this would lead to delay: PD, para 4.1. The likelihood of securing judicial continuity is also relevant to the decision whether to transfer.

A magistrates' court may transfer proceedings to another magistrates' court if this is more **18.08** convenient for the parties, taking into account any illness or disability of any of the parties and the area where the child lives.

18.09 A magistrates' court may transfer proceedings to the county court only if (art 15(1), Allocation Order):

(a) the transfer will significantly accelerate the determination of the proceedings;

(b) there is a real possibility of difficulty in resolving conflicts in the evidence of witnesses;

(c) there is a novel or difficult point of law;

(d) there are international issues or proceedings in another jurisdiction;

(e) there is a real possibility of enforcement powers beyond the powers of the magistrates' court being necessary;

(f) in private law proceedings, there is a real possibility that a children's guardian will be appointed;

(g) there is a real possibility that a party lacks capacity;

(h) there is another good reason for transfer.

18.10 A county court may transfer cases upwards or downwards. It must transfer down to the magistrates' court if it considers that none of the criteria in art 15 applies, unless there are proceedings pending in the county court. This applies to cases that have been transferred up from the magistrates' court as well as cases issued in the county court.

18.11 The county court may not transfer proceedings to the High Court unless the proceedings are exceptionally complex; the outcome of the proceedings is important to the public in general; or there is some other substantial reason for transfer. See para 18.06 above for a discussion of the issues which are likely to make a case suitable for hearing in the High Court.

Public law applications in the county court

18.12 If an application under Part III, IV, or V, CA 1989 (ie, for an order with a public law element) is to be heard in a county court, then that county court must also be a designated care centre (see art 20(2), Allocation Order).

Mediation

18.13 An applicant who intends to issue an application for a private law order must comply with the Pre-Application Protocol for Mediation Information and Assessment: Family Procedure Rules 2010 ('FPR 2010'), PD3A. See Chapter 17, para 17.200 for an explanation of the Protocol.

The Private Law Programme

18.14 The Private Law Programme (now set out at FPR 2010, PD12B) commenced in 2004 and contains best practice guidance for the conduct of private law cases in all courts. Where an application is made to the court under Part II, CA 1989, the court will apply the overriding objective to enable it to deal with the case justly, with regard to the welfare issues. The court is required to deal 'expeditiously and fairly' with every case, in ways which are proportionate to the issues. It is also required to save unnecessary expense and to allot to each case an appropriate share of the court's resources.

18.15 An essential feature of the Private Law Programme is the First Hearing Dispute Resolution Appointment (FHDRA). This will take place within four to six weeks of the issue of the application. Prior to the FHDRA, a copy of the application is sent to the Children and Family Court Advisory and Support Service (Cafcass) which must carry out initial safeguarding checks. A Cafcass officer will speak to each party prior to the hearing about safety issues only. He or she will also carry out safeguarding enquiries, including checks of local authorities and the police. Cafcass will report the outcome of the risk identification work to the court at least three days before the hearing.

The FHDRA should be attended by all parties to the proceedings and the Cafcass officer who **18.16** has carried out the safeguarding checks. The appointment will be held before a 'gateway' district judge with a family 'ticket' who will identify any immediate safety issues; identify the aim of the proceedings, including the timescale within which the aim can be achieved; identify the issues between the parties and the opportunities for resolution of those issues by appropriate referrals for support and assistance and any subsequent steps required. Wherever possible, a Cafcass officer will be available to facilitate early dispute resolution rather than providing a formal report. At the conclusion of the FHDRA the court must identify in the order the details of what has or has not been agreed and give subsequent directions for the progress of the case, the filing of evidence, and, if necessary, the preparation of a Cafcass report.

Applications for a s 8 order

A person who wishes to make an application for a s 8 order should do so by completing the **18.17** prescribed form. This will usually be in Form C100 unless the applicant must first obtain leave of the court to make the substantive application (see para 18.35 below). The rules for service of the application will be found in Part 6, FPR 2010. The application may be made to the magistrates' court, county court, or High Court, subject to it meeting the appropriate criteria (see para 18.06 above). If the applicant is in receipt of public funding then his certificate will usually contain a restriction that the proceedings should be commenced in the magistrates' court since that will normally be the cheapest route. However, if there are any other proceedings already pending in relation to the relevant children then the new proceedings should be consolidated with them so that all matters are heard together.

The categories of persons who can apply automatically for s 8 orders and those who may **18.18** apply only with leave are set out fully in para 18.35 below.

Where a question as to the child's welfare arises as part of s 8 proceedings, a court has power **18.19** to make a s 8 order of its own motion in spite of the fact that no application has been made for such an order: s 10(1)(b).

B   PROCEDURE

The procedure to be adopted in proceedings under the CA 1989 is set out in Part 12, FPR **18.20** 2010.

It is noticeable that the court is encouraged to take an inquisitorial role, in an effort to play **18.21** down the adversarial nature of the proceedings. The court is expected to take control of the timetable for hearings, to make directions as to the evidence to be filed, to make directions as to the conduct of the proceedings generally, and to call for welfare reports where necessary. There is now much more emphasis on written material and on disclosure by each party of its evidence in advance of the hearing so that the real issues involved in the case are clear. It is hoped that this will help to avoid the all-too-familiar scenario whereby advocates waste time during a hearing in following unproductive lines of examination and cross-examination which do not go to the heart of the issues between the parties.

18.22   The procedure to be adopted once a local authority decides to apply for a care or supervision order is governed by the public law outline (FPR 2010, PD12A), which is discussed in detail in Chapter 20, para 20.33. The Protocol aims to ensure that care cases are dealt with as justly, expeditiously, and fairly as possible. The key principles underlying the Protocol are that there should be judicial continuity, active case management by the court, consistency by the stand-ardization of steps to be taken in preparing, and a case management conference in each care case to enable the judge to identify the issues and fix the timetable for all further directions and hearings.

Allocation of functions within the courts

18.23   Which type of case will be heard by a judge, district judge, magistrate(s), or justices' clerk? The allocation of cases to certain categories of the judiciary within the High Court and county court is governed by the Family Proceedings (Allocation to Judiciary) Directions 2009 ('FP(AJ) D 2009'). The schedule to the FP(AJ)D 2009 allocates specified classes of proceedings to speci-fied classes of judge in specified circumstances.

County court care centres

18.24   Care centres will be staffed by:

   (a) designated family judges;
   (b) nominated care judges;
   (c) nominated care district judges.

They will hear the following types of cases:

   (i)   transferred/issued public law cases;
   (ii) contested matrimonial applications;
   (iii) adoptions;
   (iv) occupation and non-molestation orders.

County court family hearing centres

18.25   Family hearing centres will be staffed by:

   (a) nominated family judges;
   (b) all district judges.

They will be able to hear the following cases:

   (i)   contested matrimonial and s 8 applications;
   (ii) adoptions;
   (iii) occupation and non-molestation orders.

Divorce county courts

Divorce county courts will be staffed by: **18.26**

(a) non-nominated circuit judges;
(b) all district judges.

They will have 'district judge jurisdiction' only.

County courts

Ordinary county courts will be staffed by: **18.27**

(a) non-nominated circuit judges;
(b) all district judges.

They will have no involvement in family proceedings save for applications for injunctions.

Family proceedings courts

Family proceedings courts hearing CA 1989 applications will be staffed by family proceedings   **18.28**
panels of magistrates. They will hear the following types of cases:

(a) public law cases;
(b) private family proceedings (outside divorce).

A single justice may sit as the family proceedings court: r 2.6, FPR 2010. However, his or her
powers to make orders are restricted by FPR 2010, PD2A. In particular, unless a rule, Practice
Direction, or other enactment provides otherwise, a single justice may not make the decision
of a magistrates' court at the final hearing of an application for a substantive order: for example,
a s 8 order on notice, placement order, adoption order, or care order. Even when the single
justice has power to make an order or direction, he must refer the matter to a magistrates'
court if he considers, for whatever reason, that it is inappropriate to perform the function:
r 2.10, FPR 2010.

There are certain functions which the justices' clerk may perform on his own, without any   **18.29**
magistrates at all: see the Justices Clerks Rules 2005. These include the power to give, vary, or
revoke directions as to:

(a) timetable;
(b) variation of time allowed by Rules;
(c) attendance of child;
(d) appointment of guardian ad litem or solicitor;
(e) service of documents;
(f) submission of evidence, including experts' reports;
(g) preparation of welfare reports;
(h) transfer from magistrates' court vertically or horizontally;
(i) consolidation of cases.

Availability of public funding

The availability of public funding under the Community Legal Service scheme for CA 1989   **18.30**
proceedings is fully set out in Chapter 2. However, it is important to remember that for most

private law children cases (under Parts I to III, CA 1989) the applicant will be required to attend a mediation meeting with a mediator to determine whether the case is suitable for mediation before any public funding may be made available for representation (for further discussion of mediation see Chapter 3). On the other hand, there is no such requirement to attend a meeting with a mediator for public law children cases (under Parts IV and V, CA 1989).

18.31   Where the court is considering making an order for costs against a publicly funded individual, it must take into account the matters in s 11, Access to Justice Act 1999. In *R v R (Costs: Child Case)* [1997] 2 FLR 95, the Court of Appeal held that the judge should adjourn the question of the father's ability to pay costs in connection with CA 1989 proceedings until after the conclusion of ancillary relief proceedings since at that stage the court would have a better idea of his resources.

Forms of application

18.32   Part 5, FPR 2010 makes provision for applications under the CA 1989 to be made by way of a simple application. There are prescribed forms for each type of application, and the forms are to be found in FPR 2010, PD5A. The forms are designed to extract the essential information from the applicant at an early stage. They also provide litigants with essential information about the conduct of their case, for example as to the importance of obtaining legal advice and as to the right to file an answer to an application.

Withdrawal of an application

18.33   Once an application has been made it may only be withdrawn with the leave of the court: r 29.4(2), FPR 2010. An application for leave can be made orally to the court, provided that the parties are present. Otherwise there must be a written request setting out the reasons for the request. It must be served on all parties. The court can grant the request provided that the parties consent, the guardian (if there is one) has had an opportunity to make representations, and the court thinks fit. Instead of granting the request, the court may direct that a date be fixed for the hearing of the request.

18.34   The court must consider an application for leave to withdraw just as carefully as any other application in respect of a child in proceedings under the CA 1989. The court has a statutory duty to have regard to the welfare of the child, including the duty to hear expert evidence from the guardian (*Re F (A Minor) (Care Order: Withdrawal of Application)* [1993] 2 FLR 9). Although the statutory checklist in s 1(3) does not apply to an application for leave to withdraw, it is available to the court as an aide-memoire (*London Borough of Southwark v B* [1993] 2 FLR 559). However, the paramountcy of the child's welfare principle under s 1(1) does apply and the court must look at each case on its facts to see if there is some 'solid advantage to the child to be derived from continuing the proceedings': *London Borough of Southwark v B* (above). For an example of the application of the test see *Re N (Leave to Withdraw Care Proceedings)* [2000] 1 FLR 134 where the court refused the local authority's application for leave to withdraw care proceedings.

Requests for leave to bring proceedings

As was explained in para 18.18, in some circumstances the CA 1989 requires a person to **18.35** obtain leave before commencing proceedings, for example applications by grandparents for s 8 orders. The procedure in Part 18, FPR 2010 is used for such applications. The applicant must submit an application notice which states what order is being requested, with brief reasons, and attaches a draft of the order being sought: r 18.7. It must contain either a request for a hearing or a request that the application be dealt with without a hearing: PD18A. Where the application is for permission to apply for an order, a draft of the substantive application must be included with the application notice.

Respondents

Those persons who must be made respondents to an application are set out in tabular form **18.36** at r 12.3, FPR 2010. Reference should be made to the rule for details of the respondents to a particular application but in most cases the respondents will include:

(a) every person whom the applicant believes to have parental responsibility for the child;
(b) where the child is the subject of a care order, every person whom the applicant believes to have had parental responsibility immediately prior to the making of the care order;
(c) if the application is to extend, vary, or discharge an order, the parties to the proceedings leading to the original order which the applicant seeks to have extended, varied, or discharged;
(d) in certain proceedings, the child himself.

Parties

The rules concerning the addition and removal of parties are to be found in r 12.3(2) to (4), **18.37** FPR 2010. Where a person with parental responsibility requests to be joined as a party, the court must join him. Otherwise the court has discretion as to whether to add or remove a party.

Where a number of different parties are putting forward essentially the same case, serious **18.38** consideration should be given to the degree of separate representation of those parties that is strictly necessary: *Birmingham City Council v H (No 3)* [1994] 1 FLR 224.

There is no statutory guidance as to the factors which the court should take into account in **18.39** making its decision as to whether to give leave for a person to be joined as a party. It would appear that s 1(1), CA 1989 does not apply in this context: *North Yorkshire County Council v G* [1993] 2 FLR 732; *G v Kirklees MBC* [1993] 1 FLR 805. However, even though the applicant does not expressly seek leave to apply for a s 8 order it would appear that the factors in s 10(9) nevertheless apply: *G v Kirklees MBC* (above); *North Yorkshire County Council v G* (above). The court is not precluded from considering all the circumstances of the case, including the overall merits of the case for a s 8 order, since if the applicant has no reasonable prospects of success there is no point in joining him as a party: *North Yorkshire County Council v G* (above).

From 6 April 2010, the guidance in the authorities must be read subject to the overriding **18.40** objective contained in r 1.1, FPR 2010.

Service

18.41   The applicant must serve a copy of the application in the appropriate form, together with Form C6 which sets out the date, time, and place for a hearing or directions appointment, on each respondent at least 14 days before the hearing or appointment: r 12.8, FPR 2010 and PD12C.

18.42   Once service has been effected the applicant must lodge at court a statement of service in Form C9 confirming the date of service, method of service, documents served, and giving details of the party on whom service was effected.

Persons who must be given written notice

18.43   At the same time as effecting service of the application on the relevant respondents the applicant must give written notice of the application and of the date, time, and place of the hearing or directions appointment to those persons set out in FPR 2010, PD12C, para 3.1. They include:

(a)   the local authority providing accommodation for the child;

(b)   persons who are caring for the child at the time when the proceedings are commenced;

(c)   if the child is in a refuge, then the person providing the refuge;

(d)   every person whom the applicant believes:

(i)   to be named in a current court order with respect to the child (unless the applicant believes the order is not relevant to the present application);

(ii)   to be a party in pending proceedings in respect of the child (unless the applicant believes the pending proceedings not to be relevant to the present application);

(iii)   to be a person with whom the child has lived for a period of at least three years prior to the application;

(e)   in special guardianship proceedings, the appropriate local authority.

The Children and Family Court Advisory and Support Service

18.44   In family proceedings, Cafcass is responsible for safeguarding and promoting the welfare of children, giving advice to any court about any application made to it in such proceedings, arranging for children to be represented, and providing information, advice, and other support for children and their families (ss 11, 12, 15, and 16, Criminal Justice and Court Services Act 2000). The person responsible for preparing a Cafcass report (formerly a 'welfare report') will usually be the 'children and family reporter' and the person appointed to represent a child in public law proceedings will usually be the 'children's guardian'. In some complex private law proceedings an officer of Cafcass (or some other appropriate person) may be appointed to represent the child; depending on the child's role within the proceedings, this person is known as the child's guardian or 'litigation friend' (formerly 'guardian ad litem'): rr 16.5 and 16.24, FPR 2010. Important guidance in relation to the appointment of a children's guardian in private law proceedings is to be found in FPR 2010, PD16A. The National Standards for the Children and Family Court Advisory and Support Service set out a framework of service principles and standards, including a rigorous complaints procedure. It can be found at <http://www.cafcass.gov.uk>.

Cafcass report

A Cafcass report will usually be ordered where there are to be contested s 8 proceedings.   **18.45**
Cafcass and local authorities are under a duty to provide reports as requested (s 7(5)), but a
local authority may delegate the task to someone who is not a member of its staff, for example
a children's guardian. The person undertaking the report is referred to as a 'welfare officer':
r 16.33(1), FPR 2010—previously, a 'children and family reporter.' The court may refer the
case of its own motion to a welfare officer for investigation (s 7(1)). A party has the right to
question the welfare officer about his oral or written advice: r 16.33(5), FPR 2010.

It normally takes several weeks (or even months) for a Cafcass report to be prepared. The party   **18.46**
wishing for the report may find that if he delays his request for a report for too long the court
may take the view that the advantages to the court of having the report for the hearing are
outweighed by the disadvantages to the child of having to wait too long for a resolution of
the case; in that instance the court would refuse the request for the report, in the interests of
the child.

The welfare officer will be able to inspect the court file relating to the case on which there will,   **18.47**
of course, be copies of all the statements filed in relation to the dispute. He will therefore be
aware of what the issues between parties are. He will see both parties (often on several occasions) preferably in their homes and with and without the children present. The impression
that the officer forms of a parent is vital and the client must therefore be warned to cooperate
with the officer fully and make him or her welcome. The officer will also see the children on
their own if they are old enough for this to be of benefit. In addition, he will make whatever
other enquiries seem to be appropriate in the particular case. For example, he may visit the
children's school as problems at home are often reflected in behaviour at school; he may see
other relations; he will contact any social workers who have been involved with the family;
he may speak to the family's general practitioner, etc. Having carried out his investigations,
the children and family reporter will prepare what is usually a lengthy report for the court setting out the investigations he has made and the conclusions he has reached. The report may
make a recommendation as to which orders the court should make.

It will be noted that Cafcass reports often contain a lot of what would traditionally be classed   **18.48**
as hearsay evidence (eg 'I spoke to the child's form-teacher who told me that she is often distressed at school the day after a contact visit with her father'). The court will receive such evidence in children's cases and attach to it whatever weight it thinks fit (see para 18.91 below).
The parties' solicitors should receive copies of the report prior to the hearing so that they can
take instructions from their clients on it and review the witnesses that they were intending to
call in light of the investigations the children and family reporter has made. It may be necessary to cross-examine the officer if, for example, the officer has misreported conversations
with the client or has made a clear recommendation in favour of the other party on grounds
which the solicitor feels to be unsound: *Re I and H (Contact: Right to Give Evidence)* [1998] 1
FLR 876. If the children and family reporter does make recommendations which are in favour
of the other party, the solicitor should consider seriously with the client whether he wishes
to proceed with his application. Looking at things realistically, it is almost always an uphill
battle to obtain a residence order if the welfare officer is against you. Where the judge concludes that the children and family reporter's enquiries are inadequate because the officer has

not assessed the relationship between the children and each parent individually in a natural setting (ie, their home), the judge may order a fresh hearing with a new welfare report.

18.49 The importance of the Cafcass report cannot be underestimated. In *Re W (Residence)* [1999] 2 FLR 390, the Court of Appeal reminded judges of the value of such reports, since the children and family reporter has the primary task of assessing factual situations and attachments. In consequence, judges should not depart from the recommendations of an experienced welfare officer without giving reasons for doing so and allowing the officer an opportunity to respond to any misgivings which the judge might have about the officer's approach.

18.50 The welfare officer is not required to attend hearings in respect of which his report has been made or in the course of which his report is due to be considered unless the court so orders, but the court officer must notify the officer of any direction given at a hearing at which he was not present.

18.51 If the report is not available before the hearing, it will certainly be disclosed on the day and practitioners should ensure that they ask for sufficient time to go through it thoroughly with their client before embarking on the hearing.

Appointment of children's guardian

18.52 Reference was made to the role of the children's guardian in Chapter 20, paras 20.91 ff.

18.53 Section 41(1), CA 1989 requires the court in any 'specified proceedings' (ie, proceedings of a public nature—care orders, supervision orders, emergency protection orders, etc) to appoint a guardian for the child concerned *unless* it is satisfied that it is not necessary to do so in order to safeguard his interests. By s 41(2), CA 1989 the appointment of and duties of the guardian are to be regulated by rules of court. The appropriate rules will be found in Part 16, FPR 2010.

18.54 Section 122, Adoption and Children Act 2002 ('ACA 2002') has inserted into s 41 a new subs (6A) so as to include within the category of proceedings which may be 'specified for the time being . . . by rules of court' (ie, proceedings in which the court must appoint a guardian for the child unless satisfied that it is not necessary to do so in order to safeguard his interests) any proceedings for the making, varying, or discharging of an order under s 8, CA 1989 (ie, residence, contact, specific issue, and prohibited steps orders). This reflects the growing pressure for the appointment of children's guardians in certain private law children cases, for example bitterly contested residence or contact disputes, where children frequently have particular interests and standpoints which do not coincide with or cannot be adequately represented by the parents (*Re H (Contact Order) (No 2)* [2002] 1 FLR 22). Although the court already has power (see Chapter 17, paras 17.22 ff) to appoint a children's guardian in such cases, it will be enshrined in statute rather than merely in statutory instrument.

18.55 In carrying out his duties (whether in public law or private law proceedings) the children's guardian is to have regard to the 'delay principle' set out in s 1(2), CA 1989, that is, that there is a presumption that delay in hearing a case will be prejudicial to the welfare of the child concerned. This emphasizes the need for the guardian to complete as quickly as possible any necessary enquiries and reports. Furthermore, the guardian is enjoined to have regard to the 'checklist' of 'welfare factors' set out in s 1(3), CA 1989 when carrying out his duties.

The obligations of the children's guardian are extensive and include the following: **18.56**

(a) to appoint a solicitor to represent the child (unless this has already been done) and to instruct that solicitor, unless the child is of sufficient age and understanding to instruct a solicitor himself;

(b) to advise the court whether any person might have an interest in becoming a party to the proceedings or in making representations to the court;

(c) to attend all hearings (including directions hearings);

(d) to advise whether the child is of sufficient understanding for such purposes as the service of documents, refusal to submit to a medical or psychiatric examination or assessment, attendance at court etc;

(e) to advise the court of the wishes and feelings of the child in respect of any relevant matter;

(f) to advise as to the appropriate forum for, and timing of, the proceedings;

(g) to advise as to the options available to the court and as to the suitability of each option;

(h) to deliver interim and final written reports as directed by the court.

The rules provide for the inspection by the children's guardian of local authority records   **18.57**
as allowed by s 42, CA 1989. For example, in *Re T (A Minor) (Guardian ad Litem: Case Record)*
[1994] 1 FLR 632, the guardian was entitled to see case records prepared by the local authority
giving detailed information concerning prospective adopters and to include the relevant
information derived from it in his report to the court. The rules also allow the guardian, either
of his own motion or at the direction of the court, to obtain such professional assistance as
he thinks appropriate.

It is generally expected that a children's guardian will be appointed in *most* of the cases to   **18.58**
which s 41, CA 1989 applies (ie, in 'specified proceedings' as set out in s 41(6)). In this context
'specified proceedings' include any proceedings:

(a) in relation to an application for a care order or a supervision order;

(b) in which the court has given a direction under s 37(1) and has made, or is considering whether to make, an interim care order or supervision order;

(c) on an application for the discharge of a care order or the variation or discharge of a supervision order;

(d) in which the court is considering whether to make a residence order with respect to a child who is the subject of a care order;

(e) with respect to contact between a child who is the subject of a care order and any other person;

(f) in which the court is considering making an order under Part V, CA 1989, for example emergency protection order, child assessment order, education supervision order etc;

(g) on an appeal against the orders at points (a) to (f) above.

Solicitor for the child

The rules require the children's guardian to appoint a solicitor for the child unless an appoint-   **18.59**
ment has already been made. In that event the solicitor is required to represent the child 'in
accordance with instructions received from the children's guardian': r 16.29(1), FPR 2010.

18.60   However, provision is made for the solicitor to receive instructions from the child personally. This will take place if the solicitor considers, having taken into account the views of the children's guardian, that:

(a)   the child wishes to give instructions which conflict with those of the guardian; and

(b)   that he is able, having regard to the degree of his understanding, to give such instructions on his own behalf: r 16.29(2).

See, for example, *Re H (A Minor) (Care Proceedings: Child's Wishes)* [1993] 1 FLR 440, where a 15-year-old boy had sufficient understanding to instruct his own solicitor in care proceedings but had been denied the opportunity to do so; his solicitor had been in error in accepting instructions from the children's guardian rather than from the boy himself. Where the child does part company with the guardian in such circumstances then the guardian will continue to participate in the proceedings to such extent as the court directs. (See also *Mabon* v *Mabon* [2005] 2 FLR 1011.) He may be invited to remain involved as *amicus curiae*. The role of *amicus curiae* in these circumstances has been defined in *Re H (A Minor) (Role of Official Solicitor)* [1993] 2 FLR 552 to include the authority to carry out such investigations and enquiries as the court requires, to receive all papers and reports, to be able to apply for such directions as he thinks fit. The *amicus curiae* will not become a party to the proceedings. He remains an independent adviser to the court.

18.61   See Chapter 20, para 20.91 for further discussion of the appointment of a solicitor for a child in proceedings for a care or supervision order.

Directions appointments

18.62   The provisions governing directions appointments are set out in Parts 12 and 27, FPR 2010 and the associated Practice Directions. The court's general case management powers are set out in Part 4. The procedure for applications within ongoing proceedings is in Part 18. The rules allow for a preliminary hearing or 'directions appointment' at which the court can give directions for the subsequent conduct of the proceedings. There can be several directions appointments. They can take place of the court's own motion or as a result of a request made by one of the parties. A party should be given 'reasonable notice' of a directions hearing: r 12.14(6)(a); minimum notice periods for certain applications are specified in the rules themselves or in PD12C, para 2.1. In urgent cases a request for directions can (with leave) be made orally or without notice to the other parties, or both: r 12.16 and PD12E, FPR 2010. The matters which can be dealt with include (r 12.12):

(a)   timetable for the proceedings and the management of the case;

(b)   varying time limits;

(c)   service of documents;

(d)   joinder of parties;

(e)   preparation of welfare reports and a direction that the children and family reporter responsible for preparing the report is to attend the final hearing to assist the court and to give oral evidence, if necessary;

(f)   submission of evidence, including experts' reports;

(g)   appointment of children's guardian/solicitor or litigation friend;

(h)   attendance of child;

(i)   transfer of case to another court;

(j)   consolidation with other proceedings.

The parties must comply with FPR 2010, PD 27A, Practice Direction—Family Proceedings: **18.63** Court Bundles. The provisions of this Practice Direction apply to all hearings and directions appointments listed for more than one hour in all courts other than family proceedings courts. Failure to comply with the Practice Direction may result in the case being taken out of the case, or a 'wasted costs' order in accordance with Part 48.7, CPR 2010: PD27A, para 12.1.

Where time estimates are given to the court in the course of directions hearings or otherwise, **18.64** care must be taken to ensure that provision is made for judicial reading time, the length of the opening address, the likely time to be taken in respect of judicial pre-reading, the evidence of each witness, the number and likely length of closing speeches, and time for preparing and delivering judgment: PD27A, para 10.1.

All public law childcare cases are now governed by the Public Law Proceedings Guide to **18.65** Case Management, PD12A, which is discussed in Chapter 20, paras 20.33 ff. The question of whether to instruct experts will be subject to particular scrutiny and will be governed by the Practice Direction—Experts and Assessors in Family Proceedings, FPR 2010, PD25A. The Practice Direction is designed to draw together all the threads that have emerged through case law and practice. It sets out comprehensive guidance and is discussed in greater detail in Chapter 20, para 20.106.

Timing

A recurring theme of the CA 1989 is the avoidance of delay in proceedings wherever possible. **18.66** There is a mandatory requirement that whenever proceedings are adjourned the court *must* fix a date for reconvening: r 12.13(1), FPR 2010. The aim of these provisions is to prevent the proceedings from lying dormant through the delay of the parties or their advisers.

Attendance at hearing/directions appointment

All parties, including the child (if he is a party), *must* attend a directions appointment of **18.67** which they have had notice unless the court directs otherwise: r 12.14(2), FPR 2010.

Where the child is a party then proceedings will take place in his absence if: **18.68**

(a)   the court considers it to be in the interests of the child, having regard to the matters to be discussed or the evidence likely to be given at the hearing or directions appointment; and

(b)   the child is represented by a children's guardian or solicitor.

In practice, the child will very rarely attend court. **18.69**

The court must not begin a case in the absence of a respondent unless: **18.70**

(a)   it is proved that he had reasonable notice of the hearing; or

(b)   the circumstances of the case justify proceeding.

If the respondent appears but the applicant does not then the court can refuse the application, **18.71** or, if it has sufficient evidence, it can proceed in the absence of the applicant.

18.72   If neither the applicant nor the respondent appear then the court may refuse the application.

18.73   In the High Court and county court most hearings and directions appointments will take place in chambers. In the family proceedings court there is provision for hearings and directions appointments to take place in private.

18.74   Media attendance at hearings in the High Court and county court is governed by FPR 2010, PD27B, and in the family proceedings court by PD27C.

Documentary evidence

18.75   Great emphasis is placed upon the need for advance disclosure of evidence in proceedings under the CA 1989: see FPR 2010, r.12.19(2), Part 22, and PD22A. Each party is required to file and serve not only written statements of the oral evidence he intends to adduce at the hearing, but also copies of any documents upon which he intends to rely. The rules are very clear upon the requirement that at a hearing a party *may not adduce* evidence or seek to rely upon a document which has not been disclosed in advance to the other parties, except with the leave of the court. Statements of witnesses must be dated and signed by the person making the statement and must contain a declaration that the maker believes the statement to be true.

18.76   'In advance' means by such time as the court/justices' clerk directs, or in the absence of such a direction, before the hearing.

18.77   The practitioner should note that in s 8 proceedings a party must file no document other than as required or authorized by the rules without leave of the court: r 12.19(2). The aim of this rule is to prevent information being set down in writing which may serve only to inflame the situation between the parties and thus prevent a sensible settlement of the matter. If it becomes clear at a later stage that the matter is not going to be settled then the court can direct that further evidence be filed in readiness for a contested hearing.

18.78   Practice Direction (Family Proceedings: Court Bundles) (Universal Practice to be Applied in All Courts Other Than the Family Proceedings Court), FPR 2010, PD27A governs the preparation and arrangements for lodging with the court any bundles of documents for use in court proceedings. See para 18.63 above for further details.

18.79   In public law proceedings the local authority is required to file a care plan with the court and the parties (s 31A, CA 1989). A local authority circular dated 12 August 1999 entitled *Care Plans and Care Proceedings under the Children Act 1989* (LAC(99)29) sets out the ingredients to be contained in care plans. All public law childcare cases are governed by the public law outline which is discussed in Chapter 20, para 20.33.

Matters to be included in a statement in support of an application for a residence order

18.80   As and when it becomes necessary for further evidence to be filed then it would be advisable for the party applying for the residence (or indeed other s 8) order to seek permission under r 12.19, FPR 2010 to file a witness statement dealing not only with the merits of his own application but also with any matters raised by the other party in his own application/statement.

Great care must be taken over the preparation of a party's statements. The court will read **18.81**
them before it hears the application and they will therefore colour the court's initial approach
to the case. For this reason it is important that statements are reasonably comprehensive and
read clearly. The following matters should be covered if possible (adapted as appropriate for
the nature of the application and the matters in issue):

(a) The proposed living arrangements for the child (where he will live, who else will be
     living there, who will look after him when the parent is not available, etc). If the parent
     proposes to move in the foreseeable future, his proposed new arrangements should also
     be covered. The more definite they are, the better. Indeed, if the parent can actually be
     installed in the new accommodation before the hearing it will be helpful as the welfare
     officer may then have an opportunity to visit the accommodation and report on it to the
     court. It is particularly important that a parent should investigate and, if possible, try to
     arrange alternative accommodation if his present circumstances are unsuitable for the
     children. If he is awaiting council accommodation he should be in a position to produce
     to the court a letter from the council dealing with his place on the waiting list and his
     prospects of obtaining housing.

(b) The proposed arrangements for school. If the parent is seeking a transfer of residence to
     him, he should say whether the child can stay at the same school or, if this is not possible,
     he should state what alternative arrangements are available. This will mean him doing
     some homework himself in visiting the schools in his area, checking whether they can
     take the child, etc. If he does make this effort, it will help to give the impression that he is
     a conscientious and caring parent and really does wish to have the child living with him.
     If the child is below school age, opportunities for nursery education, playgroups, etc in
     the parent's area should be investigated.

(c) Where the parent lives with or has a close relationship with a new partner, the statement
     should inform the court how the child gets on with the new partner.

(d) If there are any problems over the child's health, these should be outlined in the
     statement and, if possible, a medical report should be exhibited.

(e) The parent's attitude to contact and also that of the child should be dealt with. For example,
     it will clearly help a parent's application for a residence order if he has had frequent regular
     contact with the child for prolonged periods and the child has enjoyed it. It will also be in
     his favour if he is prepared to facilitate generous contact between the child and the other
     parent if he obtains a residence order. The courts are disapproving of parents who try to
     turn the child against the other parent or to disrupt contact arrangements.

(f) Any views that the child has expressed about residence and contact. Obviously, what is
     said on this score will be viewed cautiously by the court, particularly if the child is young.
     However, it is worth mentioning in the statement if the child has made more than a
     throwaway remark.

(g) Any worries that the parent has about the care the other parent is giving/would give
     to the child. It must be emphasized that it is advisable to avoid an endless catalogue of
     minor grumbles about the other parent's standard of care. In particular, it is not generally
     appropriate to go into the question of who is to blame for the breakdown of the mar-
     riage or to detail the circumstances in which the marriage broke down. Throwing mud at
     the other parent only encourages mudslinging in return and simply irritates the court.

However, if there are *genuine* worries that really do relate to the children and not to the unfortunate situation between the parents, these must be set out fully in the statement.

(h) If the other party's statement has already been served, the statement should incorporate comments on the matters contained in it if the maker of the statement has any to make.

18.82 The most important statements in a dispute over residence or contact are obviously from the parties themselves. However, each side is free (with permission) to file and serve statements from supporting witnesses if appropriate.

Expert evidence: examination of child

18.83 No person may cause a child to be medically or psychiatrically examined or otherwise assessed for the purpose of the preparation of expert evidence for use in proceedings, *except* with the leave of the court: see r 12.20(1), FPR 2010. If such an examination or assessment is made without the leave of the court then that evidence cannot be adduced in the proceedings without the leave of the court.

18.84 All public law childcare cases are governed by the public law outline which is discussed in Chapter 20, para 20.33. The question of whether to instruct experts in such cases will be governed by the Practice Direction—Experts and Assessors in Family Proceedings, FPR 2010, PD25A. It sets out comprehensive guidance and is discussed in greater detail in Chapter 20, para 20.106.

18.85 Practitioners should take note that if a party, having obtained the leave of the court, has commissioned an expert's report, the contents of which are relevant to the future of the child in question, the report must be disclosed: there is no concept of litigation privilege in Children Act proceedings, which are essentially non-adversarial: *Re L (Police Investigation: Privilege)* [1996] 1 FLR 731. The position in relation to expert reports commissioned without the need to seek leave (eg a medical report on an adult which does not involve disclosure of the court papers or examination of the child) is less clear: see the discussion in *Vernon v Bosley (No 2)* [1998] 1 FLR 304.

Other evidence

18.86 The solicitor should consider in good time whether any evidence other than that of the party should be obtained for the hearing. For example, where someone other than the parent (eg a new spouse or a grandparent) is going to assist in the care of the child, there must be evidence from that person. If a parent is concerned about the standard of care that the other party would provide or about his or her lifestyle, consideration should be given to obtaining evidence from independent witnesses on these points. For example, the child's school might be approached in a case where it is alleged that the child is not properly fed, clothed, and kept clean. However, in determining whether to call further witnesses, it must be borne in mind that the welfare report is likely to deal with a number of the matters that are of concern and it may be possible to rely simply on this without calling further evidence. A final decision as to this can only be taken once the Cafcass report has been seen.

18.87 Generally speaking it is not a good tactical move to call a string of witnesses unless their evidence really does further the client's case. The solicitor will have the advantage of seeing the potential witnesses and evaluating their evidence for himself. A statement should be prepared for each of those who are to give evidence and should preferably be filed at court and served on the other side before the hearing. In addition, unless the other side indicate that they accept the evidence of the witness, the witness should be warned to attend the hearing. In particular it is vital that (whatever the attitude of the other side to the evidence) anyone who is to help to look after the child is present at court to give oral evidence. If there is a last-minute witness, it may be possible to call oral evidence at the hearing without having filed and served a statement previously provided that the court gives leave.

Sometimes a potential witness may be reluctant to get involved. The solicitor should be wary of such witnesses—their evidence can often turn out to be less valuable than the client expects. **18.88**

Hearing

Most hearings before the High Court or county court will be in chambers, and hearings before the family proceedings court will normally be held in private. Rule 12.21, FPR 2010 provides that: **18.89**

(a) the court may give directions as to the order of evidence and speeches;
(b) unless the court directs otherwise, the parties and children's guardian should usually adduce evidence in the following order:
    (i)   applicant;
    (ii) any party with parental responsibility for the child;
    (iii) other respondents;
    (iv) children's guardian;
    (v)   the child, if he is a party and there is no children's guardian.

Hearing children cases in England and Wales in private does not breach Art 6, European Convention for the Protection of Human Rights and Fundamental Freedoms (*B v UK and P v UK* [2001] 2 FLR 261). The right of the media to attend hearings in family proceedings is contained in FPR 2010, PD27B and PD27C. **18.90**

Hearsay evidence

The Children (Admissibility of Hearsay Evidence) Order 1993 allows evidence given 'in connection with the upbringing, maintenance or welfare of a child' to be admissible notwithstanding any rule of law relating to hearsay. However, the weight to be given to such evidence will be at the discretion of the judge. **18.91**

Power of court to direct investigation by local authority

If, during the course of hearing proceedings for a s 8 order (or, indeed, in the course of any family proceedings, as defined by s 8(3)), it becomes apparent to the court that the circumstances of the child may merit the making of a care or supervision order, then the court has power to direct the local authority to investigate (s 37(1)). All public law childcare cases, **18.92** which includes cases in which a s 37 direction is made, are governed by the public law outline (see Chapter 20, para 20.33).

18.93 The procedure for making a s 37 direction is contained in r 12.17, FPR 2010. As soon as practicable after the direction is made the court officer will serve it on all parties to the proceedings, and on the appropriate local authority. The local authority must allocate the request to a social services team manager within 24 hours of receiving the order: PD12A. Any assessment undertaken should be completed within 35 days. The local authority must report to the court in writing (r 12.17(5)) and where it decides not to apply for a care or supervision order it should set out the reasons for its decision in the report.

Appeals

18.94 Appeals will only be allowed where the decision of the lower court is wrong, or unjust because of a serious procedural or other irregularity in the proceedings: r 18.12, FPR 2010.

18.95 An appeal against the making of an order by a family proceedings court, or against the refusal of the magistrates to make an order will lie to a judge of the county court: s 94(1), CA 1989 and Access to Justice Act 1999 (Destination of Appeals) (Family Proceedings) Order 2011. Permission to appeal is not required.

18.96 An appeal against the decision of a district judge will usually be made to the judge of the court in which the decision was made: Access to Justice Act 1999 (Destination of Appeals) (Family Proceedings) Order 2011. Permission to appeal is required, unless the appeal is against a committal order or a secure accommodation order: r 18.3(2), FPR 2010. Permission should first be requested orally from the lower court: PD30A, para 4.2. If refused, the appellant may renew the application to the appeal court. Permission may be given only where the court considers that the appeal would have a real prospect of success, or there is some other compelling reason why the appeal should be heard: r 18.3(7).

18.97 An appeal from the district judge to the judge will not be conducted by way of rehearing unless it is in the interests of justice to do so: r 18.12. Fresh evidence will not be admitted unless the court orders otherwise: r 18.12(2), and see the principles in *Ladd* v *Marshall* (1954) FLR Rep 422.

18.98 Appeals against the decision of a judge of the county court or the High Court lie to the Court of Appeal and are governed by CPR 1998, Part 52.

Procedure

18.99 The procedure for conducting appeals from a magistrate or district judge to a judge is set out in FPR 2010, Part 30 and PD30A. The appellant must file and serve on the parties the following documents:

(a) a written notice of appeal, setting out the grounds upon which he relies and seeking permission where this is required (r 18.4);

(b) a copy of the order appealed against;

(c) a copy of any order giving or refusing permission to appeal, together with the court's reasons;

(d) a transcript or note of judgment or, in a magistrates' court, written reasons for the decision;
(e) any documents which the appellant reasonably considers necessary for the determination of the appeal.

Note that s 55, Access to Justice Act 1999, restricts the right to more than one appeal in most civil cases. Section 55(1) provides that where an appeal is made to a county court or the High Court in relation to any matter, and on hearing the appeal the court makes a decision in relation to that matter, no appeal may be made to the Court of Appeal from that decision unless the Court of Appeal considers that:

(i) the appeal would raise an important point of principle or practice; or
(ii) there is some other compelling reason for the Court of Appeal to hear it.

Time limits

The time limits for filing and serving notice of appeal are: **18.100**

(a) generally, within 21 days after the determination against which the appeal is brought;
(b) for appeals against interim care orders or interim supervision orders, seven days;
(c) otherwise, such other time as the court may direct.

Respondents to appeals

A respondent who wishes to contend: **18.101**

(a) that the decision of the court below should be varied; or
(b) that the decision of the court below should be affirmed on grounds other than those relied upon by that court; or
(c) by way of cross-appeal that the decision of the court below was wrong in whole or in part, must, within 14 days of receipt of notice of the appeal, file and serve on all other parties to the appeal a notice in writing, setting out the grounds upon which he relies: r 18.5, FPR 2010.

Procedure for interim applications

(a) Public funding: the question of costs must be resolved before embarking on an interim **18.102** application. If the matter is truly urgent, application can be made for an emergency certificate to cover the interim application. However, the solicitor may find the Legal Services Commission reluctant to grant such funding unless there are very special circumstances (eg where the other party has snatched the child from the care of the client and refuses to return him). If no emergency certificate is forthcoming, the solicitor will have to await the granting of a certificate for Legal Representation before taking action.
(b) The normal method of application for an interim order will be by filing the appropriate application form and asking the court for an early hearing date before a nominated family judge. The hearing itself will be in chambers and is likely to be brief. It follows the normal pattern, but any evidence given by the parties and witnesses is likely to be short. The court should be slow at an interim hearing to alter the status quo or to make any order which would have the effect of pre-judging the final decision. Other directions can be requested if they are required (eg a direction that the parties should file statements within a certain period).

Confidentiality of documents

18.103   FPR 2010, PD12G sets out the rules relating to the confidentiality of documents in family proceedings heard in private and involving children. It sets out in the form of a table those parties and other specified people who may disclose certain information from the proceedings to other specified people for specific purposes without needing the permission of the court or being in contempt of court. The court retains its inherent power to authorize or restrict disclosure of information in any particular case (s 12, Administration of Justice Act 1960). Any disclosure that falls outside the circumstances set out in the table requires the permission of the court.

Costs in family proceedings

18.104   It is important to note that costs in family proceedings are now governed by the Civil Procedure Rules 1998 ('CPR 1998'). The Family Proceedings (Miscellaneous Amendments) Rules 1999 apply the main parts of the costs rules under the CPR 1998 to family proceedings. Much of the detail will be found in the related Practice Directions. For the purposes of the family law practitioner, the following are the important areas of the CPR 1998 governing the practice and procedure relating to costs:

(a) Part 43—Scope of Costs Rules and Definitions.
(b) Part 44—General Rules about Costs.
(c) Part 47—Procedure for Detailed Assessment of Costs etc.
(d) Part 48—Special Cases.

Enforcement of a s 8 order

18.105   The enforcement of s 8 orders is discussed in more detail in Chapter 17, paras 17.150 (residence orders) and 17.175 (contact orders).

18.106   Section 34, Family Law Act 1986 ('FLA 1986') empowers the High Court, county courts, or a family proceedings court in private law proceedings where an order has been made to authorize an officer of the court or a constable to take charge of a child and deliver him to the person in whose favour the original order was made. Section 34 may only be used, however, where the court is satisfied that the original order requiring the giving up of the child has been served on the relevant party and that it has been disobeyed.

18.107   Where a family proceedings court has made a residence order then this can be enforced under s 63(3), Magistrates' Courts Act 1980 against the party in breach of it as if the order had required the person concerned to produce the child, even though the order did not specifically say so: s 14(1), CA 1989. This enables the enforcement of the order under s 34(1) and (3), FLA 1986.

18.108   The application for enforcement under s 34, FLA 1986 is made in Form C3 and it should be made on notice unless there is an urgent need to make the order without notice. The application should be supported by evidence. The order issued by the court will be in Form C31.

18.109   It is possible to obtain an *ex parte* order under the inherent jurisdiction of the court for the Tipstaff to seek and recover a child in appropriate cases (see further, Chapter 17, para 17.209).

Finally, the failure of a person to obey a court order or undertaking given to the court is a contempt which can be punished by way of imprisonment, fine, or sequestration of assets.

Best Practice Guidance

Practitioners may find it helpful in the preparation of Children Act cases to refer to the *Best* **18.110**
Practice Guidance of June 1997 which is taken from the Children Act Advisory Committee
Handbook of Best Practice in Children Act Cases and is set out in Part V of *The Family Court
Practice* (Jordan Publishing).

C   KEY DOCUMENTS

Children Act 1989   **18.111**
Family Procedure Rules 2010 (SI 2010/2955)

D   USEFUL WEBSITES

The National Standards for the Children and Family Court Advisory and Support Service   **18.112**
    <http://www.cafcass.gov.uk>

19

PREVENTING THE REMOVAL OF A CHILD FROM THE JURISDICTION AND TRACING A LOST CHILD

A   FAMILY LAW ACT 1986

19.01 The Family Law Act 1986 ('FLA 1986') considerably reduces the problems that can arise when a child is taken out of the jurisdiction of the English courts to another part of the United Kingdom. The FLA 1986 has been amended by sch 13, paras 62 to 71, Children Act 1989 ('CA 1989'). The FLA 1986, in its amended form, establishes a procedure whereby a 'Part I order' made in relation to a child under 16 in one part of the United Kingdom will be recognized in any other part of the United Kingdom as having the same effect as if it had been made by a local court. It is possible to register a 'Part I order' in the appropriate court in another part of the United Kingdom. Once this has been done, one can apply to that court for the order to be enforced as if it were one of the court's own orders (see Chapter V, Part I, FLA 1986). For the meaning of 'Part I order' and for details of the other rules as to jurisdiction to make s 8 orders under the FLA 1986, see Chapter 17, para 17.108. However, note that Part I orders include s 8 orders (other than one varying or discharging a s 8 order) and certain orders made in the exercise of the inherent jurisdiction of the High Court with respect to children.

B   REMOVAL FROM THE UK

Child Abduction Act 1984

Section 1(1), Child Abduction Act 1984 ('CAA 1984'), as amended by sch 12, para 37, CA 1989 **19.02** makes it a criminal offence for a person 'connected' with a child under 16 to take or send the child out of the United Kingdom without the appropriate consent.

The following are 'connected' with the child: **19.03**

(a)   a parent of the child;
(b)   in the case of a child whose parents were not married to each other at the time of his birth, a person whom there are reasonable grounds for believing to be the father of the child;
(c)   a guardian of the child;
(d)   a special guardian of the child;
(e)   a person in whose favour a residence order is in force with respect to the child;
(f)   a person who has custody of the child.

The consent that is needed is from the following:

(1)   (a)   the child's mother;
      (b)   the child's father, if he has parental responsibility for him;
      (c)   any guardian of the child;
      (d)   any special guardian of the child;
      (e)   any person in whose favour a residence order is in force with respect to the child;
      (f)   any person who has custody of the child; or
(2)   the leave of the court granted under or by virtue of any provision of Part II, CA 1989; or
(3)   if any person has custody of the child, the leave of the court which awarded custody to him.

A person does *not* commit an offence under CAA 1984 if he takes or sends a child out of the   **19.04** United Kingdom without the appropriate consent *if*:

(a)   he is a person in whose favour there is a residence order in respect of the child; and
(b)   he takes or sends the child out of the United Kingdom for a period of less than one month; or
(c)   he is a special guardian of the child and he takes or sends the child out of the United Kingdom for a period of less than three months;

unless he does so in breach of the terms of an order made under Part II, CA 1989 (s 4A, CAA 1984).

Section 1(5), CAA 1984 provides that a person does not commit an offence by doing anything   **19.05** without the consent of another person whose consent is technically required if:

(a)   he does it in the belief that the other person:
      (i)   has consented; or
      (ii) would consent if he was aware of all the relevant circumstances; or

(b) he has taken all reasonable steps to communicate with the other person but has been unable to do so; or

(c) the other person has unreasonably refused his consent.

However, point (c) above does *not* apply if:

(a) the person who refused to consent is a person:
  (i) in whose favour there is a residence order in force with respect to the child; or
  (ii) who is a special guardian of the child; or
  (iii) who has custody of the child; or

(b) the person so taking or sending the child is doing so in breach of an order made by a court in the United Kingdom.

For the purposes of CAA 1984 the terms 'guardian of a child', 'special guardian', 'residence order', and 'parental responsibility' have the same meaning as in the CA 1989.

19.06 Note that there are special modifications of s 1 for certain children, for example those who are in the care of local authorities, detained in a place of safety, remanded to local authority accommodation, or the subject of an order relating to adoption (see s 1(8) and the schedule to CAA 1984).

19.07 By virtue of s 2, CAA 1984, a person who is *not* the parent, guardian, someone with a residence order in respect of the child, or someone with custody of the child commits an offence if, without lawful authority or reasonable excuse, he takes or detains a child under 16 so as:

(a) to remove him from the lawful control of any person having lawful control of him; or

(b) to keep him out of the lawful control of any person entitled to lawful control of him.

19.08 A person charged under s 2, CAA 1984 has a defence if he can show that, at the time of the alleged offence:

(a) he believed that the child was at least 16; or

(b) in the case of a child of unmarried parents, he had reasonable grounds for believing he was the child's father.

19.09 Although the provisions of CAA 1984 may be a psychological deterrent to anyone contemplating abducting a child and taking him abroad, the Act itself does not establish any practical safeguards to prevent the removal of the child. What it has done, however, is to prompt the setting up of a 'port alert' system which does offer more concrete help.

The port alert system

General

19.10 The port alert system is described fully in FPR 2010, PD12F, Part 4. It is operated by the police.

19.11 The police provide a 24-hour service and, in conjunction with immigration officers at the ports, will attempt to prevent the unlawful removal of a child from the country. The National Ports Office can be contacted on 020 7230 4800.

Eligibility for assistance under the system

Before they will institute a port alert for a child, the police will need to be satisfied: **19.12**

(a) That there is a real and imminent danger of the child being removed. 'Imminent' means within 24 to 48 hours and 'real' means that the port alert is not just being sought as an insurance.

(b) That:
   (i)   the child is under 16; or
   (ii)   the child is a ward (the police should be shown evidence of this, for example confirming the wardship, an injunction, or, in an urgent case, a sealed copy of the originating summons in wardship); or
   (iii) in the case of a child of 16 or over who is not a ward of court, there is in force a residence order relating to the child or an order restricting or restraining his removal from the jurisdiction; or
   (iv)   there are grounds for suspecting an offence under CAA 1984 will be committed.

Means of seeking police help

An application for assistance in preventing a child's removal from the jurisdiction must be   **19.13**
made by the applicant or his legal representative to a police station. Application should normally be made to the applicant's local police station but, in urgent cases, any police station will suffice. The police require quite a lot of detail to be given when assistance is requested, for example likely travel details and information about the child, the applicant and the person likely to remove the child from the jurisdiction. Reference should be made to PD12F, para 4.7 for a complete list of the details that should be given if possible. Where a court order has been obtained in relation to the child, it should be produced to the police even where the child is under 16 and a court order is not strictly required.

How the system works

If the police are satisfied that the port alert system should be used, the child's name will be   **19.14**
entered on a stop list for four weeks. The ports will be notified direct, and police and immigration officers will attempt to identify the child and prevent his removal from the country. After four weeks the child's name will automatically be removed from the stop list unless a further application is made.

Passports

The Identity and Passport Service (IPS) will take action to prevent the issue of a UK passport only   **19.15**
where it has been served with a court order expressly requiring a passport to be surrendered or expressly prohibiting the issue of a passport.

The law on the surrender of passports is statutory and found in s 37, FLA 1986. The section   **19.16**
provides that where there is in force an order prohibiting or restricting the removal of a child from the United Kingdom or from any part of it, the court that made the order and appropriate courts in other parts of the United Kingdom may require any person to surrender any UK passport which has been issued to or contains particulars of the child.

19.17   In any case where such an order is made, the IPS must be served immediately with a copy of the order. The details of the IPS and a specimen form of letter are set out in PD12F, para 4.10.

C   TRACING A LOST CHILD

Allowing publication of information about a child

19.18   If a child is missing, the court has power to permit the publication of information about the child to enable him to be traced. If it is felt that publicity would help, the judge should be asked to lift reporting restrictions to enable information such as a description of the child, a photograph of him, a description of the adult thought to be accompanying him, details concerning his disappearance, and anything known about where he may be to be published: FPR 2010, PD12F, para 4.15.

Disclosure of addresses by government departments

19.19   The court can request certain government departments to provide information as to where a missing child might be: FPR 2010, PD6C. The request must certify that the child cannot be traced and that the child is believed to be with the person whose address is sought. The request may be made to any government department; the most likely to be in a position to assist are the Department of Social Security, the National Health Service Central Register (administered by the Office for National Statistics), the Passport Office, and the Ministry of Defence (where the person sought is serving or has recently served in HM Forces.) PD6B sets out the details which will be required by each government department before the request can be complied with.

19.20   The Inland Revenue, for reasons of data protection legislation, will only comply with orders for disclosure made in the High Court or the Principal Registry of the Family Division. For guidance, see PD6B.

Seeking information as to child's whereabouts: s 33, Family Law Act 1986

19.21   Section 33, FLA 1986 (as amended by sch 13, para 62, CA 1989), provides that all courts have power in proceedings for or relating to an order made under s 8, CA 1989, to require any person whom they have reason to believe may have information relevant to where a child is to disclose that information to the court. The appropriate form to be completed is Form C4.

Recovering a child through s 34, Family Law Act 1986

19.22   Where a person has not returned a child in accordance with a residence or contact order, the court can be asked to make a further order authorizing an officer of the court (eg a solicitor) or a police constable to search for, take charge of, and deliver the child to him, thus giving effect to the residence or contact order (s 34, FLA 1986). However, an order under s 34 can be granted only once the original order to give up the child has been served and disobeyed. Application for such an order is made on Form C3.

Recovering a child through the inherent jurisdiction

If the applicant has good reason to believe that the person who has control of the child is **19.23** likely to try to hide the child or remove him from the jurisdiction on becoming aware of the applicant's attempts to recover the child, then it may be appropriate for the applicant to apply for an order without first giving notice to the other side (ie, *ex parte*) under the inherent jurisdiction authorizing the Tipstaff to 'search and find' the child. The Tipstaff is an officer of the High Court and has authority to arrest and bring before a court any person who obstructs him in the execution of an order of the High Court. Any such order should be carefully drafted so as to make it clear to the Tipstaff exactly what is required of him. For example, the order should specify the person, or local authority (if appropriate), to whom the Tipstaff should 'hand over' the child once he has secured his return.

Flight information

Where a person seeks an order for the return of a child who is about to arrive in England by air **19.24** he will probably wish to have information to enable him to meet the aeroplane. The applicant should ask the judge to include a direction in his order that the airline operating the flight and the immigration officer at the relevant airport should supply the appropriate information to the applicant. Where the applicant already has an order for the return of the child he should apply without first giving notice to the other side to a judge for the appropriate direction to be added to the order: FPR 2010, PD12O.

D   KEY DOCUMENTS

Child Abduction Act 1984 **19.25**
Family Law Act 1986
Children Act 1989

20

CHILDREN IN LOCAL AUTHORITY CARE

A INTRODUCTION—CHILDREN AND LOCAL AUTHORITIES

Only one route into care

A child may only be received into the care of a local authority as a result of a court order, and **20.01** upon the statutory 'threshold' criteria set out in s 31(2), Children Act 1989 ('CA 1989') having been satisfied. An interim care order may be made, for a limited period, where there are reasonable grounds for believing that the statutory criteria are met: s 38. In both cases, the fact that the threshold criteria are or may be satisfied does not automatically mean that a care order should be made. The court must go on to consider whether such an order, which amounts to an interference by the state in family life, is necessary in order to safeguard the child's welfare.

Human Rights Act 1998

The Human Rights Act 1998 ('HRA 1998') incorporated into domestic law the European **20.02** Convention for the Protection of Human Rights and Fundamental Freedoms (ECHR). Article 8, ECHR guarantees the right to respect for private and family life. Article 8(2) permits interference by a public authority with an individual's private and family life only where the interference is in accordance with the law and necessary for the purposes specified in the Article. There is need for proportionality between the interests of the applicant and the interests of the community. The existence of this guarantee is of crucial importance in public law childcare cases in determining in what circumstances a child can properly be taken into the care of a local authority.

If such interference is justified the court must also consider whether it is proportionate to the **20.03** aim of protecting the rights of the child concerned (*Re B (Care: Interference with Family Life)* [2003] 2 FLR 813). The task of the domestic court when faced with a complaint under Art 8(1) is to review the decisions taken under the ECHR by other public authorities and compare them with the case currently before it. Where the rights of parents and those of a child are at stake, the child's interests are the paramount consideration. If any balancing of interests is necessary, the child's interests must prevail (*Yousef* v *The Netherlands* [2003] 1 FLR 210).

When a local authority plans to take a child into care, it must ensure that the procedure at all **20.04** stages is transparent and fair, both in and out of court. Article 8 requires the local authority to involve parents fully in the decision-making process, at all stages of the child protection procedure, whether before, during, or after the making of a care order (*Re G (Care: Challenge to Local Authority's Decision)* [2003] 2 FLR 42). See further under para 20.64 below.

Adoption and Children Act 2002

The Adoption and Children Act 2002 ('ACA 2002') has made amendments to the CA 1989. **20.05** The main changes affecting the public law relating to children (which will be referred to in more detail at appropriate points in the text) include:

(a) *Extended definition of 'harm'*—s 120, ACA 2002 extends the definition of 'harm' in s 31(9), CA 1989 to include, for example, impairment suffered by hearing or seeing the ill-treatment of another.

(b) *Care plans*—s 121, ACA 2002 inserts a new s 31A, CA 1989 which provides that in all public law cases in which a local authority seeks a care order in respect of a child it must prepare a care plan (to be known as a 's 31A care plan'). Furthermore, the local authority is required to keep the care plan under review and make changes as and when necessary, even after a care order has been made and implemented.

(c) *Review of cases of 'looked-after' children*—s 118, ACA 2002 amends s 26(2)(e), CA 1989 to create a 'looked-after' children reviewing officer, so that even after the making of a care order the officer will participate in the review process and will have power to refer the case to the Children and Family Court Advisory and Support Service (Cafcass) where appropriate. Cafcass will have power to take proceedings on behalf of the child.

(d) *Advocacy services*—s 119, ACA 2002 inserts a new s 26A, CA 1989 to place a duty on local authorities to provide assistance to adults and children wishing to make representations under ss 24D and 26, CA 1989 about the way the authority has discharged its functions.

The general duty of the local authority

20.06   Local authorities are placed under a general duty to:

(a) safeguard and promote the welfare of children within their area who are in need; and
(b) so far as it is consistent with that duty, to promote the upbringing of children by their families

by providing a range and level of services appropriate to those children's needs: s 17(1).

20.07   Thus, the CA 1989 emphasizes that the prime responsibility for the upbringing of children lies with their parents. The intention is that the state should be ready to help parents to discharge that responsibility, especially if it lessens the risk of family breakdown. Services to families in need of help should be arranged in voluntary partnership with parents, so far as possible. If those services include looking after the child away from home then the underlying principle is that close contact should be maintained between the child and his family and, if appropriate, the family should be reunited as soon as possible.

20.08   A child is taken to be 'in need' if he is unlikely to achieve or maintain, or to have the opportunity of achieving or maintaining, a reasonable standard of health or development without the provision for him of services by a local authority under Part III, CA 1989, or if he is disabled: s 17(10).

20.09   'Family', in relation to a child in need, includes any person who has parental responsibility for the child and any other person with whom he has been living: s 17(10).

20.10   'Development' means physical, intellectual, emotional, social, or behavioural development: s 17(11).

20.11   'Health' means physical and mental health: s 17(11).

20.12   The specific duties placed on local authorities are set out in sch 2, Part I, CA 1989 and include, for example, the provision of family centres; but lack of space precludes exploring these issues further.

Duty to accommodate children in need

A duty is imposed on local authorities to accommodate children in need in the following **20.13** circumstances:

(a) where there is no person with parental responsibility for him;

(b) where he is lost or has been abandoned; or

(c) where the person who has been caring for him is prevented (whether or not permanently, and for whatever reason) from providing him with suitable accommodation or care (s 20).

A child 'accommodated' by the local authority (but not the subject of a care order) may be removed by his parents at any time. The only way in which a local authority can assume 'parental responsibility' for a child is by applying for, and being granted, a care order. This reflects the aim of Parliament that the transfer to a local authority of the legal powers and responsibilities of caring for a child should only be done by a full court hearing following due legal process. Thus, the application of emergency powers to remove a child at serious risk (eg by way of an emergency protection order), which necessarily cannot be preceded by a full court hearing, should be of short duration and subject to court review.

A child who is accommodated by a local authority becomes 'looked after' in the same way **20.14** as a child who is in care, and the local authority owes the same duties to children in both categories: see para 20.19 below.

The child's view

The CA 1989 stipulates that wherever possible the local authority should consider the wishes of **20.15** the child before providing him with accommodation. It should give due consideration to such wishes as it has been able to ascertain (having regard to his age and understanding): s 20(6).

If the child is over 16, the CA 1989 effectively gives the child complete autonomy in that he **20.16** may consent to being provided with accommodation by the local authority even though:

(a) the person(s) with parental responsibility for him objects (s 20(11)); and

(b) the person with parental responsibility is able to provide the child with accommodation (s 20(4)).

Parental removal

Once a child is accommodated by a local authority, then any person with parental respon- **20.17** sibility may *at any time* remove the child from the local authority accommodation: s 20(8). There are only two exceptions:

(a) Where a person in whose favour a residence order has been made in respect of a child, or who has care and control of the child by virtue of an order made in the exercise of the inherent jurisdiction of the High Court (s 20(9)) or by virtue of an existing order (sch 14, para 8(4)) *agrees* to the child being looked after by the local authority (s 20(9)). If there are two such persons then *both* must agree: s 20(10).

(b) Where the child has reached 16 and *agrees* to being so accommodated: s 20(11).

If the local authority wishes to prevent the child from being removed from local authority **20.18** accommodation it has only two choices:

(a) to apply to the court for a care order, by satisfying the s 31(2) statutory grounds; or

(b)   to apply to the court for an emergency protection order under s 44(1); this will be suitable only where the case is urgent.

Duties of local authorities in relation to children 'looked after' by them

20.19   A child is 'looked after' by a local authority for the purposes of the CA 1989 if he is:

(a)   in local authority care by virtue of a care order; or

(b)   provided with accommodation by the local authority (for a continuous period of more than 24 hours) under a voluntary arrangement: ss 22(1) and 105(4).

General duties

20.20   When a local authority looks after a child, s 22(3) places upon that authority a general duty:

(a)   to safeguard and promote his welfare, including a duty to promote his educational achievement (s 22(3A)); and

(b)   to make such use of services available for children cared for by their own parents as appears to the authority reasonable in his case.

The local authority must act as a 'good parent'. *Before* making decisions about the child the authority is required by s 22(4) to ascertain the wishes and feelings of the following persons:

(i)   the child;

(ii)   the child's parents;

(iii) any person who is not a parent of the child but has parental responsibility for him;

(iv) any other person whose wishes and feelings the authority consider to be relevant.

20.21   Once the local authority actually engages in the process of *making* the decision, s 22(5) requires them to give consideration:

(a)   to the wishes and feelings of those persons listed above; and

(b)   to the child's religious persuasion, racial origin, and cultural and linguistic background.

Provision of accommodation and maintenance

20.22   Once the local authority is looking after a child it is under a duty to provide him with accommodation and to maintain him: ss 22A and 22B.

20.23   There is a statutory *presumption* that an authority looking after a child must make arrangements enabling him to live with one of the following:

(a)   a parent;

(b)   a person who is not a parent but has parental responsibility;

(c)   a person in whose favour a residence order was in force immediately before a care order was made; or

(d)   a relative, friend, or other person connected with him;

unless those solutions would not be reasonably practicable or consistent with his welfare: s 22C.

20.24   Once the child is the subject of a care order that presumption is reversed.

Contact between the child and his family

Once a local authority is looking after a child it must endeavour, so far as is practicable and **20.25** consistent with the child's welfare, to promote contact between the child and the following persons:

(a) his parents;
(b) any person who is not a parent but has parental responsibility for him;
(c) any other person connected with him: sch 2, para 15(1).

For further discussion of parental contact with children in care see para 20.75 below.

Advice and assistance for certain children

Where a child is being looked after by a local authority the authority is under a duty to 'advise, **20.26** assist and befriend him' with a view to promoting his welfare when he ceases to be looked after by that authority (s 24A).

Review of cases

The CA 1989 requires local authorities to conduct at regular intervals a general review of the **20.27** progress of each child who is being looked after or provided with accommodation by them in accordance with the Review of Children's Cases Regulations 1991.

The CA 1989 also requires local authorities to provide a review procedure, with an independ- **20.28** ent element, to resolve disputes and complaints raised when a child, his parents, anyone with parental responsibility for him, or a local authority foster parent is unhappy with the arrangements made for the child's care (s 26(3)). See the Children Act 1989 Representations Procedure (England) Regulations 2006.

Section 118, ACA 2002 has introduced in s 26(2)(e), CA 1989 (requirement to consider dis- **20.29** charge of a care order) an amendment to create a looked-after children independent review- ing officer. The functions of the independent reviewing officer (IRO) are to participate in the process of reviewing the care plan and revising it as necessary, to monitor the local authority's functions in respect of the review, and to refer the case to Cafcass if he considers it appropriate to do so. The detailed provisions are contained in the Review of Children's Cases (Amendment) (England) Regulations 2004 (SI 2004/1419) and *Independent Reviewing Officer's Guidance* (Department for Education and Skills, 2004) ('the DfES Guidance') avail- able at <http://www.dres.gov.uk/adoption>. IROs have power to refer cases they are unable to resolve to their satisfaction to Cafcass Legal, which may start court proceedings against the local authority seeking an order requiring it to put right its failings in relation to the care plan. It is intended that all looked-after children will have an IRO. Cafcass Legal can only accept referrals from IROs and their options are to: reject the referral; attempt to resolve the matter by mediation; refer the matter to another agency; or, bring civil proceedings against the local authority. If further proceedings under CA 1989 are required, Cafcass Legal refer the case back to the children's guardian from the care proceedings (Children and Family Court Advisory and Support Service (Reviewed Case Referral) Regulations 2004). There is an explanatory Cafcass Practice Note, 'Cases Referred by Independent Reviewing Officers' dated 8 June 2004 and available at <http://www.justice.gov.uk>. If a civil action is brought against the local authority, one of the social work practitioners in Cafcass Legal will act as the child's litigation friend. The options for civil action are: judicial review proceedings; a compensation claim; or a freestanding HRA 1998 application.

20.30   The second stage of the reviewing system depends on action being taken by Cafcass as and when it decides that there is a need to return a case to court for further scrutiny by a judge.

20.31   The remedy available under ss 7 and 8, HRA 1998. Section 7, HRA 1998, provides a mechanism for 'victims' of an alleged breach of Convention rights to make complaints about acts of a public authority which are unlawful as being incompatible with Convention rights. There are two routes to bring such a complaint. The first is through legal proceedings in any court or tribunal in which the proceedings are brought by or at the instigation of a public authority (s 7(6)). The second route is by making a separate claim under s 7(1)(a) in the High Court (or Administrative Court) for judicial review. Where the court finds that an act of a public authority is unlawful it has power to grant such relief or remedy, or make such order, within its powers as it considers just and appropriate (s 8, HRA 1998). Damages may be awarded, but only by a court with jurisdiction to do so (s 8(2), HRA 1998). Therefore, if a local authority conducts itself in a manner which infringes the Art 8 rights of a parent or child, the court may grant appropriate relief on the application of a victim of the unlawful act (*Re S (Minors) (Care Order: Implementation of Care Plan); Re W (Minors) (Care Order: Adequacy of Care Plan)* [2002] 1 FLR 815).

Advocacy services

20.32   Section 119, ACA 2002 inserts a new s 26A, CA 1989. This places a duty on local authorities to provide assistance to adults and children who wish to make representations under ss 24D and 26, CA 1989, about the way the local authority has discharged its functions. This includes arranging for that adult or child to have assistance by way of representation.

B   THE PUBLIC LAW OUTLINE: FPR 2010, PD12A

20.33   The Public Law Outline sets out the steps which must be taken in any application for a care or supervision order and, as far as practicable, to all other public law proceedings. Key features of the outline are:

(a)   The Timetable for the Child: each case will have a timetable for the proceedings set by the court in accordance with the Timetable for the Child, which will include significant legal, social, and educational events in the child's life.

(b)   Judicial continuity: each case is allocated to one or not more than two case management judges who are responsible for every case management stage in the proceedings.

(c)   Active case management by the court.

(d)   Consistency and standardization.

20.34   The Public Law Outline places emphasis on the 'pre-proceedings' stage of an application, imposing requirements on the local authority to carry out an initial and core assessment before issuing proceedings in all but the most urgent cases. Parents must be informed of the local authority's intention to issue proceedings in a Letter Before Proceedings which sets out the local authority's concerns and the steps which the parents are expected to take in order to address them.

Once the proceedings have been issued, the Public Law Outline sets out steps that must be **20.35** taken by the parties and the court as follows.

Stage 1—Issue and the First Appointment

When a decision is made to apply for a care or supervision order the local authority must file **20.36** with the court an application in Form C1 and set out in Form C13 a summary of the facts and matters relied upon to satisfy the threshold criteria. On the day the application is filed the court must issue the application. It must also give standard directions on issue, fixing a time and date for the First Hearing, which must be not later than day 6. The court must appoint a guardian (unless it is satisfied that it is not necessary to do so to safeguard the child's interests) and solicitor for the child.

By day 3 Cafcass is expected to allocate the case to a children's guardian.

At the First Appointment the court will make arrangements, if necessary, for a contested hear- **20.37** ing; confirm the Timetable for the Child; identify any additional parties; scrutinize the care plan; and give standard directions, including the listing of a Case Management Conference (no later than day 45) or, if appropriate, an Early Final Hearing.

Stage 2—Case Management Conference

No later than two days before the Case Management Conference there must be an advocates' **20.38** meeting held in order to prepare the draft Case Management Order, to identify experts, and to draft questions for them. A draft of the Case Management Order must be filed with the case manager or case management judge by 11 am on the day before the Case Management Conference.

At the Case Management Conference the court will review the Timetable for the Child; con- **20.39** sider case management directions; scrutinize the care plan, and check compliance with the Experts Practice Direction (PD25A). The court will list an Issues Resolution Hearing and, where necessary, a warned period for the Final Hearing.

Stage 3—Issues Resolution Hearing

An advocates' meeting must take place between two and seven days before the Issues **20.40** Resolution Hearing. The advocates must prepare case summaries setting out their positions and file a draft Case Management Order with the case manager or case management judge by 11 am on the day before the Issues Resolution Hearing.

At the Issues Resolution Hearing the court's objective will be to resolve and narrow issues, **20.41** and to undertake final case management. The court will give directions for filing of an agreed threshold document or identification of the facts and issues remaining to be determined; final evidence and care plan; the guardian's case analysis and recommendations; witness templates and skeleton arguments. It will list or confirm a final hearing.

Stage 4—Final Hearing

20.42   Where one of the allocated case management judges or a family proceedings court has heard a substantial factual issue or there has been a 'preliminary hearing' to determine findings of fact it is necessary for the same judge/magistrates who conducted that hearing to conduct the Final Hearing.

C   CARE AND SUPERVISION ORDERS

20.43   The statutory provisions governing care and supervision orders are set out in Part IV, CA 1989. The main features of the statutory scheme are as follows:

(a)   The court may make a care order only if it is satisfied that:
    (i)   the statutory 'threshold' criteria in s 31(2) have been met; *and*
    (ii)   the child's welfare demands that a care order be made.

(b)   Care orders may be made on specific application or in the course of 'family proceedings'.

(c)   The family proceedings court, county court, and High Court all have jurisdiction to make care orders. However, most care proceedings will commence in the family proceedings court. For further details as to the allocation of work between the courts, see Chapter 18, para 18.01.

(d)   The local authority assumes parental responsibility for the child on the making of a care order and any existing s 8 orders terminate. However, other persons having parental responsibility for the child will not be divested of it. They will 'share' parental responsibility with the local authority.

(e)   There is a statutory presumption that the authority will allow the child in care to have contact with his parents and other specified persons. Section 34, CA 1989 contains the mechanisms for determining and enforcing the existence and levels of such contact.

(f)   When an application for a care order has been issued, the court has power (subject to the threshold criteria being satisfied) to make either a care or a supervision order.

(g)   The court may make interim orders during the course of care proceedings.

Who can apply for a care or supervision order?

20.44   The application for a care order may be made by:

(a)   any local authority; or
(b)   an authorized person (s 31(1)).

So far the only 'authorized person' is the NSPCC. However, there is provision for the Secretary of State to name others in due course.

20.45   No one else may initiate care proceedings. With one exception, the court itself may not make a care or supervision order without an application first having been made by the local authority. The exception is that where the court forms the view within other family proceedings that it may be appropriate for a care or supervision order to be made, it may direct the local authority to investigate pursuant to s 37(1), and at the same time make an interim care or supervision order: s 38(1)(b). However, if the authority investigates but chooses not to make an application, the court has no power to make a further care/supervision order.

No care order may be made with respect to a child who has reached the age of 17 (or 16 if the **20.46** child is married): s 31(3).

What must the local authority do before making an application?

Where a local authority suspects that a child in their area has suffered significant harm or is **20.47** likely to do so then it must investigate fully the circumstances of the child so that it can decide whether any action should be taken to 'safeguard or promote the child's welfare': s 47(1). *Before* making a decision the authority must (so far as is reasonably practicable) ascertain the wishes and feelings of the child, his parents, anyone else with parental responsibility (eg a guardian), and any other person whose wishes and feelings the authority considers to be relevant: s 22(4). The duty to consult could be waived on the basis that it was not 'reasonably practicable' if the circumstances of the child required urgent action which might be prejudiced by such consultation; for example, where the parents are likely to run away with the child if they are informed in advance that an application for a care order is to be made.

Who are the respondents in care proceedings?

The persons who must be made respondents to an application for a care or supervision order **20.48** are defined in r 12.3, Family Procedure Rules 2010 ('FPR 2010'). They are as follows:

(a) every person whom the applicant believes to have parental responsibility for the child;
(b) where the child is the subject of a care order (ie, in the course of an application for a supervision order), every person whom the applicant believes to have parental responsibility immediately prior to the making of the care order;
(c) in the case of an application to extend, vary, or discharge an order, the parties to the proceedings leading to the order which it is sought to have extended, varied, or discharged;
(d) the child.

Who may be a party to care proceedings?

Anyone can make a request that he be joined as a party, or cease to be a party to care proceedings. **20.49** The court will deal with the request in accordance with the procedure set out in rr 18.1 to 18.13, FPR 2010 and PD18A. If a person with parental responsibility for the child requests to be made a party the court must grant the request: r 12.3(2). If the natural father of the child concerned wishes to participate as a party in care proceedings then he should generally be allowed to do so, even if he does not have parental responsibility, unless there are justifiable reasons for not so joining him: *Re B (Care Proceedings: Notification of Father without Parental Responsibility)* [1999] 2 FLR 408.

In *Re W (Discharge of Party to Proceedings)* [1997] 1 FLR 128 the court discharged the children's **20.50** natural father from the proceedings. In that case the father had been convicted of the murder of the children's half-sister, was serving a sentence of life imprisonment, had never seen the younger child and had not seen the elder child for over four years. Although it was a very serious matter to prevent a natural parent from being a party, the facts of this case justified it. In very exceptional circumstances, the court has power to make a declaration that the local authority need not comply with its duty to provide information about proceedings to a parent and to consult him or her before issuing: *Re C (Care: Consultation with Parents not in Child's Best Interests)* [2006] 2 FLR 787.

The threshold criteria

20.51   Section 31, CA 1989 states that a court may make a care or supervision order *only* if it is satisfied that:

(a) the child is suffering, or likely to suffer, significant harm; *and*
(b) the harm, or likelihood of harm, is attributable to:
  (i)   the care given to the child, or likely to be given to him if the order is not made, not being what it would be reasonable to expect a parent to give to him; or
  (ii) the child's being beyond parental control.

Grounds (a) and (b) are cumulative. Both must be satisfied, although ground (b) may be satisfied by either of its sub-paragraphs. The expression 'if [the court] is satisfied' envisages that the court must be judicially satisfied on proper material. The legal burden of establishing the relevant conditions rests on the applicant for a care order: *Re H and R (Child Sexual Abuse: Standard of Proof)* [1996] 1 FLR 80. Once the grounds have been made out then the court moves on to the second limb of its decision-making exercise. Before completing its determination of the case the court must abide by the dictates of s 1, CA 1989, that is to say:

(a) the child's welfare is the paramount consideration (s 1(1)); and
(b) in considering the welfare of the child the court must apply the statutory checklist of factors set out in s 1(3); and
(c) the court must bear in mind the general principle in s 1(2) that there is a presumption that any delay in determining the matter is likely to prejudice the welfare of the child; and
(d) the court must not make an order unless it considers that making it would be better for the child than making no order at all: s 1(5).

Definition of terms used in s 31(2)

20.52   For the purposes of the CA 1989 the following terms used in s 31(2) are defined in s 31(9) as follows:

'Harm' means ill-treatment or the impairment of health and development. (Note: the meaning of harm has been extended to include, for example, impairment suffered by hearing or seeing the ill-treatment of another.)

'Development' means physical, intellectual, emotional, social, or behavioural development.

'Health' means physical or mental health.

'Ill-treatment' includes sexual abuse and forms of ill-treatment which are not physical.

'Significant' is not defined in the CA 1989, but it will obviously be construed by the lawyer with reference to the *de minimis* principle. The layman should be warned not to equate 'significant' with 'substantial'. Where the question of whether the harm suffered by the child is 'significant' turns upon the child's health or development, then his health or development is to be compared with that which could reasonably be expected of a similar child: s 31(10). Thus, a subjective stance is to be adopted in relation to the particular characteristics and disabilities of this particular child. Thereafter, an objective test is to be applied as to whether the standard of his health and development is a standard which could reasonably be expected of a child with similar characteristics.

'Care' in s 31(2)(b)(i) is not defined, but it has been held to go beyond physical care and to include the emotional care which a reasonable parent would give a child; in the case of a child who has been abused, that includes listening to the child and monitoring his words and actions so that a professional assessment can be carried out: *Re B (A Minor) (Care Order: Criteria)* [1993] 1 FLR 815.

Meaning of present and future harm

Meaning of 'is suffering' significant harm   The requirement in s 31(1)(a) that the child   **20.53**
'is suffering' significant harm falls to be examined on the date at which the local authority initiated the procedure for protection under the Act. In other words, the threshold criteria will be satisfied if, at the time of the local authority's decision to take the temporary measures to protect the child from immediate harm which leads to the application for the care or supervision order in due course, the child is suffering or likely to suffer significant harm: *Re M (A Minor) (Care Order: Threshold Conditions)* [1994] 3 All ER 298. However, the local authority does not have to be in possession of all the information it wishes to rely upon at the date of the application. Evidence-gathering continues after proceedings have begun and later acquired information as to the state of affairs at the relevant date can be taken into account: *Re G (Care Proceedings: Threshold Conditions)* [2001] 2 FLR 1111.

Meaning of 'likely to suffer' significant harm   The meaning of 'likely harm' was referred   **20.54**
to by the Law Commission in *The Law on Child Care and Family Services* (Cm 62, 1987, para 60) as follows:

> It is intended that 'likely harm' should cover all cases of unacceptable risk in which it may be necessary to balance the chance of harm occurring against the magnitude of that harm if it does occur . . . the court will have to judge whether there is a risk and what the nature of the risk is.

The meaning of 'likely to suffer' in s 31(2) should not be equated with 'on the balance of prob-   **20.55**
abilities'. The court is not applying a test to events which had happened in the past and then deciding on the balance of probabilities whether such events had in fact happened; instead, the court is looking to the future where all it can do is to evaluate the chance that the child will suffer significant harm in the future if the care order or supervision order is not made. The word 'likely' means a 'real possibility, a possibility that cannot sensibly be ignored having regard to the nature and gravity of the feared harm in the particular case': *Re H and R (Child Sexual Abuse: Standard of Proof)* (para 20.51 above); see also *Re B (Care Proceedings: Standard of Proof)* [2008] 2 FLR 141.

The relevant date for assessing the 'likelihood of harm' is the date upon which the local   **20.56**
authority initiated protective arrangements for the relevant child, provided that those protective arrangements have been continuously in place from the time of the authority's intervention and initiation until the date when the court finally disposes of the case: *Southwark LBC v B* [1998] 2 FLR 1095; *Re M (A Minor) (Threshold Conditions)* [1994] 2 FLR 577 (HL). Therefore, the relevant date is the same for both limbs of the criterion (ie, for present and for future harm) set out in s 31(2)(a), CA 1989.

Cause of the harm, or likely harm

20.57   Ground (b), in its alternatives, requires the court to find the cause for the harm, or likely harm. In relation to ground (b)(i), that is, that the care being given to the child is not that which one would expect a reasonable parent to give him, the court must look to the standard of care which the child obtains, or is likely to obtain if the care order is *not* made. It must evaluate that standard of care and then ask the following question: is that standard below that which it would be reasonable to expect the parent of *such* a child to give him? The intention is that the court should focus upon the characteristics of the particular child and that the child's *needs* be assessed subjectively. However, the standard to be applied to the care being given to that particular child is an objective one.

20.58   The phrase 'attributable to' in s 31(2)(b) connotes a causal connection between the harm or likelihood of harm, on the one hand, and the care or likely care or the child's being beyond parental control, on the other hand. The connection need not be that of a sole, or dominant, or direct cause and effect; a contributory causal connection suffices. For instance, if a parent entrusts a child to a third party without taking the precautionary steps a reasonable parent would take to check the suitability of the third party, and subsequently the third party injures or sexually abuses the child, the harm suffered by the child may be regarded as attributable to the inadequate care of the parent as well as of the third party: *Lancashire County Council v B* [2000] 1 FLR 583, per Lord Nicholls at p 585C–E.

20.59   To be within s 31(2)(b)(i) the care given or likely to be given must fall below an objectively acceptable level. That level is the care a reasonable parent would provide for the child concerned. Therefore, an absence of a reasonable standard of parental care need not imply that the parents are at fault: for example, it may be that for reasons beyond their control the parents are not able to provide a reasonable standard of care for the child: *Lancashire County Council v B*, para 20.58 above, per Lord Nicholls at p 585F–G. In the *Lancashire* case the child was looked after by several people, including a childminder. The child suffered serious non-accidental injury causing significant harm and triggering an application by the local authority for a care order in relation to the child. The evidence was such that it was not possible to say whether the parents or the childminder was the perpetrator. The House of Lords interpreted s 31(2)(b)(i) and stated that the phrase 'care given to the child' refers primarily to the care given to the child by a parent or parents or other primary carers. Where the care is shared, the task for the court is to establish, if possible, the perpetrator of the harm. If the court can go no further than to establish that there is a 'pool' of possible perpetrators, which may include a non-parent (such as a childminder), the threshold is nevertheless crossed: *Re O and N: Re B* [2003] 1 FLR 1169. This means that parents who may be wholly innocent face the possibility of losing their child. Once the threshold conditions have been crossed the court will, of course, go on to consider whether to exercise its discretionary power to make a care order or supervision order.

20.60   It was argued in the *Lancashire* case that keeping the child concerned in foster care infringed the rights of the child and her parents to respect to their right to family life as guaranteed by Art 8(1), ECHR. The argument put forward was that once the local authority realized that it could not prove that the child was injured by either of the parents it should have withdrawn the proceedings and reinstated the child with the parents. However, the House of Lords held (at p 591B–C) that the steps taken by the local authority were no more than the steps reasonably necessary to pursue the legitimate aim of protecting the child from further injury and that therefore the local authority in this case had acted within the exception set out in Art 8(2), ECHR.

In relation to ground (b)(ii) the relevant question for the court is this: is the child beyond **20.61** parental control? The parent may not necessarily be at fault for this ground to be satisfied. For example, the parent may have tried to discipline the child only to find that the child will not accept it. A parent in such a position cannot force the local authority to bring proceedings in respect of the child. If he informally requests the authority to do so and it refuses then his only remedy is by way of judicial review.

Care plans

Section 124, ACA 2002 inserted a new s 31A, CA 1989. It places a statutory duty on the local **20.62** authority to prepare a care plan (known as a 's 31A care plan') in every case in which it seeks a care order. However, the duty does not apply where only an interim care order is sought. The local authority is required to keep the care plan under review and to make changes as and when necessary. The care plan should accord so far as possible with *The Children Act 1989 Guidance and Regulations* (HMSO), vol 3, para 2.62, as supplemented by the local authority circular of 12 August 1999 (LAC(99)29), *Care Plans and Care Proceedings under The Children Act 1989*. The local authority circular seeks to cover practice and policy matters and to improve the consistency between local authorities in relation to the style, format, and level of detail set out in care plans.

The care plan is of vital importance because it sets out the local authority's plans for the child's **20.63** future care and gives reasons as to why a particular placement or course of action has been chosen. It should consider achievable timescales for the implementation of the plan. Where care plans are needed at an interim stage in the care proceedings they will not necessarily represent the local authority's confirmed views for the final hearing as circumstances may (and often do) change. Therefore the first page of the care plan should distinguish clearly between interim care plans for interim hearings and complete care plans for final hearings. The procedure to be adopted once a local authority decides to apply for a care or supervision order is governed by the Public Law Outline (FPR 2010, PD12A), which is discussed in detail in paras 20.33 ff above. Where the local authority decides to make an application to the court it will be necessary to satisfy the court that an order would be better for the child than making no order at all. An interim care plan should be prepared, filed, and served so as to be available to the court for the first hearing. The interim plan should include details of:

(a) the aim of the plan and a summary of the social work timetable;
(b) a summary of the child's needs and how these are to be met;
(c) implementation and management of the plan.

A separate plan is needed for each child who is the subject of the care proceedings, even where siblings with very similar needs are concerned in the same proceedings. See *Re J (Minors) (Care Plan)* [1994] 1 FLR 253 for useful judicial guidance as to the making of a care plan.

Duty to keep parents properly involved in planning process

It is essential that the local authority keeps the parents properly involved in the planning pro- **20.64** cess when care proceedings are initiated and the care plan is being formulated (*Re S (Minors)*

(Care Order: Implementation of Care Plan); Re W (Minors) (Care Order: Adequacy of Care Plan) [2002] 1 FLR 815). A failure to do so may leave it open to the parents to bring an application under the ss 6, 7, and 8, HRA 1998, for breaches of Art 6 (right to a fair trial) and Art 8 (right to respect for private and family life) *(Re C (Care Plan: Human Rights Challenge)* [2002] Fam Law 790; *Re G (Care: Challenge to Local Authority's Decision)* [2003] 2 FLR 42; *Venema v The Netherlands* [2003] 1 FLR 552).

Where adoption is the preferred option

20.65 If the local authority takes the view that adoption is the probable option then it needs to advise the court of the likely steps and timescales required to implement the care plan.

Twin-track planning and concurrent planning

20.66 In *Re D and K (Care Plan: Twin Track Planning)* [1999] 2 FLR 872, Bracewell J highlighted the problems which arise for the court in cases where the local authority recognizes from an early stage that its care plan presents options of rehabilitation within the natural family or permanency outside the family but fails to address the option of an adoptive placement until shortly before the substantive court hearing. The result is that the court is handicapped at the hearing by a lack of information as to the availability of adoptive parents; in the event that the court makes a care order and approves the care plan to place the child outside the natural family in an adoptive placement then there is a substantial delay whilst the child is considered and approved by the adoption and fostering panel and a suitable adoptive placement is identified. Where the local authority is considering two options comprising rehabilitation of the child to his natural family within a strictly limited timescale or adoption outside the family then, particularly in the case of babies or young children, the authority and children's guardian have a duty to seek to prevent delay by clearly identifying the options available to the court by twin-track planning as opposed to sequential planning. In such cases it is vital that the local authority should make it absolutely clear to the natural family as early as possible that it is considering these two options and that enquiries are proceeding on a twin track so that the court can be presented at the final care hearing with properly researched options in order to prevent delay. See *Best Practice Guidance of June 1997*, paras 7–12, which is helpfully set out in Part V of *The Family Court Practice*.

20.67 In appropriate cases, the authority may be able to proceed using 'concurrent planning', a form of planning which is distinct from twin-track planning. 'Concurrent planning' describes a scheme whereby the local authority chooses foster parents who are trained and willing to foster children on the basis that they work with the natural family towards rehabilitation, but who, in the event that rehabilitation is ruled out, wish to adopt the children. The aim is to reduce the number of moves a child experiences in care, and to reduce temporary placements so that children can achieve permanence, whether rehabilitated with their family or with the foster family, with minimum disruption. Contact between carers and birth children is encouraged and there is openness between the parties about the primary aim of rehabilitation with the alternative secondary plan of permanent placement. It is vital in such cases that the two options are clearly explained to the natural family from the outset and that they are reassured that it in no way pre-empts the outcome of the care proceedings. Not every case will be suitable for such placement. Generally, it is likely to apply to babies or young children where there are some but by no means optimistic prospects of rehabilitation to the natural family.

Whenever care proceedings are commenced the court should be proactive at an early directions hearing, requiring the authority to establish whether twin-track planning and/or concurrent planning are suitable and giving appropriate directions.

Effect of care orders

Local authority obtains parental responsibility under a care order

While a care order is in force with respect to a child, the local authority has parental responsibility for him: s 33(3). However, parents do *not lose* their parental responsibility as a result of a care order being made: s 2(5). The parents share parental responsibility with the local authority, although the authority has the power to determine, largely, the extent to which a parent, special guardian, or guardian of the child may meet his parental responsibility for the child: s 33(3)(b). However, s 33(4) directs that the local authority should not limit the extent to which the parent exercises his parental responsibility for the child *unless* it is satisfied that it is necessary to do so in order to safeguard or promote the child's welfare. Furthermore, s 33(5) states that where a parent has de facto care of the child then he may do what is reasonable in all the circumstances to safeguard or promote the child's welfare (see also s 3(5)). **20.68**

However, there are certain things which the local authority has no right to do even if it has a care order in respect of a child, since those matters remain the prerogative of the parents. The authority may not: **20.69**

(a) bring the child up in a different religion from that in which he would have been brought up if the order had not been made: s 33(6)(a). However, the child could choose to practise a different religion if he was of sufficient age and understanding, since he is entitled to be consulted by the authority about such matters: s 22(4) and (5);
(b) agree or refuse to agree to the making of an adoption order in respect of the child (s 36(b)(ii));
(c) appoint a guardian for the child (s 33(6)(b)(iii)).

Care order discharges all existing s 8 orders

A care order has the effect of discharging all existing s 8 orders (ie, residence, contact, prohibited steps, and specific issue orders). There is a separate scheme under s 34 which provides for parental contact with children in care (see para 20.75 below). **20.70**

Restriction of change of name and removal from the jurisdiction

While a care order is in force, s 33(7) provides that no person may: **20.71**

(a) cause the child to be known by a new surname; or
(b) remove him from the United Kingdom;

without *either*:

(i) the written consent of every person who has parental responsibility for the child; or
(ii) the leave of the court.

However, the above consent is not necessary if the authority wishes to remove the child from the jurisdiction for periods of less than one month: s 33(8)(a).

Local authority power to place child with his parents

20.72 Section 23(4), (5), and (6) gives the local authority power to place a child in its care with one or both of his parents. See the Placement of Children with Parents etc Regulations 1991. The case of *Re D (Care: Natural Parent Presumption)* [1999] 1 FLR 134 emphasizes that there is a strong presumption that where it is possible to place a child in care with his natural parent then that is the course which should be taken, unless there are compelling factors to override the presumption.

Duties of local authority towards a child in its care

20.73 The duties of local authorities in relation to children looked after by them apply equally to a child in their care by virtue of a care order. Those duties have already been discussed at para 20.19 above.

No power to attach conditions to care order

20.74 The court has no power to attach to a care order conditions binding on a local authority (save those under s 34 as to contact), since Parliament has entrusted the administration of care orders to local authorities. The task of the court is to scrutinize the local authority's care plan and then to decide whether it is in the interests of the child to make a care order: *Re J (Minors) (Care: Care Plan)* (para 20.63 above). If it is, then it falls to the local authority to decide how the child's care should be managed. It is not, therefore, possible for a court to make a care order with a requirement that the local authority is to place the child with the parents: *Re T (A Minor) (Care Order: Conditions)* [1994] 2 FLR 423 (CA). See further para 20.62 above.

Parental contact with children in care

20.75 Schedule 2, para 15, CA 1989 places a duty upon local authorities to 'endeavour to promote contact' between any child they are looking after (note that 'looking after' includes children being looked after by virtue of a care order) and the following persons:

(a) his parents;
(b) those who have parental responsibility for him (eg guardians); and
(c) any relatives, friends, or other persons connected with him.

This duty applies in all cases *unless* contact is not reasonably practicable or is not consistent with the child's welfare.

20.76 The court has no power to make a s 8 order (other than a residence order) whilst a child is in the care of a local authority: s 9(1). However, the CA 1989 sets out a special scheme in s 34 which enables the court to make orders directing or refusing contact with children in care.

20.77 Where the child is the subject of a care order s 34(1) imposes a statutory presumption that the local authority must allow the child to have reasonable contact with:

(a) his parents;
(b) any guardian or special guardian of his;
(c) any person who by virtue of s 4A has parental responsibility for him (ie, step-parents with parental responsibility);

(d) where there was a residence order in force with respect to the child immediately before the care order was made, the person in whose favour the residence order was made; and

(e) where, immediately before the care order was made, a person had care of the child by virtue of an order made in the exercise of the High Court's inherent jurisdiction, that person.

Section 34 makes the duty enforceable in the courts.

When may a s 34 contact order be made?

A s 34 contact order may be made at the same time as the care order itself or later: s 34(10). **20.78** Before making the care order the court must consider the arrangements which the authority has made, or proposes to make, for arranging contact between the child and the persons to whom s 34 applies: s 34(11). Therefore, in the course of care proceedings all parties should be prepared to present evidence and make submissions about contact. Indeed, the local authority is under a duty in the course of care proceedings to present to the court a care plan dealing with the matters set out in *The Children Act 1989 Guidance and Regulations*, vol 3, ch 2, para 2.62, which include 'arrangements for contact and reunification': *Re J (Minors) (Care: Care Plan)* (para 20.63 above). See further details relating to care plans at para 20.62 above.

However, where the court considers an application for contact with a child in care the court **20.79** can require the local authority to justify its long-term plans to the extent only that the plans exclude contact between the parent and the child. On the other hand, where the application for contact is, in effect, an attempt to set aside a care order then the parent must show a change of circumstances which requires further investigation and consideration of the local authority's plan, and it would be only in unusual cases that a parent would succeed with such an application: *Re B (Minors) (Care: Contact: Local Authority's Plans)* [1993] 1 FLR 543.

Who may apply for contact under s 34?

The following persons may make an application under s 34 that the court make such order as **20.80** it considers appropriate with respect to the contact which is to be allowed between the child and the *person named in the order*:

(a) the local authority (s 34(2));
(b) the child (s 34(2)).

The following persons may make an application under s 34 that the court make such order as it considers appropriate with respect to the contact which is to be allowed between the child and *that person*:

(i) any of the persons listed in para 20.77(a) to (e) above: s 34(3)(a);
(ii) anyone else who has first obtained the leave of the court to make an application (s 34(3)(b)), for example grandparents and siblings may wish to retain contact with the child in care.

Power of the court to attach conditions to a s 34 order

Section 34(7), CA 1989 makes provision for the court to attach to a s 34 contact order such **20.81** conditions as it considers appropriate. It is open to the court to specify the timing, nature, and duration of the contact, if necessary, provided that such specification does not in effect constitute a review by the court of the implementation of the local authority's care plan: *Re S (A Minor) (Care: Contact Order)* [1994] 2 FLR 222. Section 34 is sufficiently wide to enable the court to make what is, in effect, an interim contact order at the same time as a care order, with a specific provision for a further hearing with a view to making further provision for contact at the subsequent hearing: *Re B (A Minor) (Care Order: Review)* [1993] 1 FLR 421.

Prohibition of contact with a child in care

20.82 If the local authority or the child wish to apply to the court to prohibit contact between the child and the persons set out in para 20.77(a) to (e) above, the appropriate section to use is s 34(4), for example to prevent contact between a child and a parent who has sexually abused him. It is not open to anyone other than the local authority or the child to apply for such a *prohibition* on contact. For example, if a mother took the view that the child's father should not have contact with the child while he is in care then she could not apply for an order under s 34(4); she would have to rely upon the authority sharing her anxieties about contact and making the application in its own right.

20.83 The authority may refuse to allow contact that would otherwise be required by virtue of s 34(1) or by an order under s 34 if:

(a) it is satisfied that it is necessary to do so to promote the child's welfare; and
(b) the refusal:
    (i) is decided upon as a matter of urgency; *and*
    (ii) does not last for more than *seven* days: s 34(6).

Where the authority exercises its power to refuse to allow contact with a child in care then it must adopt the procedure set out in the Contact with Children Regulations 1991. Those Regulations require that the authority notify the following persons, in writing, of its decision:

(a) those listed in s 34(1);
(b) the child, if he is of sufficient understanding; and
(c) any other person whose wishes and feelings the authority considers to be relevant.

In the notification the authority should give its reasons for the decision, its date, its duration, and the remedies available in case of dissatisfaction.

20.84 The same principles apply where:

(a) the authority decides to depart from the terms of any agreement as to contact made with the person in relation to whom the s 34 order was made; or
(b) the authority intends to vary or suspend arrangements made, *other than under a s 34 order*, with a view to affording any person contact with a child in care.

Where the authority wishes to refuse contact with a child in care for more than seven days then, after following the procedure outlined above, it must apply to the court for an order allowing it to refuse contact for a longer period. The court has a complete discretion under s 34(4) to authorize the refusal of contact for as long as it considers it to be for the child's welfare: *West Glamorgan County Council v P (No 1)* [1992] 2 FLR 369. However, where the child is the subject of an interim care order then contact between the child and his parents should be continued until the substantive hearing wherever possible, so that the court hearing the interim applications does not reach a firm conclusion which effectively decides the final outcome of the case: *A* v *M and Walsall Metropolitan Borough Council* [1993] 2 FLR 244.

Where the court has to determine an application by the local authority for the permanent **20.85** cessation of contact between the child in care and his parents then the court must start with the presumption of continuing parental contact. If, on a s 34(4) application, the judge concludes that the benefits of contact outweigh the disadvantages of disrupting any of the local authority's long-term plans which are inconsistent with such contact, the judge must refuse the local authority's application; such action does not amount to monitoring or scrutinizing the local authority's plan, but is the discharge by the court of the duty which Parliament has placed upon the court by s 34(4): *H* v *West Sussex County Council* [1998] 1 FLR 862; *Re D and H (Care: Termination of Contact)* [1997] 1 FLR 841; *Re T (Termination of Contact: Discharge of Order)* [1997] 1 FLR 517; *Re E (A Minor) (Care Order: Contact)* [1994] 1 FLR 146; *Re B (Minors) (Care: Contact: Local Authority's Plans)* (para 20.79 above). The Court of Appeal observed in *Re E (A Minor) (Care Order: Contact)* (above) that even where the criteria in s 31 are satisfied, contact may still be of great importance to the long-term welfare of the child. It could give the child the security of knowing that his parents loved him and were interested in his welfare and avoid any damaging sense of loss to the child in seeing himself as abandoned by his parents. Contact could also enable a child to commit himself to a substitute family with the seal of approval of his natural parents and give the child the necessary sense of family and personal identity. Contact, if maintained, is therefore capable of reinforcing and increasing the chances of success of a permanent placement, whether on a long-term fostering basis or by adoption.

However, there will be cases in which the cessation of contact between parent and child is **20.86** necessary: see, for example, *Birmingham City Council* v *H (No 3)* [1994] 1 FLR 224.

An order under s 34(4) is permissive and not mandatory. Once an order under s 34(4) is in **20.87** place authorizing refusal of contact, the local authority must continue to keep the issue of contact under review. Contact must be permitted again where the local authority considers that the circumstances which led to its original concern about contact no longer exist.

Variation and discharge of s 34 contact orders

The court may vary or discharge any s 34 order on the application of: **20.88**

(a) the person named in the order;
(b) the authority; or
(c) the child concerned (s 34(9)).

Where a person other than a local authority has made a s 34 application and that application has been refused, that person may not make a similar application in respect of the *same* child until at least *six months* have elapsed since the refusal, unless he has first obtained the leave of the court: s 91(17). Before restricting or terminating contact under s 34, the court must consider the local authority's care proposals: *Re D and H (Care: Termination of Contact)* (para 20.85 above).

A s 34 contact order must be discharged if the care order to which it relates is discharged. **20.89** A s 8 contact order could be made instead in the course of the proceedings dealing with the discharge of the care order: s 10.

Care/supervision order procedure

20.90   The procedure to be adopted in all applications for care or supervision orders is now governed by the Public Law Outline at FPR 2010, PD12A.

Representation of the child

20.91   The court is under a duty to appoint a children's guardian for a child for the purpose of 'specified proceedings' *unless* it is satisfied that it is not necessary to do so in order to safeguard the child's interests: s 41(1). 'Specified proceedings' are defined in s 41(6) and include:

(a) applications for care and supervision orders;

(b) proceedings in which the court has given a direction under s 37(1) and has made, or is considering whether to make, an interim care order;

(c) applications to discharge care or supervision orders;

(d) appeals against care or supervision orders.

The above are just *some* of the relevant categories of proceedings to which the duty applies. The practitioner is referred to s 41(6) for the remainder of the list.

20.92   The method of appointing a children's guardian is set out in Chapter 18, para 18.52, together with a description of his role and duties towards the child. The procedure is set out in FPR 2010, Part 16.

20.93   The court may appoint a solicitor to represent the child provided that:

(a) he is not already represented by one; and

(b) one of the conditions in s 41(4) is satisfied: s 41(3). The conditions are that no children's guardian has been appointed for the child, that the child has sufficient understanding to appoint a solicitor and wishes to do so, or that it appears to be in the child's best interests for him to be represented by a solicitor.

Once appointed the solicitor must represent the child in accordance with the rules of court.

20.94   There is also provision for a children's guardian to appoint a solicitor for the child. This topic is further discussed in Chapter 18, para 18.59.

Jurisdiction and procedure

20.95   Proceedings with a public law element (eg applications for care orders, supervision orders, s 34 contact orders, emergency protection orders) must, as a general rule, be issued in the family proceedings court (there is an exception where proceedings in relation to the child are already underway, in which case the application for a public law order must be issued in that court). However, the family proceedings court, county court, and High Court all have concurrent jurisdiction, and are all capable of hearing public law cases in appropriate circumstances (note that only 'nominated care judges' may hear cases with a public law element in the county court).

20.96   Initially, the clerk to the justices (or the justices themselves) will make a decision as to the level of court at which the matter is to be tried. The criteria for transferring the proceedings upwards to the county court or High Court are set out in the Allocation and Transfer of Proceedings Order 2008. The criteria for transferring the case include factors such as the forensic or legal complexity of the case or the involvement of a question of general public interest. For an outline on the topic of the transfer of proceedings, see Chapter 18, para 18.07.

If a party is dissatisfied with the decision reached by the family proceedings court as to the **20.97** level of court at which the matter is to be tried, he may apply for a transfer before the district judge of the relevant county court: rr 2.7 and 12.12, FPR 2010. Note that this is by way of application only; it is not by way of appeal from the magistrates' decision. The district judge may then make his own decision as to the level of court before which the case is to be heard.

The application

The general procedure for applications is to be found in FPR 2010, Part 12. The persons who are **20.98** to be made respondents to proceedings and the persons who are to be notified of proceedings are set out in tabular form in r 12.3. The rules for service are set out in Part 6.

Withdrawal of an application

The general rules apply. See Chapter 18, para 18.33. **20.99**

The court has given useful guidance on this type of application. In *Re N (Leave to Withdraw* **20.100** *Care Proceedings)* [2000] 1 FLR 134 the local authority, supported by the parents, sought to withdraw its application for a care order. However, the children's guardian opposed the application to withdraw on the basis that the child's welfare demanded a full hearing of the matter. The court refused the local authority's application, saying that the welfare of the child was paramount when deciding this issue. The guardian should think long and hard before opposing an agreement between the local authority and the parents, but had a duty to put his view before the court. The local authority should have consulted the guardian before taking the decision to withdraw the proceedings. The court also considered the impact of Art 8(2), ECHR; Art 8(2) makes it clear that interference by public authorities with the parents' right to respect for their private and family life is only justified and necessary if it fulfils a pressing social need. In this case, the guardian had shown a pressing social need for intervention and the court made it clear that where there is a real risk to a child the law will not allow the potential harm actually to occur before taking action.

Timetable

Section 32, CA 1989 reflects the general principle of the Act that delay in proceedings is likely **20.101** to be prejudicial to the child's welfare. It requires the court hearing applications under Part IV to draw up a timetable with a view to disposing of the application without delay. It also enables the court to give directions to ensure that the timetable is adhered to. The relevant rules of court which deal with the timing of proceedings are to be found in r 12.13, FPR 2010. The aim of these provisions is to prevent the proceedings from lying dormant through the delay of the parties and their advisers.

The hearing

A hearing before the High Court or county court will be in chambers and a hearing before the **20.102** family proceedings court may be held in private.

Attendance of parties For the general rules as to the attendance of parties at hearings or **20.103** directions appointments, see Chapter 18, para 18.67. In the course of hearing any application made under Part IV or V, CA 1989 (eg for a care order, supervision order, s 34 contact order, emergency protection order etc), the court has a discretion to order the attendance of the child at any stage in the proceedings: s 95(1). Where it believes that such an order will not be, or has not been, complied with the court may authorize a constable or other named person to enter and search premises in order to take charge of the child and to bring him to court: s 95(4)(a). Furthermore, the court may order anyone whom it believes to be in a position to bring the child to court to do so, or to order a person with information as to the whereabouts of the child to disclose it to the court: s 95(4)(b). However, in *Re C (A Minor) (Care: Child's Wishes)* [1993] 1 FLR 832, Waite J said that young children (in this case a girl aged 13) should be discouraged from attending High Court appeals from the justices in family proceedings. Where the children's guardian proposes to arrange for a young child to be present at an appeal he should give the question very careful thought beforehand and be prepared, if necessary, to explain his reasons to the judge.

20.104   **Factors to be considered by the court**   The various factors which the court must consider when hearing contested proceedings of this nature are set out fully in Chapter 17, paras 17.11 ff. In general, the court must bear in mind that the child's welfare is paramount. In doing so, it must apply the statutory checklist of factors contained in s 1(3), and must have regard to the principle that any delay in deciding the case is likely to be prejudicial to the welfare of the child. Finally, the court must have regard to the whole range of orders available to it (and not just the one applied for), but must not make any order unless satisfied that to make an order would be better for the child than making no order at all: s 1(5).

20.105   The 'child' to whom s 34(3) applies is the child in care, in respect of whom an order is sought. The question to be determined relates to that child's upbringing and it is that child's welfare which must be the court's paramount consideration. The fact that the parent is also a child does not mean that both the parent's and the child's welfare are paramount and that each had to be balanced against the other, since no question is to be determined as to the parent's upbringing (*Birmingham City Council* v *H (No 3)* (para 20.86 above)).

20.106   **Expert evidence**   The question of whether to instruct experts will be governed by the Practice Direction—Experts and Assessors in Family Proceedings, FPR 2010, PD25A.

20.107   The objective of the Practice Direction is to provide the court with early information to enable it to determine whether it is necessary to ask an expert to assist the court:

(a) to identify, narrow, and where possible agree the issues between the parties;
(b) to provide an opinion about a question that is not within the skill and experience of the court;
(c) to encourage the early identification of questions that need to be answered by an expert;
(d) to encourage disclosure of full and frank information between the parties, the court, and any experts instructed.

The overriding duty of an expert in family proceedings is to the court and this takes precedence over any obligation to the person from whom he has received instructions or by whom he is paid (para 3.1). The particular duties an expert may have are set out in para 3.2.

20.108   Any party who proposes to ask the court for permission to instruct an expert must carry out enquires and file and serve a written proposal including details of the identity and qualifications of the expert, his availability, the relevance of the evidence sought to be adduced, and whether the evidence can properly be obtained by the joint instruction of the expert by two or more parties: paras 4.1 and 4.3.

Where the court gives permission to instruct an expert, the party or parties instructing must **20.109** set out in a letter of instruction the context in which the opinion is sought and any specific questions which the expert is required to answer. Detailed guidance on the content of the letter of instruction is contained in PD25A, para 4.5 and a specimen letter of instruction is included as an Annex.

The expert's report must be addressed to the court and must include the information pre- **20.110** scribed in para 3.3 including:

(a) the details of his qualifications and experience;
(b) the substance of his instructions;
(c) details of any literature or research he has relied on;
(d) where there is a range of opinion on the question, summarize the range of opinion and give reasons for the opinion expressed;
(e) summarize his conclusions and opinions.

Any party wishing to ask supplementary questions of an expert to clarify the report must put them in writing in accordance with r 25.6, FPR 2010.

The court may at any stage direct a discussion between experts in accordance with r 25.12. **20.111** The purpose of the experts' discussion or meeting is:

(a) to identify and discuss the expert issues in the proceedings;
(b) where possible, to reach an agreed opinion on those issues.

The court may direct that following a discussion between the experts they must prepare a statement for the court setting out the issues on which they agree and disagree, and giving the reasons for any disagreement: r 25.12(3). Where a party refuses to accept an expert agreement, he must inform the court and the other parties in writing within ten business days after the discussion or meeting of his reasons for refusing to accept the agreement: PD25A, para 7.1.

Expert attendance at a final hearing is governed by PD25A, paras 8.1 to 9.1. **20.112**

Documentary evidence The general rules as to the need for the advance disclosure of **20.113** documentary evidence are discussed in Chapter 18, para 18.73. However, the procedure to be adopted once a local authority decides to apply for a care or supervision order is now governed by the Public Law Outline (FPR 2010, PD12A.) The preparation and disclosure of documentary evidence is tightly controlled by the court. There is no concept of litigation privilege in Children Act proceedings and so expert reports prepared for the purpose of the proceedings must be disclosed, even if the contents are unfavourable: see Chapter 18, para 18.85.

Oral evidence In the course of any proceedings under Part IV or V, CA 1989 (eg applications **20.114** for care orders, supervision orders, s 34 contact orders, emergency protection orders, etc) no one is excused from giving evidence on any matter, or answering any question put to him in the course of giving his evidence, on the ground that doing so might incriminate him or his spouse of an offence. However, any statement or admission made in such proceedings is not admissible in proceedings for an offence other than perjury (see ss 98 and 48(2), CA 1989).

20.115 **Welfare reports**   The question of welfare reports is dealt with fully in Chapter 18, para 18.44.

20.116 **Split hearings**   Where there are crucial issues of disputed fact (eg allegations of sexual abuse), the court may give a direction that those issues be determined first, within a discrete 'fact-finding' hearing, before issues of welfare and overall disposal are considered. Once those issues have been determined, a further substantive hearing can be fixed to consider more fully the outcome which would best serve the child's welfare. It is imperative that those cases which are suitable for a split hearing should be identified as early as possible by the court, with the assistance of the local authority and the children's guardian: *Re S (Care Proceedings: Split Hearing)* [1996] 2 FLR 773. Where findings of fact are made on preliminary issues at a split hearing there is jurisdiction to hear an appeal against them if those findings are of crucial importance to the final decision: *Re B (Split Hearings: Jurisdiction)* [2000] 1 FLR 334. Note that a decision of the court is treated as a final decision for the purpose of an appeal if it '(a) is made at the conclusion of part of a hearing or trial which has been split into parts; and (b) would, if made at the conclusion of that hearing or trial, be a final decision under para. (2)(c)' (Access to Justice Act 1999 (Destination of Appeals) Order 2000 (SI 2000/1071)). Article 1(2)(c) of the Order defines a 'final decision' as a decision of a court that would finally determine (subject to any possible appeal or detailed assessment of costs) the entire proceedings whichever way the court decided the issues before it.

20.117 It is important that the same judge or Bench of magistrates should hear both parts of a split hearing.

Interim orders

20.118 Despite the presumption that delay in proceedings is likely to prejudice the welfare of the child concerned, there will be occasions when an adjournment of care proceedings is unavoidable. For example, the parties may need time in which to prepare their cases properly, or the children's guardian may need time in which to investigate and report on the child's circumstances. It is important that in appropriate cases the court can control the case by way of interim orders until all the relevant material is before the court to enable it to make a final order: *C v Solihull Metropolitan Borough Council* [1993] 1 FLR 290; *Hounslow LBC v A* [1993] 1 FLR 702; *Re J (Minors) (Care: Care Plan)* (para 20.63 above). The effect of an interim care order is the same as a full order (eg the authority obtains parental responsibility and there is a presumption that it will allow reasonable contact between the child and his parents), except where express provision is made to the contrary: *A v M and Walsall Metropolitan Borough Council* (para 20.84 above). The two main differences between full and interim orders are in respect of their duration (see para 20.126 below) and in respect of the directions which the court may make (see para 20.127 below).

20.119 The court has power under s 38, CA 1989 to make an interim care or interim supervision order where:

(a) proceedings are adjourned on an application for a care or supervision order; or
(b) the court gives a direction under s 37(1) (ie, that the local authority is to investigate the child's circumstances).

20.120 The power to make an interim order must not be exercised unless the court is satisfied that there are *reasonable grounds for believing* that the statutory criteria in s 31(2) are satisfied with respect to the child concerned. The court does not have to be satisfied that the s 31(2) grounds actually *exist*, since that would defeat the purpose of an adjournment and require the authority to prove its case on the first hearing. In effect, the authority has to show a prima facie case. In addition, the court must consider the three fundamental principles contained in s 1 before making an interim order, that is to say:

(a) the child's welfare is the paramount consideration: s 1(1);
(b) any delay in determining the proceedings is likely to prejudice the welfare of the child: s 1(2); and
(c) the court must not make any order unless it considers that making an order would be better for the child than making no order at all: s 1(5).

The purpose of an interim order is normally to hold the balance so as to cause the least pos-   **20.121** sible harm to the child and to avoid, where possible, pre-determining the outcome of the proceedings: *Re H (A Child) (Interim Care Order)* [2003] 1 FCR 350. Where the interim care plan is for the child's removal, the court must be satisfied that the removal or continued removal is proportionate to the risk of harm to which she would be exposed if she were allowed to return to the parents' care: *Re B (Interim Care Order)* [2010] 2 FLR 283. When considering an application for an interim care order the court must consider, if the interim threshold is met, whether it is in the child's best interests for an order to be made, and the satisfaction of the interim threshold criteria does not necessarily mean there should be an order: *Re A (Children) (Interim Care Order)* [2001] 3 FCR 402.

When a court has heard all the available evidence at a final hearing but is still considering   **20.122** whether to make a further interim care order rather than a final care order, it must approach any such decision with extreme caution. The court must be aware of the danger of using an interim care order as a means of exercising judicial supervision and of diminishing the general principle of avoiding delay. Section 38 is primarily designed to cater for the situation prior to a final hearing where a case needs to be adjourned because it is not ready for trial. In some cases the action necessary in the interests of children requires steps into the unknown. Provided that the court is satisfied that the local authority is alert to the difficulties which might arise in the execution of its care plan, the function of the court is not to seek to oversee the plan but to entrust its execution to the local authority. If the care plan represents the only practical course of action for the children then it would be artificial for the court to make an interim order since to do so would represent an attempt to exercise a supervisory jurisdiction over matters entrusted to the local authority: *Re D (Simultaneous Applications for Care Order and Freeing Order)* [1999] 2 FLR 49; *Re J (Minors) (Care: Care Plan)* (para 20.63 above); *Re P (Minors) (Interim Order)* [1993] 2 FLR 742. The court cannot oversee the implementation of a care plan once a care order has been made. This can cause problems in the following cases:

(a) where the court is left with the choice of accepting an unsatisfactory care plan or refusing to make a care order;
(b) where the local authority makes a substantial change to the care plan after the final care order has been made.

As the law stands at present the latter can only be challenged by judicial review or by an   **20.123** application to discharge a care order. However, see para 20.27 above, 'Review of cases', which describes the role of IROs under s 26(2)(e), CA 1989. Once a care order has been made, the duties of the reviewing officer will encompass a review of the care plan concerning the child and the revision of that plan as necessary in the circumstances of each particular case. The officer will have power to refer the case to Cafcass where appropriate. Cafcass will have power to take proceedings on behalf of the child. The introduction of IROs was implemented partly to meet the criticism that the inability of the court to oversee the implementation of a care plan may be subject to challenge under the HRA 1998.

20.124   Article 6, ECHR in particular guarantees the right to a fair trial; in childcare cases this would include sufficient procedural protection of parents' interests throughout the process: *W* v *UK* (1987) 10 EHRR 29, paras 77 and 82. Where administrative decisions have the effect of interfering with family relationships, Art 8, which guarantees the right to respect for family life, includes the need for fair procedures to be put in place when such administrative decisions are taken: *McMichael* v *UK* (1995) 20 EHRR 205; *Scott* v *UK*, application no 34745/97.

20.125   If the court is hearing an application for a care or supervision order but decides, instead, to make a residence order, the court *must* make an interim supervision order as well *unless* it is satisfied that the child's welfare will be satisfactorily safeguarded without an interim supervision order: s 38(3).

Duration of interim orders

20.126   An interim care or supervision order will last for a maximum initial period of eight weeks, or any shorter time ordered by the court: s 38(4). The court may extend the order for a further period of four weeks (s 38(5)), and thereafter at four-weekly intervals. However, an interim care order must be used for its intended purpose and not simply extended to provide the court with continuing control over the actions of the local authority: *Re L (Sexual Abuse: Standard of Proof)* [1996] 1 FLR 116. In any event, the court must draw up a timetable with a view to disposing of the case without delay, and it is to be hoped that the duration of interim orders will thus be kept as short as possible. In fixing the period of the interim order the court can take into account whether any party opposed to the order was in a position to argue his case in full: s 38(10). Where all parties consent, an interim care order may be renewed without a hearing.

Directions made under an interim order

20.127   When a court makes a full care order, responsibility for the care plan passes to the local authority and, subject to making orders for contact under s 34, the court has no jurisdiction to give directions as to the child's welfare and upbringing. In *Re B (A Minor) (Care Order: Review)* (para 20.81 above) the family proceedings court purported to grant a care order with the provision that the court would review the operation of the care order, progress in the care plan, and contact six months after the date of the order. On appeal, Thorpe J held that the court had no power, once a care order had been made, to monitor the operation of the care order by the local authority. This approach was confirmed by the Court of Appeal in *Re T (A Minor) (Care Order: Conditions)* [1994] 2 FLR 423. However, the court did have power under s 34 to make an interim contact order at the same time as the care order with a specific provision for a further hearing with a view to making further provision for contact at the subsequent hearing. See also *A* v *Liverpool City Council* [1982] AC 363; *Re B (Minors) (Care: Contact: Local Authority's Plans)* (para 20.79 above); and *Kent County Council* v *C* [1983] 1 FLR 308. However, when it makes an *interim* care or supervision order the court may give directions as to the medical or psychiatric examination or other assessment of the child: s 38(6). For example, in *Re O (Minors) (Medical Examination)* [1993]

1 FLR 860 the family proceedings court made an interim care order and directed under s 38(6) that the children be tested to determine whether they were HIV positive. Furthermore, in *Berkshire County Council* v *C* [1993] 1 FLR 569 the family proceedings court made an interim care order, directed the local authority to arrange for the child to be assessed by a social worker, and further directed that the assessment was to commence on or before a specific date. The court had power to make a mandatory direction of this type, even after being told by the local authority that such a worker would not be available for some time due to lack of resources, because the court had taken proper account of the practical consequences for the local authority of such a direction and because on the facts of the case the decision was plainly right.

What is directed under s 38(6) must clearly be an examination or assessment *of the child,*   **20.128** including, where appropriate, his relationship with his parents, the risk that they may present to him, and the ways in which those risks may be avoided or managed. Any services which are provided for the child and his family must be ancillary to that aim. They must not be an end in themselves (*Re G (Interim Care Order: Residential Assessment)* [2006] 1 FLR 601—the court had no power to make an order the main purpose of which was to provide a continuing course of psychotherapy to the mother with a view to giving her the opportunity to change sufficiently to become a safe carer for the child).

A direction can be to the effect that no medical or psychiatric examination or other assess-   **20.129** ment of the child is to take place: s 38(7). If the child is of sufficient understanding to make an informed decision he may refuse to submit to such an examination or assessment: s 38(6).

A direction may be varied at any time on the application of a qualified applicant: s 38(8).   **20.130** A direction made under s 38(6) can be appealed: *Re O (Minors) (Medical Examination)* (para 20.127 above).

Exclusion requirements in interim care orders

Where the court decides to make an interim care order it may safeguard the child by includ-   **20.131** ing in the order a provision excluding from the home the 'relevant person' who is putting the child at risk: s 38A.

Meaning of 'exclusion requirement'   An exclusion requirement is any one or more of the   **20.132** following provisions (s 38A(3)):
(a) that the relevant person must leave a dwelling-house in which he is living with the child;
(b) that the relevant person is prohibited from entering a dwelling-house in which the child lives;
(c) that the relevant person is excluded from a defined area in which a dwelling-house in which the child lives is situated.

Conditions to be met for exclusion requirement   Section 38A(1), CA 1989, provides that   **20.133** the court may include an exclusion requirement in an interim care order:
(a) on being satisfied that there are reasonable grounds for believing that the circumstances with respect to a child are as mentioned in s 31(2)(a) and (b)(i); and
(b) the conditions in s 38A(2) are satisfied.

It is important to note that the ground contained in s 31(2)(b)(ii), which enables a court to make a care or supervision order where a child is beyond parental control, is not mentioned in limb (a) above, and therefore it would not be possible to include an exclusion requirement in an interim care order which was made on that ground only. Furthermore, the court must have actually decided to make an interim care order before considering the need for an exclusion requirement.

20.134   The conditions laid down in s 38A(2), which must be met before an exclusion requirement can be made, are that:

(a)   there is reasonable cause to believe that if the relevant person is excluded from the child's home then the child will cease to suffer, or cease to be likely to suffer, significant harm; and

(b)   another person living in the same house (whether or not he or she is a parent of the child):
(i)   is able and willing to give the child the care which it would be reasonable to expect a parent to give him; and
(ii)   consents to the inclusion of the exclusion requirement.

20.135   **Duration of exclusion requirement**   The court can provide that the exclusion requirement itself is to have effect for a shorter period than the other provisions in the interim care order: s 38A(4). However, the court has power on an application to vary or discharge the interim care order to extend the period specified for the exclusion requirement if it thinks fit: s 38A(7). The exclusion requirement automatically ceases to have effect if the local authority removes the child from the home to other accommodation for a continuous period of more than 24 hours: s 38A(10).

20.136   **Power of arrest attached to exclusion requirement**   The court can attach a power of arrest to the exclusion requirement, and where it does so it may provide that the power of arrest is to have effect for a shorter period than the exclusion requirement: s 38A(5) and (6). Where a power of arrest is attached, a constable may arrest without warrant anyone whom he has reasonable cause to believe to be in breach of the requirement.

20.137   The court has power on an application to vary or discharge the interim care order to extend the period so specified for the power of arrest if it thinks fit: s 38A(7).

20.138   The power of arrest may be varied or discharged on the application of the 'relevant person' excluded by the requirement, any person with parental responsibility for the child, the child himself, or the designated local authority: s 39(3B).

20.139   **Discharge, extension, and variation of exclusion requirement**   The drafting of s 39 does not state clearly who is entitled to apply for the discharge or variation of an exclusion requirement. The section seems to draw a distinction between (a) discharge and (b) variation of exclusion requirements. It would appear that three categories of people may apply for discharge of the requirement: a person with parental responsibility; the child himself; the designated local authority: s 39(1). It is not clear whether those three categories of people may also apply for the variation of the requirement.

20.140   The 'relevant person' to whom the exclusion requirement applies specifically has the right to apply for the variation of the interim care order insofar as it imposes the exclusion requirement: s 39(3A). On such an application the court has the power to vary or discharge the order insofar as it imposes the exclusion requirement.

20.141   The application to discharge would be made to the court which made the order incorporating the exclusion requirement or to the court to which the case had been transferred.

Procedure   The procedure to be adopted in relation to cases involving exclusion require-   **20.142**
ments is to be found in r 12.28, FPR 2010.

The principal points to note are as follows: **20.143**

(a) Where the applicant seeks the inclusion of the exclusion requirement, she is required to
    prepare a separate statement of evidence in support of such application and to serve this
    together with a copy of the order containing the exclusion requirement on the person in
    respect of whom the exclusion requirement has been made: r 12.28(2).
(b) Where the court includes the exclusion requirement in an order of its own motion,
    there is no requirement for the applicant to produce a statement of evidence in support:
    r 12.28(7).

Final orders   Exclusion requirements cannot be attached to final care orders. The expecta-   **20.144**
tion is that the proposed carer should in the meantime have taken steps to exclude the abuser
in the long term, and if the carer has not been able to do this then she should not expect the
court or the local authority to do it for her.

Undertakings relating to interim care orders

Wherever a court has power under s 38A, CA 1989, to include an exclusion requirement in   **20.145**
an interim care order the court may instead accept an undertaking from the relevant person:
s 38B. The undertaking would normally be to leave the property within a specified time,
although it could contain other terms. However, the court cannot attach a power of arrest to
any such undertaking: s 38B(2). Where an undertaking is given to the court then:

(a) it will be enforceable as if it were an order of the court (s 38B(3)(a)); and
(b) it will cease to have effect if, while it is in force, the local authority removes the child
    from the house from which the relevant person is excluded to other accommodation for
    a continuous period of more than two hours (s 38B(3)(b)).

Discharge of care orders

A care order, other than an interim care order, will remain in force until the child reaches 18   **20.146**
unless determined earlier: s 91(12). The other ways in which it might be terminated or discharged are as follows:

(a) when the court makes a residence order in respect of a child in care the care order will be
    discharged automatically: s 91(1);
(b) when the court makes an adoption order the care order will be discharged automatically:
    s 46(2), ACA 2002;
(c) when a successful application is made under s 39(1) to discharge the order. Such an appli-
    cation may be made by:
    (i)   any person with parental responsibility for the child; or
    (ii) the child; or
    (iii) the relevant local authority.

A child does *not* require leave to make an application to discharge a care order: *Re A (Care*   **20.147**
Order: Discharge Application by Child) [1995] 1 FLR 599. When the court considers whether to
discharge a care order it simply applies the welfare criteria set out in s 1, CA 1989. There are

no additional criteria to be considered as there are when the court considers whether to *make* a care order.

20.148 Upon an application to discharge a care order the court can consider an application to substitute the care order with a supervision order: s 39(4). When it considers such an application the court is relieved of the exercise of deciding whether the s 31(2) grounds are made out: s 39(5).

20.149 When an unsuccessful application has been made for the discharge of a care order or for its substitution with a supervision order, no repeat applications may be made for a period of six months following that disposal of the matter, except with the leave of the court: s 91(15).

Supervision orders

20.150 Up until now only passing mention has been made of supervision orders. It is now proposed to examine them in more detail.

When may a supervision order be made?

20.151 The court may make an order placing a child under the supervision of a local authority or a probation officer pursuant to s 31(1) provided that:

   (a) the court is satisfied that the statutory grounds in s 31(2) are made out in relation to the child concerned; and
   (b) the making of the supervision order is for the welfare of the child: s 1.

20.152 Many of the rules relating to care orders apply equally to supervision orders:

   (a) an application can only be made if the child is under 17 (or under 16, if married): s 31(3);
   (b) any delay in the determination of the application will be presumed to prejudice the welfare of the child, and therefore a timetable should be drawn up for the speedy disposal of the proceedings: s 32;
   (c) the court may take the initiative and direct the local authority to investigate the circumstances of the child pursuant to s 37(1) in order that the authority might decide whether to make an application for a supervision (or care) order;
   (d) interim supervision orders may be made on the same principles as interim care orders (see para 20.131 above);
   (e) the provisions relating to children's guardians apply equally to proceedings for a supervision order as they do to care order proceedings: s 41(1);
   (f) the same rules apply to the variation and discharge of supervision orders as for care orders (s 39 and see para 20.146 above).

20.153 When deciding whether to make a care order or a supervision order in a case where the balance between the two is equal, the court should take the least interventionist approach: *Re D (Care Order or Supervision Order)* [2000] Fam Law 600. The court should ask itself whether:

   (a) the stronger order is needed to protect the child;
   (b) the risks could be met by a supervision order;
   (c) there is a need for the speed of action that a care order allows the local authority;
   (d) the parent could properly protect the child without sharing parental responsibility with the local authority;
   (e) parental cooperation could only be obtained through the more draconian care order;

(f) the child's needs could be met by advising, assisting, and befriending the child rather than by sharing parental responsibility for him;

(g) there have been any improvements seen by objective observers during the current proceedings which would indicate the future; and

(h) consider the range of powers available under a supervision order, including its duration.

The choice between a care order and a supervision order has to be considered in the context **20.154** of the HRA 1998 and the ECHR. In each case, a court must decide whether the making of a supervision order is a proportionate response to the risk presented: *Re O (Supervision Order)* [2001] 1 FLR 923; *Re C (Care Order or Supervision Order)* [2001] 2 FLR 466. For a more detailed comparison between care orders and supervision orders see para 20.163 below.

Effect of supervision order

(a) The supervising officer does not acquire parental responsibility for the child. **20.155**

(b) The supervisor's duties are set out in s 35(1). His main duties are to advise, assist, and befriend the supervised child and to take such steps as are reasonably necessary to give effect to the order. Where the supervision order is not wholly complied with or the supervisor considers that it may no longer be necessary then he may consider whether to apply to the court for the variation or discharge of the order (s 35(1)(c)): see *Re V (Care or Supervision Order)* [1996] 1 FLR 776).

(c) The making of a supervision order brings to an end any earlier care or supervision order made in respect of that child which would otherwise continue in force: sch 3, para 10.

Duration of supervision order

A supervision order will last for an initial period of one year, but the supervisor may apply to **20.156** the court to have it extended for a period of up to three years in total, beginning with the date on which the order was first made (sch 3, para 6). If the authority takes the view, towards the end of the three-year period, that the supervision order is still necessary then it will have to apply to the court again and prove that the s 31(2) grounds are still in existence.

Power to give directions to supervised child

A supervision order may (pursuant to sch 3, para 2) require the supervised child to comply **20.157** with directions given by the supervisor to:

(a) live at a particular place for a particular period of time;

(b) present himself to specified persons at specified times and places;

(c) participate in specified activities at specified times.

Although the court has power to give directions to a supervised child, for example that the child should comply with directions given by the supervisor as to his place of residence, the supervising authority has no way in which to enforce the order. If the child refused to comply, the local authority would have to bring the matter back to court under s 35 or apply to the court for a variation of the supervision order: *Re R and G (Minors) (Interim Care or Supervision Orders)* [1994] 1 FLR 793.

The supervisor has no power to give directions in respect of any medical or psychiatric treat- **20.158** ment for the child: sch 3, para 2(3). Such directions can only be given by the court: sch 3, para 4 and see para 20.161 below.

Imposition of obligations on responsible persons

20.159   The CA 1989 enables obligations to be imposed upon 'responsible persons' (sch 3, para 1), provided that the person concerned *consents* to those obligations.

20.160   A 'responsible person' in relation to a supervised child means:

(a) any person with parental responsibility for the child; and

(b) any other person with whom the child is living (eg step-parents).

The obligations can be to take all reasonable steps to:

(i)   ensure that the child complies with his supervisor's directions; and

(ii) ensure that the child complies with any requirements in the supervision order, for example to attend for medical and psychiatric treatment.

The parent can apply to the court to have any requirement affecting him varied: s 39(2) and (3).

Psychiatric and medical examination

20.161   A supervision order may require a child to submit to a medical or psychiatric examination, or to do so from time to time as directed by his supervisor, provided that:

(a) the child *consents* to it (where he is of sufficient understanding to make an informed decision): sch 3, para 4(4)(a); and

(b) satisfactory arrangements have been made for the examination: sch 3, para 4(4)(b); and

(c) the order must require that the examination be conducted by a specified medical practitioner at a specific place: sch 3, para 4(2).

In *Note: Re HIV Tests* [1994] 2 FLR 116, Singer J directed that any application to submit a child to a blood test where it appeared that the child might be HIV positive should be made only to a High Court judge in the Family Division, whether in public law or private law proceedings.

Psychiatric and medical treatment

20.162   When a court makes or varies a supervision order it may include a requirement that the child shall submit to psychiatric or medical treatment by a registered medical practitioner at a specific place: sch 3, para 5. Before including such a requirement the court must be satisfied:

(a) on the evidence of an appropriate medical practitioner that the treatment is justified; and

(b) that the child consents to it (where he is of sufficient understanding to make an informed decision); and

(c) that satisfactory arrangements have been made for the treatment.

The medical practitioner may seek a variation of the requirement (eg where he feels that the treatment should continue for longer than the specified period) by submitting a written report to the supervisor to that effect. Thereupon, the supervisor must refer the report to the court and the court can make an order cancelling or varying the requirement: sch 3, para 5(7).

Comparison between care orders and supervision orders

A very useful summary of the differences between care orders and supervision orders is to be   **20.163**
found in *Re S (J) (A Minor) (Care or Supervision Order)* [1993] 2 FLR 919, as follows:

(a) When deciding whether to make a care order or a supervision order the court needs to be
     clear as to what the future risks are. This requires a careful scrutiny of what has happened
     in the past so that a view of the future risks can be formed.

(b) A supervision order is capable of providing a great deal of protection. It can guarantee
     access into the child's home, supported by a warrant under s 102 if necessary. There can
     be a care plan. An emergency protection order is available if there is a need to remove
     the child in an emergency. The child can be kept on the 'at risk' register so that the local
     authority is required to conduct periodic reviews.

(c) The concept of parental responsibility is at the heart of the difference between a care
     order and a supervision order. A care order means that a local authority can take over
     virtually all the parental responsibility functions if satisfied that it was necessary to do so
     in order to safeguard or promote the child's welfare. A supervision order does not deprive
     the parents of parental responsibility and does not endow the local authority with paren-
     tal responsibility. Section 34 enables the local authority to control contact between the
     child and other people where a care order has been made.

(d) When a care order is made then a duty is imposed upon the local authority under s 22 to
     safeguard the welfare of the child. A supervision order carries with it no such duty, and the
     obligation to keep the child safe remains with the parent who has parental responsibility.

(e) Under a supervision order the supervisor has a duty under s 35 to advise and assist the
     supervised child, but not the parent.

(f) A care order places a local authority in a better position to enforce its requirements than
     a supervision order. For example, it has power to remove the child when it is no longer
     considered to be safe. Under a supervision order, information and access must be given
     to the supervisor, which can be enforced by a warrant under s 102; that is, the only part
     of the arrangement which is given any specific sanction. Thus, where a grave risk exists
     in relation to a child the court should make a care order.

(g) The court must look at the case as a whole and determine its views as to the risk of both
     physical and emotional harm to the child, and then decide whether, in light of the grav-
     ity of the case, the local authority ought to have extra duties imposed on it.

In *Re D (A Minor) (Care or Supervision Order)* [1993] 2 FLR 423 there had been a history of non-   **20.164**
accidental injury to children, culminating in the death of a child whilst in the care of the
father who was subsequently imprisoned for cruelty offences. The court held that a care order
rather than a supervision order should be made in relation to a child born to the father's new
partner. The protection of the child was the decisive factor and it overrode the local authority's view that a supervision order would have been adequate because the child was thriving
and a care order would undermine the cooperation of the parents with social services.

Care and supervision orders at the instigation of the court

It may happen that whilst the court is engaged in hearing family proceedings (eg an applica-   **20.165**
tion for a s 8 order), it becomes apparent that a care or supervision order may be necessary.

In those circumstances the court may direct the local authority, pursuant to s 37(1), to investigate the circumstances of the child. Thereupon, the court will normally adjourn the matter in hand (and perhaps make an interim care or supervision order in the meantime: see para 20.118 above) while the authority conducts its investigation and compiles a report.

20.166   If the authority, in due course, decides *not* to apply for a care or supervision order it must inform the court of the reasons for that decision. It must also tell the court of any services or assistance it has provided, or intends to provide, for the child and his family, and of any other action it has taken, or will take: s 37(3). Furthermore, it must consider whether it would be appropriate to review the case at a later date: s 37(6).

D   PUBLIC FUNDING

20.167   The availability of public funding for CA 1989 proceedings under the Community Legal Service scheme is dealt with fully in Chapter 2, para 2.74. The practitioner will remember that whereas, for most private law children cases (under Parts I to III, CA 1989) the applicant will be required to attend a meeting with a mediator to determine whether the case is suitable for mediation before any public funding may be made available for representation, there is no such requirement to attend a meeting with a mediator for public law children cases (under Parts IV and V, CA 1989).

E   APPEALS

20.168   The question of appeals is dealt with fully in Chapter 18, para 18.94. However, there are certain cases relating to appeals in public law proceedings which are important.

(a)   The family proceedings court has no inherent power to grant a stay of execution pending an appeal. If an appeal is being considered against a care order and a stay is required then the proper course is immediately to apply to the appeal court: *Re J (A Minor) (Residence)* [1994] 1 FLR 369.

(b)   When an appeal court is considering whether to give leave for fresh evidence to be adduced at the appeal hearing the question to be asked is: does the evidence lead to a different conclusion from that which would otherwise prevail, that is, does it throw a different light on the matter? The court must act cautiously in relation to the new evidence since it cannot test the evidence: *Hounslow LBC v A* [1993] 1 FLR 702.

(c)   Appeals in cases where an interim care order has been granted ought not to be made unless there are the very strongest grounds for interfering with the interim order: *Re M (Minors) (Interim Care Order)* [1993] 2 FLR 406.

(d)   In *Re M (A Minor) (Appeal: Interim Order) (No 1)* [1994] 1 FLR 54 the judge refused an application for a care order. The local authority appealed and the judge made an interim care order pending the hearing of the appeal. The Court of Appeal held that it was better that the interim care order should be extended so that the child remained where she was until the appeal hearing. It was not the job of the court to prejudge what the Court of Appeal would do, other than in cases which were hopeless.

(e) Note that s 55, Access to Justice Act 1999, restricts the right to more than one appeal in most civil cases. Section 55(1) provides that where an appeal is made to a county court or the High Court in relation to any matter, and on hearing the appeal the court makes a decision in relation to that matter, no appeal may be made to the Court of Appeal from that decision unless the Court of Appeal considers that:

  (i) the appeal would raise an important point of principle or practice; or

  (ii) there is some other compelling reason for the Court of Appeal to hear it.

F   KEY DOCUMENTS

Children Act 1989   **20.169**
Human Rights Act 1998
Adoption and Children Act 2002
European Convention for Human Rights and Fundamental Freedoms 1950
CAFCASS Practice Note, 'Cases Referred by Independent Reviewing Officers' dated 8 June
    2004 and available at <http://www.dca.gov.uk>

21

EMERGENCY PROTECTION OF CHILDREN

A INTRODUCTION

Part V, Children Act 1989 ('CA 1989') contains a code for the protection of children. It aims **21.01** to ensure that proper protective action can be taken in respect of children whilst providing proper procedures to enable parents and others connected with the child to challenge such action before the court. The main orders available under the statutory scheme are as follows:

(a) Local authorities are placed under a positive duty to investigate cases of suspected child abuse and to decide upon the appropriate action to take: s 47 and sch 2, para 4.

(b) If parents refuse to cooperate with the local authority's assessment of a child whom it has reasonable cause to suspect is suffering, or is likely to suffer, significant harm then a 'child assessment order' is available to enable the authority to complete its enquiries: s 43.

(c) The CA 1989 introduced 'emergency protection orders' to provide for the emergency protection of children. The grounds upon which they may be granted are tightly defined. Parents and others can challenge the making of an emergency protection order if they are present at the hearing; if they are not, then they can seek a discharge of the order from the court: ss 44 and 45.

(d) 'Police protection': powers are available to enable the police to detain a child for the purpose of protecting him: s 46.

(e) 'Recovery orders' are available to facilitate the recovery of children who have been abducted while the subject of a care, emergency protection, or recovery order: s 50.

B CHILD ASSESSMENT ORDERS

The 'halfway house' of a child assessment order is available to cover the situation where **21.02** the local authority suspects that the child may be at risk of significant harm, but not at immediate risk requiring his removal or detention (eg in a hospital) under an emergency protection order, and his parents or others responsible for him refuse to cooperate with the authority's attempts to make an assessment of the child: s 43. The order aims to allow the authority to complete its assessment so that it can decide whether to take further action in respect of the child. Where the court hears an application for a child assessment order it may, instead, make an emergency protection order if it is satisfied that the circumstances of the case warrant it: s 43(4).

The application

Only a local authority or 'authorised person' may apply for a child assessment order. The **21.03** court may make an order if, but only if, it is satisfied that:

(a) the applicant has reasonable cause to suspect that the child is suffering, or is likely to suffer, significant harm;

(b) an assessment of the state of the child's health or development, or of the way in which he is being treated, is required to enable the applicant to establish whether the child is suffering, or is likely to suffer, significant harm; and

(c) it is unlikely that the assessment will be made, or be satisfactory, without a child assessment order.

Before making a child assessment order the court must also have regard to the 'welfare' and 'presumption of no order' principles set out in s 1 (see Chapter 17, paras 17.04 ff).

21.04 The application should always be made on notice at a full hearing in which the parties are able to participate, so that it can be challenged at that stage. Article 6, European Convention for the Protection of Human Rights and Fundamental Freedoms (ECHR) guarantees a right to a fair trial; this implies a right to give evidence.

21.05 The court has power to prevent a further application being made by particular persons (including a local authority) without the court's leave, or to refuse to allow a further application within six months without leave: s 91(14) and (15).

Parties

21.06 An application can be made in respect of a child under the age of 18. (Note: it is not subject to the age 17 limit applicable to care and supervision orders.) Those who must be respondents to child assessment order proceedings and those who must be notified of the proceedings are set out in r 12.3(1), Family Procedure Rules 2010 ('FPR 2010').

21.07 The persons who must be made respondents are:

(a) every person the applicant believes to have parental responsibility for the child;
(b) where the child is the subject of a care order, every person the applicant believes to have had parental responsibility immediately prior to the making of the care order;
(c) where the application is to extend, vary, or discharge an order, the parties to the original proceedings when the order was made;
(d) the child;
(e) any other person *may* be made a respondent, provided that he has first obtained leave of the court: r 12.3(3).

Commencement and duration

21.08 The court may allow up to a maximum of seven days for the assessment, and the order must specify the date by which the assessment is to begin: s 43(5).

Effect of child assessment order

21.09 The main effects of a child assessment order are as follows:

(a) Parental responsibility does not vest in the applicant by virtue of an order being made.
(b) The order requires any person in a position to do so to produce the child to the person named in the order so that the assessment may take place, and requires him to comply with any other directions contained in the order: s 43(6).
(c) The order authorizes the carrying out of the assessment in accordance with the terms of the order: s 43(7).

(d) The child to whom the order relates may refuse to consent to the assessment if he is of sufficient understanding to make an informed decision: s 43(8).

(e) Child assessment orders may run alongside s 8 orders (but will not be required where a care, supervision, or emergency protection order is in force as the local authority will have parental responsibility for the child if it holds any one of these orders).

Directions

The court is empowered to attach directions to the child assessment order. For example, the **21.10** court may wish to limit the extent of the assessment to a medical examination; it may wish to direct that a particular medical practitioner conduct the examination; it may wish to direct that specific persons be present during an examination and so forth. Furthermore, where it is necessary for the child to be kept away from home for the purposes of the assessment (eg in hospital), then tight conditions are imposed as to the circumstances in which this may be done and provision is made for contact between the child and persons connected with him during that time: s 43(9) and (10).

Variation and discharge of child assessment orders

Provision is made for an application to the court for a child assessment order to be varied or **21.11** discharged: see s 43(12). Those who may apply include:

(a) the child;
(b) his parents;
(c) any other person with parental responsibility for him;
(d) any other person caring for him;
(e) any person in whose favour a contact order is in force with respect to the child;
(f) any person allowed to have contact with the child under a s 34 contact order.

Appeals

The provisions for appealing from a child assessment order are the same as those for appealing **21.12** any order made under the CA 1989 (see Chapter 18, para 18.94).

C   EMERGENCY PROTECTION ORDERS

Who may apply—and on what grounds?

There are three categories of applicants and different grounds apply to each category: **21.13**

(a) 'Any person' may apply for an emergency protection order under s 44(1)(a). The court may only grant the order under this ground if it is satisfied that there is reasonable cause to believe that the child is likely to suffer significant harm if either:
   (i) he is not removed to accommodation provided by or on behalf of the applicant; or
   (ii) he does not remain in the place where he is then being accommodated.

(b) A local authority may apply on the ground set out in point (a) above *or* it may, instead, rely on the ground set out in s 44(1)(b), that is to say:

  (i) enquiries are being made with respect to the child under s 47(1)(b); and

  (ii) those enquiries are being frustrated by access to the child being unreasonably refused to a person authorized to seek access *and* that the applicant has reasonable cause to believe that access to the child is required as a matter of *urgency*.

(c) An 'authorised person' (the meaning of which is the same as for the purposes of s 31, that is, at the moment only the NSPCC has this status) may apply on the ground set out in s 44(1)(c) if he can show that:

  (i) he has reasonable cause to believe that a child is suffering, or is likely to suffer, significant harm;

  (ii) he is making enquiries with respect to the child's welfare; and

  (iii) those enquiries are being frustrated by access to the child being unreasonably refused to a person authorized to seek access *and* the applicant has reasonable cause to believe that access to the child is required as a matter of *urgency*.

'Harm' and 'significant harm' are defined in s 31(9) and (10) and have already been discussed in Chapter 20, para 20.52. Note that the meaning of harm has been extended to include, for example, impairment suffered by hearing or seeing the ill-treatment of another.

21.14 A 'person authorised to seek access' is defined in s 44(2)(b) as:

(a) in the case of a local authority—an officer of the authority or a person authorized by it to act on its behalf in connection with its enquiries;

(b) in the case of an 'authorised person' that person.

Without notice applications

21.15 An application for an emergency protection order may be made without notice. However, an emergency protection order is a draconian order which involves a significant interference with the family's Art 8 rights. In *X Council v B (Emergency Protection Orders)* [2005] 1 FLR 341, Munby J gave guidance as to the way in which such applications should be approached. The court held that there are unusual and exceptional cases (of which this was an example) in which an *ex parte* application is appropriate, but adequate evidence must be presented and a proper note of the hearing prepared by the local authority and made available to the parents. In all such cases: (a) the summary removal of a child from his parents requires exceptional justification and proof of imminent danger; (b) no emergency protection order should be longer than absolutely necessary to protect the child; (c) supporting evidence must be full and compelling; (d) less drastic alternatives (eg a child assessment order) must be considered; and (e) where an emergency protection order is made, arrangements for reasonable contact under s 44(13) must be driven by the needs of the family and not be stunted by lack of resources.

21.16 In *Re X (Emergency Protection Orders)* [2006] 2 FLR 701, McFarlane J held that the guidance in *X Council v B* (para 21.15 above) was 'required reading' for any Bench hearing an application for a without notice emergency protection order, and that this case should be copied and put before the Bench in every such case.

Effects of an emergency protection order

The effects of an emergency protection order are as follows: **21.17**

(a) The court can direct any person who is in a position to do so to comply with any request to produce the child to the applicant: s 44(4)(a).

(b) The court can authorize:
   (i) the removal of the child at any time to accommodation provided by or on behalf of the applicant; or
   (ii) the prevention of the child's removal from any hospital, or other place, in which he was being accommodated immediately before the making of the order: s 44(4)(b).

(c) The emergency protection order gives the applicant parental responsibility for the child for the duration of the order: s 44(4)(c). However, the applicant should only take such action in meeting his parental responsibility as is reasonably required to safeguard or promote the welfare of the child (having particular regard to the duration of the order): s 44(5).

(d) The court has power under s 44(6) to make directions as to:
   (i) the contact which is, or is not, to be allowed between the child and any named person; and
   (ii) the medical, psychiatric, or other assessment of the child.

Duration of emergency protection order

An emergency protection order may have effect in the first instance for a maximum of eight   **21.18**
days: s 45(1). The court may extend the order once only for a period of up to seven days (s 45(6)), but *only* if the applicant has parental responsibility for the child as a result of the emergency protection order *and* is entitled to apply for a care order with respect to the child (ie, only local authorities and the NSPCC at the moment). The extension should only be granted if the court has reasonable cause to believe that the child is likely to suffer significant harm if the order is not extended: s 45(4), (5), and (6).

Who should be informed?

Rule 12.3(1), FPR 2010 sets out those persons who should be informed of an application for   **21.19**
an emergency protection order.

Parental contact

The court may give directions as to the contact which is, or is not, to be allowed between the   **21.20**
child and any named person: s 44(6)(a).

Furthermore, the applicant is under a duty, while the emergency protection order is in force,   **21.21**
to allow the child reasonable contact (subject to any direction of the court under s 44(6)) with the following persons (s 44(13)):

(a) his parents;

(b) any person who is not a parent but has parental responsibility for him;

(c)   any person with whom he was living immediately before the making of the order;

(d)   any person in whose favour a contact order is in force with respect to him;

(e)   any person who is allowed to have contact with the child by virtue of an order under s 34; and

(f)   any person acting on behalf of any of those persons.

The contact provisions may not be challenged (s 45(10)).

Challenging an emergency protection order

21.22   An emergency protection order may be challenged by any of the following persons (s 45(8)):

(a)   the child;

(b)   any parent of his;

(c)   any person who is not a parent of his but who has parental responsibility for him;

(d)   any person with whom he was living immediately before the making of the order.

21.23   Any application for the order to be discharged may be made at any time. The right to apply to discharge is not available where the prospective challenger was given notice of the hearing at which the order was made and was present at that hearing (or at a hearing as a result of which the period of the order was extended): s 45(11). The reason for this is that no challenge should be allowed if it could have been made at the time of the application for the order.

21.24   There is no right to appeal against the making of, or refusal to make, an emergency protection order, or against any direction given by the court in connection with such an order: s 45(10) and *Essex County Council* v *F* [1993] 1 FLR 847. If the magistrates act unreasonably in connection with such proceedings then the only available remedy would appear to be judicial review: *Re P (Emergency Protection Order)* [1996] 1 FLR 482. In the future it is possible that this area of the law will be the subject of challenge under the Human Rights Act 1998. See the comments made in para 21.04 above.

Returning the child

21.25   The applicant has a duty to return the child if it appears to him that it is safe for the child to be returned or that it is safe for the child to be allowed to be removed from the place in question: s 44(10) and (11). However, the applicant may remove the child again under the same order, provided that the order remains in force and it appears to him that a change in the circumstances of the case makes it necessary for him to do so: s 44(10) and (12).

Exclusion requirements in emergency protection orders

21.26   The court may include an exclusion requirement in an emergency protection order in certain circumstances. To a large extent the same rules apply as when the court includes an exclusion requirement in an interim care order, including the rules relating to the attachment of a power of arrest and the acceptance by the court of undertakings. Those rules are set out in Chapter 20, paras 20.131 ff. There are, however, some differences in the conditions which must be met

before the court can include an exclusion requirement in an emergency protection order. The relevant conditions are that:

(a) there is reasonable cause to believe that if a person ('the relevant person') is excluded from a dwelling-house in which the child lives:
  (i) in the case of an order based on s 44(1)(a), the child will not be likely to suffer significant harm, even though the child is not removed or, as the case may be, does not remain; or
  (ii) in the case of an order based on s 44(1)(b) or (c), the enquiries will cease to be frustrated; and
(b) another person living in the dwelling-house (whether or not a parent of the child):
  (i) is able and willing to give the child the care which it would be reasonable to expect a parent to give him; and
  (ii) consents to the inclusion of the exclusion requirement.

Otherwise, ss 44A, 44B, and 45(8A) and (8B) contain provisions identical (*mutatis mutandis*) to those set out in Chapter 20, para 20.131, in respect of exclusion requirements included in an interim care order.

D   POLICE PROTECTION

The police have important powers under s 46. Where a constable has reasonable cause to believe that a child would otherwise be likely to suffer significant harm, he may: **21.27**

(a) remove the child to suitable accommodation and keep him there; or
(b) take reasonable steps to prevent the removal of the child from any hospital, or other place, in which he is then being accommodated.

The s 46 power to remove a child can be exercised even where an emergency protection order   **21.28**
is in force in respect of the child. However, where a police officer knows that an emergency protection order is in force he should not exercise the s 46 power unless there are compelling reasons to do so (*Langley* v *Liverpool City Council* [2006] 1 FLR 342).

Duration of police protection

A child may not be kept in police protection for a period of more than 72 hours: s 46(6). As soon as   **21.29**
practicable after taking the child into police protection the constable must ensure that the appropriate enquiries into the case are undertaken by the police officer designated for this purpose. After completing his enquiries the designated officer must release the child unless there is still reasonable cause to believe that the child would be likely to suffer significant harm if released: s 46(3)(e) and (5). The constable who initially took the child into police protection has a duty to inform various persons, including the local authority, the child, the child's parents, and persons with parental responsibility for the child, of, amongst other things, the steps that have been taken and the reasons for them. The full extent of those duties are set out in s 46(3) and (4).

Parental responsibility

21.30   Neither the constable concerned nor the designated officer acquires parental responsibility for the child whilst he is in police protection. However, the designated officer must do what is reasonable to promote the child's welfare, bearing in mind the short duration of the period of police protection: s 46(9) and s 3(5).

Contact with the child

21.31   The designated officer must allow the following persons to have contact with the child during the period of police protection, provided that *in his opinion* it is both reasonable and in the child's best interests:

(a)   the child's parents;

(b)   anyone else who has parental responsibility for the child;

(c)   anyone with whom the child was living immediately before he was taken into police protection;

(d)   a person who has a contact order in his favour relating to the child;

(e)   anyone acting on behalf of the persons listed in points (a) to (d) above: s 46(10).

E   RECOVERY ORDERS

21.32   A court may make a 'recovery order' in respect of a child, pursuant to s 50 where:

(a)   the child is in care, in police protection, or is the subject of an emergency protection order: ss 50(2) and 49(2); and

(b)   there is reason to believe that the child:

   (i)   has been unlawfully taken away, or is being unlawfully kept away from the 'responsible person'; or

   (ii)   has run away or is staying away from the 'responsible person'; or

   (iii)   is missing.

Who can apply?

21.33   The court may make a recovery order only on the application of the following persons:

(a)   a person with parental responsibility for the child by virtue of a care order or emergency protection order; or

(b)   where the child is in police protection, the designated officer: s 50(4).

Effect of recovery order

A recovery order will have the following effects (s 50(3)): **21.34**

(a) it operates as a direction to any person who is in position to do so to produce the child on request to any authorized person;

(b) it authorizes the removal of the child by any authorized person;

(c) it requires any person who has information as to the child's whereabouts to disclose that information, if asked to do so, to a constable or an officer of the court;

(d) it authorizes a constable to enter any premises specified in the order and search for the child, using reasonable force if necessary.

F   KEY DOCUMENTS

Children Act 1989 **21.35**
Family Procedure Rules 2010 (SI 2010/2995)

PART IV
MONEY AND PROPERTY

22

THE HOME: PREVENTING A SALE OR MORTGAGE

A   THE PROBLEM

The major asset owned by the parties to a marriage or civil partnership is usually their home. **22.01** For each party, this represents both a roof over his or her head and a capital investment. Whilst the marriage or civil partnership is satisfactory they are likely to discuss and agree any step that is to be taken in relation to the home, such as selling it or mortgaging it. However, once the relationship begins to founder, the danger arises that without consulting the other party to the relationship, one party will engage in dealings in relation to the house which will jeopardize either the roof over the other's head or his or her financial interest in the property.

Example 1 The parties purchase a house in 1984 with the aid of a mortgage. It is conveyed into the husband's sole name. By 2000 the marriage is on the rocks and the wife petitions for divorce making a comprehensive claim for application for financial orders. She is living in the house but she goes away for two months to see her sister in Australia. Whilst she is away, the husband puts the property on the market and sells it. By the time the wife returns the proceeds of sale have been dissipated. She has lost both the roof over her head and any prospect of having the home transferred to her in proceedings under s 24, Matrimonial Causes Act 1973 ('MCA 1973') or of receiving under s 23 a lump sum payment of a share in the proceeds.

Example 2 Instead of selling the house, the husband grants a second mortgage of it to a bank as security for a substantial loan. Provided he keeps up the repayments on both mortgages, this does not prejudice the wife's occupation of the property but it clearly does affect her financial interest in the house. Not only the first but also the second mortgage will have to be discharged from the proceeds of sale if the house is sold before the mortgagees have been fully repaid, thus substantially reducing the equity in the house available for distribution between the parties.

If the husband falls behind with the mortgage instalments, the wife's occupation of the house may also be endangered if the mortgagees seek to enforce their rights in relation to the property.

22.02 This chapter sets out what can be done to prevent problems of this type arising. It is assumed that the solicitor acts for a wife who wishes to prevent her husband from dealing with the property. The same principles would apply if the roles were reversed. References to spouses also include civil partners.

B   HOUSE IN JOINT NAMES

Protection against sale or mortgage by one spouse

Generally

22.03 If the house is in the joint names of both spouses the wife will automatically be protected against the husband selling the property without her consent. As she is a joint tenant of the legal estate, the property cannot be conveyed or transferred unless she joins in the conveyance or transfer.

22.04 In theory it might be possible for the husband to use the house as security for a loan without the consent of the wife. In practice, however, it would be hard for him to find anyone willing to lend on this basis because the security provided by such arrangements would be inadequate. Thus, the wife is unlikely to have anything to fear from this quarter either.

Consent obtained by misrepresentation, fraud, or 'actual undue influence'

22.05 If the wife is a party to the mortgage or sale, the transaction will in most cases bind her interest. It may be, however, that her consent has been obtained by fraud, misrepresentation, or 'actual undue influence' on the part of the husband. Each will require a wife to provide cogent evidence of the deceit, particularly in the case of fraud. Where actual undue influence is alleged, the complainant must prove affirmatively that she entered into the transaction not of her own free will but as a result of the undue influence used against her.

22.06 Stress and anxiety caused by external pressure is not enough. What is needed is some sort of fraud, victimization, or coercion.

'Presumed undue influence' between husband and wife and similar relationships

22.07 The well-known case of *Barclays Bank* v *O'Brien* [1994] 1 FLR 1 set out legal principles aimed at providing protection to a wife in a situation where she had consented to the matrimonial home being used as a surety in order to support the husband's business debts. That protection took the form of presuming undue influence on the part of the husband if the wife was able to establish certain facts, and then fixing the lender with 'constructive notice' of that influence when the lender sought possession of the home. The lender was then required to satisfy the court that certain steps had been taken to ensure that the wife was not in fact the victim of such influence.

In *Royal Bank of Scotland* v *Etridge (No 2) and other appeals* [2001] 4 All ER 449 the House of Lords went to considerable lengths to clarify this complex area of law and to deal with practical uncertainties produced by *Barclays Bank* v *O'Brien*. **22.08**

In the leading speech, Lord Nicholls confirmed that a rebuttable presumption will become operative as a general rule depending upon the nature of the alleged undue influence, the personality of the parties, their relationship, the extent to which the transaction cannot be readily accounted for, and all the circumstances of the case. Typically, in the case of 'surety wives' the complainant must adduce sufficient evidence of the fact that she placed trust and confidence in the husband and that the transaction is not readily explicable by the relationship of the parties. This second requirement does not have to constitute 'manifest disadvantage', merely that the transaction cannot be reasonably or ordinarily accounted for. **22.09**

If the evidential burden upon the wife is discharged, then the transaction is presumed to have been procured by undue influence unless the lender can rebut the presumption. His Lordship's reasoning was that in these circumstances the lender ought to have known that the wife's agreement was not truly her own. Lord Nicholls went to considerable lengths to detail the steps that a lender must take in order to rebut the presumption and thereby enforce the mortgage against the wife. **22.10**

Lenders are 'put on enquiry' in every case where the relationship between surety and debtor is non-commercial. The lender must take reasonable steps to satisfy itself that the practical implications of the proposed transaction have been brought home to the wife, in a meaningful way, so that she enters the transaction with her eyes open so far as the basic elements are concerned. A meeting with the wife is not normally required and, ordinarily, it will be reasonable for the lender to rely upon confirmation from a solicitor that she has been advised appropriately. In order to ensure that its position is protected, the lender should take the following steps: **22.11**

(a) It should write to the wife, informing her that for its own protection it will require written confirmation from a solicitor acting for her that both the nature of the documents and the implications of the transaction have been fully explained to her. She should be informed that thereafter she will not be able to dispute that she is legally bound by the transaction.

(b) The wife should be requested to nominate a solicitor who, if she wishes, can be the same one that is acting for the husband. The bank should not proceed until it has received an appropriate response directly from the wife.

(c) Where the bank is unwilling to explain the husband's financial affairs to the wife, it should provide sufficient and adequate disclosure to the solicitor. The extent of this will depend on the facts of the case. Obviously, the consent of the husband will be required before confidential information is disclosed.

(d) Where the bank suspects that the husband has misled the wife as to the nature of the transaction, it should inform the solicitor of this.

(e) A letter of confirmation, as detailed below, should be obtained from the solicitor.

It is not necessary that the solicitor should act solely for the wife, as cost and familiarity of the family solicitor are important factors. The solicitor's legal and professional duties, assumed when accepting instructions to advise the wife, are owed to her alone. The solicitor should consider whether there is any conflict of duty or interest.

22.12 Lord Nicholls specified that the core duties owed to the wife by the solicitor are:

(a) to explain the reason that the solicitor has become involved;

(b) to explain that, if the bank decides to commence possession proceedings, the lender will rely upon the solicitor's involvement to counter any suggestion of undue influence;

(c) to obtain instructions from the wife that she wishes the solicitor to act for her and then to advise her on the legal and practical implications of the proposed transaction.

22.13 Assuming such instructions are forthcoming, the content of that advice will typically contain:

(a) an explanation of the nature of the documents and the practical consequences they will have for the wife if she signs them;

(b) the seriousness of the risks involved;

(c) the purpose of the proposed facility, its amount, and its principal terms;

(d) whether the bank may increase the amount of the facility, or change its terms, or grant a new facility without reference to her;

(e) the amount of the wife's liability under the guarantee;

(f) a discussion of the wife's financial means, including her understanding of the value of the property being charged;

(g) whether there are any other assets out of which repayment can be made if the husband's business fails;

(h) importantly, that the wife has a choice and that the decision is hers and hers alone;

(i) the solicitor should check whether the wife wishes to proceed and whether the wife is content that the solicitor write to the bank to confirm that the documents, the nature of the transaction, and the implications have been explained to her. Alternatively, the wife may wish the solicitor to negotiate better terms with the bank.

22.14 The solicitor's discussion with the wife should take place at a face-to-face meeting in the absence of the husband and should be presented in non-technical language. The bank ought to have provided all the information required by the solicitor. If it has not, the solicitor ought to decline the confirmation sought by the bank.

22.15 Their Lordships noted that the decision over whether to proceed is the wife's and that, as a general rule, the obligation on the solicitor was not to veto the proposed transaction but merely to provide the wife with reasoned advice. Where, however, it was glaringly obvious that the transaction was procured as a result of undue influence on the part of the husband the solicitor should decline to act for her further.

22.16 Lord Nicholls confirmed that the position will be unaltered where the husband stands as surety to the wife's debts. The same will also apply in the case of unmarried couples, heterosexual or homosexual, where the lender is aware of the relationship. Importantly, cohabitation is not essential (see *Massey* v *Midland Bank plc* [1995] 1 All ER 929 at 933, per Steyn LJ).

In the subsequent case of *National Westminster Bank plc* v *Amin and Another* [2002] 1 FLR 735, **22.17** which involved the question of whether a defence of undue influence between a son and his parents who spoke only Urdu should be struck out, the House of Lords noted that the instructions received by a solicitor who had been retained by the bank raised serious questions which should be aired at trial. These included the limited extent of the instructions provided by the couple, the solicitor's communications to the lender, the fact that the lender knew that the couple did not speak English, and that they were especially vulnerable to exploitation. The case was remitted for trial.

'Presumed undue influence' and other types of relationships

In *Etridge No 2*, Lord Nicholls made it clear that in certain types of relationship where one **22.18** party acquires influence over another who is vulnerable and dependent the law will adopt a sternly protective attitude where a gift is made by the vulnerable person which cannot be readily explained. Where the complainant can demonstrate both the existence of the relationship and the transaction, the law will presume, irrebuttably, that one party had influence over the other. The complainant need not prove that he or she actually reposed trust and confidence in the other party. Examples of the types of relationship include parent and child, guardian and ward, trustee and beneficiary, and solicitor and client.

Providing for the possibility of death before divorce

Generally

The solicitor must give some thought as to what will happen to the wife's share in the property **22.19** should she die before the parties are divorced and questions of financial provision resolved. If husband and wife are joint tenants in equity, the wife's interest will pass to her husband on her death by virtue of the right of survivorship. If they are tenants in common, the husband will still probably obtain the wife's share, perhaps under a will made by the wife in his favour at a time when the marriage was running smoothly, or otherwise under the statutory provisions governing intestacy (see Part IV, Administration of Estates Act 1925, as amended). This may be perfectly acceptable to some clients; others are so embittered by the breakdown of the marriage that they wish to prevent their spouse from benefiting in any way from their death. However, the husband may be able to make a claim against the wife's estate for family provision by virtue of the Inheritance (Provision for Family and Dependants) Act 1975 (see Chapter 25, Section F). The matter must therefore be discussed with the client and, if she does not wish her property to pass to her husband, the solicitor must consider:

(a) whether there is or may be a beneficial joint tenancy, in which case he should consider serving notice of severance; *and*
(b) whether it is necessary to advise the client to make a will/a new will.

The question of a beneficial joint tenancy is dealt with below; the question of making a will is dealt with in Chapter 25.

Severance of the joint tenancy to avoid right of survivorship

22.20 The basic principles as to joint tenancies are as follows:

(a) Where property is conveyed into the names of more than one person, there is always a joint tenancy of the legal estate. The equitable interests in the property may be held on a joint tenancy or as tenants in common.

(b) If a joint tenancy exists in equity as well as in law, on the death of one joint tenant the other joint tenant will automatically become entitled to his beneficial interest in the property by virtue of the right of survivorship.

(c) If the equitable interests are held as tenants in common, there is no right of survivorship and the equitable interest of the deceased tenant in common will pass in accordance with his will or according to the intestacy provisions if he has not made one.

22.21 One of the difficulties facing the solicitor in a matrimonial case is how to determine whether there is a joint tenancy in equity. If:

(a) the conveyance or transfer to the parties expressly provides that they are to hold the equitable interest as tenants in common; *or*

(b) a separate declaration of trust has been made to this effect; *or*

(c) a note or memorandum of severance is endorsed on or annexed to the conveyance to the parties or an appropriate restriction entered on the proprietorship register,

this is conclusive evidence that there is an equitable tenancy in common and therefore no right of survivorship—once a tenancy in common, always a tenancy in common. In such circumstances, there is no need to serve a notice of severance but the solicitor should not forget to consider whether it is necessary to make a will/new will for the client. There is no point in going to the trouble of checking up on the right of survivorship only to overlook the fact that the client's spouse will be entitled to the property anyway under her will or by virtue of the intestacy provisions.

22.22 The solicitor will not always be in a position to find out about the equitable interest in the house (eg a building society may hold the title deeds and may not be prepared to release them without the consent of the other party). If he is unable to find out what the position is or finds that there was originally an equitable joint tenancy which has apparently not been severed, the only safe course is to consider serving a notice of severance: see s 36(2), Law of Property Act 1925. When considering whether to sever, however, it must be borne in mind that not only will severance of the joint tenancy prevent the client's share in the property passing to her spouse on her death, it will also prevent her becoming automatically entitled by survivorship to his share in the property on his death. This disadvantage must be weighed against the advantages of severance. For an interesting case of a spouse trying to hedge her bets, see *Kinch v Bullard* [1999] 1 FLR 66.

22.23 If the solicitor decides, in consultation with the client, that it would be appropriate to serve notice of severance, care should be taken over the wording of the notice. Service of an unconditional notice of severance could be taken as an admission by the client that there *is* an equitable joint tenancy and that the parties are entitled to the equitable estate in equal shares. An admission of this nature could be prejudicial (eg in s 17, Married Women's Property Act 1882 proceedings or when the operation of the Legal Services Commission's statutory charge came to be considered). Therefore, if there is any doubt at all as to whether there is an equitable joint tenancy, the notice of severance should be drafted in such a way that it is clear that no admission is made that there is a joint tenancy, but that if there is one the intention is to sever it. Again it is important that the solicitor should not stop at service of notice of severance—he must then consider whether there is any need to make a will/new will.

Note that while the issue of an application under s 17, Married Women's Property Act 1882 **22.24** will automatically sever an equitable joint tenancy (*Re Draper's Conveyance* [1969] 1 Ch 486), issue and service of a divorce petition containing a prayer for property adjustment will not: *Harris* v *Goddard* [1983] 1 WLR 1203, [1983] 3 All ER 242.

C HOUSE IN SOLE NAME OF ONE SPOUSE

The powers of the spouse who is the legal owner to sell, mortgage, etc

Theoretically the spouse or civil partner who is the legal owner (whom we are assuming to **22.25** be the husband) has the power to deal as he pleases with the property. However, although the husband may feel that he is sitting pretty because he is the sole legal owner, that is not, of course, the end of the story. The wife may have rights in relation to the property; in particular:

(a) she will have a right of occupation (known as 'home rights') by virtue of the Family Law Act 1996 ('FLA 1996'); *and*
(b) she may have a beneficial interest in the property, normally arising because she has made a contribution to the purchase price.

If the appropriate steps are taken on the wife's behalf, these rights can afford her a substantial measure of protection against her husband selling or mortgaging the property. However, banks which are lending on the security of a mortgage over the matrimonial home will inevitably ask the wife to consent to the charge being granted. If the wife gives consent then she will only be able to deny the bank's priority by arguing that her consent was vitiated by virtue of undue influence or fraud in accordance with the principles set out in paras 22.03 to 22.18 above.

Home rights (s 30, Family Law Act 1996)

When the rights arise

By virtue of s 30(1), where one spouse or civil partner is entitled to occupy a dwelling-house **22.26** by virtue of a beneficial estate or interest or contract or by virtue of any enactment giving him or her the right to remain in occupation, and the other spouse/civil partner is not so entitled, the spouse/civil partner not so entitled has 'home rights' in relation to the house.

These rights arise if the dwelling-house is, or has been, or was intended to be the family home **22.27** (s 30(7)). A spouse/civil partner has no home rights in respect of, for example, a holiday cottage owned by the other spouse/civil partner. The definition of 'dwelling-house' contained in s 63 also includes any caravan, houseboat, or structure which is occupied as a dwelling.

22.28   Section 30(9)(a) and (b) provides that, for the purpose only of determining whether he or she has home rights under s 30, a spouse/civil partner who has an equitable interest in a dwelling-house or in the proceeds of sale thereof, not being a spouse in whom is vested (solely or as a joint tenant) a legal estate or legal term of years absolute in the house, is to be treated as not being entitled to occupy the house by virtue of that equitable interest.

Example A dwelling-house is purchased partly from the savings of a husband, partly from his wife's savings, and partly on mortgage. It is conveyed into the sole name of the husband. Both spouses move in and live in the property as their matrimonial home. The husband is entitled to occupy the house because he owns it. The wife has almost certainly got an equitable interest in the property by virtue of her initial contribution to the purchase price. Nevertheless, because she has no legal estate, s 30(9) means that she is treated as if she is not entitled to occupy the house by virtue of her equitable interest. The situation therefore falls within s 30(1) and she is entitled to home rights.

Meaning of 'home rights'

22.29   Where the spouse/civil partner with home rights is in occupation of the house already, her rights of occupation amount to a right not to be evicted or excluded from the house or any part of it by the other spouse/civil partner except with leave of the court given by an order under s 33: s 30(2)(a).

22.30   If she is not in occupation, her home rights amount to a right with the leave of the court to enter into and occupy the house: s 30(2)(b).

Termination of home rights

22.31   Normally home rights are brought to an end by:

(a)   the death of the other spouse/civil partner; *or*

(b)   the termination (other than on death) of the marriage, except to the extent that an order under s 33(5) otherwise provides (see Chapter 36 on occupation orders).

However, where there is a matrimonial dispute or the parties are estranged, the court has power to direct that the home rights should continue despite either of these events occurring: s 33 or 35. The order to this effect will be made under s 33.

22.32   In fact, the court has a very wide power under s 33 to deal with the question of occupation of the matrimonial home on the application of either spouse/civil partner during the marriage/civil partnership (eg the court can not only order the continuation of home rights post-decree, it can also terminate or suspend the right of either spouse/civil partner to occupy the house during the marriage/civil partnership). Further, under s 35 the court may make an occupation order in favour of a former spouse with no existing right to occupy.

How do home rights protect a wife/civil partner against sale or mortgage?

22.33   It is all very well for a wife/civil partner to have the benefit of home rights under the FLA 1996 but how do these rights protect her if her husband attempts to sell or mortgage the house over her head? In reality the protection is limited unless her rights are registered as a charge against the property. It is therefore the solicitor's duty to take the necessary steps to register his client's home rights as soon as he is consulted in relation to her matrimonial or civil partnership problems.

The rules are as follows: **22.34**

(a) The wife/civil partner's home rights are a charge on the other party's estate or interest in the property concerned: s 31, FLA 1996.
(b) They should be protected as follows:
   (i) in case of unregistered land, by the registration of a Class F land charge against the name of the husband in the register of land charges: s 2, Land Charges Act 1972;
   (ii) in the case of registered land, by the entry of a notice in the Charges Register as an agreed notice on Form HRI under Part 4, Land Registration Act 2002 ('LRA 2002'). It is no longer possible to register a caution to protect home rights: s 31(11), FLA 1996.

If a wife is entitled to a charge in respect of two or more dwelling-houses, only one can be **22.35**
registered at any one time: sch 4, para 2. Note that notice of the charge is automatically provided to the registered proprietor and no request for withholding notice to the owner will be
considered. Receipt of such notice may provoke a violent reaction and clients should be fully
advised of the protection available to them under the FLA 1996. The Land Registry will hold
any application made for a period of one week to give the applicant wife an opportunity to
consider the likely effect of her application.

Where the legal title to the property is vested in the sole name of the husband, it is likely **22.36**
that the wife's solicitor will be denied access to the title deeds to check the position. In order
to determine whether the land is registered or unregistered a search of the Index Map at
the District Land Registry can be carried out using form SIM. The result of the search
will indicate whether the land in question is registered and give the title number for identification purposes if registered. Land Registry Direct (http://www.landregistry.gov.uk) is a
web-based service providing a facility to obtain official copy entries of the title and make
searches online.

Generally the registration of home rights provides effective protection. The prospective pur- **22.37**
chaser or mortgagee will carry out a search prior to completion and will uncover the wife's or
civil partner's rights at that stage if he has not learned of them before. He will immediately go
back to the vendor to find out how he proposes to deal with the problem. In fact a contract for
the sale of a house affected by a registered charge must include a term requiring cancellation
of the registration before completion: sch 4, para 3(1). If the wife will not agree to her charge
or notice being cancelled, the vendor will be in breach of contract and the purchaser will
withdraw from the deal, leaving the wife or civil partner to enjoy her home rights in peace.

The wife with a beneficial interest

It is not uncommon for a wife or civil partner to have a beneficial interest in the home even **22.38**
though her name is not on the property register or the title deeds. The usual reason for such
a beneficial interest is that the spouse concerned has contributed to the purchase price of the
house directly (eg by providing part of the deposit or making mortgage repayments). A wife
with a beneficial interest in the home can register her home rights in the normal way and
should be able to protect both her financial interest and her occupation of the home by thus
preventing a sale/mortgage of the property except on her terms. But what if she omits to register
her home rights? Has she any independent rights arising from her beneficial interest?

Overreaching provisions

22.39   Where property is held by the husband on trust for both himself and his wife (or for his wife alone), a trust of land will automatically be imposed.

22.40   Where property subject to a trust of land is sold, the purchaser, if he knows of the trust of land, will insist that the purchase money is paid to two trustees because in this way he can ensure that the conveyance overreaches all the equitable interests under the trust of land, leaving him with the property free of obligation. Where the wife's interest is recognized on the deeds or in a separate declaration of trust, the overreaching provisions should therefore ensure that she will get the money that represents her beneficial interest (because, unless her husband has the second trustee in his pocket, her share will be paid to her by the trustees), even if she has omitted to register her home rights and thus cannot prevent the sale itself or insist on living in the property after it is sold. The overreaching provisions apply whether the property is registered or unregistered (see *City of London Building Society* v *Flegg* [1988] AC 54, [1987] 3 All ER 435).

22.41   Where a wife has a beneficial interest under an implied, resulting, or constructive trust (eg where she has made substantial payments towards the acquisition of the home), a mortgagee or prospective purchaser may be unaware of this, as her rights are unlikely to appear on the register or on the title deeds. Her position is therefore vulnerable, as the mortgage money, or proceeds of sale, may be paid to the husband, who might then disappear without accounting to the wife for her share. In two situations, the wife's legal position is particularly weak:

(a)   Where the mortgagee is seeking to enforce a mortgage entered into at the date of acquisition of the property. The wife's beneficial interest will be deemed, as a matter of law, to be subject to, and bound by, the mortgage: *Abbey National Building Society* v *Cann* [1990] 1 All ER 1085.

(b)   Where the mortgagee is seeking to enforce a mortgage entered into subsequent to the date of acquisition of the property, and the wife either knew, or should have known, of the mortgage at the time it was entered into. In such circumstances, the wife is expected to inform the mortgagee of her rights, and in the event of her failure to do so, she will be estopped from later asserting a claim against the mortgagee: *Bristol & West Building Society* v *Henning* [1985] 1 WLR 778.

22.42   Subject to this, a wife whose beneficial interest is not overreached may still be protected against a sale or mortgage quite independently of the question of registration of her matrimonial home rights. The protection she may have in these circumstances will differ according to whether the land is registered or unregistered.

Beneficial interest in registered land as an overriding interest

22.43   A sale or mortgage of registered land takes effect subject to any *overriding interest* existing at the date of completion of the transaction in question, whether or not the purchaser or mortgagee has notice of the overriding interest. If a wife is in actual occupation of the property (ie, physically present there), whether or not her husband is also living there, her beneficial interest can constitute an overriding interest under s 70(1)(g), Land Registration Act 1925. This was established by the House of Lords in *Williams & Glyn's Bank Ltd* v *Boland* [1981] AC 487, [1980] 2 All ER 408. There will be no overriding interest if enquiry is made of the wife and her rights are not disclosed.

In the context of a sale or mortgage by a party whose spouse has an overriding interest under **22.44** s 70(1)(g), as the *Boland* case illustrates, this means that the purchaser or mortgagee will be bound by the wife's equitable interest in the property which is not only a financial burden on the property but also gives her a right to possession.

Example (The facts of *Williams and Glyn's Bank Ltd v Boland*.) The husband was the registered proprietor of the matrimonial home. Both he and the wife had contributed to the purchase price of the property and they were therefore equitable tenants in common. Both spouses lived in the matrimonial home. Without the wife's knowledge, the husband mortgaged the house to the bank under a legal mortgage. The bank did not enquire of the husband or the wife before taking the mortgage whether the wife had any interest in the property. The husband defaulted on the mortgage and the bank took proceedings for a possession order which initially they obtained. The wife appealed to the Court of Appeal and the possession order was discharged on the basis that the wife, being in actual occupation of the property, had an overriding interest within s 70(1)(g). The Court of Appeal held that the bank had taken the mortgage subject to the overriding interest and the wife was entitled to remain in possession against them. The bank's appeal to the House of Lords was dismissed.

Note that, before agreeing to lend in respect of a property, banks and building societies now **22.45** tend to ask all those who are occupying or are going to occupy the property to sign a document under seal stating that any rights they have or may acquire in relation to the property are postponed to those of the bank or building society. If the wife has entered into such an agreement it may adversely affect her rights as against the bank or building society.

Boland now has to be considered in the light of the LRA 2002 which created a number of **22.46** important qualifications to the principle. A person can now only protect an unregistered interest to the particular piece of land of which she is in actual occupation (see sch 3, LRA 2002). Any other connected parcels of land are not overreached. Another new and important limitation is that the unregistered interest will not override where the occupation was not obvious to the purchaser on a reasonably careful inspection *and* where the purchaser had actual knowledge of the unregistered interest at the time of the disposition. The fact that the purchaser could have discovered the interest on reasonable enquiry is not enough—he must actually know about it for the interest to override: sch 3, para 2(c).

Beneficial interest in unregistered land and notice

The wife with a beneficial interest in unregistered land has no prospect of establishing an **22.47** overriding interest since the concept is peculiar to registered land. Her rights depend instead upon the doctrine of notice. Unless the purchaser or mortgagee has actual or constructive notice of the wife's equitable interest at the time of the disposition, he will not be bound by it: *Caunce v Caunce* [1969] 1 WLR 286, [1969] 1 All ER 722. In *Caunce v Caunce* the court took the view that the mere fact that the wife is resident in the property with the husband does not fix the purchaser/mortgagee with notice. However, this view is now seriously outmoded. Whether a purchaser/mortgagee has actual or constructive notice of the wife's interest is a question of fact in each case: *Kingsnorth Finance Co Ltd v Tizard* [1986] 1 WLR 783, [1986] 2 All ER 54. Where the purchaser/mortgagee is held to have notice, the wife may be able to enforce her rights in the property against him.

Registration of pending land action

22.48   Where proceedings are begun in relation to the matrimonial/civil partnership home (eg under s 17, Married Women's Property Act 1882 or under s 24, MCA 1973), a pending land action can be registered in the case of unregistered land. This protects the wife's interest in the property in much the same way as the registration of a Class F land charge save that, whereas the wife would normally have to agree to a Class F land charge being cancelled once decree absolute comes through, the registration of a pending land action will protect her until the dispute in relation to the property is settled.

22.49   Note also that a pending land action can be registered in relation to a property that was never or has never been intended to be the matrimonial home—a situation in which no Class F land charge can be registered. In the case of registered land, the appropriate way to prevent dealings with the land where an action is pending would appear to be by lodging a caution in the Proprietorship Register.

D   BANKRUPTCY AND THE FAMILY HOME

22.50   The security of the matrimonial home will be threatened in the event of either spouse (we shall assume, here, the husband) being declared bankrupt. The question will then arise whether the wife (and children) can continue to live in the home, or whether the property should be sold to pay off the landlord's creditors.

22.51   The husband's property will vest in his trustee in bankruptcy. However, his wife's home rights (under the FLA 1996) will bind the trustee and the creditors if they are duly registered, as will any rights the wife has by reason of her having a legal or beneficial interest in the home. Nevertheless, the trustee will be able to apply for an order for sale of the property (under s 14, Trusts of Land and Appointment of Trustees Act 1996) in the bankruptcy proceedings.

22.52   Where the order for sale is sought by the trustee in bankruptcy (as is usually the case), certain factors have to be considered by the court. These are listed in s 25 and sch 3, para 23, Trusts of Land and Appointment of Trustees Act 1996 which inserted a s 335A into the Insolvency Act 1986. On such an application the court will make such order as it thinks just and reasonable having regard to:

    (a) the interests of the bankrupt's creditors;
    (b) where the application is made in respect of a dwelling-house which has been the home of the bankrupt or the bankrupt's spouse or former spouse—
       (i)   the conduct of the spouse or former spouse so far as contributing to the bankruptcy,
       (ii) the needs and financial resources of the spouse or former spouse, and
       (iii) the needs of any children;
    (c) all the circumstances of the case other than the needs of the bankrupt. (s 335A(2))

22.53   Section 335A(3) states that if an application is made for an order of sale more than one year after the bankrupt's estate vested in the trustee, the court shall assume that, unless the circumstances are exceptional, the interests of the bankrupt's creditors outweigh all other considerations.

In applications for sale of the matrimonial home by a trustee in bankruptcy or by a bank as chargee, the interests of the creditor will generally prevail, unless there are exceptional circumstances.

A practical example of how narrow this exception is can be seen in the case of *Dean v Stout* **22.54** *(The Trustee in Bankruptcy of Dean)* [2005] EWHC 3315 where the former matrimonial home had been purchased in the names of the husband and his brother, both of whom had been made bankrupt. The wife continued to live in the property with the children for a further seven years. At the time that the husband's trustee in bankruptcy applied for an order for sale a large proportion of the debts had been discharged by the wife. She had also paid off the husband's other creditors and the mortgage. She argued that by managing to do this, combined with the modest value of the property and the presence of the children that the trial judge had been wrong to find that there were no exceptional circumstances. The High Court judge disagreed. Typically, exceptional circumstances related to the personal circumstances of one of the joint owners, such as a medical condition, should be outside the usual 'melancholy consequence of debt and improvidence'.

23

KEEPING UP WITH THE MORTGAGE OR RENT

A   GENERAL

23.01 The importance of keeping up with the mortgage repayments or rent on the matrimonial home in spite of the breakdown of the marriage need hardly be stressed. If arrears are allowed to accumulate, there is a danger that the mortgagee or landlord will take action which could ultimately lead to the parties losing their home.

Example Husband and wife are joint owners of the matrimonial home. There is a mortgage in favour of a building society. Repayments are £100 per month and have always been made by the husband as the wife is not working. The marriage fails and the husband leaves to live with another woman. He ceases to pay the mortgage instalments. The wife cannot pay the instalments herself as she has no income. No payments are made for six months. The building society becomes concerned and presses for payment. It threatens to bring proceedings for possession in order to sell the property if payments are not resumed together with some payment each month off the arrears.

B   STEPS THAT CAN BE TAKEN

Contacting the mortgagee/landlord

23.02 Where the client is in difficulties with mortgage instalments or rent, it is often a good idea to contact the mortgagee/landlord straight away to explain the position and to outline what the client proposes to do to alleviate it (eg she may be intending to make application for maintenance from her husband or to seek state benefits). Provided that it appears that the problem is capable of solution within a reasonable period of time, most building societies and banks are prepared to be patient, as are some landlords.

Seeking financial help

State benefits

It is possible for rent or the interest repayments on a mortgage to be met by state benefits (see **23.03** Chapter 24). The solicitor should consider whether his client is likely to be entitled to any benefit and, if so, advise her how to go about making a claim. The claim should be made as soon as possible—the situation will be harder to deal with if arrears have been allowed to build up.

Where mortgage interest is to be covered by state benefits, arrangements will have to be made **23.04** in relation to the capital repayments. The mortgagee may be prepared to agree to these being suspended temporarily; if not, the client will have to scrimp and save on other outgoings in order to be able to discharge the payments.

Maintenance

An application for periodic payments from the client's spouse should be considered. If the client **23.05** is to continue to discharge the mortgage payments herself, she can ask the court to take this into account in fixing the amount of her maintenance. Applications for maintenance can be made in the family proceedings court under the Domestic Proceedings and Magistrates' Courts Act 1978 and in the county court under the Matrimonial Causes Act 1973 ancillary to proceedings for divorce, nullity, or judicial separation or under s 27 (see Chapters 29 ff and 26).

Submitting to a possession action

The client may, in fact, be prepared to leave her home if she can be rehoused by the local **23.06** authority. If she moves out voluntarily, she will have to take her normal place in the queue. If, on the other hand, she is turned out of the house as a result of a possession order made by the court, the council is more likely to rehouse her straight away. For this reason it may be necessary for the client to allow the mortgagee/landlord to take proceedings for possession and to submit to the making of a possession order.

C SPECIAL PROVISIONS OF THE FAMILY LAW ACT 1996

Payment of other spouse/civil partner outgoings

Where a spouse/civil partner has home rights in relation to a dwelling-house or any part of **23.07** it, any payment that that spouse makes towards the other spouse's liability for the rent, rates, or mortgage payments or other outgoings affecting the house is as good as if the other spouse had made the payment himself: s 30(3).

Example Mr Simpkins is the tenant of a flat where he lives with his wife. The marriage breaks down and Mr Simpkins walks out and stops paying the rent. His wife pays the rent instead.

Her payment is as good as payment from Mr Simpkins would have been. The landlord cannot refuse Mrs Simpkins's payments and use the tenant's non-payment of rent as the ground for possession proceedings.

It is only necessary to rely on s 30(3) where the spouse is not herself a tenant or an owner with a right to tender payment.

Where a mortgagee takes action to enforce his security

Notice of enforcement action

23.08   Where a spouse has registered a Class F land charge or notice or caution, a mortgagee bringing an action for enforcement of his security must serve notice of action on that spouse if she is not a party to the action: s 56(2).

Joinder of spouse as a party

23.09   A spouse who is enabled by s 30(3) to meet the mortgagor's liabilities under the mortgage (see para 23.07 above) can apply to the court to be made a party to an action brought by the mortgagee to enforce his security and will be entitled to be a party if:

(a)   she has applied to the court before the action is finally disposed of;

(b)   the court sees no special reason against her being joined and is satisfied that she may be expected to make such payments or do such other things in or towards satisfaction of the mortgagor's liabilities or obligations as might affect the outcome of the proceedings: s 55(3).

Example Mr Michaels is the sole owner of the matrimonial home which is subject to a mortgage in favour of a building society. He leaves his wife and goes abroad where he cannot be traced. He ceases to make any mortgage repayments. Although s 30(3) enables his wife to make the payments, Mrs Michaels cannot afford to do so immediately after the separation as she is not working. She refuses to seek state benefits on principle. The building society is informed of the position and allows the arrears to mount for six months. Thereafter it presses for payment and ultimately takes proceedings for possession to enable it to exercise its power to sell the property to recoup the mortgage debt. Mrs Michaels has registered a caution against dealing and therefore is entitled to receive notice of the proceedings by virtue of s 56(2). She may apply to the court to be joined as a party to the action. The court orders that she should be a party as she has just obtained a sufficiently well-paid job to enable her to meet the normal mortgage repayments and pay off a small amount from the arrears each month, in which circumstances the court would be unlikely to grant immediate possession.

Security of tenure with rented property

23.10   Under the Rent Act 1977 and the Housing Acts 1985 and 1988, a tenant's security of tenure is dependent on his remaining in possession or occupation of the property. Section 30(4), Family Law Act 1996 ('FLA 1996') ensures that security of tenure will not be prejudiced when the tenant moves out, provided his spouse continues to live in the property. Her possession or occupation will be treated as his, thus protecting not only his rights in relation to the home but also hers (which are dependent on his). This would include a dwelling-house which has not yet been, but is intended to be, a home (*Gull* v *Gull* [2007] EWCA Civ 900).

However, if the spouse who is the tenant actually surrenders the tenancy when he leaves, the **23.11** remaining spouse will lose her home rights unless she has already registered them under s 31, FLA 1996. If there has been no such registration of rights, the remaining spouse would appear to have no defence to possession proceedings instituted by the landlord: *Sanctuary Housing Association* v *Campbell* [1999] 2 FLR 383.

Where the spouses are joint tenants of the matrimonial home and one of them terminates the **23.12** joint tenancy against the will of the other, the tenancy is nevertheless brought to an end: *Bater* v *Greenwich LBC* [1999] 2 FLR 993; *Newlon Housing Trust* v *Alsulaimen* [1998] 2 FLR 690.

In any situation where the unilateral act of one joint tenant is capable in law of destroying the **23.13** interests of both, the vulnerable tenant who would be prejudiced by such notice should seek from the other an undertaking not to serve notice prior to the court's determination of the issue. The undertaking should be served on the landlord as well as on the departing tenant. Where the tenant concerned is unwilling or unable to give an undertaking, an application could be made for an injunction, which would also be served on the landlord as well as on the departing tenant.

24

WELFARE BENEFITS

A INTRODUCTION

This chapter deals with the following welfare benefits: **24.01**

(a) income support and jobseeker's allowance;

(b) working tax credit;

(c) child tax credit;

(d) housing benefit;

(e) child benefit.

The law on benefits is to be found in various statutes and regulations and is immensely detailed. It is not possible to deal with each benefit comprehensively in a book of this type. The aim of this chapter is to give the practitioner a broad outline of the provisions, first so that he can advise his client whether it is worth his while making further enquiries of the Department for Work and Pensions (DWP) or local authority with a view to making a claim and, secondly, so that he will be aware of how maintenance and other payments to the client from his or her spouse or former spouse will affect his or her entitlement to benefit.

24.02 Should a specific problem arise over the client's benefit, the solicitor can find out more about the rules of entitlement from specialist books on welfare benefits (eg the Child Poverty Action Group handbooks). The rates of benefit are raised regularly and care must be taken to find out whether the figures given in this chapter are still applicable at the time of reference. Where examples are given, the figures used are those in force from 5 April 2011.

24.03 The working tax credit and child tax credit are in fact administered by HM Revenue and Customs. However, details are included in this chapter since, for many, the credits will be perceived as a form of welfare benefit.

24.04 This chapter largely considers the position when a marriage has broken down. However, the same principles apply on the breakdown of a civil partnership: s 254 and sch 24, Civil Partnership Act 2004.

PART 1   INCOME SUPPORT AND JOBSEEKER'S ALLOWANCE

B   INTRODUCTION

24.05 The law relating to income support is to be found in the Social Security Contributions and Benefits Act 1992, which consolidated much of the previous legislation in the field and (among other things) the Income Support (General) Regulations 1987 (SI 1987/1967), as amended. It should be noted that in social security law the regulations are extremely important as they set out the fine detail of each benefit.

24.06 Income support is a cash benefit to help people who do not have enough money to live on. People receiving income support will automatically be entitled to other valuable benefits, for example exemption from certain NHS charges, free school meals, full housing and council tax benefits. These are known as 'passport' benefits.

24.07 The Jobseekers Act 1995 introduced, with effect from 7 October 1996, a new benefit known as the jobseeker's allowance. It replaced unemployment benefit and also income support for claimants who are required to be available for work. Income support continues to be paid to claimants who are not required to be available for work (eg a lone parent of a child under 16).

24.08 In order to be eligible for a jobseeker's allowance claimants are required to enter an agreement under which they are obliged to take whatever steps are considered appropriate towards finding suitable work or retraining.

24.09 Essentially, the allowance is means-tested and payable at the same rate as personal allowances for income support, except that a higher rate of allowance will be available for a maximum period of six months to claimants who have the necessary contribution level (Class 1) and sign the agreement.

For the purpose of this chapter reference will be made to income support on the basis that the **24.10** client is not required to be available for work.

C INCOME SUPPORT

Who can claim?

Claimants must: **24.11**

(a) Be at least 16.

(b) Be habitually resident in the United Kingdom and present in Great Britain.

(c) Not be engaged in remunerative work for more than 16 hours per week and not have a partner who is engaged in remunerative work for more than 24 hours per week. A partner is someone to whom the claimant is married, or with whom he or she lives as if married to them.

(d) Not be receiving 'relevant education'. A child or young person is treated as receiving 'relevant education' if he is receiving full-time non-advanced education or, although not receiving such education, is treated as a child for the purposes of child benefit. In certain circumstances a young person who is in relevant education may nevertheless be entitled to income support, for example where he is responsible for a child under the age of 16. In such cases he must also satisfy the other conditions of entitlement to income support.

(e) Have no income or an income which does not exceed the 'applicable amount' (an amount fixed by Parliament based upon basic living expenses).

(f) Not have capital exceeding £16,000. Capital of less than £6,000 will be completely ignored.

Entitlement to income support

In order to be entitled to income support the claimant must satisfy a means test to ensure that **24.12** his income is not above the level prescribed by law as the amount necessary for a person to live on. The income of the whole family will be taken into account in assessing entitlement. If the claimant is working for 16 hours or more each week, or has a partner who is working for 24 hours or more each week, then he or she will not normally be entitled to income support. For the purposes of this assessment the 'family' includes a married couple (who are married to each other and are members of the same household) or an unmarried couple (a man and woman who are not married to each other but are living together as husband and wife or a same-sex couple).

Calculating the claimant's income

For the purposes of establishing entitlement to income support the claimant's weekly income **24.13** is calculated as follows:

(a) Take the claimant's net (not gross) weekly income—'income' includes periodical payments made to the claimant or his or her children (whether made voluntarily, under a court order, or Child Maintenance and Enforcement Commission calculation), lump-sum orders (whether or not payable by instalments), statutory sick pay, statutory maternity payments, and child benefit.

(b) Add to it any 'tariff income' the claimant may receive from capital. This arises if the claimant's capital exceeds £6,000; if so, then each complete £250 in excess of £6,000 (but not exceeding £16,000) is treated as a weekly income of £1.

(c) Certain sums will be disregarded in the calculation of earnings. The rules in relation to this are complex and the practitioner should refer to the appropriate regulations for full details. An example is the first £20 per week of any child maintenance payment.

Disregarded capital

24.14 As stated above, savings and capital which the claimant and his partner have or are deemed to have exceeding £16,000 will exclude him from income support. Capital includes savings, premium bonds, shares, items of value, coin collections, etc. Personal possessions such as wedding rings will be disregarded unless they have been clearly bought into order to circumvent the calculation. In those circumstances they will be valued at the current market value or surrender value.

24.15 Certain types of capital can be disregarded. The most important are the claimant's dwelling home, regardless of its value or the sale proceeds of any previous home of the claimant which he intends to use to buy a new home within 26 weeks (or such longer period as may be needed).

Amount of income support

24.16 If the claimant is entitled to income support, then the following are the amounts to which he is entitled:

(a) if the claimant has no income, the amount of income support is the 'applicable amount';

(b) if the claimant has income, the amount of income support is the difference between the claimant's income and the 'applicable amount'.

24.17 Ordinary 'applicable amounts' fall into four categories:

(a) a 'personal allowance' for the claimant and his partner (if there is a partner), and an allowance for any child or young person that the claimant and his partner look after;

(b) a 'family premium' if the claimant is a member of a family of which at least one member is a child or young person;

(c) special 'premium payments' for groups of people with special expenses (eg associated with disability);

(d) 'housing costs payments' to cover certain costs of accommodation not met by housing benefit.

24.18 The Social Security (Income Support and Claims and Payments) Amendment Regulations 1995 (SI 1995/1613) came into force on 2 October 1995. They amend the regulations in respect of help with housing costs in circumstances where the claimant has a mortgage. The position is as follows:

(a) If the loan was taken out *before* 2 October 1995, the claimant will receive no assistance with the payment of the mortgage for the first eight weeks of the claim, 50 per cent of the housing costs will be paid for the next 18 weeks, and full housing costs after 26 weeks in receipt of income support.

(b) If the loan was taken out *after* 1 October 1995, the claimant will receive no assistance for 39 weeks of the claim but full housing costs will be paid after 39 weeks in receipt of income support.

A 13-week waiting period applies if the claim for income support was made after 4 January **24.19** 2009 and the claimant is entitled to some benefit or the claimant or partner were getting pension credit. If this waiting period applies then the upper limit for eligible loans is £200,000. A claimant can only receive assistance for a maximum of two years.

It is important to emphasize that the 'assistance with housing costs' amounts to assistance **24.20** with the payment of mortgage interest *only* and, since 10 April 1995, in respect of the first £100,000 of the loan (unless the 13-week waiting period applies).

Because no assistance is offered with the payment of the capital element of the mortgage or **24.21** with premiums for any linked endowment policy, it is imperative that clients are advised to inform the mortgage lender of the position as soon as a claim for income support is made. It may be possible to negotiate interest-only payments for a limited period or the conversion of an endowment mortgage into an ordinary repayment one using the surrender value (if any) of the policy to reduce the capital debt.

Current rates of benefit

The rates of benefit change regularly, and the practitioner should ascertain the appropriate **24.22** rates at the time of reference.

The rates as at 5 April 2011 are as follows: **24.23**

(a) Personal allowances
    (i) Single
        aged 18–24: £51.85
        aged 25 or over: £65.45
    (ii) Lone parent
        under age 25: £65.50
        aged 25 or over: £79.10
    (iii) Couple
        married or cohabiting (both aged 18 or over): £102.75
    (iv) Dependent children until day before 20th birthday: £57.57
(b) Premiums
    (i) Family: £17.40
    (ii) Lone parent: £13.65
    (iii) Disability (depending on circumstances): £28.00–53.65

How to claim income support

24.24 The income support scheme is administered by Job Centre Plus, an agency of the DWP. Enquiries about entitlement should be made to the claimant's local Job Centre. The normal method of applying for benefits is to fill in the appropriate form which should be sent or delivered to the local office. An interview will usually be arranged to determine the claimant's circumstances unless the claimant has claimed income support before. The 'decision maker' will then determine whether the claimant is eligible for benefit and, if so, how much.

24.25 If the claimant is not required to be available for work, benefit is generally paid automatically into a claimant's bank account. There are provisions for certain of the claimant's expenses to be paid direct if he gets into difficulties (eg gas and electricity bills).

24.26 Where income support includes an amount for mortgage interest, this part of the benefit is normally sent direct to the lender.

Appeal and review

24.27 If the claimant feels he has been wrongly refused benefit or that benefit has been fixed at too low a level, he should write to the DWP asking for a revision on the basis that the decision maker did not know about or made a mistake about some material fact, or that there has been a change in the circumstances on which the decision was based. If the outcome of the request for a revision is still not satisfactory, consideration can be given to appealing to an appeal tribunal. There is a right of appeal from any decision of the decision maker be it the original decision whether to grant benefit or a revision decision (including a decision by the decision maker to refuse to carry out a revision at all). Written notice of appeal must be given within one month of the decision against which appeal is made. There will be a tribunal hearing and the decision will be sent to the claimant.

24.28 A further appeal by the claimant or the adjudication officer on a point of law may be possible to the Social Security Commissioners provided permission is granted. The chairman of the tribunal should be asked for permission to appeal and, if he refuses it, an application for permission can be made to a Commissioner.

24.29 If there is a point of law involved, the claimant or the Secretary of State may then be able to appeal from the Commissioner to the Court of Appeal. Permission to do this is required. The Commissioner can grant permission and, if he refuses, application for permission can be made to the Court of Appeal.

D   THE SOCIAL FUND

24.30 The social fund was set up by s 32, Social Security Act 1986. The object of payments from the social fund is to meet special needs which are not catered for by other benefits. The question of whether or not a payment will be made is decided by a social fund officer, who has a wide discretion. The most usual form of payment will be a loan. There are powers to make 'budgeting loans' which are interest-free and help to spread the cost of large one-off expenses over a longer period, 'crisis loans' which are interest-free and are for living expenses or items needed urgently, and 'community care grants'. Typically eligibility depends upon a recipient receiving income support, pension credit, or income-based jobseeker's allowance for 26 weeks. The levels of the loans vary from £100 to £1,000 depending on the circumstances. Other forms of payment available include a maternity payment to help to buy necessities for a baby and funeral grants. Applications for payments from the social fund should be made to the claimant's local DWP office.

PART 2 TAX CREDITS

E INTRODUCTION

Major changes in this area came into force in April 2003 with the introduction of the child tax credit and the working tax credit, under the Tax Credits Act 2002, replacing working families tax credit.   **24.31**

F THE CHILD TAX CREDIT

The credit

The child tax credit ('CTC') replaces the child-based elements in income support, jobseeker's allowance, working tax credit, disabled person's tax credit, and the current children's tax credit. CTC is designed to provide financial support for families with children. The claimant for CTC is not required to be working.   **24.32**

CTC is claimed from HM Revenue and Customs. However, child benefit remains unchanged: the procedure for making a claim remains as previously and the benefit continues to be paid as a separate payment.   **24.33**

Who can claim?

To claim CTC, the applicant must live in the United Kingdom and be responsible for at least one child or a 'qualifying young person' who is aged between 16 and 18 and is receiving full-time education (up to A level or NVQ level 3) or has left full-time education but does not have a job or training place and has registered with the careers service. From April 2006, 19-year-olds completing a non-advanced course also qualified.   **24.34**

Responsibility for a child

To be responsible for a child means having the child 'normally living' with the applicant and, if care of the child is shared between parties living in different households (eg as the result of a shared residence order), CTC will be paid to the party having 'the main responsibility' for   **24.35** the child. If that cannot be agreed, the Revenue (which takes responsibility for paying CTC) will determine the position.

Calculating child tax credit

24.36 The amount of CTC payable depends upon the applicant's income for the previous tax year and awards will last for 12 months. The amount may be adjusted during the year to take account of changes in income but rises of up to £2,500 in the current tax year will be ignored. Where the applicant is married or cohabits with another person, their incomes will be aggregated to determine the amount of CTC payable.

24.37 Income is calculated by adding all gross earned and unearned income including benefits in kind and state benefits but excluding child benefit, working tax credit, housing and council tax benefit, and student loans, etc. Maintenance from a former spouse and children's income are ignored, so child support payments are not taken into account.

24.38 Where the applicant is in receipt of income support or income-based jobseeker's allowance, the maximum amount of CTC will be payable. To calculate the amount of CTC to which an applicant is entitled, it is necessary to add together the appropriate 'elements', namely 'the family element', 'the baby element', and 'the child element'.

24.39 Annual CTC rates are £545 for the family element and for the baby element (this is payable if there is a baby in the family below the age of one) and £2,555 for the child element.

24.40 These are the maximum rates of CTC payable. A claimant will be eligible for them if her income is at or below the threshold of £6,420. If her (and her partner's) income is over that threshold then the maximum amount is reduced at the rate of 41 pence for every pound of income above the threshold. If the income is above a second threshold of £40,000 then the family element is tapered off at the rate of 41 per cent. This means that everyone will receive some element of CTC if the total income is less than £48,175.

G   THE WORKING TAX CREDIT

The credit

24.41 The working tax credit ('WTC') is a payment to top up the earnings of working people on low incomes and is available to employees and the self-employed. It lasts for one year and is calculated on the basis of the applicant's income in the previous tax year. The amount payable depends upon eligibility for various elements (eg couple and lone parent element, etc) but the basic element is an annual rate of £1,920.

Who can claim?

24.42 The applicant must be present in Great Britain and be working. In certain circumstances (eg if the applicant is aged 25 or over and works for at least 30 hours per week or the applicant is aged 16 or over, works for at least 16 hours per week, and has a disability which puts the applicant at a disadvantage in obtaining employment), WTC can be claimed by the childless applicant.

WTC is paid in addition to any CTC to which the applicant may be entitled. The claimant's **24.43** annual income is compared with the 'income threshold figure'. This is £6,420 at 5 April 2011. If the claimant's income is below that figure the maximum amount of WTC will be payable. What is paid depends upon the claimant's circumstances. The 'basic' element of £1,920 for 2011–2012 will always be paid, as may a couple or lone parent element of £1,950 and an element if the hours worked each week amount to 30 or more in which case a further £790 is paid.

If the family's income exceeds £6,420 the maximum WTC is reduced by 41 per cent of the **24.44** excess until it disappears.

Childcare costs

As well as being entitled to WTC, an applicant may, depending on his or her income, be able **24.45** to obtain extra help towards the costs of registered or approved childcare—this is known as the 'child care costs element'.

The child care costs element is worth up to 70 pence in tax credit for every £1 per week spent **24.46** on approved childcare. The claimant must be a lone parent or, where there is a joint claim, both members of the couple must be working more than 16 hours per week. Eligible childcare is childcare provided by registered childminders, nurseries, or other approved childcare.

PART 3   HOUSING BENEFIT

The law on housing benefit is to be found in the Social Security Contributions and Benefits **24.47** Act 1992 and the Housing Benefit (General) Regulations 1987, as amended. The scheme is in the form of rent rebates funded and administered by housing authorities. The benefit is non-contributory and is available to those on low income who pay rent in the public or private sector.

H   WHO QUALIFIES?

In order to qualify for housing benefit the claimant must be liable to make payments in **24.48** respect of a dwelling which he occupies as his home. In general only one home is allowed.

The following people will be treated as if they are 'liable to make payments in respect of a **24.49** dwelling':

(a) the person who is liable to make those payments or his partner;

(b) a person who has to make the payments if he is to continue to live in the home, because the third party who is liable to make the payments is not doing so; in this case the claimant must have been the former partner of the defaulting third party, or some other person whom it is reasonable to treat as liable to make the payments.

I   WHAT PAYMENTS WILL BE MADE?

24.50   Housing benefit is payable for rent, and the appropriate maximum housing benefit to which the claimant is entitled is calculated by reference to the amount of the claimant's 'eligible rent'.

'Eligible rent'

24.51   The amount of the claimant's 'eligible rent' means those periodical payments which the claimant is liable to make in respect of the dwelling which he occupies as his home. Such payments include the following: rent; payments in respect of a licence or permission to occupy the dwelling; mesne profits; payments for use and occupation of the dwelling; service charges which are a condition of the right to occupy the dwelling.

24.52   The amount of the claimant's 'eligible rent' is the total rent which the claimant is liable to pay, minus charges for water, sewerage, and certain ineligible service charges.

24.53   If the rent is registered and the rent which the claimant is liable to pay is limited to the registered rent, then the claimant's 'eligible rent' cannot exceed the amount of the registered rent.

Reduction of 'eligible rent' and maximum housing benefit

24.54   The amount of the claimant's 'eligible rent' may be reduced by an 'appropriate' amount if the assessment officer considers that:

(a) the claimant is occupying a dwelling that is too large for the requirements of the claimant and those who also occupy that dwelling; or

(b) the rent payable for the claimant's dwelling is unreasonably high for the area in which the property is situated.

24.55   In this situation the claimant's maximum housing benefit will be calculated with reference to the 'eligible rent' as reduced by the 'appropriate' amount.

J   AMOUNT OF HOUSING BENEFIT

24.56   A payment of housing benefit will be made if:

(a) the claimant has no income; or

(b) the claimant's income does not exceed the 'applicable amount'.

The applicable amount

The applicable amount appropriate for the claimant and his family includes personal allow- **24.57** ances and premiums which are almost the same as those used for calculating income support.

Assessing the claimant's income and capital

Having ascertained the amount of a claimant's 'applicable amount', the next step is to ascer- **24.58** tain his income and capital in order to determine whether his income exceeds his weekly applicable amount.

Where the claimant is a member of a family, the income and capital of any member of that **24.59** family will be treated as the income and capital of that person. The capital of a child or young person who is a member of the claimant's family will not be treated as the capital of the claimant, but special rules will apply where the child or young person has capital in excess of £6,000. The practitioner is referred to the regulations for full details.

The claimant's income is assessed as follows: **24.60**

(a) Calculate the claimant's weekly earnings (the sums that will be counted as part of the claimant's earnings are clearly set out in the regulations and the practitioner is referred to them. They include, for example, WTC and CTC).

(b) Add to it any tariff income from capital—where the claimant's capital exceeds £6,000, it will be treated as equivalent to a weekly tariff income of £1 for each complete £250 in excess of £6,000 but not exceeding £16,000.

(c) Certain sums will be disregarded in assessing the claimant's income. The rules in relation to those sums are complex and the practitioner is referred to the regulations for details. However, sums to be disregarded include, among other things, child maintenance and £25.00 a week of a lone parent earnings. It should be noted that where the claimant is in receipt of income support the whole of his income will be disregarded.

Effect of capital on housing benefit

Where a claimant's capital exceeds £16,000 he will be disqualified from any entitlement **24.61** to housing benefit. Certain sums will be disregarded in assessing what does and does not amount to capital.

Appropriate maximum housing benefit

The appropriate maximum housing benefit consists of 100 per cent of the claimant's eligible **24.62** rent.

In each case there will be a deduction, where appropriate, in respect of a non-dependent **24.63** person who resides with the claimant, ranging from £9.40 a week where the non-dependant is not working to £60.60 where the non-dependant has a gross weekly income of £382.00 or more. The rates of the relevant weekly deductions are updated regularly, and practitioners should ascertain the appropriate rate at the time of reference.

Where the claimant's income exceeds the applicable amount

24.64 The amount of housing benefit to which the claimant is entitled will be reduced in certain circumstances. This will happen when the claimant's income exceeds 'the applicable amount' (ie, the relevant income support level). The reduction is approximately 65 pence for every pound by which the claimant's income exceeds the income support level.

How is the benefit paid?

24.65 Where the claimant is a tenant of the local authority (or its successor social housing landlord), housing benefit will reduce the amount of rent payable so that no money will pass through the tenant's hands. Conversely, where the claimant is a private tenant, housing benefit will usually be paid direct to the landlord.

K   COUNCIL TAX BENEFIT

24.66 Council tax benefit is paid by local authorities although it is a national scheme and the rules are mainly determined by DWP regulations. Details of the scheme are contained in the Council Tax Benefit (General) Regulations 1992 (SI 1992/1814, as amended). The basic conditions for eligibility are that the claimant's income is low enough and their savings and other capital do not exceed £16,000. Council tax benefit operates in a similar way to housing benefit, save that the benefit will be reduced by approximately 20 pence for each pound by which the claimant's income exceeds the relevant income support level. An income support claimant is eligible for a 100 per cent reduction in respect of the council tax; for others, the council tax will be reduced appropriately.

24.67 Detailed guidance on the rules relating to council tax liability, valuations, reductions, discounts, and benefits may be found in CPAG's *Council Tax Handbook*.

PART 4   CHILD BENEFIT

24.68 The law on child benefit is to be found in the Social Security Contributions and Benefits Act 1992 and the various child benefit regulations.

L   CHILD BENEFIT

General

24.69 Child benefit is a standard weekly amount and as at 6 April 2011 is £20.30 for the only, elder, or eldest child and £13.40 for each subsequent child paid to the person (normally but not necessarily a parent) who is responsible for a child.

Definition of a child

Child benefit is payable in respect of: **24.70**

(a) all children under 16;
(b) children of 16 to 20 who are still in full-time non-advanced (ie, not above A level or NVQ level 3) education (amended by the Child Benefit Act 2005).

Child benefit is not paid for children at university, training for professional qualifications, **24.71** apprenticed, etc, or for children in full-time employment.

When a child under 20 leaves school, child benefit will generally still be payable for him until **24.72** the start of the new term after he has left, that is, right through the school holidays, unless he gets a full-time job or a training place.

Person responsible

A person is responsible for a child if either: **24.73**

(a) he has the child living with him; *or*
(b) he contributes to the child's maintenance at a weekly rate of not less than the rate of child benefit.

More than one person may count as responsible for one child but benefit will only be paid to **24.74** one person. There are rules for determining who should receive the benefit if more than one person claims it. If the child is living with both his parents (whether they are married or not), his mother will be the one entitled to claim the benefit. If the child is not living with both parents, the person with whom he is living (whether a parent or not) will have first claim to the benefit. If the household in which the child is living comprises a parent and a non-parent (eg his mother and her boyfriend), the parent will naturally have priority over the non-parent.

Example 1 Cedric is 16 and is still at school doing A levels. He lives with his mother and father, Mr and Mrs Conn. Child benefit will be payable in respect of Cedric. As he is living with both his parents, both parents qualify as responsible for him. His mother is the one who has the prior claim to benefit, although if she wants Mr Conn to receive the benefit, he can apply enclosing her written statement that she does not wish to claim the benefit herself.

Example 2 Dennis is 5. His parents, Mr and Mrs Drabble, have split up. Dennis is living with his mother who is cohabiting with Mr Eves. Mr Drabble pays voluntary maintenance for Dennis of £30 per week. Child benefit is payable in respect of Dennis. Mr Drabble, Mrs Drabble, and Mr Eves can all claim to be responsible for him (Mrs Drabble and Mr Eves because he is living with them and Mr Drabble because he contributes to Dennis's maintenance). Mrs Drabble and Mr Eves have the prior claim to the benefit over Mr Drabble because Dennis is living with them. As between Mrs Drabble and Mr Eves, Mrs Drabble has the prior claim because she is Dennis's parent.

Making a claim

A form on which to claim child benefit can be obtained from the DWP. If the claimant is **24.75** seeking to have the benefit transferred from someone else who has priority, he will have to provide with the claim form a statement from the person with priority that she does not want to claim the benefit herself. If he is seeking to have the benefit transferred on the basis that he now has priority, three weeks will have to elapse after the claim is made before the transfer can take place.

Payment of benefit

24.76 Child benefit is tax-free. However, it forms part of the recipient's income for the purposes of income support but not for WTC.

PART 5   STATE BENEFITS AND MARRIAGE OR CIVIL PARTNERSHIP BREAKDOWN

M   RELEVANCE OF STATE BENEFITS IN DETERMINING APPROPRIATE MAINTENANCE

24.77 A spouse or civil partner cannot normally rely on the fact that his family will be eligible for state benefits as relieving him from his obligation to maintain them. The relevance of state benefits in an application for periodical payments after divorce is discussed in Chapter 31.

N   MAINTENANCE VERSUS STATE BENEFITS: PROS AND CONS FOR THE RECIPIENT

24.78 It quite often happens that one spouse, usually the wife, is on benefit (usually income support) and the other spouse is earning but not at a very high rate. Where it is unlikely that maintenance from the husband will be fixed at a rate significantly more than the wife would be receiving by way of state benefits, it must be remembered that if the wife is taken off benefit she may lose not only the weekly amount of cash benefit but also the other benefits to which she is automatically entitled by virtue of the fact that she is on income support, for example housing benefit, free school meals, and prescriptions, etc. On top of this, she will lose her opportunity to claim payments from the social fund as she could have done had she remained on income support.

24.79 It follows that sometimes it may pay the wife to receive slightly less maintenance in order to stay on benefit and this possibility must be kept firmly in mind when advising on the level of maintenance which would be acceptable and in presenting applications for periodical payments to the court.

O   LUMP SUMS AND INCOME SUPPORT

A lump sum payment which is in reality a form of capitalized maintenance will be counted as   **24.80**
income of the family for income support purposes and will prevent the family from receiving
benefit for a period of time.

There does, however, seem to be some leeway over certain lump sums where what is really   **24.81**
happening is that the recipient is realizing her interest in a capital asset owned by her solely
or by her and her spouse jointly and sold/divided up/retained by the other spouse on the
breakdown of the marriage. Thus, the following types of lump sum will be regarded as capital
and will therefore only put a stop to the family's entitlement to benefit if the family has more
than £16,000 capital altogether:

(a) A lump sum ordered by the court or agreed between the parties as representing the capi-
    talization of an interest in joint property or property held by the other party solely; for
    example, £2,000 paid by the husband to the wife representing her interest in the family
    car and the furniture in the matrimonial home which he has kept.
(b) A lump sum ordered by the court or agreed between the parties representing the alloca-
    tion of or division of money held in banks, building societies, or similar.
(c) A sum derived from the proceeds of sale of the matrimonial home or intended to com-
    pensate the claimant for her loss of interest in the home (such a sum will not be counted
    as capital for at least six months).
(d) Payments in kind. The court does not have power in financial proceedings to order one
    spouse to purchase any item for the other spouse so the most that could be done would
    be for him to give an undertaking to do so.

P   WELFARE BENEFITS AND CIVIL PARTNERS

Section 254 and sch 24, Civil Partnership Act 2004 places civil partners in the same position   **24.82**
as spouses, and same-sex cohabitants in the same position as opposite-sex cohabitants, in
respect of the welfare benefits discussed above. The relevant regulations have been amended
accordingly.

These provisions mark a significant change for same-sex couples whether or not they are reg-   **24.83**
istered civil partners. Previously, such couples were not treated as a single economic unit and
hence their income and capital was not aggregated.

Guidance on what amounts to 'cohabitation' was laid down in *Kimber* v *Kimber* [2000] 1 FLR   **24.84**
383 and includes, for example, a shared home, stability and a degree of permanence in the
relationship, a sexual relationship, and public acknowledgement of the relationship.

25

THE QUESTION OF WILLS

A   CIVIL PARTNERSHIPS

25.01 The Civil Partnership Act 2004 ('CPA 2004'), sch 4, provides that the position of civil partners and spouses will be the same in respect of each other's estate. In summary:

(a) The provisions of the Wills Act 1837 ('WA 1837') are extended to civil partnerships. This means that a will is revoked upon the testator entering into a civil partnership. The same effects will flow from dissolution or nullity of the partnership as flow from divorce and nullity in respect of a marriage. The same rules as for married couples will apply in relation to witnesses to wills and as to the priority over children in distribution of the estate.

(b) A civil partner may obtain probate or letters of administration on the intestacy of their deceased partner and has priority over the public trustee.

(c) A civil partner will have the same rights and priority upon the intestacy of their deceased partner as a surviving spouse. This means that they will be entitled to personal chattels,

£200,000, plus half of the residue absolutely; or, if the deceased left issue, then the surviving partner would be entitled to personal chattels, £125,000, plus a life interest in half the residue. The surviving partner would also have the same rights as a surviving spouse to capitalize any life interest and to acquire the family home.

(d) A civil partner will have the same rights under the Inheritance (Provision for Family and Dependants) Act 1975 as a surviving spouse. The quantum of such a claim is not limited to reasonable maintenance. The court must have regard to what financial provision would have been awarded upon a dissolution of the civil partnership. Cohabitation prior to the civil partnership ceremony is likely to be taken into account in determining the length of the partnership for this purpose (*CO v CO (Ancillary Relief: Pre-marriage Cohabitation)* [2004] 1 FLR 1095). Furthermore, in relation to such claims:

   (i) former civil partners have the same rights as former spouses, which end upon a subsequent marriage or civil partnership;

   (ii) a child of the family of a civil partnership has the same rights as a child of a marriage;

   (iii) same-sex cohabitants have the same rights as heterosexual ones, so that they no longer have to show a dependency (*Ghaidan* v *Godin-Mendoza* [2004] 2 FLR 600). It is necessary to show at least two years' cohabitation up to the time of death.

(e) The proceeds of a life insurance policy for the benefit of a civil partner or the children will not form part of the estate (s 70, CPA 2004). Civil partners will be presumed to have an unlimited insurable interest in the life of each other (s 253, CPA 2004).

For the purposes of this chapter, any reference to 'spouse' or 'partner' will include 'civil part-   **25.02**
ners'; any reference to 'marriage' will include 'civil partnerships'; any reference to 'divorce' and 'nullity' will include nullity and dissolution of civil partnerships.

B   THE NEED TO CONSIDER WHAT WILL HAPPEN ON CLIENT'S DEATH

When the solicitor is consulted by a client who is experiencing matrimonial difficulties or (in   **25.03**
the case of the unmarried client) problems with her cohabitant, or problems with their civil partner, it is most important for the solicitor to consider with her what is to happen to her property should she die.

The first matter to investigate is what the present position would be were she to die today.   **25.04**
If the client and her spouse/partner own land (eg the home) as joint tenants, the spouse/ partner would be entitled to the whole of the property on the client's death by virtue of the right of survivorship. In the case of a married client, the chances are that her spouse would also end up with a good deal of her remaining estate by virtue of her will if she has made one and otherwise by virtue of the intestacy provisions. What would happen to the balance of the estate in the case of a cohabitant would depend on whether she had made a will benefiting her partner. If so, the partner would clearly benefit in accordance with the terms of the will; if not, property would pass in accordance with the intestacy provisions under which the partner would have no entitlement.

Having ascertained what would happen to the client's property under the present arrangements,   **25.05**
the solicitor should find out whether this is what the client wants. Some people are content for

their spouse/cohabitant to continue to benefit after their death despite the breakdown of the relationship, for example for the sake of the children or because they have no one else to whom they wish to leave their property. Others wish to take all possible steps to deprive their partner of any benefit, for example because they now wish to benefit a new girlfriend/boyfriend or child or because they are embittered over the breakdown of the marriage/relationship.

C   THE EFFECT OF MARRIAGE ON A WILL

25.06   Before considering the effect of marital breakdown on existing testamentary documents, it is important to realize the effect which marriage itself may have had on an earlier will. By s 18, WA 1837, a will is revoked by the marriage of the testator. This rule does not apply, however, to invalidate dispositions in the will in exercise of a power of appointment (see s 18(2), unless the property appointed would, in default of appointment, pass to the testator's personal representative), or (more significantly) where it appears from a will that at the time it was made the testator was expecting to be married to a particular person *and* that he intended that the will should not be revoked by the marriage then again the rule does not apply: s 18(3), as applied to wills made on or after 1 January 1983.

D   THE EFFECT OF DIVORCE, JUDICIAL SEPARATION, AND NULLITY ON SUCCESSION

25.07   Certain events, such as divorce, automatically affect existing wills and entitlement on intestacy. The rules are set out in the following paragraphs and they should be borne in mind when considering the position with the client.

The effect of divorce or nullity on a will

25.08   Section 18A, WA 1837 (as inserted by the Administration of Justice Act 1982 and amended by s 3, Law Reform (Succession) Act 1995) provides that, unless the contrary intention appears in the will, the granting of a decree absolute of divorce or nullity will have the following effects on the will of either spouse:

(a) Any appointment in the will of the testator's former spouse as executor or as executor and trustee of the will is ignored. Similarly, a testamentary provision conferring a power of appointment on a spouse is revoked on divorce or annulment of the marriage.

(b) The former spouse is treated as having died at the date of dissolution or annulment of the marriage so that any devise or bequest to the former spouse automatically lapses.

The property that would have passed to the former spouse will either become part of the residue and pass to whoever is entitled to the residuary estate or, if the gift to the former spouse is a residuary gift, will pass according to the intestacy provisions. If it is intended to rely simply on s 18A, the solicitor must be careful to check with the client that the result will fit in with her wishes. It may be, for example, that she was originally very happy for the Society for the

Assistance of Beleaguered Budgerigars to benefit from her residuary estate when it was likely to be in the region of £250. She is not likely to be anxious to endow the Society with her entire estate worth £50,000.

Note that divorce and nullity have no effect on the right of survivorship. Thus, any property **25.09** which, at the time of her death, the deceased still holds as a joint tenant with her former spouse will pass automatically to her former spouse by survivorship despite the termination of the marriage. This underlines the necessity to consider serving a notice of severance where a joint tenancy exists or may exist (see Chapter 22, para 22.20).

Note also that a decree of judicial separation has no effect on a will. **25.10**

The effect of divorce or nullity on intestacy

Where a marriage is void or has been annulled or dissolved by decree absolute of nullity or **25.11** divorce, on the death intestate of either party to the marriage, the other party will have no right to any part of the estate under the intestacy provisions. This is because he or she no longer qualifies as a surviving spouse. However, the former spouse (who has not married someone else) may be able to make a claim for family provision against the estate pursuant to s 1(1)(b), Inheritance (Provision for Family and Dependants) Act 1975.

The effect of judicial separation on intestacy

Whilst a decree of judicial separation is in force and the separation is continuing, if either **25.12** party dies intestate his or her real and personal estate will devolve as if the other party had been dead: s 18(2), Matrimonial Causes Act 1973.

E   STEPS TO BE TAKEN

In the light of the client's instructions, either or both of the following steps may be necessary: **25.13**

(a)   service of notice of severance of joint tenancy (see Chapter 22, para 22.20);
(b)   drafting of will/new will.

If the will/new will is drafted before a decree of divorce or nullity is granted and contains a provision benefiting the client's spouse or appointing him executor or executor and trustee, the solicitor should take care to make it clear in the will (if it be the case) that the provisions are intended to be effective even after divorce/nullity. If this is not done, s 18A, WA 1837 will obviously nullify the provisions relating to the spouse.

F   INHERITANCE (PROVISION FOR FAMILY AND DEPENDANTS) ACT 1975

If the client's instructions are to take steps to deprive her spouse/cohabitant of substantial ben- **25.14** efit from her estate, she should be warned that, whatever steps are taken, her spouse/cohabitant may ultimately be able to secure a share in her estate by means of an application under the Inheritance (Provision for Family and Dependants) Act 1975. A spouse is a favoured class of applicant under this jurisdiction as he can claim whatever is reasonable in all the circumstances. A cohabitant's claim is much more tightly proscribed (see further Chapter 13, para 13.10).

25.15 Applications under the Act are made on the ground that the disposition of the deceased's estate effected by her will or by the intestacy rules (or by a combination of both) is not such as to make reasonable financial provision for the applicant. In some cases, the client may be well advised, despite her feelings, to make some limited provision for her spouse herself in her will in an attempt to rule out the possibility of him subsequently applying to the court under the Act for provision. At least this way she may be able to dictate her own terms rather than leaving the matter at large for the court to resolve after her death. The procedure for applications under the Inheritance (Provision for Family and Dependants) Act 1975 is governed by the Civil Procedure Rules 1998 ('CPR 1998'). The claim must be brought within six months of the date upon which representation is taken out and is usually made by the Part 8 CPR 1998 procedure.

25.16 Note that a former spouse may still apply under the 1975 Act, provided that he or she has not remarried. However, it is possible to attempt to preclude such an application during the course of proceedings for a financial order (see Chapter 30, para 30.146).

G   IMPORTANCE OF CONSIDERING SUCCESSION

25.17 The importance of considering succession can be illustrated by an example.

Example Mr and Mrs Heap are joint tenants of the matrimonial home 'Inglefield'. Mr Heap makes a will leaving £50,000 to his wife and the residue of his estate (which he anticipates will be small) to his old school. Mrs Heap does not make a will. There are no children.

The marriage runs into difficulties. Mrs Heap petitions for divorce but no decree has yet been pronounced. If Mr Heap died today, his share in Inglefield would pass to Mrs Heap by survivorship. The balance of his estate excluding Inglefield would be worth £25,000 and this would pass to Mrs Heap by his will.

If Mrs Heap died today, her share in Inglefield would pass to Mr Heap by survivorship and the rest of her estate (worth £10,000) would pass to him under the intestacy provisions.

If nothing is done to alter the present position, decree absolute of divorce will automatically produce the following results:

(a) On Mr Heap predeceasing Mrs Heap:
  (i)   his share in Inglefield will still pass to Mrs Heap by survivorship;
  (ii) the gift in the will to Mrs Heap will lapse and the balance of his estate (£25,000) will therefore pass to his old school.
(b) On Mrs Heap predeceasing Mr Heap:
  (i)   her share in Inglefield will still pass to Mr Heap by survivorship;
  (ii) the balance of her estate (£10,000) would still pass under the intestacy provisions but *not* to Mr Heap who would no longer qualify as a spouse. If she has a surviving parent or parents, they would be the ones to benefit. If not, other relatives would inherit her estate.

Neither Mr nor Mrs Heap wishes the other to benefit by his/her death before or after the divorce. Mr Heap wishes to leave a slightly larger sum to his old school and the balance of his estate to his girlfriend, Miss Maybury. Mrs Heap wishes to leave her estate to her sister. The following steps should be taken by their solicitors:

(a) The joint tenancy in relation to Inglefield should be severed with the effect that, on the death of either party, his or her interest in the property will pass with his or her estate.

(b) A new will should be made for Mr Heap.

(c) A will should be made for Mrs Heap.

When the new wills are being drafted, each party's solicitor should consider with him or her whether a will leaving nothing to his or her spouse would be reasonable or whether it would be a good idea to make some limited provision for the spouse in an attempt to rule out the possibility of future litigation under the Inheritance (Provision for Family and Dependants) Act 1975. This consideration is likely to be more important for Mr Heap, who has a considerably larger estate than Mrs Heap.

If either party does decide to leave money or property to his or her spouse and the will is to become effective before decree absolute, care should be taken to express in the will the intention that the provision concerning the spouse will continue after the decree is granted.

H   APPOINTING A GUARDIAN FOR CHILDREN

The solicitor should consider with the client whether it is appropriate to make provision in the will for the appointment of a guardian for her minor children. Section 5, Children Act 1989 enables parents and special guardians to appoint guardians to take their place after their death. Unless the child is living under a residence order with the parent who dies, the appointment will not take effect until there is no surviving parent with parental responsibility. Such appointments will be valid if made in writing, dated, and signed at the direction of the person making the appointment and in the presence of two witnesses. This is a departure from the old rules whereby such appointments were only valid if made by deed or will. For further discussion about guardianship, see Chapter 17, para 17.93. **25.18**

26

SECTION 27, MATRIMONIAL
CAUSES ACT 1973

A   GROUNDS FOR APPLICATION

26.01   Section 27, Matrimonial Causes Act 1973 ('MCA 1973') provides that applications may be
made for maintenance and/or lump sum orders by either party to a marriage (the applicant)
on the grounds that the other party (the respondent) either:

(a) has failed to provide reasonable maintenance for the applicant; *or*
(b) has failed to provide, or to make proper contribution towards, reasonable maintenance
     for any child of the family: s 27(1).

B JURISDICTION

The court has jurisdiction under s 27 if: **26.02**

(a) the applicant or respondent is domiciled in England and Wales at the date of the application; *or*
(b) the applicant has been habitually resident in England and Wales throughout the year ending with the date of the application; *or*
(c) the respondent is resident in England and Wales on the date of the application: s 27(2).

(See Chapter 6 for the meaning of domicile, habitual residence, etc.)

C ORDERS THAT CAN BE MADE

General

The court can make one or more of the following orders against the respondent: **26.03**

(a) that he shall make periodical payments or secured periodical payments to the applicant;
(b) that he shall pay the applicant a lump sum;
(c) that he shall make periodical payments (secured or unsecured) for the benefit of a child to whom the s 27 application relates, to the child himself, or to the applicant or such other person as the court specifies (provided that the court retains jurisdiction);
(d) an order that the respondent shall pay the child or the applicant or such other person as the court specifies a lump sum for the benefit of the child: s 27(6).

These orders are identical to the financial provision orders under s 23, MCA 1973 made after **26.04** divorce, nullity, or judicial separation (see Chapter 29). Just as is the case under s 23, the amount of any periodical payments or lump sum ordered is within the court's discretion although the court must take into account specified factors (see paras 26.12 ff below). There is no financial limit on the amount of the lump sum that can be ordered. The court has power to order that the lump sum should be paid by secured or unsecured instalments if it thinks fit: s 27(7). The court is also able to specify the duration of any periodical payments order it makes subject to certain limitations which are set out below.

In contrast to the position on divorce, etc, the court does not have power to make property **26.05** adjustment orders.

Limitations on orders relating to children and duration of orders generally

The limitations on the orders that can be made to or for the benefit of children and the dura- **26.06** tion of orders are basically the same as those applicable to financial provision orders under s 23. In particular, it must be remembered that in most cases the court is prevented by the Child Support Act 1991 ('CSA 1991') from making orders for periodical payments for children, whether secured or unsecured. It may only make such orders in relation to children where the case falls within one of the exceptions to the general rule (see Chapter 35 for a full account of the provisions of the CSA 1991).

Limitations on orders relating to children

26.07   The restrictions imposed by s 29(1) and (3), MCA 1973 on the making of financial provision orders in favour of children who have attained the age of 18 apply also to s 27 (see Chapter 29, paras 29.18 ff for the provisions of s. 29(1) and (3)). The restriction is disapplied by virtue of s 29(3)(b) where there are 'special circumstances'. In *C v F (Disabled Child: Maintenance Orders)* [1998] 2 FLR 1 it was held that special circumstances may include physical or other handicap, and the expenses attributed to the child's disability should be taken into account in the broadest sense.

Duration of orders under s 27

26.08   The provisions of ss 28 and 29, MCA 1973 relating to the duration of periodical payments orders apply to s 27 periodical payments orders for spouses and children. These provisions are dealt with in Chapter 29.

26.09   Note that whereas orders for periodical payments made after divorce, etc can normally date back to the date of the petition, in the case of periodical payments ordered under s 27, backdating can be to the date of the originating application for relief under s 27.

26.10   The fact that there is a subsequent decree of divorce, nullity, or judicial separation has no effect on the orders made under s 27.

26.11   However, if the marriage is dissolved or annulled and the spouse in whose favour the s 27 order was made remarries, the s 27 order will automatically cease to have effect except in relation to any arrears which might have accrued up to the date of the remarriage: s 28(2).

D   FACTORS TO BE CONSIDERED ON AN APPLICATION UNDER S 27

26.12   The factors to be considered on a s 27 application are virtually the same as those to be considered on an application under s 23.

In relation to orders for a spouse

26.13   In deciding whether the respondent has failed to provide reasonable maintenance for the applicant and what order, if any, to make in her favour, the court shall have regard to all the circumstances of the case including the s 25(2), MCA 1973 criteria. Where an application is also made under s 27 in respect of a child who is under 18, first consideration shall be given to the welfare of the child while a minor: s 27(3). (For the matters mentioned in s 25(2), see Chapter 31.)

26.14   Note that there are minor differences between the approach under s 27 and that under s 23:

(a)   Under s 23, first consideration must always be given to the welfare of any child of the family under 18 whether any application is made in respect of the child or not: s 25(1).

Under s 27, first consideration is given to the child's welfare only if an application is made in respect of him under s 27.

(b) Section 25(2)(c), which provides that the court must take into account the standard of living enjoyed by the family before the breakdown of the marriage is modified so that, in s 27 cases, the court must take into account the standard of living enjoyed by the family before the failure to provide reasonable maintenance for the applicant: s 27(3B).

(c) Section 25(2)(h) (consideration of benefits lost, such as pensions) is confined to proceedings for divorce or nullity and cannot therefore apply in s 27 cases.

In relation to orders for a child

It must be remembered that in most cases the court is prevented by the CSA 1991 from making orders for periodical payments for children, whether secured or unsecured. It may only make such orders in relation to children where the case falls within one of the exceptions to the general rule (see Chapter 35 for a full account of the provisions of the CSA 1991). **26.15**

In deciding whether the respondent has failed to provide, or to make proper contribution towards, reasonable maintenance for a child of the family in respect of whom an application under s 27 has been made and what order, if any, to make under this section in favour of the child, the court is to have regard to all the circumstances of the case including the matters mentioned in s 25(3)(a) to (e), MCA 1973. If the child to whom the application relates is not a child of the respondent, the court must also have regard to the matters mentioned in s 25(4), MCA 1973 (s 27(3A)). (For the matters mentioned in s 25(3) and (4), reference should be made to Chapter 31, paras 31.84 ff.) **26.16**

There is one minor alteration to the terms of s 25(3) in order that it should fit the circumstances of a s 27 application. This is to s 25(2)(c) which deals with the standard of living enjoyed by the family before the breakdown of the marriage. This must be read as if it referred to the standard of living enjoyed by the family before the failure to provide, or to make proper contribution towards, reasonable maintenance: s 27(3B). **26.17**

Approach in practice

In practice, what the court is likely to do when faced with a s 27 application is to decide what order it would have made had it been considering the case under s 23 after a divorce and then to compare what it would have ordered with what the respondent has actually been paying. If his provision does not measure up, the court can be expected to make an order for periodical payments and/or lump sum payments for the applicant and any children of the family in substantially the same terms as the order it would have made had the application been for a financial order under s 23. **26.18**

Expenses that can be the subject of lump sum orders

The power to order a lump sum is wide enough to enable the court to order a lump sum for any reason whatsoever. It is specifically provided by s 27(7) that an order may, amongst other things, be made for the payment of a lump sum to cover liabilities or expenses reasonably **26.19** incurred in maintaining the applicant or any child of the family to whom the application relates before the making of the application.

E PROCEDURE

26.20 The application is made to a divorce county court on Form D50C, contained within PD5A of the Family Procedure Rules 2010. The form must be accompanied by a Statement in Support confirmed by a statement of truth. Public funding is available for proceedings for financial orders under s 27, MCA 1973. The detailed provisions relating to public funding under the Community Legal Service scheme are to be found in Chapter 2. Preliminary advice may be available by way of Legal Help with the possibility of General Legal Help for the institution of proceedings. However, proceedings under s 27 come within the definition of 'family matters' for the purposes of public funding and therefore the applicant will be required to attend family mediation before any application may be made for publicly funded representation.

26.21 Section 27 applications are usually dealt with by a district judge and the hearing can be expected to be much the same as the hearing of an application under s 23 after a divorce. See Chapter 30 for a general account of the procedure in applications for financial orders.

F INTERIM ORDERS

26.22 Where it appears to the court that the applicant or any child of the family to whom the s 27 application relates is in immediate need of financial assistance but it is not yet possible to determine what order, if any, should be made on the application, the court can make an interim order for maintenance, that is, an order requiring the respondent to make to the applicant until the determination of the application such periodical payments as the court thinks reasonable: s 27(5). Note that there is no power to order interim periodical payments to be made to the child direct or to any person other than the applicant for the benefit of the child.

G VARIATION OF S 27 ORDERS

26.23 It must be remembered that in most cases the court is prevented by the CSA 1991 from making orders for periodical payments for children, whether secured or unsecured. It may only make such orders in relation to children where the case falls within one of the exceptions to the general rule (see Chapter 35 for a full account of the provisions of the CSA 1991). Subject to those matters it may be that an order for periodical payments made under s 27 can be varied under s 31, MCA 1973, as can the instalment element of an order for the payment of a lump sum by instalments.

H   SECTION 27 COMPARED WITH DOMESTIC PROCEEDINGS AND
MAGISTRATES' COURTS ACT 1978

It will have been noted that the grounds for an application under s 27 are the same as two   **26.24**
of the grounds for an application in the family proceedings courts for an order under s 2,
Domestic Proceedings and Magistrates' Courts Act 1978 ('DPMCA 1978') that is, s 1(a) (failure
to provide reasonable maintenance for the applicant) and s 1(b) (failure to provide/contribute
properly towards reasonable maintenance for a child of the family).

It follows that the applicant intending to rely on failure to maintain has a choice whether to   **26.25**
proceed in the family proceedings courts under DPMCA 1978 or in the divorce county court
under s 27, MCA 1973. In practice, by far the majority of applications appear to be made in
the family proceedings courts but the solicitor must consider what is best for his particular
client in each case.

The following points must be borne in mind: **26.26**

(a) The grounds for an order under s 27 relate only to failure to maintain whereas the appli-
     cant for an order under s 2, DPMCA 1978 can rely alternatively on behaviour or desertion:
     s 1(c) and (d), DPMCA 1978. If, therefore, there is doubt about proving failure to maintain
     but a possibility of making out one of the other grounds it may be prudent to apply in the
     family proceedings court alleging, as an alternative, behaviour or desertion.
(b) The grounds for jurisdiction are more restrictive under DPMCA 1978. This simply means
     that the solicitor must check that the family proceedings court would have jurisdiction
     in a particular case. If not, he may still be able to bring the case under s 27.
(c) The orders that can be made under s 2, DPMCA 1978, although basically the same as
     those available under s 27 are, in fact, more restricted as follows:
     (i)   No secured periodical payments can be ordered under s 2, DPMCA 1978; they can
           under s 27.
     (ii) There is an upper financial limit of £1,000 on a lump sum ordered under s 2, DPMCA
           1978; there is no limit under s 27.
(d) The powers under the two Acts to make interim orders differ significantly in the following
     ways:
     (i)   Under s 19, DPMCA 1978 (the section dealing with interim orders), the family
           proceedings court has power to make an interim maintenance order requiring the
           respondent to make periodical payments direct to a child of the family under 18 or
           to the applicant for the benefit of the child. Under s 27, interim periodical payments
           are limited to the applicant only.
     (ii) Section 27 is far more generous than s 19, DPMCA 1978 about the duration of inter-
           im orders. Interim orders under s 27 can go on until the determination of the s 27
           application, however long it takes for that application to be heard. Interim orders
           under s 19, DPMCA 1978 can only be made for a period of up to three months in
           the first instance and, although they can be extended, can only be extended so that
           they continue for a maximum of three months more (a total of six months in all,
           maximum). If it takes longer than six months for the case to be heard, the applicant

and child will cease to be entitled to any interim payments. It is to be hoped that this will rarely prove a problem in practice as six months should be ample time in most cases for the application to be disposed of by a final order.

In fact, the apparent choice facing the applicant may, in any event, be determined for her by the Legal Services Commission if she is reliant upon public funding. Unless good grounds can be shown for seeking an order under s 27, it is likely that the applicant will be expected to pursue what will probably be the less expensive course of an application to the family proceedings court and that her application for funding for s 27 will be turned down on the basis that she should seek funding by way of representation for the family proceedings courts.

27

SEPARATION AND MAINTENANCE AGREEMENTS

A THE DIFFERENCE BETWEEN SEPARATION AND MAINTENANCE AGREEMENTS

The essence of a separation agreement is that the parties agree to live apart. A separation **27.01** agreement may, however, include all manner of other terms dealing with maintenance, family property, arrangements for the children, etc.

An agreement which deals with the payment of maintenance by one spouse to or for the **27.02** benefit of the other and/or the children but not with the separation of the parties is sometimes referred to as a 'maintenance agreement'; there may or may not be other terms in the agreement as well as provision for maintenance. This general use of the term should not be confused with maintenance agreements as defined in s 34(2), Matrimonial Causes Act 1973 ('MCA 1973').

27.03   By virtue of s 34(2), a 'maintenance agreement' is any agreement in writing made between the parties to a marriage, being:

(a) an agreement containing financial arrangements, whether made during the continuance or after the dissolution or annulment of the marriage; or

(b) a separation agreement which contains no financial arrangements in a case where no other agreement in writing between the same parties contains such arrangements.

'Financial arrangements' means provisions governing the rights and liabilities towards one another when living separately from the parties to a marriage (including a marriage which has been dissolved or annulled) in respect of the making or securing of payments or the disposition or use of any property, including such rights and liabilities with respect to the maintenance or education of any child, whether or not a child of the family.

B   LIKELY CONTENTS OF SEPARATION AGREEMENTS

27.04   There are very few restrictions on the contents of a separation agreement and agreements are therefore likely to vary considerably depending on the circumstances of each case. The following are examples of matters commonly dealt with:

(a) *Agreement to live apart*: the agreement of the parties to a marriage to live apart is central to a separation agreement. The spouses frequently also agree not to molest each other.

(b) *Maintenance*: the spouses often agree that one spouse (usually the husband) will pay maintenance of a certain amount to or for the benefit of the other spouse and/or the children. Where the recipient is in receipt of income support the Child Maintenance and Enforcement Commission (CMEC) will determine the level of financial support to be provided by the absent parent in respect of his natural child. On the other hand, in non-benefit cases it is possible for the parties to reach agreement on the level of support to be provided. However, such an agreement would not prevent the carer parent from subsequently requesting CMEC to carry out a maintenance assessment. Once such an assessment is made it will override the original agreement: s 9(2) and (3), Child Support Act 1991.

     Care must be taken in drafting agreements to pay maintenance. In particular, thought must be given as to when the obligation to pay maintenance under the agreement should terminate. It is possible to draft an agreement to pay maintenance that will create an obligation that will continue irrespective of whether the parties start to live together again or get divorced and despite the remarriage or cohabitation of the payee or even the death of the payer. If such an open-ended commitment is what the parties want, all well and good. Generally, however, the payer will be anxious to limit his obligations and the relevant clauses should therefore make clear the events that will bring the duty to pay maintenance to an end.

(c) *Property*: the spouses may also reach agreement over what is to become of the family property. This is less common than an agreement over maintenance.

(d) *Arrangements for the children*: the agreement may provide for where, and with whom, any children of the family are to live and for any arrangements as to contact.

C   WHAT A SEPARATION AGREEMENT CANNOT DO

A separation agreement must provide for *immediate* separation. Spouses cannot enter into a   **27.05**
valid agreement to provide for their legal rights in case they should separate at any stage in
the future as this is contrary to public policy.

However, a couple who have already separated but who want to attempt a reconciliation are   **27.06**
free to negotiate a reconciliation agreement containing provisions as to what will happen
should they separate again in the future. As soon as they separate, the appropriate terms will
become effective.

D   THE FORM OF A SEPARATION OR MAINTENANCE AGREEMENT

A separation or maintenance agreement is a contract just like any other contract. It can be   **27.07**
made orally or in writing or even by conduct although if the agreement covers more than
simple separation it is prudent to record the terms of the agreement in writing so that they
are beyond dispute.

The normal contractual rules apply to determine whether a binding agreement exists, that   **27.08**
is, the court will look for offer and acceptance, for an intention to create legal relations, and
for consideration. However, consideration may be lacking in a maintenance agreement. An
agreement by the payee not to seek further or different provision by making application to
the court is void (*Hyman* v *Hyman* [1929] AC 601) and cannot therefore constitute good consideration for a promise to pay maintenance. Unless there are clearly other covenants which
are binding on the payee, it is therefore recommended that a maintenance agreement should
be embodied in a deed to ensure that it is binding.

Note that a separation or maintenance agreement can be void for mistake or fraud and can   **27.09**
be set aside on the grounds of misrepresentation, duress, or undue influence. In order to preclude future problems of this type over the validity of the agreement, it is therefore desirable
that both parties to the agreement should receive separate legal advice.

E   EFFECT OF A SEPARATION AGREEMENT

Apart from the specific matters upon which agreement is reached, a separation agreement   **27.10**
will:

(a) release both spouses from their duty to cohabit with each other thus preventing either of
     them from alleging that the other is in desertion;
(b) provide evidence that the parties looked upon the marriage as at an end (necessary to
     prove separation for divorce and judicial separation; see *Santos* v *Santos* [1972] Fam 247,
     [1972] 2 All ER 246 and para 4.36) and as to the date of their separation;

(c)   if the agreement also makes provision for maintenance and the payer fulfils his obligations in this respect, be rebuttable evidence against a claim on the basis of his failure to provide reasonable maintenance.

F   ADVANTAGES OF A SEPARATION OR MAINTENANCE AGREEMENT

27.11   The possibility of a formal separation or maintenance agreement is sometimes overlooked by solicitors who tend only to consider making an application to court for financial provision. Such an agreement does, however, have some advantages, for example:

(a)   An agreement is flexible—it can include any terms which the parties wish subject to very few limitations.

(b)   Financial matters often cause some of the most bitter disputes between couples after marriage breakdown. If its terms are observed, an agreement may serve to take the heat out of the breakdown of the marriage and will enable both parties to know where they stand. It provides a means of resolving financial and other problems formally but without the need to have recourse to court, which can be expensive and can also encourage the parties to draw up battle lines.

It should be pointed out, however, that there are disadvantages of a separation agreement in comparison with a court order, notably:

(i)   It is not so easy to enforce (for enforcement of agreements, see para 27.12 below; for enforcement of court orders, see Chapter 33, para 33.02).

(ii)   It cannot achieve the same degree of finality as a court order. The jurisdiction of the court to entertain future financial and property applications (eg after divorce) cannot be ousted by an agreement.

(iii)   While variation by the court can be sought if the agreement can be classed as a maintenance agreement within s 34, MCA 1973, if the agreement falls outside the definition, it can only be varied by consent. Court orders for periodic payments are always variable by subsequent order.

G   ENFORCEMENT

27.12   A separation or maintenance agreement is enforceable in the same way as any other contract. Thus an action can be brought for damages (eg if the breach alleged is a failure to pay maintenance, damages equal to the arrears of maintenance could be sought), and the equitable remedies of specific performance and an injunction to prevent a breach of a negative clause of the agreement are also available.

H IMPACT OF SUBSISTING SEPARATION AGREEMENT OR MAINTENANCE AGREEMENT ON FINANCIAL ARRANGEMENTS AFTER DIVORCE, ETC

The fact that there is a subsisting maintenance or separation agreement dealing with finance **27.13** and/or property does not preclude either party making a comprehensive application for financial provision in conjunction with divorce, nullity, or judicial separation even if that party undertakes in the agreement not to seek further provision from the court (an undertaking which will be void). However, the existence of the agreement will be one of the factors for the court to take into account under s 25, MCA 1973 when it considers the application for financial orders (see Chapter 31).

28

SECTION 17, MARRIED WOMEN'S PROPERTY ACT 1882 AND TRUSTS OF LAND

A   INTRODUCTION

Section 17, Married Women's Property Act 1882 provides a procedure for determining the **28.01** property rights of spouses, of formerly engaged couples, and of certain divorcees without relying on the court's powers to grant financial orders after divorce.

Because s 17 proceedings are relatively rare these days, this chapter does not go into either the **28.02** law or the procedure in any depth. The reader is referred to the main practitioners' textbooks on family law and on property and trusts law for further information.

B   THE BASIC PROVISION

Section 17 provides that, in any question between husband and wife as to the title to or pos- **28.03** session of property, either party may apply in a summary way to a High Court or county court judge who may make such order with respect to the property in dispute and as to the costs of the application as he thinks fit.

C   POSSIBLE APPLICANTS

The following can make application under s 17:   **28.04**

(a)   either party to a marriage during the marriage: s 17;

(b)   civil partners provided that the application is made within three years of the dissolution or annulment (s 66, Civil Partnership Act 2004);

(c)   either party to a marriage within three years of the dissolution or annulment of the marriage: s 39, Matrimonial Proceedings and Property Act 1970;

(d)   engaged couples within three years of the termination of the engagement: s 2(2), Law Reform (Miscellaneous Provisions) Act 1970. The section affords relief even where the promise to marry was not enforceable because the promisor was already married: *Shaw* v *Fitzgerald* [1992] 1 FLR 357.

Note that s 17 does not assist cohabitants for whom no special procedure presently exists for determining property disputes. Where a dispute arises between cohabitants, therefore, the only means of resolving it is unfortunately by relying on the general jurisdiction of the county court or High Court. The exact nature of the application that should be made depends on the circumstances of the case but the following forms of relief may be sought: an order declaring and enforcing a trust; an order for sale under s 14, Trusts of Land and Appointment of Trustees Act 1996; an order granting possession of real property; injunctions and damages for wrongful interference with goods (where chattels are in dispute).

D   WHAT PROPERTY IS COVERED?

28.05   Application can be made under s 17 to resolve disputes over all manner of property including, for example, houses and land, money, shares, furniture, jewellery, and even items of very little financial value such as holiday souvenirs, garden tools, photograph albums.

28.06   Although most disputes concern property which is in the possession of one or the other party, it is not essential for either party to have the property in his or her possession at the time of the application. By s 7, Matrimonial Causes (Property and Maintenance) Act 1958, application can be made where it is alleged:

(a)   that the other party has had in his possession or control property to which the applicant was partly or wholly beneficially entitled even though he no longer has the property; *or*

(b)   that the other party has or has had in his possession or control money representing the proceeds of sale of property to which the applicant was wholly or partly entitled.

E   WHAT ORDERS CAN BE MADE?

Orders declaring parties' property rights

28.07   Section 17 is a procedural provision only. It empowers the court to determine in a summary way what the parties' rights in particular property *are* as a matter of strict law and to declare them accordingly. There is no power under s 17 to make orders *adjusting* property rights such as the court can make under s 24, Matrimonial Causes Act 1973 ('MCA 1973').

Order for sale

28.08   The court also has power under s 17 to order a sale of the disputed property (see para 28.34 below).

F   ORDINARY TRUST PRINCIPLES GENERALLY APPLY IN DETERMINING DISPUTES

28.09   Statutory provision has been made for one or two problems that have arisen frequently in disputes between husband and wife (see below). However, on the whole, the same principles apply in determining property disputes between spouses and others under s 17 as apply to disputes between total strangers. Thus, the courts will generally apply normal trust principles though with the assistance of numerous authorities in the reports illustrating how these principles have been interpreted in family situations (eg in disputes between husband and wife under s 17 or, more commonly these days, between cohabitants in a trust action).

G   DISPUTES OVER LAND

Principles to be applied

The leading cases in relation to disputes over the beneficial ownership of land are *Pettitt* v   **28.10**
Pettitt [1970] AC 777, [1969] 2 All ER 385; *Gissing* v *Gissing* [1971] AC 886, [1970] 2 All ER 780;
and *Lloyds Bank plc* v *Rosset* [1991] 1 AC 107, [1990] 1 All ER 1111. The principles set out in
this section derive largely from these decisions of the House of Lords.

Examples of the types of problem that arise

Example 1 The matrimonial home was purchased in the sole name of the husband. The   **28.11**
wife claims to have a beneficial interest in the property because she has paid for substantial
improvements to be made to the property.

Example 2 Miss James and Mr Harris are engaged. They buy a house to be their home after they
are married. The house is transferred into Mr Harris's sole name but both parties contribute
equally to the deposit, legal fees, and mortgage instalments. The engagement is broken off.
Miss James claims to have a beneficial interest in the property by virtue of her contribution
to the purchase price.

Example 3 The matrimonial home was purchased in the joint names of husband and wife.
The wife claims that, as she put up the deposit and her earnings have been used to pay the
mortgage instalments, the whole beneficial interest in the house belongs to her.

The need to establish a trust

Where one party claims to be entitled to a greater share in the house than the legal title sug-   **28.12**
gests, he or (more usually) she must establish that the legal estate in the property is held on
trust for her to the extent that she alleges she is beneficially entitled. Thus, for instance, in
Example 2 above, Miss James would no doubt argue that Mr Harris holds the legal estate in the
house on trust for herself and himself in equal shares and in Example 3, the wife would have
to establish that the parties hold the legal estate on trust for her absolutely.

Express and implied trusts

A trust may be express or implied. Implied trusts are generally subdivided into resulting and   **28.13**
constructive trusts.

Express declaration on documents of title

In determining whether a trust exists, the first step is to examine the documents of title.   **28.14**
The conveyance or transfer (TR1 form) will obviously stipulate who is to hold the legal estate.
The beneficial interest may or may not be mentioned specifically.

If the conveyance or transfer stipulates not only who is to hold the legal estate but also who   **28.15**
is entitled to the beneficial interest in the property (eg 'to Joe Bloggs and Mildred Bloggs as

beneficial joint tenants' or 'to Joe Bloggs and Freda Walker as tenants in common in equal shares'), that concludes the question of beneficial ownership of the property unless it can be shown that the statement in the conveyance was the result of fraud or a mistake or that there has subsequently been a fresh agreement varying the position. The same is true where a separate deed of trust has been prepared dealing with the beneficial interest in the property (*Goodman* v *Gallant* [1986] Fam 106).

Example The matrimonial home is purchased in the joint names of husband and wife. The conveyance is expressed to be to H and W 'as joint tenants in law and equity'. Although W has never worked, and the whole of the purchase price has been provided by the husband, H cannot argue that he is entitled to the whole beneficial interest in the property, as the express declaration in the conveyance is conclusive: see *Goodman* v *Gallant* [1986] Fam 106, [1986] 1 FLR 513 and *Barclays Bank plc* v *Khaira* [1993] 1 FLR 343.

Note, however, that s 37, Matrimonial Proceedings and Property Act 1970 can operate to entitle a spouse to a larger interest in the property by virtue of improvements that he or she has effected to the property subsequently, and this provision will override the terms of the conveyance or transfer.

28.16   In *Stack* v *Dowden* [2007] UKHL 17, the House of Lords considered the position where a property was held in the joint names of two cohabitants in law but there was no declaration as to how the beneficial interest was held. The result was that in a domestic relationship between a cohabiting couple, a transfer into joint names with no declaration of trust gives rise to a beneficial joint tenancy in the absence of any evidence to the contrary. In other words, where the property is held by Joe Bloggs and Mildred Smith as joint tenants in law a court will presume that they are also joint beneficial tenants unless one of them can show that there was an agreement or understanding that they would not hold in anything other than equal shares.

28.17   In *Jones* v *Kernott* [2011] UKSC 53 the Supreme Court recently revisited the judgment in *Stack* v *Dowden*. The justices have confirmed that there remains a 'heavy presumption' in favour of an equal share of the beneficial interest where the legal estate is held in joint names. That presumption can only be rebutted by evidence that the parties intended something different, the intention being inferred by a court from the parties' actual agreement, discussions, or conduct at the time that the property was purchased. It is, however, possible for any such intention to change, which is what had occurred in *Jones* v *Kernott*, following Mr Kernott's departure from the shared home and his subsequent failure to pay anything towards the joint mortgage over a period of 14 years. The justices referred to this as an 'ambulatory trust'. It was also clarified that if the presumption is rebutted, the court will then go on to consider how the respective interests should be quantified. The court should do its best on the available evidence to work out by inference what the parties themselves intended. If that is not clear then it is permissible for a court to impute an intention so that 'each is entitled to the share which the court considers fair having regard to the whole course of dealing between them in relation to the property'.

The implication of a trust

28.18   Where the conveyance or transfer deals with the legal estate only and is silent as to the beneficial interests in the property, at first sight the beneficial interest goes with the legal estate.

Thus, where the conveyance or transfer says, for example, 'to Joe Bloggs in fee simple', Joe Bloggs is on the face of it entitled to the whole beneficial interest in the property. Where the conveyance or transfer consigns the legal estate to a husband and wife jointly, they are at first sight jointly entitled to the beneficial interest. However, these presumptions can be displaced by evidence of disparate financial contributions to the purchase of the property, or of express discussions between the spouses.

In *Carlton* v *Goodman* [2002] 2 FLR 259, Ward LJ reminded practitioners of the need to sit pur-   **28.19**
chasers down, explain the differences between a joint tenancy and a tenancy in common, find out what the purchasers want, and then expressly declare in the transfer how the beneficial interest is to be held. This is reinforced by the Land Registration Rules 1925, which require a declaration of trust where land is to vest in persons as joint proprietors whether on first registration or on registration of a dealing. Even if the parties do not go so far as an express declaration of trust or agreement, their conversations can still be taken into account as part of their conduct (see para 28.23 below).

It was thought, at one time, that the provisions of s 53, Law of Property Act 1925 would cause   **28.20**
difficulties for the informal creation of trusts in the family context. Section 53(1)(b) provides that a declaration of trust respecting any land or interest in land must be manifested and proved in writing signed by some person who is able to declare such a trust. Section 53(1)(c) goes further and requires that a disposition of an equitable interest or trust subsisting at the time of the disposition must be in writing signed by the person disposing of it or his agent or by will. However, the requirements of the section do not affect the creation or operation of resulting, implied, or constructive trusts (s 53(2)), thereby giving the courts a way around the strict provisions of s 53, so that it is rare for a claimant in a family situation to fail to establish a trust simply because there is no written evidence of it (see, however, *Midland Bank plc* v *Dobson* [1986] 1 FLR 171, which makes it clear that it can still happen).

Resulting trust: direct financial contribution

It had long been recognized that a spouse who had made a financial contribution towards   **28.21**
the acquisition of property would, in the absence of some other arrangement being intended, obtain a beneficial interest in the house commensurate to the contribution made. This is traditionally referred to as the doctrine of resulting trust and it gave rise to a presumption.

This presumption no longer applies following *Jones* v *Kernott* in 'normal' cohabitation cases   **28.22**
where both parties are paying the mortgage. The more appropriate vehicle is that of a constructive trust (see below). The resulting trust may however remain where there is some element of a business relationship between the parties; the precise extent of its present application has yet to be confirmed.

Constructive trust: parties' common intentions

In *Lloyds Bank* v *Rosset* [1991] 1 AC 107, Lord Bridge summarized the principles for the imposition   **28.23**
of a constructive trust as follows:

> The first and fundamental question which must always be resolved is whether, independently of any inference to be drawn from the conduct of the parties in the course of sharing the house as their home and managing their joint affairs, there has at any time prior to acquisition, or exceptionally at some later date, been any *agreement*, *arrangement* or *understanding* reached between

them that the property is to be shared beneficially. The finding of an agreement or arrangement to share in this sense can only, I think, be based on evidence of *express discussions* between the partners, however imperfectly remembered and however imprecise their terms may have been. Once a finding to this effect is made it will only be necessary for the partner asserting a claim to a beneficial interest against the partner entitled to the legal estate to show that he or she has acted to his or her *detriment* or significantly altered his or her position in *reliance* on the agreement in order to give rise to a constructive trust or proprietary estoppel. (Emphasis added.)

28.24   Examples of the operation of constructive trusts can be found in two decisions of the Court of Appeal, both of which concerned unmarried cohabitants. In *Eves* v *Eves* [1975] 1 WLR 1338, the man explained that the legal estate was to be vested in his sole name because the woman was under 21, and that otherwise the house would have been put into their joint names. The woman relied on this by doing a considerable amount of building work to the house (wielding a sledge hammer and operating a cement mixer). She thereby obtained a share in the home. In *Grant* v *Edwards* [1986] 2 All ER 426, the man told the woman that the only reason the house was not being acquired in their joint names was because to do so might prejudice the divorce proceedings to which she was then party. In the course of living with him, she made substantial, albeit largely indirect, financial contributions from her own earnings, which enabled him to meet his obligations under the mortgage. The Court of Appeal held that she thereby obtained a half share in the house. (See also *H* v *M (Property: Beneficial Interest)* [1992] 1 FLR 229.)

Improvements

28.25   Section 37, Matrimonial Proceedings and Property Act 1970 makes it clear that a share in property can be acquired by carrying out, helping with, or paying for improvements. It provides that where a husband or wife (or a partner to an engagement by virtue of s 2(1), Law Reform (Miscellaneous Provisions) Act 1970 makes a *substantial* contribution in money or money's worth to the improvement of real or personal property in which, or in the proceeds of sale of which, either or both of them has or have a beneficial interest, the contributor shall, subject to any contrary agreement between them, be treated as having acquired a share or an enlarged share in the beneficial interest by virtue of his or her contribution. The proportion of the share/increased share acquired is dependent on the parties' agreement at the time or, in default of agreement, will be determined by the court as it thinks just in all the circumstances: see *Passee* v *Passee* [1988] 1 FLR 263, [1988] Fam Law 132; *Thomas* v *Fuller-Brown* [1988] 1 FLR 237, [1988] Fam Law 53; and *Risch* v *McFee* [1991] 1 FLR 105. It is important to note that this provision applies to spouses and engaged couples only. It does not apply to cohabitants.

Example   Mr and Mrs Couch are looking for a new home. They find a row of three dilapidated cottages which are suitable for conversion and buy them. Mr Couch puts up the purchase money and the cottages are conveyed into his name. The Couches carry out much of the renovation work themselves. They re-roof the property, Mr Couch going up on the roof and Mrs Couch loading up the tiles on the conveyor at the bottom for him. They knock down several internal walls, both wielding a sledge hammer and wheeling away the stone although there are certain bits that Mr Couch has to lift as his wife is not strong enough. They install new window frames which Mrs Couch paints and glazes while Mr Couch installs central heating. Mrs Couch pays for the property to be professionally rewired. There is no doubt that Mrs Couch will acquire a beneficial interest in the property by virtue of her hard work and her payment for the rewiring.

H THE OWNERSHIP OF CASH AND ASSETS OTHER THAN LAND

As with land, entitlement to cash and other assets generally depends on the intention of the parties. A number of matters that commonly cause difficulty are dealt with below. **28.26**

Housekeeping money

Section 1, Married Women's Property Act 1964 provides that if any question arises as to the right of a husband or wife to money derived from any allowance made by the husband for the expenses of the matrimonial home or for similar purposes, or to any property acquired out of such money, the money or property shall, in the absence of any agreement between them to the contrary, be treated as belonging to the husband and the wife in equal shares. **28.27**

Example Mr Hill pays his wife £75 housekeeping each week. She manages to save £15 a week and, at the end of the year, buys a Victorian button-back chair with the savings. Nothing is said by either party as to who the savings from the housekeeping or the chair belong to. Section 1 therefore dictates that the chair belongs to the parties equally.

Joint accounts

The ownership of a joint account and of property purchased from it depends on the intention of the parties. **28.28**

In some cases, the proper inference is that the parties are pooling their resources and intend that the account and any assets acquired from it shall belong to them jointly: see, for example, *Jones* v *Maynard* [1951] 1 All ER 802. In other cases, one party provides all the funds and a joint account is only opened as a matter of convenience, in which case the funds in the account and any property bought with them belong to the spouse who put up the money unless there is specific agreement about particular items purchased: see, for example, *Heseltine* v *Heseltine* [1971] 1 WLR 342. In other cases it may be that assets bought from the joint account belong solely to the spouse making the purchase: see, for example, *Re Bishop* [1965] 1 All ER 249. **28.29**

Wedding presents and other gifts

Naturally each spouse owns the items that were given to him or her personally, for example as birthday presents. **28.30**

28.31   Who owns the wedding presents and other gifts to the parties jointly will depend on the intention of the donor. However, in the absence of other evidence, the court may be inclined to find that wedding presents in particular belong to the spouse whose side of the family donated them: *Samson* v *Samson* [1960] 1 All ER 653, [1960] 1 WLR 190.

Property purchased before marriage

28.32   Property purchased by one of the spouses before the marriage without a view to the marriage will normally belong to that spouse absolutely. It is possible, however, for that spouse subsequently to give the property or a share in it to the other spouse. Again, it is a question of intention.

I   FIXING THE SIZE OF EACH PARTY'S SHARE IN THE DISPUTED PROPERTY

28.33   As stated above at para 28.17, if the applicant succeeds in establishing the presence of a beneficial interest, the next task will be to quantify that share. A declaration of trust as part of the conveyance will normally be determinative of the share in the absence of fraud or mistake. If, however, there is no such declaration, the court will consider all of the available evidence. Contributions to the running of the house can also be considered in the exercise of working out what the parties' shared intention was. Where there is insufficient evidence to arrive at an answer then the court must do its best to provide (or impute) an answer. Where it is forced to do so then the test is that 'each is entitled to that share which the court considers fair having regard to the whole course of dealing between them in relation to the property': Chadwick LJ in *Oxley* v *Hiscock* [2005] Fam 211, para 69, approved of in *Jones* v *Kernott*.

Example (The facts of *Oxley* v *Hiscock*.) When the couple first cohabited Mrs Oxley purchased property in her sole name using, in part, money from Mr Hiscock. That property was sold and proceeds were used to buy another property, this time in Mr Hiscock's sole name. The effective contributions to the purchase price of £126,000 were £36,000 by Mrs Oxley, £60,000 by Mr Hiscock, and the remaining £30,000 raised on a mortgage. There was no declaration setting out the parties' respective beneficial shares and there had been no discussions between them. Both, however, worked on the house for a number of years and contributed to household expenditure. Following their separation Mrs Oxley applied under s 14, Trusts of Land and Appointment of Trustees Act 1996 for a declaration that each party held equal shares in the property. It was held that the parties' conduct was such as to justify the implication of a beneficial interest. After examining all of the circumstances a fair division of the proceeds of sale was 60 per cent to Mr Hiscock and 40 per cent to Mrs Oxley.

J   ORDERS FOR SALE

The court has power to order a sale of the disputed property. Where there is a dispute over who **28.34** is to have possession of a jointly owned chattel, the court can therefore order that the item in question be sold and the proceeds divided between the parties in accordance with their shares. The threat of sale of a cherished item (usually, of course, for considerably less than the parties feel that the garden gnomes or whatever the item is, are worth to them) is usually sufficient to introduce a more rational attitude as to who should have what.

The power is more important in relation to the matrimonial home. Where land is jointly **28.35** owned, the owners of the legal title hold the land as joint tenants and trustees of land: Trusts of Land and Appointment of Trustees Act 1996 ('TOLATA 1996'). Any interested party may make an application to the court under s 14, TOLATA 1996 for an order for sale or other order concerning the land, which may include a declaration of the nature or extent of that party's interest in the land in question.

The court is not bound to order a sale. In deciding what order or orders to make the court is **28.36** required to consider a number of factors, set out in s 15, TOLATA 1996:

(a)   the intentions of the parties who established the trust;
(b)   the purposes for which the property is held;
(c)   the welfare of any minor who occupies the land as his home;
(d)   the interests of any secured creditor of any beneficiaries; and
(e)   the wishes of the owner of the equitable interest in the land.

Whether a sale will be ordered is a question for the court's discretion but basically depends **28.37** on whether the underlying purpose of the trust is continuing: *Re Buchanan-Wollaston's Conveyance* [1939] Ch 738, [1939] 2 All ER 302. The court will therefore look to see why the house was bought. The normal purpose is to provide a home. In cases of this type, where there are no children (or no children living at home), the purpose of the trust will come to an end on the breakdown of the relationship and a sale will therefore normally be ordered. In contrast, where the house is still needed to provide a home for the children, the court is unlikely to order a sale.

K   PROCEDURE

The relevant rules are contained in rr 8.13 to 8.17, Family Procedure Rules 2010. Application **28.38** is to the High Court or county court and should use the Part 18 procedure.

L   PRACTICAL IMPORTANCE OF S 17

Where one of the parties has commenced or contemplates proceedings for divorce, nullity, **28.39** or judicial separation, it is generally a waste of time and money for the court to investigate their strict property rights in an application under s 17. It is preferable to rely on the much wider powers of the court under ss 23, 24, 24B, 25B, and 25C, MCA 1973, which will enable the court to do broad justice between the parties.

28.40   There are, however, cases where the strict property rights of the parties have to be determined under s 17. The following situations are examples:

(a)   Where the parties have only ever been engaged.

(b)   Where the spouses do not want or cannot get a decree of divorce, nullity, or judicial separation.

(c)   Where a claim is made on behalf of a spouse who has remarried without making an application under the MCA 1973 and is therefore debarred.

(d)   Where one spouse is adjudicated bankrupt, his property vests in his trustee in bankruptcy to be administered for the benefit of his creditors. It may be necessary for the other spouse to seek a declaration of the parties' strict property rights under s 17 in order to prevent the trustee in bankruptcy laying claim to property that is legally hers.

(In the case of points (a) and (c), it is important to note the time limit in para 28.04 above.)

29

FINANCIAL ORDERS AVAILABLE

A   INTRODUCTION

29.01 An important task for a solicitor is to assist the parties in settling their financial and property affairs so that the family assets are fairly distributed following the dissolution of the marriage or civil partnership.

29.02 It is rare for the parties to have resolved all such matters satisfactorily before separation. Subsequent negotiations may lead to an agreement to be embodied in a consent order as a record of the settlement—this can be extremely cost effective.

29.03 Where agreement cannot be reached, however, it will be necessary to commence proceedings for a financial remedy, that is, for orders dealing with income, property, and other capital assets and, most importantly today, pensions.

29.04 This chapter explains the types of financial orders which are available in divorce proceedings and their principal characteristics.

29.05 Financial proceedings were referred to as 'ancillary relief', that is, financial relief which is ancillary to the petition for divorce. However, the term has been discarded by the Family Procedure Rules 2010 which substitutes it with the term 'application for a financial order'.

29.06 The position on dissolution of a civil partnership is considered in Chapter 14 and summarized at the end of this chapter.

B   MAINTENANCE PENDING SUIT: S 22, MATRIMONIAL CAUSES ACT 1973

The nature of maintenance pending suit

29.07 An order for periodical payments in favour of a party to a marriage can only become effective once a final decree has been granted in the proceedings, be it proceedings for divorce, nullity, or judicial separation. However, it is quite likely that one or other spouse will be in financial difficulties as a result of the breakdown of the marriage and will not be able to wait for money until after a final decree has been granted. Maintenance pending suit exists therefore to bridge the gap between the commencement of the proceedings and final determination of the proceedings and is essentially a temporary measure. The order will be for the regular payment of a sum of money by one spouse to the other normally at weekly or monthly intervals.

29.08 An order can be made so that the applicant is able to pay legal fees, since these are 'recurring' expenses of an income nature and come within the meaning of 'maintenance': *A v A (Maintenance Pending Suit: Provision for Legal Fees)* [2001] 1 FLR 377 and confirmed in *G v G (Maintenance Pending Suit: Costs)* [2003] 2 FLR 71. Another example of the court awarding a significant sum (£33,000 per annum plus school fees) by way of maintenance pending suit is *M v M (Maintenance Pending Suit)* [2002] 2 FLR 123.

Who can apply?

29.09 Either party to the marriage can apply. It is immaterial whether they are the petitioner or the respondent in the proceedings.

Applications cannot be made by or on behalf of children. This is because they are not necessary—   **29.10**
in contrast to the position in relation to periodical payments for the parties, periodical payments can be granted to or for a child of the family at any time after the petition is filed to become effective immediately, but it is now virtually always the case that financial support for children will be dealt with by a maintenance calculation carried out by the Child Maintenance Enforcement Commission or by a maintenance agreement reached between the parties.

When available

The court can make an order for maintenance pending suit at any time after the petition has   **29.11**
been filed until a final decree has been granted (ie, decree absolute in divorce or nullity proceedings or the one and only decree in the case of judicial separation).

Duration of order

An order for maintenance pending suit can be made for such term as the court thinks reason-   **29.12**
able beginning not earlier than the date of the presentation of the petition and ending with the determination of the suit (ie, the decree of judicial separation or decree absolute of divorce or nullity or, in all cases, the dismissal of the suit). Orders for maintenance pending suit can therefore be backdated from the date on which they are made as far as the date of presentation of the petition if the court thinks fit. Reference should be made to Chapter 30, para 30.139 for the guidelines as to when the court will decide to backdate an order.

Maintenance pending suit distinguished from interim periodical payments

There is often confusion between maintenance pending suit and interim periodical pay-   **29.13**
ments. Whereas the former is ordered to tide a spouse over until such time as the court has power to make a periodical payments order and is only effective up to decree absolute, the latter is essentially a temporary periodical payments order in favour of a spouse made at a time when the court *has* power to order periodical payments but is not yet in a position to make a final decision on the appropriate rate (eg because the respondent's accounts are still in the course of preparation or the court does not have an appointment available for a full hearing). Interim periodical payments are dealt with more fully at paras 29.84 ff.

C   LONG-TERM ORDERS: SS 23, 24, AND 24B, MATRIMONIAL CAUSES ACT 1973

Orders available

The following long-term financial orders are available: **29.14**

(a) financial provision orders (s 23), that is, periodical payments, secured periodical payments, and lump sums (including pension attachment orders under ss 25B and 25C);

(b) property adjustment orders (s 24), that is, transfer of property, settlement of property, and variation of settlement;

(c) pension sharing orders under s 24B.

In whose favour

Parties to the marriage

29.15 As a general rule the court can make any of the orders listed at para 29.14 above in favour of a party to the marriage. However, pension sharing orders are not available in proceedings for a decree of judicial separation (s 24B(1)).

Children of the family

29.16 Subject to certain age limits, the court may also make any of the orders listed at para 29.14 in favour of a child of the family (defined in Chapter 7, para 7.32). This does not necessarily mean that the child will receive money or property directly into his own hands. The court can order the payment of money or transfer of property to someone else for the benefit of the child.

29.17 A detailed account of the impact of the Child Support Act 1991 ('CSA 1991'), as amended, is set out in Chapter 35, but it should be noted at this stage that although the court retains power to make lump sum and property adjustment orders in favour of children of the family, generally speaking, the court no longer has power to make a periodical payments order in favour of such a child (see s 8, CSA 1991). However, there are some exceptions to this, the most important being the power of the court to make a periodical payments order in favour of a child of the family who is not the natural child of the prospective payer. There are some other important exceptions fully set out in Chapter 35.

29.18 The age limits on orders for children are set out in s 29, Matrimonial Causes Act 1973 ('MCA 1973'). The general rule is that no financial provision or transfer of property order shall be made in favour of a child who has attained the age of 18 (s 29(1)). However, by virtue of s 29(3) orders can be made for children who are 18 or over if either:

(a) The child is or will be (or if a financial provision order or transfer of property order were made would be) receiving instruction at an educational establishment or undergoing training for a trade, profession, or vocation whether or not he is also (or will also be) in gainful employment.

Example The parents of a child are divorced. At the age of 18 the child goes to university. A periodical payments order can be made in her favour as she is receiving instruction at an educational establishment.

(b) There are special circumstances justifying the making of an order.

Example Bernard is a child of the family. He is 20 but he suffers from Down's syndrome and he has a mental age of about 6. He lives with his mother, the petitioner. The court can order the respondent to make financial provision for Bernard or to transfer property to him on the basis that there are special circumstances.

Note that there is no age limit on the making of orders requiring a settlement of property to be made for the benefit of a child or varying a settlement for the benefit of a child. Further, there appears to be no upper age limit on the payment of maintenance for the benefit of a child of the family provided that the conditions laid down in s 29(3) are met.

The nature of the orders

Periodical payments (s 23(1)(a) and (d), Matrimonial Causes Act 1973)

An order for periodical payments will be for the payment of a regular sum of money by one **29.19** spouse to the other or to or for a child of the family (where the court retains jurisdiction), normally at weekly or monthly intervals.

Secured periodical payments (s 23(1)(b) and (e), Matrimonial Causes Act 1973)

Having decided that a spouse or a child of the family (where the court retains jurisdiction) is **29.20** entitled to periodical payments, the court may feel that it is necessary to take steps in advance to ensure that he will actually receive the sum ordered and will not be burdened with problems over enforcement. This can be done by means of a secured periodical payments order.

The way in which a secured order operates varies from case to case depending on the exact **29.21** terms of the order and the assets used as security. In some cases, the assets serving as security produce an income which is used to pay the periodical payments ordered. In other cases, assets which do not produce an income are used as security. The idea in cases of the second type is that the spouse against whom the order is made, let us say the husband, makes the periodical payments from his own income in the normal way, but if he defaults the assets stand charged with the amount of the unpaid periodical payments which the wife can therefore be sure of recovering by enforcing her charge.

Example 1 (Income-producing assets.) The court orders the husband to secure to the wife the annual sum of £5,000 upon his entire shareholding in three companies. The income by way of dividends from the shares is used to provide the wife with the annual sum of £5,000. If the husband paid the maintenance from other sources of income, the dividend income would continue to belong to him.

Example 2 (Assets which do not produce income.) The court orders the husband to secure to the wife the annual sum of £5,000 to be charged upon the freehold property Rose Cottage, Lake View, Gullswater (the husband's holiday cottage). As long as the husband pays the wife the annual sum of £5,000, the holiday property will be unaffected. Should he default at any stage, the amount of the arrears will form a charge over the property which the wife can seek to realize by forcing a sale of the property.

While the order for secured periodical payments is in force, the husband cannot dispose of the assets forming the security. Indeed, in a case such as Example 1, he may feel that the court might as well have ordered him to transfer the assets to the wife outright as he may be deprived of all the benefits of owning the property while the order is in force if the entire income is required for the payment of the secured order.

However, secured periodical payments do have the important advantage for the husband that **29.22** once the secured order comes to an end the assets revert to him to do with as he pleases.

In reality, secured periodical payments orders are rarely made, save in cases where there is evi- **29.23** dence of persistent non-payment of maintenance in the past, where the maintenance payer is resident abroad, or has an unreliable source of income.

Lump sums (s 23(1)(c) and (f), Matrimonial Causes Act 1973)

29.24   A lump sum order is, as its name suggests, an order for the payment of a specified sum of money. Payment of the whole sum at once may be required or the payment of the lump sum can be extended over a period of time as the court has the power to provide for payment by way of instalments (s 23(3)(c)), as was demonstrated in *R v R (Lump Sum: Repayments)* [2004] 1 FLR 928 where the husband was ordered to make lump sum payments of £30,000 immediately together with 240 monthly instalments in a sum equivalent to the wife's obligations under a 20-year mortgage. Such an arrangement would survive any remarriage by the wife (because it related to the payment of a capital sum) and would be varied, if necessary, under s 31(2)(d), MCA 1973.

29.25   The court can order that the payment of the instalments be secured to the satisfaction of the court (s 23(3)(c)). Security will be provided in the same way as with secured periodical payments (see para 29.20).

29.26   If the lump sum is not to be paid in full immediately (eg where it is to be paid in instalments or where the payer is given a period of time to raise it), the court can order that the amount deferred or the instalments shall bear interest at a rate specified by the court and for a period specified by the court not commencing earlier than the date of the order (s 23(6)). When obtaining an order for a lump sum payment within a specified time limit, consideration should be given to the inclusion of a clause requiring the payment of interest in the event of default, as provided for by s 23(6). A claim for interest should not be pursued, however, where the value of benefits (maintenance and housing costs) received under the interim provisions of the order exceed the value of interest which would otherwise be payable until the lump sum payment is made: *H v H (Lump Sum: Interest Payable)* [2006] 1 FLR 327.

29.27   It should be noted, however, that a lump sum order (or an order for sale under s 24A, MCA 1973 of assets to produce the lump sum) cannot be made on an interim basis at a time when the application for financial orders has not been set down for a substantive hearing. A better course of action in such circumstances is to apply for an order under s 17, Married Women's Property Act 1882 for a declaration as to ownership of property with an order for sale being available by virtue of s 7(7), Matrimonial Causes (Property and Maintenance) Act 1958; *Wicks v Wicks* [1998] 1 FLR 470 (CA) (see Chapter 27).

29.28   In practice, a lump sum order is a very useful and flexible form of provision. It can, for example, be used to compensate one party for the transfer to the other party of his interest in the matrimonial home, the house contents, savings, investments, or an endowment policy.

29.29   It can also be used to enable one party to meet liabilities or expenses reasonably incurred in maintaining that party or a child of the family: s 23(3), MCA 1973. Although only one lump sum may be ordered, and therefore it is important to ensure that it is for the correct amount, it may be intended that the lump sum is to fulfil a number of different *purposes*. For example, in *Duxbury v Duxbury* [1987] 1 FLR 7, the wife received a large lump sum which was intended, amongst other things, to provide funds for new accommodation and to be invested to provide her with an income. Similarly, in *Hobhouse v Hobhouse* [1999] 1 FLR 961, a multipurpose lump sum order was made.

29.30   Further, where there is evidence that a periodical payments order will be disregarded a lump sum order may be made in order to put an end to the expensive process of enforcement: *Fournier v Fournier* [1998] 2 FLR 990.

Transfer of property (s 24(1)(a), Matrimonial Causes Act 1973)

The court can order one spouse to transfer to the other spouse or to or for the benefit of the   **29.31**
children, any property to which he is entitled either in possession or reversion. Transfer
of property orders are most commonly used in relation to the title to the family home, for
example where the court orders the husband to transfer the house from his sole name into
the wife's name or, where the house is in joint names, to transfer his share in it to the wife.
However, there are all sorts of other property which can also be made the subject of an order,
for example a car, furniture, a holiday cottage, a tenancy, title to a building held by one spouse
as an investment and presently let, shares, and choses in action, for example copyright.

Settlement of property (s 24(1)(b), Matrimonial Causes Act 1973)

The court can order one spouse to settle property to which he is entitled for the benefit of the   **29.32**
other spouse or the children. One example of the use of this power is the making of a *Mesher*-
type of order ordering that the family home be held on a trust of land, the house not to be sold
until the youngest child reaches 17.

The power could also be used, for example, to order one spouse to set up a trust fund out of   **29.33**
capital perhaps to benefit the wife for life or until remarriage and thereafter for the children
or, alternatively, for the wife for life and thereafter to revert to the husband.

Variation of settlement (s 24(1)(c) and (d), Matrimonial Causes Act 1973)

The court can vary for the benefit of the parties or of the children of the family any ante-   **29.34**
nuptial or post-nuptial settlement made on the parties to the marriage (including such
settlement made by will or codicil). Where property is bought in contemplation of marriage
during the parties' engagement and is subsequently used as the family home, it is likely to
be regarded as being subject to an ante-nuptial settlement which will not be affected by an
intervening tenancy: *N v N and F Trust* [2006] 1 FLR 856.

Variation of a post-nuptial settlement can include, for example, varying the terms of a trust to   **29.35**
give the wife 30 per cent of the husband's shares in a company which formed the basis of the
trust: *C v C (Variations of Post-nuptial Settlement: Company Shares)* [2003] 2 FLR 493.

Furthermore, the interest of either spouse in such a settlement can be extinguished or reduced.   **29.36**

Pensions in financial proceedings

Introduction   After the family home, the most valuable asset which a party to a marriage is   **29.37**
likely to have is his or her pension.

The courts have extensive powers to deal with the pension asset in financial proceedings: **29.38**
pension attachment orders were introduced on 1 August 1996 and pension sharing orders on
1 December 2000 (under provisions contained in the Welfare Reform and Pensions Act 1999
('WRPA 1999'), amending the MCA 1973).

29.39   **Section 166, Pensions Act 1995**   Section 166 of the 1995 Act amended the MCA 1973 by the addition of ss 25B, 25C, and 25D. The chief characteristics of ss 25B, 25C, and 25D are as follows:

(a)   *The importance of the pension asset*

Section 25B(1) states that the matters to which the court is to have regard under s 25(2) (discussed fully in Chapter 31) include:

(i)   any benefits under a pension arrangement which a party to the marriage has or is likely to have; and

(ii)   any benefits under a pension arrangement which, by reason of the dissolution or annulment of the marriage, a party to the marriage will lose the chance of acquiring.

Thus the court's duty to give full consideration to pension rights is reinforced.

Further, s 25B(1) goes on to state that, in considering benefits under a pension arrangement, there is no requirement to consider only those benefits which will be available 'in the foreseeable future'. Hence, the court is permitted to take account of such benefits irrespective of the length of time before the pension becomes payable.

(b)   *Pension attachment orders*

When the court is exercising its powers under s 23, MCA 1973 in proceedings for divorce, nullity, or judicial separation, it may order that *once the pension becomes payable* the person responsible for the pension arrangement (ie, the trustees or managers of the fund) pay part of the pension income and/or lump sum available under the pension to the other party to the marriage in question: s 25B(4), MCA 1973. This means that one party may benefit from the other's pension long after the marriage is dissolved.

This arrangement is known as a 'pension attachment order' and is a method of securing periodical payments and/or lump sum orders against a pension—it is not a separate form of financial provision but payment of the benefits is deferred until the pension becomes payable.

It should be noted that, unlike the position with 'normal' periodical payments, payments of income derived from the pension are taxable in the hands of the recipient: s 347A(2), Income and Corporation Taxes Act 1988.

Many occupational pension schemes in particular provide for benefits to be paid if an employee dies prematurely before retirement. These benefits are called 'death in service benefits' and may also be attached: s 25C(1), MCA 1973, thus providing some financial security for the surviving former spouse. It should be noted, however, that children may not specifically benefit from this type of order.

Further, the court may require the person with pension rights to nominate the other party to the marriage as the person to whom death-in-service benefits should be paid: s 25C(2)(b), MCA 1973 (but see *T* v *T* [1998] 1 FLR 1072 below).

It is important to understand that MCA 1973 contains no guidance as to the circumstances in which an attachment order would be appropriate or as to the amount of the pension income, lump sum, or death-in-service benefits to be attached: this is entirely a matter for the court's discretion. The only restriction is that the amount to be attached must be expressed as a percentage of the payment due to the person with pension rights: s 25B(5). This requirement also applies where the pension is already in payment.

Case law developments on pension attachment orders The first reported case on pen-   **29.40**
sion attachment orders was *T* v *T* [1998] 1 FLR 1072. The judgment of Singer J in the Family
Division of the High Court was important because it clarified a number of points, as follows:

(a) The MCA 1973 does not compel the court to compensate for pension loss. The court's
     obligations are limited to considering whether orders for periodical payments, secured
     provision, or lump sum are appropriate and then to examine how pension considera-
     tions should affect the terms of the orders to be made.
(b) The pension attachment order (whether in respect of pension income or lump sum or
     both) may be varied by a subsequent court order: s 31(2)(dd), MCA 1973.
(c) The order attaching the pension income will cease to have effect on the death or remarriage
     of the recipient. (It would appear that the lump sum order may remain payable, despite the
     remarriage of the recipient, but it would be open to the pension holder to seek to have this
     aspect of the order varied under s 31(2)(dd) on the grounds of a change in circumstances
     (namely the remarriage of the recipient) since the order was originally made.)

In *T* v *T*, Singer J refused to make attachment orders in respect of the husband's pensions on   **29.41**
the grounds, first, that the former wife was receiving a substantial lump sum at the time of
the financial proceedings and, secondly, she was to receive significant periodical payments
which could be varied in due course.

The judge recognized, however, that the former wife would be prejudiced in the event of the   **29.42**
husband's premature death before retirement because the periodical payments would terminate. He accepted that the death-in-service benefits may not form part of the husband's estate
and therefore would not be susceptible to an application by the wife for support under the
Inheritance (Provision for Family and Dependants) Act 1975. He also acknowledged that to
require the husband to nominate his former wife as the beneficiary of death-in-service benefits
might not be effective since the trustees had a discretion to disregard the nomination.

The judge, therefore, protected the income position of the former wife by making an attach-   **29.43**
ment order in respect of death-in-service benefits by requiring the trustees of the pension
fund to pay to the wife a lump sum equal to ten times the annual maintenance in the event
of the husband's premature death.

By contrast, in *Burrow* v *Burrow* [1999] 1 FLR 508, Cazalet J upheld the attachment order relat-   **29.44**
ing to the lump sum to be derived from the pension arrangement while setting aside a similar
order made by the district judge in respect of the pension income.

The judge considered that the lump sum order recognized past contributions made by the   **29.45**
parties by ensuring an equal division of the capital assets. He held that the attachment order
in respect of the pension income was unnecessary because the wife was to retain her entitlement to periodical payments in any event. Accordingly, once the pension became payable
and the needs of the parties were known, the periodical payments order could then be varied,
if required.

In this case, the judge went on to state that there was no need to provide for the attachment of   **29.46**
death-in-service benefits because the wife retained an insurance scheme to protect her and, in
addition, her potential claim against the husband's estate had also been preserved.

29.47 The drafting of pension attachment orders is complex and care needs to be taken to ensure that the recipient is as fully protected as possible. This is discussed fully in Chapter 30.

29.48 **The problems with pension attachment orders** Pension attachment orders involve a number of practical difficulties, including, in particular:

(a) The arrangements undermine the principle of once-and-for-all settlements embodied in clean break orders (because of the continuing commitment to make provision once the pension becomes payable).

(b) Attachment is necessarily a speculative exercise since it will usually be impossible to predict either the respective needs of the parties at the time the pension becomes payable, or the value of the asset to be divided, these difficulties being highlighted by Cazalet J in *Burrow* v *Burrow* (1999) discussed at para 29.44.

(c) Where the attachment order relates to a private or money purchase pension scheme (where, eg, a self-employed individual is contributing to a scheme to provide a pension in retirement) the court has few, if any, powers to ensure that the individual continues to contribute to the scheme or retires by a specified age.

In practice, pension attachment orders have proved to be unpopular and will probably only be considered where the pension fund is of little value at the time of the financial proceedings but is expected to increase significantly in value by the date of retirement.

29.49 **The solution: pension sharing orders** A better solution to deal with the pension asset, is to enable the court to make an order sharing the pension asset *at the time* of the financial proceedings. Such arrangements are now contained in the WRPA 1999, which came into force on 1 December 2000.

29.50 Section 19, WRPA 1999 states that sch 3 amends the MCA 1973 to enable the court to make pension sharing orders. Further, sch 4, WRPA 1999 amends the MCA 1973 in respect of attachment orders.

29.51 The definition of a pension sharing order is found in s 21A(1), MCA 1973 which provides as follows:

(1) A pension sharing order is an order which:
  (a) provides that one party's
    (i)   shareable rights under a specified pension arrangement, or
    (ii) shareable state scheme rights
    be subject to pension sharing for the benefit of the other party, and
  (b) specifies the percentage value to be transferred.

29.52 The principal features of the pension sharing order (s 24B, MCA 1973):

(a) The order is not available retrospectively and is therefore only available where the petition for divorce or nullity is filed at court on or after 1 December 2000.

(b) The order may not be made in proceedings for a decree of judicial separation: s 24B(1).

(c) The order will not take effect before the grant of the decree absolute: s 24B(2).

(d) The order may be varied but only *before* the decree absolute has been granted: s 31(2)(g). The order will not then take effect until the application to vary has been dealt with.

(e) While pension sharing orders will be available in respect of occupational, personal, and state earnings related pension schemes (all of which are 'pension arrangements' under s 46(1), WRPA 1999), the basic state pension scheme may not be the subject of an order.

    A pension sharing order may not be made in respect of a pension already subject to a pension sharing order in relation to the marriage in question (ie, it is not possible for a pension sharing order to be made on two occasions to benefit the same party to the marriage); nor may a pension sharing order be made in any event where the pension is already subject to an attachment order: s 24B(4) and (5), MCA 1973. To do otherwise would prejudice the party who is to benefit from the attachment order.

(f) It is not possible for a party to a marriage to have both a pension sharing order and attachment order in respect of the *same* pension. Hence, where a party to a marriage obtains a pension sharing order, there can be no attachment of death-in-service benefits in respect of the same pension under s 25C (as happened in *T* v *T*, discussed at paras 29.39–29.41). This fact may make it more sensible to seek a pension attachment order in certain circumstances, for example where the dependent former spouse is caring for young children and death-in-service benefits would help to compensate for the loss of periodical payments on the premature death of the paying former spouse.

(g) The question of whether to seek a pension sharing order is complex, and the involvement of an independent financial adviser will be crucial to determine the best solution in the circumstances. Such an adviser must have a suitable qualification in order to conduct pension transfer business. A suitable adviser may be found by contacting the Personal Finance Society, 20 Aldermanbury, London EC2V 7HY (tel: 020 7417 4471).

The pension sharing order in practice This book cannot discuss in detail the complexities   **29.53** of pension sharing in practice and practitioners are referred to specialist texts such as *Pension Sharing in Practice* by David Salter (Family Law). However, set out below is an introduction to the mechanics of the pension sharing order.

When the court decides to make a pension sharing order, the transferor's pension scheme   **29.54** will be debited with a specified amount and the transferee will be entitled to a credit of that amount. In essence, the transferor loses a percentage of his or her pension fund which is reduced in value and the transferee acquires a pension fund of his or her own.

As with any other form of financial remedy, no obligation is placed on the court to make a   **29.55** pension sharing order nor is there any guidance in the MCA 1973, as amended, as to the circumstances in which the order will be made nor as to the percentage of the fund to be debited. These are matters for judicial discretion, bearing in mind the factors to be considered in s 25, MCA 1973 which are discussed fully in Chapter 31.

The percentage of the fund to be debited is a percentage of the cash equivalent of the trans-   **29.56** feror's relevant benefits on the valuation date. The 'valuation date' is to be specified by the court, but the date must not be earlier than one year before the date of the petition or later than the date on which the court is exercising its power: reg 3(1)(a) and (b), Pensions on Divorce (Provision of Information) Regulations 2000 (SI 2000/1048).

When a pension sharing order is made the person responsible for pension arrangements (ie,   **29.57** the trustees or managers of the scheme) are given a period in which to transfer the specified percentage of the fund. This is known as 'the implementation period' and is four months beginning on the date on which the order takes effect or on the day on which the trustee receives the order and prescribed information, whichever is the later. The prescribed information is contained in reg 5, Pensions on Divorce (Provision of Information) Regulations 2000. The information includes names and addresses of the parties concerned, dates of birth, National Insurance numbers, etc; all relevant information to enable the person responsible to carry out the necessary transfer.

29.58 **The transferee receives a pension credit** The transferee cannot receive 'cash in hand' to spend as he or she pleases. The intention behind the legislation is to provide the transferee with some degree of security in old age.

29.59 Schedule 5, WRPA 1999 explains what may happen to the transferred fund. Essentially, where the pension arrangement is a *funded* occupational pension scheme or a personal pension scheme, the trustee for the scheme is required to offer to transfer the fund to a scheme of the transferee's choice. This scheme could be the one of which the transferee is already a member so that the effect of the transfer will be to boost the value of his or her fund. Alternatively, the transferee could become a member of the original scheme so that an internal transfer takes place. If the transferee fails to make a choice within a specified period, the trustee will decide on the destination of the pension credit.

29.60 Where the pension arrangement is unfunded (ie, where the present contributors to the scheme are in effect paying the pensions of those retired from the scheme) and is a public service pension scheme, external transfer is not permitted for obvious reasons. However, where the scheme in question has been closed to new members, the transferee will be offered membership of an alternative public service scheme.

29.61 Where the pension arrangement is unfunded but is not a public service scheme, the person responsible for the administration of the scheme has an absolute right to insist on an internal transfer: external transfer is available in limited circumstances laid down in the Pensions Sharing (Implementation and Discharge) Regulations 2000.

29.62 Where the pension sharing order relates to the state earnings related pension scheme, the position is governed by s 49(1), WRPA 1999. Put simply, the transferor's entitlement is reduced by the amount of the debit and the transferee becomes entitled to an additional pension because of the pension credit which has been transferred to him or her.

29.63 **The statutory charge and pension orders** Where either an attachment order or pension sharing order is made, a lump sum may in effect be transferred from one party to the marriage to the other. The question then arises as to whether the statutory charge may attach to the lump sum. The basic position is as follows. An attachment order in respect of pension income will be exempt since it is regarded as a form of maintenance. However, an attachment order in respect of a lump sum is not exempt from the statutory charge which will apply assuming that the other conditions are fulfilled (eg that the assisted person has 'recovered' or 'preserved' the asset). However, interest will not accrue from the date of the order because the charge has not been postponed. The charge and interest will apply only once the lump sum has been received. Because the Legal Services Commission has nothing on which to secure the charge in the meantime, it is difficult for it to protect its position and therefore the Commission will look to satisfy the charge from other assets which may have been recovered or preserved. If the other assets are inadequate to meet the charge, notice in writing of the Commission's interest in the lump sum must be given to the person responsible for the pension arrangement.

By contrast, guidance issued by the Legal Services Commission makes it clear that a lump sum **29.64** received by way of a pension sharing order is exempt from the statutory charge.

Offsetting   The amendments to MCA 1973, set out above, demonstrate the extensive powers **29.65** now available to the court in dealing with the pension asset.

Do not fall into the trap, however, of believing that in every case where there is a pension asset **29.66** in financial proceedings a pension order will be made. Often, the client with valuable pension rights will be anxious to preserve those rights intact and, where this is the case, will offer to the other party to the marriage other capital assets (eg the family home and/or other investments and savings) to compensate for the loss of a share of the pension—this is called an 'offsetting order' and is very common in practice. Care should be taken with orders of this type, however. Where offsetting is planned, it must be remembered that the pension asset is very different from other capital assets in that the party with pension rights has little control over the final value of the pension fund or how it is invested to provide him or her with a lump sum or income in retirement (usually a significant part of the fund must be used to purchase an annuity).

Further, even with a final salary pension scheme (where benefits depend on length of service **29.67** and the individual's salary at retirement) the pension fund may suffer a shortfall and be unable to produce the anticipated benefits. It is essential therefore to try, as far as possible, to ascertain the viability of the client's pension provision before embarking on an offsetting arrangement and to ensure that the pension asset is not valued unrealistically.

When are the orders for financial provision available?

In favour of a spouse

The basic rules   All the orders set out in para 29.14 above can be made in favour of a spouse **29.68** on granting a decree nisi of divorce or nullity or a decree of judicial separation (except that an order under s 24B, MCA 1973 cannot be made in proceedings for a decree of judicial separation) or at any time thereafter (ss 23(1) and 24(1)). Note that the fact that orders can be made at any time after granting a decree means that there are no time limits on the making of an application for a financial order. Therefore a spouse could, at least in theory, make an application for a financial order out of the blue ten years after the divorce or could suddenly decide to pursue an application made in the initial stages of the divorce which has remained dormant for years. This is confirmed in *Twiname* v *Twiname* [1992] 1 FLR 29 (CA). In practice there are a number of reasons why this is unlikely to be profitable and may indeed be impossible:

(a) Rule 9.4, Family Procedure Rules 2010 ('FPR 2010') dictates that the petitioner's application for financial relief is to be made in her petition. If an application is not made as required by this rule, permission of the court will be needed before it can be made and the passage of time between the beginning of the matrimonial proceedings and the application for permission may increasingly influence the court against granting permission.

(b) If the court first comes to consider an application for a financial remedy an unusually long time after the parties have been granted a decree, it will be influenced adversely by the lapse of time in exercising its discretion as to what orders to make. The court will certainly want to know how the applicant has supported him or herself in the meantime and what has prompted the application at this time.

(c) Repeat applications for a financial remedy are not possible (see below).

Financial orders made on or after granting a decree nisi of divorce or nullity cannot take effect until the decree is made final (ss 23(5) and 24(3)). The gap between the commencement of the matrimonial proceedings and the decree nisi is filled by maintenance pending suit (see para 29.07 above). Under r 9.8, FPR 2010 a spouse may apply for periodical payments at the same rate as an order for maintenance pending suit provided that a decree nisi has been made and that at or after the date of the decree nisi an order for maintenance pending suit is in force. Orders made on or after granting a decree of judicial separation can become effective immediately.

29.69 **Repeat applications** Once the court has dealt with an application for a financial remedy on its merits (ie, by making an order of the type sought or by dismissing the application), it usually has no future jurisdiction to entertain applications by that spouse for the same type of financial relief. The most that the court can do is to vary or discharge the original order (if it is an order which is capable of variation—see, eg, *Minton v Minton* [1979] AC 591) but in doing so the court may now commute a periodical payments order by a single lump sum payment, a property adjustment order, and/or a pension sharing order: s 31(7A) MCA 1973 and discussed more fully in Chapter 31.

Example 1 The petitioner makes a comprehensive application for financial provision in her petition. After the divorce the court orders that the family home should be transferred to her absolutely and that all her other claims to financial provision should be dismissed. The petitioner cannot come back to the court in two years' time when she has lost her job and is short of money asking for periodical payments or, indeed, for any other form of financial provision against the respondent. The court dealt with her application for all forms of financial provision on its merits after the divorce; she cannot revive the claims that were then dismissed and the one order that she was granted, being a transfer of property order, is not variable.

Example 2 The petitioner makes a comprehensive application for financial provision in her petition. After the divorce the court orders that the respondent should make periodical payments at the rate of £100 per week for the petitioner. As the respondent has no capital assets whatsoever the petitioner's other claims for a financial order are dismissed. A year after the order the respondent has a substantial win on the lottery and the petitioner wishes to claim a share. She cannot do so as her claims for a lump sum and for property adjustment orders have been dismissed. The best she can do is to seek a variation of the periodical payments order under s 31, MCA 1973 and invite the court, if appropriate, to terminate the periodical payments order and replace it with a lump sum, property adjustment order, and/or pension sharing order, if appropriate.

The fact that the court's original order was made by consent does not affect the principles governing repeat applications (see, eg, *Minton v Minton* above).

29.70 There are two ways round the rule about repeat applications:

(a) If it appears that one spouse may come into a worthwhile sum of money (as yet of an uncertain amount) in the not-too-distant future, instead of the court pressing on to deal with the other spouse's application for a financial order immediately after the divorce, it would be possible (at her suggestion) for the court to adjourn some or all of her financial order applications to be heard at a later date when the position is clearer. In the case of *M T v M T (Financial Provision: Lump Sum)* [1992] 1 FLR 362, the court considered the line of cases dealing with the adjournment of financial remedy cases. It was held that on an application for a lump sum order in circumstances where there was a real possibility of capital from a specific source becoming available in the near future, and where an order for an adjournment was the only means whereby justice could be done to the parties, there was a discretionary jurisdiction to order an adjournment of the application. On the unusual facts of *M T* v *M T* (above) the wife's lump sum application was adjourned until the death of her then 83-year-old father-in-law since at that time the husband would have real prospects of inheriting substantial wealth and otherwise the wife would be permanently without capital to buy even a modest property.

In *D* v *D (Lump Sum Order: Adjournment of Application)* [2001] 1 FLR 633, for example, the wife's application for a lump sum order to invest in a pension fund was adjourned until assets could be disposed of to produce the necessary capital. It is likely, however, that the court will only adjourn the financial proceedings for a limited period—in *Roberts* v *Roberts* [1986] 1 WLR 1437, Wood J indicated that the longest period a court should adjourn an application should be four to five years.

(b) Where one spouse, say the petitioner, seeks periodical payments against the other but a periodical payments order is not appropriate in light of the parties' financial circumstances at the date of the hearing, instead of permanently debarring the petitioner from seeking periodical payments against the respondent by dismissing her claim, the court can preserve her entitlement to periodical payments in the future by making a nominal order for periodical payments against the respondent. This is an order for the payment of a nominal sum (say £1 per annum) to the petitioner by way of periodical payments which the petitioner can seek to have varied under s 31 to a worthwhile sum should circumstances change in the future.

Example When the petitioner's application for periodical payments is considered the respondent is out of work through no fault of his own. The petitioner is tied to the house with young children and cannot work. If the respondent were working, a periodical payments order would clearly be appropriate. The court can make an order for nominal periodical payments to the petitioner which she can seek to have increased when the respondent gets a job. It could also require him to undertake to the court to inform the wife (perhaps through her solicitors) when he does return to work.

Nominal orders used to be made almost as a matter of course not only where the respondent was presently unable to make periodical payments because of his financial circumstances but also where the petitioner was not at the time in need of periodical payments because of her circumstances, for example where she was working.

Further, where an attachment order is made in respect of pension income, it must be supported by a periodical payments order under s 23, MCA 1973 even if the sum involved is nominal. It should be recognized, however, that in recent years courts have come to think more in terms of a clean break order between the parties where the parties can work. This approach is reinforced by the provisions of s 25A, MCA 1973 (see Chapter 31). A clean break order is one where the parties' claims against each other are dealt with on a once-and-for-all basis, in such a way that neither is allowed to return to the court in the future in an attempt to vary or revive an earlier claim. The terms of s 25A are that it is the duty of the court to consider whether it would be appropriate to make a clean break. In other words, the court must consider whether to make a clean break although there is no presumption in favour of one. So, there is more likely to be a clean break for a young childless wife than an older wife with children where her prospects of becoming financially self-sufficient are much less.

In favour of a child of the family

29.71 (a) *Financial provision orders* These can be made in favour of a child of the family in certain circumstances at any stage after the commencement of the proceedings (s 23(1) coupled with s 23(2)(a)). Section 23(4) expressly provides that the power to make financial provision orders for a child can be exercised from time to time. Unlike the position with regard to spouses, therefore, an application for financial provision for a child can never be finally dismissed and repeat applications for financial provision orders can be made provided that the child concerned is still within the age limits for the order sought (see para 29.18 above).

Even if the petition is dismissed, provided that this happens after the beginning of the trial, the court can make financial provision orders in relation to a child of the family on dismissing the petition or within a reasonable period after dismissal (s 23(2)(b)). This is not possible in the case of an application for an order in favour of a spouse.

(b) *Property adjustment orders* These can be made for the benefit of a child of the family on granting a decree nisi of divorce or nullity or a decree of judicial separation or at any time thereafter. As there is no express power to make such orders from time to time, it would appear that the child is in the same position as a spouse in relation to repeat applications—once the child's application has been dealt with on its merits no further application for an order of the same type can be made.

Orders made on or after a decree of judicial separation become effective immediately. Orders made on or after granting a decree nisi of nullity or divorce do not take effect until the decree is made absolute (s 24(3)).

Who can make the application

Parties to the marriage

29.72 Either party to the marriage can apply for any of the orders listed in para 29.14 above on behalf of himself or herself or on behalf of a child of the family.

Children of the family

29.73 Where he has been given permission to intervene in the cause for the purpose of applying for financial provision, the child himself can apply for any of the orders listed in para 29.14 (r 9.10, FPR 2010).

Others on behalf of a child

29.74 Apart from the parties to the marriage and the child himself, there are various other people empowered by r 9.10, FPR 2010 to apply for financial orders in respect of a child of the family, for example the child's guardian or any person in whose favour a residence order has been made with respect to a child of the family.

Duration of periodical payments and secured periodical payments order (ss 28 and 29, Matrimonial Causes Act 1973)

In favour of a spouse

Subject to s 25A(2) (duty of court to consider making order for fixed term only, see below **29.75** in this paragraph and also Chapter 31, paras 31.24 ff), an order for periodical payments or secured periodical payments for a spouse can last for whatever period the court thinks fit with these limitations:

(a) Commencement of the term: the term shall not begin earlier than the date of the making of an application for the order (s 28(1)(a)). This provision enables the court, if it sees fit, to backdate its order for periodical payments or secured periodical payments to the date of the making of the application (see Chapter 30, para 30.139 for guidelines in relation to backdating of orders). A petitioner's application will normally have been made in her petition and the court therefore has the power to backdate an order in her favour to the date of the presentation of the petition.

   If the respondent files an answer he will normally make his claim for periodical payments in his answer. The FPR 2010 do not lay down rules as to when a respondent who does not file an answer should make his application for financial orders (see Chapter 30, paras 30.38 ff). His application will be made at whatever stage in the proceedings his solicitor sees fit by filing a notice of application in Form A and an order for periodical payments or secured periodical payments can be backdated to the date on which this notice was filed.

(b) End of the term: the court cannot make an order for a term defined so as to extend beyond:
   (i) The remarriage of the party in whose favour the order is made (this provision applies only, of course, to cases of divorce and nullity as remarriage is clearly out of the question in a case of judicial separation). Note that remarriage of the paying spouse will not have any direct effect on the periodical payments or secured periodical payments order. However, where the paying spouse remarries this may constitute a change in his circumstances that would justify his making an application for a reduction in the rate of the order (see Chapter 34 with regard to variation). *Or*
   (ii) In the case of an unsecured periodical payments order, the death of either of the parties to the marriage, or, in the case of a secured periodical payments order, the death of the spouse in whose favour the order is made. (Note that in contrast to a straightforward order for periodical payments, a secured order can continue beyond the death of the paying spouse.)

Subject to these limitations the court can leave the periodical payments order open-ended if it thinks fit. On the other hand, the court can make the order for a limited period. The court has always been able to do this but s 25A, MCA 1973 draws particular attention to this power by directing the court, when exercising its power to make periodical payments orders in favour of a spouse, to consider whether it would be appropriate to make the order only for a limited period such as would be sufficient to enable the payee to adjust to being self-supporting.

Where the court makes such an order in favour of a party to the marriage, it may direct that **29.76** that party shall not be entitled to apply under s 31 for the order to be varied by extending the term (s 28(1A)).

Example 1 ('Open-ended' order.) 'It is ordered that the respondent do make periodical payments to the petitioner for herself during their joint lives until she shall remarry or until further order at the rate of £x per week payable weekly in advance.'

Example 2 ('Fixed term' order.) 'It is ordered that the respondent do make periodical payments to the petitioner for herself at the rate of £x per month payable monthly in advance for a period of one year from the date of this order or during their joint lives or until the petitioner shall remarry or until further order whichever period shall be the shortest. And it is directed that the petitioner's right to make any further application in relation to the marriage of the petitioner and the respondent for an order under s. 23(1)(a) and (b) of the MCA 1973, shall stand dismissed.'

The case of *Richardson* v *Richardson* [1993] 4 All ER 673 is a warning to all practitioners to ensure that where the periodical payments order is intended to be of limited duration, the order contains a clause expressly prohibiting the payee from seeking to extend the term. Failure to include such a clause will mean that the court retains jurisdiction to vary the order, although it may impose a time limit on the extended order: *Richardson* v *Richardson (No 2)* [1996] 2 FLR 617 (CA).

29.77   In practice, however, recent case law suggests that the court will be unlikely to extend an order where the payer has a legitimate expectation that his obligation to make periodical payments will end by a specified date unless the circumstances are exceptional: *Fleming* v *Fleming* [2004] 1 FLR 667.

Special provisions with regard to children

29.78   Section 29(2) provides that the term specified in a periodical payments or secured periodical payments order in favour of a child (in cases where the court retains jurisdiction despite the CSA 1991) may begin with the date of the making of the application or at any later date (so backdating is possible), but:

(a)   shall not extend, in the first instance, beyond the child's next birthday after he attains school-leaving age unless the court considers that in the circumstances of the case the welfare of the child requires that it should extend to a later date. As the present school-leaving age is 16 this means that when first granted most periodical payments orders will be expressed to be 'until the said child shall attain the age of 17 years or further order'. If it is clear that the child will not be leaving education at the first possible opportunity, for example where it is certain that the children will be staying on at school to do A levels, the court should be asked specifically to grant the order to last until the child is 18 instead; *and*

(b)   shall not in any event extend beyond the date of the child's eighteenth birthday unless s 29(3) applies. Reference should be made to para 29.18 above for the full provisions of s 29(3). Basically, it enables the court to make orders in favour of children who are over 18 if they are being educated or there are special circumstances.

29.79   The death of the paying spouse will bring a periodical payments order in favour of a child to an end unless it is secured (s 29(4)). Remarriage of either spouse will not affect orders in favour of a child.

D   ORDERS FOR SALE: S 24A, MATRIMONIAL CAUSES ACT 1973

The power to order sale

Where the court makes (a) a secured periodical payments order, (b) a lump sum order, or (c) a   **29.80** property adjustment order, on making the order or at any time thereafter the court may make a further order for the sale of property in which or in the proceeds of sale of which either or both of the parties to the marriage has or have a beneficial interest either in possession or reversion.

Consequential and supplementary provisions

The sale order may contain whatever consequential or supplementary provisions the court   **29.81** thinks fit (s 24A(2)). Two forms of consequential or supplementary provision are specially mentioned in the subsection:

(a)   a requirement that a payment be made out of the proceeds of sale (s 24A(2)(a)); *and*

(b)   a requirement that the property be offered for sale to a particular person or class of persons specified in the order (s 24A(2)(b)).

Directions as to the conduct of the sale (eg as to whose solicitor should be in charge of the conveyancing and how the sale price is to be fixed) can be given under the s 24A(2) power and will usually be necessary.

When effective

(a)   Not before decree absolute: if an order for sale is made before decree absolute, it will not   **29.82** become effective until after the decree is made absolute (s 24A(3)).

(b)   Suspended orders: the court can specifically direct that the order (or a particular provision of it) shall not take effect until a particular event has occurred or a specified period has elapsed.

Examples

(a)   Order for sale enabling capital provision to be made: the order for sale may be made at the   **29.83** same time as the secured periodical payments, lump sum, or property adjustment order, timed to take effect before it as an enabling measure.

   Example 1 The court orders that the matrimonial home which is in the respondent's name be sold (the s 24A(1) order) and a sum equal to half the net proceeds of sale be paid by the respondent to the petitioner (a lump sum order).

(b)   Order for sale as an enforcement measure: alternatively the spouse in whose favour a secured periodical payments, lump sum, or property adjustment order has been made already may need to return to court for an order for sale as a means of enforcement if the original order has not been complied with.

Example 2 The court orders the respondent to pay to the petitioner a lump sum of £10,000 within three months of the date of the order. The respondent fails to comply within the three-month period. The petitioner applies for an order for sale of certain of the respondent's assets and payment of £10,000 from the proceeds to her.

(c) Not available as a means of varying a property adjustment order: the power to order a sale cannot, however, be used to vary a property adjustment order (*Norman* v *Norman* [1983] 1 All ER 486).

Example 3 (The facts of *Norman* v *Norman*.) In 1979 in financial proceedings after a divorce, the registrar (now district judge) made a property adjustment order under s 24(1)(b) settling the matrimonial home on trust for sale (now on a trust of land) on the husband and wife equally, the sale to be postponed until the youngest child ceased to receive full-time education or training, whereupon the property would be sold and the proceeds divided equally between the husband and wife. In 1982, when one child still remained in full-time education, the husband applied for an order for immediate sale of the house so that he could buy himself a mobile home. The court held that there was no jurisdiction under s 24A(1) to grant the order for sale which would in effect vary the original property adjustment order by substituting an earlier sale date.

E   INTERIM ORDERS

29.84   Pending the final determination of an application for a financial order and subject to r 9.7, FPR 2010 (which lays down the procedure to be followed and is described in Chapter 30), the district judge has power to make an interim order upon such terms as he thinks just.

29.85   By far the most common form of interim order is an interim periodical payments order:

(a) Interim periodical payments for children: in virtually all cases the court will not have jurisdiction to make such an order (s 8, CSA 1991).

(b) Interim periodical payments for a spouse: interim periodical payments for a spouse can be ordered in divorce and nullity cases at any time on or after granting decree nisi to become effective after decree absolute (in judicial separation, interim periodical payments can be ordered and become effective as soon as the single decree is granted). An interim order should be sought when financial matters cannot be finally resolved until some time after decree absolute. The gap between commencement of the proceedings and decree of judicial separation/decree absolute can be filled by maintenance pending suit.

Occasionally, however, an interim lump sum order will be made as happened in *Askew-Page* v *Page* [2001] Fam Law 794 to meet expenses and liabilities incurred by a mother on behalf of her children.

F FINANCIAL PROVISION AND CIVIL PARTNERSHIP

Where a civil partnership is dissolved or annulled, or a separation order is made, either party **29.86** may apply to the court for orders for financial provision: Chapters 3 and 4 and schs 5, 6, and 7, Civil Partnership Act 2004 ('CPA 2004').

Section 72(1), CPA 2004 states that sch 5 'corresponds to provision made for financial relief in **29.87** connection with marriages by Part 2 of the Matrimonial Causes Act 1973'.

In practice, the court may therefore make any of the orders discussed in this chapter except **29.88** a pension attachment order. Where, however, one partner's pension scheme provides for the payment of a lump sum in the event of that partner's death, the court may direct the person responsible for the pension arrangement to pay the whole or part of that sum, when it becomes due, to the other civil partner: sch 5, Part 4, para 26, CPA 2004.

As with financial proceedings in relation to spouses, the orders do not take effect until the **29.89** dissolution or nullity order has been made final or the separation order granted.

Further pension sharing orders are not available in proceedings for a separation order, mirror- **29.90** ing the position for spouses.

G CHAPTER SUMMARY

1. Part II, MCA 1973 provides a regime for dealing with financial and property matters in **29.91** proceedings for a decree of divorce, nullity, or judicial separation.

2. Unsecured or secured periodical payments orders are designed to provide a regular income for a spouse or child of the family (where the Child Support Agency has no jurisdiction).

3. A lump sum order can be made to distribute capital assets such as savings and the like. Its other important use is in an offsetting arrangement where one party to the marriage 'buys out' the interest of the other in the family home or pension asset by making a lump sum payment.

4. Property adjustment orders are available to deal with the future of the family home and other real or personal property owned by the parties.

5. Pension assets may be redistributed through pension sharing or attachment orders.

6. The above orders do not take effect in relation to spouses until a decree of judicial separation or a decree absolute of divorce or nullity has been granted.

7. Virtually the same orders are available to civil partners with similar principles applying as to when the orders may be applied for and take effect.

30

PROCEDURE FOR AN APPLICATION FOR A FINANCIAL REMEDY

A INTRODUCTION

The procedure for making application to court for a financial order is contained in the Family **30.01** Procedure Rules 2010 ('FPR 2010').

This chapter explains the procedure for making the application and the pre-action protocol **30.02** to be observed. It emphasizes the need for the exchange of information about each spouse's financial circumstances to be on a full and frank basis and explains the procedure where such disclosure is not forthcoming.

Many parties resolve the distribution of the assets by negotiation and agreement with **30.03** the settlement embodied in a consent order. The procedure for this arrangement is discussed.

Responsibility for drafting a consent order lies with the solicitor. Considerable care is needed **30.04** if pitfalls are to be avoided. Guidance on drafting such orders is included in the chapter. Appeals and methods of challenging orders are discussed below at para 30.120.

The procedure for making claims for financial provision for civil partners is briefly explained. **30.05** At the end of the chapter you will find a flowchart to guide you through the complex procedure.

B THE COST OF THE APPLICATION

Public funding

The solicitor will no doubt have assessed whether his client is eligible for Legal Help when first **30.06** consulted by his client in relation to the divorce. He can give preliminary advice on ancillary matters under the scheme. However, it will be necessary for him to make an application on his client's behalf for a certificate to cover financial proceedings (see Chapter 2, especially on the reference to mediation). Funding to take the application to court, assuming that mediation is unsuccessful, will be by a certificate for General Family Help in the first instance. Such a certificate extends to all steps up to and including the financial dispute resolution hearing, and any interim financial application dealt with before or at that hearing.

30.07   The solicitor should also remind the client of the potential impact of the Legal Services Commission's statutory charge when making the application.

Private cases

30.08   If the client is not eligible for public funding, the solicitor is required to give him some estimate of the potential cost of the financial proceedings, or, if this is not possible, he should at least warn the client that they may be very expensive. He should consider whether he needs to take a payment on account to cover the cost of preliminary work and disbursements. Whether he insists on this will depend on the normal practice of the firm and his knowledge of the individual client. Certainly, the client would be expected to provide money for the payment of disbursements as the case progresses (see Chapter 1).

C   PROTECTING THE APPLICANT PENDING THE MAKING OF AN ORDER

30.09   One of the first matters that the solicitor should consider is whether the client's interests are adequately protected pending the making of a financial order. Could the other spouse sell the matrimonial home over his client's head, for instance? Will his client's assets pass by will or on intestacy to the respondent if she dies before everything is resolved? Where the solicitor does not feel his client's interests are sufficiently secure, he should consider steps such as severing the joint tenancy or registering a charge or notice under the Family Law Act 1996 or a pending land action. Reference should be made to Chapter 22 where these matters are dealt with more fully.

D   THE PROCEDURE FOR A FINANCIAL REMEDY

Introduction

30.10   The rules governing financial relief procedure are contained in Part 9, FPR 2010.

30.11   Practice Direction 9A offers guidance on the practical application of the Rules and contains a pre-action protocol outlining the steps that the parties should take to seek and provide information from and to each other prior to the commencement of the proceedings. Compliance with the Protocol is expected and non-compliance may be reflected in costs penalties.

30.12   The aim of the Protocol is 'to ensure that applications should be resolved and a just outcome achieved as speedily as possible without costs being unreasonably incurred'.

The scope of the Protocol

The Protocol is intended to cover all claims for financial relief. Practitioners are reminded **30.13** that, in considering the options of pre-application disclosure and negotiation, there may in fact be an advantage in having a court timetable and court-managed process. There is a warning to the profession that exercising the option of pre-application disclosure and negotiation can carry risks of excessive and uncontrolled expenditure and delay. Pre-application disclosure and negotiation should be encouraged only where both parties agree to follow this route and disclosure is not likely to be an issue, or has been adequately dealt with in mediation or otherwise.

Practitioners are also urged to keep under review whether it would be appropriate to suggest **30.14** mediation/collaborative law as an alternative to solicitor negotiation or court-based litigation.

Further, making an application to court should not be regarded as a hostile step or last resort **30.15** but 'rather as a way of starting the court timetable, controlling disclosure, and endeavouring to avoid the costly final hearing and the preparation for it' (para 4). However, such an application should only be made where there is no reasonable prospect of a settlement, for example where protracted negotiations by correspondence have been inconclusive.

The first letter

While recognizing that it is difficult to prescribe a specimen first letter since the circumstances **30.16** of the parties to an application for a financial order will be so different, the tone of the first letter is very important: therefore the guidance in para 5 of the Protocol must be followed. This states that consideration must be given to the impact of any correspondence on the reader and, in particular, the parties. Irrelevant issues should be avoided, as should contents which cause the recipient of the letter to adopt an entrenched or hostile position.

The client should approve the first letter in advance. Solicitors writing to an unrepresented **30.17** party should always recommend that he seeks independent legal advice and enclose a second copy to be passed to any solicitor instructed. A reasonable time limit for a response should be included—usually 14 days.

All correspondence should focus on the clarification of claims—protracted correspondence **30.18** should be avoided (para 13), as should 'trial by correspondence'.

Disclosure

The Protocol emphasizes that disclosure of all material facts, documents, and other relevant **30.19** information must be full and frank. This is regarded as being fundamental if the parties are to seek to clarify and identify the issues between them. Practitioners are required to explain to clients in clear terms the nature of the duty and the possible consequences of breach of that duty. It is important to remember that the duty is ongoing and therefore details of material changes after initial disclosure must be given to the other party.

30.20 The Protocol indicates that if parties carry out voluntary disclosure before the issue of proceedings, the parties should provide the information and documents using Form E (see para 1230) as a guide to the format of the disclosure. Hence, documents should be disclosed only to the extent that they are required by Form E. Excessive and disproportionate costs should not be incurred.

30.21 Are there any circumstances in which it is safe not to insist on full and frank disclosure? The answer is 'no'—to avoid the risk of later difficulties. However, where the parties are communicating fully, cooperating well, and a realistic and sensible offer has been made, the entire procedure set out above may not be insisted upon. Such an approach would only be appropriate where the client was satisfied that he or she had a good knowledge of the financial position of the other party and considered that rigorous insistence on further disclosure of minor matters might be counter-productive, leading to undesirable delay and excessive costs.

Expert evidence

30.22 The Protocol provides that the principle of proportionality must be borne in mind at all times. It is unacceptable for the costs of any case to be disproportionate to the financial value of the subject matter of the dispute. Parties are strongly urged therefore to obtain a valuation from a single expert (this principle being reinforced by Baron J in *P v P (Financial Relief: Illiquid Assets)* [2005] 1 FLR 548 who commented that it would have been much better (and significantly cheaper) if one expert had been instructed to report on an unbiased basis to the court. In this case, each party had instructed an accountant who had valued one of the principal assets, a series of family companies, from different perspectives so that their evidence to the court was inevitably coloured).

30.23 Where one party wishes to instruct a valuer at a pre-action stage, he should give to the other party a list of names of one or more experts in the relevant speciality whom he considers suitable to instruct. Within 14 days the other party may indicate any objection and, if so, supply a list of experts whom he considers to be more suitable.

30.24 If no agreement is reached as to the identity of a suitable expert, the parties must consider the costs implications of instructing their own expert. Where the costs implications are significant, it may be better for the court to decide the issue in the context of the proceedings.

30.25 In any event, where each party instructs an expert, the parties should be encouraged to agree that the reports will be disclosed so that areas of agreement and disagreement may be identified as early as possible.

30.26 In the event of a single expert being jointly instructed, the following requirements must be complied with:

   (a) the parties should agree a joint letter of instruction;
   (b) the parties must disclose whether they have already consulted that expert about the assets in issue;
   (c) the costs will normally be shared equally;
   (d) the expert report should comply with Part 25, FPR 2010.

30.27 Irrespective of there being single or joint valuations, it must be established that the expert is prepared to answer reasonable questions raised by either party.

E   THE PROCEDURE IN DETAIL

The overriding objective

This mirrors the provisions of Part 1, Civil Procedure Rules 1998 and is contained in r 1.1, FPR   **30.28**
2010. The overriding objective is to enable courts to deal with cases justly, having regard to
any welfare issues involved.

Rule 1.1(2) explains the meaning of 'to deal with a case justly', including as far as practicable: **30.29**

(a) ensuring that it is dealt with expeditiously and fairly;
(b) dealing with the case in ways which are proportionate to the nature, importance and
complexity of the issues;
(c) ensuring that the parties are on an equal footing;
(d) saving expense; and
(e) allotting to it an appropriate share of the court's resources, while taking into account the
need to allot resources to other cases.

The court must seek to give effect to the overriding objective when it: **30.30**

(a) exercises any power given to it in the FPR 2010; or
(b) interprets any rule: r 1.2.

The court is also obliged to further the overriding objective by 'actively managing cases'   **30.31**
(r 1.4), and this is stated to include:

(a) encouraging the parties to cooperate with each other in the conduct of the proceedings;
(b) identifying the issues at an early date;
(c) deciding promptly which issues need full investigation and hearing and which do not
and the procedure to be followed in the case;
(d) regulating the extent of disclosure of documents and expert evidence so that they are
proportionate to the issues in question;
(e) encouraging the parties to use an alternative dispute resolution procedure if the court
considers that appropriate and facilitating the use of such procedure;
(f)   helping the parties to settle the whole or part of the case;
(g) fixing timetables or otherwise controlling the progress of the case;
(h) making use of technology; and
(i)   giving directions to ensure that the trial of a case proceeds quickly and efficiently.

The parties to the proceedings are under a corresponding duty to help the court to further
the overriding objective (r 1.3) and therefore compliance with timetables and willingness to
negotiate a settlement will be expected.

The court now has a duty actively to manage each case in accordance with the overriding   **30.32**
objective. It has considerable discretion as to how it applies the core principles. For example,
the phrases 'the importance of the case' and 'the complexity of the issues' indicate that not
all cases turn on the value of the assets alone but on how such assets as there are should be
distributed between the parties.

30.33   Under the general principles of the pre-action protocol, already referred to, para 8 requires the parties to bear in mind the overriding objective and that 'the procedures which it is appropriate to follow should be conducted with minimum distress to the parties and in a manner designed to promote as good a continuing relationship between the parties and any children affected as is possible in the circumstances'.

Making the application

30.34   As with private law Children Act applications, the pre-application protocol set out in PD3A of the FPR 2010 applies. This requires a potential applicant (except in certain specified circumstances), to consider with a mediator whether the dispute may be capable of being resolved through mediation. The court will expect all applicants to have complied with the Protocol before commencing proceedings and will expect any respondent to have attended a Mediation Information and Assessment Meeting, if invited to do so. If court proceedings are taken, the court will wish to know at the first hearing whether mediation has been considered by the parties. In considering the conduct of any relevant family proceedings, the court will take into account any failure to comply with the Protocol and may refer the parties to a meeting with a mediator before proceedings continue further.

30.35   Section 26, MCA 1973 provides that where a petition for divorce, nullity, or judicial separation has been filed, then, proceedings for orders for financial relief may be begun at any time after the filing of the petition.

30.36   However, with the exception of an order for maintenance pending suit, no other order for the benefit of the other party to the marriage takes effect until the grant of the decree absolute in proceedings for divorce or nullity or the decree of judicial separation: ss 23(5) and 24(3), Matrimonial Causes Act 1973 ('MCA 1973').

Petitioner's application

30.37   Rule 9.4, FPR 2010 provides that any application by a petitioner for a 'financial order' (as defined in r 2.3) may be made in an application for a matrimonial or civil partnership order, or at any time after an application for such an order has been made. The application will then be 'activated' by filing Form A at the court.

The importance of making a comprehensive claim for financial relief

30.38   It is usually advisable to make the fullest possible claim for financial relief in the petition/answer or Form A (despite the fact that it may seem inappropriate at the time to claim, eg, periodical payments from a spouse who is unemployed or a lump sum from a spouse with no capital assets) for the following reasons:

   (a)   Circumstances can change between the initiation of the application and the hearing, and the spouse who was impecunious when an application for financial orders was made in the petition may, by the date of the hearing, have obtained a lucrative job or won the lottery. It is obviously in the interests of all concerned that the court should have the fullest possible powers to resolve the case at the hearing.

   (b)   The client must be prevented from falling into the remarriage trap. Section 28(3) provides that if a party to a marriage remarries after a decree of divorce or nullity, that party shall not be entitled to *apply* for a financial provision order or for a property adjustment order in his or her favour against the other party to the former marriage.

A party who may want to remarry can, however, preserve her claim for lump sum and property adjustment orders by making them before remarriage, in which case he or she will be able to pursue the claims after remarriage. (This is confirmed in *Re G (Financial Provision: Liberty to Restore Application for Lump Sum)* [2004] 1 FLR 997.) Nothing can be done, of course, to preserve a claim for periodical payments, which will always cease on remarriage in any event (s 28(1) and (2), MCA 1973).

The petitioner who later wishes to make a claim for a financial remedy that should have been made in her petition in accordance with PD5A, FPR 2010 will, in most cases, need the permission of the court to make the claim.

Respondent's application

Respondent filing an answer   Rule 9.4 also applies to a respondent who files an answer, **30.39** save that, of course, it is in his answer that he must make his financial relief claims.

Respondent not filing an answer   A respondent who does not file an answer (and this **30.40** will apply in the majority of cases) may make his application for financial orders by notice in Form A. There are no particular requirements as to when Form A should be filed. In theory, therefore, a respondent can file Form A months or years after the decree has been granted.

However, delay in filing Form A can prejudice a respondent's financial relief claims—in par- **30.41** ticular the client may fall into the remarriage trap (see para 30.38 above), or may find the court reluctant to grant relief if the lapse of time has led the petitioner to believe that no claim will be made. It is therefore suggested that the solicitor should make it his practice to file a notice in Form A claiming the full range of financial relief as a matter of course in the early stages of the main proceedings, and certainly before decree absolute.

Making the application where no claim has been made in the prayer in the petition or **30.42** **answer**   Where no claim has been made in the prayer to the petition or in the answer to the petition then an application may be made subsequently by permission of the court by notice in Form A.

Proceeding with the application made in the prayer in the petition or answer

Rules 9.4 and 9.12 govern the procedure where the application for financial relief is made **30.43** comprehensively in the prayer to the petition or in the answer to the petition.

The application form   PD5A provides that the notice of intention to proceed with the **30.44** application for financial relief is made by notice in Form A, the notice being filed in a county court or registry of the High Court in which the petition was filed.

The contents of Form A   Rule 9.13 requires that where there is an application for a prop- **30.45** erty adjustment order relating to land, the notice in Form A must identify the land and state whether it is registered or unregistered and, if registered, the Land Registry title number, giving particulars, so far as is known to the applicant, of any mortgage of the land or any interest in it.

30.46   **Other documents to be filed**   In addition to Form A (and a copy for service on the respondent), the following documents should be taken to the court (normally the divorce county court where the proceedings were commenced) to be issued/filed:

(a) Where the client is publicly funded:

    (i)   a copy of the certificate for General Family Help or representation;

    (ii) a notice of issue of the certificate.

(b) Notice of acting if the solicitor is not already on the court record (if the divorce proceedings have been handled under the Legal Help scheme so far, the solicitor will not be on the court record).

(c) A fee (currently £240).

(d) A copy of any family proceedings court maintenance order currently in force in respect of a spouse or child.

Further, if the applicant is seeking periodical payments or secured periodical payments for children, Form A must state whether the petitioner/respondent is applying for payment:

(a) for a step-child or children;

(b) for top-up maintenance over and above that payable under a Child Support Maintenance Calculation (see Chapter 35);

(c) to meet expenses arising from a child's disability;

(d) to meet educational or training expenses for a child;

(e) to cover a situation where the Child Support Act 1991 ('CSA 1991') does not apply because the carer parent, the non-resident parent, or the child in question is not habitually resident in the United Kingdom;

(f) for any other reason (eg to reflect a written agreement under s 8(5), CSA 1991).

Steps to be taken by the court

30.47   Once Form A has been filed at the court, the court is required to:

(a) fix a first appointment not less than 12 weeks and not more than 16 weeks after the date of filing Form A and to give notice of the date to the applicant;

(b) serve a copy of the notice on the respondent within four days of the filing of Form A: r 9.12.

A notice in Form C is sent by the court to both parties and advises them of the date of the first appointment and lays down a timetable of the steps to be taken before the first appointment.

30.48   In line with the principle of active case management, no court appointment may be cancelled except with the court's permission and, if cancelled, the court must immediately fix a new date: r 9.12(3).

30.49   The applicant must serve on the respondent a notice of issue of public funding and a notice of acting, where appropriate.

30.50   In the weeks before the first appointment, a considerable amount of work has to be undertaken by the solicitor both in terms of collating information and of assessing the conduct of the case in future.

The preparation of the financial statement in Form E

The layout of Form E

Rule 9.14 requires that both parties to the application, at the same time and not less than 35 days before the first appointment, exchange with each other and file at the court a financial statement in Form E. This is a complex form running to some 27 pages requiring a comprehensive account of the financial circumstances of the party making the statement. The statement requires details, amongst other things, of the personal and family history, the financial resources, liabilities and needs of the maker of the statement, together with details of future marriage plans, and an indication of the nature of the orders applied for or sought.   **30.51**

The documents to be annexed to Form E

The form must have attached to it the documents specified in the statement, but no others. Documents include, for example, the last three payslips and a form P60, a mortgage statement, a property valuation, bank and building society statements for the last 12 months, the surrender value of any endowment policy. The Schedule of Documents to Accompany Form E is a reminder in tick box form of the documents to be attached with an opportunity to indicate if the documents are attached, not applicable, or are to follow.   **30.52**

Rule 9.30 applies where an application is made in Form A and the applicant or respondent is likely to have any benefits under a pension arrangement.   **30.53**

Within seven days of receiving details of the date of the first appointment, a party with pension rights must request the person responsible for each pension arrangement to furnish details of the arrangement. The information to be provided includes a valuation of the pension rights, details of whether the person responsible for the pension arrangement offers membership to a person entitled to a pension credit, the types of benefit which would be available under such membership and the position on charges (Pensions on Divorce etc (Provision of Information) Regulations 2000).   **30.54**

The reason for this rule is to ensure that pension details are sought from the person responsible for the pension arrangement as early as possible in the financial relief process: some pension providers (eg the NHS and the Teachers' Pension Agency) can take anything up to three months to provide the relevant information.   **30.55**

A copy of the above information together with the name and address of the person responsible for each pension arrangement must be sent to the other party to the marriage by the person with pension rights within seven days of receipt: r 9.30(3).   **30.56**

The above steps are not required where the person with pension rights has already obtained or requested a valuation.   **30.57**

If the required documents, indicated above, cannot be attached to Form E, they must be served on the other party at the earliest opportunity and copies of the documents must be filed at the court with a written explanation setting out the reasons for the failure to send the documents with Form E: r 9.14(3). The parties are not permitted disclosure or inspection of any other documents before the first appointment.   **30.58**

30.59 Clearly, it is sensible to begin the collection of information and documents required in the statement before filing Form A in order to be as well prepared as possible. This is especially the case where the solicitor anticipates that he will be acting for the respondent in the proceedings and therefore has little control over when the application is to be made. A period of, at most, 11 weeks to collect and collate information may be insufficient especially when documents must be obtained from a variety of sources.

30.60 The reason for the requirement that certain documents be attached to Form E is so that, if possible, the first appointment may be used as a Financial Dispute Resolution appointment and this would not be possible in the absence of vital documents.

Completing Form E

30.61 For the main part, completion of Form E is relatively straightforward. It is a matter of completing those Parts which are relevant to the client's case. It is inevitable that a number of Parts of the form will not be completed at all. For example, where the client is an employee and has no self-employed earnings, Part 2, paras 2.11 and 2.16 may be safely ignored.

30.62 In para 3.1.1, the client must give details of his or her expenditure from income. In some so-called 'big money' cases, full details have been omitted on the grounds that the client is sufficiently wealthy to be able to afford any periodical payments order which the court is likely to make, making detailed disclosure unnecessary. Such an approach was heavily criticized in *McFarlane* v *McFarlane, Parlour* v *Parlour* [2004] 2 FLR 893, Thorpe LJ indicating that the court is entitled to have a full picture both of the client's income and expenditure in order properly to deal with the application for financial relief.

30.63 Guidance on the proper completion of Form E was given by Nicholas Mostyn QC sitting as a Deputy High Court Judge in *W* v *W (Financial Provision: Form E)* [2004] 1 FLR 494. A number of points emerge from the judgment but of particular importance are the following:

(a) a contingent liability (eg moneys set aside to meet the cost of potential damages in litigation unconnected with the financial proceedings) should be mentioned in the calculations at para 3.2.1 if, on the balance of probabilities, the maker of the statement and his legal advisers are satisfied that the liability will arise;

(b) where a spouse has remarried, his or her assets should not be treated as assets jointly owned with the new spouse: to do otherwise would be to reduce the assets available for distribution in relation to the first marriage.

30.64 It is suggested that particular care is needed, however, with the completion of paras 4.3, 4.4, and 5.1. Since the House of Lords' decision in *White* v *White* [2000] 3 WLR 1571 (discussed fully in Chapter 31), contributions of both a financial and non-financial kind (eg domestic contributions such as running the home and caring for the children) have achieved a greater significance and it is sensible in completing para 4.3 to highlight these. Furthermore, one party may seek to argue that his or her contribution has been so significant (eg by making a major contribution to the family wealth) that greater weight should be given to this contribution. An indication of this argument can be set out in para 4.3.

30.65 As for para 4.4, dealing with issues of conduct, the guidance in Form E makes it clear that conduct will only be taken into account in exceptional circumstances. This is in line with case law discussed in Chapter 31. Nevertheless, it is possible to indicate at para 4.4 that conduct will be raised in financial proceedings, the nature of that conduct and the effect it might reasonably have on the outcome of those proceedings. For example, if it is alleged that the husband disposed of significant savings and investments without the knowledge or consent of the wife, it may be possible to argue on her behalf that the family home, as the remaining family asset, should be transferred to her sole name (but see *K v K (Financial Relief: Management of Difficult Cases)* [2005] 2 FWR 1137).

In the writer's view, particular caution is needed in completing para 5.1. The paragraph seeks **30.66** an indication of the type of financial order(s) sought. It may be difficult to be specific at this stage in the absence of the financial statement of the other spouse. It may be sensible, therefore, to be non-committal unless the identity and value of all assets are already known or the client has a clear view as to an appropriate settlement. In essence, do not sell the client short!

Once completed, Form E must be signed by the maker of the statement and sworn to be true: **30.67** r 9.14(1).

Mutual exchange of Form E

In order for the application to be dealt with as expeditiously as possible, Form E must be **30.68** exchanged and filed not less than 35 days before first appointment.

The requirement for simultaneous exchange of Form E is to prevent either side from trying **30.69** to gain an advantage over the other. However, the Rules are silent as to the steps to be taken if one party fails to cooperate.

It is suggested that the party whose statement has been prepared within the prescribed time **30.70** limit should file Form E at court in any event, in a sealed envelope marked 'Not to be opened until the Respondent's Form E is filed', but not serve the document on the other side. An application should then be made to the district judge, without notice to the other side, for an order that the respondent file and exchange his Form E within a prescribed period. A penal notice should be attached to the order and costs should be applied for (see para 30.90 below). The order should be served personally on the recalcitrant party.

If the order is not complied with, it becomes impossible to prepare for the first appointment **30.71** (see para 30.81 below) and it will be necessary to seek an adjournment of the first appointment usually at the first appointment itself. The court should be asked to assess the wasted costs and require the respondent to pay these within a short, prescribed period.

Where Form E is served by the respondent without the required documents, this may be **30.72** dealt with in the questionnaire (see paras 30.84 ff below) and possibly reflected in an order for costs against the respondent at the first appointment.

Service of Form A and Form E on other parties

Where the application is made for a variation of an ante-nuptial or post-nuptial settlement, **30.73** r 9.13 requires a copy of Form A to be served on the trustees of the settlement.

Where the property in the proceedings is subject to a mortgage, a copy of Form A must be **30.74** served on any mortgagee mentioned in the application and the mortgagee may apply to the court for a copy of the applicant's financial statement in Form E. The mortgagee may file a statement in answer to the application within 14 days after service or receipt of the statement but will rarely do so in practice.

30.75 Similarly, where the notice in Form A seeks a pension sharing order under s 24B or a pension attachment order under ss 25B and/or 25C, MCA 1973, the applicant must serve a copy of the notice in Form A on the person responsible for the pension arrangement: r 9.30.

30.76 Where the application is for a *pension attachment order*, additional information laid down in r 9.33 must be sent to the person responsible for the pension arrangement. This includes, among other things, an address for service, and an address of a bank, building society, or other place to which payment is to be sent.

30.77 In these circumstances, the person responsible for the pension arrangement may, within 21 days after service, require the applicant to provide him with a copy of para 2.13 of the applicant's Form E. The applicant must then provide the document not less than 35 days before the date of the first appointment, or within 21 days of being required to do so, whichever is the later.

30.78 Paragraph 2.13 of Form E deals with the pension position of the applicant. The person responsible for the pension arrangement is not entitled to see details of the applicant's other financial circumstances.

30.79 Under r 9.33(5) the person responsible for the pension arrangement may then send to the court, the applicant, and the respondent a statement in answer. This step must be taken within 21 days of receipt of a copy of para 2.13 of Form E.

30.80 Further, under r 9.13 the applicant is required to file at the court a certificate of service of all persons who have been served with Form A (other than the respondent) at or before the first appointment.

Preparation for the first appointment

30.81 Rule 9.14(5) requires that at least 14 days before the first appointment, each party must file with the court and serve on the other party:

(a) a concise statement of the issues between the parties;

(b) a chronology (as to the history of the marriage and the divorce proceedings);

(c) a questionnaire setting out by reference to the concise statement of issues any further information and documents requested from the other party, or a statement that no information or documents are required;

(d) a notice stating whether that party will be in a position at the first appointment to proceed on that occasion to a Financial Dispute Resolution ('FDR') giving reasons. The purpose and structure of the FDR is explained at para 30.103 below.

PD9A requires the parties to exchange an agreed case summary, a schedule of assets, and details of any directions sought by the parties including, where appropriate, the name of any proposed expert.

The concise statement of issues

This is an important document and its principal purpose is to identify the issues in the case. **30.82** Since Form E concludes with an opportunity for each party to indicate the terms of the order sought by them, it should be possible to establish the issues without difficulty. The document should be concise and avoid unnecessary details.

An example of a matter which should be highlighted in the statement of issues is when the **30.83** respondent husband is arguing that he should not be required to make periodical payments for his wife and the wife is contending that maintenance is essential.

The questionnaire

In line with the principle of active case management, the parties are not permitted to ask **30.84** for information or documents on an informal basis once the application for financial relief has been filed. Hence, the questionnaire is important and, having received the other party's Form E, time will be spent deciding what information or documents should be requested, if any, and drafting the questionnaire.

At the risk of stating the obvious, the starting point will be to check that the other spouse **30.85** has provided all the relevant documents. If not, these should be requested. Remember to concentrate on *relevant* documents—requesting receipts for expenditure from several years ago is unlikely to be very productive!

What is made clear by Baron J in *K v K (Financial Relief: Management of Difficult Cases)*, referred **30.86** to at para 30.65 above, is that, if the solicitor considers that insufficient relevant information has been given, enquiries must be pursued rigorously in the questionnaire (and if necessary, at the next court hearing). It is not acceptable 'simply [to] wait to use the absence of information as a forensic ambush at trial'.

Following the approach of Coleridge J in *OS v DS (Oral Disclosure: Preliminary Hearing)* [2005] 1 **30.87** FLR 675, Baron J acknowledged that 'in some cases continual orders for disclosure can be counter-productive and it is better to have an oral hearing ...' (the purpose being for the oral examination of the recalcitrant party on matters where disclosure has not been forthcoming).

F THE FIRST APPOINTMENT

Rule 9.15, FPR 2010 governs the conduct of the first appointment which has the objective of **30.88** 'defining the issues and saving costs'. Both parties must personally attend the first appointment unless the court orders otherwise: r 9.15(8). Further, the person responsible for the pension arrangement is entitled to be represented at the first appointment where he has filed a statement in answer.

The district judge will have read the documents filed and has a number of duties at the first **30.89** appointment laid down in r 9.15:

(a) He must determine the extent to which any questions seeking information or documents requested in r 9.14(5)(c) must be answered or produced, giving directions for the production of such further documents as may be necessary. It is helpful to the court in producing replies to the other party's questionnaire to reproduce the original question and then add the reply so that a comprehensive document is created. This saves the court having to locate the question in one document and the reply in another.

In determining, for example, the additional information required, the district judge may by virtue of r 21.2 FPR 2010 order the disclosure of documents from a person who is not a party to the proceedings where disclosure is necessary to dispose fairly of the proceedings or to save costs. Obviously, the court's decision is going to be guided by the need to act proportionately.

(b) The district judge may give directions about the valuation of assets (including the joint instruction of joint experts), the obtaining and exchanging of expert evidence, the evidence to be adduced by each party, and further chronologies or schedules to be filed by each party.

(c) Where the parties are not able to reach an agreement on financial and property matters, the district judge must also direct that the case be referred to a FDR appointment unless he concludes that a referral is not appropriate in all the circumstances. This may arise, for example, where the parties are in dispute on a point of principle and need a formal determination of the issue from a district judge. The question of the extent to which an inheritance should be available for distribution is an example of such a dispute. Where this is the case, he must direct one or more of the following:

  (i)   that a further directions appointment be fixed;
  (ii) that an appointment be fixed for the making of an interim order;
  (iii) that the case be fixed for a final hearing and, where that direction is given, the district judge must determine the judicial level at which the case must be heard.

(d) Further, he may make an interim order where an application was made for such an order to be dealt with at the first appointment.

(e) Where the case is referred to a FDR appointment, the district judge may require the parties to file and serve skeleton arguments and/or schedules of assets prior to the FDR.

(f) He must consider whether to make a costs order in respect of the hearing under r 28.3(5) FPR 2010, having regard to all the circumstances and the extent to which each party has complied with the Rules, especially in respect of the requirement to send documents with Form E.

G   A NOTE ON COSTS

30.90   In order to comply with certain aspects of the overriding objective, in particular, those of saving expense and dealing with the case in a way proportionate to the amount of money involved, etc, it is necessary for the parties involved to understand throughout the extent of the costs incurred both to date and in respect of particular applications to the court.

30.91   Hence, by r 9.17, FPR 2010 at *every* court hearing or appointment each party must produce to the court an estimate in Form H of the costs and disbursements incurred by him up to the date of that hearing or appointment. This means that the court and the party will be aware of the 'running total' of costs incurred. This document is also disclosed to the other party.

Not less than 14 days before a final hearing each party must provide full particulars of all costs **30.92** to enable the court to take full account of the parties' liabilities for costs when deciding the final outcome (r 9.27(2)). The relevant form is Form H1.

Rule 28.3 provides that the general rule in financial remedy proceedings is that the court will **30.93** not make an order requiring one party to pay the costs of another party. This is subject to the proviso in r 28.3(6) that a costs order may be made at any stage in the proceedings where the court considers it appropriate to do so because of the conduct of a party in relation to the proceedings (either before the proceedings start or during the course of the proceedings).

To assist the court in deciding whether an order for costs should be made, r 28.3(7) requires **30.94** the court to have regard to the following:

(a) any failure by a party to comply with the Rules, any order of the court, or any Practice Direction which the court considers relevant;
(b) any open offer to settle made by a party;
(c) whether it was reasonable for a party to raise, pursue, or contest a particular allegation or issue;
(d) the manner in which a party has pursued or responded to the application or a particular allegation or issue;
(e) any other aspect of a party's conduct in relation to the proceedings which the court considers relevant; and
(f) the financial effect on the parties of any costs orders.

In practical terms, this means that an order might be made in the following circumstances: **30.95**

(a) where there has been non-compliance with the Rules or a direction or order of the court (see, eg, the Practice Direction on Court Bundles at PD27A);
(b) where there has been disproportionate pursuit of an issue which turns out to be irrelevant;
(c) where there has been unjustifiable delay in giving full disclosure.

It is vital to know that there are exceptions to the 'general rule'. The exceptions are interim **30.96** applications such as maintenance pending suit and interim periodical payments order. Also excluded are appeals, applications for financial provision for children under sch 1, Children Act 1989, and enforcement proceedings. Costs in these excluded remedies are subject to the court's discretion (sometimes referred to as a 'clean sheet' position). In cases of this nature, courts need to start somewhere and as the unsuccessful party is usually regarded as the one responsible for the generation of costs then that is often a decisive factor in the exercise of the court's discretion (see, eg, *Baker* v *Rowe* [2010] 1 FLR 761).

H   INTERIM ORDERS

Rule 9.7, FPR 2010 deals with interim orders. It is recognized that the long delay before the **30.97** date of the first appointment may cause hardship where the applicant needs immediate financial support in the form of periodical payments. Rule 9.7(1) therefore permits *either* party to apply at *any stage of the proceedings* for an order for maintenance pending suit, interim periodical payments, or an interim variation order.

30.98   The wording of r 9.7(1)indicates that the proceedings for a financial order must have begun and therefore one of the parties will have filed Form A.

30.99   The procedure is that set out in r 30. To make an application for an interim order, a notice of application is filed at the court A copy of the notice of application must be served forthwith on the respondent: r 30.8.

30.100   It is likely, of course, that at this stage neither party will have filed Form E. The applicant is therefore required to file with the application and serve on the other party a draft of the order requested and a short sworn statement explaining why the order is necessary and giving the necessary information about his means: r 9.7(4).

30.101   Not less than seven days before the hearing, the other party must file with the court and serve on the other party a short sworn statement about his means unless he has already filed Form E: r 9.7(4).

30.102   To determine the application the court will adopt normal principles using the factors under s 25, MCA 1973 (see Chapter 31).

I   THE FINANCIAL DISPUTE RESOLUTION APPOINTMENT

30.103   The FDR appointment is a relatively recent innovation, dealt with in r 9.17.

30.104   The FDR appointment will normally take place when all the evidence has been exchanged and the court and the parties are able to identify the issues.

30.105   The FDR appointment is a 'meeting held for the purpose of discussion and negotiation', r 9.17(1). The process is seen as reducing the tension which inevitably arises in a family dispute and facilitating settlement of those disputes. The parties must personally attend the FDR appointment unless the court orders otherwise (r 9.17(10)) and must use their best endeavours to reach agreement on the matters in issue between them (r 9.17(6)). The FDR appointment gives the parties an opportunity to put their fundamental positions to the district judge and for him to make such comments as may be helpful to assist in arriving at a settlement.

30.106   In addition to complying with any direction given at the first appointment, not later than seven days before the FDR appointment, the applicant must file with the court details of all offers and proposals and responses to them: r 9.17(3). This includes proposals or responses made on a 'without prejudice' basis.

30.107   The appointment is then conducted on a privileged basis so that the parties have the reassurance that nothing can be repeated at a later date, for example at a final hearing if no settlement is reached.

30.108   Although the Rules are not explicit on the point, it is clearly the function of the district judge to help the parties to settle their dispute by eliminating unrealistic expectations and giving a general indication of how the court would be likely to approach the particular circumstances of the case.

If a settlement cannot be achieved, the district judge or judge hearing the FDR appointment is not permitted to have any further involvement with the application, other than to direct a further FDR appointment, make a consent order, or a further directions order: r 9.17(2). **30.109**

Where there is no agreement, all offers, proposals, and responses to them must, at the request of the party who filed them, be returned to him and not retained on the court file: r 9.17(5). **30.110**

The FDR appointment may be adjourned from time to time and, at its conclusion, the court may make an appropriate consent order. If that is not appropriate because a settlement has not been reached, the court must give directions for the future conduct of the proceedings including, for example, the filing of evidence and fixing a final hearing date: r 9.17(9). **30.111**

Where agreement has been reached but a consent order cannot be obtained at court that day, the following is suggested: **30.112**

(a) Do not leave the court building without, at the very least, 'heads of agreement' containing all relevant terms and undertakings, signed by the parties, their legal representatives, and initialled as approved by the judge. This is known as a 'Rose agreement', following *Rose* v *Rose* [2002] 1 FLR 978. This will be an unperfected order.

(b) The heads of agreement must be detailed—not simply broad terms. In particular, care must be taken with the terms of any undertakings (see paras 30.133 ff) which may be vital to the working of the order but which the court cannot compel a party to give.

(c) If the final order is not drafted and approved at the FDR, ensure that a date is fixed within about 28 days for a five-minute appointment at which the order can be approved or any *Rose*-style problems explored. The hearing should be listed as an adjourned FDR.

J   PREPARATION FOR THE FINAL HEARING

In preparing for the final hearing, which will be necessary if the FDR appointment has not succeeded and there is little prospect of a consent order, attention must be paid to the FPR 2010 and a number of Practice Directions. A fair degree of common sense is also required! **30.113**

It is suggested that the following matters should be covered: **30.114**

(a) In addition to complying with directions made at the FDR, the solicitor should spend some time isolating the issues in the case and ensuring that he can prove any disputed factual matters that may have a bearing on the district judge's decision.

(b) Preparation of the bundle of documents. Preparation of the bundle of documents is now governed by PD27A. This Practice Direction has to be complied with in High Court proceedings, proceedings in the Principal Registry of the Family Division, and at all hearings in family proceedings except for family proceedings courts.

The term 'hearing' is defined as 'all appearances before a judge or district judge whether with or without notice to other parties and whether for directions or for substantive relief': para 2.2. Further, the Practice Direction applies whether the bundle is being lodged for the first time or being re-lodged for a further hearing.

However, the Practice Direction does not apply in the following circumstances:

(i)   cases listed for an hour or less in the Principal Registry or a county court;

(ii)   the hearing of an urgent application if and to the extent that it is impossible to comply with it (para 2.4).

The following is a summary only of the Practice Direction.

Responsibility for preparation of the bundle lies with the applicant or, where the applicant is a litigant in person, with the first respondent who is not a litigant in person: para 3.1.

If possible, the contents of the bundle should be agreed by all parties and in any event the bundle should be paginated and indexed: para 3.2.

The bundle should be contained in one or more A4-size ring binders or lever arch files. Each is to be clearly marked on the front and spine to identify the case, the court, the hearing date and time, and, if known, the name of the judge hearing the case: paras 5.1 and 5.2.

As for the contents of the bundle, the documents must be in chronological order from the front of the bundle, paginated, and indexed and divided into separate sections as follows:

(i)   preliminary documents and any other case management documents required by any other Practice Direction;

(ii)   applications and orders;

(iii) statements and affidavits (which must be dated in the top right hand corner of the front page);

(iv)   care plans (where appropriate);

(v)   experts' reports and other reports;

(vi)   other documents, divided into further sections, as may be appropriate: para 4.1.

At the commencement of the bundle there must be inserted the following documents (these are known as the preliminary documents):

(i)   an up-to-date summary of the background to the hearing limited, if possible, to one A4 page;

(ii)   a statement of the issue or issues to be determined (1) at the hearing and (2) at the final hearing;

(iii) a position statement of each party including a summary of the order or directions sought (1) at the hearing and (2) at the final hearing;

(iv)   skeleton arguments, if appropriate, with copies of all authorities relied on;

(v)   a list of essential reading for that hearing: para 4.2.

Paragraphs 4.3, 4.4, and 4.5 set out additional requirements for the preparation of the preliminary documents including, for example, giving the date of preparation of the document and the date of the hearing for which it was intended, comprehensive cross-referencing of the documents which should be agreed by all parties. Where that is not possible, the fact of disagreement and their differing contentions should be set out at appropriate places in the document.

Further, para 10.1 requires an agreed time estimate to be inserted at the front of the bundle which separately specifies:

(i)   the time estimated to be required for judicial pre-reading;

(ii) the time required for hearing all evidence and submissions;

(iii) the time estimated to be required for preparing and delivering judgment.

The time estimate is to be prepared on the basis that before they give evidence, all witnesses will have read all relevant filed statements and reports.

Paragraph 10.2 sets out the procedure if there is a change in the time estimate once the case is listed for hearing while para 11 deals with the situation where a case is to be taken out of the list.

According to para 6.1, the party preparing the bundle shall provide a paginated index to all parties not less than four working days before the hearing, irrespective of whether the bundle has been agreed. Counsel is to receive a paginated bundle by those instructing him or her not less than three working days before the hearing (para 6.2) and the bundle (with the exception of the preliminary documents if and insofar as they are not then available) is to be lodged at the court not less than two working days before the hearing or at such other time as may be specified by the judge (para 6.3).

Paragraph 6.4 provides that the preliminary documents are to be lodged no later than 11 am on the day before the hearing and, where the hearing is before a High Court judge whose identity is known, the documents should also be sent by email to the judge's clerk.

Paragraph 7 sets out in detail how and where the bundle is to be lodged at court with specific additional requirements, set out in para 8, to be followed for cases being heard in the Principal Registry of the Family Division at First Avenue House or at the Royal Courts of Justice.

What is clear, at para 12, is that, where there is a failure to comply with any part of the Practice Direction, the judge is authorized to remove the case from the list or put the case further back and he may also make a 'wasted' costs order against the party at fault.

It will be apparent from the above that now a trial bundle is to be lodged and then re-lodged as the case progresses. Paragraphs 9.1 and 9.2 deal with this by requiring the person responsible for the bundle to retrieve it immediately on completion of the hearing. If that is not practicable, the bundle must be collected from the court within five working days, otherwise it may be destroyed.

Before the bundle is re-lodged in readiness for the next hearing, it must be updated and all superseded documents (eg outdated summaries and chronologies) are to be removed (para 4.7).

(c) A calculation of both parties' tax positions should be prepared with copies for the other side and the district judge. This is likely to be limited now to an indication of any capital gains tax liability which a party may incur in carrying out the order.

(d) It is suggested that, where there are children of the family in respect of whom the Child Support Agency is likely to carry out a maintenance calculation, the solicitor should make the calculation to establish his client's future liability since this will have an impact on the outcome of the application.

(e) It is of enormous help to the court if the solicitor or barrister prepares a schedule summarizing the income and outgoings, together with the assets and liabilities of his client as they stand at the date of the hearing. This enables the district judge, at a glance, to see the basic parameters of the financial information. It is becoming common practice for the schedule of assets to be divided into two parts, namely total assets without pension and a separate statement of the pension cash equivalent transfer value (CETV). The pension figures should be divided to show the sum which may be taken as a lump sum and the date on which that could happen, and the balance which would provide an income stream.

Example

Mrs A:	age 42
Mr A:	age 45
Samantha:	age 12 (resides with Mrs A)
Tom:	age 10 (resides with Mrs A)

SCHEDULE OF INCOME AND ASSETS
Mrs A: Income and Outgoings

Mrs A's income (net of tax and National Insurance)	£20,000 pa
Mrs A's outgoings (itemized on separate sheet)	£25,000 pa

Mr A: Income and Outgoings

Mr A's income (net of tax and national insurance)	£35,000 pa
Mr A's outgoings (itemized on separate sheet)	£20,000 pa

Capital Assets (joint)

House: value: £250,000 [Mortgage: £30,000]	Equity:	£220,000
Endowment Policy	Surrender value:	£25,000
Shares × 100 (£50 each)	Value:	£5,000
Building Society account		£450
	TOTAL:	£250,450

Capital Assets (Mrs A)

Jewellery	£10,000
Premium Bonds	£750
Bank account (fluctuating balance)	£1,000
Pension	£35,000
TOTAL:	£46,750

Capital Assets (Mr A)

Sailing boat	£15,000
Painting (original oil)	£3,000
Bank account (fluctuating balance)	£1,200
Pension (CETV)	£85,000
TOTAL:	£104,200

Debts (joint)

Bank loan	[outstanding]	[£6,000]
Credit card debts	[outstanding]	[£3,000]
	TOTAL OUTSTANDING:	£9,000

Summary of assets

TOTAL ASSETS:	£401,400
TOTAL LIABILITIES:	£9,000
BALANCE:	£392,400

(f) The division of chattels should not be overlooked. In *K v K* (para 30.65 above), Baron J recommended that the division of chattels should be accomplished before the final hearing, with a clear schedule indicating who is to receive what. Where this is not possible, a Scott schedule should be drawn up with the items marked as agreed or remaining in dispute. The schedule should set out in very short form the reasons why any particular item is sought.

(g) As indicated in para 30.109 above, where the FDR appointment does not lead to a settlement and costs order, the district judge may give appropriate directions for the future conduct of the proceedings. This may include filing further evidence about the finances of the parties or specific outstanding issues. In the majority of cases such further evidence should be unnecessary because of the nature of the information in Form E and the replies to questionnaires. Nevertheless, in *W v W (Ancillary Relief: Practice)* [2000] Fam Law 473, Wilson J indicated that in cases of greater wealth it would be helpful for the evidence to be broadened by narrative sworn statements.

(h) As stated above, r 9.27 requires each party 14 days before the final hearing to file with the court and serve on the other party a statement in Form H1 giving full details of all costs in respect of the proceedings incurred or expected to be incurred. This is to enable the court to take account of the parties' liabilities for costs when deciding what order (if any) to make for financial provision.

Form H1 is a far more comprehensive document than Form H. It requires the solicitor over three pages to detail the costs incurred at each stage of the case. Since it takes time to complete and may be a disproportionate exercise, consideration should be given to asking the district judge to dispense with this requirement. This should be done at the conclusion of the FDR hearing and, if the request is granted, Form H (discussed in para 30.91 above) would be completed instead.

(i) The procedure in preparation for a final hearing also requires some specific steps to be taken prior to the hearing.

Where a date is fixed for the final hearing, the applicant is required to file with the court and serve on the respondent an open statement which sets out concise details, including the amounts involved, of the orders he proposes to ask the court to make. This must be done not less than 14 days before the date fixed for the final hearing: r 9.28(1).

This is known as 'an open proposal'. The respondent is then required to file with the court and serve on the applicant an open statement which sets out concise details, including the amounts involved, of the orders he proposes to ask the court to make. This step must be taken not more than seven days after the service of the applicant's statement: r 9.28(2).

These steps are designed to promote a settlement even where this has not been achieved by the FDR appointment.

(j) At the risk of stating the obvious, it must be stressed that the practitioner should think out *in advance* what matters are covered adequately in his client's financial statement and what further evidence he will need to elicit from her at the hearing. Similarly, thought must be given to cross-examination—the art is to put telling questions pleasantly and in knowing what not to ask and when to stop. This is easier if a brief list has been made in advance of the points that need to be put to the witness.

(k) In the average case, the housing needs of the parties is the principal concern. It is useful, therefore, to obtain details from estate agents to demonstrate the cost of suitable accommodation, letters from the council setting out details of waiting lists, and, perhaps most importantly, an indication from the present mortgagee as to its willingness to rearrange the mortgage or to lend additional amounts and so on.

(l) Negotiations should be carried on right up to the last minute. The client may be saved a substantial sum in costs if a contested hearing can be averted.

___

K   THE HEARING

The hearing itself

30.115   The hearing will almost always be before a district judge. It will be held in the district judge's chambers and will be private. In theory, the procedure should follow the normal pattern (applicant opens the case and calls evidence, respondent calls evidence, respondent addresses the district judge, applicant addresses the district judge). Many district judges do require proceedings to be run in this traditional manner. Others are prepared/prefer to adopt a much more informal approach. It is not unknown for the district judge to start off the proceedings by letting the parties know what he has in mind having read their financial statements and open proposals and inviting comment and discussion before going on to hear evidence and argument. Sometimes this produces agreement between parties without a fully contested hearing. Even if it does not, it is often valuable to the advocate in giving him an idea as to how the district judge's mind is working—it helps to know what aspects of the client's case do not appeal to the district judge and what points are particularly troubling him.

30.116   The important thing to remember is to cover all relevant points concisely. Often evidence is one of the least important parts of the case as the district judge knows much of what he needs to know already from Form E and any sworn statement filed. Some points should, however, be made here on addressing the district judge, which may be a good deal more important.

30.117   The applicant's advocate must be prepared to open the case formally, outlining to the district judge the history of the matter (although often he will have gleaned this from his preliminary reading of the papers) and explaining what order it is that his client wants. It is a help to get matters clear in one's own mind before the hearing by preparing a timetable of the case so far (date of marriage, birth of children, separation, petition, etc).

30.118   When it comes to addressing the district judge in closing the case, it is not often useful to indulge in a review of the evidence that the district judge has just heard, although important points can be brought out if necessary. It can, however, be a great help to put to the district judge the types of orders that the advocate submits may be appropriate, outlining how his suggestions (and any suggestions made by the other side) would work in practice, for example what effect they would have on the parties' tax positions, on income support entitlement, and on the statutory charge. Where maintenance is concerned, it is also helpful to draw to the district judge's attention how the proposed order would (or would not) enable both parties to meet their reasonable outgoings. From time to time it may be necessary to cite authorities on a legal point, but on the whole financial relief cases depend upon their own facts and authorities are not therefore particularly useful.

The district judge may make a bald announcement of his decision or he may give a short **30.119** judgment. A careful note should be taken of what he says as it can be important if an appeal is made against his order or if an application is made for a variation of the order at a later stage.

L CONSENT ORDERS

The importance of attempting to settle financial remedy disputes without incurring the costs **30.120** of a contested hearing cannot be stressed too heavily. There is no point in fighting over £750 if a costs bill of £1,000 is run up in the process. Furthermore, a continuing battle over financial relief does nothing to help the parties get over the breakdown of their marriage and resolve other difficulties, for example over children.

Just as each party has a duty to make full disclosure of all material facts to the court hearing an **30.121** application for a financial order, each party has a duty to make full and frank disclosure of all material facts to the other party during negotiations which may lead to a consent order (see the case of *Livesey* v *Jenkins* [1985] 2 WLR 47).

The solicitor should not be frightened therefore to seek from the other party all the informa- **30.122** tion that he considers to be necessary in order to advise his client whether a proposed settlement is acceptable.

Rule 9.26, FPR 2010 should ensure that relevant facts are disclosed. This rule deals with the **30.123** procedure for seeking a consent order for financial relief. The procedure where agreement is reached before the hearing date of the financial order applications is as follows:

(a) If agreement is reached before either party has filed a notice in Form A, application should be made by one or the other party in Form A for an order in the agreed terms and, in accordance with r 9.26, there should be lodged with the application two copies (although many courts require three) of a draft of the order, one of which must be endorsed with a statement signed by the respondent signifying his agreement. Presumably, if agreement is reached after Form A has been filed, the applicant should simply lodge the endorsed draft order with the court requesting that the district judge should make an order in these terms. It is essential to check with the client that the draft order reflects the terms of settlement to prevent errors.

(b) Section 33A, MCA 1973 provides that, on an application for a consent order for financial relief, the court may, unless it has reason to think that there are other circumstances into which it ought to enquire, make an order in the terms agreed on the basis only of the prescribed information furnished with the application.

Rule 9.26 prescribes the information that must be furnished. It requires that there shall be lodged with the application a statement of information in Form D81 relied on in support of the application. Importantly, if there is one statement then both parties must sign it. If each party files their own statement then each will require the signatures of both.

Matters that must normally be incorporated include details of the duration of the mar- **30.124** riage (or civil partnership), ages of the parties, and any children of the family; an estimate in summary form of the approximate amount or value of the capital, income resources, and value of any benefits under a pension arrangement which either party has or is likely to have, including the most recent valuation provided by the pension arrangement and, where relevant, of any minor child of the family; details of what is intended with regard to the occupation or disposal of the matrimonial home and what is intended with regard to accommodation of both parties and minor children; whether either party has remarried, or presently intends to remarry or cohabit (or form a civil partnership) confirmation that, where appropriate, the mortgagee of the property and/or the person responsible for the pension arrangement has been served with notice of the application and has not objected within 14 days (in the case of the mortgagee) or 21 days in the case of the pension provider.

30.125   Under the FPR 2010 a special procedure exists where a proposed consent order includes a pension sharing order. Where the parties have, for example, reached their own agreement about a pension share without Form A having been served, by virtue of r 9.32, before providing the court with the necessary information, the party with the pension rights must request the information set out in Section C of the Pension Inquiry Form from the pension provider. The provider must, on receipt of that request, provide the information sought. There is no need to have the approval of the pension provider to the proposed pension sharing order.

30.126   The position is slightly different where the parties' proposed consent order includes a pension attachment order. The requirements are set out in r 9.34. In those circumstances the parties must serve on the pension provider a copy of the application for a consent order, a draft of the proposed order, and the further information required under r 9.33(1).

30.127   In the case of a consent order including a pension attachment order, the pension provider may object within 21 days following service upon them. The client needs to be warned that the court retains a discretion to refuse to make the order in the proposed terms, especially if it takes the view that the provision for the other spouse is inadequate. It is sensible therefore to explain the reasons for the particular terms of the order under 'any other especially significant circumstances' rather than leaving the court to guess and raise concerns.

30.128   Where agreement is reached only at the door of the court, r 9.26(5) enables the court to dispense with the lodging of the draft of the order and a statement of information and to give directions for the order to be drawn and the information that would otherwise be required in the statement of information to be given in such manner as it sees fit.

30.129   It is incumbent upon the solicitor to make sure that the order is carefully drafted so as to embody what the parties have agreed upon comprehensively, leaving no room for future doubt.

M   SOME POINTS ON DRAFTING FINANCIAL ORDERS

Introduction

30.130   There are a number of reasons for becoming familiar with the requirements of a well-drafted order dealing with financial provision. First, many claims for a financial remedy are eventually agreed. It is the responsibility of the solicitor to incorporate the terms of the settlement in a consent order to be submitted to the court for approval and sealing before its terms can be implemented. Secondly, often the solicitor is asked to approve a draft order submitted by the other party's solicitor and it is important to know how the document should be drawn up so that any amendments can be made. Thirdly, it is not uncommon for a district judge, at the conclusion of his judgment, to outline the terms of the order and require the solicitors or counsel to draft the order for his approval.

The form of the order

Most financial orders are made up of two elements: **30.131**

(a) the preamble; and
(b) the body of the order.

The preamble

The main purpose of the preamble is to record essential elements in the financial settlement **30.132** which the court has no power to order because of the restrictive wording of the MCA 1973.

The preamble may indicate the basis upon which certain provision is to be made (eg that **30.133** periodical payments are to be made on the basis that the recipient uses them to pay specified outgoings). In addition the preamble may contain a number of undertakings.

An undertaking is a promise to the court to do certain things. Breach of an undertaking is a **30.134** contempt of court and can be enforced in a similar way to an order.

An undertaking may be used to deal with matters which the court cannot expressly order. It **30.135** is important to distinguish between an undertaking to do something and an undertaking to use best endeavours to achieve a particular outcome. The latter form of undertaking is used where the cooperation or consent of a third party is required, for example the petitioner may give an undertaking to use her best endeavours to secure the release of the respondent from his covenants under the mortgage. Obviously this arrangement requires the consent of the mortgage lender over whom the petitioner has no control. By contrast, the performance of other undertakings will be well within the power of the person giving them. Such undertakings include, for example:

(a) to make mortgage payments;
(b) to pay contributions in respect of a personal pension;
(c) to pay other debts or outgoings.

An example of such an undertaking is set out below:

> And upon the Petitioner undertaking as from the date of the order:
> (a) To pay or cause to be paid the mortgage to the Wessex Building Society and all other liabilities relating to the property known as 28 Acacia Avenue, Ambridge, Wessex.
> (b) To use her best endeavours to procure the release of the Respondent from any liability under the mortgage in favour of the Wessex Building Society and in any event to indemnify the Respondent against all such liability.

30.136   To ensure that an undertaking is enforceable it is recommended that the undertakings are recorded on a general form of undertaking (usually available from the court office). The form contains standardized warnings in the form of a penal notice. The person giving the undertaking should sign it in front of the judge who will have checked that they understand the promises that they are making, understand the nature of an undertaking, and that, if a breach is proved, that the result may be a fine or imprisonment. Once the person giving the undertaking has signed the general form of undertaking it should be sealed by the court and then personally served. The fact of service would normally be evidenced by an affidavit of service.

30.137   The preamble can also be used to set out the history of the division of the family assets which has already taken place. For example, it may record that the family home has already been sold and the net proceeds of sale divided equally between the parties. Further, the preamble may explain the rationale of aspects of the order. For example, it may record that one party is taking responsibility for discharging outstanding family debts (and that is why he or she is to receive an enhanced lump sum payment).

The body of the order

30.138   This will deal with those aspects of the financial settlement which the court has power to order.

Periodical payments

30.139   (a)   The order must indicate the following:
  (i)   to whom and by whom is the payment to be made;
  (ii)   the amount of the payment;
  (iii)   whether the payment is to be made weekly, monthly, or annually;
  (iv)   whether the payment is to be made in advance or in arrears;
  (v)   the date on which payment is to begin;
  (vi)   the events which will bring payment to an end.

(b)   *Backdating an order for periodical payments*: there is power to backdate periodical payments orders to the date of the making of the application (see Chapter 29). If an order is backdated, the payer is instantly in arrears in respect of the payments due prior to the hearing. For this reason, the court will be reluctant to backdate unless the payer has actually been making voluntary periodical payments in the run-up to the hearing which can be offset against the arrears. Care must be taken therefore to ensure that the payer is given credit for any payments he may have made between the date to which the order is backdated and the date on which the order is made. Where such credit is given, it has the effect of reducing the arrears (or even extinguishing them).

(c)   *Registration of periodical payments order in a magistrates' court*: this means that the order will be paid and enforced through the magistrates' court and that any application for a variation will have to be made to that court except if there are already proceedings to vary another aspect of the order in a different court. It also means that the diversion procedure can be used with regard to social security benefits (see Chapter 24). An application for registration should certainly be considered where it appears that payment under the order may be erratic.

Lump sums

In addition to the order specifying the details of the amount to be paid and the date of pay- **30.140**
ment, it is important to specify the rate of interest to be paid should default occur.

The clause would read as follows: **30.141**

> The Respondent do within 28 days of the date of this order pay or cause to be paid to the Petitioner
> a lump sum of £10,000, interest to accrue at the rate of x per cent per annum calculated on a daily
> basis in the event of default.

Property adjustment orders

Such orders normally deal with the future of the family home but can also determine the **30.142**
disposal of personal property, for example house contents, cars, and investments and savings. The precise terms of the property adjustment order will depend on how the assets are to
be disposed of but set out below is a non-exhaustive list of matters to be considered with the
more usual types of order.

(a) *Outright transfer of the family home*: the order must include provision for the transfer of
the legal and equitable interest in the property and a date or event for transfer. This is
essential to determine whether default has occurred.

(b) *Deferred trust*: here the property will remain in joint names or be transferred into the joint
names of the parties to hold the legal estate as trustees and the order will then include
provisions to regulate the trust.
    The following matters must be dealt with:
    (i) a statement as to who is to have the exclusive right to occupy the property until
    sale;
    (ii) identifying the 'triggering' events for the sale to occur, for example of the youngest
    child of the family attaining the age of 17 years, or on the death or remarriage of the
    occupying party (whichever occurs first);
    (iii) provision as to how the net proceeds of sale are to be calculated and an indication of
    the division of the net proceeds between the parties;
    (iv) determining who is to be responsible for the cost of repairing and insuring the prop-
    erty in the meantime;
    (v) who is to pay for any costs associated with implementing the terms of the order (eg
    the cost, if any, of preparation of the transfer documents).

(c) *Deferred charge*:
    (i) if necessary the order will require the transfer of the legal estate into the sole name of
    the occupying party, the transfer to be completed by a specified date;
    (ii) the occupying party will also be required to execute a charge in favour of the
    non-occupier to ensure that he receives payment of a sum representing a specified
    proportion of the net value of the property.

The legal charge is a comprehensive document which not only regulates the occupation of
the property (eg preventing the occupying party from remortgaging the property without the
consent of the other party), but specifies the triggering events for the statutory power of sale
to arise.

Orders for sale

30.143 Where there is to be an immediate sale of assets the order must of course specify the division of the net proceeds of sale and indicate which party is to have responsibility for the conduct of the sale (this is particularly important where one party is likely to be uncooperative) and which estate agent is to be instructed.

30.144 For more detail on orders relating to the family home, see Chapter 31.

Pension attachment orders

30.145 These orders, made under ss 25B and 25C, MCA 1973 and described in Chapter 29, require careful drafting.

30.146 The following points should be noted:

(a) The attachment order may relate to a personal, as distinct from an occupational, pension. Here responsibility for payment of the pension contributions lies with the pension holder. The court has no power to order that payments be made to increase the value of the pension fund. The pension holder could therefore be required to give an undertaking to the court, recorded in the preamble to the order, to continue to make such payments (and, arguably, to increase them on an annual basis in line with inflation or by a specified percentage).

(b) The order cannot take effect until the pension becomes payable. The court is unable to order that the pension holder retire by a specified date, and therefore it is imperative that the preamble to the order contains an undertaking from the pension holder to retire by a certain date or take the benefits under a personal pension arrangement by a specified date.

(c) For a lump sum to be payable on maturity of the pension, a proportion of the pension fund must be commuted (ie, pension benefits are exchanged for a tax-free single lump sum payment). Under s 25B(7), MCA 1973, the court may order the pension holder to commute a proportion of the pension fund to provide a lump sum for the benefit of the receiving party. What the court is not able to do is to order the pension holder *not* to commute the pension fund, and yet such action will reduce the pension income otherwise payable and, in consequence, the benefit of any order attaching the pension income. The solution is to incorporate an undertaking into the preamble in which the pension holder agrees to commute a specified proportion of the pension benefits only.

(d) While the order attaching the pension income will end on the remarriage of the receiving party, this is not the case with the payment of a lump sum which has been attached. The pension holder may consider this to be unjust, and unless it can be demonstrated that payment of a lump sum at the time of the maturity of the pension is simply part of the process of the redistribution of capital assets, as happened in *Burrow v Burrow* [1999] 1 FLR 508, it is sensible to include a provision in the order allowing the lump sum payment to lapse on the remarriage of the receiving party;

(e) the order attaching the pension income is seen as a form of periodical payments order made under s 23, MCA 1973. In consequence it is essential that the body of the order contains a periodical payments order (for a nominal amount). This will enable the receiving party, if appropriate, to seek a prospective variation of the attachment order, to become effective on the retirement of the pension holder.

The terms of a pension sharing or pension attachment order

Rule 9.35 requires that where such an order is to be made, the body of the order must contain **30.147** a statement that there is to be provision by way of pension sharing or pension attachment in accordance with the annex to the order and be accompanied by an annex containing information which will be determined by whether a pension sharing or pension attachment order is made. Where provision is made in relation to more than one pension arrangement there must be an annex for each pension arrangement.

The information in the annex (Form P1)—pension sharing order

The detailed information is set out in the annex and includes, among other things, details **30.148** of the court making the order and of the transferor and transferee, details sufficient to identify the pension arrangement concerned, the specified percentage required to create the pension debit and pension credit, details as to who is to pay the costs of implementing the order, the date on which the order takes effect, and whether there is to be an internal or external transfer, etc.

Most importantly, the annex indicates that, before making the pension sharing order, the **30.149** court must be satisfied that the person responsible for the pension arrangement has provided the information required by reg 4, Pensions on Divorce, etc (Provision of Information) Regulations 2000 (SI 2000/1048) and that in consequence there is a power to make a pension sharing order.

The information in the annex (Form P2)—pension attachment order

The detailed information is similar to that contained in Form P1. The annex enables the par- **30.150** ties to set out the precise terms of the order (eg the percentage of the pension income to be paid to the recipient). In addition, however, the annex must also prescribe what the person responsible for the pension arrangement is required to do and details of addresses where payment is to be made.

Clean break orders

Where the parties have agreed that there should be a clean break order (see Chapter 31, **30.151** paras 31.24 ff), the order should be drafted in such a way that the arrangement works on a mutual and comprehensive basis, as demonstrated in the clause set out below:

> Upon compliance with paragraphs 1 and 2 of this order and upon compliance by the Respondent with his undertaking herein the Petitioner's and the Respondent's claims for financial provision and property adjustment orders do stand dismissed, and it is directed that neither party shall be entitled to apply to the court thereafter for an order under s. 23(1)(a), (b) or (c), s. 24, s. 24A, s. 24B or ss. 25B and C of the Matrimonial Causes Act 1973 as amended or substituted nor under the Married Women's Property Act 1882.
>
> Pursuant to the Inheritance (Provision for Family and Dependants) Act 1975, s. 15, the court considering it just so to order, neither the Petitioner nor the Respondent shall be entitled on the death of the other to apply for an order under s. 2 of that Act.

It should be noted that where the order contains provision for pension sharing, claims should **30.152** not be dismissed until the pension sharing order takes effect so that the non-member party is left with a claim against the member's estate under the 1975 Act, if the member dies during the implementation process.

Costs

30.153 The issue of costs is considered at paras 30.90 ff. However, it may be necessary to ask the court to direct that a detailed assessment of costs is carried out.

30.154 Where a client is publicly funded, such a direction should be requested to enable costs to be recovered from the Community Legal Service Fund.

30.155 Remember the need to try to ensure that the Legal Services Commission will agree to the postponement of the charge where property has been recovered or preserved for the publicly funded client (see Chapter 2).

Liberty to apply

30.156 This provision should be included to enable either party to seek guidance from the court in respect of the interpretation and/or implementation of the order if difficulties subsequently arise. However, note that this provision does not enable the parties to return to court for a variation of some of the substantive parts of the order.

30.157 The liberty to apply provision is essential in orders relating to property. For example, it enables the matter to be referred back to the district judge for execution of the transfer, or for an order for possession if one party refuses to cooperate. Similarly, it can be relied on if one party fails to sign an assignment of a life policy, or refuses to sell when the triggering event occurs in respect of property held on a trust of land (see Chapter 33).

N   APPEAL

30.158 Where an order is made after a contested hearing in front of the district judge, either party may appeal, if dissatisfied, to a circuit judge. Note that the appeal period is 21 days from the date of the district judge's order (see r 30.4(2)(b), FPR 2010). Furthermore, the appellant must set out his grounds of appeal in his notice of appeal in Form N161. Those grounds are contained in r 30.12(3); an appeal will succeed where the decision of the lower court was wrong or unjust because of a serious procedural or other irregularity in the proceedings in the lower court.

30.159 Note that permission to appeal must be sought from the trial judge immediately after the decision to be appealed (r 30.3(1)). A basis for the appeal must be set out at that stage. Permission to appeal will only be given where the court considers that the appeal would have a real prospect of success or there is some other compelling reason why the appeal should be heard (r 30.3(7)). Where the trial judge refuses permission, the person seeking permission may make a further application for permission in writing (in practice as part of the appeal notice at section 4) to the appeal court. Where the appeal court, without a hearing, refuses permission to appeal, the person seeking permission may request the decision to be reconsidered at a hearing (r 30.3(4)). Note that that request must be made within seven days.

30.160 It is important to be aware that where a party's advocate considers that there has been a material omission from the judgment then that advocate must bring it to the court's attention before the order is perfected. Similarly, if permission to appeal is sought on that basis then the trial court must consider whether there has been a material omission and adjourn for that purpose if necessary and where it is persuaded that there has been such an omission, provide an addition to the judgment (see PD30A, para 4.6).

Oral evidence or fresh evidence will not be admitted on appeal unless either it was not avail-   **30.161**
able at the trial to the party seeking to rely on it, or that reasonable diligence would not have made it available and that it would have formed a determining factor in, or an important influence on, the outcome of the case.

Appeal is normally to a circuit judge, except in the Principal Registry of the Family Division   **30.162**
where the appeal is heard by a judge of the Family Division. Appeals which involve issues of complexity or gravity (eg allegations of deception or fraud or material non-disclosure, etc) should be dealt with in the High Court.

If you are bringing an appeal or responding to one then it is essential that the Practice Direction   **30.163**
to Part 30, FPR 2010 is studied closely. It sets out the various documents that must be lodged with the appeal notice and provides rules for the filing of an appeal bundle.

O   CHALLENGING FINANCIAL ORDERS MADE BY CONSENT

Procedure

Consent order are also capable of being set aside but only in very limited circumstances.   **30.164**
Those circumstances are where the parties' agreement was reached on the basis of a serious mistake by one of the parties, or as a result of fraud or serious misrepresentation, where one party's apparent consent had not been freely given or in circumstances where one party had not disclosed all the material facts to the other and this had led the court to make an order substantially different from that which it would otherwise have made (eg see *T* v *T (Consent Order: Procedure to Set Aside)* [1997] 1 FCR 282, and, for a case where the Court of Appeal refused to set aside, stating that the policy of the law is to encourage a clean break, *Harris* v *Manahan* [1997] 1 FLR 205).

Prior to the FPR 2010 consent orders were usually challenged by applying for a rehearing pur-   **30.165**
suant to Order 37, r 1 of the County Court Rules. Under this provision the judge has power on an application made within 14 days (or later with permission) to order a rehearing where no error of the court at the hearing is alleged. The rehearing will be on the basis of a considera-tion of the documents only. In the High Court where the application would be to set aside the original order, there is no specific time limit for the application to set aside to be made, but two weeks would normally be regarded as the time for application.

At the time of writing it is, unfortunately, not clear whether the FPR 2010 apply to the County   **30.166**
Court Rules and therefore whether this route remains viable.

Appeal out of time

Events may occur shortly after the order is made which have the effect of undermining the   **30.167**
basis on which the order was made. In these circumstances it would be inappropriate to apply for a rehearing (in the case of a county court order) or to have the order set aside (in the case of

a High Court order) since the event in question occurred *after* the order was made. Nor could there be a conventional appeal, since it would be impossible to argue that the judge had made an error on the facts before him.

30.168 The solution is to apply to the court for permission to appeal out of time.

30.169 The criteria to be met are set out in *Barder* v *Barder (Caluori intervening)* [1988] AC 20, as follows:

(a) that new events have occurred since the making of the order which invalidate the basis, or fundamental assumption, upon which the order was made so that, if permission to appeal out of time were given, the appeal would be certain, or very likely, to succeed;

(b) that the new events have occurred within a relatively short time of the order having been made;

(c) the application for permission to appeal should be made reasonably promptly in the circumstances of the case;

(d) granting of permission to appeal out of time should not prejudice third parties who have acquired, in good faith and for valuable consideration, interests in the property which is the subject matter of the relevant order.

30.170 The first two conditions above were demonstrated in *Reid* v *Reid* [2004] 1 FLR 736 where the wife died two months after a consent order had been made. Her early death justified permission to appeal out of time and enabled the court to make a more generous order in favour of the husband while ensuring that the wife's estate retained some capital.

30.171 The fact that there had been a delay of three months between the death of the wife and the making of the application did not fall foul of the requirement to act promptly. However, an application for permission to appeal out of time will fail where there is an unjustified delay in making the application (eg a period of approximately four years in *Burns* v *Burns* [2004] 3 FCR 263).

30.172 Guidance on the application of the above principles in practice has been offered by the Court of Appeal in *Williams* v *Lindley* [2005] 2 FLR 710. In particular, where it is found that a supervening event (in this case, the wife's remarriage) has invalidated the original order, then reassessment by appeal out of time would be appropriate. The reassessment would include a full consideration of all the factors in s 25, MCA 1973 and not simply a consideration of what assets the parties had at the time of the hearing and what their current value is.

30.173 Hence, practitioners need to ensure that in drafting the application to appeal out of time:

(a) the application should clearly identify the supervening event;

(b) explain why the event would produce a fundamentally different result had it been anticipated at the time of the original order; and

(c) clearly indicate the effect the supervening event has (i) on the original order and (ii) on what happens subsequently.

P FINANCIAL REMEDIES AND CIVIL PARTNERSHIP

30.174 The procedure described above also applies to financial proceedings brought where a civil partnership is to be annulled or dissolved or where a separation order is applied for: r 9.1, FPR 2010.

FLOWCHART

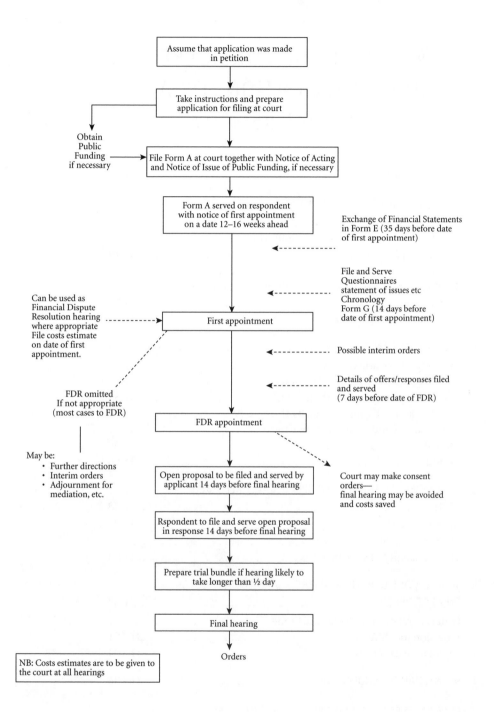

Assume that application was made in petition

Take instructions and prepare application for filing at court

Obtain Public Funding if necessary

File Form A at court together with Notice of Acting and Notice of Issue of Public Funding, if necessary

Form A served on respondent with notice of first appointment on a date 12–16 weeks ahead

Exchange of Financial Statements in Form E (35 days before date of first appointment)

File and Serve Questionnaires statement of issues etc Chronology Form G (14 days before date of first appointment)

Can be used as Financial Dispute Resolution hearing where appropriate File costs estimate on date of first appointment.

First appointment

Possible interim orders

FDR omitted If not appropriate (most cases to FDR)

Details of offers/responses filed and served (7 days before date of FDR)

May be:
• Further directions
• Interim orders
• Adjournment for mediation, etc.

FDR appointment

Open proposal to be filed and served by applicant 14 days before final hearing

Court may make consent orders— final hearing may be avoided and costs saved

Rspondent to file and serve open proposal in response 14 days before final hearing

Prepare trial bundle if hearing likely to take longer than ½ day

Final hearing

Orders

NB: Costs estimates are to be given to the court at all hearings

31

FACTORS TO BE CONSIDERED IN AN APPLICATION FOR A FINANCIAL REMEDY

A   INTRODUCTION

The court has a very wide discretion about which orders to make on an application for a **31.01** financial remedy. Section 25, Matrimonial Causes Act 1973 ('MCA 1973') directs that all the circumstances of the case should be taken into account and it has been stressed by the courts that every case has to be dealt with individually on its own facts.

This chapter sets out the s 25, MCA 1973 considerations that must be taken into account and **31.02** explains a number of principles derived from case law that provide guidance in such applications. It should be appreciated at the outset that the MCA 1973 does not indicate what type of financial order should be made in particular circumstances nor does it give guidance on how a financial award should be quantified.

This is a matter for the judge to decide, bearing in mind: **31.03**

(a) the types of orders available;
(b) the s 25 factors;
(c) the relevant case law; and
(d) the facts of the particular case.

This area of family law requires patience and attention to detail. It is important to remember **31.04** that there is usually more than one possible outcome in an application for a financial order: learn to develop arguments to justify the settlement you are seeking.

In practice, knowledge of the likely approach of the local county court(s) is invaluable. **31.05**

Many of the reported cases referred to below involve 'big money' where the courts have to **31.06** determine the destination of surplus assets. While the judges in these cases emphasize that the general principles laid down in such cases are of general application, it is important to remember that, in many cases, the assets for distribution will be so limited that the courts will be hard pressed to ensure that even the basic needs of the parties (for accommodation and the like) will be met. Priority will inevitably be given in these circumstances to the needs of the party who has the care of any minor children of the family.

Nevertheless, it is essential to understand the principles which underpin the approach of the **31.07** courts as set out by the House of Lords in *White* v *White* [2000] 2 FLR 981 and in *Miller* v *Miller; McFarlane* v *McFarlane* [2006] UKHL 24.

In very basic terms they are as follows: **31.08**

(a) the aim is to achieve a fair outcome in which discrimination plays no part;
(b) fairness is not necessarily the same thing as equality of provision;
(c) where a judge is considering departing from equality he should cross-check his tentative views against the 'yardstick of equality'.

Sometimes, where the property involved is clearly matrimonial in nature, the yardstick of equality is a starting point and not just a cross-check. Such property is likely to be divided equally, regardless of which party actually owns it or the length of the marriage; equal division only usually being offset by a parties' particular needs or when one party needs to be compensated for relationship-generated financial loss.

31.09   The MCA 1973 contains three underpinning principles which inform a court how it should exercise its powers; those being need, compensation, and sharing.

31.10   'Need' speaks for itself and while the parties' needs will probably have been generated by the marriage (such as accommodation needs of the primary carer for the children of the marriage), there is no requirement that they are. So, needs arising from age or disability are an example of this. Need trumps the other principles; in other words if there are only sufficient assets to meet the parties' needs then the principles of compensation and sharing fall away.

31.11   Compensation is more subtle. As Lord Nicholls said in *Miller*:

> this is aimed at redressing any significant prospective economic disparity between the parties arising from the way they conducted their marriage. For instance, the parties may have arranged their affairs in a way that has greatly advantaged the husband in terms of his earning capacity but left the wife severely handicapped so far as her own earning capacity is concerned. (para 13)

Compensation is therefore of particular importance in periodical payments applications and applications to vary.

31.12   Sharing, in this context, means that when a couple marry they share the fruits of the marriage between them, both financial and otherwise, and therefore it follows that the wealth belongs to each of them. The principle of sharing strongly applies to matrimonial property. Its application is of less relevance in the case of non-matrimonial property.

31.13   It should be stressed that these various principles elucidate the 'philosophy' behind financial provision. They are not a statutory code as set out in s 25.

B   THE S 25 FACTORS

General duty

31.14   The court's general duty on all applications for financial orders is set out in s 25(1) as follows:

> It shall be the duty of the court in deciding whether to exercise its powers under section 23, 24, 24A or 24B above and, if so, in what manner, to have regard to all the circumstances of the case, first consideration being given to the welfare while a minor of any child of the family who has not attained the age of eighteen.

31.15   In *Suter* v *Suter* [1987] 2 FLR 232, the Court of Appeal underlined that the welfare of the children was to be given first consideration but was not the overriding consideration. Thus, the task for the court was to consider all the circumstances, always bearing in mind the important first consideration of the welfare of the children, and then to try to attain a financial result that was just between husband and wife.

31.16   Ensuring that a child was suitably accommodated in reasonable travelling distance to his school amounted to giving the child's needs first but not paramount consideration so that the statutory duty was properly carried out: *Akintola* v *Akintola* [2002] 1 FLR 701.

31.17   It should be noted that the duty is limited to the child of the family: it does not extend to other children who might be affected by the outcome of an application for a financial order, such as children from new relationships entered into by either spouse.

The provision 'all the circumstances' can include the existence of a pre-nuptial agreement. **31.18**
Such agreements have been accorded increasing importance in financial proceedings. This
slow development has now been approved by the Supreme Court in the recent case of
Radmacher v *Granatino* [2010] UKSC 42. As a result a court should give effect to a nuptial
agreement that is freely entered into by each party with a full appreciation of its implications unless in the circumstances prevailing it would not be fair to hold the parties to their
agreement. The type of consideration that a court would have regard to are questions such
as whether one party to the agreement placed the other under excessive pressure to enter
the agreement. The parties' age and maturity might also be relevant and whether either had
been in previous relationships. Another important factor might be whether the marriage
would have gone ahead with or without the agreement. The Supreme Court confirmed that
on entering such an agreement it was not necessary for each party to be aware of the precise
detail of the assets owned by the other: 'what is important is that each party should have all
the information that is material to his or her decision, and that each party should intend that
the agreement should govern the financial consequences of the marriage coming to an end'
(para 69). As far as the relevance of events occurring after the agreement are concerned, the
length of the marriage, the parties' respective needs when assessed against the agreement, the
importance of the principles of sharing and compensation are the types of issues that may
render the agreement to be unfair, or partially unfair.

Specific matters to consider in an application for provision for a spouse

Section 25(2), MCA 1973 directs the court in particular to have regard to the following **31.19**
matters when dealing with an application for a financial order:

(a) the income, earning capacity, property, and other financial resources which each of
the parties to the marriage has or is likely to have in the foreseeable future, including
in the case of earning capacity any increase in that capacity which it would in the
opinion of the court be reasonable to expect a party to the marriage to take steps to
acquire;

(b) the financial needs, obligations, and responsibilities which each of the parties to the marriage has or is likely to have in the foreseeable future;

(c) the standard of living enjoyed by the family before the breakdown of the marriage;

(d) the age of each party to the marriage and the duration of the marriage;

(e) any physical or mental disability of either of the parties to the marriage;

(f) the contributions which each of the parties has made or is likely in the foreseeable future
to make to the welfare of the family including any contribution by looking after the
home or caring for the family;

(g) the conduct of each of the parties, if that conduct is such that it would in the opinion of
the court be inequitable to disregard it;

(h) in the case of proceedings for divorce or nullity of marriage, the value to each of the
parties to the marriage of any benefit which, by reason of the dissolution or annulment
of the marriage, that party will lose the chance of acquiring.

In *Piglowska* v *Piglowski* [1999] 2 FLR 763 the House of Lords indicated, amongst other things, **31.20**
that with the exception of the consideration of the children of the family there was no hierarchical order to the factors: each is of equal value and must be considered in turn.

Pensions

31.21   Section 25B, MCA 1973 inserted by s 166, Pensions Act 1995 provides as follows:

> 25B.—(1) The matters to which the court is required to have regard under section 25(2) above include—
>
> (a) in the case of paragraph (a), any benefits under a pension arrangement which a party to the marriage has or is likely to have, and
>
> (b) in the case of paragraph (h), any benefits under a pension arrangement which, by reason of dissolution or annulment of the marriage, a party to the marriage will lose the chance of acquiring,
>
> and, accordingly, in relation to benefits under a pension arrangement, section 25(2)(a) above shall have effect as if '*in the foreseeable future*' were omitted.

The effect of this amendment is to enable the court to take into account any pension benefits which a party to a marriage has accrued irrespective of the length of time before the pension becomes payable.

Specific matters to consider on application for provision for a child

31.22   Section 25(3) directs the court to have regard in particular to the following matters when dealing with an application for a financial order for a child of the family:

(a)   the financial needs of the child;

(b)   the income, earning capacity (if any), property, and other financial resources of the child;

(c)   any physical or mental disability of the child;

(d)   the manner in which he was being and in which the parties to the marriage expected him to be educated or trained;

(e)   the considerations mentioned in relation to the parties to the marriage in paras (a), (b), (c), and (e) of subs (2) above.

These factors are now far less important due to the advent of the Child Support Act 1991 ('CSA 1991'), but will still be considered where the application relates to a lump sum or property adjustment order. They must, of course, be considered where provision is sought for a child who is not the natural child of the prospective payer, or in the other categories of cases where the court still retains jurisdiction to make orders for the maintenance of children (see Chapter 35 for further details).

31.23   Furthermore, where the application relates to a child of the family who is not the child of the party against whom an order is sought, the court must also have regard:

(a)   to whether that party assumed any responsibility for the child's maintenance, and, if so, to the extent to which, and the basis upon which, that party assumed such responsibility and to the length of time for which that party discharged such responsibility;

(b)   to whether in assuming and discharging such responsibility that party did so knowing that the child was not his or her own;

(c)   to the liability of any other person to maintain the child (s 25(4)).

The clean break approach

Section 25A, MCA 1973 deals with the concept of clean break orders. A clean break order **31.24** is one that achieves a once-and-for-all settlement between the parties to the marriage by dismissing any outstanding claims for financial orders at the time of making the order and preventing them reviving such claims in the future.

What s 25A has done is to oblige the courts to give thought to achieving a clean break between **31.25** the parties in every case of divorce or nullity whether the parties suggest it or not, and to give the court the power to dictate a clean break by dismissing a party's application for periodical payments without his or her consent if appropriate.

Section 25A(1) obliges the court, when exercising its powers in relation to a spouse on or after **31.26** divorce or nullity, to consider whether it would be appropriate to exercise those powers so as to achieve a clean break between the parties as soon after the decree as the court thinks just and reasonable.

Section 25A(2) applies to cases where the court decides to make a periodical payments or **31.27** secured periodical payments order in favour of a spouse on or after divorce or nullity. It obliges the court to consider, in particular, whether it would be appropriate to make an order for a fixed term only of sufficient length to enable the spouse in whose favour the order is made to adjust without undue hardship to being financially independent of the other party. This may be appropriate where, for example, there are young children but the wife is trained or experienced, or plans to acquire a skill and can be expected to go back to work when the children are old enough, or where a wife who has been working part time through choice needs time to arrange to work full time and adjust to the prospect. This may, of course, be a highly speculative exercise and the court must look carefully at the particular circumstances of the case.

In *McFarlane* v *McFarlane* (para 31.07 above), the House of Lords upheld the wife's appeal and **31.28** removed the five-year time limit imposed by the Court of Appeal on the periodical payments order made in her favour, stating that the five-year term was 'most unlikely to be sufficient to achieve a fair outcome and indicating that the onus should be on the payer, rather than the payee, to seek a variation as future circumstances changed'.

Nevertheless, s 25A(3) enables the court to impose a clean break between the parties when **31.29** it considers that no continuing obligation to make or secure periodical payments should be imposed on either spouse in favour of the other. In such a case, the court can dismiss an application for periodical payments or secured periodical payments without the consent of the applicant and, to put the matter beyond doubt, direct that the applicant shall not be entitled to make any further application in relation to that marriage for a periodical payments or secured periodical payments order.

The Court of Appeal has over the years given guidance as to the circumstances in which a **31.30** clean break order will be appropriate or inappropriate, stating that it is not usually appropriate to provide for the termination of periodical payments in the case of a woman in her mid-forties. In *C* v *C (Financial Relief: Short Marriage)* [1997] 2 FLR 26 the Court of Appeal held that a court should not decide upon a term without evidence to support its conclusion: 'facts supported by evidence must, therefore, justify a reasonable expectation that the payee can amounted to £16 million of which £12 million had been inherited by the husband. The wife was awarded 32 per cent of the overall assets.

31.43   The debate as to which assets should be subject to division in financial proceedings continues. At the outset, it should be emphasized that, in the majority of financial cases, this exercise is academic for reasons highlighted in the introduction. However, where the assets exceed needs, the matter has to be explored. In the leading speeches of Lord Nicholls and Lady Hale in *Miller* v *Miller; McFarlane* v *McFarlane* (para 31.07 above), both judges agreed that the source of an asset is a relevant issue in determining how it should be allocated or shared.

31.44   In broad terms, 'matrimonial property' tends to include assets that have come into existence during the marriage and also items that are shared between the parties during the marriage, such as the matrimonial home, cars, life insurance policies, etc. As already set out above, the principle of sharing applies to matrimonial property so that, in very general terms, such assets are normally divided equally, subject to the parties' needs and any relationship-generated compensation.

31.45   'Non-matrimonial property' tends to be assets that a party owned prior to the marriage, inheritances or assets that came into existence after the marriage such as subsequent performance bonuses. It is important to repeat, however, that merely because an asset is 'non-matrimonial' does not mean that it is not included in the pot; nevertheless, its origin is relevant to whether one party should receive more than the other party. The principle of sharing does not apply quite so readily to non-matrimonial property. However, the length of the marriage, the nature of the asset, and other such matters must be considered.

31.46   On a practical note, the difficulty of classification highlights the need for pre-nuptial agreements, at the very least to identify the nature and value of assets brought by each party into the marriage.

31.47   Entitlements under an insurance policy that could be surrendered or is likely to mature anyway in the foreseeable future can be taken into account. Pension and lump sum entitlement on retirement can be considered irrespective of the length of time which must elapse before the pension becomes payable.

31.48   The court will pay attention to the fact that not all assets are readily realizable. A businessman, for example, may not be able to draw substantial capital sums out of his business without affecting its liquidity; indeed, he may not even be able to withdraw his entire income entitlement each year as profits may need to be ploughed back as working capital. The court would not make an order that would cause a spouse to lose his livelihood, for example by forcing him to sell his business. If the other spouse's contribution to a business should be recognized, this will have to be done in some other way, for instance by giving her a greater share in the family's other assets such as the family home or by ordering a lump sum payment to her to be made by instalments, the instalments being at such a level that the husband can afford to pay them from income without prejudicing his business interests.

31.49   Account may be taken of property and income of a cohabitant or new spouse (see paras 31.54 ff) and property acquired after separation if it is necessary to do so to achieve a fair outcome: *A* v *B (Financial Relief: Agreements)* [2005] 2 FLR 730.

31.50   Note that where there is doubt as to a party's future prospects, it may be worth considering seeking an adjournment until such time as the position becomes clearer if it appears that this will not delay matters unduly or prejudice either side, as happened in *D* v *D (Lump Sum: Adjournment of Application)* [2001] 1 FLR 633. However, courts do prefer to achieve certainty at the time of the hearing, if possible, and it has been held that it would be wrong to adjourn an application for a lump sum payment for more than four or five years (*Roberts* v *Roberts* [1986] 2 All ER 483).

As far as pensions are concerned as a type of asset to be taken into account, the value of the **31.51** pension is normally quantified by an actuarial computation known as a cash equivalent transfer value (CETV). If the pension is in payment the computation is referred to as a cash equivalent benefit value (CEB). Either of those values must be obtained from the pension provider by the party that holds the pension as part of the process of financial disclosure. The relevant information is inserted into Form E. In simple terms, the valuation figures indicate the cost of purchasing a corresponding future annuity. Be careful, however, with the valuation of certain schemes such as those belonging to members of the police force or civil service: sometimes the CETV might not fully reflect the true value. In some cases it may be worth taking expert advice from a pensions specialist.

The other point to make is that the pension asset is different from other capital assets: it is not **31.52** a cash fund over which the parties may have complete control but, according to Thorpe LJ in *Cowan* v *Cowan* [2001] 2 FLR 192, a pension fund 'is no more and no less than a whole life fixed rate income stream'. Hence, in *Maskell* v *Maskell* [2003] 1 FLR 1138, Thorpe LJ criticized the circuit judge for aggregating the value of the pension fund with the other assets since only 25 per cent of the husband's fund could be taken as capital, the balance having to be taken as an income stream. Thorpe LJ commented 'he simply failed to compare like with like'.

So, how is a court likely to treat the existence of a pension? All that can usefully be said is that **31.53** context is everything. It may be that in a long marriage one of the parties has accumulated a large pension pot in a scheme that has a host of associated benefits. As such, it is likely to fall to be considered as one of the 'fruits of the matrimonial partnership', a phrase coined by Lady Hale in *Miller*. If the other party has no pension provision, a normal approach would be to share the fund between the parties. Matters become more complicated where one party started the pension many years before the marriage and perhaps started to draw upon the pension during the marriage having received a lump sum. One simple approach often used is to calculate the number of years of the marriage that fall within the accumulation of the pension and then share a corresponding proportion. This approach, however, ignores the fact that pensions tend to increase exponentially as they mature. This is again something that may merit consideration by a pensions expert. A similar stance might be appropriate where each party has a pension but where the values differ as do the benefits. Where they wish to equalize the income from those pensions when they fall to be paid, then only an expert is able to calculate the appropriate sharing necessary.

Needs, obligations, and responsibilities

Needs and obligations vary from household to household. Invariably, however, both spouses **31.54** will need a roof over their heads and the spouse who has the care of the children will have a particularly pressing need for a home for the family. This factor is likely to be of crucial importance in the court's decision. The court will also look at each party's regular outgoings (fuel bills, rent, council tax, water rates, mortgage, food, hire-purchase debts, payments following a maintenance calculation under the CSA 1991, etc) and then consider what are the reasonable such outgoings in the circumstances. What is reasonable will obviously vary from case to case—someone travelling a mile to work each day may be expected to use a bicycle or walk if money for the family is tight, whereas a person who travels many miles in the course of his job can fairly expect to do so in a relatively comfortable car. The court's approach to each party's regular expenditure will have to be realistic—it may be wholly unreasonable for one party to be purchasing an expensive television on hire-purchase where the other party does not even have enough money for food, but, once the party has entered into the commitment, there is very little that can be done about it and the continuing obligation to pay will have to be taken into account.

31.55   Although the abstract prospect of remarriage is not relevant, where one or the other party has actually remarried or formed a new relationship, this will have to be taken into account as it will obviously have an effect on his needs and obligations and possibly also on his resources. He may be in a better position than if he had remained single (eg where the new partner has substantial means), or the new relationship may burden him with more responsibilities, particularly if there is a child of the new family. Where the new partner is earning or has resources, the proper course is to take these into account not as a figure to add to the spouse's own income and resources but on the basis that the partner's resources release the spouse from obligations he would otherwise have had towards her (and in some cases also from expenditure on himself) and therefore free a greater part of his income or property for distribution by way of financial relief.

The standard of living enjoyed by the parties

31.56   Briefly, two points are to be made here. First, the court is no longer under a duty to apply the minimal loss principle and to endeavour to place the parties in the position in which they would have been if the marriage had not broken down.

31.57   Secondly, while courts are to recognize the standard of living enjoyed by the parties during the marriage, Lord Nicholls in *Miller* (para 31.07 above) deprecated any attempt to extend the scope of this to include the concept of 'legitimate expectations' stating that 'both hopes and expectations, as such, are not an appropriate basis to assess financial needs'.

Age of parties and duration of marriage

31.58   Age can have an important bearing on the court's decision. Where the parties are young when the marriage breaks down, it may be reasonable to impose a clean break between them immediately if there are no children, or to expect the wife to make her way on her own within a period of time (granting her a periodical payments order for a fixed term, for instance) where she is looking after children. Furthermore, young spouses are likely to have a greater capacity to borrow money than those in their fifties or over. This can be taken into account when deciding what is to be done about lump sum and transfer of property orders. Thus, where the parties are young it may be possible, for instance, to transfer the matrimonial home to the wife who is looking after young children and to expect the husband to raise capital on mortgage to purchase alternative accommodation for himself; in contrast, the older husband with no prospect of obtaining a mortgage will need some capital to rehouse himself.

The court is less likely to expect a wife in her late forties or fifties to go out and get a job **31.59** (particularly if she has not worked since getting married or having children) than a younger wife brought up in the tradition of working wives and mothers. It can also be taken into consideration that parties who are nearing retirement are likely to need to preserve their capital for when they stop work and will therefore be less able to transfer assets or make lump sum payments than younger people who have time to build up provision for their retirement over the course of their working lives.

The length of the marriage is also a highly important factor—the longer the marriage, the **31.60** more each party is likely to have contributed to it and the harder it will be for them to achieve independence again when it breaks down.

Miller was itself a short marriage case of two years and nine months involving no children. **31.61** The husband was a wealthy fund manager worth some £30 million. The wife received £5 million at the first hearing, approximately 17 per cent. The Court of Appeal confirmed that award and the husband's second appeal to the House of Lords was dismissed.

Applying the underlying principles of need, compensation, and sharing, the House of Lords **31.62** said that in a short marriage where there were no children a party's need would probably not exceed the need for a 'gentle transition' into self-sufficiency (para 158). There is little place for compensation in a short marriage. The position is different, however, in terms of the principle of sharing. Lady Hale said that the principle is 'applicable as much to short marriages as to long marriages. A short marriage is no less a partnership of equals than a long marriage. The difference is that a short marriage has been less enduring. In the nature of things this will affect the quantum of the financial fruits of the partnership' (para 7). The speeches differ in how the principle of sharing is to be applied. What is apparent, however, from the result is that the wife shared in a relatively small proportion of the wealth that the husband created during their short marriage. Lady Hale, having stated that the husband's business profits during the marriage were not matrimonial property as such, did say that she was still entitled to 'some share in the considerable increase of the husband's wealth during the marriage' (para 158).

Miller does clarify that even in short marriages the matrimonial assets (eg the home, cars, **31.63** insurance policies, etc) are likely to be divided equally as a result of the principle of sharing. In practice, however, a court is likely to take a far firmer view about what qualifies as a matrimonial asset. Take the case of a former matrimonial home which had been previously in the sole possession of one of the parties for some years perhaps following an earlier marriage; fairness may dictate that the principle of sharing does not apply.

Obviously, where children are present the length of the marriage is far less relevant as the **31.64** children's principal carer is likely to have considerable financial needs which will trump the other principles.

Courts have also had to determine what weight, if any, should be attached to extensive pre- **31.65** marital cohabitation. Since s 25(2)(d), MCA 1973 refers to 'the duration of the marriage', the plain words of the statute are ignored if account is taken of pre-marital cohabitation at this point in the exercise. On the other hand, fairness demands that, on occasions, due weight is given to pre-marital cohabitation especially where that cohabitation moves seamlessly to marriage. It is suggested that a better approach is to consider pre-marital cohabitation either as part of 'all of the circumstances of the case' under s 25(1) or as an aspect of 'contribution' or (positive) conduct under s 25(2)(f) and (g), respectively. Certainly, in *CO* v *CO (Ancillary Relief: Pre-marriage Cohabitation)* [2004] 1 FLR 1095, Coleridge J held that, to ignore a committed, settled period of cohabitation would fly in the face of the duty of the court to have regard to all the circumstances of the case.

Contributions

31.66   In *White* v *White* (para 31.07 above), Lord Nicholls emphasized that, especially in a long marriage (that is generally taken to mean marriages of ten years or longer), both parties make different and significant contributions. He held that it was wholly wrong to discriminate against the party to the marriage who has remained at home caring for the children and household while the other party may have been the principal breadwinner.

31.67   It is important to note that the wording of s 25(2)(f) also refers to contributions likely to be made in the foreseeable future to the welfare of the family. Hence, even where the duration of the marriage is relatively short, the financial award can be calculated to include that future important contribution.

Conduct

31.68   Conduct is a vexed question in financial proceedings.

31.69   In practice, however, the courts appear to treat the issues of conduct as they have always done so that it will be taken into account only if it is 'obvious and gross' (a phrase derived from *Wachtel* v *Wachtel* [1973] 1 All ER 829, and interpreted in *West* v *West*, see Example 2 below, as meaning 'of the greatest importance'). Thus in the majority of cases the court will continue to take the view that a certain amount of unpleasantness can be anticipated on both sides when a marriage is breaking down, possibly including an element of violence and that such matters should not affect the outcome of financial applications.

31.70   From time to time the conduct of one or the other party will stand out in some way and demand consideration. Examples of conduct which has been thought relevant in past cases are given below. Standards change, however, and the facts of cases are always different, so examples should be used simply to get a feel of the attitude of the courts, not as precedents dictating what is and is not relevant conduct.

31.71   At the risk of stating the obvious, the task for the court when dealing with allegations of conduct is twofold:

(a)   Is the conduct of a kind which it would be inequitable for the court to ignore? *and*

(b)   What effect should the conduct, if taken into account, have on the outcome of the application?

Example 1   (*Jones* v *Jones* [1975] 2 All ER 12.) Wife seriously attacked by husband after decree absolute with a razor causing continuing disability rendering her virtually unemployable; whole house transferred to her from joint names.

Example 2 (*West* v *West* [1977] 2 All ER 705.) Short marriage, wife refused to join husband in the home he had provided and lived at her parents' home instead. Wife's conduct found obvious and gross and, despite the fact there were two children of the marriage living with her, her financial provision was substantially reduced.

Example 3 (*Kyte* v *Kyte* [1987] 3 All ER 1041.) Husband was a manic depressive and wife connived at his suicide attempts with a view to gaining as much of the husband's assets as possible. Wife's conduct found to be gross and obvious so that it would be inequitable to ignore it, and accordingly her financial provision was reduced but not extinguished.

The point is often taken by a husband that it is unreasonable to expect him to make provision for his wife when she has committed adultery or formed a continuing relationship with another man. Unless it takes place in particularly aggravated circumstances (eg having an affair with the husband's father, see *Bailey* v *Tolliday* (1982) 4 FLR 542), the simple fact that the wife has committed adultery will not generally affect her entitlement to a financial order. **31.72**

An example of the relevance of conduct is to be found in the case of *B* v *B (Financial Provision: Welfare of Child and Conduct)* [2002] 1 FLR 555 where Connell J ordered that the family home be transferred into the sole name of the wife. He recognized that such an award reflected the wife's ongoing contribution to the care of the child but the principal reason for the order was the husband's conduct which the judge considered it would be inequitable to disregard. The conduct included the husband's failure to disclose that he had removed moneys from the jurisdiction, the effect being to prevent the court from having a meaningful say in the disposal of the moneys, and his abduction of the child which had led to a conviction for child abduction and a sentence of 18 months' imprisonment. **31.73**

More recently, in *H* v *H (Financial Relief: Attempted Murder As Conduct)* [2006] 1 FLR 990, Coleridge J had to consider what impact on the financial order the conduct of the husband should have where that conduct comprised a conviction for the attempted murder of the wife, and a refusal either to consent to the sale or letting of the family home. The wife had been compelled to leave the property because she was unable to cope with the memories which the property evoked. **31.74**

In awarding the wife the family home and the bulk of the assets, Coleridge J held that the conduct was not simply of a type which it would be inequitable to disregard but it was at the very top end of the scale. The conduct here was not merely a backdrop to the s 25, MCA 1973 exercise: it had seriously affected her mental health, had almost destroyed her earning capacity, and had deprived her of financial and parenting support from the husband. **31.75**

The fact of non-disclosure of financial matters will often entitle the court to draw adverse inferences and reflect its displeasure in both the financial remedy and the order for costs: *Al-Khatib* v *Masry* [2002] 1 FLR 1053. In this case, the award also reflected the fact that the husband had abducted the children to Saudi Arabia. In addition to a significant lump sum payment, the wife received a further £2.5 million to fund her litigation costs to secure the return of the children. **31.76**

The 'gross and obvious' test was reaffirmed in *Miller*. Lord Nicholls said that **31.77**

> in most cases, fairness does not require consideration of the parties' conduct. This is because in most cases misconduct is not relevant to the bases on which financial relief is ordered today.

Where, exceptionally, the position is otherwise, so that it would be inequitable to disregard one party's conduct, the statute permits that conduct to be taken into account (para 65).

D   OTHER CIRCUMSTANCES NOT SPECIFICALLY REFERRED TO IN S 25

31.78   Section 25 is not an exhaustive catalogue of the circumstances that are to be taken into account on an application for a financial order. This section lists additional matters which, among others, may be relevant.

Agreements

31.79   It can happen that on or after the breakdown of the marriage the parties reach an agreement on property and finance and make it a term of the agreement that no claims will be made thereafter for any further or different financial provision.

Example   Soon after separating, husband and wife agree that the wife will be allowed to remain in the family home until the children are grown up and that it will thereafter be sold and the proceeds divided equally between them. The wife agrees never to make any claim for periodical payments for herself and the husband agrees to maintain the children at the rate of £60 per week per child, the figure to be increased periodically to keep pace with inflation.

The wife changes her mind about the agreement and wants to seek a transfer of the house into her name and/or periodical payments for herself after decree nisi of divorce is granted.

31.80   While a party cannot be bound by a promise not to apply to the court, the court *can* take into account the making of the agreement as part of the conduct of the parties under s 25 (see *Edgar v Edgar* [1980] 3 All ER 887). As the Court of Appeal pointed out in *Edgar*, the district judge will decide what weight to give to the agreement by considering the circumstances surrounding the making of it (eg was there undue pressure on one side, bad legal advice, inadequate knowledge?), the conduct of both parties in consequence of it, and any important change of circumstances unforeseen or overlooked at the time of making the agreement. These principles were reconfirmed in *Xydhias* v *Xydhias* [1999] 1 FLR 683 and followed in *A* v *B (Financial Relief: Agreements)* [2005] 2 FLR 730. However, in *Xydhias* the Court of Appeal also stated that the existence of a financial agreement between the parties to a marriage does not avoid the need for the court to exercise its discretion under s 25 to explore the circumstances leading to the agreement and to determine whether it should stand.

31.81   Munby J reviewed the whole line of authorities in *X* v *X (Y and Z intervening)* [2002] 1 FLR 508 in deciding whether a wife could resile from an agreement under which, in consideration for various concessions in relation to divorce proceedings, the husband was to receive a lump sum payment of £500,000. The husband had complied with his obligations under the agreement and applied to the court for the wife to show cause why the terms of the agreement should not be converted into an order of the court. Munby J concluded that the agreement should be upheld: the wife had not been disadvantaged and had received 'the most expert legal advice'. Munby J held that s 25 required the court to ensure that a fair outcome had been achieved between the parties. The fact that the parties had reached an agreement was an

important factor and where the agreement was formally drawn up following competent legal advice, the agreement should be upheld by the court unless there were 'good and substantial grounds' for concluding that an injustice might otherwise be done to one of the parties. As in so many recent cases, Munby J concluded by indicating that, so far as it is consistent with its obligations under s 25, the court should aim to achieve finality between the parties.

The tax implications of orders

The tax implications of a proposed order may be important. For example, the court will need **31.82** to know if the husband will have to bear a considerable amount of capital gains tax in selling assets to raise a lump sum—it may reduce the lump sum payable to take account of this or choose to make a different order with less severe tax consequences. Expert accountancy evidence is likely to be necessary.

The availability of state benefits

The court is not generally entitled to take into account the fact that the applicant for a finan- **31.83** cial remedy is on income support and that she is therefore unlikely to derive any real advantage from the order that can be made in her favour (see, eg, *Peacock v Peacock* [1984] 1 All ER 1069), except where the available financial resources are very limited and an order would result in the husband being left with a sum that would be inadequate to meet his own financial commitments (see, eg, *Delaney v Delaney* [1990] 2 FLR 457).

E SPECIAL CONSIDERATIONS WITH REGARD TO PARTICULAR TYPES OF ORDER

Orders in relation to the family home

Family home owned by one or both parties

Common orders   The home is often one of the most substantial assets that the parties have **31.84** and is therefore generally the focus of financial disputes. Although the court has the power to resolve the question of the home in whatever manner it thinks appropriate, in practice there are several types of order which frequently crop up:

(a) immediate sale and division of the net proceeds of sale;
(b) transfer of the house into the sole name of one spouse, with or without a charge in favour of the other spouse or an immediate payment of a lump sum in his favour in respect of his interest;
(c) sale of house postponed, proceeds to be divided between the spouses on eventual sale.

Importance of securing homes for all concerned   What will normally be at the forefront **31.85** of the district judge's mind is the question of homes for both parties and particularly for the children. This consideration is likely to override all others and in particular will undoubtedly take precedence over strict property rights. For example, in *M v B (Ancillary Proceedings: Lump Sum)* [1998] 1 FLR 53 the Court of Appeal stated that every effort should be made to deal

with the need to provide a home for minor children of the family. This approach is confirmed in *B* v *B (Financial Provision: Welfare of the Child and Conduct)* [2002] 1 FLR 555 where Connell J ordered the outright transfer of the former family home in order to meet the need of the child of the family to be housed to a reasonable standard. In essence, therefore, the principal carer requires a home from the resources available and ideally the parent having regular contact with the children should be allocated sufficient moneys to acquire accommodation where contact may be enjoyed.

31.86   **When will immediate sale be appropriate?**   The following are illustrations of the types of situation in which the court may be prepared to order immediate sale of the family home:

(a)   Where the equity in the family home is sufficiently large to be divided between the parties and to enable them both to buy somewhere new, not necessarily of the same size and standard as the family home but with adequate accommodation for their needs. In working out what the equity is and whether it is sufficient, account must be taken not only of any outstanding mortgage on the property, but also of the estate agent's and conveyancing fees that will arise on a sale and new purchase and of removal costs. Furthermore, in the case of a publicly funded client, the effect of the Legal Services Commission's statutory charge must be borne in mind (see Chapter 2); if the Legal Services Commission has (or will have when the proceedings are over) a charge over a party's house, that charge *may* have to be redeemed and repaid on sale of the property thus reducing the sum available to that party.

On the plus side, the court will take into account the availability of loans and mortgages to assist the parties in their new purchases.

Example 1   Husband and wife live in a five-bedroomed house which they bought 20 years ago in their joint names. The children have all grown up and left home. The wife is living in the property on her own whilst the husband is in rented accommodation. The house is worth £200,000 and there is an outstanding mortgage of £10,000. The equity in the property is therefore £190,000 less the costs of sale. To be on the safe side, these are estimated at £5,000 and the available equity is taken to be £185,000. The court takes the view that this would be sufficient to enable both parties to purchase suitable accommodation for one person with enough room for the children and their families to come to stay and in the same locality as the family home. The sale of the family home is ordered, with equal division of the net proceeds.

Example 2   Husband and wife are both in their thirties. There are two children. The husband is a businessman with a healthy income. The wife works part time as a receptionist to fit in with the children. The family home is in joint names. It is worth £400,000 but there is a substantial mortgage of £100,000. The wife is to have a residence order in respect of the children. The equity in the house will be in the region of £300,000 after repayment of the mortgage and payment of expenses. The Legal Services Commission will have a statutory charge over the wife's share in the property for her publicly funded costs of £8,000 but it is anticipated that they would agree to the charge being transferred to another house. The wife is unable to obtain a mortgage. Equal division of the equity would give her only £150,000 and, as she shows to the court by bringing estate agents' particulars to the hearing, this would not be enough to enable her to buy a three-bedroomed property in the area where the

children go to school. She estimates that she requires £200,000 to buy a suitable property. The husband, on the other hand, can obtain a mortgage of up to £200,000. The court therefore orders that the house should be sold and that the husband should receive one-fifth of the proceeds (£60,000, which should be enough, together with a mortgage, to enable him to purchase a house for himself) and the wife four-fifths £240,000). Because the wife is doing rather well out of the house, the level of her maintenance payments is reduced considerably from what she would otherwise have been granted. The court may conclude that there should be no maintenance payments to her. This is possible because she can buy a property outright and will therefore have no mortgage or rent.

(b) Where one party has already got suitable alternative accommodation and the house can be sold and the proceeds divided enabling her to realize some capital from it but leaving the other spouse with sufficient to purchase accommodation.

Example After the breakdown of the marriage the wife goes to live with another man in his four-bedroomed detached house taking with her the two children of the family. The husband has continued to reside in the family home; sale would free approximately £20,000. The wife would like the property to be sold so that she can buy furniture and furnishings for her new home which her cohabitant has allowed to run to seed since his wife died. The court orders that the family home be sold and the proceeds divided equally. The wife's share of £10,000 would not be enough to enable her to purchase alternative accommodation but she has, of course, no need to do so because she looks upon her cohabitation as a long-term venture. £10,000 is enough to enable the husband to pay a deposit on a new house for himself. He can raise the balance of the purchase price on mortgage. The wife's claim to periodical payments for herself is dismissed in view of her cohabitation with the other man who is in a good job.

(c) Where there is not enough money to pay for the mortgage and other outgoings on the family home. In this situation, there is no choice but to sell the home even if this means one or the other party seeking housing association or other rented accommodation when they have been accustomed to owning their own home.

Example Both husband and wife are working, taking home about £250 per week each. The husband is living with his parents, while the wife has continued to live in the family home since the separation but she cannot afford to run it or to make the mortgage repayments on it—neither could the husband. There is very little equity in the house (only about £4,500 before the expenses of sale, etc are deducted). There is no alternative to a sale of the house which will produce hardly anything for division between the parties. What this means in practice is that the husband will have to go on living with his parents and the wife will have to move into rented accommodation.

Note that where one party wants a sale and the other does not, the party who wants to stay can attempt to raise capital to buy the other spouse out. The court can make an order to this effect by requiring the house to be transferred into the sole name of one spouse in return for the payment of a lump sum, amount stipulated, to the other spouse (see para 31.87 below). This will only be possible, of course, where the spouse has borrowing power or can lay his hands on realizable assets.

31.87   **Transfer into name of one spouse**   There are infinite variations of the orders of this type that can be made. What is usually involved is that the house is transferred into the name of the spouse who is living there either:

(a)   on immediate payment of a lump sum to the other spouse as compensation for losing his interest; *or*

(b)   on the other spouse being given a charge over the property for a proportion of the proceeds of sale realizable when the owner chooses to sell the property (while a charge for a fixed sum of money is normally undesirable as it will be whittled away by inflation, it is possible for the charge to be for a fixed amount but index-linked by reference to the property prices index for the area in which the property is situated—this is seen by some commentators as fairer to both parties);

(c)   outright with no charge or lump sum (although in such cases, it is usual for the transferring spouse to be compensated in some other way for the loss of his interest, eg, by his maintenance liability for his spouse being wiped out).

Whether an immediate lump sum can be ordered depends on the ability of the spouse who will be staying on to raise the necessary capital. Whether a charge is feasible depends on whether the transferor can afford to wait to realize his capital interest in the home (eg does he need money now to buy somewhere to live or has he already obtained alternative accommodation?) and also, whether, after the charge is ultimately paid off, the transferee will still have enough to buy a new home. It is possible for the charge to be made realizable not only on the sale of the home but also on the happening of other events such as the remarriage of the transferee or her cohabitation for more than six months. Where this is done, the order will operate very much like a *Mesher* order (described in para 31.89 below).

31.88   Outright transfer with no capital compensation may seem harsh but the idea of, for example, shaking off continuing liability for maintaining a spouse in return for a transfer can appeal, particularly where the transferring spouse has already secured accommodation for himself or has sufficient capital from other sources or borrowing power to buy somewhere else. In particular circumstances, it may even be appropriate to deprive one spouse of his interest in the family home with little or no reduction in maintenance payments or other compensation—it is really a question of who needs what. Furthermore, any mortgage will be transferred into the sole name of the transferee (provided that the mortgage lender which has provided the mortgage agrees to this step). This releases the transferor from his covenants under the mortgage and enables him more easily to obtain a mortgage for the purchase of alternative accommodation.

Example 1   Husband is living with his new girlfriend in her house. Wife and the two young children continue to live in the family home, a two-bedroomed bungalow with an equity of approximately £30,000. The mortgage repayments on the bungalow are £200 per month. The wife works part time but does not earn much. The court orders that the bungalow should be transferred into the sole name of the wife. The husband is ordered to pay the wife maintenance for herself fixed at a rate sufficient to cover the mortgage repayments and water rates on the family home.

In all probability the level of financial support to be provided by the husband for the two children will be determined by a maintenance calculation carried out by the Child Support Agency.

Example 2 Husband goes to live temporarily with his parents. Wife continues to live in the family home which is subject to a very small mortgage. Both parties are earning but the wife earns considerably less than the husband. The mortgage lender is happy for the wife to take over the existing mortgage repayments and for the husband to be released from his covenants in relation to the mortgage. They are also prepared to lend the wife a further £5,000. The court orders that the home should be transferred to the wife and that she should pay the husband £5,000 in respect of his interest therein (in fact, £5,000 representing about one-quarter of the equity in the property). This will provide the husband with a deposit and he can obtain a mortgage for the balance of the purchase price of another property. The wife's claim to periodical payments is dismissed.

Mesher-**type order**   An order preserving both parties' interests in the family home but post-   **31.89**
poning sale until certain specified events, has come to be called a '*Mesher* order' after the case of *Mesher* v *Mesher and Hall* decided in 1973 but reported at [1980] 1 All ER 126.

The beauty of the *Mesher* order is that it enables the court to escape from a difficult situation—   **31.90**
it does not force the wife and children (if there are any) on to the street immediately nor does it totally deprive the husband of his capital asset. It is a particularly useful arrangement where the lender refuses to release a party from his covenants under the mortgage deed. Because of this it was seized upon as the ideal answer and such orders were widespread in the mid 1970s.

In 1978, however (see, eg, *Martin* v *Martin* [1977] 3 All ER 762 and *Hanlon* v *Hanlon* [1978] 1   **31.91**
WLR 592), the Court of Appeal voiced disapproval of the universal use of *Mesher* orders. It was pointed out that this type of order simply stores up trouble for the future. Families do not, of course, split up when the youngest child leaves school and a family home is often needed for considerably longer. Even when the children have grown up, the wife will need somewhere to live. What the *Mesher* order does in putting off the evil day is to force the wife into the property market to look for another house when she is least able, probably in her forties with poor employment prospects (particularly if she has not worked for some time), and possibly vulnerable emotionally because her children are growing up and need her less.

In *Clutton* v *Clutton* [1991] 1 All ER 340, the Court of Appeal decreed that where there is doubt   **31.92**
as to the wife's ability to rehouse herself, on the statutory charge taking effect, then a *Mesher* order should not be made. However, such an order did provide the best solution:

> where the family assets are amply sufficient to provide both parties with a roof over their heads if the family home were sold, but nevertheless the interests of the children require that they remain in the matrimonial home. In such a case it may be just and sensible to postpone the sale until the children have left home, since, *ex hypothesi*, the proceeds of sale will then be sufficient to enable the wife to rehouse herself. In such a case the wife is relatively secure.

Where the non-occupier retains an interest in the equity of the former family home (whether   **31.93**
by charge or continuing joint ownership), it has become common practice for the division of the proceeds of sale to be on an equal basis—this seems appropriate in the light of the high level of financial support likely to be required of the non-resident parent following a maintenance calculation by the Child Support Agency and the yardstick of equality.

Rented homes

31.94   **Transfer under s 24**   Most tenancies are 'property' for the purposes of s 24, MCA 1973 and the court can therefore make an order that one spouse should transfer the tenancy to the other (*Hale* v *Hale* [1975] 1 WLR 931 (private sector tenancy); *Thompson* v *Thompson* [1975] 2 All ER 208 (council tenancy)). It does not matter whether the tenancy is for a fixed term or periodic (eg weekly). The court may also make an order transferring a housing association tenancy: *Akintola* v *Akintola* [2002] 1 FLR 701. Transfer of an assured, protected, or secure tenancy can be ordered and, whereas normally assignment of a secure tenancy would cause it to cease to be a secure tenancy, assignment pursuant to an order under s 24 does not have this effect (s 91, Housing Act 1985).

31.95   The court is only likely to order a transfer of a tenancy under s 24 if there is no prohibition against assignment or the landlord agrees to the transfer.

31.96   Statutory tenancies (ie, under the Rent Act 1977) are *not* property within s 24 and no order can therefore be made for such a tenancy to be transferred. However, statutory tenancies are covered by sch 7, Family Law Act 1996 (see para 31.97 below).

31.97   **Transfer under sch 7, Family Law Act 1996**   Quite apart from the power under s 24 to order the transfer of tenancies, sch 7, para 2 empowers the court, on granting a decree of divorce, nullity, or judicial separation or at any time thereafter, to order the transfer of a protected, statutory, secure, or assured tenancy (under the Housing Act 1988) from one spouse to the other (or from joint names into one spouse's sole name) and to order that a statutory tenant shall cease to be entitled to occupy and the other spouse shall be deemed to be the statutory tenant. The landlord must be given the opportunity to be heard before the court makes an order under the schedule (sch 7, para 14(1)).

31.98   The court may make the order only if the dwelling-house is or was the family home (sch 7, para 4).

31.99   In deciding whether to make the order the court must have regard to all the circumstances of the case, including:

(a)   the circumstances in which the tenancy was granted to either or both spouses, or the circumstances in which either or both became a tenant;

(b)   the matters set out in s 33(6)(a) to (c) of the Act (see Chapter 36);

(c)   (not relevant to spouses—see Chapter 13 for details in respect of cohabitants);

(d)   the suitability of the parties as tenants: sch 7, para 5.

31.100   On making such an order (known as a Part II order) the court may direct that the transferee make a payment to the transferor. It must have regard under sch 7, para 10(4) to all the circumstances of the case, including:

(a)   the financial loss which would otherwise be suffered by the transferor as a result of the order;

(b)   the financial needs and financial resources of the parties;

(c)   the financial obligations which the parties have or are likely to have in the foreseeable future, including financial obligations to each other and to any relevant child.

Where the court considers a payment to be appropriate, it may direct that the payment be deferred (wholly or partly) until a specified date or the occurrence of a specified event, or that the payment be made by instalments: sch 7, para 10(2). It should be noted that any payment received in this way is exempt from the statutory charge: reg 44(1)(c), Community Legal Service (Financial) Regulations 2000.

Provision for children

Periodical payments

Following the coming into force of the CSA 1991, there are fewer occasions when the court **31.101** will have jurisdiction to make a periodical payments order for the benefit of a child of the family. The court retains jurisdiction where the child to be supported is not the natural child of the prospective payer but has been treated by the prospective payer as a child of the family. It is clear now that courts apply a formula similar to that used by the Child Maintenance and Enforcement Commission (CMEC) to determine the level of periodical payments to be made.

The court also retains jurisdiction to make a periodical payments order for the benefit of a **31.102** child who has specific needs, for example a disability (as happened, eg, in *C v F (Disabled Child: Maintenance Order)* [1998] 2 FLR 1), or a need to be educated in a certain way. It is expected that the level of payments to be ordered in such cases will be linked to the needs of the child, balanced against the resources of the payer to meet those needs.

Other provision for children

It is not common for orders other than periodical payments orders to be made for children **31.103** (eg transfers of property to them or lump sums). No doubt the reason for this is that there is enough difficulty sharing the parties' capital between the two of them without trying to cut the cake into even smaller slices for the children as well. Nevertheless, where there is money to spare, or the children have special needs, it may be appropriate for the court to make a lump sum order in their favour.

Payment of expenses

It must be noted that the court does not have power in financial proceedings to order a spouse **31.104** to make payments to third parties (except for the benefit of the children). However, it is usually possible to find a way round this. For example, the court cannot order a husband to make the mortgage repayments on the former matrimonial home but it can step up the maintenance that he has to pay for the wife to include an element to cover the mortgage repayments. Nor can the court order a husband or wife to take out an insurance policy to make provision for the other spouse in the event of his or her death but it could, for example, order him or her to provide a lump sum that the spouse could use to make his or her own provision. Nor can the court order a spouse to pay the parties' joint debts or repay a loan from the other spouse's parents but it could order him to pay a lump sum to the other spouse to cover the parties' debts so that she can pay off the debts herself if he is not to be trusted to do so voluntarily.

31.105   As explained in Chapter 30, para 30.137, an alternative method of ensuring that the other spouse will pay money to third parties is to accept an undertaking from him to that effect if he is prepared to give it. The undertaking is set out as a preamble to the order. If the spouse breaches the undertaking, the ultimate sanction is committal to prison. A further alternative is that the order recites that it is made on the basis that the party will be responsible for certain debts. If he fails to pay it is not possible to seek to enforce the payment of the debts but variation of the original order can be sought and his non-payment will be clear evidence of a change in circumstances since it was made.

F   MAINTENANCE PENDING SUIT

31.106   The court is not directed to take the s 25 factors into account on an application for maintenance pending suit, simply to make such order as it thinks reasonable (s 22, MCA 1973). The court's calculation will, of necessity, be rather rough and ready. The district judge will not normally have the advantage of a very full hearing nor will all the income and outgoings of each party necessarily be ascertained by that stage. What the district judge has to do, therefore, is to take into account the income, outgoings, and needs of each party as they appear at the time and make an order that will tide the applicant over until the final hearing without causing undue hardship to the respondent. It is quite likely that the sum ordered as maintenance pending suit will be rather less than the applicant can ultimately expect by way of a full periodical payments order.

G   CIVIL PARTNERSHIPS AND ORDERS FOR FINANCIAL PROVISION

31.107   Provisions found in sch 5, para 21, Civil Partnership Act 2004 ('CPA 2004') largely replicate those found in s 25, MCA 1973 in setting out the factors to be considered by the court in determining an application for financial orders.

31.108   It remains to be seen, however, how the above provisions will be interpreted in practice, although it can be anticipated that, at least initially, the present case law will be applied to civil partnerships.

31.109   The duration of the civil partnership is likely to mean that the case law on seamless cohabitation will be highly relevant.

31.110   Further, sch 5, para 23, CPA 2004 retains the clean break philosophy which has been incorporated wholesale into civil partnership.

31.111   As for pre-partnership agreements, these are unenforceable if they seek to restrict or oust the jurisdiction of the court so that the weight to be attached to the terms of the agreement will depend on all the circumstances of the case. It is important to remember, however, that there is no concept of a lifelong arrangement in civil partnership, as there is in marriage, and hence arguably greater justification in the parties seeking to organize their financial affairs before forming a civil partnership.

32

PREVENTING AND SETTING ASIDE DISPOSITIONS UNDER SECTION 37, MATRIMONIAL CAUSES ACT 1973

A   INTRODUCTION

The court has powers under s 37, Matrimonial Causes Act 1973 ('MCA 1973') to prevent a   **32.01**
spouse from wriggling out of his obligations by divesting property and income to a suitable
accomplice or by transferring it out of the country.

Under s 37 the court has power where financial relief proceedings are brought by one spouse   **32.02**
(the applicant) to prevent the other spouse (the respondent) from making a disposition or to
order him to set aside a disposition that he has made.

B   REQUIREMENT OF FINANCIAL RELIEF PROCEEDINGS

32.03   In order to qualify for an order under s 37 the applicant must have brought proceedings for financial relief against the respondent.

32.04   The following applications are classed as financial relief proceedings:

(a)   for maintenance pending suit;

(b)   for any financial provision order for a spouse or a child of the family;

(c)   for any property adjustment order for a spouse or a child of the family;

(d)   for a pension sharing order for a spouse;

(e)   for a pension attachment order;

(f)   for an order under s 27 (failure to provide reasonable maintenance) for a spouse or a child of the family;

(g)   for most forms of variation of financial orders under s 31;

(h)   for alteration of a maintenance agreement under s 35.

C   ORDERS THAT CAN BE MADE

Preventing a disposition

32.05   If the court is satisfied that the respondent is about to make any disposition or to transfer out of the jurisdiction or otherwise deal with any property with the intention of defeating a claim for financial relief, it may make such order as it thinks fit to restrain him from so doing or otherwise for protecting the claim: s 37(2)(a).

Example Mrs Watson has petitioned for divorce. Her petition includes a comprehensive prayer for financial provision. She learns that her husband intends to transfer all the funds that he has in his bank account with Lloyds Bank in Grimsby to a bank account in his new girlfriend's name in Switzerland. Mrs Watson may apply for an order freezing her husband's bank account.

Setting aside a disposition

Disposition to defeat claim

32.06   Section 37(2)(b) deals with the situation where the respondent has disposed of assets *before* the applicant's application for financial orders is dealt with.

32.07   If the court is satisfied:

(a)   that the respondent has made a reviewable disposition with the intention of defeating the claim for financial relief; *and*

(b)   that if the disposition were set aside financial relief or different financial relief would be granted to the applicant,

it may make an order setting aside the disposition: s 37(2)(b).

Example Before the financial hearing, Mrs Watson also discovers that her husband has transferred his valuable shareholdings in two companies to his girlfriend. Mrs Watson can apply to have the transfer set aside if she can show that this will make a difference to her claim.

Disposition to prevent enforcement

Where the court has already made a financial order against the respondent, if it is subsequently satisfied that he has made a reviewable disposition with the intention of defeating the order, that disposition may be set aside by virtue of s 37(2)(c). **32.08**

In *Trowbridge* v *Trowbridge* [2003] 2 FLR 231, the former wife had been awarded a lump sum payment in financial proceedings which had not been paid. In the meantime, the former husband had invested moneys in a house vested in the sole name of his new wife. The Chancery Division held that the former husband had intended to impede enforcement of the lump sum order and the payments in respect of his new wife's property could be set aside. The judge went on to declare that the former husband had acquired a beneficial interest in his second wife's home by way of a constructive trust. The former wife was then permitted to register a charge on the former husband's share of the property for the amounts still owed to her under the terms of the lump sum order. **32.09**

Consequential directions

Unscrambling a disposition that has already been made is rarely straightforward so the court is given power by s 37(3) to make such consequential directions as it thinks fit in conjunction with an order under s 37(2)(b) or (c). **32.10**

Example The court makes an order setting aside a conveyance of 10 Acacia Avenue, made by the respondent to his brother who was fully aware of the applicant's claims and of the respondent's intention to prevent the applicant from obtaining any share in the family home by the sale. The brother paid £10,000 for the property. The court can direct that this sum should be repaid to him.

D   DEFINITIONS

Various terms used in s 37 require further definition. **32.11**

'Defeating' the applicant's claim

Any reference in s 37 to 'defeating' a person's claim for financial relief is a reference to: **32.12**

(a) preventing financial relief from being granted to that person or to that person for the benefit of a child of the family; *or*
(b) reducing the amount of any financial relief which might be granted; *or*
(c) frustrating or impeding the enforcement of any order which might be or has been made by way of financial relief: s 37(1).

Presumption of intention

32.13 Section 37 is concerned with respondents who *intend* to defeat financial relief claims and orders. It is not always easy to prove the intention behind a disposition or intended disposition (*Mubarak* v *Mubarak and Others* [2007] EWHC 220 (Fam)). Section 37(5) therefore provides that in certain circumstances, the respondent will be presumed to intend to defeat the applicant's claim for financial orders. Thus where:

(a) the disposition or other dealing in question:
   (i)   is about to take place; *or*
   (ii) took place less than three years before the date of the application under s 37; *and*
(b) the court is satisfied that the disposition would have the consequence or has had the consequence of defeating the applicant's claim;

it is presumed that the respondent has made or is about to make the disposition with the intention of defeating the applicant's claim for financial relief.

32.14 If the presumption arises it is then up to the respondent to show that he did *not* intend to defeat the applicant's claim. If the presumption does not arise, the burden of proving intention will be on the applicant.

'Disposition'

32.15 Section 37(6) provides that the term 'disposition' includes any conveyance, assurance, or gift of property of any description by instrument or otherwise except any provision contained in a will or codicil. The meaning of 'property' is not defined but it is not restricted to property in England and Wales; it also includes real and personal property situated abroad (*Hamlin* v *Hamlin* [1986] Fam Law 11, [1986] 1 FLR 61). However, the surrender of a tenancy is not a disposition and therefore once it has been made it cannot be set aside under s 37(2)(b) or (c). If it appears that a tenancy or joint tenancy is about to be surrendered, then in the absence of an undertaking by the person about to surrender that he will not do so, the person seeking to prevent the surrender should make an application to restrain the surrender under s 37(2)(a). Any such undertaking or order should be served on the landlord (*Bater* v *Greenwich LBC* [1999] 2 FLR 993).

'Reviewable disposition'

32.16 A disposition that has already been made will only be set aside if it is a reviewable disposition. 'Reviewable disposition' is defined in s 37(4) to comprise *any* disposition made by the respondent *unless* it was made:

(a) for valuable consideration other than marriage; *and*
(b) to a person who, at the time of the disposition, acted in relation to it in good faith and without notice of any intention on the part of the respondent to defeat the applicant's claim for financial relief.

Thus a sale to a purchaser who paid good money and had no idea of the respondent's intention to defeat his wife's claim cannot be set aside.

Procedure

In order to restrain an anticipated disposal under s 37(2)(a) the applicant should, in accord- **32.17**
ance with r 9.6, Family Procedure Rules 2010 ('FPR 2010') follow the Part 18 procedure under
those Rules. This requires an application on Form FP2, together with a draft of the order
sought.

It may be the case that the application has to be made immediately to the court to seek an **32.18**
order without the respondent being aware of it. In those circumstances, r 9.6(2), FPR 2010
provides that an application to prevent a disposition can be made without notice to the
respondent.

Where a without notice order is made (or even if the application is dismissed) r 18.10 requires **32.19**
that a copy of the application notice, any evidence in support, and the order made be served
on the respondent and all parties to the proceedings unless otherwise ordered by the court.
The court order must contain a statement of the right of the respondent or any other party to
make an application to set aside or vary the order (r 18.10(3)).

If the powers provided to the county court under s 37 are insufficient to meet the needs of a **32.20**
particular situation then consideration should be given to the application for an injunction
being issued in the High Court which has far more extensive powers available to it under its
inherent jurisdiction. For example, in *Roche* v *Roche* [1981] Fam Law 243 the husband was
soon to receive an award of damages in his claim for personal injury. This fell outside the definition of 'property' under s 37 but did not stop the High Court issuing a freezing injunction
under its inherent jurisdiction.

E   PREVENTING AND SETTING ASIDE DISPOSITIONS AND CIVIL PARTNERSHIP

Provisions virtually identical to those set out above are found in sch 5, paras 74(2), (3), and (4), **32.21**
and 75(3), Civil Partnership Act 2004 to protect one civil partner from transactions planned
or entered into by the other for the purposes of defeating a claim for financial relief.

33

COLLECTION AND ENFORCEMENT
OF FINANCIAL ORDERS

A   INTRODUCTION

33.01 This chapter deals in outline only with the means of enforcing financial orders. The practitioner is referred to standard textbooks for further details. It is assumed throughout the chapter that it is the wife who seeks to enforce an order against the husband, but the principles would be no different were the roles reversed.

B   ENFORCING ORDERS FOR THE PAYMENT OF MONEY

33.02 There are the following considerations where the wife seeks to enforce an order for the payment of money (usually an order for periodical payments or for the payment of a lump sum):

(a) Payments made direct between the parties: unless the court directs that the periodical payments order should be registered in the family proceedings court, maintenance payments under the order will be made direct between the parties and not through the court. Lump sums will also be paid between the parties direct. It is therefore up to both parties to keep a record of payments made/received in case there are problems in the future. One of the most convenient ways of ensuring that there is a record of payment and guarding against default is for the payments to be made through the bank by cheque in the case of a lump sum and by standing order in the case of periodical payments.

(b) Under the new provisions of r 33.3, Family Procedure Rules 2010 ('FPR 2010') an application to enforce an order for the payment of money must be made in a notice of application (Form D11) which shall state the amount due under the order, showing how the amount is arrived at and be verified by a statement of truth. The application should specify the suggested method of enforcement. An alternative is to apply under r 33.3(2)(b) using Form D50K, requesting the court to order such method of enforcement as the court may consider to be appropriate.

(c) Permission of the court is required to enforce arrears more than 12 months old. Where a party wishes to enforce arrears that are more than 12 months old, permission to enforce the arrears must be sought: s 32, Matrimonial Causes Act 1973 ('MCA 1973') using Form D11.

(d Methods of enforcement available: the methods of enforcement available include the following:

(i) Judgment summons (rr 33.9 to 33.18, FPR 2010)—the wife applies for a judgment summons which requires the husband to attend before a judge to be examined as to his means. At the hearing the judge will make such order as he thinks fit in relation to the arrears/outstanding lump sum. There is power to commit the husband to prison for non-payment, but any committal order made will normally be suspended on condition that the husband pays the amount due by a specified date or by specified instalments.

The application in Form D62 must be supported by a sworn statement confirming the amount said to be owed, with a breakdown of how the sums claimed are calculated (r 33.3(1)). Unlike the other methods of enforcement, if there are arrears of over 12 months, the application to enforce those arrears must be included in the same application. A copy of the order to be enforced should be exhibited. Once issued, the judgment summons itself (Form D63) must be personally served on the debtor not less than 14 days prior to the hearing and should be accompanied by the evidence relied upon (r 33.11). The summons will require the debtor to attend court. Rule 33.14 states that no person may be committed on an application for a judgment summons unless he fails to attend an adjourned hearing or where the creditor is able to prove that the debtor has had the means to pay the sum since the date of the original order and has refused or neglected to pay that sum. The fact that the original order was made by consent is a good starting point in terms of proving that the debtor had the means to pay (see *Topping* v *Topping* [2008] EWCA Civ 1142. The burden of proof is upon the creditor and the standard is the criminal standard, that is, beyond reasonable doubt.

(ii) While a bankruptcy order is not generally made as a means of enforcing a lump sum order in family proceedings, such an order will be made in exceptional circumstances (see, eg, *Levy* v *Legal Services Commission* [2001] 1 FLR 435). It should be noted that r 12.3, Insolvency Rules 1986 (SI 1986/1925) was amended by Insolvency (Amendment) Rules 2005 (SI 2005/527), effective from 1 April 2005, so that lump sum orders and costs orders are now provable debts in bankruptcy proceedings. This means that the debt owed to the wife will take its place among the other debts in the bankruptcy and she will receive a proportion of the proceeds of the bankruptcy in the settlement of the debt.

(iii) Section 24A sale order—if she is seeking to enforce a lump sum order, the wife can consider seeking an order for sale of property under s 24A, MCA 1973 (with a consequential direction that the proceeds of sale or part of them should be paid to her).

(iv) The usual enforcement methods, such as warrant of execution, attachment of earnings, charging order, and third party debt order.

C   THE MAINTENANCE ENFORCEMENT ACT 1991

33.03   The Maintenance Enforcement Act 1991 ('MEA 1991') improves the method of collecting and enforcing maintenance payments for spouses and children. The MEA 1991 provides for the High Court or county court to specify that payments of maintenance be made by standing order or some other method, or by attachment of earnings. However, unlike the position in the family proceedings court, the direction as to the method of payment in the county court may only be given on a later occasion on an application by the interested party or on the court's own motion.

33.04   The MEA 1991 provides that in the family proceedings court the court must specify that payments be made direct from the debtor to the creditor, through the court, by standing order or similar method, or by attachment of earnings.

33.05   The MEA 1991 was an interim measure to improve the mechanics of maintenance collection and enforcement pending the coming into force fully of the Child Support Act 1991 ('CSA 1991'). However, it will continue to be used even though the CSA 1991 is now in force because it deals with *all* maintenance payments and not simply child maintenance payments.

D   REGISTRATION OF A PERIODICAL PAYMENTS ORDER IN THE FAMILY PROCEEDINGS COURT

33.06   On or at any time after making a periodical payments order, the High Court or county court may direct that it shall be registered in a family proceedings court with the result that it will be paid and enforced through that court (see further, Chapter 30, para 30.139).

E   ENFORCEMENT OF PROPERTY ADJUSTMENT ORDERS

33.07   Property adjustment orders are most commonly made in relation to the family home. Let us take as an example an order that the husband should transfer the family home (which is in his name) to the wife. In order that the necessary conveyance or transfer can be effected, the husband's cooperation will be required. What if he refuses to execute the required documents?

The answer is simple. The wife can apply to the court for an order that unless he does so within a specified time, the document be executed by a district judge of the court instead: s 39, Senior Courts Act 1981 in the High Court and s 38, County Courts Act 1984 in the county court.

If it is anticipated that there may be a problem over the drafting of the necessary documents **33.08** (rather than over execution of them), the court can direct that the matter be referred to one of the conveyancing counsel of the court for him to settle the proper instrument to be executed by all necessary parties. Where the order is made in proceedings for divorce, nullity, or judicial separation, the court may also, if it thinks fit, defer the grant of the decree in question until the instrument has been duly executed: s 30, MCA 1973.

Where the court has ordered a sale of property under s 24A, MCA 1973, and one party refuses **33.09** to cooperate with the sale process by, for example, refusing to give vacant possession of the property, it is possible to make an application to the court requiring the recalcitrant party to give up possession so that the sale will proceed: r 9.24, FPR 2010.

F ENFORCEMENT AND CIVIL PARTNERS

The above methods of enforcement are available to civil partners where the court has made a **33.10** financial provision order of some type.

34

VARIATION OF FINANCIAL ORDERS

A   THE SCOPE OF S 31

Orders that can be varied

34.01 Under s 31, Matrimonial Causes Act 1973 ('MCA 1973'), the court has wide powers to vary certain types of orders made previously. Those orders are:

(a) any order for maintenance pending suit or interim maintenance;

(b) any periodical payments or secured periodical payments order (though see paras 34.03 ff with regard to fixed term orders);

(c) some orders providing for the payment of a lump sum by instalments (see the Court of Appeal decision in *Westbury* v *Sampson* [2002] 1 FLR 166);

(d) a deferred lump sum made under the 'earmarking' provisions;

(e) a pension attachment order;

(f) an order for a settlement of property or for a variation of settlement which was made on or after a decree of judicial separation (such an order can, however, only be varied where application is made in proceedings for the rescission of a decree of judicial separation or in subsequent divorce proceedings);

(g) an order for settlement or sale of property made under s 24A(1), MCA 1973;

(h) a pension sharing order made before decree absolute.

Note that it makes no difference to the court's powers of variation that the original order was made by consent.

Although this chapter deals with the variation of orders made in financial proceedings, an **34.02** order made on a s 27, MCA 1973 application (failure to provide reasonable maintenance, see Chapter 26) for periodical payments or for interim maintenance or for the payment of a lump sum by instalments is equally variable. The case of *Burrow* v *Burrow* [1999] 1 FLR 508 clarifies the point that an order 'earmarking' pension provision is an order under s 23 and is therefore capable of variation under s 31 (see s 31(2)(b) and (e)).

Orders that cannot be varied

There is no power to vary an order for the transfer of property made under s 24(1)(a), MCA **34.03** 1973 nor, except in limited circumstances where the order has been made on judicial separation, an order under s 24(1)(b), (c), or (d) for the settlement of property or varying an antenuptial or post-nuptial settlement or extinguishing the interest of either party to the marriage in such a settlement.

There is no power to vary the amount of a single lump sum payment (made under s 27 or s 23). **34.04**

Where the court has, in connection with divorce or nullity, granted periodical payments for **34.05** a fixed term in favour of a party to the marriage, it may specify that that party shall not be entitled to apply under s 31 for an extension of the fixed term: s 28(1A). *Jones* v *Jones* [2000] 2 FLR 307 confirmed that the application to vary a fixed-term periodical payment order must be issued during the life of the order. It did not matter that the hearing took place once the order had expired.

B   PROCEDURE

The application is commenced in exactly the same way as an application for a financial **34.06** remedy. Form A commences the application to vary and, upon receipt, the court will provide the usual directions requiring the parties to complete Form E.

Even where the application merely seeks an upward or downward variation of a periodical **34.07** payments order it is appropriate that all parts of Form E are completed and accompanied by the usual financial disclosure. One small exception to this might be the need to seek formal valuations of pensions or businesses if those valuations appear to be irrelevant to the substance of the application. That is a matter for the court to consider at the First Appointment along with the extent of the parties' questionnaires.

The court will list a Financial Dispute Resolution appointment in exactly the same way as **34.08** a first application for a financial remedy. Where there is no agreement, the application will continue to a final hearing. The 'general rule' for costs applies (see r 28.3(5), FPR 2010, above Chapter 30).

C   WHAT CAN THE COURT DO ON A VARIATION APPLICATION?

34.09   On a variation application the court has power to vary or discharge the order concerned or to suspend any provision of the order temporarily and to revive any provision so suspended: s 31(1), MCA 1973. The most common applications for variation are by the recipients of periodical payments who seek to have their payments increased and by payers who seek to have their payments reduced.

34.10   Where the court has made an order for maintenance of some type (maintenance pending suit, interim maintenance, and periodical payments, secured or unsecured), it has power to remit arrears due under the order in whole or in part: s 31(2A).

34.11   Provisions contained in sch 8, Family Law Act 1996 ('FLA 1996') amended s 31, MCA 1973 so as to introduce new powers in s 31(7B), MCA 1973 to enable the court, in dealing with variation proceedings, to make a 'compensating' lump sum or property adjustment order so that a 'clean break' may be achieved at that stage.

34.12   As a general rule, the court has no power to make a property adjustment order or a lump sum order on an application for variation of a periodical payments order or secured periodical payments order in favour of a spouse: s 31(5), MCA 1973. However, the 'clean break' provisions give the court further powers after the dissolution of a marriage in cases where:

(a)   it discharges a periodical payments order or secured periodical payments order made in favour of a party to the marriage (s 31(1)); or

(b)   it varies such an order so that the payments under the order are required to be made or secured only for such further period as is determined by the court: s 31(7A).

34.13   By virtue of its powers in s 31(7B) the court may substitute one of the following orders when it discharges a periodical payments order:

(a)   an order for the payment of a lump sum in favour of a party to the marriage;

(b)   one or more property adjustment orders in favour of a party to the marriage (provided that each falls within different subsections of s 21(2)(a) to (d): see s 31(7E)), in other words one property transfer order, one settlement of property, and one variation of settlement;

(c)   one or more pension sharing orders;

(d)   a direction that the party in whose favour the original order discharged or varied was made is not entitled to make any further application for:

(i)   a periodical payments order, secured periodical payments; or

(ii)   an extension of the period to which the original order is limited by any variation made by the court.

Any lump sum order so made can be ordered to be paid by instalments, deferred, or secured and to carry interest at the discretionary rate under s 22A(7) and (8): see s 31(7C) and (7D).

34.14   In practical terms it is not therefore possible to have a 'clean break' of capital provision while an order for periodical payments is in existence. Clients will have to be warned that, while an order for periodical payments is in force, it will always be possible for a court to make an order requiring the paying party to make capital provision for the receiving party as compensation for the termination or variation of periodical payments. The court has power to make such an order 'of its own motion' regardless of whether one or other of the parties has made an application for such an order.

D   FACTORS TO BE TAKEN INTO ACCOUNT ON A VARIATION APPLICATION

In exercising its powers to vary under s 31, MCA 1973, the court is directed by s 31(7) (as   **34.15**
amended by the Matrimonial and Family Proceedings Act 1984 and sch 8, FLA 1996) to have
regard to all the circumstances of the case, the first consideration being given to the welfare
while a minor of any child of the family under 18. The circumstances of the case include any
change in any of the matters to which the court was required to have regard when making
the order to which the application relates (ie, the s 25, MCA 1973 factors; see Chapter 31)
and, in a case where the party against whom the order was made has died (a situation that
normally only arises on an application for variation of secured periodical payments), the
circumstances of the case shall also include the changed circumstances resulting from his or
her death. As well as having power to bring periodical payments to an end immediately, the
court has power, on a variation application, to limit the future term of the periodical payments or secured periodical payments order to such term as will be sufficient to enable the
payee to adjust to the termination of the payments without undue hardship and must always
give consideration to exercising this power in all variation applications concerning periodical
payment orders (secured and unsecured) made on or after a decree of divorce or nullity. It is
particularly important to realize that, as a result of the amendments to s 37 made by sch 8, FLA
1996, the court, when considering the application, may look to capital accumulated by the
parties after the divorce, since it is entitled in variation proceedings to take a fresh look at the
evidence of the parties' means as they stand at the date of the variation application. It is not
restricted to the evidence of the parties' means as they stood at the date of the original order.

The court's general approach was recently considered by the President in *VB* v *JP* [2008] 1 FLR   **34.16**
742. He confirmed that an element of compensation for ongoing career disadvantage could
indeed play some part in a subsequent application for a variation of periodical payments
orders. On the facts of the case, however, there was no need to calculate a separate element
for such compensation. He said his task was to quantify the wife's needs (generously assessed)
against the background of the standard of living during the marriage, the husband's considerably increased income, and the reduced availability to the wife of a substantial proportion of
the child maintenance originally provided. He increased the wife's periodical payments from
£33,000 to £65,000 per annum and backdated it to the date of her Form E.

   VB was a case where there was agreement that the periodical payments should continue for
the parties' joint lives. As can be seen above, however, the court now has the power to capitalize periodical payments. Where such capitalization is achievable (the payer having access to
such a lump sum and the payee being able to adjust her affairs so that a lump sum will meet
her ongoing needs once and for all) the court will quantify the sum to be paid. In *Pearce* v
Pearce [2003] 2 FLR 1144 Thorpe LJ set out a three-stage test:

(a) first, decide what if any variation it would make to the original periodical payments
     order;

(b) next, decide on what date those payments should commence;

(c) finally, apply the *Duxbury* tables to calculate the appropriate sum. Those tables contain
     actuarial calculations depending on the age and sex of the recipient along with the period
     during which the payments would be otherwise made. They can be found in a number of
     practitioners' guides including *At A Glance* (FLBA) and *Matrimonial Property and Finance*
     (Duckworth, Family Law). The tables are intended only as a guide to the court; the judge
     may add to or subtract from the award to some degree.

35

CHILD SUPPORT

A   INTRODUCTION

The Child Support Act 1991 ('CSA 1991') came into force in April 1993. It is largely in the form   **35.01**
of a framework: the detailed provision is contained in numerous regulations, some of which
have been significantly amended. This chapter is designed to explain the basic principles of

the Act, but throughout the book reference has been made to the Act and the implications of its provisions have been indicated. For further detail the practitioner is advised to consult a specialist textbook on the subject (eg Roger Bird, *Child Support: The New Law*, 6th edn (Family Law, 2009)). In particular, the Act's impact on the law relating to applications for financial orders, and the position of cohabitants is discussed.

35.02   The CSA 1991 has been significantly amended by the Child Support, Pensions and Social Security Act 2000 ('CSPASSA 2000') which provides the present formula for the calculation of child support.

35.03   Despite those reforms, the child support regime and the Child Support Agency, which had responsibility for the administration of the regime, remained subject to considerable scrutiny and criticism. In 2006 the government published proposals for further reform which advocated giving greater autonomy to parents to make their own arrangements for child support (even where the carer parent is claiming state benefits of some kind), and strengthening enforcement powers where the parents cannot agree on the level of child support or where default in providing adequate child support occurs. The result was the Child Maintenance and Other Payments Act 2008 ('CMOPA 2008') which at the time of writing is only partly in force. The CMOPA 2008 abolished the Child Support Agency, replacing it with the Child Maintenance and Enforcement Commission (CMEC). It also alters the child support formula from its present net income calculation to a gross calculation—at the time of writing that change is not yet in force. The most recent proposals set out in the government's response to a consultation paper entitled *Strengthening families, promoting parental responsibility: the future of child maintenance* (Cm 8130, July 2011) indicates that the government is likely to incentivize parents to agree their own child support arrangements by making a charge for access to government enforcement measures or by potentially making the parents' agreement enforceable in the courts.

35.04   In the meantime, the regime described in this chapter remains in force and is applicable to all cases arising since 3 March 2003.

35.05   Cases arising before that date are dealt with under the original child support regime which is discussed fully in specialist practitioner texts (see above). Although it was initially intended that pre-March 2003 cases would be brought into the new scheme (a process described as 'migration'), on 9 February 2006 the Secretary of State announced an indefinite postponement of migration.

B   THE PURPOSE OF THE 1991 ACT

35.06   The aim of the CSA 1991 is to establish a regime to ensure that non-resident parents (whether or not married) make a significant contribution to the financial support of their natural children.

35.07   It is important to note the following:

   (a)   The provisions of s 23, Matrimonial Causes Act 1973 ('MCA 1973') still remain available for the financial support of a child by a step-parent who has treated the child as a child of the family.

(b) In *any* case where an order for a lump sum, property adjustment, or transfer or settlement of property for the benefit of a child is required, application must be made to the court in the usual way (see MCA 1973 and sch 1, Children Act 1989 ('CA 1989')).

C   SOME BASIC DEFINITIONS

The 'qualifying child'

The natural child is described in the CSA 1991 as a 'qualifying child', and the term is defined **35.08** in s 3(1) so that a child is a 'qualifying child' if: '(a) one of his parents is, in relation to him, a non-resident parent; *or* (b) both of his parents are, in relation to him, non-resident parents'. The term includes an adopted child and a child born to a married couple by artificial insemination by donor, unless it is proved that the husband did not consent to the treatment (s 28(2), Human Fertilisation and Embryology Act 1990).

The provisions of the CSA 1991 apply to a child who is under the age of 16, or under the age **35.09** of 19 and receiving full-time, non-advanced education (ie, education at school). The Act does not apply if the child is or has been married or is a civil partner: s 55(2), CSA 1991, amended by the Civil Partnership Act 2004 ('CPA 2004').

The 'non-resident parent'

This term is defined in s 3(2), CSA 1991 as follows: **35.10**

The parent of any child is a 'non-resident parent', in relation to him, if:

(a) that parent is not living in the same household with the child; and
(b) the child has his home with a person who is, in relation to him, a person with care.

The 'person with care'

This term is defined in s 3(3) as follows: **35.11**

a person:

(a) with whom the child has his home;
(b) who usually provides day to day care for the child (whether exclusively or in conjunction with any other person); and
(c) who does not fall within a prescribed category of person.

Parents, guardians, or a person in whose favour a residence order has been made in respect of the child can never come within 'a prescribed category of person': s 3(4).

For the purposes of the CSA 1991 a local authority is not normally a person with care (reg **35.12** 21(1), Child Support (Maintenance Calculation Procedure) Regulations 2000 (SI 2001/157)) and a procedure to enable a local authority to recover the cost of caring for a child is contained in the CA 1989. For the purpose of this chapter it will be assumed that the person with care is the other parent of the child, who will be referred to as the 'carer parent'.

D   THE DUTY TO MAINTAIN

35.13   This is laid down in s 1(1), CSA 1991 in the statement 'each parent of a qualifying child is responsible for maintaining him'.

35.14   Further, in s 1(3) it is provided that 'where a maintenance calculation made under this Act requires the making of periodical payments, it shall be the duty of the non-resident parent with respect to whom the calculation was made to make those payments'.

35.15   In order to give effect to this statutory duty a Child Support Agency was established, and it has extensive powers to trace non-resident parents, to investigate their means and to calculate, collect, and enforce child maintenance payments.

35.16   Because of amendments to s 44, CSA 1991 the Agency's jurisdiction to carry out maintenance calculations is extended to cover non-resident parents who are not habitually resident in the United Kingdom but are in certain classes of occupation including, for example, the diplomatic service, overseas civil service, and HM forces, or who are employed by employers described in the Child Support (Information, Evidence and Disclosure and Maintenance Arrangements and Jurisdiction) (Amendment) Regulations 2000 (SI 2001/161). Essentially, this covers employees who work outside the United Kingdom, but whose payment arrangements are made by their employers in the United Kingdom.

E   THE CALCULATION OF CHILD MAINTENANCE

35.17   The CSPASSA 2000 amends substantially Part I, sch 1, CSA 1991 in prescribing the calculation of child maintenance.

The calculation

35.18   The level of child maintenance is to be determined by calculating the income of the non-resident parent. No account is taken of the income or other resources of the carer parent even where there is a significant disparity in earning capacity.

The calculation process

35.19   The level of maintenance to be paid depends upon which rate of payment is applicable given the financial circumstances of the non-resident parent.

35.20   In calculating the level of child maintenance to be provided by the non-resident parent, the following questions must be asked:

(a)   Which rate is to apply (ie, basic, reduced, flat, or nil rates)?
(b)   When the basic or reduced rate applies, what sum is payable?
(c)   How is the flat rate calculated?
(d)   In what circumstances does the nil rate apply?
(e)   Should there be apportionment of the figure in (b) above?

(f) Is care shared? If so, should it lead to a reduction in the level of maintenance to be paid by the non-resident parent?

The application and calculation of the basic rate

The basic rate will be the one applicable to most families when the non-resident parent is **35.21** working. The basic rate is a specified percentage of the net income of the non-resident parent, dependent upon the number of qualifying children to be maintained, namely:

(a) 15 per cent where the non-resident parent has one qualifying child;
(b) 20 per cent where he has two qualifying children;
(c) 25 per cent where he has three or more qualifying children: sch 1, Part 1, para 2(1), CSA 1991.

On the face of it, therefore, the calculation of maintenance is simple. If the non-resident parent earns £400 per week net, he will pay £60 for one child and £100 for three or more children, irrespective of the ages or individual needs of the children concerned. Net weekly income is defined in Part 1 of the schedule to the Child Support (Maintenance Calculations and Special Cases) Regulations 2000 (SI 2001/155) as any remuneration (including overtime and bonuses) or profit derived from employment, together with working tax credit, if paid to the non-resident parent, less income tax, Class 1 or Class 2 and Class 4 National Insurance contributions, and any contributions to an occupational or personal pension scheme, except where the scheme is intended to provide a capital sum to discharge a mortgage secured on a non-resident parent's home in which case 75 per cent of the contribution may be deducted.

While investment income is ignored, an income derived from a pension is included. **35.22**

In *Smith v Secretary of State for Work and Pensions and another* [2006] UKHL 35, by a majority **35.23** decision, the House of Lords held that, in calculating a self-employed trader's income for child support purposes, no deduction for capital allowances should be made. The decision had a significant impact on the non-resident parent's income to be subject to the child support calculation. The non-resident parent had, during the period 1 April 2000–31 March 2001, made a taxable profit (before capital allowances) of £169,520, reduced by capital allowances of £148,628 to the sum of £20,892 on which he was charged income tax. Disregarding the capital allowances enhanced the non-resident parent's net income for CMEC purposes and substantially increased the level of child support payable to the carer parent.

The ceiling on net weekly income Although initially it was the view of the government **35.24** that there should be no limit on the income, a percentage of which could be taken in child maintenance, it did not oppose an amendment to the legislation proposed in the House of Lords which now has the effect of ignoring any net income of the non-resident parent which exceeds £2,000 per week (sch 1, Part 1, para 10(3), CSA 1991). Thus, very high earners have some measure of protection under the CSA regime.

Position where the non-resident parent has a child at home with him The CSA 1991, sch 1, **35.25** Part 1, para 2(2) deals with the situation where the non-resident parent has a child at home with him (eg a child of a new relationship or the child of a new partner) for whom he or his partner receives child benefit. Schedule 1, Part 1, para 10C(4) defines the term 'partner' as follows:

(a) if they are a couple, the other member of that couple (this is further defined in para 10C(5) to mean a man and a woman who are married to each other and members of the same household, or who are not married to each other but are living together as husband and wife or two people of the same sex who are civil partners of each other and are members of the same household or two people of the same sex who are not civil partners of each other but are living together as if they were civil partners (amended by sch 24, Part 1, CPA 2004)).

(b) if the person is a husband or wife by virtue of a valid polygamous marriage, another party to the marriage who is of the opposite sex and is a member of the same household.

In such circumstances, allowance is made for 'any other relevant children' in calculating the level of maintenance for the qualifying child. No account is taken of any income of the new partner or of the 'relevant children'.

35.26 The allowance which is made is by way of a percentage deduction from the net weekly income of the non-resident parent before the basic rate is calculated. The percentages are:

(a) 15 per cent, where he has one relevant other child;
(b) 20 per cent, where he has two relevant other children;
(c) 25 per cent, where he has three or more relevant other children.

If, therefore, the non-resident parent has a net weekly income of £400 and one relevant other child, 15 per cent is first deducted from his net weekly income, leaving £340 available to support the qualifying child. Hence, the qualifying child receives maintenance at the rate of £51.00 per week, not £60.00, which would have been payable if there had been no relevant other child.

35.27 This reform recognizes the variety of domestic relationships which exist today while giving some preference to the first family.

The application and calculation of the reduced rate

35.28 The reduced rate is designed to recognize that low wage earners need a disproportionate percentage of their income to meet their basic living expenses. Such a rate is payable where neither the flat rate nor the nil rate applies and the non-resident parent's net weekly income is less than £200 but more than £100.

35.29 According to reg 3, Child Support (Maintenance Calculations and Special Cases) Regulations 2000, the reduced rate is an amount calculated as follows:

$$F + (A \times T)$$

where F is the flat rate liability applicable to the non-resident parent (ie, £5.00) (see para 35.30 below); A is the amount of the non-resident parent's net weekly income above £100 but not exceeding £200; and T is the percentage determined in accordance with Table 35.1.

Table 35.1 Determining the percentage 'T'

	1 qualifying child of the non-resident parent				2 qualifying children of the non-resident parent				3+ qualifying children of the non-resident parent			
Number of relevant other children of the non-resident	0	1	2	3+	0	1	2	3+	0	1	2	3+
parent T(%)	25	20.5	19	17.5	35	29	27	25	45	37.5	35	32.5

PART V
DOMESTIC VIOLENCE

The authors are indebted to Paul Mallender and Jane Rayson in the preparation of this Part.

36

OCCUPATION ORDERS

(c)   was at any time intended by the applicant and a person with whom he or she is associated to be their home.

Clearly, it is important to note, first, the wide range of potential applicants for an order under s 33; and, secondly, the fact that the dwelling-house need not be presently occupied by the applicant as a pre-condition to seeking the order.

Example Mary is a single parent and the tenant of a council flat. She agrees to let her brother stay with her following the breakdown of his marriage. Initially, things go well and Mary appreciates having the extra cash provided by the board and lodging he pays. However, following service on him of his wife's divorce petition, his behaviour becomes increasingly unpredictable culminating in a violent attack on Mary, witnessed by her young daughter. Mary asks him to leave, but he refuses to do so, saying that he has nowhere else to go. Mary could seek an occupation order under s 33 because:

(a)   she is entitled to occupy the property;
(b)   the property has been the home of her and her brother (albeit for a short period of time, but no time scale is prescribed under the Act); and
(c)   the respondent is someone with whom she is associated (they are relatives (s 62(2)).

At the very least, Mary would be advised to seek a regulatory order requiring her brother to leave the property and to stay away from the area in which the flat is situated.

What a s 33 order may contain

36.08 A s 33 order may contain any of the following provisions:

(a)   enforcing the applicant's entitlement to remain in occupation as against the respondent;
(b)   requiring the respondent to permit the applicant to enter and remain in the dwelling-house;
(c)   requiring the respondent to permit the applicant to enter and remain in part of the dwelling-house;
(d)   regulating the occupation of the dwelling-house by either or both parties;
(e)   prohibiting, suspending, or restricting the exercise by the respondent of his right (whether by virtue of a beneficial estate or interest, contract, or enactment) to occupy the dwelling-house;
(f)   restricting or terminating the respondent's home rights;
(g)   requiring the respondent to leave the dwelling-house;
(h)   requiring the respondent to leave part of the dwelling-house;
(i)   excluding the respondent from a defined area in which the dwelling-house is included: s 33(3).

Because orders containing any of the above provisions effectively regulate the occupation of the home, they are sometimes referred to as regulatory orders, as opposed to declaratory orders which declare or extend existing rights and grant rights.

The test for regulatory orders

Section 33(6), FLA 1996 provides that in deciding whether to make any of the above regula- **36.09**
tory orders under s 33(3) the court shall have regard to all the circumstances including:

(a) the housing needs and housing resources of each of the parties and of any relevant child;
(b) the financial resources of each of the parties;
(c) the likely effect of any order, or of any decision by the court not to exercise its powers
      under s 33(3), on the health, safety, or well-being of the parties and of any relevant child;
(d) the conduct of the parties in relation to each other and otherwise: s 33(6)(a), (b), (c), and (d).

In accordance with s 33(7), the court must make an order if it appears that the applicant or any **36.10**
relevant child is likely to suffer significant harm attributable to conduct of the respondent if
an order is not made, unless it appears that:

(a) the respondent or any relevant child is likely to suffer significant harm if the order is
      made; and
(b) the harm likely to be suffered by the respondent or the child in that event is as great as,
      or greater than, the harm attributable to conduct of the respondent which is likely to be
      suffered by the applicant or child if the order is not made.

This is known as 'the balance of harm test'.

The test explained

In cases where the question of significant harm does not arise, the court has *power* to make an **36.11**
order taking into account the four factors considered above (ie, housing needs and housing
resources, financial resources, health, safety or well-being, and conduct).

However, in cases where there is a likelihood of significant harm and the balance comes down **36.12**
in favour of the applicant, the power becomes a *duty* (the section uses 'shall', therefore it is
mandatory) and the court must make an order. If both parties are able to establish significant
harm, but neither is able to show greater harm, then the court still has the power to make an
appropriate order, but is not under a duty to do so.

It is very likely that in cases where it can be established that there is a risk of significant harm **36.13**
to a child, the child's interests will become in effect the paramount consideration since it is
that factor which will have imposed a duty on the court to make an order.

The reported cases provide some guidance as to how these provisions are applied in practice. **36.14**
In *Chalmers v Johns* [1999] 1 FLR 392 there had been assaults by the mother on the father and
the father on the mother. The mother left the family home, taking their 7-year-old daughter
with her. The mother applied for an occupation order. The court at first instance made the
order, but it was subsequently set aside by the Court of Appeal. In allowing the appeal, the
court held that in deciding whether to make an order under s 33 the court had first to consider whether, if the order were not made, the applicant or any relevant child would be likely
to suffer significant harm attributable to the conduct of the respondent. If the answer was
'yes', then, under s 33(7), the court had to make the order unless the harm to the respondent
or the child if the order were made was likely to be as great or greater. If the answer was 'no',
then the court had a discretion based on the s 33(6) factors. On the facts of this case, neither

the mother nor the child were likely to suffer 'significant harm' attributable to the conduct of the father if the order were not made and therefore the case was one for the exercise of the s 33(6) discretion. The court must first consider s 33(7) and only if the balance of harm test is *not* satisfied in favour of the applicant should it move on to consider s 33(6).

36.15   Under s 33(7), significant harm must be attributable to the respondent's conduct. The court should concentrate on the effect of the conduct of the respondent, rather than on his or her intention. The 'balance of harm' test is a comparison of the harm which would be suffered by the applicant and any relevant child if the order were not made with that which would be suffered by the respondent and any relevant child if the order were made. The discretionary exercise under s 33(6) is precise and is governed by the factors specified in the checklist.

36.16   In the case of *B v B* [1999] 1 FLR 715 the court refused to make an occupation order in favour of the applicant wife where the wife had left the matrimonial home as a result of the husband's violence towards her, taking their baby daughter with her. The husband remained in the property with his 6-year-old son from a previous marriage. The court applied the 'balance of harm' test and held that the husband's child would suffer more harm if an order were made than the wife and baby if it were not.

36.17   In *Banks v Banks* [1999] 1 FLR 726 the court held that it would be wrong to make an order excluding the 79-year-old wife from the home she shared with her 75-year-old husband even though the wife's behaviour towards the husband had been verbally and physically aggressive. The wife suffered from manic depression and dementia, had been hospitalized, and was ready to return home. The husband sought to exclude her. The court found that her behaviour did not significantly threaten the husband's health and that the strain of her continuing to live in the same house as him would not cause him significant harm. It held that the harm caused to the wife if the order were made would be significantly greater than the harm caused to the husband if it were not.

36.18   In *Re Y (Child)* [2000] FCR 470 the court stated that occupation orders were not to be used to resolve deadlock in proceedings for a financial order, particularly in a case where the parties could be accommodated in separate quarters within the home and cross-undertakings given by each party not to molest the other seemed to be effective. However, in *G v G (Occupation Order)* [2011] 1 FLR 687 the Court of Appeal (refusing the excluded spouse permission to appeal) held that the provisions of s 33(6) should not be used as a straightjacket where immediate separation was not only beneficial but necessary. An occupation order was made where alternative accommodation was readily available to the excluded spouse, even though there was no allegation of violence.

'Harm', etc defined

36.19   'Harm' is defined in s 63, FLA 1996. In relation to a person who is 18 or older, 'harm' means 'ill-treatment or the impairment of health' and in relation to a child it means 'ill-treatment or the impairment of health or development'.

36.20   'Ill-treatment' includes forms of ill-treatment which are not physical. In the case of a child, the phrase includes sexual abuse.

36.21   'Health' includes physical and mental health.

36.22   'Development' means physical, intellectual, emotional, social, or behavioural development.

Preparation of the case

Clearly, it will be of assistance to the court if the applicant's witness statement deals with each **36.23** of the matters listed in s 33(6) separately following a paragraph on the general background to the case. It should be clear from the statement whether the applicant is seeking to establish significant harm under s 33(7).

In particular, as far as the applicant is concerned, a paragraph setting out what is alleged to **36.24** constitute significant harm will be extremely helpful since, assuming that the court is satisfied that the likelihood of significant harm has arisen and there is no attempt on the part of the respondent to rebut this or to show suffer greater significant harm on the other side of the 'balance of harm' equation, an occupation order must be made.

By contrast, if acting for the respondent in a case where significant harm is alleged by the **36.25** applicant, it would be sensible to deal with this specifically in the respondent's statement, in particular seeking to demonstrate any significant harm suffered by the respondent or a relevant child and the effect on the respondent or child should an order be made.

Mental capacity for submission to the jurisdiction

Because the respondent to an occupation order is at risk of committal if the order is breached, **36.26** it is important to establish the degree to which he understands the nature of the court's jurisdiction and the concept of contempt. In *P v P (Contempt of Court: Mental Capacity)* [1999] 2 FLR 897 the husband was deaf and dumb, had limited vision, and an average IQ, but was not suffering from mental illness or impairment. On 29 occasions he breached an injunction with a power of arrest attached prohibiting him from returning to the former matrimonial home where the wife lived. The husband applied for a discharge of the order. The wife applied for the husband's committal to prison for his breaches of the order. The Court of Appeal held that a comprehension of the nature of the court's jurisdiction and of the concept of contempt was not a prerequisite for contempt or for the making of an order. It was sufficient for the contemnor to understand that an order had been made forbidding him to do certain things and that if he did them he would be punished. The court made no order on the committal but the injunction was extended for six months with a power of arrest attached.

Duration of the order

Section 33(10) provides that orders under s 33 may be for a specified period, until the occur- **36.27** rence of a specified event or until further order. There is therefore no maximum duration of the order.

If the applicant has family home rights and the respondent is the other spouse or civil partner, **36.28** an order under this section made during the marriage may provide that those rights are not to be brought to an end by:

(a) the death of the other spouse/civil partner; or
(b) the termination (otherwise than by death) of the marriage/civil partnership;
provided that the court considers that in all the circumstances it is just and reasonable to make the direction: s 33(5) and (8).

F   OCCUPATION ORDER WHERE NEITHER SPOUSE OR CIVIL PARTNER IS ENTITLED TO OCCUPY

Characteristics of the order

36.47   This is dealt with in s 37 and permits the court to make a regulatory order only. The provisions of s 33(6) and (7) apply. Because the parties are spouses or civil partners the court is under a duty to make the order if the balance of harm test is established by the applicant. See paras 36.14 ff above for case law concerning the 'balance of harm' test.

36.48   Although neither party is entitled to occupy the property, it must be or have been either the matrimonial home or the civil partnership home. The order must be limited so as to have effect for a specified period not exceeding six months, but may be extended on one or more occasions for a further specified period not exceeding six months.

Relevance to practice

36.49   Applications of this type will be comparatively rare since in most cases at least one of the parties will be entitled to remain in occupation of the dwelling-house. The Law Commission identified two circumstances in which an application might be made, namely in the case of squatters and of bare licensees.

36.50   It will also be noted that it is not sufficient for the purposes of an application that the parties *intended* to use the dwelling-house as a matrimonial home.

G   POSITION WHERE NEITHER COHABITANT NOR FORMER COHABITANT IS ENTITLED TO OCCUPY

36.51   An application may be made for a regulatory order only under the provisions of s 38.

Factors to be considered

36.52   In deciding whether to exercise its powers the court must consider all the circumstances including:

(a) the housing needs and housing resources of each of the parties and of any relevant child;

(b) the financial resources of each of the parties;

(c) the likely effect of any order on the health, safety, or well-being of the parties and of any relevant child;

(d) the conduct of the parties in relation to each other and otherwise and the questions mentioned in s 38(5).

36.53   In other words, the court must consider the 'balance of harm' test, but because the applicant is a non-entitled cohabitant or former cohabitant the court retains a discretion as to whether to make the order sought. See paras 36.14 ff above for recent case law concerning the 'balance of harm' test.

Duration of the order

Under s 38(6), the order is limited for a specified period not exceeding six months but may be **36.54** extended on one occasion for a further period not exceeding six months.

H ANCILLARY ORDERS WHERE AN OCCUPATION ORDER IS MADE UNDER SS 33, 35, OR 36

Section 40 provides that the court, on making an occupation order under s 33, 35, or 36 (or **36.55** at any time thereafter), may make an ancillary order imposing certain obligations on either party (eg as to the repair and maintenance of the dwelling-house or as to the payment of rent, mortgage, or other relevant outgoing) or requiring the payment of rent to the party who has been excluded. Further, the court may grant either party possession or use of furniture or other contents of the dwelling-house and impose a requirement that reasonable care is taken of them. Such an order lasts for as long as the occupation order.

In deciding whether to exercise its powers and, if so, in what manner, the court shall have **36.56** regard to all the circumstances of the case including:

(a) the financial needs and financial resources of the parties; and
(b) the financial obligations which they have or are likely to have in the foreseeable future, including financial obligations to each other and any relevant child: s 40(2).

The difficulty, however, with s 40 is that there is no procedure for enforcing compliance: see *Nwogbe v Nwogbe* [2000] 2 FLR 744. Section 40 will only be of assistance, therefore, where a respondent is likely to comply without the need for enforcement.

I PROCEDURAL GUIDE

Where to find the rules

The rules governing applications for non-molestation and occupation orders are set out in **36.57** Part 10, Family Procedure Rules 2010 ('FPR 2010').

The fee

On making an application for a non-molestation order or occupation order in the county **36.58** court or family proceedings court a fee of £60 is payable irrespective of whether the applicant is publicly funded.

Only one fee is payable when an application is made for both types of order at the same time: **36.59** Family Proceedings Fees Order 1999 (SI 1999/690) as amended.

Where is the application to be made?

Introduction

36.60   The provisions are set out fully in the Allocation and Transfer of Proceedings Order 2008 (SI 2008/2836). The principal features of the Order are set out below.

Choice of venue

36.61   Generally speaking, an application for an order under Part IV may be commenced in a county court (ie, a designated divorce county court, a family hearing centre, or a care centre) or a family proceedings court. For the purpose of Part IV proceedings the Principal Registry of the Family Division of the High Court is to be treated as a county court.

36.62   However, there are some important exceptions to note:

(a)   A family proceedings court shall not be competent to entertain any application, or make any order, involving any disputed question as to a party's entitlement to occupy any property (however that might arise) unless it is unnecessary to determine the question in order to deal with the application or make the order. Further, the magistrate may decline jurisdiction in any proceedings if he considers that the case can more conveniently be dealt with by another court: s 59, FLA 1996.

(b)   The family proceedings court has no jurisdiction to deal with applications for the transfer of tenancies on divorce or on the separation of cohabitants: s 53 and sch 7, para 1.

(c)   Applications for the grant of leave under s 43 (where the applicant is a child under the age of 16) should be commenced in the county court: FPR 2010, PD10A.

Funding the application

36.63   The provisions for funding an application for an occupation order are the same as those which apply to applications for non-molestation orders and are set out in full in Chapter 37, para 37.08.

Normal procedure in the county court

36.64   A free-standing application for an occupation order or a non-molestation order is to be made in Form FL401. If applicants are concerned about giving their address on the application form, they may leave the form blank and complete Confidential Address Form C8.

36.65   It is recognized that the applicant may not know all the details requested on the application form and this should be stated wherever it applies.

36.66   The form should be signed by the applicant and dated.

36.67   Where the application is made in other proceedings which are pending, the application is likewise to be made in Form FL401.

36.68   The application in Form FL401 shall be supported by a witness statement signed by the applicant and containing a statement of truth: r 10.2(1), FPR 2010. Where the application is made without notice, the witness statement must set out the reasons why notice has not been given: r 10.2(4).

Procedure where the applicant is a child under the age of 16

The application for permission should be made using the Part 18 procedure: FPR 2010, **36.69** PD10A.

Procedure for a without notice (*ex parte*) application

The application is made in Form FL401 but the statement must set out reasons why notice **36.70** was not given: r 10.2(4).

Service of the application

On the respondent

The application on notice (together with the witness statement and notice of proceedings **36.71** and guidance in Form FL402) shall be served by the applicant on the respondent personally not less than two days before the date on which the application will be heard: r 10.3(1)(i).

The court may abridge the period: r 10.3(1)(ii). **36.72**

Where the applicant is acting in person, personal service of the application shall be effected **36.73** by the court if the applicant so requests: r 10.3(2).

Service on third parties

Where an application is made for an occupation order under s 33, 35, or 36, FLA 1996 a copy **36.74** of the application shall be served by the applicant by first-class post on the mortgagee or, as the case may be, the landlord of the dwelling-house with a notice in Form FL416 informing him of his right to make representations in writing or at any hearing: r 10.3(3).

Statement of service

The applicant is required to file a certificate of service after he has served the application: **36.75** r 10.3(4). This gives details of the identity of the person served and sets out how service was effected.

The hearing

In the High Court and county court, the hearing will be in private unless the court directs **36.76** otherwise: r 10.5.

A record of the hearing is to be issued in Form FL405 and the order made in Form FL404. **36.77**

The precise wording of the occupation order depends, of course, on the section under which **36.78** the order was made.

Service of the order

An order obtained without notice

A copy of the order obtained without notice, a copy of the application, and of the witness **36.79** statement must be served by the applicant on the respondent personally: r 10.6(1)(b).

The order made on notice

36.80 A copy of an order made after a hearing of which both sides received notice must be served by the applicant on the respondent personally: r 10.6(1)(a).

36.81 Further, when an occupation order is made under s 33, 35, or 36, FLA 1996 a copy of the order must be served by the applicant on the mortgagee or, as the case may be, the landlord of the dwelling-house in question: r 10.6(3).

The applicant acting in person

36.82 In these circumstances, service of a copy of any order made must be effected by the court if the applicant so requests: r 10.6(2). The method of service to be employed by the court is not indicated in the Rules.

J   ENFORCEMENT

Introduction

36.83 Enforcement of an occupation order or of an undertaking is dealt with in s 47 and sch 5, FLA 1996 with provision for remand for medical examination and reports contained in s 48.

36.84 Where the order is made on notice, the court is required to attach a power of arrest to specified provisions of an occupation order where it appears that the respondent has used or threatened violence against the applicant or a relevant child, unless the court is satisfied that in all the circumstances of the case the applicant or child will be adequately protected without such a power of arrest: s 47(2). In *P v P* (Court of Appeal, 21 January 2000, unreported) the attaching of a power of arrest to an occupation order was not found to be justified where the last incident of physical violence had occurred more than four years previously and where the occupation order removed the most serious harm that had been found to exist.

36.85 If the criteria for a power of arrest is satisfied, the court is under an obligation to attach a power of arrest—it is not a matter of discretion.

36.86 Where the order is made without notice, the court is given a discretion to attach a power of arrest if it appears to the court that:

(a) the respondent has used or threatened violence against the applicant or a relevant child; and

(b) there is a risk of significant harm to the applicant or child attributable to conduct of the respondent if the power of arrest is not attached immediately: s 47(3).

36.87 In *JH v RH* [2001] 1 FLR 641 the court held that a power of arrest could properly be attached to an occupation order made against a 17-year-old child if the statutory criteria were made out.

The power of arrest in practice

Where a power of arrest is attached to one or more of the provisions ('the relevant provisions') **36.88** of the order:

(a) the relevant provisions must be set out in Form FL406 and the form must not include any provisions of the order to which the power of arrest was not attached; and

(b) a copy of the form must be delivered to the officer for the time being in charge of any police station serving the area for the applicant's address or to any other police station as the court may specify: r 10.9, FPR 2010.

The copy of the form detailing the provisions must be accompanied by a statement showing **36.89** that the respondent has been served with the order or informed of its terms (whether by being present when the order was made or by telephone or otherwise): r 10.10(2).

It is the responsibility of the applicant to deliver the documentation to the police, unless **36.90** the order was served by the court after a request by a litigant in person, in which case it is the responsibility of an officer of the court to ensure that the police are properly informed: r 10.10(3).

Similarly, when the relevant provisions of the order are varied or discharged the proper officer **36.91** at the court must immediately inform the police officer who received the form and deliver a copy of the order to that officer: r 10.10(5).

Where a power of arrest is attached to specific provisions of the order a constable may arrest **36.92** without warrant a person whom he has reasonable cause to suspect to be in breach of any such provision: s 47(6).

The respondent must then be brought before the relevant judicial authority within 24 hours **36.93** beginning at the time of his arrest. When the 24-hour period is being calculated, no account is taken of Christmas Day, Good Friday, or any Sunday. See *President's Practice Direction: Family Law Act 1996—Attendance of Arresting Officer* [2000] 1 FLR 270.

The 'relevant judicial authority' depends upon the court which made the original order. For **36.94** example, if the order was made by a county court, the relevant judicial authority is a judge or district judge of that or any other county court. If the order was made in a magistrates' court, the relevant judicial authority is any magistrates' court: s 63(1), FLA 1996.

All courts may remand respondents if the matter is not disposed of forthwith (see below). **36.95**

When an arrested person is brought before the relevant judicial authority, the attendance of **36.96** the arresting officer will not be necessary unless the arrest itself is in issue. A written statement from the officer about the circumstances of the arrest should normally be sufficient. In those cases where the arresting officer was also a witness to the events leading to the arrest and his evidence about those events is required, arrangements should be made for him to attend at a subsequent hearing to give evidence.

The proceedings should be listed for hearing within 14 days of the date on which the respondent **36.97** was arrested and he must be given not less than two business days' notice of the adjourned hearing: r 10.11(3), FPR 2010.

Issue of a warrant

36.98   If, at any time, the applicant considers that the respondent has failed to comply with an order to which no power of arrest has been attached, he may apply to the relevant judicial authority for the issue of a warrant substantiated on oath for the arrest of the respondent: s 47(8) and (9), FLA 1996. The court will issue the warrant if it has reasonable grounds for believing that the respondent has failed to comply with the order. An application for the issue of a warrant for the arrest of the respondent is to be made in Form FL407 and the warrant must be issued in Form FL408. The warrant will be executed by the bailiffs attached to the county court.

Remands

36.99   Schedule 5, FLA 1996 gives the High Court and county courts powers to remand corresponding to those which apply in magistrates' courts under ss 128 and 129, Magistrates' Courts Act 1980. In county courts, the powers may be exercised by a judge or a district judge. The powers are as follows.

Remand in custody or on bail

36.100   Where a court has power to remand the respondent under s 47 it may:

(a)   remand him in custody; or

(b)   remand him on bail, either:

   (i)   by taking a recognizance from him (with or without sureties), such recognizance to be 'conditioned' in accordance with sch 5, para 2(3): or

   (ii)   by fixing the amount of the recognizances with a view to their being taken subsequently (and in the meantime committing the person to custody): sch 5, para 2(1).

36.101   If bail is granted, the court may require the remanded person to comply with 'such requirements' as appear to the court to be necessary to ensure that he does not interfere with witnesses or otherwise obstruct the course of justice: s 47(12).

The period of remand

36.102   A period of remand may not exceed eight clear days unless:

(a)   the person is remanded on bail and both he and the applicant agree to a longer period;

(b)   a case is adjourned under s 48(1) for a medical examination and report to be made, when the court may remand for the period of adjournment (but see the limitations in s 48, below): sch 5, para 2(5).

Further remand

36.103   If the court is satisfied that a remanded person is unable, because of illness or accident, to appear at the relevant time, he may be remanded in his absence (and the eight days' time limit does not apply): sch 5, para 3(1). Otherwise, a person may be remanded in his absence by the court's enlarging his recognizance and those of any sureties to a later date: sch 5, para 3(2).

36.104   For the avoidance of doubt, sch 5, para 3(2) specifically provides that a person brought before the court after remand may be further remanded.

Remand for medical examination

Where the court has reason to consider that a medical report will be required, it may remand **36.105** a person to enable a medical examination and report to be made. A remand must not exceed four weeks at a time, or three weeks if the remand is in custody: s 48(2) and (3).

Section 48(4) gives to the civil courts powers similar to those of the Crown Court to make an **36.106** order under s 35, Mental Health Act 1983, remanding for a report on the mental condition of the respondent where there is reason to suspect that the person arrested is suffering from mental illness or severe mental impairment.

If the case is adjourned the court may remand the respondent on bail or in custody. If the **36.107** remand is on bail the proceedings may not be adjourned for longer than eight clear days unless both the applicant and the respondent agree to a longer adjournment. The bail may be conditional, for example that the respondent does not interfere with witnesses or obstruct justice. If the respondent is remanded in custody, the maximum duration of the remand is eight clear days at a time. Remand in custody may be for the specific purpose of obtaining medical reports on the respondent.

The court may adjourn the proceedings without considering what penalty should be imposed. **36.108** Such an adjournment may be subject to conditions with which the respondent must comply. If there is a breach of the conditions, the matter may be restored for further consideration.

Committal proceedings

Committal in the county court is governed by sch 2, CCR Ord 29, CPR 1998, as amended by **36.109** r 33.7, FPR 2010. In the High Court committal is governed by sch 1, RSC Ord 52, CPR 1998. The general rule is that committal hearings will be held in public.

An order may not be enforced by way of committal unless it has been endorsed with a penal **36.110** notice: r 10.12, FPR 2010.

The application for the issue of a committal order ('notice to show good reason') is made on **36.111** Form N78 (county court) or by Part 8 claim form (High Court). It must:

(a) specify the provisions of the order or undertaking which have been disobeyed or broken;
(b) identify separately and numerically the ways in which it is alleged that the order or undertaking has been disobeyed or broken;
(c) be supported by an affidavit (sworn statement) by the applicant setting out the grounds for the application. Unless the court agrees to dispense with the need for service, the notice and affidavit must be served personally on the respondent.

A fee of £80 is payable in the High Court or county court.

Committal proceedings are always important since they affect the liberty of the individual **36.112** alleged to have acted in contempt of a court order. Consequently, it is vital that such proceedings are conducted by way of a proper hearing. It is highly desirable to have written allegations of the breaches alleged placed before the judge, even if the constraints of time mean that these must be in manuscript form (*Manchester City Council* v *Worthington* [2000] Fam Law 147).

36.113 When a committal order is made otherwise than in public or a courtroom open to the public, it must be announced in open court at the earliest opportunity (*President's Direction* [1998] 1 FLR 496). The announcement must include:

(a) the name of the party committed;

(b) the nature of the contempt of court (in general terms); and

(c) the length of the period of committal to prison.

Where a committal order is suspended for so long as the contemnor complies with a separate order expressed to last 'until further order' it will be valid even though its effect is to suspend a sentence of imprisonment indefinitely (*Griffin* v *Griffin* [2000] Fam Law 451). The order must be on Form N79 (county court) or Form A85 (High Court). Failure to draw up an order on the correct form will amount to a fundamental defect in procedure (see *Couzens* v *Couzens* [2001] 2 FLR 701—where a suspended order which had not been drawn up on Form N79 could not be activated on the wife's subsequent application following further serious breaches by the husband).

36.114 In *Begum* v *Anam* [2004] EWCA 578 the Court of Appeal set aside a committal order following a hearing in the respondent's absence. The application had been served on the respondent while he was serving a prison sentence and he was therefore unable to obtain legal advice or obtain a production warrant so that he could be present. These failings breached the respondent's right to a fair trial under Art 6, ECHR. The Court of Appeal said that in these circumstances the judge should have adjourned the hearing until a later date.

Attachment of a penal notice

36.115 Rule 10.12, FPR 2010 also provides that CCR Ord 29, r 1 (preserved in sch 2, CPR 1998) shall have effect as if for para (3) (a copy of the injunction served on the respondent must be endorsed with a penal notice informing him or her that disobedience of the order would constitute a contempt of court and render him liable to be committed to prison) there were substituted the following:

> (3) At the time when the order is drawn up, the proper officer shall
>   (i) where the order made is (or includes) a non-molestation order; or
>   (ii) where the order made is an occupation order and the court so directs,
> issue a copy of the order endorsed with or incorporating a notice as to the consequence of disobedience, for service in accordance with paragraph (2) [ie, personal service on the respondent].

In other words, a penal notice *must* be attached to a non-molestation order and may be attached to an occupation order if the court so directs. The purpose of this provision is to ensure that the respondent is aware of the consequences of breach of the order.

Powers of the court on a committal application

36.116 Before imposing any form of penalty, a deliberate act or failure to act, with knowledge of the terms of the order, must be proved.

36.117 Because the alleged contemnor's liberty is at stake, the standard of proof is the criminal standard. The alleged contemnor has the right to choose not to give evidence: *Hammerton* v *Hammerton* [2007] 2 FLR 1133.

If a breach is proved, county courts and the High Court have power to sentence the respond-   **36.118**
ent to be committed to prison for up to two years or to impose a fine, or both: s 14, Contempt
of Court Act 1981. There is no limit to the amount of the fine which the court may impose:
Hale v *Tanner* [2000] 2 FLR 879. If the court is considering the imposition of a prison sentence,
it must take into account the effect of the sentence on the children of the family and on the
financial position of the respondent.

Consideration should also be given to whether the prison sentence should be suspended   **36.119**
(which may be for a specified period or on terms and conditions laid down by the court):
s 50(1), FLA 1996; sch 1, RSC Ord 52, r 7(1), CPR 1998. In the event of a further breach the
court has power to decide whether to impose the prison sentence at that point.

In any event, if a prison sentence is imposed, the length of sentence must be clearly specified.   **36.120**
The court cannot sentence the respondent to prison for an indefinite period.

The general principle has been that the imposition of a prison sentence in family proceedings   **36.121**
should only be used as a last resort: *Ansah* v *Ansah* [1977] 2 All ER 638 (CA). However, in the
case of *N* v *R (Non-molestation Order: Breach)* [1998] 2 FLR 1068 the Court of Appeal clearly
stated that orders must be obeyed. Here the court substituted an immediate custodial sentence for a suspended custodial sentence where the application was to commit for a serious
breach of a non-molestation order.

The jurisdiction of the court to impose an immediate custodial sentence is confirmed in   **36.122**
Wilson v *Webster* [1998] 1 FLR 1097. In *P* v *P (Contempt of Court: Mental Capacity)* [1999] 2 FLR
897, the Court of Appeal held that, provided a recalcitrant respondent understood what he
was forbidden to do and that if he disobeyed the order he would be punished, the order would
be enforced. In *Hale* v *Tanner* [2000] 2 FLR 879 the Court of Appeal dealt with the question
of the appropriate length of a prison sentence where there had been persistent breaches of a
non-molestation order. The court recognized that there was a lack of guidance in sentencing
for contempt of court and Hale LJ set out the following general guidelines:

(a) Imprisonment was not to be regarded as the automatic response to the breach of an order,
     although there was no principle that imprisonment was not to be imposed on the first
     occasion.
(b) Although alternatives to imprisonment were limited, there were a number of things the
     court should consider, in particular where no violence was involved.
(c) If imprisonment was appropriate, the length of the committal should be decided without
     reference to whether it was to be suspended.
(d) The seriousness of the contempt had to be judged not only for its intrinsic gravity but also
     in light of the court's objectives both to mark its disapproval of the disobedience to the
     order and to secure compliance in the future.
(e) The length of the committal should relate to the maximum available, that is, two years.
(f) Suspension was possible in a wider range of circumstances than in criminal cases, and
     was usually the first way of attempting to secure compliance with the order.
(g) The court had to consider whether the context was mitigating or aggravating, in particular
     where there was a breach of an intimate relationship and/or children were involved.
(h) The court should consider any concurrent proceedings in another court, and should
     explain to the contemnor the nature of the order and the consequences of breach.

The Court of Appeal held in this case that a sentence of six months' imprisonment, suspended for one year, was excessive and should be reduced to 29 days, although the period of suspension was considered to be appropriate.

36.123   In reaching its decision, the court was influenced by the fact that there had been no immediate threat of violence. It was rare even in more serious breaches for a sentence as long as six months to be imposed and in this case the appellant had admitted the allegation, had not been present when the order was made, had received no legal advice or warning of the penalties for breach, and was the mother of a young child.

36.124   In *H* v *O* [2005] 2 FLR 329 a father appealed against a sentence of 12 months for three breaches of a non-molestation order. One of the breaches involved a physical attack on the person caring for the child. The other two breaches related to verbal abuse and threatening behaviour. The Court of Appeal held that the level of sentencing under the FLA 1996 did not fully reflect contemporary requirements and opinion. Parliament and society now regarded domestic and other violence associated with harassment and molestation as demanding rather more condign deterrent punishment than formerly. In cases of actual or threatened violence, sentences under the FLA 1996 should not be manifestly discrepant with sentences passed in the Crown Court for comparable offences, such as under the Offences Against the Person Act 1861. In this case the Court of Appeal took the view that the seriousness of the breaches was aggravated because the carer of the child had been assaulted and that the father had shown no remorse. The sentence was, however, reduced to nine months in view of the fact that it was a first offence.

36.125   In *Robinson* v *Murray* [2006] 1 FLR 364 the Lord Chief Justice said that where a course of domestic violence or molestation warranted a sentence towards the top of the range, it was appropriate to bring civil or criminal proceedings under the Protection from Harassment Act 1997 where a maximum of five years' imprisonment was available. He also reiterated that domestic and other violence related to harassment or molestation should be viewed rather more seriously than had previously been the case.

Applications to purge contempt

36.126   Regardless of the length of the sentence imposed, a contemnor has the right to apply to the court to 'purge' his contempt. The application must be made in writing and attested by the governor of the prison or principal officer. The court has no jurisdiction on an application to purge a contempt to suspend an unserved balance of a prison sentence for any period. There are only three possible outcomes of an application to purge a contempt, namely immediate release, deferred release at a later date, or refusal: *Harris* v *Harris* [2002] 1 FLR 248 (CA)).

K   KEY DOCUMENTS

36.127   Family Law Act 1996
Family Procedure Rules 2010
Civil Procedure Rules 1998, Schs 1 and 2

37

NON-MOLESTATION ORDERS

A INTRODUCTION

37.01 Part IV, Family Law Act 1996 ('FLA 1996') has been in force since 1 October 1997. It provides a simple and unified system designed to offer protection from domestic violence. Protection is provided to those who fall within the class of 'associated persons' and includes provision for powers of arrest to be attached to orders, the granting of orders on a 'without notice' basis, and considerable flexibility over how the family home is to be occupied.

B THE ORDERS AVAILABLE

37.02 Two forms of order are available in all courts having jurisdiction in family matters. The orders are 'occupation orders' and 'non-molestation orders'. Non-molestation orders are dealt with in this chapter. Occupation orders are dealt with in Chapter 36. There are two significant differences between the orders:

(a) a non-molestation order is far easier to obtain than an occupation order, because it involves only a limited interference with the respondent's rights because it simply prohibits behaviour which he should not have been exhibiting anyway;
(b) breach of a non-molestation order is a criminal offence, whereas breach of an occupation order can be dealt with only as a contempt of court within the civil jurisdiction.

A non-molestation order

37.03 A non-molestation order means an order containing either or both of the following provisions:

(a) a provision prohibiting the respondent from molesting another person who is associated with the respondent;
(b) a provision prohibiting the respondent from molesting a relevant child (s 42(1)).

The term 'molestation' is not defined in the FLA 1996. It has been held that 'molestation' includes any conduct which can properly be regarded as such a degree of harassment as to call for the intervention of the court: *Horner* v *Horner* [1982] Fam 90. In colloquial terms, it means 'pestering': *Vaughan* v *Vaughan* [1973] 3 All ER 449.

37.04 In *C* v *C* [2001] EWCA Civ 1625 it was stressed that the judge must be satisfied on the balance of probabilities that judicial intervention is required to control the behaviour which is the subject matter of the complaint before the court. The form that that behaviour takes is also an important consideration.

The case of *C* v *C* [1998] 1 FLR 554 confirms that a non-molestation order should only be **37.05** made where there was some conduct which harassed and affected the applicant. It was not appropriate to seek a non-molestation order to prevent an invasion of the applicant's privacy by the publication of an article which related to the marriage and relationship between the applicant and his former wife and which he feared might damage his reputation. In *Banks* v *Banks* [1999] 1 FLR 726 the court held that it would be wrong to make the wife subject to a non-molestation order where the abuse to which the wife had subjected the husband was a symptom of her mental condition and was something over which she had no control. A non-molestation order would serve no practical purpose in such circumstances, even if the wife were capable of understanding it.

C   ASSOCIATED PERSONS AND RELEVANT CHILD

In determining whether a client will be able to obtain a non-molestation order the first matter **37.06** to be ascertained is whether the applicant or respondent are associated or, where it is a child who is to be protected, whether the child is a 'relevant' child.

Associated persons

The list of 'associated persons' appears in s 62(4) and (5). **37.07**

The definition

Persons are 'associated' with each other if: **37.08**

(a) They are married: s 62(3)(a).
(b) They are or have been civil partners of each other: s 62(3)(aa).
(c) They have been married: s 62(3)(a).
(d) They are cohabitants or former cohabitants (ie, two persons who, although not married to each other, are or were living together as husband and wife or (if the same sex) in an equivalent relationship): ss 62(1)(a) and 62(3)(b), which should be interpreted generously so as not to exclude borderline cases: *G* v *F (Non-molestation Order: Jurisdiction)* [2000] Fam Law 519.
(e) They live in the same household or have lived in the same household: (s 62(3)(c)) otherwise than by reason merely of one of them being the other's employee, tenant, lodger, or boarder.
(f) They are relatives: s 62(3)(d). 'Relative' is defined by s 63, the interpretation section, to include the following:

father	stepson
mother	stepdaughter
stepfather	grandmother
stepmother	grandfather
son	grandson
daughter	granddaughter

of a person *or* of that person's spouse or former spouse, civil partner, or former civil partner; and

brother	aunt
sister	niece
uncle	nephew

(whether of the full blood or of the half blood or by affinity) of a person *or* of that person's spouse or former spouse, civil partner, or former civil partner.

It should be noted that cohabitants and former cohabitants are treated as though they were married to each other or in a civil partnership, for the purpose of the above definition.

(g) They have agreed to marry one another (whether or not that agreement has been terminated): s 62(3)(e).

(h) They have entered into a civil partnership agreement (as defined by s 73, Civil Partnership Act 2004 ('CPA 2004') (whether or not that agreement has been terminated): s 62(3)(eza).

(i) They are parents of the same child: s 62(3)(f).

(j) They have or have had parental responsibility for the same child: (s 62(3)(f)) (unless one of those persons is a body corporate—s 62(6)). The most obvious example of a body corporate in this context would be a local authority which would of course acquire parental responsibility for a child upon the making of a care order: s 33(3)(a), Children Act 1989 ('CA 1989').

(k) They are parties to the same family proceedings (other than proceedings under the FLA 1996): s 62(3)(g). The exception to this is where one of the parties is a body corporate, for example a local authority: s 62(6).

(l) They have or have had an intimate personal relationship with each other which is or was of significant duration.

Same-sex couples

37.09 By virtue of the CPA 2004 and the Domestic Violence, Crime and Victims Act 2004 ('DVCVA 2004') the protection afforded to members of same-sex couples (whether in a civil partnership or not) now mirrors that which was available to either married, cohabiting, or formerly cohabiting couples of the opposite sex.

Associated persons in adoption

37.10 In recognition of the fact that strong feelings (and hence the need for injunctive relief) may arise in connection with adoption proceedings, the FLA 1996 provides that when a child has been adopted, freed for adoption, or subject to a placement order, the natural relatives of such a child and the child's new adoptive carers shall be 'associated persons' for the purposes of the Act: s 62(5).

Relatives

37.11 The mere fact that an applicant seeks protection from a relative is not, in itself, necessarily enough to engage the FLA 1996. The nature of the dispute must be of a 'domestic' type.

37.12 In *Chechi* v *Bashier* [1999] 2 FLR 489 the applicant was subjected to violence at the hands of his brother and nephew following a dispute concerning land in Pakistan. It was held that the family relationship was merely incidental and therefore fell outside the intended ambit of the FLA 1996. Civil proceedings were the appropriate means of resolving the dispute.

In *Rafiq* v *Muse* [2000] 1 FLR 820 a mother obtained non-molestation injunctions against her **37.13** son and after successive breaches of the injunctions he was imprisoned for six months.

Relevant child

By s 62(2) a 'relevant child' in relation to any proceedings under the FLA 1996 means: **37.14**

(a) any child who is living with either party to the proceedings;
(b) any child who might reasonably be expected to live with either party to the proceedings;
(c) any child in relation to whom an order under the Adoption Act 1976 or the Adoption and Children Act 2002 is in question in the proceedings;
(d) any child in relation to whom an order under the CA 1989 is in question in the proceedings;
(e) any other child whose interests the court considers relevant.

Engaged couples or same-sex couples who have entered into a civil partnership agreement

Where proceedings are based on the fact that the parties have entered into an agreement to **37.15** marry or become civil partners, no application for an occupation order or a non-molestation order may be made if a period exceeding three years has expired since the date of termination of the agreement: ss 33(2) and 42(4).

This is one of the few examples in this Part of the Act of the right to make an application being **37.16** time-limited.

Section 44 prescribes what constitutes an agreement to marry or form a civil partnership. The **37.17** agreement must be evidenced in writing or evidenced by the gift of an engagement ring or other gift in contemplation of marriage or civil partnership or by a ceremony entered into by the parties in the presence of one or more witnesses assembled for the purpose of witnessing the ceremony.

The agreement to marry or form a civil partnership need not itself be in writing, but there needs **37.18** to be some evidence in writing of an agreement to marry—for example, a press announcement or wedding/civil partnership invitations.

D   NON-MOLESTATION ORDERS

Introduction

The court's power to make a non-molestation order is contained in s 42. The order may refer **37.19** to molestation in general, to particular acts of molestation, or to both. The order may be made for a specified period or until further order (thus ensuring considerable flexibility) and may be varied or revoked.

37.20   The order may be made on application as a free-standing application or by the court of its own motion in 'family proceedings' where it considers that the order should be made for the benefit of any other party to the proceedings or any relevant child.

Conditions

37.21   In determining whether a client will be able to obtain a non-molestation order under the FLA 1996, the first matter to be established is whether the applicant and respondent are 'associated persons' (see paras 37.07 ff above) or the person to be protected is a 'relevant child'.

The test for a non-molestation order

37.22   In deciding whether to exercise its powers and, if so, in what manner, the court shall have regard to all the circumstances, including the need to secure the health, safety, and well-being:

(a)   of the applicant or the person for whose benefit the order would be made; and
(b)   of any relevant child: s 42(5).

In practice, therefore, an applicant will have to provide evidence of molestation, that he or she (or a relevant child) needs protection and that, on the balance of probabilities, judicial intervention is required to control the respondent's behaviour (*C* v *C* (above)).

What amounts to molestation?

37.23   There is no statutory definition of 'molestation' contained in the FLA 1996 and courts are guided by case law which establishes that the term includes, but is wider than, violence: see *Davis* v *Johnson* [1979] AC 264 per Viscount Dilhorne: 'Violence is a form of molestation, but molestation may take place without the threat or use of violence and still be serious and inimical to mental or physical health.' In *Vaughan* v *Vaughan* (para 37.03 above) the court considered a dictionary definition of molestation, namely 'to cause trouble; to vex; to annoy; to put to inconvenience'. In other cases repeated telephoning has amounted to molestation as has the positioning of embarrassing notices in public places.

Duration of non-molestation orders

37.24   Non-molestation orders are usually made for periods of six months or one year, depending on the seriousness of the molestation.

37.25   Where the application is made without notice, it may be appropriate to make the order for a period of six to 12 months notwithstanding that the court will fix an on notice hearing much sooner than that, usually within a week: this means that if the order is confirmed at the on notice hearing, there is no need for a new order to be re-drawn and re-served. However, different courts have different approaches and some judges prefer to make a without notice non-molestation order only for a very short period until it can be reconsidered at an on notice hearing.

Family proceedings

Family proceedings are defined in s 63 as any proceedings under: **37.26**

(a) the inherent jurisdiction of the High Court in relation to children;
(b) Part II and Part IV, FLA 1996;
(c) Matrimonial Causes Act 1973 ('MCA 1973');
(d) Adoption and Children Act 2002;
(e) Domestic Proceedings and Magistrates' Courts Act 1978;
(f) Part III, Matrimonial and Family Proceedings Act 1984;
(g) Parts I, II, and IV, CA 1989;
(h) s 54, Human Fertilisation and Embryology Act 2008;
(i) schs 5 to 7, CPA 2004.

By the operation of s 42(3), FLA 1996 the court may specifically make a non-molestation order   **37.27**
in proceedings in which the court has made an emergency protection order which includes
an exclusion requirement under s 44, CA 1989 (see Chapter 21). That specific inclusion in
the definition of 'family proceedings' is necessary because proceedings under s 44, CA 1989
(for an emergency protection order) are not proceedings under Part I, II, or IV, CA 1989—s 44
being contained in Part V, CA 1989—and are therefore not 'family proceedings'.

Where a non-molestation order is made in other family proceedings, the order ceases to have   **37.28**
effect if those proceedings are withdrawn or dismissed: s 42(8).

E   APPLICATIONS BY CHILDREN

Section 43(1) permits a child under the age of 16 to apply for a non-molestation order or   **37.29**
an occupation order, provided he has obtained leave of a High Court judge. The court may
grant leave only if satisfied that the child has sufficient understanding to make the proposed
application.

It will be unusual for a child to seek a non-molestation order and even more unusual for a   **37.30**
child to be entitled to apply for an occupation order since a minor child has no capacity to
hold a legal estate in land and, therefore, will be unable to demonstrate an entitlement to
occupy the dwelling-house (a precondition to an application under s 33). In exceptional
cases, however, the applicant child may of course have a beneficial interest in the land under
a trust and therefore have an entitlement to occupy in consequence.

'Sufficient understanding'

The issue of the sufficiency of a child's understanding was considered by the House of Lords   **37.31**
in *Gillick* v *West Norfolk and Wisbech Area Health Authority* [1986] AC 112. It was held that the
parental right to decide whether medical treatment could be given to a child under 16 terminated if and when the child achieved a sufficient understanding and intelligence to enable
her to understand fully what was proposed. Lord Scarman used the phrase (at p 188A): 'the
attainment by a child of an age of sufficient discretion to enable him or her to exercise a wise
choice in his or her own interests'.

Practice

37.32　Any application for a non-molestation or occupation order made by a child under the age of 16 should be started in the county court: art 6, Allocation and Transfer of Proceedings Order 2008. The procedure to be followed is the Part 18 procedure: para 2.1, PD10A, Family Procedure Rules 2010 ('FPR 2010').

F　ORDERS MADE WITHOUT NOTICE

37.33　Section 45, FLA 1996 provides for the making of both occupation and non-molestation orders without notice having first been given to the other side (in circumstances where the court considers it just and convenient to do so: s 45(1)). The section goes on to prescribe the factors which the court must take into account in addition to all the circumstances of the case. These are set out in s 45(2) as follows:

(a)　any risk of significant harm to the applicant or a relevant child, attributable to conduct of the respondent, if the order is not made immediately;

(b)　whether it is likely that the applicant will be deterred or prevented from pursuing the application if an order is not made immediately; and

(c)　whether there is reason to believe that the respondent is aware of the proceedings but is deliberately evading service and that the applicant or a relevant child will be seriously prejudiced by the delay involved—

  (i)　where the court is a magistrates' court, in effecting service of proceedings, or

  (ii)　in any other case, in effecting substituted service.

It should be noted, however, that there is a fundamental difference between the granting of a without notice non-molestation order and a without notice occupation order. The former is often granted to give an applicant immediate protection as such an order does not infringe upon a respondent's legal rights, it merely prevents him from doing something that he should not be doing. The same reasoning does not apply to a without notice occupation order which would directly encroach upon a respondent's legal rights. For this reason, occupation orders are seldom granted on a without notice basis.

37.34　When the court does make an order without notice to the other side, it must give the respondent an opportunity to make representations at a full hearing as soon as just and convenient: s 45(3).

G　UNDERTAKINGS

37.35　Undertakings are a very useful mechanism in that if agreed they save time and the client walks away from the court without an order or findings of fact having been made against him.

37.36　In s 46 statutory recognition is given to this common practice of the courts of accepting undertakings. Accepting an undertaking is possible where the court has power to make an occupation order or non-molestation order or both. An undertaking is enforceable as if it were an order of the court: s 46(4).

However, the court shall not accept an undertaking instead of making a non-molestation **37.37** order in any case where it appears to the court that the respondent has used or threatened violence against the applicant or a relevant child, and that for the protection of the applicant or child it is necessary to make an order so that any breach may be punishable as a criminal offence: s 46(3A).

H   VARIATION AND DISCHARGE OF ORDERS

General

Either the respondent or the applicant may apply to court to vary or discharge an occupation **37.38** or non-molestation order: s 49(1).

Court's own motion

Where a court has made a non-molestation order of its own motion under s 42(2)(b), the **37.39** court itself may vary or discharge the order, even though no separate application has been made to do so: s 49(2).

I   PROCEDURAL GUIDE

Where to find the rules

The rules governing applications for non-molestation and occupation orders are set out in **37.40** Part 10, FPR 2010.

The fee

On making an application for a non-molestation order or occupation order in the county **37.41** court or family proceedings court a fee of £60 is payable irrespective of whether the applicant is publicly funded.

Only one fee is payable when an application is made for both types of order at the same time: **37.42** Family Proceedings Fees Order 1999 (SI 1999/690) as amended.

Where is the application to be made?

Introduction

The provisions are set out fully in the Allocation and Transfer of Proceedings Order 2008 **37.43** (SI 2008/2836). The principal features of the Order are set out below.

Choice of venue

37.44 Generally speaking, an application for an order under Part IV may be commenced in a county court (ie, a designated divorce county court, a family hearing centre, or a care centre) or a family proceedings court. For the purpose of Part IV proceedings the Principal Registry of the Family Division of the High Court is to be treated as a county court.

37.45 However, there are some important exceptions to note:

(a) A family proceedings court shall not be competent to entertain any application, or make any order, involving any disputed question as to a party's entitlement to occupy any property (however that might arise) unless it is unnecessary to determine the question in order to deal with the application or make the order. Further, the magistrate may decline jurisdiction in any proceedings if he considers that the case can more conveniently be dealt with by another court: s 59, FLA 1996.

(b) The family proceedings court has no jurisdiction to deal with applications for the transfer of tenancies on divorce or on the separation of cohabitants: s 53 and sch 7, para 1.

(c) Applications for the grant of leave under s 43 (where the applicant is a child under the age of 16) should be commenced in the county court: FPR 2010, PD10A.

Funding the application

The private client

37.46 Where the client is ineligible for public funding, it will be necessary to advise the client of the fee (para 37.41 above) and the likely costs involved in making the application.

37.47 A payment on account should be obtained, at least to pay for the preparation of the case and to provide the court fee.

The publicly funded client

37.48 Under the Legal Services Commission's Funding Code, which governs the availability of public funding for family matters, great emphasis is placed on mediation as a means of resolving disputes. For many family matters a client must attend an assessment of suitability with a recognized mediator before an application can be made for General Family Help and for Legal Representation. However, there are a number of occasions when it will not be necessary for the client to attend an assessment appointment. These include, amongst other things, where Legal Representation should be granted as a matter of urgency and where there is a history of civil proceedings or police investigation into domestic abuse within the previous 12 months. Full details are set out in para 20.16 of the Funding Code.

37.49 A certificate authorizing Legal Representation may be applied for in emergency situations, for example in cases where protection from domestic violence is required (see Chapter 2). This will be necessary because a certificate for General Family Help cannot cover the cost of legal representation at a final contested hearing. Where a certificate for General Family Help is already in existence, authority to provide Legal Representation may be obtained from the Commission by seeking an amendment to the existing certificate, otherwise a fresh certificate must be sought. Application to the Commission is made by completion of form CLS APP3.

Emergency Representation is only available as part of Legal Representation and it does not **37.50** apply to any other level of service. Whilst a certificate for Emergency Representation should reduce the inevitable delay associated with the grant of a certificate for Legal Representation, it will be necessary not only to satisfy the standard criteria for Legal Representation but also to demonstrate that the certificate should be granted as a matter of urgency because it appears to be in the interests of justice to do so.

Paragraph 12 of the Funding Code: Decision Making Guidance states that the application **37.51** may be urgent if any of the following circumstances apply and there is insufficient time for an application for a substantive certificate to be made and determined:

(a) representation (or other urgent work for which Legal Representation would be needed) is justified in injunction or other emergency proceedings, including an order under Part IV, FLA 1996;
(b) representation (or other urgent work for which Legal Representation would be needed) is justified in relation to an imminent hearing in existing proceedings; or
(c) a limitation period is about to expire.

Emergency Representation is unlikely to be granted unless: **37.52**

the likely delay as a result of the failure to grant emergency representation will mean that either:

(a) there will be a risk to the life, liberty or physical safety of the client or his or her family or the roof over their heads; or
(b) the delay will cause a significant risk of miscarriage of justice, or unreasonable hardship to the client, or irretrievable problems in handling the case; and in either case there are no other appropriate options to deal with the risk.

(Para 12.2, Funding Code: Decision Making Guidance.)

Paragraph 20.32, Funding Code: Decision Making Guidance contains details of how public **37.53** funding is made available in proceedings seeking an injunction, a committal order, or other orders for the protection of a person from harm (other than public law children proceedings). Some of the principal points are as follows:

(a) The Commission will not require proceedings under Part IV, FLA 1996 to be commenced or conducted in any particular venue.
(b) Where matrimonial proceedings are in existence or are to be commenced then any application under Part IV may be made in those proceedings. Where there is an existing certificate capable of amendment to cover proceedings under Part IV an application must be made for an amendment rather than for a fresh certificate.
(c) Any certificate covering proceedings under Part IV will cover obtaining a final order including, if appropriate, applying for a without notice order prior to that.
(d) Certificates will generally cover a non-molestation order and/or occupation order although, where appropriate, certificates will be issued covering a non-molestation order only. If cover is being sought to apply for an order, it will be necessary to consider to what extent the remedy sought is available within the provisions of Part IV and whether the application to the court is likely to succeed, having regard to the factors to be considered by the court.

(e) An occupation order may impose financial obligations. The scope of the certificate will extend to those aspects without the need for a specific amendment.

Any recovery or preservation in proceedings under Part IV is exempt from the operation of the statutory charge. It would, however, generally be reasonable to expect substantial financial provision issues to be adjourned for consideration in other more appropriate proceedings, for example financial provision within divorce or judicial separation.

37.54 **Non-molestation orders (Part IV)**   Where the parties are 'associated persons', Legal Representation to take non-molestation proceedings is likely to be refused:

(a) unless a warning letter has first been sent (unless the circumstances make this inappropriate);

(b) unless the police have been notified and have failed to provide adequate assistance;

(c) if the conduct complained of is not of a trivial nature, took place within the last two or three weeks, and there is a likelihood of repetition.

37.55 Legal Representation to defend proceedings is likely to be refused if the matter could reasonably be dealt with by way of an undertaking. The fact that the court must consider whether to attach a power of arrest where the applicant has used or threatened violence against the applicant or a relevant child does not of itself justify the grant of representation.

37.56 **Occupation orders (Part IV)**   Legal Representation to take occupation order proceedings is likely to be refused:

(a) unless the parties and property qualify to be covered by an order;

(b) unless an order is likely to be considered necessary by the court in all the circumstances, including the 'greater harm' test (see Chapter 36, para 36.11);

(c) if the respondent has already left voluntarily and does not wish to return;

(d) if the applicant has been out of occupation for some time and there are no other issues to justify the proceedings.

37.57 Legal Representation to defend proceedings is likely to be granted if there has been a without notice order made with no opportunity for the respondent to contest it and it would be unreasonable for the order to stand. However, Legal Representation to defend proceedings is likely to be refused if the respondent is already out of the property, has no good reason to return, and there are no other issues to justify the grant of representation.

Normal procedure in the county court

37.58 A free-standing application for an occupation order or a non-molestation order is to be made in Form FL401. If applicants are concerned about giving their address on the application form, they may leave the form blank and complete Confidential Address Form C8.

37.59 It is recognized that the applicant may not know all the details requested on the application form and this should be stated wherever it applies.

37.60 The form should be signed by the applicant and dated.

37.61 Where the application is made in other proceedings which are pending, the application is likewise to be made in Form FL401.

The application in Form FL401 shall be supported by a witness statement signed by the **37.62** applicant and containing a statement of truth: r 10.2(1), FPR 2010. Where the application is made without notice, the witness statement must set out the reasons why notice has not been given: r 10.2(4).

Procedure where the applicant is a child under the age of 16

The application for permission should be made using the Part 18 procedure: FPR 2010, **37.63** PD10A.

Procedure for a without notice (*ex parte*) application

The application is made in Form FL401 but the statement must set out reasons why notice **37.64** was not given: r 10.2(4).

Service of the application

The application on notice (together with the witness statement and notice of proceedings **37.65** and guidance in Form FL402) shall be served by the applicant on the respondent personally not less than two days before the date on which the application will be heard: r 10.3(1)(i).

The court may abridge the period: r 10.3(1)(ii). **37.66**

Where the applicant is acting in person, personal service of the application shall be effected **37.67** by the court if the applicant so requests: r 10.3(2).

Statement of service

The applicant is required to file a certificate of service after he has served the application: **37.68** r 10.3(4). This gives details of the identity of the person served and sets out how service was effected.

The hearing

In the High Court and county court, the hearing will be in private unless the court directs **37.69** otherwise: r 10.5.

A record of the hearing is to be issued in Form FL405 and the order made in Form FL404. **37.70**

Service of the order

An order obtained without notice

A copy of the order obtained without notice, a copy of the application, and of the witness **37.71** statement must be served by the applicant on the respondent personally: r 10.6(1)(b).

The order made on notice

A copy of an order made after a hearing of which both sides received notice must be served by **37.72** the applicant on the respondent personally: r 10.6(1)(a).

The applicant acting in person

37.73 In these circumstances, service of a copy of any order made *must* be effected by the court if the applicant so requests: r 10.6(2). The method of service to be employed by the court is not indicated in the Rules.

J ENFORCEMENT

Breach of a non-molestation order

37.74 A person who without reasonable excuse does anything that he is prohibited from doing by a non-molestation order is guilty of an offence: s 42A(1), FLA 1996. The offence is only committed if the person is aware of the order (ie, if the order was made without notice, after it has been served): s 42A(2).

37.75 Breach of a non-molestation order is an arrestable offence. Once arrested, it will be for the CPS to decide whether to charge the person with the offence. The court has no power to attach a power of arrest to a non-molestation order.

37.76 An offence of breaching a non-molestation order is triable either in the magistrates' court or the Crown Court. The maximum term of imprisonment (in the Crown Court) is five years: s 42A(5)(a).

37.77 The civil court's power to commit a respondent for breach of a non-molestation order coexists with the criminal jurisdiction. As there is no power of arrest, an applicant will have to apply to the county court on application for a committal in a notice to show cause in Form N89. An applicant may apply for a warrant for the respondent's arrest: s 47(8). Conduct in respect of which a person has been convicted cannot, however, be the subject of a separate committal application: s 42A(4).

Breach of an undertaking

37.78 Where the court has accepted an undertaking instead of making a non-molestation order, breach of the undertaking is not a criminal offence and will therefore fall to be enforced by the family court in the same way as other civil orders and undertakings: see Chapter 36, para 36.83.

K KEY DOCUMENTS

37.79 Family Law Act 1996
Family Procedure Rules 2010

38

FORCED MARRIAGE PROTECTION ORDERS

A   INTRODUCTION

The Forced Marriage (Civil Protection) Act 2007 ('FM(CP)A 2007') introduced a new Part IVA, **38.01** Family Law Act 1996 ('FLA 1996'). It gives the High Court and certain specified county courts the power to make a forced marriage protection order, which is an order designed either to protect a person from being forced into a marriage or to protect a person who has, already, been subjected to a forced marriage. The county courts thus far designated as forced marriage county courts are Birmingham, Blackburn, Bradford, Bristol, Cardiff, Derby, Leeds, Leicester,

Luton, Manchester, Middlesbrough, Newcastle-upon-Tyne, Romford, Willesden, and the Principal Registry of the Family Division.

38.02   The Forced Marriage Unit is a joint initiative between the Foreign and Commonwealth Office and the Home Office. It offers advice and assistance to those who may be at risk of forced marriage and maintains statistics on the use of Forced Marriage Protection Orders (FMPO).

38.03   Prior to the implementation of the FM(CP)A 2007, protection was available to those at risk of a forced marriage only through the High Court's inherent jurisdiction to prevent vulnerable adults. There was disagreement about the extent to which this jurisdiction was available to assist adults who were legally competent. The FM(CP)A 2007 has removed that uncertainty by making the remedy available whether or not the person in question has capacity.

B   WHAT IS A FORCED MARRIAGE?

38.04   It has repeatedly been emphasized that there is a distinction to be drawn between cases of forced marriage and the concept of a (consensually) arranged marriage, which is the norm in some cultures.

38.05   A forced marriage is defined by s 63A, FLA 1996 as follows:

> For the purposes of this Act, a person ('A') is forced into a marriage if another person ('B') forces A to enter into a marriage (whether with B or another person) without A's free and full consent.

38.06   It does not matter whether B's conduct is directed against A, B, or another person: s 63A(5). 'Force' includes coercion by threats or other psychological means (and related expressions are to be read accordingly): s 63A(6).

C   FORCED MARRIAGE PROTECTION ORDERS

38.07   A FMPO is an order made for the purposes of protecting:

(a) a person from being forced into a marriage or from any attempt to be forced into a marriage; or

(b) a person who has been forced into a marriage: s 63A(1).

38.08   In considering whether to make a FMPO the court must have regard to 'all the circumstances including the need to secure the health, safety and wellbeing of the person to be protected': s 63A(2). In ascertaining that person's well-being, the court must in particular have such regard to the person's wishes and feelings (so far as they are readily ascertainable) as it considers appropriate in the light of the person's age and understanding: s 63A(3).

38.09   The terms of a FMPO are not defined in the FLA 1996 and the court's powers are wide. The order may contain such prohibitions, restrictions, or requirements, and such other terms as the court considers appropriate. In particular, the terms may relate to conduct outside the jurisdiction, and may affect any person including those who are not respondents and those who are not involved in forcing the marriage: s 63B(2). Examples given of other types of involvement include aiding, abetting, counselling, procuring, encouraging, or assisting another person to force a person to enter into a marriage.

D   APPLICATION AND PROCEDURE

The rules relating to applications for FMPOs are contained in Part 11, Family Procedure Rules   **38.10** 2010 ('FPR 2010'). To a large extent they mirror the rules for applications under Part IV, FLA 1996 (non-molestation and occupation orders); see Chapters 36 and 37.

The court may make a FMPO: **38.11**

(a)   on application;
(b)   without an application but of its own motion, within family proceedings where a person who would be a respondent to any proceedings for a FMPO is a party to the current proceedings: s 63C(6).

'Family proceedings' has the same meaning as for proceedings under Part IV, FLA 1996: see s 63(1), FLA 1996.

The applicant

An application may be made as of right by: **38.12**

(a)   the person who is to be protected by the order; or
(b)   a relevant third party.

Any other person may apply with the leave of the court.

The 'relevant third party' means a person specified by order. At present, the only specified   **38.13** 'relevant third party' for FMPO applications is the local authority: Family Law Act 1996 (Forced Marriage) (Relevant Third Party) Order 2009 (SI 2009/2023). The Ministry of Justice has issued guidance to the local authority in relation to FMPO applications, available at <http://www.justice.gov.uk>.

Where the person to be protected is a child, he may make the application without leave but   **38.14** the provisions of r 16.6(1) and (3), FPR 2010 will apply to the application. Therefore the child must act through a guardian or litigation friend unless a solicitor considers that he has the capacity to give instructions, or the court gives leave.

In considering an application for leave by any other person, the court must have regard to all   **38.15** the circumstances including:

(a)   the applicant's connection with the person to be protected;
(b)   the applicant's knowledge of the circumstances of the person to be protected;
(c)   the wishes and feelings of the person to be protected so far as they are reasonably ascertainable and so far as the court considers it appropriate, in light of the person's age and understanding, to have regard to them: s 63C(4), FLA 1996.

Where an application for leave is granted, the court must inform the applicant, respondent, person to be protected, and any other person directed by the court: r 11.3(3), FPR 2010.

Applications without notice

38.16 The court may, where it considers that it is just and convenient to do so, make a FMPO on an *ex parte* (the FLA 1996 uses the old term) basis.

38.17 In deciding whether to make an order *ex parte*, the court must have regard to all the circumstances including:

(a) any risk of significant harm to the person to be protected or another person if the order is not made immediately;

(b) whether it is likely that an applicant will be deterred or prevented from pursing an application if an order is not made immediately; and

(c) whether there is reason to believe that—

(i) the respondent is aware of the proceedings but is deliberately evading service; and

(ii) the delay involved in effecting substituted service will cause serious prejudice to the person to be protected or (if a different person) an applicant: s 63D(2).

38.18 Where an order is made on an *ex parte* basis, a return date hearing on notice to all parties must be listed as soon as is just and convenient. Personal service must be effected on the respondent(s) no less than two clear days before the hearing unless time for service is abridged: r 11.4, FPR 2010.

38.19 Note that where an application is made without notice, it must be supported by a *sworn* statement: r 11.2(2). This is different from the requirements for applications for FLA 1996, Part IV orders, where there is no requirement that the statement should be sworn.

Transfer

38.20 The court may transfer the proceedings to another court of its own initiative or on the application of a party or of the person who is the subject of the proceedings: r 11.5.

Joinder and removal of parties

38.21 Any person may be joined or removed as a party at any time, by application of any person or of the court's own motion: r 11.6(1) and (4).

Service of application and order

38.22 Where the application is made on notice, a copy of the application and order must be served on:

(a) all respondents;

(b) the person who is the subject of the proceedings (if not the applicant or a respondent);

(c) any other person directed by the court;

no less than two clear days before the hearing date: rr 11.4(1) and 11.7(3). Where the person who is the subject of the proceedings is a child or a person who lacks capacity, the court will give directions about the persons who are to be served: r 11.4(5).

After an order has been made, the applicant must serve it personally on the respondent(s),   **38.23**
the person who is the subject of the proceedings, and any other person named in the order:
r 11.7(3). Where the applicant is acting in person and so requests, or where the court has made
the order of its own initiative, the court must serve it: r 11.7(4).

It is good practice to direct (where appropriate) that the order should be served on: **38.24**

(a)   the Forced Marriage Unit;
(b)   the UK Border Agency;
(c)   the Identity and Passport Service;
(d)   the relevant local authority;
(e)   the appropriate police authority;
(f)   the relevant embassy.

Duration of the order

A FMPO may be made for a specified period or until varied or discharged: s 63F, FLA 1996.   **38.25**

Disclosure of information/public interest immunity

The issue of disclosure of sensitive material to other parties may be of relevance in a forced   **38.26**
marriage case. Rule 11.7(2), FPR 2010 provides that the court has a discretion to withhold any
submission made to it, or evidence produced, in order to protect the person to be protected
or any other person, or for any good reason. Where the information has been provided by an
informant to the police, they may request that the source of the information is withheld on
public interest immunity grounds, in order to protect the informant.

In *A Chief Constable* v *YK, RB, ZS, SI, AK and MH* [2010] EWHC 2438 (Fam), the President gave   **38.27**
guidance in relation to the use of special advocates in such circumstances. The use of special
advocates will be rare in the extreme, but may be used in order to prevent the disclosure of
material where it may put a party or another person at risk, while preserving the Art 6 rights
of all parties.

The hearing

Any hearing relating to an application for a FMPO must be in private unless the court   **38.28**
otherwise directs: r 11.7(1).

E   ENFORCEMENT

Power of arrest—applications on notice

38.29   Where the application has been made on notice and the court considers that the respondent has used or threatened violence against the person being protected or otherwise in connection with the matters being dealt with by the order, it *must* attach a power of arrest to one or more provisions of the order unless it considers that, in the circumstances of the case, there will be adequate protection without such a power: s 63H(2), FLA 1996.

Power of arrest—*ex parte* applications

38.30   Where the application has been made *ex parte*, the court *may* attach a power of arrest to one or more provisions of the order if:

(a)   it considers that the respondent has used or threatened violence against the person being protected or otherwise in connection with the matters being dealt with by the order; and

(b)   it considers that there is a risk of significant harm to a person, attributable to conduct of the respondent, if the power of arrest is not attached immediately: s 63H(4).

38.31   Where a power of arrest is attached to one or more of the provisions ('the relevant provisions') of the order:

(a)   the relevant provisions must be set out in Form FL406A and the form must not include any provisions of the order to which the power of arrest was not attached; and

(b)   a copy of the form must be delivered to the officer for the time being in charge of any police station serving the area for the applicant's address or to any other police station as the court may specify: r 11.12, FPR 2010.

38.32   The copy of the form detailing the provisions must be accompanied by a statement showing that the respondent has been served with the order or informed of its terms (whether by being present when the order was made or by telephone or otherwise): r 11.12(2).

38.33   It is the responsibility of the applicant to deliver the documentation to the police, unless the order was served by the court after a request by a litigant in person, in which case it is the responsibility of an officer of the court to ensure that the police are properly informed: r 11.12(3).

38.34   Similarly, when the relevant provisions of the order are varied or discharged the proper officer at the court must immediately inform the police officer who received the form and deliver a copy of the order to that officer: r 11.12(4).

38.35   Where a power of arrest is attached to specific provisions of the order a constable may arrest without warrant a person whom he has reasonable cause for suspecting to be in breach of any such provision: s 63I(2), FLA 1996.

38.36   The respondent must then be brought before the relevant judge within the period of 24 hours beginning at the time of his arrest. When the 24-hour period is being calculated, no account is taken of Christmas Day, Good Friday, or any Sunday: s 63I(3) and (4).

All courts may remand respondents if the matter is not disposed of forthwith (see below).   **38.37**

The proceedings should be listed for hearing within 14 days of the date on which the respondent   **38.38**
was arrested and he must be given not less than two business days' notice of the adjourned
hearing: r 11.14(3), FPR 2010.

Issue of a warrant

If, at any time, the applicant or the person who is the subject of proceedings considers that the   **38.39**
respondent has failed to comply with an order to which no power of arrest has been attached,
he may apply for the issue of a warrant substantiated on oath for the arrest of the respondent:
s 63J(2), FLA 1996. The court will issue the warrant if it has reasonable grounds for believing
that the respondent has failed to comply with the order.

Where an application for a warrant is made by any other person it shall be treated in the first   **38.40**
instance as an application for leave: r 11.13(2), FPR 2010.

Remands

Schedule 5, FLA 1996 gives the High Court and county courts powers to remand correspond-   **38.41**
ing to those which apply in magistrates' courts under ss 128 and 129, Magistrates' Courts Act
1980. In county courts, the powers may be exercised by a judge or a district judge. The powers
are as follows.

Remand in custody or on bail

Where a court has power to remand the respondent under s 63K, FLA 1996 it may: **38.42**

(a) remand him in custody; or
(b) remand him on bail, either—
   (i) by taking a recognizance from him (with or without sureties), such recognizance to
        be 'conditioned' in accordance with sch 5, para 2(3), or
   (ii) by fixing the amount of the recognizances with a view to their being taken subse-
        quently (and in the meantime committing the person to custody): sch 5, para 2(1).

If bail is granted, the court may require the remanded person to comply with 'such require-   **38.43**
ments' as appear to the court to be necessary to ensure that he does not interfere with witnesses
or otherwise obstruct the course of justice: s 63K(5).

The period of remand

A period of remand may not exceed eight clear days unless: **38.44**

(a) the person is remanded on bail and both he and the applicant agree to a longer period;
(b) a case is adjourned under s 63L for a medical examination and report to be made, when
     the court may remand for the period of adjournment (but see the limitations in s 63L(2)
     and (3) at para 38.47 below): sch 5, para 2(5).

Further remand

If the court is satisfied that a remanded person is unable, because of illness or accident, to   **38.45**
appear at the relevant time, he may be remanded in his absence (and the eight days' time limit

does not apply): sch 5, para 3(1). Otherwise, a person may be remanded in his absence by the court's enlarging his recognizance and those of any sureties to a later date: sch 5, para 3(2).

38.46 For the avoidance of doubt, para 3(2) specifically provides that a person brought before the court after remand may be further remanded.

Remand for medical examination

38.47 Where the court has reason to consider that a medical report will be required, it may remand a person to enable a medical examination and report to be made. A remand must not exceed four weeks at a time, or three weeks if the remand is in custody: s 63L(2) and (3).

38.48 Section 63L(5) gives to the civil courts powers similar to those of the Crown Court to make an order under s 35, Mental Health Act 1983, remanding for a report on the mental condition of the respondent where there is reason to suspect that the person arrested is suffering from mental illness or severe mental impairment.

Enforcement by way of committal proceedings

38.49 RSC Ord 52 and CCR Ord 29 apply to forced marriage cases as they do to applications for non-molestation and occupation orders: Part 33, FPR 2010 and see Chapter 36, para 36.109.

F   OTHER REMEDIES

38.50 Part IVA, FLA 1996 does not affect any other protection or assistance available to a person in connection with a forced marriage: s 63R. Other remedies may include criminal proceedings and civil remedies under the Protection from Harassment Act 1997 or Part IV, FLA 1996. In addition, where the person to be protected is a child, there may be a wide variety of orders available, including public law orders where the local authority is of the view that a care order or emergency protection order may be appropriate.

38.51 In addition the High Court continues to have available its inherent jurisdiction to make orders in an appropriate case where a statutory power is insufficient. In *B v I (Forced Marriage)* [2010] 1 FLR 1721 Baron J used the inherent jurisdiction of the High Court to pronounce a decree of nullity following a forced marriage, notwithstanding that the time limit for a nullity petition on the grounds of a lack of consent had expired.

INDEX